CONSTRUCTING QUALITY SOFTWARE

IFIP Working Conference on
Constructing Quality Software
Novosibirsk, USSR
23-28 May 1977

Organized by
Technical Committee 2
(Programming)

With the cooperation of

Working Group 2.1
(ALGOL)
Working Group 2.3
(Programming Methodology)
Working Group 2.4
(Machine Oriented Higher-Level Languages)

International Federation for Information Processing

NORTH-HOLLAND PUBLISHING COMPANY
AMSTERDAM•NEW YORK•OXFORD

CONSTRUCTING QUALITY SOFTWARE

Proceedings of the IFIP Working Conference on Constructing Quality Software

edited by

P.G. HIBBARD
Carnegie-Mellon University
Pittsburgh, Penn. USA

and

S.A. SCHUMAN
IRIA - Laboria
Rocquencourt, France

1978

NORTH-HOLLAND PUBLISHING COMPANY
AMSTERDAM • NEW YORK • OXFORD

ISBN: 0 444 85106 2

Published by:
NORTH-HOLLAND PUBLISHING COMPANY
AMSTERDAM•NEW YORK•OXFORD

Sole distributors for the U.S.A. and Canada:
Elsevier North-Holland, Inc.
52 Vanderbilt Avenue
New York, N.Y. 10017

Library of Congress Cataloging in Publication Data

IFIP Working Conference on Constructing Quality Software, Novosibirsk, Russian S.F.S.R., 1977.
Constructing quality software.

Includes index.
1. Electronic digital computers--Programming--Congresses. 2. Programming languages (Electronic computers)--Congresses. I. Hibbard, P. G. II. Schuman, S. A. III. International Federation for Information Processing. IV. Title.
QA76.6.I188 001.6'425 78-2739
ISBN 0-444-85106-2

PRINTED IN THE NETHERLANDS

Foreword

Several criteria enter into determining the *quality* of a software product, including:

- validity (with respect to its stated specifications)
- integrity (under all possible conditions of usage)
- efficiency (relative to the complexity of the task)
- clarity (of both its structure and its function)

It has long been recognized that the ability to achieve a proper balance amongst such (not necessarily compatible) objectives depends primarily upon the way in which the programs are constructed. The degree of success is largely determined by the *techniques* employed during program development and by the *tools* used to support this process (where the programming language is merely the most traditional of these tools).

This volume contains the proceedings of an IFIP Working Conference, the purpose of which was to survey the state-of-the-art in these domains and to assess the potential impact of recent research in a variety of related subject areas.

The conference took place on 23-28 May 1977 in Novosibirsk, USSR, with the Siberian Division of the Academy of Sciences of the USSR acting as host. Their invitation was particularly appreciated, since this opportunity to hold an international technical meeting at the Novosibirsk Science Centre, "Akademgorodok", afforded an excellent and perhaps unique forum for scientific interchange between East and West.

This Working Conference was sponsored by the IFIP Technical Committee 2 on Programming, and organized in cooperation with Working Group 2.1 on ALGOL, Working Group 2.3 on Programming Methodology and Working Group 2.4 on Machine-Oriented Higher-Level Languages. In keeping with the goals of the conference, participants were drawn primarily from the international research community.

The immediate, tangible outcome of that occasion is represented by this book. It is first of all the product of the individual authors, who contributed the substance of the conference in the form of original technical papers, together with a number of pertinent position papers which served to stimulate discussion. It is hoped that the interest (and potential impact) of this record will be further enhanced by the inclusion of edited transcripts of these discussions; this is an attempt to convey to the reader some part of the overall perspective which was developed during the conference.

It is necessary to acknowledge the contribution of the Programme Committee, which devoted considerable collective effort to shaping both the style and content of the technical program, despite the fact that many of its members were in the end unable to be present. Much of the support required during this organizational phase was generously provided by IRIA.

We must also make special mention of the members of the Local Organizing Committee, who not only set the stage for a pleasant and interesting week with their exceptionally warm welcome, but also managed to make transcripts of the discussions available during the conference itself, overcoming seemingly insurmountable linguistic problems in the process.

In the editing of the discussions we have consistently tried to preserve the intentions of the different speakers, as well as the spirit in which their remarks were made. [Expletives, however, have been deleted.] All editorial comments are enclosed within square brackets in the text of the discussions. To avoid tedious repetitions, we have chosen to indicate comments which occur frequently by special symbols, as follows:

☺ General audience laughter
👍 General audience approval
👎 General audience disapproval

Gratefully we acknowledge the assistance received from many sources during our task, in particular: from D. Josephson and B. McCauley, without whom the transcripts would never have appeared in a form which we could edit; from C.M.H. and SPELL, whose widely differing proof-reading talents were equally indispensible; from I. Durham, whose indefatigable efforts produced the text of the discussions in its final form; from PUB, whose unfathomable intricacies we are no nearer to understanding; from CMU, whose generosity made these proceedings possible; and from all those, too numerous to mention, who contributed time and effort to see us through our task.

🖕 Finally, we salute the good people of the Oakland Original, purveyors of editorial prerogative, to whom we dedicate the last word in brackets: 🖕.

P. G. H.
S. A. S.

Table of Contents

Part 3: Language Constructs and their Role

Session 3a

Session 3b

Part 4: The Programming Language as a Tool

Session 4a

Session 4b

Welcoming Remarks

Ladies and gentlemen, dear colleagues:

On behalf of the Præsidium of the Siberian Division of the Academy of Sciences of the USSR, and of the Organizing Committee, I would like to welcome the participants coming to Novosibirsk from 15 different countries for the IFIP Working Conference on Constructing Quality Software.

In our field, this is the first international professional meeting of its kind to be held in this country. It is an honour for a scientific organization to act as host for such a conference, and we have taken part in its preparation with great interest and enthusiasm. We also hope that the decision by IFIP to hold this conference at Novosibirsk reflects, to some extent, a recognition of our modest contribution to the field of programming.

We, as the local organizers, have already gained a great deal simply by having you, distinguished specialists, here in Akademgorodok. The reciprocal benefit will not be achieved automatically, but we sincerely hope that the quality of our technical work at this conference will be on the same level as the quality that we seek to achieve in our software.

"Quality" is not only the middle word in the title of the conference. It is really the heart of the matter, the focus for the most sensitive issues in programming: efficiency and reliability, usefulness and comprehensibility, elegance and logical coherence. That is why it is such a complex subject for logical analysis, and why it remains such an elusive goal in engineering practice. But for these same reasons, it is an extremely pertinent and provocative topic to discuss, however difficult it may be to come to constructive conclusions.

I wish everyone a very pleasant and productive stay during this week, as we now turn to our technical programme.

A. P. Ershov

Constructing Quality Software, P.G. Hibbard/S.A. Schuman (eds.)

TOWARDS RELIABLE REAL-TIME SOFTWARE

Jiří Demner, Jaroslav Král
Institute of Computation Techniques, Prague
Czechoslovakia

This paper gives a brief account of our experience in designing and implementing a real-time software system of significant size, serving to control a machine tool shop with automated stock handling. The shop consists of thirty numerically-controlled machine tools.

The paper deals with the problems encountered in design, project organization and documentation. The methods used allowed us to produce more than 20 000 lines of assembly language in 8 man years (including design), with no conceptual errors and with less than 20 bugs to be removed during testing.

1. INTRODUCTION AND DESIGN OBJECTIVES

In mid-1974, the programmers of the Institute of Computation Techniques (ICT) were confronted with the task of implementing the software for the control system. Prior to that date, there had been no experience with real-time control software at ICT. We were to provide the programs for 30 numerically-controlled machine tools (to be managed by the system) and the software for automatically controlling the stocks and transport of materials. The purpose of the system is to supply all of the machines with materials and tools, using auxiliary stocks if necessary. The system includes input/output places, checkpoints and tool preparation stations. We refer to the whole system as NCS (Numerically Controlled Shop).

The complexity of the software was estimated, quite correctly, to be approximately equivalent to that of a moderate sized compiler.

Due to the situation at ICT, a significant number of good programmers were able to take part in the implementation, but the majority of them could only devote a quarter of their time to this effort. From this, it followed that we should have to form a quite large team, since the work had to be finished in a short period of time.

The situation was further complicated by the fact that, in the first period, we had no computer on which to debug our programs. Moreover, for a variety of reasons, no real-time operating system nor any real-time programming language would be available as a programming tool for this project. So we concluded that there was only one way of successfully implementing this system: careful design, good team organization and very good documentation. At that time, we knew of the works of Mills and of the results achieved at Novosibirsk.

2. PROBLEMS IN DESIGN OF THE SYSTEM

Work on the software for the project was, from the beginning, complicated by three factors: (i) we started our work when most of the hardware subsystems had already been not only designed, but partly constructed; (ii) the system involved a lot of original hardware; (iii) the hardware was supplied by several different groups (realizing various subsystems) and there was, in fact, no leader (or system group) carefully coordinating the work. The software group had therefore to assume the role of the system group. Such a situation was not altogether satisfactory; the absence of overall direction for the project and its implementation caused a lot of difficulties.

Other problems, discussed below, we believe to be rather common to all large real-time systems. In the last year we took part in some similar projects and the difficulties encountered were analogous, although not so severe.

The first problem is communication between people of different specialties. Mutual understanding is the first necessity for cooperation. The difficulty comes from the fact that the thinking habits, symbols, professional jargon and feelings as to what is and is not important are completely different.

There is only one way out: to use natural language as a basis. This way was also deemed preferable because, in this application, control actions could very well be described in ordinary language. The solution seemed to be obvious, but we were surprised how difficult it is for an engineer to describe the function of a set of circuits, comprising thousands of transistors, in a clear and complete way. Moreover if the function is algorithmic in nature, he always wants to use flowcharts which are, as a rule, incomplete and/or inappropriate.

Initially we believed that the problems in this area were caused by failures in overall project coordination. From experience with other projects, however, we now believe the reasons to be deeper. It is not easy to describe one's intentions, with all necessary detail, in a non-algorithmic but clear fashion when using only natural language augmented by occasional symbolic notations, as in professional papers. This requires proper structuring of the problem, dividing it into small subproblems with clearly defined functions and interfaces with other subproblems etc. In other words, it necessitates something like "structured description", which must be used if we want to use "structured programming". This fact has also been pointed out by Domolki and his group.

Another source of resistance was the feeling that we can do nothing unless we use a formal language; natural language doesn't seem "scientific" enough. However, everyday language or the non-algorithmic language of scientific papers (as used, for instance, in comments to algorithms in the Communications of the ACM) can very well be used.

Professional jargons, like the language of switching circuits, flowcharts etc., only help us to design a "structure" having certain properties, but they provide no means for testing whether or not we have realized the desired function. In programming, the proof that a procedure realizes a given function is known as verification. If we use a formal language as the everyday vehicle for thinking, the real objective can easily be forgotten for some time. If we only return to the original intention during the process of bringing the system up ("debugging"), the consequences can be disastrous. We consider this to be the main source of endless debugging and/or failures. We had come to this conclusion by an analysis of the less successful parts (in this respect) of an ALGOL 68 compiler; our experience with real-time software confirmed it. It must be mentioned moreover that in complex systems, aims and subaims must often be changed, as we find out that they cannot be effectively realized on lower levels. This is also the case with structured programming.

As a result, much of the effort went into convincing the hardware people to describe the interface between subsystems in a reasonable way. At the same time we developed the main ideas for the software architecture, for organizing our work and for its documentation. These latter points will be discussed below.

3. ARCHITECTURE OF THE SOFTWARE

The software architecture was based upon the concept of processes. Each process was to be implemented by a subprogram that is not reentrant (which was dictated by the computer hardware). Conceptually, the algorithm for each process is viewed as an indivisible action (with some exceptions - see the notion of alarm). On the machine level the algorithm can be interrupted by a peripheral device, but control always returns to the interrupted algorithm. Any process can require the call (start) of other processes, but this requirement cannot delay the process initiating the call. For every call, the permitted time delay, the conditions under which the call can take place and the actual parameters are specified. Global variables are used for process communication; no wait/restart (P/V) operations are available. In addition one process can kill another, this being used to handle an alarm when the response from a peripheral device fails to come in the required time.

This concept is easily implementable, adequately covers the needs for the system to be produced and allows the work to be divided into subsystems which can be realized almost independently. This in turn makes it possible for a large group of programmers to work on the project. The main drawback is that such a method requires a lot of processor time to verify the conditions for all items (events) in the system queues. In the case discussed the drawback was not important. The details of the software structure will be given in a separate paper (see also Kral, Demner, Moudry (1976)).

The use of conditions (mentioned above) which must be satisfied before the algorithm associated with a process is activated proved to be a very flexible and powerful programming tool. It allows the many complex dependencies in the controlled system to be expressed in a clear fashion.

The design phase took more time than the actual programming. We believe that it would have been better to have devoted even more time to cleaning up the design. The lead programming group was responsible for the design. Most of the problems were caused by the fact that programmers entered the overall project too late.

4. ORGANIZATION OF THE WORK

In project organization, two interdependent problems must be solved: (i) the organization of the team; and (ii) the procedure for passing from the specification of a program to its implementation.

For the organization of the team, we adopted the principle of "lead pairs" (Mills). The design group is headed by the first programmer and his "second in command". This group leads the whole project, is responsible for the overall design, specifies the functions of software subsystems to be realized by other programming groups, coordinates changes of interfaces if necessary and programs the central algorithms. The design group is supported by several programming groups. One of these, the system group, is responsible for the integration of the system into the standard operating system and/or for the use and modification of standard programs such as drivers. Programming groups receive their tasks from the design group, implement the corresponding programs and give them back to the design group which, with the help of the service group, sees that the program realizes the required function. The design group then integrates the program into the system.

Aside from its own local variables, each programming group may only make use of globals specified as arguments or results, and of explicitly passed formal parameters. In addition, there are conventions for the use of identifiers and some instructions and "programming tricks" are simply forbidden. Moreover, every program must be well commented (see below).

The service group maintains the documentation, coordinates access to the computer (keypunching, help in running programs) and provides the necessary drawings, typing etc.

Each group is headed by a lead pair, with tasks like those described by Mills. Such an organization is especially appropriate when the team consists of many good programmers. In our case there were at some times more than 15 people involved in the project. This organization allows personal preferences to be taken into account, and it could well be used for even larger projects (since the programming groups could have their own, internal hierarchy). The crucial problem is to identify subproblems which leave each programmer with enough room for creative work. The requirements on the design group can at times be too high, but it seems that this could be avoided by careful planning of the work.

5. PROJECT DOCUMENTATION

Several different forms of documentation were adopted for this project:

(1) Newsletters. They contained the main points of the project definition, description of the computers, prescribed or recommended programming practices, standards for program documentation (comments),

description of the tasks of the programming groups, user manuals (for the system user) etc. Some of these newsletters were used as final documentation.

(2) Card Indexes. The card indexes were used to keep cross references (unfortunately we could not use a computer for this purpose), latest functions and/or modifications etc. Two different indexes were kept:

(2a) Large Card Index. This index primarily contained the description of the processes and/or supervisory programs, as well as of the main data structures. Each card contained:

(a) the name of the process, program or data structure;
(b) a detailed description of its purpose and function;
(c) specification of parameters and their structure;
(d) usage of globals (if any) and their purpose;
(e) cross references (usage and purpose);
(f) auxiliary information.

(2b) Small Card Index. This latter primarily contained the description of common (global) variables, their purpose and cross references. These card indexes could be kept in a computer, but it is advisable that they be created during the design phase, at the time when no program is yet written. Careful updating is of utmost importance. The card indexes allow easy changes and provide good documentation of the subtasks of the programming groups.

(3) Programs. Comments within the programs contained:

(a) a description of the function of the program units (similar to that provided by the Large Card Index), not only for the main program but also for the local routines, data structures, etc.;

(b) a description of the algorithm, in an ad hoc high-level language similar to PASCAL or to a subset of ALGOL 68, even though the programs were in assembly language.

6. RESULTS AND CONCLUSION

The methods described in this paper made it possible to write the control software in one year, with a team of more than fifteen people. Each programmer participated in the project in addition to his other duties, devoting one quarter of his time to it on the average. The only exception was the lead pair of the design group. The whole system works satisfactorily. There were only 18 errors which had to be removed by the usual debugging procedures; almost half of these were in the disc driver which was written in a hurry. During use of the system only one minor software error was discovered. These results were obtained in spite of the fact that, because of gaps in the hardware design, some parts of the software had to be modified after the fact. The usual situation was that the required modification was carried out, with no errors, in one or two days. These modifications were non-trivial, since they involved mutually dependent changes in several places.

We believe that the approach adopted here is applicable to substantially larger projects, there being no limitation on the size of the programming groups which can again be hierarchically organized like the team discussed above. This organization can be adapted to the personal likes and dislikes of the team members, as well as to their individual abilities.

Such an approach also has some weak points. Its success is highly dependent on the qualities of the lead pair in the design group, especially the chief programmer. Moreover it requires a high degree of discipline on his part. It sometimes seems to him that it would be both better and quicker to implement the designed algorithms directly, without any help and without so much time-consuming and disagreeable documentation work. This leads very quickly, however, to a situation where the chief programmer is overburdened, making modifications very difficult indeed.

We do not think the approach described here is completely new. Such a team structure is probably present implicitly, i.e., without any explicit organizational plan, in many programming efforts. Nevertheless, we found nowhere in the literature a description of the particular combination of methods utilized in this project.

We do not think that the conditions for the approach discussed would be present in all situations. Our situation can be characterized as follows.

(i) The project seemed to be too complicated to use a single "chief programmer" team.

(ii) The project was headed by a very good main programmer, who was able to make right decisions in almost all programming situations, and who was able to write main parts of the resulting software system.

It is likely that in still larger projects, and/or if the abilities of the main programmer were weaker, the concept of the "head committee" led by a system designer would be used (see Hammersley, 1976).

REFERENCES

Baker, F. T. and Mills, H. D. (1973). Chief programmer teams. Datamation 19, pp. 58-61.

Ershov, A. P. Private communications.

Domolki, B. Private communication.

Aron, J. D. The super-programmer project, in Software Engineering Techniques, Buxton, J. N. and Randell, B. (eds.).

Demner, J. (1975). A model of the software team effective organization (written in Czech). Acta Polytechnica, IV, Sci. Conf., pp. 71-81.

Kral, J., Demner, J. and Moudry, J. (1976). Real time software (in Czech). Proc. SOFSEM Conference, VVS OSN, Bratislava, pp. 175-193.

Hammersley, P. (1976). Team organization in integrated software projects, in ECI Conference Proceedings, Lecture Notes on Computer Science 4, Springer V., pp. 263-275.

Demner and Král : Discussion

Kurki-Suonio: It seems to me that many of the problems in project documentation were caused by the low level of the tools you were using. A project of that size already justifies the development of better tools, at least a machine-oriented high-level language. Would you care to comment on this?

Král: An assembler seemed to be the only possibility for us. You see, I think that the main problem in this area, at least to me and to the people I know, is that the function, the intention, must be well formulated. In this respect no programming language can help you. You can avoid for example the use of an assembler, but all these other things must be written or supported in some way. You can write programs in some integrated programming system (like the one being constructed in Bratislava, which will also be reported on here), but documentation must be done in some way like the one I've described. I mean function specification, interface description, and so on.

Kurki-Suonio: In a project of this size my experience is that the development of tools speeds up the project so much that it doesn't cost any more to develop those tools.

Král: We decided to use assembly language partly because we were unable to develop tools in time and we had no experience to be able to design the tools properly. Wrong tools can be worse than none. I want to say that in this case we spent half of the time in refinement of functions, interfaces, etc. We think that even that was too short a period. The coding took only half of the time. Note also that we have used some abstract tools in assembly programming, although we didn't freeze them in a high-level language.

Nehmer: You have made a statement about program errors found within your system. If I remember correctly, you said that you found 20 errors within 20,000 lines of assembly code. Do you feel that it is good enough to stay with these low-level development tools for a project of the size you described?

Král: I don't think that. I only wanted to show that we were able to produce a small number of bugs. We were obliged to use an assembler. I think that our efforts to avoid bugs in such systems were successful and could be used in high-level languages as well.

Ershov: You say that about 20,000 lines of code were written in two years by a team of 15 people. Using the concept of man-months this does not look impressive. I would like to know how many of these 15 people actually wrote the code.

Král: The situation is that during the first year we were involved in the project refinement. The coding started the second year and there were about 15 people involved, including secretaries, people in data preparation, etc. Coding took three to four man years. During this period we had to rewrite substantial parts of the system due to some mistakes in the hardware. And these modifications were made, as a rule, without errors. It is important not to count only the lines which were written, but also the ones which were not written due to good design. The estimates made by a software house were 60,000 lines and more than 20 man years.

Correll: You have stressed that the quality of the product depends critically on the main programmer. What happens if the main programmer leaves the project for any reason?

Král: I've said that we used the concept of lead pairs: main programmer and second in command. The second in command knows all the details and he also writes some programs, so it would be possible to continue the work if the main programmer left the project. It is true that there would be some difficulties in that case. We estimate that the delay would be approximately two or three months.

Correll: One must have some communication in addition to newsletters, natural language descriptions and so on.

Král: The members of each group were in personal contact all the time. I cannot imagine what delay would be caused if the contacts were missing.

Dewar: It would appear that the competence of the people involved is much more a determining factor than the organizational approach which is adopted. Your suggestion that there is some sort of trade-off does not seem to be justified by any empirical evidence.

Meyer: You mentioned the loss of programming creativity in highly structured team organization. This seems to me to be a very serious problem. I think that most of what Mills has written about programming team organization can be interpreted as a way to justify, by scientific or pseudo-scientific arguments, the classical hierarchical organization of enterprises; that is, to disguise political and sociological problems as scientific problems. My question is whether you know of any team organization which you think would lead to a highly structured programming product, without destroying that individual creativity which is, I think, a big part of the pleasure in programming?

Král: In this approach we were able to make room for creativity because the groups were good. We separated the program into pieces and gave each group scope for creative work. It's not impossible, but it is very difficult to do in general. It is a necessary condition, however, in order to interest good programmers in the work.

Turski: First of all, I'm not so sure that I'm in support of programmers' creativity. In Polish we have an expression "cheerful creativity", which describes a system that is full of incoherent elements. I'm always under the impression that the major objective of managers of team work is to curb the individual programmer's creativity. It leads the product astray when every programmer builds a temple to his creativity, forgetting the base objectives he is to fulfil. Well, it's a necessity, because of a psychological pressure, that we give everyone an opportunity to show his creativity in the work. But I don't believe it is a sensible policy to encourage creativity in team programmers' work during the implementation stage. Creativity for creativity's sake is just wrong. [👍 and 👎, concurrently.]

Constructing Quality Software, P.G. Hibbard/S.A. Schuman (eds.)

Computerized Safeguarding of Nuclear Power Plants: A Case for Reliable Software

J. Nehmer
Kernforschungszentrum Karlsruhe
Institut für Datenverarbeitung in der Technik
Postfach 3640, D-7500 Karlsruhe, Germany

G. Goos
Universität Karlsruhe
Institut für Informatik II
Postfach 6380, D-7500 Karlsruhe, Germany

Abstract: Using a computer for safeguarding the operation of a nuclear power plant requires extreme reliability of both hardware and software. We discuss how the desired software reliability may be achieved using techniques which are presently available. It appears that conventional software is of little help because of its unsystematic growth and unmanageable complexity. Dedicated systems, which are specifically tailored, are much less complex. A possible structure for a reliable, dedicated system is explained and the necessary language elements are discussed.

1. The Safeguarding Problem

The correctness and reliability of software is a key problem in safety-oriented computer applications such as traffic control, plant operation or air traffic control. In this paper we discuss the experience gained during the design of a computer system for safeguarding the operation of a nuclear power plant. The nuclear reactor is a sodium-cooled fast breeder. A prototype of this reactor has been under construction in Germany since 1974.

The nuclear process takes place within the reactor core which consists of 205 nuclear fuel elements. The primary cooling circulation, containing pure sodium as the coolant, cools each fuel element individually. This is achieved by channeling the main cooling stream through 205 tubes, each surrounding one particular fuel element. The operation of the reactor is safeguarded by controlling the temperature of the coolent. If the temperature exceeds some upper boundary, the reactor is shut down.

The temperature is controlled in two different ways in order to increase the reliability. First, the temperature of the main sodium stream is controlled by a conventional analog controller, called the global safeguard system. However, local disturbances of fuel elements may cause damage even before the disturbance is detected by the global safeguard system (at least our current theoretical insights do not exclude this case). In order to reduce the risk of a reactor accident caused by local disturbances, a second safeguard method is employed. In this method the sodium temperature at the exhaust port of each fuel element is monitored individually. An upper limit for the temperature of each fuel element is calculated using the average temperatures of the actual measure and specific parameters which are derived from fuel element characteristics. This can only be performed by a computer. Its basic task is to measure the temperature at the coolant exhaust port of each fuel element periodically every 800 msec. After comparing the temperature of each fuel element with an individual upper limit a binary signal is computed. A positive signal means that no abnormal conditions have been detected at the 205 fuel elements. It will enable the reactor to continue operation for the next period of 800 msec. In case of a negative or missing signal the reactor has to be shut down.

The following additional constraints must be met:

(1) The computer must shut down the reactor in _all_ cases of abnormal fuel element temperature. This is a _safety_ constraint. The probability that--due to computer malfunctions--a dangerous reactor condition will remain undetected should be as close to zero as possible. (For technical reasons it will never exactly be zero.)

(2) The tolerable rate of reactor shutdowns caused by a nonoperational or malfunctioning computer system is less than one in 6000 hours (about nine months). This is an _availability_ constraint.

Both constraints require stringent MTBF-standards to be met by the hardware equipment as well as the reliable functioning of the software under all relevant operational conditions. A technical supervisory board (TÜV), an independent agency, has to approve the system before it can start operation. This is the same organization which periodically checks safety requirements on cars, airplanes and all types of public transport. The case is particularly important because this is the first time that a computer system is to be submitted to such public scrutiny. Therefore, the case may set a crucial precedent for similar computer applications.

In this paper our primary objective is to give an example of a computer application where software reliability is of utmost importance. All theoretical methods for achieving reliability are practically relevant here. We also discuss why a "traditional" solution based on the standard software of a computer manufacturer did not pass the technical supervisory board. As an alternative we discuss how to solve the problem by a _dedicated approach_. It utilizes only tools specifically tailored for this application. Additional complexity that could be caused by properties of the software required for other purposes is removed.

Note that the reliability of the solution has to be shown not only to the experts but also to the public. In each solution of the problem this non-technical constraint has to be carefully considered.

2. Computer Configuration and Software Functions

From theoretical estimates [13] it is known that the availability and safety requirements can only be met by providing a certain redundancy at the hardware level. As a suitable hardware configuration a symmetric 3-computer system was chosen (fig. 1). To avoid a reactor shutdown in case of a broken thermocouple, each computer is connected to the fuel elements of the reactor core via a separate set of thermocouples.

The program flow within each computer is synchronized by an external timer (also redundantly constructed), which provides five timing signals $T_0 \ldots T_4$. They mark relevant execution stages within the 800 msec. safeguard cycle. At each stage the three computers must arrive at a well defined state of computation. The three computers are operating

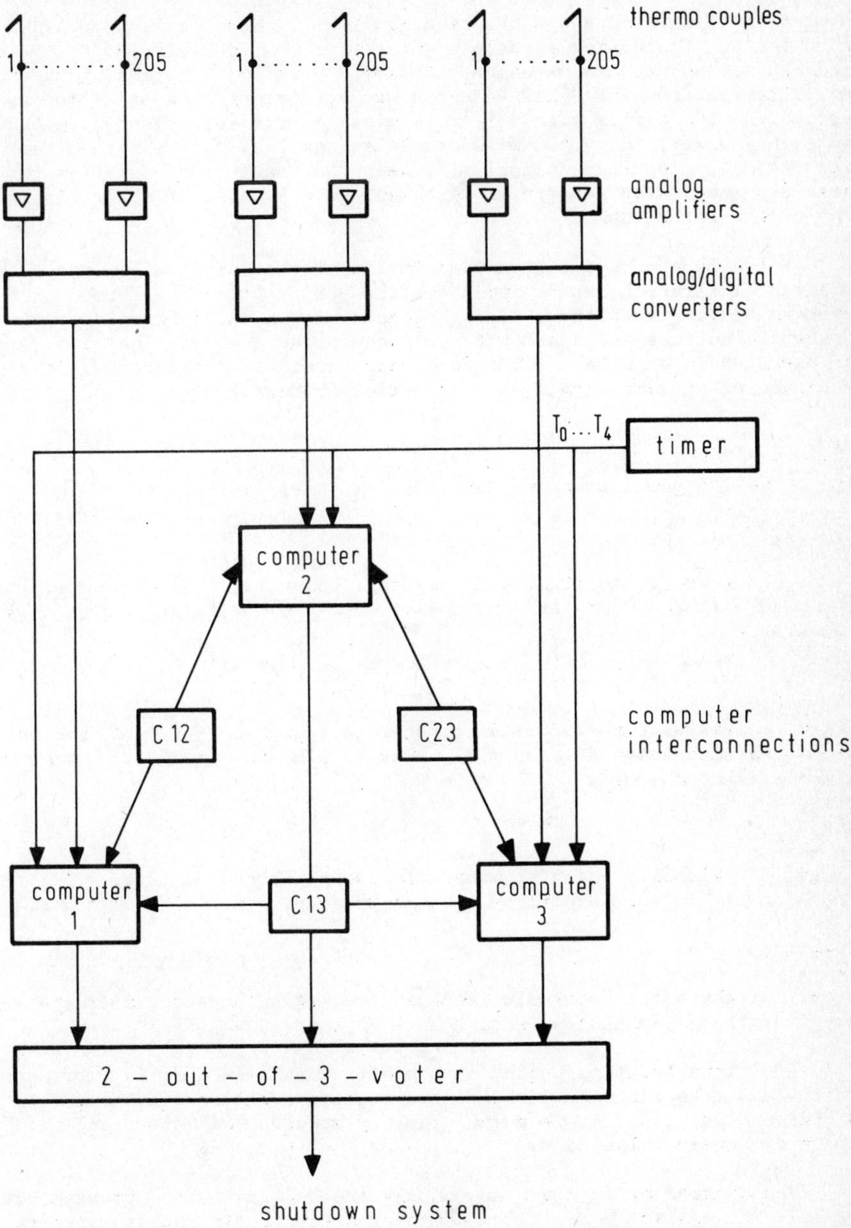

Fig.1 Hardware configuration of the safeguard system

symmetrically, running the identical software. Nevertheless program execution <u>between</u> the timing signals might differ considerably due to the varying sets of input data on which they are operating. The individual votes of all three computers will be output to a 2-out-of-3 majority voter after arrival of the timing signal T_4. (A missing vote is treated as a negative vote.) Finally, the voter will create a signal as the result of the majority voting. A positive signal will keep the reactor in operation for the next 800 msec. The reactor will be shut down by a negative or missing signal at the voter input.

Below is a more detailed description of the software, based on the diagram of figure 2, which indicates the actions to be performed by the program between successive timing signals within one safeguard cycle. If possible, actions which are not assigned to the same vertical line should be executed in parallel. Therefore each vertical line describes the sequence of actions within one sequential process.

$T_0 \ldots T_1$:

Input the 205 temperature measures (A).

$T_1 \ldots T_2$:

Output of measures to righthand computer (output 1). Input of measures from the lefthand computer (input 1). Gauge, plausibility check of own measures (B).

$T_2 \ldots T_3$:

Output of measures to lefthand computer (output 2). Input of measures from righthand computer (input 2). Gauge, plausibility check of measures from lefthand computer (C).

$T_3 \ldots T_4$:

Gauge, plausibility check of measures from righthand computer (D). Calculation of the vote according to some underlying decision criteria (E).

$T_4 \ldots T_0$:

Output of the vote. Periodic computer checks, such as register check, check of the I/O-channels, etc.

Additionally, time consuming computer checks such as a memory check which cannot be finished within one safeguard cycle, are performed in a background process. It is a low priority process which runs only if there is nothing else to do.

The diagram of figure 2 shows only the "steady state" program activities. The restart of a failed computer after repair and its integration into the system without disturbing the operation of the remaining two computers requires a restart procedure not shown in the diagram. It is also assumed that the whole program system is resident in the main storage.

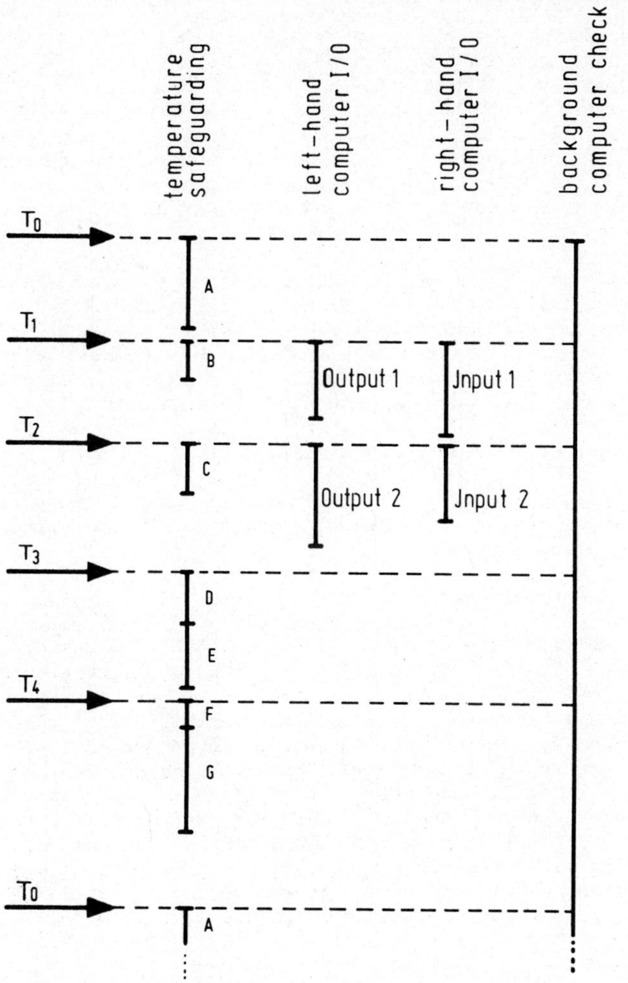

A temperature input
B gauge, plausibility checks of own measures
C gauge, plausibility checks of measures from right hand computer
D gauge, plausibility checks of measures from left hand computer
E calculation of vote
F vote output
G periodic computer checks

Fig. 2 Program activities over a period of 800 msec

3. The Validation Strategy and its Impact on the Software Design

The design of a system which solves our problem depends critically on how we are to validate that the safety and availability constraints are met, i.e., show that the system behaves reliably. The whole software construction process must be directed toward this goal. Consequently the choice of an appropriate validation strategy was discussed at the very beginning of the project.

As an obvious first step, suggested by the fault-tolerant three-computer configuration, one could ask for distinct implementations by independent programmer teams for each computer (cf. also [17]). Since it is highly improbably that two or even three programs contain the same logical or clerical error, the probability is increased that the system functions correctly. Further discussion showed that the increase in reliability is not worth the increased costs of constructing and maintaining three systems. Therefore this idea was not pursued further.

Theoretically a rigorous formal proof of the correctness of the software would be the ideal validation technique. In practice, however, this idea was rejected for several reasons.

To begin with, it was impossible to obtain a complete formal specification of the problem. Besides the usual technical difficulties, this impossibility is a natural consequence of the unsatisfiable requirement that the system behave safely under <u>all</u> conditions, even in the case of hardware malfunctions. This requirement is very common in most real time applications. It distinguishes them from purely mathematical problems in which "correctness" and "reliability" of a solution have almost the same meaning. We consider here applications for which the software is reliable, if it will not only perform its intended task correctly but also respond "appropriately" to hardware malfunctions. In our case the intended task of the computer consists of safeguarding the temperature of the fuel elements. However, large parts of the software are devoted to handling all kinds of hardware failures. These software extensions can only gradually approach the stated safety and availability constraints because a complete specification of the responses to all--basically unpredictable--hardware failures appears impossible at this time.

Even if we had a formal specification we could only partially solve our problem because it would have been impossible to demonstrate the correctness of the specification. Through verification only implementation errors are caught. It is often overlooked that verification is unable to prevent errors contained in the specification on which the program is based. It has been estimated that roughly 50% of all logical program errors fall into this class and hence, are not detected by verification methods.

Similarly, a complete validation requires that we demonstrate not only the absence of design errors but also the absence of all kinds of clerical errors which may have occurred during compiling, copying or loading of the system.

At the time when the validation strategy had to be decided upon (1975) the most serious reason against formal verification was that no one could convincingly demonstrate that he could correctly verify a system of the size which we had to consider. To get the verification process correct, whether by hand or by computer, still seems to us (even in 1977) to be the most serious problem for applying verification methods in practice [10].

As a result we finally decided to validate the system by testing. An exhaustive test is nearly as difficult as a complete proof of a program. Therefore we were focusing our attention on the more realistic case of a partial program validation in order to avoid unpredictable delays of the project. Testing offers some advantages for partial program validation over verification. First, it is a well tried technique which has been successfully applied to large programs. In addition to this, testing provides for gradual reduction of program errors when increasing the number of significant test cases.

The use of testing as the basic validation technique does not automatically exclude verification. On the contrary, some properties of the system, e.g., the absence of time dependent errors cannot be tested; they must be proven. More generally, all measures which serve to reduce the number of test cases, such as moving checks from run-time to compile-time, etc., are of interest. We return to this point in section 5.

The decision for testing results in three general software requirements:

- Since test case generation still requires manual intervention, its success depends strongly on the readability and understandability of the code. Therefore it was deemed necessary to write the software in a high-level language. The language should restrict programming to "safe" constructs. This would also reduce the number of test cases. A set of guidelines should assist in structuring, implementing and documenting the software, in the hope of producing in a well structured, easy to understand program system [18]. Notice, however, that the use of a high-level language raises the problem of compiler validation.

- Classical test techniques such as path analysis [9] assume reproducible program behavior and demand the whole software to be free of time dependent errors caused by interactions between parallel processes [1]. As mentioned before, the absence of time dependent program errors has necessarily to be checked by verification.

- A modular program structure was considered essential for a systematic testing of the whole system. Since modules are the components to be tested separately from one another, they should be small for easier understanding. Furthermore, interacting modules should have simple interfaces in order to facilitate simple test environments.

Even if we had formally verified the system, this proof would have been believable to computer scientists, but not necessarily to the technical supervisory board and the public. The members of this board are usually engineers. The traditional validation method in civil and electrical engineering is testing. Naturally these engineers believe more in the value of the methods that they have successfully applied over the years than in such "strange" methods as verification. In public opinion, testing is also the more straightforward approach for system validation.

Right now it seems nearly impossible to convince people that mathematical formulas are a better insurance against computer malfunctions than "to run it and see what happens."

4. The Traditional Software Approach

"Normal" process control applications are usually solved by employing the software development tools and basic support software, such as a real-time operating system, available from computer manufacturers. This approach is referred to as the traditional approach and was tried first.

In the case considered, a real-time operating system and a macro assembler were available. The manufacturer also offered FORTRAN but preference was given to the macro assembler to avoid validating a compiler. Furthermore, with respect to validation it was felt that FORTRAN did not add essential improvements to the assembler solution.

In the attempt to meet the design goals, the traditional approach was rejected for the following reasons:

(1) Modularization was obviously not one of the primary design goals of the operating system. It seemed to be impossible to break the system into smaller units with simple, well-defined interfaces, which could be tested independently of one another. Furthermore, since it seemed a hopeless task to get a precise picture of the interactions between software components, no assumption about the absence of time dependent errors could be justified by inspection of the operating system.

(2) The second reason was insufficient documentation of the operating system. Combined with inadequate modularization, this reduced the chance of fully understanding the effect (and, in particular, the side effects) of every instruction of the operating system. The use of an assembly language as the implementation language greatly contributed to the non-readability and non-understandability of the code.

(3) The third reason concerned the layout of the operating system interface. Missing generality in the function definitions, too many parameters and the non-homogenous growth of the system resulted in a highly complex pattern of use. The development of clearly structured application software on that base was virtually impossible.

By way of explanation, we consider a call to the operating system in more detail. It requires five different types of parameters:

a. the name of a function
b. a timing parameter, specifying the timing of the execution of the function (for example, a duration of 5 seconds with a period of 10 minutes, etc.)
c. type of synchronization applied to signal the end of the function execution (implicit, explicit by special synchronization primitives)
d. a chaining parameter, specifying a chain of successive calls to the operating system
e. the actual parameters of the function itself.

An analysis showed that parameter types b, c and d were special synchronization mechanisms extending each call to the operating system. Since the semaphore functions P and V were also contained in the repertoire of the operating system, four synchronization mechanisms were offered all together. To make matters worse, the synchronization mechanisms could not be used freely. Their use depended on the way functions had been implemented in the operating system and the actual system configuration. As a consequence, to every function description in the users' manual was appended a list of exceptions explaining under what circumstances certain values could not be assigned to certain parameters. Thus, the users' manual (describing only the interface to the operating system but not its internal structure) consisted of 400 pages.

In our opinion this amount of information exceeds by far the size which is manageable and therefore understandable. As a consequence, the correct use of the operating system could not be assured.

It is interesting to notice that for the same reasons, namely

- overparameterization,
- nonhomogenous growth of a system not intentionally based on an open-ended design and
- unsystematic, voluminous descriptions,

some new language definitions would also be adequate for the application under discussion [21].

It is an interesting question whether we would have arrived at the same conclusion if the existing standard software from a manufacturer was well structured, well documented and reliable. First we think that this is a rather hypothetical case. It will probably not happen for operating systems to come within the next few years. Even in the case that an operating system with these properties were available <u>now</u>, we doubt that it would be approved by the technical supervisory board. Many people have reservations about general purpose systems which, in addition to the problem in question, also support an unforeseeable number of other applications. They fear that such universality may have ramifications which can cause trouble in extreme situations. The argument that the most reliable solution is a system which exactly performs the desired functions (but nothing more) is difficult to refute.

5. The Dedicated Software Approach

As an alternative to the traditional approach we propose to tailor the whole system to the specific needs of the particular application. We avoid the use of existing standard software such as operating systems, utility packages and software development tools, because they usually do not meet the particular requirements of the applications. Specific construction tools are developed instead.

Aside from the other advantages mentioned, the size of the resulting system can be reduced considerably when compared to the traditional approach. This should eventually lead to a corresponding reduction of the validation efforts. The most important property of a dedicated system is of a non-technical nature. In the course of the project it became apparent that a suspicious public can never be satisfied by an approach which merely convinces (and is understood by) a few experts. The public would only trust a system if the construction principles applied were plausible to non-computer experts, too. We believe that this social constraint rules out the use of general purpose operating systems in applications like the one discussed here.

Constructing a dedicated system does not necessarily mean developing every new application from scratch. A library of elementary system modules could serve as a basis for the construction of tailored software systems instead.

In addition to the general requirements listed in section 3, the following guidelines were put forward.

- Use of hierarchical program structure [3, 7] for reduction of program complexity. It also helps to reduce the probability of global deadlocks.

- Shift of as many checks as possible from run time to compile time. They should include such steps as: checking the interfaces between modules, checking on potential storage overflow, detection of potential deadlocks, etc. In particular, synchronization should be expressed by appropriate language constructs to avoid time dependent errors caused by wrong or missing synchronization and to assist the compiler in their detection.

- An integrated language approach should be applied to the total software, i.e., the same language should be used throughout the implementation of the whole system.

A possible solution of our problem following these guidelines is presented in the next section.

6. A System Structure Based on the Dedicated Approach

We describe here the overall design of a dedicated system for the reactor safeguard problem. Such a design is presently being implemented by industry. Our presentation is purely descriptive and mainly serves as a basis for the language and system requirements explained in the following section. We do not claim "completeness" of these requirements with respect to the class of real-time applications considered.

The whole program system is subdivided into three layers (figure 3). The interfaces between these layers can be thought of as abstract machines defined by a set of functions implemented on the lower level abstract macine. The three layers are termed application program (layer 2), kernel (layer 1) and hardware adaption (layer 0).

The structure of the application program (layer 2) is shown in figure 4. It was implemented by direct transformation of the diagram of figure 4 into appropriate software structuring elements (available at this level of abstraction) like processes and monitors.

To systematically prevent time dependent errors, monitors [8] were used for the synchronization of internal processes. A different synchronization mechanism is assumed for handling external asynchronous alarms, such as clocking alarms, etc. The virtual timer process in figure 4 uses this mechanism in order to synchronize itself to the timer signals $T_0 \ldots T_4$.

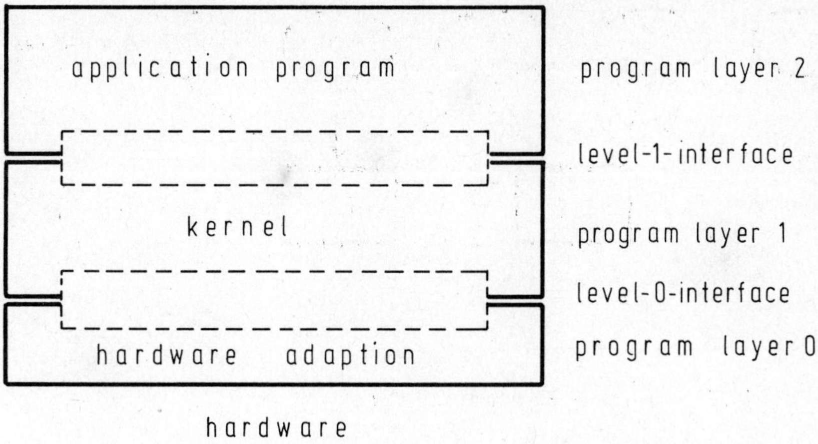

Fig. 3 Overall system structure

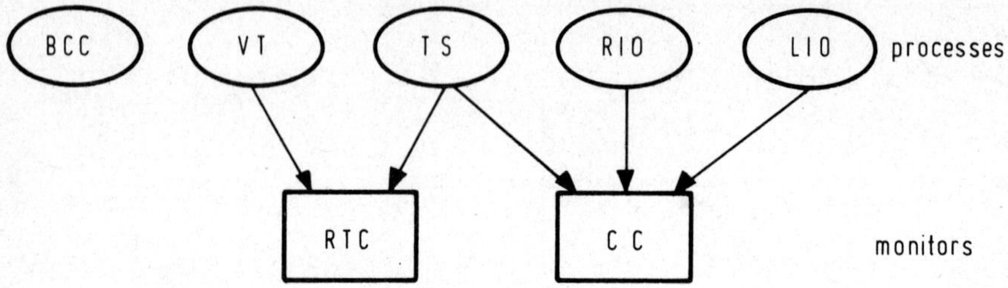

BCC background computer check

VT virtual timer

TS temperature safeguarding

RIO right-hand I/O

LIO left-hand I/O

RTC real time control

CC communication control

Fig. 4 Structure of program layer 2

A low level I/O-mechanism is needed for supporting buffered input/output on physical devices and channels in a uniform way.

Exceptional conditions detected during program execution, such as hardware failures (e.g., parity check, unknown operation code), software failures detected by hardware (e.g., division by zero, protection violation) and software failures detected by software (e.g., violation of the specified range of an array subscript) should be signaled to the program module in which the exception was found.

The kernel (program layer 1) implements a fixed number of processes and provides such functions as process management functions, synchronization functions, I/O functions and exception handling at the level-1-interface, as used by the application program. The kernel is constructed upon a virtual machine which was developed by generalizing common principles from mini- and microcomputer architecture. This will provide for high portability.

The purpose of the hardware adaption (program layer 0) is to adapt the virtual machine defined by the level-0-interface to the actual hardware of a specific target machine. We estimate the size of this layer to be less than 500 machine instructions.

7. Language and System Requirements

We discuss here features which go beyond the capabilities of the sequential part of common high-level languages such as ALGOL 68 and PASCAL.

On the application level (program layer 2) the following language features are required. They address specific problems of parallel processing, input/output and exception handling.

a) Parallel and Real Time Processing

Four types of mechanisms are desirable:

- The usual functions for high level scheduling of a process such as start, stop, continue, terminate are mandatory.
- Additionally we need functions for low level scheduling, especially the ability to assign priorities to processes in order to meet specific response time requirements [19].
- For synchronizing internal processes the monitor concept [8] has been found most appropriate. Compared to more primitive synchronization tools such as semaphores, monitors reduce the potential chance of time dependent errors and increase the readability of programs.
- A special synchronization mechanism should assist in handling external, asynchronous alarms such as clocking alarms, upper bound temperature alarms, etc. These are representative of a class of asynchronous interrupts specific to real-time applications. Similarly to the attention key of a terminal, but in contrast to I/O-interrupts, these external alarms are virtually unexpected. Such alarms may be very frequent. Therefore a more efficient synchronization tool such as private semaphores is necessary. In order to avoid misuse of this primitive

concept, P-operations should be allowed only through a "safe" language construction. The corresponding V-operations are issued by the underlying abstract machine in response to the occurrence of external alarms.

ALGOL 68 does not contain monitors, and synchronization must be described by semaphores. Therefore, ALGOL 68 does not supply the appropriate language level for our application. CONCURRENT PASCAL solves this problem but does not contain semaphores for handling external alarms.

Notice that in most real-time applications people argue for the need of functions for the creation and deletion of processes. We could not find any case where these features are actually needed. It is our strong feeling that this does not reflect a real requirement in real-time applications, but rather a lack of abstraction in the programming methods used.

b) Input/Output

It should be possible to perform, in an uniform and machine independent way, direct operations on different types of physical devices and channels.

This could be achieved by the definition of generalized classes of I/O-devices with associated operations. The concept of abstract data types seems to be the appropriate mechanism to make the functions available at the interfaces between program layers.

c) Exception Handling

For handling exceptional situations, a mechanism to propagate exceptions from "inner" to "outer" modules is required to handle the case of an inner module being unable to handle the exception [16].

The application level leads to the following functions at the level-1-interface:

- process management functions,
  such as start, stop, continue, terminate,

- process synchronization functions,
  such as P, V, wait, signal,

- functions for logical i/o,
  such as read, work, status, control,

- exception handling functions,
  such as on_exception, off_exception [15].

These functions usually form the innermost layer of an operating system, referred to as the kernel.

In general, the language level for describing the kernel should be simpler than the language level for the application program. In particular, the abstract notion of processes and the associated synchronization mechanisms cannot be used within the kernel. In order to use the language for programming the whole kernel efficiently, the requirements for the underlying virtual machine should essentially correspond to the functional power of present day computers. This will ensure that very little software remains to be written in machine dependent languages.

Figure 5 shows the modular and hierarchical structure of the kernel (program layer 1). The four modules provide the primitives upon which the functions of the level-1-interface are constructed [14, 15]. They can be construed as components of a system library, which are only included in an actual implementation if needed.

The same language can be used for writing program layers 1 and 2 if it provides semantic extensibility comparable to EUCLID and BALG [5]. Such a mechanism in the programming language would allow the use of pre-defined functions and data types (including abstract data types) in one layer while their semantics are derived from the implementation within the lower layer. The split between specification and implementation parts of a program in LIS [12] provides similar features.

8. Conclusion

The main purpose of the paper was to show a practical case where software reliability is of utmost importance. We also discussed why the choice of construction and validation techniques not only has to satisfy a few experts but also has to convince a skeptical public. For this reason the dedicated approach, based on tailoring the software to the specific needs of the application, was considered most promising.

The software validation will proceed in four stages [6]:

- Static program and data flow analysis with development of program graphs on the basis of modules,

- Module test based on appropriate test case selection derived from the program graphs,

- Partial system test applied to one of the three target computers,

- Integrated system test applied to the three-computer system.

An open question remains about the validation of the compiler and other support software used to generate the final system generation (such as the linker, load module generator, etc.). In the safeguard application the size of the compiler and associated development tools was estimated to be roughly four times as large as the actual application. It will be an expensive undertaking to reach the stage where the software construction tools can be used reliably. But the increase in reliability will certainly justify the enormous initial effort.

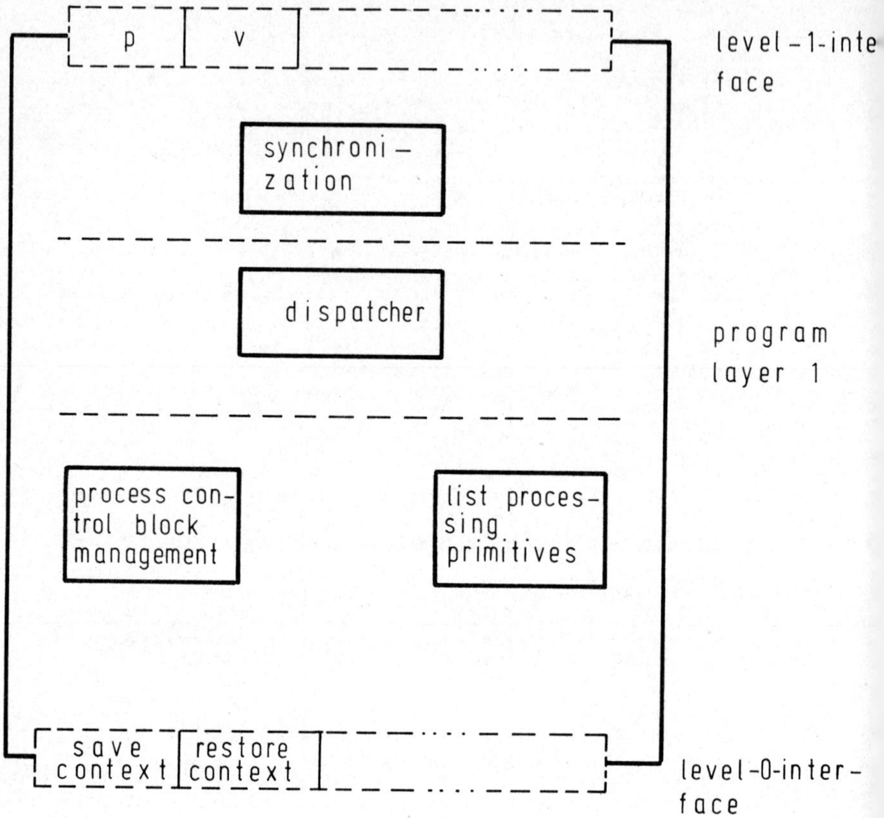

Fig. 5 Internal structure of the program layer 1

References:

[1] P. Brinch Hansen:
Operating System Principles
Prentice Hall, Englewood Cliffs (NY) 1973

[2] P. Brinch Hansen:
Concurrent PASCAL Report, Information Science,
California Institute of Technology, July 1975

[3] O. J. Dahl:
Hierarchical Program Structures in: Structured Programming
Academic Press, New York 1972

[4] W. Floh:
Sicherheitstechnische Forderungen an Prozessrechner
im Reaktorschutz
Atomwirtschaft, 223-226 (1972)

[5] G. Goos:
Einige Eigenschaften der Programmiersprache BALG
Informatik-Fachberichte 1, 90-100 (1976)

[6] W. Geiger, U. Voges:
Eine Prüfstrategie für sicherheitsrelevante
Prozessrechner-Software
Informatik-Fachberichte 7, 479/488 (1977)

[7] A. N. Habermann, L. Flon, L. Cooprider:
Modularization and Hierarchy in a Family of Operating Systems
CACM 19, 266-272 (1976)

[8] C. A. R. Hoare:
Monitors: An Operating System Structuring Concept
CACM 17, 549-557 (1974)

[9] J. C. Huang:
An Approach to Program Testing
ACM Comp. Survey 7, 113-128 (1975)

[10] S. L. Hantler, J. C. King:
An Introduction to Proving the Correctness of Programs
ACM Computing Surveys 8, 331-354 (1976)

[11] W. C. Hetzel:
Program Test Methods
Prentice Hall, Englewood Cliffs, New Jersey 1972

[12] J. D. Ichbiah et al.:
The System Implementation Language LIS,
Reference Manual CII, 4549 E/EN, July 1975

[13] U. Jüngst, H. Werner:
Unverfügbarkeit und Zuverlässigkeit von BESSY
Atomwirtschaft, 610-614 (1975)

[14] J. Nehmer:
Dispatcher Primitives for the Construction of Operating System Kernels
Acta Informatica 5, 237-255 (1975)

[15] J. Nehmer:
Betriebssysteme für Kleinrechner
Angewandte Informatik 1, 1-14 (1977)

[16] D. L. Parnas:
Response to Detected Errors in Well-Structured Programs
Dept. of Computer Science, Carnegie-Mellon University 1972

[17] B. Randell:
System Structure for Software Fault Tolerance
IEEE Trans. on Software Engineering, 220-232 (1975)

[18] U. Voges:
Aspects of Design, Test and Validation of the Software for a Computerized Reactor Protection System
2nd International Conference on Software Engineering, San Francisco (Oct. 1976)

[19] N. Wirth:
Towards a Discipline of Real Time Programming
ACM Conference on Language Design for Reliable Software
Raleigh, North Carolina, March 1977

[20] Series of papers on the Special Issue:
Software Testing
IEEE Transactions on Software Engineering, 194-231 (1976)

[21] Draft Proposed ANS FORTRAN
Sigplan Notices 11, No. 3 (1976)

Nehmer and Goos : Discussion

Schuman: Considering the sensitivity of this application, can you elaborate upon the process of "convincing the public"? What does the public "need to know" and how do they express that they are satisfied? [☺]

Nehmer: In this context, the public is represented by a German government organization, the Technical Supervisory Committee. This committee consists basically of engineers, who are not highly sophisticated computer scientists. The techniques they use to validate systems are testing methods in use for a long time, the same that they use to test electrical circuits and other things. They are very well educated and very well trained in these techniques. I do not see any reason why they should change to new validation techniques which do not offer well understood improvements over well established disciplines.

Schuman: Is this the first time that a government body has set out to validate or certify a hardware-software system in its entirety?

Nehmer: It's the first time it's been tried in Germany.

Peck: You mentioned the public objection to the use of standard software, presumably software produced by the manufacturer. However this is, of course, the software which many people have used and which has been greatly tested. Surely, there must be public objection also to the use of ad hoc software, that is software developed just for the purpose and which still has to be tested.

Nehmer: I think that was a confusion. I did not say the public objected to standard software. In the first attempt, standard software from the manufacturer was used to solve the problem. It was basically a decision of the Technical Supervisory Committee not to use standard software. My point about the public was that the public in Germany is highly suspicious of formal verification methods. It is difficult to make them believe that a mathematical formalism should be a better proof than "try it and see what happens". [☺]

Bell: One of the reasons you gave for not using standard manufacturer's software was that there wasn't a higher-level language with good real-time facilities. I think that if you had looked thoroughly, you would have found a number of them, including extensions of some standard languages, to handle real-time control. Furthermore, my opinion is that for any fixed amount of money your goals of having the most reliable possible software system would have been better met by building on tested, proven software products because the amount of money that is spent by manufacturers in the testing and validation is probably much more than any user group is going to spend.

Nehmer: I think that is basically true, but if you talk about money you must consider that the whole reactor costs roughly 10^9 DM, so the software costs are very low compared with the costs of the whole reactor installation. You can easily put three times more effort into the project than for normal applications. My personal opinion is that the standard software from computer manufacturers is not as reliable as we require for these types of application. Each operating system undergoes a certain development during its life-time. The system grows with time, a series of extensions is made, resulting in a system which was not intentionally designed with those extensions in mind. This gives an interface which is highly complex. This not only complicates validation of the operating system, but also inhibits a clean structure of the application software built on top of it. This seems to be typical of all manufacturers' standard software products; I do not think that this particular computer manufacturer was an exception.

Ershov: You have stated that you adopted a dedicated approach for this particular project. But from your presentation I see that the techniques which have been used were logical completeness of the design, fast reaction for real-time constraints and hardware redundancy. These seem to be rather universal techniques in such applications. Is there something else which could justify this term "dedicated approach"?

Nehmer: I would say "dedicated" refers to the fact that we start the software design from scratch, try to develop specific tools and try to structure the software specifically for this type of application. This creates requirements for languages which presently don't exist.

Holager: How much manpower did you put into this project? Developing an operating system, a compiler and your real-time software is a lot of work.

Nehmer: I forgot to mention that I mainly worked as a consultant to the industry and the various supervisory committees. The product itself is being implemented by industry. So I can't really say how many people are working on the project.

Constructing Quality Software, P.G. Hibbard/S.A. Schuman (eds.)

ON WHAT SHOULD QUALITY SOFTWARE BE CONSTRUCTED ?

R. Kurki-Suonio
University of Tampere
Department of Mathematical Sciences
and
Oy Softplan Ab
Tampere, Finland

Software quality may critically depend on the correctness and reliability of the hardware and of the programs on which it is constructed. Simple example cases are reviewed in order to illustrate the problems and attitudes involved.

The main conclusions are in warning against building on any complex pieces of software that are not under one´s own control, and advocating the use of tools and methods with which this can be avoided.

INTRODUCTION

Discussion on quality software usually concentrates on the methods and tools with which one could produce correct, reliable, maintainable, portable and efficient programs. There is a wealth of good ideas in this context, varying from general design theory to linguistic tools, programming discipline, debugging aids and formal verification methods. Compared to these ideas, the starting point of this paper is very modest and mundane: no matter how good your methodology and tools are, your systems are likely to inherit the errors, unreliabilities and inefficiences of the hardware and software on which you build. In mathematics, if one gives no proof, and this cannot be reconstructed by others, the result is not considered a firm basis on which to build. Similarly, there is not much value in proving a real-time application system, if this assumes the correctness of an operating system of which you cannot even receive source listings.

When making use of existing general-purpose software, distinction should be made between using this software as a tool and as a building block. In the former case one only has to avoid its errors and unreliabilities during one´s own work. In the latter case the building block remains as a part of the object system, which requires consideration of whether any potential situation in its use would be effected by such undesirable features. The latter type of general-purpose software is comparable to the hardware on which the object system will be run. If the user cannot be sufficiently protected against errors and unreliabilities in such black boxes in the object system, it is impossible to build quality software on them. Were the shortcomings known in advance, there would at least be a rational basis for deciding on what to build. Unfortunately, this is often not the case, and decisions have to be made on guesses and good faith.

The background of this paper is in software development in both university and commercial environments. In each case there has been explicit pursuit of the skills for producing high quality software, and the educational background of the people has been very good. Each project has been a real-life project with relatively stringent requirements for economy and schedule. In particular, I am referring to systems which contain, are parts of, or are otherwise comparable to operating systems in the sense that their reliable operation is required through extended lengths of time.

EXAMPLES

Case 1. The programmer's manual of a minicomputer warned against burning out a memory location by a jump instruction leading to itself. No harm was caused by this restriction.
Comments. This restriction raised interest for two reasons. Firstly, this was considered an unpleasant anomaly. Secondly, it was considered positive that this restriction was made explicit. Although this kind of a hardware restriction does not seem acceptable to most software people, we do not feel similar distaste for many software systems with much more severe shortcomings that have not even been documented in manuals. Furthermore, software users and high-level language programmers can be completely protected against potential consequences of this particular limitation.

Case 2. A time-sharing system, based on a dual-processor minicomputer system, was extended with the possibilities of accessing peripheral devices and with a remote batch connection to a bigger computer. During this work it was found that a particular bit in the I/O bus was always forced to 1 by the hardware when a certain peculiar combination of conditions occurred. Without correcting this feature it was impossible to achieve reliability of the extended system.
Comments. The time-sharing system was marketed as an integrated system of hardware and software. From this point of view the "error" was no error at all, as the particular conditions could never occur simultaneously in the original system. However, once the cause for the anomalous behavior was located, it was easy to correct, and the manufacturer never objected to doing this.

Case 3. During the same time-sharing system extension it was found difficult to keep up with the speed of the remote batch line, when certain relatively rare sequences of events took place in time-sharing operations. Since the response would be negative acknowledgement in such a case, renewed transmission was to be expected. In addition, occasional loss of two consecutive messages was observed in these situations, and this revealed a logical error in the communication program in the other end: if the first negative acknowledgement signal was lost, positive acknowledgement was sent afterwards.

Comments. In spite of a clear demonstration that the communication program did not meet its specifications, the manufacturer never admitted any error. Their argument was that no significant unreliability was shown when the program was used "as it was intended to be used". Notice that this was a case with clear functional specifications, against which the program could be tested.

Case 4. The same time-sharing system was claimed to be fail-safe against anything that could be done from the user's terminals, and it was reported to have been used in commercial time-sharing service for a few years without any such problems. During the first day of operation in our university, the system was repeatedly crashed by a brief Fortran program that was intended to be used as part of an application system.
Comments. Since the system could only handle sequential files, this program was simulating random access by creating a separate file for each search key. The relatively great number of files manipulated by the program caused on overflow in the free space within the operating system. Users had to learn to be cautious in dynamic generation of file names.

These examples seem to show a difference in our attitudes towards anomalies in hardware and software. In hardware these are accepted when certain requirements for the physical environment, such as temperature, ruggedness of usage, etc., are violated. Cases 1 and 2 seem to support the view that even relatively unharmful logical anomalies are considered shortcomings in hardware. It would be unheard of, for instance, if a hardware designer would deem some particular instruction sequences useless and would therefore not care to guarantee their proper operation. Such preconceived ideas of how hardware will be used, would not be felt tolerable.

In contrast, cases 3 and 4 are simple examples of the phenomenon that software designers tend to have strong ideas of how their system would or should be used. Furthermore, it is not even felt necessary to make such restrictions explicit in specifications or documentation. In some cases (case 4) this is considered a more or less irrelevant implementation detail; what it actually is, is hidden and potentially dangerous complexity in the interface between the system and its users. In other cases (case 3) there is a clear discrepancy between specifications and implementation, but the users still have to live with the situation.

Another interesting experience was in developing terminal-based applications software for a well-known minicomputer. The first of these projects was a real-time order entry system which was started from scratch, making no use of any existing programs at all. The project was completed by 4 persons in about 4 man-years, including the design and implementation of a machine-oriented high-level language in which the system was written. The result is a reliable and well-manageable system which does not rely on any software that would not be under our control. Later projects of similar nature for the same computer were based on a real-time operating system provided by the manufacturer. Several problems of reliability have arisen, and the amount of effort needed to understand the system has turned out to be much greater than expected. The average time spent by each of 15 programmers in fighting with the system has been about 2 months more than estimated. In a one-year project this is an increase of about

20 %. The possibilities of the system are, in general, much wider than what we need, but even a simple thing seems to be complicated to accomplish with it.

CONCLUSIONS

It would be inappropriate to draw far reaching conclusions on the basis of such practical experiences. However, they seem to reinforce certain views and positions, which admittedly may be tied to the present state of art and to the kind of environments where this experience comes from.

Construction of quality software obviously needs ability to build on previous work. Two ways of doing this are to use high-level tools such as languages, abstractions, etc., and to use building blocks, i.e. ready-made modules or modifiable systems. Both are ways to cope with the complexity of a family of problems. In the first case the complexity is reduced at a conceptual level, and an object system does not become more complex than necessary. In the latter case, on the other hand, the potential complexity of the whole family is contained in all object systems (to some extent at least). Notice the analogy with compilation and interpretation: object code generated from a simple program by a complex compiler should be simple, whereas an interpreter always needs to be prepared for the full potential complexity of the language.

As a conclusion, it seems that preference should be given to tools instead of building blocks whenever possible. This requires, however, much more education and intellectual ability on the part of the programmers. The main requirements for a building block - especially when it is not under your own control - are that (1) it has a well-defined interface without hidden interactions and that (2) it has clear functional specifications which do not allow for implicit assumptions about how it will be used. Unfortunately, most software does not meet either of these requirements.

ACKNOWLEDGEMENTS

I gratefully acknowledge that the sweat and tears required by these experiences were not mine but of several students and friends at the institutions mentioned above.

Kurki-Suonio : Discussion

Ershov: In my opinion you have touched the darkest point in programming, because the hardware-software interface is the point where logical abstractions end. Logical abstractions are an inherent part of programming. They allow us to have a mental picture of the corresponding system. Some of your examples show that if we come too close to this limit of logical abstraction, something unpredictable happens. What is your opinion or hope? Is it reasonable to expect that hardware manufacturers will design their hardware so as to provide a logical structure which allows us to extend the scope of the abstractions used in programs? Or will it remain the programmer's obligation to program in such a way as to keep a reasonable distance from these critical points where logical abstractions are not valid?

Kurki-Suonio: First of all I have stated that I think there are fewer problems in dealing with hardware than in dealing with software. We are somewhat happy with building on hardware, since it usually conforms to its specifications; if not, the manufacturer would correct it. But when we build on software we cannot count on this. I think that in making software, we should learn from our attitude towards hardware. We expect it to work according to its specifications even in unusual situations, and we assume it to be free of unexpected logical anomalies. As to the point of your question, I think microprogramming will have a significant effect, but I cannot tell in which direction. The basic hardware will become simpler but, on the other hand, the total complexity of basic hardware and microprograms will increase, and I am afraid that it will be harder to prove the correctness of microprograms than ordinary ones.

Constructing Quality Software, P.G. Hibbard/S.A. Schuman (eds.)

SOFTWARE QUALITY CONTROL: TECHNIQUES AND USERS' CRITERIA

W. M. Turski
Institute of Informatics
Warsaw University
Warsaw, Poland

If the correctness of a program is defined as a relation in the space of state vector transformations, then the efficiency of a program is a subrelation (or a family of subrelations) of this relation. Similarly, the integrity and clarity of a program could be defined - if at all - as (families of) subrelations of the correctness relation. Any interpretation of the notion of "software quality" obviously has to imply the correctness of the relevant programs and, perhaps, some (or all) of its more specific aspects. The point we should like to raise here is that the notion of software quality covers more ground than just correctness; indeed, that the correctness (and thus notions contingent on it) is but a projection of the quality on a constituent of the product space in which the quality forms a relation.

In order to indicate why I believe that it is insufficient to pay attention only to those attributes which are collected in the correctness space, let us consider the notion of the reliability of a program.

A standard practice of reliability investigation consists in assigning measures of reliability (i.e. positive proper fractions) to atomic constituents and then applying various calculations to arrive at the reliability of the composite object, again expressed as a number from the (zero, one) range. Counterparts of this general approach in software analysis are represented by numerous investigations reporting on "mean-time-between-failures" of software systems. It is quite symptomatic that what is taken for a "failure" in such investigations is, most often, a complete system crash, or another catastrophe manifested or monitored in the computer room or at the programmer's (or system analyst's) desk. Two most pertinent observations are in order:

1. If a program is considered correct only if its properly started execution invariably leads to the completion in a desirable state, then such a program cannot fail, unless the characterisation of desirable states is inadequate in that it admits some catastrophic ones. Disregarding, for the time being, the latter as an evident error in specifications, we may observe that in this sense correctness should imply a complete reliability.

2. In many, if not most, uses the computer-room type of failures are insignificant per se and matter only insofar as they lead to "failures" in operations (business, military, control etc.) external to the

computer and its staff. Conversly - any failure in operations fairly attributable to a misguidance resulting from a computer application, or to a lack of timely guidance, ought to be considered as a software failure, even if it is not manifested in the computer room. (Needless to say, for the sake of argument, I am assuming an imaginary world of perfect hardware).

In both instances, the notion of software failure (and hence of reliability) exceeds the framework set by a relation in the space of state vector transformations: either because specifications of "desirable" turn out to be insufficiently discriminating, or because an aspect, particular to a use, happens not to be covered by them at all. This leads to considering the reliability as a property some programs may have in one use and have not in another.

Similar arguments could be put forward for other ingredients of the very wide notion of software quality.

Consequently, any estimates of the quality of a software system must take into the account the degree to which this system satisfies its users, which implies direct concern with a context much broader than that usually considered in programming.

Of course, the same reasoning applies to other engineering products, for which we have quality standards based on criteria derived from and related to their use, but few other products being so versatile as "programs", it is much easier to identify these standards with products themselves, allowing the concrete application to enter the quality estimate via few well-defined parameters. If it is relatively easy to specify quality standards for watches, it is due to the fact that watches are used for a relatively narrow class of applications and, consequently, the criteria of quality observable in a watch application may easily be identified with the watch itself, or even translated into quality criteria of watch design and production. Programs, which have much more diversified applications than watches, hardly can be expected to possess quality criteria abstracted from the applications.

Naturally, if we consider a particular program, or to be more precise, a class of programs for a particular application, we may formulate the quality criteria relevant for this particular class of programs, and, translating them into design and implementation criteria, obtain a set of quality standards for programs of this particular class. Thus we may talk of quality standards for Algol 60 compilers, payroll systems, perhaps even for data bases (although I am not so sure about the last example!), but should not be surprised that they would be different in each case. To be sure: there is a non-empty intersection of those particular quality criteria - and it includes correctness! - but in each particular case the "specific difference" is so significant that restricting one's attention to the common part only is highly misleading.

Incidentally, we touch here upon the methodological phenomenon distinguishing software engineering from other kinds of engineering. An engineering firm specializing, e.g., in tunnel construction differs from a software house, even from a highly specialized one, in a most fundamental way. There hardly are two identical tunnels (not to mention the absurdity of a "portable tunnel"). The expenditures on tunnel design are incomparably smaller than those on its implementation and therefore most of the intellectual effort is allocated and consumed by attempts to make the implementation as simple as possible under the concrete circumstances. The economic success of a tunnel construction firm depends on its ability to do the implementation in an economical fashion. The cost of doing two similar tunnels is approximately twice as high as doing a single tunnel, regardless of how much of the design is carried over from the first one.

Even in the engineering of mass production objects (watches, computers, TV-sets, washing mashines) the material costs of replication are significant as compared with costs of the design.

In software engineering we hardly ever have to bother with costs of replication, which anyhow is seldom needed, and the costs of the design outweigh very considerably the costs of implementation. The economic viability of a software house depends on its ability to design as economically as possible, and while the tunnel drilling firm may redesign its project several times over if only it does not involve any significant changes in the implementation technology, the redesign of a software product comes precariously close to an economic disaster for a software firm.

These factors considered, we understand why programmers are trained to concentrate on qualities of the design process. Since, moreover, this process is difficult and can be excruciatingly messy, the obsessive preoccupation with the "in" aspects of it is hardly surprising. A dangerous side of programmers' preoccupation with the qualities of program design process emerges when the concern with it takes precedence over the concern with the intended use of the program, when the programmer forgets that finally it is not the program, nor even its execution, but the services it renders to the user that count. The preoccupation with program design problems becomes disastrous when problems generated in the process of program design are exported into the application, requiring that the users solve them by adjusting their activities to the dictates of programmers.

Unfortunately, instances of this disease are not uncommon, although usually it appears disguised by a veneer of "scientific" self-righteousness.

Let us take some examples. Most notions of correctness, formulated for programming, require an exact specification of the transformation to be achieved by the program and/or invariants to be preserved. The task of formulating these predicates for a specific application may very well be <u>the</u> most difficult part of the problem. It does not belong to the programmer - because he, in general, does not know enough about the application to be able to do it. But since he is taught and trained that without such clearly formulated predicates correct programming is impossible, he bullies the user into accepting a formulation that seems right and then measures his success against specifications; if the user is not satisfied - too bad for him.

All too often we teach the programmers by examples where the program design evolves by virtue of deep facts from the application area which happens to be that part of general knowledge the programmer is likely to possess as a part of his general education, thus he uses it without realizing that he is made dependent on such knowledge. Such crafty exploitation of general education in examples used for teaching deadens the awarness of the fact that the application-bound knowledge is being applied, disguises the fact that the author acts as a programmer <u>and</u> as a specialist in the application area, that the program is designed by the team of these two experts.

For centuries banks have been operating without a slightest worry about simultaneous update in master files, since ledger entries were never deleted and updates were clearly dated (at least by honest bookkeepers). Programmers have exported the ludicrous expedient of invisible, intractable change of value from the area of their professional worries (where it should have remained as one of the most embarrassing skeletons in the cupboard) into the application field. Why any user should put up with our endless thrashing about the "integrity" of data bases remains a mystery, which I can solve only by assuming a huge inferiority complex on the part of users vis a vis "modern technology".

To sum up what we have said so far:

1. The notion of software quality must encompass factors related to software use in particular environment, which seldom is fully represented in design specifications.

2. Programmers tend to measure their success against the design specifications, and formal methods of establishing correctness of programs are explicitly geared to state transform specifications.

3. Therefore: programmers are not qualified by their professional activities alone to judge the quality of software.

If this reasoning - admittedly informal and exaggerated in an attempt to redress the balance - is accepted, then we must seek some means for incresing the software quality <u>beyond those traditionally associated with programming</u>.

In general, such means may be found in users' participation in software design, verification and implementation. Of course, if we wish to go outside the realm of motherhood statements, we must devise and implement technical contents of the "user participation" principle.

Two techniques, practically tried and found successful, should be mentioned here:

1. Staged contract and payment procedure (SCPP), which seems but a managerial trick while being a powerful design policy.

2. The widespread use of incomplete specifications for control and structuring of the program design process, which is a technique enabling a quite penetrating analysis to be conducted on the level of abstraction accessible to the user.

In fact, these two techniques, briefly described in the remainder of this paper, could be nicely combined and allow the user to be an active participant in the software project carried out for him.

The SCPP, rougly speaking, consists in contracting a software system to be designed and implemented stage by stage, where the specifications and charges for each step are agreed upon at the completion of the preceding step. In order to minimize the likelihood of the customer dropping the project regardless of the successful completion of the first n stages a penalty clause should be agreed upon, requiring the customer to pay an increasingly high penalty for dropping the project "on the way", butunder normal circumstances this clause is very unlikely to be invoked.

The advantages of SCPP are equally important to the user and to the software producer: the former is never in the dark with respect to what he is going to get (since he is never more than one stage behind in understanding the development), the latter is never uncertain about the acceptability of his work nor risks being more than one stage unfunded. The whole technique can work because in software engineering there is no final implementation stage overwhelmingly expensive (in contrast to other kinds of engineering, as noted before).

The SCPP allows for realistic implementation of the "evolving specification" principle - abhorred by the programmers paid on the "whole job" basis.

Most important of all - the SCPP enforces a continous interchange between programmers and users on ever broader basis and prevents programmers from going on with design or implementation not fully understood by the user.

Assuming that programmers working under an SCPP contract apply all the necessary tools of their craft, the procedure can not adversly affect these aspects of software quality which are due to the honed methods of programming. On the other hand, the confrontation with the user coming much sooner than in case of the whole program delivery, the deficiencies of the software may be detected much earlier, thus decreasing the probability of an unexpected gross mismatch between the software and application. Since the user also learns more and more about the system while it is being developed, one can expect that quite a few details, missing from the original specification, can be brought to the attention of program developers. Should such additional information necessitate a redesign of the program, the sooner it is found out the more economical would be the redesign (assuming that the design stages are correlated with abstraction levels): the amount of wasted effort is proportional to the "distance" between the level at which the need for redesign is discovered and the level at which the redesign must be carried out.

If the user is to participate in the decision-making about consecutive stages of program development, he must understand the system description after each stage and the proposal for the development to be carried out in the next stage. It is just this need which bridges the SCPP with the technique of incomplete specifications.

Several available incomplete specification languages (DeRemer's and Kron's MIL, Teichroew's PSL, Parnas's "technique for module specification", etc.) allow to describe a program applying more or less formalized means for expressing the structure and specific interconnections between structural components which correspond to functional units of a program. Typically, the description of a functional unit would include:

-its name (intuitively suggestive of the user function it performs),

-description of the interface with other functional units (i.e. the names of those units, names of functions and other resources delivered by such units for the benefit of the unit being described, and names of services rendered by the latter for the units with which it is to be interfaced),

-a list of private resources of the unit being described (including various access rights granted to its subunits or to the foreign units),

-descriptions of the subunits (expressed in a similar fashion).

A system represented by thus described functional units and their interconnections can be verified (even automatically!) for consistency and completeness at the level of abstraction chosen for the descriptions, even though no semantics can be formally inferred from the intuitively selected names of units and resources. Therein rests the great advantage of the method. Inconsistencies and sources of incompleteness may be discovered (reported) and suitable corrections can be made within given level of abstraction, or at the worst, going to higher levels.

At the beginning of the project such incomplete specifications are supplied by the user who envisages the system in terms of functions well-understood and widely used by himself. Similarly, the interconnections and resources he names are closely related to his visualization of the system.

As the analytic (top-down) design progresses, step-wise refinements introduced by the programmer are first meant to help him (i.e. the programmer) to grasp the semantics of the terms used by the customer, and then to express it in terms of programming concepts. Even if this process cannot be continued in the analytic order down to the complete program design (and, as Stan Gill pointed out at the first NATO Software Engineering Conference, the top-down design must sooner or later be complemented by a bottom-up swing), we have a ladder of system descriptions, starting with purely application-oriented and getting closer and closer to programming-oriented. In the meantime, the intuitive semantics attached in the user's mind to names of units and resources is gradually transformed into explicit semantics of a programming language. At the same time, however, the user has a complete picture of the system before his eyes, and, if the SCPP is employed, can control the steps of refinement. If it appears that in this way it is the user (and not the programmer) who is placed the driver's seat during the software development, so much the better!

Exactly as in the case of SCPP, the use of incomplete specifications cannot hurt any techniques traditionally employed for achieving high quality of programming. The additional virtues of the method come from users' familiarity with the system as it is being developed and from the availability of an easy and relatively cheap technique of "system verification" well ahead of completion of any actual computer-oriented software.

Turski : Discussion

Ershov: It appears that you have carefully mixed in your presentation the social and professional aspects of programming on the basis that they are both human factors. So, my half-question, half-remark will also be a mixed one. I feel that there exists a kind of problem which could be called "software appreciation". There is one difficult thing with programming, that is the invisibility of programs. It seems to me that to orient the society properly with respect to software products and to educate good professionals for producing them, it is imperative to find some system for visualization of program products. I would like to mention the so-called aesthetic of the technological age. You know there are a lot people who are crazy about airplanes, cars and steamers, not just because they use them functionally. The psychology of a passenger who uses the train "unconsciously" each day is quite different from the psychology of the enthusiast, for whom the physical appearance, the different gadgets, different aspects of their design and any other components of their physical image constitute a very important psychological or even emotional aspect of his understanding and his feeling about the corresponding product. This is a very direct bridge to the profession, because the best professionals in the corresponding technical fields come from those crazy lovers of the corresponding pieces of hardware. It seems to me that something of this sort is necessary for software.

With respect to user's criteria, I find it doubtful that we can rely essentially on their front-end understanding or opinions about software products, as they relate to the front-end behavior of an integrated system. Let us take the example of literature. Certainly literature is not developed on the basis of the front-end opinions of mass readers. It's developed through literary science, through aesthetics, through a very fine understanding of style and other professional aspects not seen by everybody. The same thing has to be true with software. But software is a very unhappy product. It does not have the intuitive elegance and emotional power of literature nor, on the other hand, does it have the physical presence of hardware products. That is one of the difficult points. Please, may we have your comments.

Turski: Yes, I would be delighted to comment. In true programmer's style, I'll do it in stack order. There seems to be a world of difference between writing software and writing fiction. First of all I don't believe that literary science is conducive to making good books. Some of the best books are written by people who are semi-literate. And I never saw a reasonably good book written by any institute of literature. [☺] I don't believe any deep education is needed to write a good work of fiction. It's an internal feeling you have or you haven't, to say something to somebody else. It is false to pretend that you don't write books for readers. The very fact that you write them rather than think them means that you do hope for readers. But that's about fiction and this is not a conference on literature.

Goos: Sometimes the output of software is fiction. [☺]

Turski: With respect to software, yes, we do make invisible products. We are not alone. A surgeon does things which are invisible after the operation is completed. At least good surgeons do. It's a reflection on our society that in order to be appreciated things have to be of solid dimensions and solid weight, preferably gold plated. Yes, I do believe very firmly that the quality of software should be judged by the users and by nobody else but the users. We are not good judges of quality. Now, the notion of quality is immense. Perhaps that is a trap into which I am falling. Some components of this notion are professional, the "in" components: e.g. code conciseness, code readability, etc. They do not mean anything for the layman. No user should be concerned with readability of the code.

Král: Users have to judge software, but this has to be done by the writer of the software too, because users cannot validate, users cannot find out whether the program is correct. That they can do only by testing and we know that's no good. So the writer of a program has to validate the program. The user can only find out if it's reliable. That's one remark. A second remark is that users have to read programs, as we all know. This does not necessarily mean reading COBOL or FORTRAN code. In a better situation there is a specification, in a kind of programming language or some kind of language, which explains something about the code. This at least has to be read by users.

Holager: Just a brief comment. I think that there is a simple explanation of why programmers tend to tell the users about the internal problems of their programs. It is because we have not been able to get into the situation to which Turski referred. People have really been trying to make computer systems that just unobtrusively sit there and work and work and work, without anyone noticing them. But we have not been able to do that.

Turski: Have we really tried?

Holager: I think we have tried. I think very many people are trying and I think we are uniformly failing. That is perhaps the subject of this conference: how do we get up to the level where we are able to meet your requirements.

Dewar: I think it's important to remember that in fact we are not uniformly failing. There are many examples of very complex, very successful pieces of software written with conventional techniques. I choose for one example the fact that many telephone calls go through an extremely sophisticated computer system and the public is not even aware of its existence. I think it's a perfect example of the point which has been made. The critical factor which led to success in that particular case was that the programmers and designers of that system were intimately familiar with the requirements. They could in fact act as successful judges of the finished program. This is one of the most important components for success in software development.

Meyer: I'd like to oppose the view that we should accept work with incomplete specifications. This seems to be the attitude responsible for a large part of the present mess in the software business. If you don't have a complete specification, it just means that you haven't worked enough on it. So you shouldn't start to do anything else, other than completing the specifications.

Ross: I agree and disagree with you. Certainly the lack of discipline is where major problems have come from. I think specifications should be incomplete, although it must be a well-defined incompleteness. Merely referring to them as "incomplete" is incomplete. For example they should be structured, they should be self-consistent, etc. The idea is not to build in your own ignorance. You will learn from your first approaches to the system. If you try to specify too much before you have built anything and learned from that experience, all you will do is build problems into the system that otherwise you could have avoided. However, the "incompleteness" must be carefully controlled.

Dewar: Should specifications be incomplete? I might as well expect NASA to ask, "should the moon be a quarter of a million miles away?" The fact is that specifications are incomplete for the vast majority of problems and there is no possibility or question of making them complete, because the knowledge to make them complete just does not exist. So I think the question must be, "what do we do with incomplete specifications?"

Goos: I'd like to take issue with Turski's statement that the public should not be concerned about software as such, but only with whole systems. I think that the production of software is an engineering discipline, as is the construction of cars, tunnels, bridges, and so on. The public should be as concerned about software as it is about the safety of bridges. I don't see any difference. I believe that the public inevitably sees the mistakes made by programmers (in the case of payroll programs, sometimes very annoying mistakes). We have to distinguish between two different ways of being concerned with the quality of software: the view which is seen by the user, and the inner workings, which are mostly of interest because they have consequences on the outside. We are interested in verification of software and code readability only because those topics have consequences in economic terms or affect the users' interface.

Turski: Yes, the public is interested in the strength and reliability of the bridge but we are not making bridges; we are making planks, we are making bolts, we are making nuts. A bridge is a complete system. I never, never said that the public should not be interested in the reliability of the system. Yes, that is for the public to be interested in, but software is never delivered to the public as a complete product. It's only a component. If you buy a car you never question the reliability of one particular bolt or spring in it. [G√, but unarticulated due to ending of the session.]

Constructing Quality Software, P.G. Hibbard/S.A. Schuman (eds.)

SOME PERFORMANCE ASPECTS OF SYSTEM IMPLEMENTATION LANGUAGES

B. A. Wichmann
National Physical Laboratory, U. K.

How important is the efficiency of System Implementation Languages in constructing quality software? It is easy to exaggerate the need for efficiency and require a performance competitive with optimal hand-coding. In practice, small differences in the specification and implementation of software can make such large differences to its performance that small losses due to the use of a SIL are inconsequential. Not infrequently, the barrier to the use of a SIL is more psychological rather than technical in not wishing to risk the 'unknown'.

The paper surveys the technical problems of assessing the efficiency of SILs, with special reference to the work carried out in conjunction with members of IFIP WG 2.4. Implementation aspects are discussed which will make a language an effective tool as well as being an efficient one.

Introduction

It has been stated that the rapid improvements in modern hardware make the inefficiencies in high-level languages unimportant. However, any program which can meet a specification for less cost has an obvious advantage. One can see from the rise of the microprocessor industry the market potential from large cost improvements. Good performance is an essential component for quality software which must be taken into account during the design and coding phases.

The use of high-level languages usually means larger and slower programs - a cost against which a significant number of advantages accrue. The ease of writing, testing and maintaining software written in high-level languages is well known. These gains involve a human factor which makes measurement very difficult whereas the loss in efficiency would appear to be more easily quantified.

The classical experiment to measure the efficiency of a language is to code a program from an agreed specification in the chosen language and machine code and compare the results. Unfortunately the human factor in the form of a programmer cannot be avoided and hence the conclusions are always in doubt. In practice, the likely winner is the programmer who codes the program first in a high-level form to check the logic and to confirm that the best algorithm has been chosen, and then codes at machine level using all available tricks. It is doubtful whether such optimal coding is desirable; for each instruction should be aligned with word and page boundaries, instructions should be reordered if possible to achieve maximum overlap etc. Although such optimisation may be required for desk calculator chips produced in thousands, code of this type can hardly be called software since change without completely rewriting is rarely possible (certainly the optimality will be destroyed).

In this paper the problem of obtaining good performance is surveyed when the software is written in "System Implementation Languages" (ie high level programming languages specifically designed for writing significant software systems).

How important is efficiency?

The reduced software costs of the use of a high-level language have to be met by increased hardware in most cases. Unfortunately, the software and hardware costs are not easily separated due to the marketing policy of most main-frame manufacturers. Indeed, several manufacturers produce special 'slow' machines to meet part of the market. In one case, cutting one wire nearly doubles the performance of a computer. In these circumstances it is hard to convince the programmer that making his program run 20% faster really matters.

A common error is to believe that a program written in machine code is necessarily efficient. An inefficient implementation of a good algorithm will almost always beat a good implementation of a poor algorithm. For instance, an optimal machine coding of an N squared sort routine can easily be improved upon by a high-level version using an N log(N) algorithm. Frequent modifications to software mean that performance is unlikely to be anywhere near optimal. This is particularly true of badly structured machine code routines because the overall logic cannot be changed to suit a new environment. As an example of this, a fortuitous experiment on an NPL computer revealed that the assembler itself was half the speed it should have been (even though the program had been in regular use for 10 years). This was caused by unnecessary code conversion in the basic input routines, which was easily changed to one table look-up resulting in the expected gain.

The importance of the specification and the algorithm compared with the implementation is easily seen from operating systems. The use of a high-level language might make the operating system 20% bigger but if an improved paging algorithm can reduce backing store transfers by half, the gain will be very worthwhile.

In moving from low-level coding methods to a high-level language, both programmers and their managers will have natural worries about the consequences. Good training and experimenting with minor projects first can help this move. Performance aspects of a new SIL must also be checked, since there are many pitfalls for the unwary.

Syntax and semantics

An intuitive idea of some aspects of performance can be gained from a simple diagram, fig 1 in which every language is characterised by two parameters. The first parameter measures the syntactic power of the language, or more strictly, the compile-time components of a language. By definition, these aspects do not impinge upon the performance of the compiled program and hence are 'free'. The second parameter is the (underlying) semantics of the language which must be reflected in the complexity of the compiled code and the ability of the hardware to support this complexity.

The syntactic parameter includes names (some languages are more restrictive than others), scoping rules for names (but excluding dynamic storage allocation), flow control without labels (if-then-else etc) and so on. Shown at the highest level is 'visibility' - a technique whereby groups of names have their visibility controlled by more sophisticated methods than the ALGOL type of scope rules (see LIS (Ichbiah, et al 1976) for an example).

The semantic axis starts from the ability to perform integer arithmetic on a few locations (like some small programmable desk calculators) to mini-computers with indirection and indexing. Next one has floating point, character manipulation and then 'high-level' features such as a hardware stack, display registers, logic for multi-dimensional array access or even array operations. The axis itself (with no syntax) corresponds to the bare machine, although no doubt manufacturers would not agree as to the relative semantic power of their products.

In assessing a language, the major features of it are analysed so that its position in the diagram can be determined. This position can then be compared with that of the target hardware architecture. If the hardware lacks significant features required by the language, then this defect will be reflected in poor code produced by the compiler - typically by calls of run-time support subroutines. The gap between the requirements of the language and the target machine will be shown on the graph as a displacement on the Y axis; the language being further over than the machine, which will lie on the axis itself. Small areas of mismatch between the hardware and the language may be partly overcome by good optimisation in the compiler but as will be illustrated below, this is often not possible.

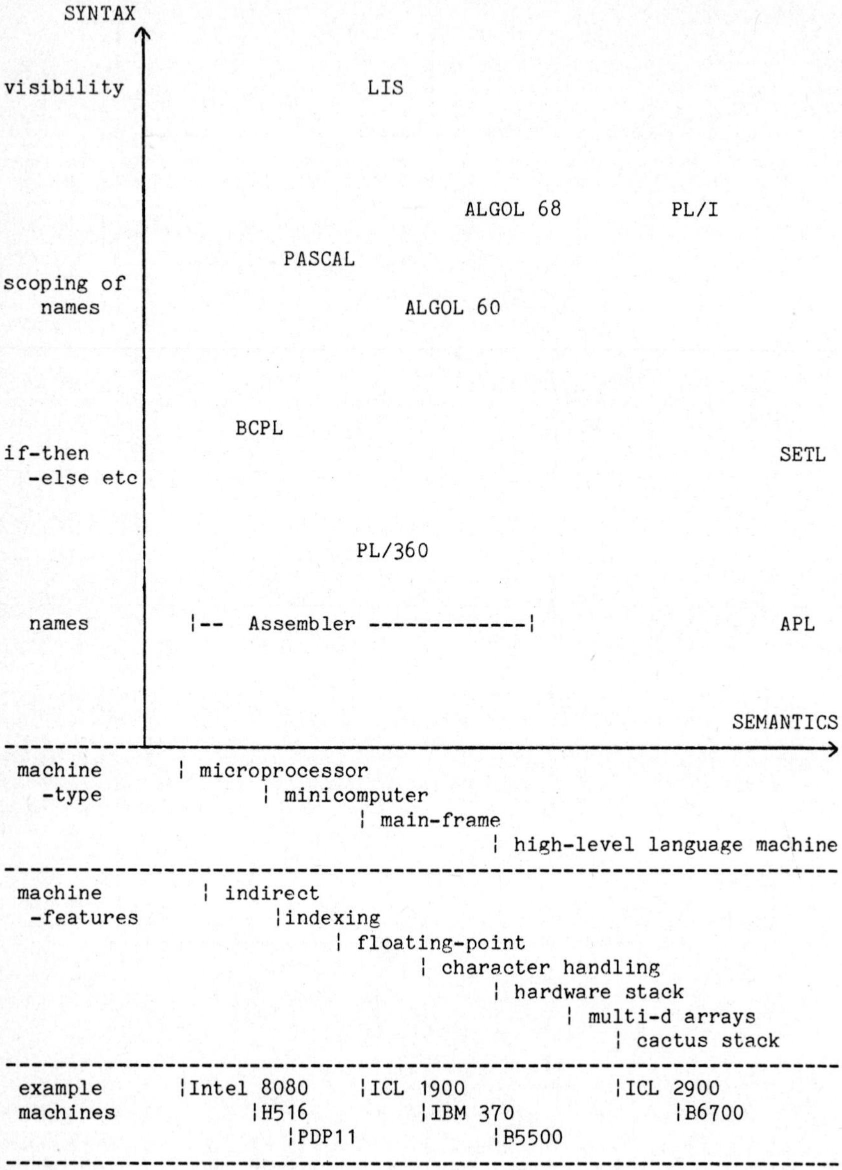
SYNTAX
visibility
LIS
ALGOL 68
PL/I
PASCAL
scoping of names
ALGOL 60
BCPL
if-then -else etc
SETL
PL/360
names
Assembler
APL
SEMANTICS
machine -type
microprocessor
minicomputer
main-frame
high-level language machine
machine -features
indirect
indexing
floating-point
character handling
hardware stack
multi-d arrays
cactus stack
example machines
Intel 8080
ICL 1900
ICL 2900
H516
IBM 370
B6700
PDP11
B5500

fig 1

Lessons from an example

A test has been designed for procedure calls in languages supporting recursion. The procedure, Ackermann's function, has been run on a wide variety of machines and compilers. The main results have been reported elsewhere (Wichmann, 1976 and 1977) and will not be repeated here. The principal performance measure was the number of machine instructions required for each call of Ackermann, which is summarised in fig 2.

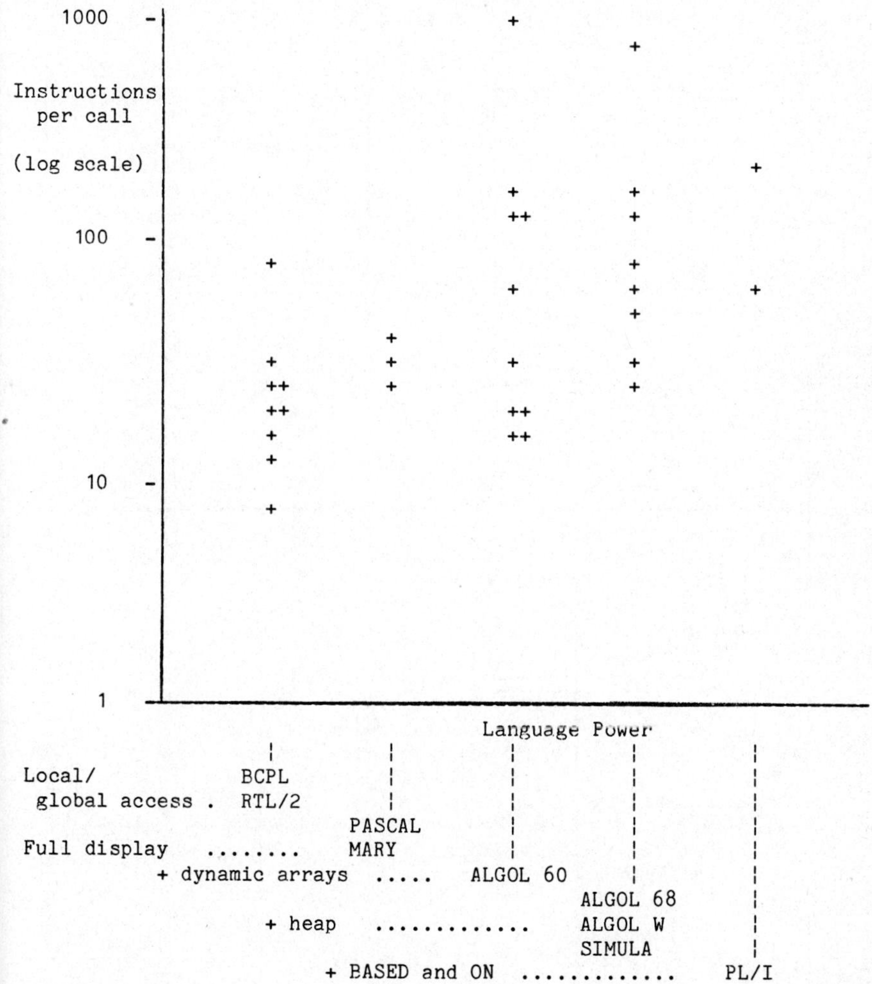

fig 2

The main conclusions from this study are as follows:

1. The quality of the implementation rather than the power of

the language is the single most important factor. Later implementations of the same language are invariably superior. The quality is largely determined by the method of handling environments and procedure parameters.

2. The main reason for some of the very poor results concerns the ALGOL 60 'thunk' mechanism and the difficulty of handling the parameters of formal procedures (which cannot be specified). Although the parameters in the test are by <u>value</u>, the poorer implementations have not taken advantage of this to generate better calling code than would be required for call-by-name.

   The call of formal procedures is 100 times less common than direct calls (Wichmann, 1973) and hence it is disastrous to let the full mechanism for formal calls degrade the straightforward case. This is, of course, a design error in ALGOL 60 in not permitting formal procedures to be specified (which has been partly overcome in Modified ALGOL, De Morgan et al 1977). It is surprising that both SIMULA and ALGOL W suffer from this defect. It is comparatively easy for a compiler to detect when a procedure can be called formally and handle that case specially.

3. The language 'power' has a small effect upon the performance. The main reason for this is that if environments are being changed, it is simple to arrange for the same mechanism to handle (for instance) variable array storage. The cost of running a heap is more difficult to avoid although the ALGOL 68-R compiler has an excellent algorithm for this. The loader determines whether a complete program requires the heap. If it does not, then six instructions to perform a stack overflow check are omitted from the procedure entry code. The DEC 10 SIMULA compiler uses a similar strategy but at run-time.

4. The main advantage of high-level language machines such as the Burroughs and ICL 2900 is to reduce the size of the program rather than reduce the number of instructions executed.

5. The minimum architecture required to support recursion is about 3 index or base registers on a conventional machine. Apart from a few mini-computers and many microprocessors, this is available and hence the majority of SILs do use a stack.

<u>Performance instability</u>

If performance in any particular area is always poor, then this is usually easy to identify and produce a cure. The cure could be a compiler enhancement, an additional optimisation strategy or a language change. Unfortunately the last option is often not open because of the volume of existing code that would need changing. A much more difficult problem is performance instability - that is, when a comparatively small change to a program can make a very large change to its performance. Typical examples of this phenomenon are a program that thrashes through being just a bit too large, and where a small change completely inhibits some otherwise very effective optimisation within a compiler. The cure is 'graceful degradation'. One must arrange every aspect of a system so that any small change has the desired small effect. A severe and not uncommon form of performance instability is when some compiler or hardware limitation is exceeded so that no small increase in a program is permitted. This is particularly common on mini-computers due to addressing limitations. Languages which only require short offsets from stack registers to access most variables can more easily accommodate some addressing limitations.

Good language design can do much to reduce the effects of performance instability. A lesson can be drawn from the elegant but inefficient call-by-name mechanism of ALGOL 60. For instance, in many programs, the value specification can be removed without affecting the action of the program - except that it may now run at half the speed. Similarly, an apparently innocuous statement such as A = B added to a PL/I program can lead to severe performance problems due to the inclusion of implicit type conversions. Language design can make the 'cost' more apparent to the programmer, but this should not be at the expense of overburdening him with excessive detail.

Storage allocation is a potential source of performance difficulties. Languages with two or more dynamic storage regimes are clearly a danger. In fact, in the case of PASCAL, ALGOL 68 and ALGOL W, good implementations are available. There are no real problems with PASCAL since garbage collection is not usually provided. So on a conventional machine, the only requirement is for a stack overflow check (this can be avoided on segmented machines by running the stack in a separate segment). The IBM 360 ALGOL W compiler allocates separate pages to a record class giving fast storage management but with the possibility of internal fragmentation. One must, of course, expect unusual circumstances to give rise to performance problems. This is illustrated by running Ackermann's function on the ICL 1900 (XALT) ALGOL 60 compiler. The run-time system claims stack space in multiples of 96 words from the supervisor, but does not return the space to avoid excessive operating system overheads. This works well enough for most ALGOL programs because the maximum stack depth is reached quickly in a few steps. This is not the case with Ackermann's function so the overheads are very large, especially since if the supervisor cannot easily find additional storage for the program it is rolled out onto backing store. It should not be thought that the time spent in the garbage collection routines represents the sole overhead of dynamic store management. At the very least, additional pointers must be kept and updated and checks made for storage overflow. A likely hidden cost is the inability of an optimising compiler to keep volatile information in registers. Hence the usually quoted cost of 20% for garbage collection in SIMULA is probably an underestimate, but the fact remains that several SIMULA implementations outclass the (poor) ALGOL 60 compilers on the same hardware.

It cannot be expected that changes in the declarative structure of a program will not make major changes to the performance. However, what appears to be a minor change can nevertheless have a major impact. Languages which allow one to specify the packing of a data structure at the bit level are prone to this. The reason is that a different alignment can easily double the number of machine instructions required for accessing. This can be partly overcome by allowing the compiler to determine the packing as in PASCAL, although this cannot be permitted for certain system tables (see below).

Some hardware architectures give rise to instabilities in performance. For instance, machines with pipe-lining are particularly sensitive to conditional jumps. In Verstege and Wichmann (1975) an example is given of a FORTRAN program which runs at a third of the speed one would otherwise expect on a 360/195 for this reason. Slaving can have similar effects, for instance, the statement option in the PL/I compiler generates a double write which can slow down a 370/165 by a factor of two (see Wortman et al 1976).

A new technique called 'throw-away compiling' devised by P J Brown (1976) is prone to instability. Intermediate code is compiled on demand at run-time and thrown away if storage is insufficient. The result is that speeds up to full machine code rates can be obtained but if the run-time structure of the program is not of the right type, then the system degrades by a factor of 10. Figures for both throw-away compiling and for SNOBOL show an interesting counter-intuitive behaviour; the systems can run more slowly if given more store.

Simple optimisation strategies can be prone to instability. For instance, allocating registers sequentially without regard to program structure can mean that an inner loop which is in the wrong position is not optimised. The CDC ALGOL 60 compiler divides code into segments regardless of structure, so that if an inner loop is by misfortune on a segment boundary, the inter-segment jumps will slow the code down by about a factor of two. Similar problems arise with base registers on the 360, but with careful design no instabilities should be noticeable.

Locality of reference

This phrase covers the access of instructions and data within a program, which should be designed to be highly structured and non-random. At the lowest level, on say a CDC 6000 Series machine, it means arranging instructions within words to minimise dummy padding instructions and to increase the potential parallellism of the program. At a higher level, good locality means using registers rather than store locations where possible.

Several machines have a hardware stack, and it is in this area that data accesses should be concentrated. The Burroughs B7700, MU5 and ICL 2900 machines slave the stack giving effective register speeds without the need for compiler optimisation. The contiguous nature of data accesses within a stack should help to avoid thrashing in a paged environment. On a 370, related data should be kept together not only to improve paging, but also to minimise base register manipulation.

In the programming language LIS (Ichbiah et al 1976), related declarations can be linked to form a 'visibility' unit. Access to declarations within this unit can be controlled to give highly structured programs. For instance, details of a name list within a compiler need only be made available to the relevant parts of the compiler. From the performance viewpoint, the importance of this technique is that it provides good locality of reference and on a 360 implementation gives the compiler an opportunity to minimise base register settings.

Data structures and addressing

The critial language design issue for data structures is the degree to which their addressing can be determined at compile time. Consider, for instance, PASCAL, ALGOL W and ALGOL 68. In ALGOL W, record classes are always allocated dynamically whereas in PASCAL it is almost always static (or strictly speaking, statically related to the stack). Arrays are essentially dynamic in ALGOL W and ALGOL 68, but static in PASCAL. Mixing arrays and records in PASCAL will never produce poor code because all the address calculation can be performed at compile time, whereas in ALGOL 68 dynamic structures must incur a penalty. In ALGOL 68 and ALGOL W, one can 'slice' a matrix to give a vector (by rows or by columns). This may be a nice facility but in consequence, with an array parameter, the address of A[i+1] is not necessarily one storage unit more than A[i]. Address calculation is more complex even if slicing is not used, since it is hard for a compiler to determine its absence (and impossible in most independent compilation systems).

The performance depends upon how the underlying semantics of data access relates to that of the target machine. If a crucial addressing mode is missing from a machine, it may double the size of the generated code to make up for the defect. Under such circumstances, a chosen SIL may not be viable in the same way that recursion is not viable on (say) a PDP8. With primitive mini-computers, interpretation may be a good solution, but otherwise radical changes will be necessary.

Optimisation of data structure accessing is rarely simple. The basic problem is that improvements usually require a different lay-out, but this cannot be done without checking every other access to the structure. Consider the following PASCAL fragment:

```
   TYPE person = RECORD
                  age, income, height : integer
                 END;
   VAR bill : person;
       group : ARRAY [ 1 .. 10] OF person;
```

The obvious implementation is to allocate three contiguous storage units for 'person'. Hence the access to group[i].income would require the calculation 3*i + 1 + <base address of group>. Multiplication may not be available on some primitive machines although this can be handled by shifting and adding (but the code size may be large). The multiplication could be avoided completely if the array group was represented as three separate arrays, the address calculation becoming i + <base address of group.income>. This is not, in general, possible because a procedure print(s : person) may be called with print(bill) as well as print(group[i]).

The interaction between the addressing provided by the machine and that required by the language is complex. Significant performance improvement can be obtained by tuning the declarations so that addressing is more efficient. Programmers who understand the underlying machine can do the tuning but only at the expense of making the code less natural and <u>less</u> efficient on other machines. Some languages are particularly susceptible to this, for instance, by adjusting the field lengths in COBOL to align with the word boundaries of the machine.

Machine orientation

A system implementation language must be in touch with the real world - this includes not only the raw hardware but an operating system and code written in other languages. A frequent technique is to have a universal mechanism, namely in-line code statements. Unless adequately controlled, this can effectively destroy the usefulness of the high-level language. Several instances can be quoted of good implementation languages which have been seriously undermined in a few programs through uncontrolled use of code statements. In one system, a good and effective improvement to a compiler could not be released because it was incompatible with the use that had been made of code statements.

The problem with machine orientation is not in providing it, but in providing it in such a way that it is used correctly. Unless detailed measurements have been made, programmers can be easily misled in identifying the time consuming parts of their programs. In consequence, code statements or other low-level features are inserted in some loops to make them 'efficient' whereas the actual advantages are minimal and the resulting code much more difficult to maintain.

Machine orientation merely to obtain efficiency seems dubious because it will make languages and programs more complex without increasing their readability. In the author's view, language features aimed at giving more efficient code should be designed in a way that is natural to the programmer. For instance, both MARY and LIS have a way of specifying that an index of a for loop is to be used to access data structures of a certain type. This means that the index can be kept in an appropriate machine format - for instance, on a 370 this may mean that it is held as a byte offset rather than an integer value. From the programmer's viewpoint, the need for an additional specification is offset by allowing the compiler to perform more static checks on the use of the index. The increased redundancy makes a better program as well as a more efficient one.

Several languages provide a method of using registers like ordinary variables. Although safe in the sense that the semantics does not change, registers are an example of global variables which can easily be misused. The danger well-known to assembler programmers is that a subroutine does not preserve a register used in the calling code. Ideally, this error should not occur because of static checks made by the compiler. The data flow analysis techniques developed by Fosdick and Osterweil (1976) could be a very powerful tool in detecting the misuse of global variables (or registers). However, the current implementation methods do not lend themselves to large systems.

Status bits from peripheral or segmentation tables are examples of externally defined data structures. Not infrequently, these are handled in a SIL by a programmer 'knowing' how the compiler will map certain data structures. This is clearly dangerous, and explicit mention of the required mapping is to be preferred (which should be isolated from the data structure itself whose semantics is more easily defined). A controlled mapping should result in a different type (or sub-type) so that a compiler can freely change the layout of uncontrolled data structures if efficiency requires it. For this reason, the use made of structures with controlled mappings must be restricted by means of strong type checks.

The space occupied by code can be reduced by increasing the declarative power of the language. For instance, several SILs provide a method for declaring the calling convention of subroutines in terms of the machine registers. This provides the programmer with a powerful tool for tuning programs but is dangerous unless special methods are available to check the life-time of registers (as noted above). The effectiveness of this technique can be judged from Ackermann's function where the Bliss/11 compiler produced the same code as the assembler expert. If such declarative power is provided for both subroutine linkage and data structure layout and also good measurement aids are available then clearly it becomes very simple to perform large scale tuning to a system.

One aspect of machine orientation must not be forgotten, namely providing an effective programming tool rather than just a compiler. All too often, diagnostic aids require knowledge of the system at the very lowest level, ie binary machine code. The author regards the following tools as essential for the construction of quality software: source text formatter, source text debugger (with complete checking), execution frequency analyser and processor utilisation analyser. Equally important, the compiler and sytem must work well within the chosen environment. Several SILs have failed in competition with assemblers merely because inadequate support has been supplied.

Conclusions

There are very few areas where SILs cannot be used to construct good quality software. Such areas are:

1. Some microprocessors which have very poor instruction sets (and where interpretation cannot be used).

2. Engineering test programs where one must generate arbitrary instruction sequences which may even be invalid.

3. Some aerospace applications with very tight constraints (but prototypes should be programmed in a high-level language).

4. Small amounts of code in conventional systems which need never be changed (e.g. software floating point package).

Hence the vast majority of systems software can be written in a SIL, providing certain problems are avoided. If the efficiency of generated code on complete programs exceeds 20% (in space or time) then several techniques discussed above can be used to improve the code. So efficiency cannot be quoted as an excuse for not using a high-level language for system work.

References

Brown, P. J. (1976). Throw-away Compiling. Software - Practice and Experience, Vol 6 pp423-434.

De Morgan, R. M, Hill, I. D, and Wichmann, B. A. (1976). Modified Report on the Algorithmic Language ALGOL 60. Comp. J. Vol 19 pp364-379.

Fosdick, L. D, and Osterweil, L. J. (1976). Data Flow Analysis in Software Reliability. Computing Surveys, Vol 8, pp305-330.

Ichbiah, J. D, Rissen, J. P, Heliard, J. C, and Cousot, P. (1976). The System Implementation Language LIS. Technical Report, 4549E1/EN, CII Louveciennes.

Verstege, P, and Wichmann, B. A. (1975). An experimental data base for computer performance information. National Physical Laboratory Report NAC62.

Wichmann, B. A. (1973). ALGOL 60 compilation and assessment. Academic Press.

Wichmann, B. A. (1976). Ackermann's Function: A study in the efficiency of calling procedures. BIT Vol 16 pp103-110.

Wichmann, B. A. (1977). How to call procedures, or second thoughts on Ackermann's Function. Software - Practice and Experience. (to appear).

Wortman, D. B, Khaiat, P. J, and Laskar, D. M. (1976). Six PL/I Compilers. Software - Practice and Experience, Vol 6 pp411-422.

Wichmann : Discussion

Ershov: I wish to make the point that any language is machine dependent. The so-called machine independent languages are just language schemes with some property left undefined. A machine oriented language is a language in which the dependency on a particular computer has been implemented. A machine orientable language is one where this dependence on a machine is singled out and taken, in some sense, as an orthogonal dimension in the language design. We have to start with a study of machine dependence in existing languages, and on the basis of this study, to develop a family of concepts concerning machine dependence and machine orientation. This is of special importance for system implementation languages.

Král: In the project I presented, we were essentially forced to use assembly language. But we think that it was a good decision in that context. This was confirmed by people from industry, who said that even when using a real-time programming language, you must, on the average, write about 30% of your program in assembler. Such programming is so difficult that it is very often better to use assembly language to program the whole system.

Mráz: We wrote in our centre a terminal system for debugging, testing and maintaining programs. The system is some 10K of lines in Concurrent PASCAL. It is also a sort of real-time system. We have in the system some 2% or 3% of assembly code and even a lot of this was written "by mistake". We found that we had an efficiency bottleneck in the system, so we rewrote some parts in assembly code but it turned out that the system was running just as slowly as it was before and the error was somewhere higher up, in the general strategy. Maybe, if we redesigned the program, we would need almost no assembly code. So I ask why is there such a great need for assembly code in real-time programs?

Ross: Our approach is to allow assembly language only in isolated subroutines, and even then, only when it is essential. Then we try to make sure that even that doesn't happen, by giving a machine-independent version of how to compile a particular one-to-one instruction. This is done by incorporating into each high-level language a library of built-in functions, which can be added to. This preserves the high-level language flavour. The compiler itself recognizes particular functions and puts these very particular instructions in the proper place. So you very seldom need to use assembly language as such at all. It works for a very tight, real-time application software, including operating system software.

Holager: Concerning assembly language versus a high-level language, I would like to comment on our experience using MARY, an ALGOL-68-like systems programming language. We found that we were able to write almost everything within that language, without any assembly code. We were able to write editors and compilers without ever stepping outside the high-level language. We sometimes had to use punning, that is to go outside the mode-checking scheme, but we never actually wrote anything similar to assembly code. We also made a multiprocessing, time-sharing operating system, containing 10 or 15 different pieces of assembly code. Most of them were just one instruction as the body of a macro definition. So, in fact, it is possible to get very, very close to not having any assembler code. Concerning the efficiency, I think that the current state-of-the-art is such that it is possible to make better programs using high-level languages than using assembly code. The compiled code will be 10 to 30% larger than the equivalent machine code, but you would never be able to produce as neat and effective an algorithm using assembler as you would do with a high-level language.

Ershov: I have a personal opinion with respect to the question raised. In my opinion, assembly language coding should be taught in universities, and not be used in developing systems. [☺]

Wichmann: A quick response with regard to teaching: I think that the use of MIXAL in Knuth's otherwise excellent volume has been a disaster. I wish somebody would rewrite this book using something else.

Goos: I think we should remember that most of the cost associated with software is maintenance cost, and that the highest percentage of maintenance cost occurs in cases where the systems were produced in assembly language. It is this point which cries out for avoiding the use of assembly language, and for restricting the teaching of assembly language to those cases where it is absolutely necessary. I see only three points. The first is that people have to learn how to generate code in a compiler; this is the most important case for which knowledge of assembly language is needed. The second is to integrate special instructions into high-level languages, as described by Ross. Thirdly, there are limitations created by a machine, where we have to employ the most efficient code. Examples appear in real-time programming but they are rare, certainly not as frequent as people usually report. Other examples may come up in micro-processor applications. But even in those cases, I believe that it would be much more useful to produce a system in a high-level language, using a cross-compiler. Consider the use of a microcomputer in a motor car and imagine, after two or three years, finding mistakes in the code and having to recall a million cars just to repair the software.

Dewar: A fourth point, I believe, should be added to that list, namely where space is very critical. There are applications routinely written in a space which I don't believe could be achieved by any high-level language. Those applications are becoming increasingly frequent, because of the advent of microprocessors. The problem there is that the entire program has to be in assembly language; it is not sufficient just to extract inner loops.

Goos: Yes, that is mentioned again and again. I believe that it is true in some cases. But most of the applications where space is critical would be better written in a high-level language and an effort made to optimize the code. Many examples show that we can come down to 90% of the space requirement by using a high-level language and optimizing the results.

Rajlich: I would like to describe one experience which we had in our institute. We used a specially tailored high-level language for a simulation project. For certain reasons, the program was later rewritten in assembly language. In the process, proper data abstractions were used in the form of a set of basic macros. As a result, runs were one hundred times more efficient than the corresponding high-level language runs and the process of writing and debugging was about half of the previous effort. After this experience, I think that in many problems, high-level languages are not the appropriate answer. Another answer might be the use of proper data abstractions. The underlying language is then immaterial.

Bell: Wichmann referred to the potential instability of higher-level languages, that is, that a small change might create quite a drastic increase in size or degradation of performance. This phenomenon occurs the other way as well. When you write in a high-level language rather than a lower-level one, the chance of making a radical improvement with a minor change is also better.

Wichmann: Yes, but the high-level language programmer, I think, ought to be able to program in a confident fashion, so that he can have some degree of confidence in the performance of his program. If its performance is very uneven, he will have to look out for dangerous features of his powerful language that he shouldn't use because they're too inefficient. Then he will be distracted from his main object of trying to write his program in an intelligent fashion.

Schlichting: I would like to point out that language design may influence performance in other ways, which may not at first be obvious. This is because most commercially produced implementations are produced on a fixed budget, the size of which is generally independent of the complexity of the language to be implemented. This means that if the language is too complex it will either suffer the fate of not being implemented, because no one can be persuaded to finance it, or the implementations which are produced will be very incomplete. For example, if some language feature causes an extra pass to be required in the compiler, then other facilities which could be provided, such as optimization or cross-references, will have to be made simpler, or omitted entirely. On the other hand, it seems to me that redundancies in languages, which help to reduce errors because they allow checking at compile-time, are also useful because they simplify the compiler and reduce the cost of syntactic and semantic analysis. I think that language designers should think carefully in these economic terms if they expect to see commercially produced implementations, and they should judge specific features according to the following criteria: what will the feature cost to implement and will this cost be justified if it results in less attention being paid to other features, what will be the distributed overheads at compile-time and run-time of having the feature, and what does the feature do for the user.

Holager: I'd like to object to Wichmann's suggestion that measurements might not be cost-effective. If we experts, assembled here, consider that the methods which have been developed are worthwhile, then we really should do measurements. We have to consider the "sales" aspect. We first have to develop the techniques and tools, which is the matter most people here are interested in; but we must also do the relevant measurements, which is an essential part of the task of "selling" them to the people we want to use them. If they turn out to save, say, half of all programming effort, then this will in the end pay for a lot of measurements.

Wichmann: I'm not going to argue against doing measurements, obviously I've done rather a lot of them myself. [☺] The point I would like to make is that very large-scale experiments with a large piece of software are likely to be so expensive and the results so inconclusive that it's unlikely to be worthwhile. However, I think that the Ackermann example shows that if you measure something simple you are likely to learn something. The measurements were worthwhile because they showed the cost of the mismatch between hardware and software.

Koster: I would like to point out another pragmatic problem, other than the cost, in comparing languages objectively. In the social sciences if you want to find out something you organize an experiment where, at the very least, you try for a single blind experiment where the subjects are left in the dark about what they are using. But then there is still the phenomenon of influence by those who are conducting the experiment. So, the best situation would be to have a double blind experiment, where even the leaders don't know what they're handing out.

Turski: That's exactly what we are doing. [☺]

Constructing Quality Software, P.G. Hibbard/S.A. Schuman (eds.)

TOWARDS IMPROVED RELIABILITY AND EFFICIENCY THROUGH HYBRIDS

Peter C. Poole
Department of Computer Science
University of Melbourne
Melbourne, Australia

A hybrid program is one composed of a mixture of codes of different types, in particular, code to be interpreted and code to be executed directly. The former can be optimised for space and the latter for speed. If the program structure is such that only a small fraction of the instructions are the most frequently executed ones, then a hybrid can make more efficient use of the machine resources than can a normal program. If the amount of each type of code can be varied by parameters set at compile time, then the hybrid form lends itself to being embedded in an interactive test bed and can therefore be used to improve the reliability of the final program.

The paper describes progress in a project to develop a hybrid form for programs written in an abstract intermediate language called Janus which has been developed as a means of achieving compiler portability. A Pascal compiler which generates Janus exists and an interactive test bed for debugging Pascal programs in a hybrid form is under development.

INTRODUCTION

A hybrid program is one which contains a mixture of different types of code, in particular, code to be interpreted and code to be executed directly. The advantage of such a structure derives from the fact that the program in this form can make more efficient use of machine resources than conventional programs. This is particularly true if the execution profile of the program is such that only a small fraction of the instructions are the most frequently executed ones. These can be translated into the directly executable form and hence optimised for speed; the remainder can be encoded in the interpretive form and optimised for space.

While the idea of mixing interpretive and directly executable code has been employed in a variety of applications, a hybrid structure has rarely been used as the target of the compilation process. One of the first applications of the technique was the "mixed" code approach (Dakin 1973) used for a portable text editor called MITEM (Poole 1971). This program was written in a simple assembly language for an abstract machine which could be translated by the macroprocessor STAGE2 (Waite 1970) into the assembly language of the target machine. The fraction of directly executable code could be varied by parameters set at compilation time to indicate which parts of the program were to be optimised for speed. It was found that a hybrid form containing 10% of directly executable instructions was about one half the size of the complete directly executable version yet was only approx. 10% more expensive with regard to CPU utilisation. Thus the program was not only more efficient with regard to space requirements but also more portable since it could be moved to machines with memories too small to hold the directly executable version.

Another advantage of the hybrid form is that the behaviour of the program during execution can be conveniently monitored by the interpreter; in fact, the structure is quite suitable for embedding in an online interactive test bed. The fraction of directly executable code can be varied to ensure that sections under test become active as soon as possible. In principle, the use of such a test bed should lead to an improvement in the reliability of programs since the developers would have convenient access to powerful testing and debugging aids. A preliminary step towards this goal was taken by Bate (1974) who developed an interactive test bed for programs written in a simple systems development language called CLSD (Calderbank 1973). The compiler for CLSD produced an intermediate language to be interpreted in the test bed set up on a large machine with a time sharing system. Cross-compilers were then used to generate directly executable code for small process control computers. Bate reported that an interactive command processor of about 500 lines of CLSD was exhaustively tested during the course of half a day. Users were very enthusiastic about the system and the general feeling was that much more reliable software could be produced now that such a tool was available.

This pilot development, based on a specialised language, suggested that such techniques could be employed to advantage with some of the languages which are in much more widespread use. A likely candidate was Pascal, particularly as a portable compiler for Pascal was being constructed (Ravenel 1975) as part of an on-going research program into the development of techniques for producing portable software. The compiler written in Pascal itself was designed to produce an abstract intermediate language called Janus (Coleman 1974). Currently, the translation of Janus is carried out via STAGE2 and a set of macro definitions which relate Janus to the target machine. Thus, the task of providing an interactive test bed for software written in Pascal reduces to whether the Janus language can be translated successfully into a form suitable for interpretation. Furthermore, to improve the portability of Janus and make the hybrid approach feasible, the design of the interpretive code must attempt to minimise the space that such code will occupy. A project to design such a code and construct an interactive test bed is currently underway at the University of Melbourne. This paper is essentially a progress report on this work.

THE JANUS ABSTRACT MACHINE

In order to justify some of the design decisions taken in defining the interpretive code, it will first be necessary to give the reader some understanding of the structure of Janus. The language is fully defined in a report by Waite (1975) which contains the complete syntactic definition of the language as well as a description of the semantics. The following summary is based on this report but describes the language in terms of the underlying abstract machine rather than by formal methods of syntax definition. Although this relies on the intuitive understanding of the reader, it does enable the flavour of the language to be conveyed more readily.

The Janus abstract machine consists of a memory and a processor. The latter contains three registers, a base register for indirect access to memory, an index register and a condition code register which may be set to the values: LT, EQ, or GT. In addition, the processor has access to an operand stack of unspecified size. It is the source of operands and the destination of results for most instructions.

The repertoire of executable instructions available in Janus may be divided into four groups.

(a) Transmission: These are used to move information around within the Janus machine. Instructions exist to transfer information from one part of the memory to another and between memory and the operand stack. Values can also be loaded into the base and index registers. A special TEST instruction provides a mechanism for transferring the condition code onto the operand stack as a boolean value.

(b) Computational: These involve the arithmetic, logical and conversion operations which take some number of operands from the stack, process them and return some number of results to the stack. This implies that the instructions are "addressless" and indeed such a form is allowed. However, if an instruction specifies an operand explicitly, then this is moved onto the stack before the processing commences. One instruction which compares its operands arithmetically is available to set the condition code.

(c) Control: These cause control to be transferred to a specified location. Transfers may be direct or indirect, conditional or unconditional but in all cases the target must be an executable instruction. Case selection is provided, a particular statement being selected on the basis of a match between an index value and a constant associated with the statement. Procedure entry and exit also fall into this class. A complete procedure call is the sequence of statements specifying both the transfer of control and the calculation of the arguments to be passed to the procedure. When control is returned to the caller from a procedure, a result may be returned on the operand stack.

(d) Allocation: The memory of the abstract machine may be allocated statically at compile time or dynamically at run time. The instructions in this group are used to manage the latter operation. Storage may be claimed (or released) from two areas, the stack (not to be confused with the operand stack) and the heap. Stack storage is released in the reverse order to which it was claimed, whilst there is no particular relationship between the allocation and release of heap storage.

The memory of the Janus abstract machine may be regarded as a collection of named operands comprising constants and variables. The latter are grouped into several different categories which reflect the storage allocation strategy and the access mechanism. The operands may be either elementary or composite. An elementary operand is one which has no structure discernible to Janus. A composite operand, on the other hand, is one which is constructed from other operands according to formation rules. Its components may be either elementary or composite but ultimately it can be described in terms of the elementary operands.

Each operand has a mode and a value. Modes may be primitive corresponding to the elementary operands or composite. Janus recognizes six pre-defined primitive modes: ADDR, BOOL, CHAR, INT, REAL and PROC. The latter specifies the entry point of a procedure and the environment within which it was declared. Additional primitive modes may be defined for particular applications but these would constitute an extension to Janus.

Composite modes which must be defined explicitly, are constructed from other modes by applying formation rules. Two such rules exist for Janus, defining the data aggregates, array and record. The definition of an array mode specifies the number and mode of the elements in an array of this class and carries an indication of how the elements are to be aligned. This enables the program to indicate to the translator the importance of storage economy as opposed to access time; i.e., whether the array is to be packed or not. The definition of a record mode establishes the displacement of each field from the beginning of the record and allows the determination of the size and alignment of the whole record.

Access to a variable in memory is made via a reference which, in its most general form, specified a base, an index and a displacement. The base is just the address of the variable in the Janus memory; the index and the displacement are respectively used to select an element of an array variable and a field of a record variable. The interpretation of the base depends upon the category of the variable which qualifies the reference. Janus supports the following categories of storage:

(i) STATIC: the base is interpreted as the absolute address in the Janus memory.

(ii) DISPn: n is an integer specifying the procedure level. When a procedure at level m is activated, a set of activation records for procedures at levels 0 to m-1 is accessible. If a reference in a procedure at level m is qualified by a DISPn category then the base is interpreted as the location of the variable within the activation record at level n ($0 \le n < m$).

(iii) LOCAL: a special case of DISPn for variables within the activation record of the current procedure. This is provided to assist optimization since these are likely to be accessed very frequently.

(iv) PARAM: base is interpreted as the location of an argument to the current non-recursive procedure.

(v) BASED: base is interpreted as a relative address in the area addressed by the Janus base register.

The reference index may contain a static component known at translate time and a dynamic component computed during execution. The static component consists of an integer expression associated with a mode identifier. The value of the expression gives the integral number of units of the mode specified.

The symbolic format of an instruction in Janus is an operator followed by (optionally) a modifier and (optionally) a specification of an operand. The operator defines a basic operation and the modifier enables a particular variant of this operation to be selected. There may also be flags attached to the operator to indicate variations from the normal operation. The "R" flag indicates that the operands at the top of the stack are to be reversed before the operator is applied; the "N" flag causes the return of results to the stack to be suppressed. If no operand is specified, then, in most cases, it is assumed to be on the operand stack. An explicit operand, on the other hand, may specify a constant, a variable or an address.

All code in a Janus program is contained in procedures which may be recursive or non-recursive; one of these is the main program at which execution commences after control is transferred from the operating system. It contains declarations of static storage which is allocated at compile time and may be initialized. During activation, each procedure has access to an activation record containing local variables and parameters which are passed to it by value. Further, it operates within an addressing environment which allows it to access certain non-local objects. All procedures must be declared. Each declaration consists of a procedure heading followed by a procedure body. The former contains the name and class of the procedure together with a description of the formal parameters. The body comprises declarations of local variables, constant definitions, label declarations and executable statements.

THE INTERPRETIVE CODE

Economy of storage was a very important aspect of the design since it was planned to use the interpretive code as the basis for a hybrid structure. Thus, it was necessary to ensure that the number of bytes occupied by such instruction was as small as possible.

In order to assess what might be a feasible reduction in size for the interpretive code compared with the directly executable form, it was first necessary to map typical Janus instructions into the latter form. On the Interdata 8/32, the target machine in this project with an architecture very similar to the IBM/360, Janus instructions, in the main, required 4 bytes (a 1-byte operation code and a 3-byte operand). Experience with previous interpretive systems has demonstrated that there is an overhead with this type of structure, for example, the interpreter itself, various lists of addresses, etc. Hence, in order to obtain a worthwhile reduction in the amount of space required by the interpretive version, it was necessary to aim at a representation which required 2 bytes per instruction.

The first step in the design of the interpretive code was to carry out a static analysis of typical Janus programs to determine the frequency with which various operator and operand types were used. Although, at the time, this analysis was performed, there was only one Janus program available, namely the Pascal compiler, nevertheless, since it contained approximately 30,000 Janus statements, it supplied a reasonable sample, albeit somewhat biased towards non-numeric processing. Table 1 lists the various operators in the Janus core set together with their frequency of occurrence in the compiler. If the operators were combined with all the possible modifiers, then the number of operation codes required would have been of the order of 140. This would require 1 byte for the operation code leaving the second byte for the operand which would clearly be too small to represent any address. If on the other hand the modifier were dissociated from the operator, then only 6 bits would be required to represent the operation codes leaving 10 for the operand. Whilst this is still too small to represent an address, it could be usefully used as an index to a table containing both the mode and the address of each operand; i.e. it is assumed that there are less than 1,024 distinct operand references in the program. In fact, as the control instructions can be treated separately, this restriction on the number of operands applies only to references to storage. The number of such distinct references including constants is about 800 in the compiler.

Janus is an extensible language and one must, therefore, allow for the possibility that the number of operation codes will be increased. This is done by assigning one of the six-bit codes to provide an instruction extension mechanism and access to a 3-byte representation. This will have very little effect on the overall reduction in size since, irrespective of the nature of the program, it is highly probable that the majority of instructions will still be those with the high frequency counts in Table 1: e.g., LOAD, STORE, JMP, RARG, CALL, etc.

The net result of the above decision is that an instruction now requires 2 bytes for each representation in the interpretive code and 4 bytes for the entry in the list of operand addresses which hereafter will be called the reference vector. This is an increase of 50% over the number of bytes required for the representation in the directly executable form. A net saving in space, therefore, will only occur when there is more than one reference to a specified operand; i.e. for two references, store requirements are the same, for three references, there is a 16% reduction and, for ten or more references, the figure approaches 50%. Again, an analysis of the compiler shows that there are 120 variables which are referenced once only and 95 variables which are referenced twice. These numbers are very small compared with the total number of references in the program (approx. 10,000) and the net saving in space is therefore considerable. Of course, access is slow using this approach since it must pass through two levels of indirection. However, this is of little consequence in view of the design criteria of storage economy.

The transmission, computational and allocation operations in Janus which involve references to operands in data storage are treated in the manner described above. The control instructions, since they only reference operands in the space of the Janus program, are treated differently as one can take into account some of the properties of their targets. For example, the targets of JMP instructions are local to the procedures in which the instructions occur. By placing a restriction that the number of labels in any one procedure should be less than 256, only 1 byte is required to index a table of label addresses. An escape mechanism could have been introduced to handle a larger number of labels but has not been at this stage since such subroutines are likely to be very rare. The remaining two bits in the instruction can then be used to represent four of the seven possible modifiers - null, EQ, LT, GT. Only one operation code needs to be assigned to transfer of control and the remaining conditional jumps for NE, LE, GE can be constructed from those already defined. The restriction on the number of labels is easily satisfied in the Pascal compiler as it would be for most programs. Of 155 procedures in the program, one has 135 labels and another, 95. Each of the remainder has less than 30 labels.

The reference vector for transfers of control can be stored at the end of the procedure code and, if the size of any one procedure is restricted to being less than 65,535 bytes, only 2 bytes are required for each entry if it is made relative to the start of the procedure. Since 4 bytes are required for a transfer of control in the directly executable form, there is a saving in space only if the label is referenced more than once. Further economies could be obtained by introducing a short jump which is relative to the current value of the program counter; i.e., the 1-byte operand is a displacement within the code space rather than an index to the reference vector.

Procedure calls are treated in a similar manner to jumps with the operand serving as an index to a list of addresses of procedures. Information can also be stored in this table to indicate whether the procedure is recursive or not and to access details of its addressing environment.

The reference vector mechanism outlined above would work smoothly if all of the storage was static; that is, allocated during translation. Dynamically allocated storage, however, creates problems. For example, access to the activation record of a procedure can be calculated at compile time only in terms of the base address of the activation record. However, this may vary at run time depending upon the path taken by control before the procedure was called. The base address of the activation record of the current procedure clearly depends upon the size of the activation records of the procedures already active when the call occurs.

The mechanism adopted to handle the dynamic allocation of storage involves determining at compile time for each procedure level the maximum number of entries in the reference vector needed for any procedure at that level. DISPØ is excluded since there is only one such activation record and it can be laid out at compile time in a similar manner to static variables and the constants. Associated with each procedure are details indicating how its activation record is to be laid out. When entry is effected to a procedure at level n , the index of the previous procedure (if any) activated at this level is preserved on a stack and the entries in the reference vector for the current procedure are constructed to point to its activation record. Note that while a procedure at level n can call another procedure at the same level, it can only reference activation records for procedures at levels 0 to n-1. Thus, no conflict of access will arise if the entries in the reference vector for the previous procedure at this level are over-written. When exit occurs from the current procedure, the entry in the reference vector for the previous procedure at this level is reconstructed since the base address of its activation record can be recovered from the stack.

TABLE 1
Static Occurrence Frequencies of Janus Operators in the Pascal Compiler

Operation	Modifier	Frequency	Description
ABORT	-	0	terminate execution due to error
ABS	REAL|INT	1	absolute value of operand to stack
ADD	REAL|INT	200	add operands
AND	BOOL	100	logical and of operands
ARG	mode	0	specify arg. for call, non-recursive
ARGLOC	ADDR	0	specify addr. as arg. for call, non-recursive
BASE	ADDR	1320	load base register
BASLOC	ADDR	15	load address to base register
BEGCAS	primitive mode	30	initiate case statement
BOOL	INT	0	convert operand to boolean
CALL	[primitive mode]	0	initiate procedure call, non-recursive
CASE	primitive mode	420	element of case statement
CHAR	INT	0	convert operand to character
CMP	primitive mode	1160	compare operands
CMPM	mode	7	compare composite operands
DIV	INT	5	divide operands, integer result
DIV	REAL	0	divide operands, real result
EQSGN	REAL|INT	0	compare signs of operands
EXOR	BOOL	0	logical exclusive or of operands
FREE	STACK|HEAP	15	release dynamic storage
GRAB	STACK|HEAP	50	allocate storage dynamically
INDEX	INT	470	load index register
INT	BOOL|CHAR|REAL	50	convert operand to integer
JMP	[condition code]	1280	transfer of control
LOAD	primitive mode	2860	load operand stack
MOD	INT	2	modulus of operand
MOVE	mode	50	transfer object in memory
MPY	REAL|INT	1	multiply operands
NEG	REAL|INT	0	change sign of operand
NOT	BOOL	60	logical complement of operands
ODD	INT	2	test if operand is even
OR	BOOL	50	logical or of operands
PROC	PROC-LEVEL	0	return address of procedure
RARG	mode	2230	specify arg. call, recursive
RARGLOC	ADDR	160	specify addr. as arg. for call, recursive
RCALL	[primitive mode]	1110	initiate procedure call, recursive
REAL	INT	0	convert operand to real
RETURN	[primitive mode]	150	exit from procedure
SETLOC	ADDR	570	load operand stack with address
STOP	-	1	terminate execution normally
STORE	primitive mode	1620	store from operand stack
SUB	REAL|INT	230	subtract operands
TEST	condition code	570	condition code to operand stack
TRAP	[condition code]	0	condition exit to environment
TRUNCN	INT	0	truncate operand
TRUNCZ	INT	0	truncate operand towards zero

Note: The | symbol on the above table separates alternatives.
[] indicates that modifier is optional.

TABLE 2

The Interpretive Code

Number	Operator	Size	
1	LOAD	2	operand to stack
2	ARG	2	specify argument for procedure
3	STORE	2	stack to operand
4	BASE	2	load base register
5	JMP	2	transfer of control
6	CMP	2	compare operands
7	CALL	2	enter procedure
8	SETLOC	2	address of operand to stack
9	TEST	1	convert condition code to boolean
10	INDEX	2	load index register
11	SUB	2	subtract operands
12	ADD	2	add operands
13	ARGLOC	2	specify address as argument for procedure
14	RETURN	1	exit from procedure
15	AND	2	logical and
16	NOT	2	logical complement
17	MOVE	2	transfer object in memory
18	GRAB	2	allocate dynamic storage
19	OR	2	logical or
20	INT	2	convert to integer mode
21	FREE	2	release dynamic storage
22	BASLOC	2	load address to base register
23	CMPM	2	compare composite mode
24	DIV	2	divide operands
25	ODD	2	test if operand even
26	MOD	2	modulus of operand
27	MPY	2	multiply operands
28	ABS	2	absolute value of operand
29	STOP	2	terminate execution
30	NEG	2	change sign of operand
31	TRUNCN	2	truncate operand
32	TRUNCZ	2	truncate operand towards 0
33	EXOR	2	logical exclusive or
34	EQSGN	2	compare sign of operands
35	BOOL	2	convert to boolean mode
36	CHAR	2	convert to character mode
37	REAL	2	convert to real mode
38	PROC	2	return address of procedure
39	TRAP	2	condition failure exit
40	NOOP	1	AND, BASE and INDEX with no operand
41	BNOOP	1	LOAD and STORE BASED, no operand
42	ZERO	1	RARG, LOAD, CMP with operand = 0
43	ONE	1	LOAD, ADD, SUB, CMP with operand = 1
44	STKOP	1	Stack operations REV, ERASE

The final list of the operation codes for the interpretive form is shown in Table 2 together with the number of bytes required for each instruction. Most of the instructions in this table come directly from Table 1. However, certain economies have been effected. The special 1-byte instructions which have no direct parallel in Table 1 have been devised on the basis of an analysis of occurrence frequencies of operands. Some instructions such as BASE and INDEX have a high frequency of utilization without an operand. Hence the extra two bits in the byte can be used to select the particular instruction which operates in this manner. Similarly, LOAD and STORE are used frequently with no operand but with a category BASED and therefore give rise to the instruction BNOOP. Other instructions such as ADD and CMP make frequent use of the constant operands 0 and 1. The operations ZERO and ONE are derived from this fact. Finally, there are the stack operations, REV and ERASE, to cater for the R and N flags of Janus. The use of these special instructions saves about 2500 bytes in the interpreted code. Should a subsequent Janus program alter this usage pattern, then extra operation codes can be allocated.

In the previous discussion very little has been said about data storage. In fact, very little can be said since the storage requirements of both the interpretive and directly executable versions are the same, indeed, both must have the same storage map for the hybrid form to operate. No saving in space can therefore be effected in this area; all reduction must take place in the core occupancy of the code itself.

CONCLUSION

At the time of writing, the design of the interpretive code is complete and Janus may be translated into a symbolic representation of this code via STAGE2. In parallel with this work, another implementation of the portable Pascal compiler is being made into directly executable code. This compiler is operational and the current measurements indicate that it requires about 100K bytes (excluding dynamically allocated storage). About 80K bytes of this space is taken up by the code. A conservative estimate suggests that the interpretive version will require about 50K for a total size of 70K, a net saving of 30%. As yet, no statistics are available about the pattern of instruction execution. However, even a 20% reduction in space requirements could be very useful when an attempt is being made to move the compiler to a smaller machine. On large machines, paging behaviour might very well be improved.

The design of the interpreter is essentially complete and coding is under way. The next step is to add the extra facilities to convert the interpreter into the test bed. It should be noted that the structure chosen for the interpretive code will greatly simplify this task. Since all operand references are indirect, flags indicating the need for special monitoring action can easily be placed in the reference vector. These can also contain pointers to the symbol tables produced by the compiler so that all diagnostic information can be output in terms of the original source symbols of the Pascal program. When such a test bed becomes operational, it will provide a very powerful tool for the development of software written in Pascal and thereby contribute to an improvement in the quality of such programs.

ACKNOWLEDGEMENTS

My thanks are due to the Software Engineering Group at the University of Colorado who distributed the software and the supporting documentation, also to Jane Owen who compiled the statistics about the Pascal compiler. This work was supported by the Australian Research Grants Committee, Grant No. F76/15583.

REFERENCES

Bate, D.J. "Design and Implementation of an Interactive Test Bed", Software - Practice and Experience, 4 (1974) 91.

Calderbank, M. and Calderbank, V.J. "A Portable Language for Systems Development", Software - Practice and Experience, 3 (1973) 309.

Coleman, S.S., Poole, P.C., Waite, W.M. "The Mobile Programming System - Janus", Software - Practice and Experience, 4 (1974) 5.

Dakin, R.J. and Poole, P.C. "A Mixed Code Approach", Computer J. 16 (1973) 219.

Poole, P.C. "Mitem User's Manual", UKAEA, Culham Laboratory, Abingdon, Berkshire, 1971.

Ravenel, B.M. "PASCALJ User's Guide and Implementation Notes", Technical Report SEG-75-3, Software Engineering Group, Department of Electrical Engineering, University of Colorado, Boulder, Colorado, 1975.

Wiate, W.M. "The Mobile Programming System: STAGE2", CACM, 13 (1970) 415.

Waite, W.M. and Haddon, B.K. "A Preliminary Definition of Janus", Technical Report SEG-75-1, Software Engineering Group, Department of Electrical Engineering, University of Colorado, Boulder, Colorado, 1975.

Poole : Discussion

Koster: As you put it in your paper, you are making use only of static information deduced from the text of the program. You can make this method much more forceful if you also make use of dynamic information obtained from running your program a number of times. In general, the use of dynamic information should be stressed more, because many more improvement techniques work on the basis of dynamic measurements. For instance, in a machine with paged memory you can try to improve the working set; in a machine which does not have paged memory you can aim at automatic overlaying based on the dynamic profile of your program. Would you comment on that?

Poole: It is just the process of dynamic analysis which is used to determine which parts of a program are to be optimized for space and which parts for speed. Once one has produced the interpretive form of a system, it is very easy to introduce statistics-gathering code in order to determine the execution profile of the program. I suggest, that if one looks into the future, it should be possible to produce compilers which, according to parameters supplied by the user, will generate code optimized either for space or speed. One could generate fully interpretive code initially, for execution on the test bed. Once sections of the program have been checked out, they could be turned into directly executable code and speeded up by a factor of 10 to 20. Hence they would not slow down the rest of the debugging process.

Hibbard: I'd like to point out that there is a FORTRAN compiler which exists, written by Hansen of Carnegie-Mellon University, which generates "dumb code" at first, and then dynamically recompiles and reoptimizes the code when it discovers the most frequently executed parts of the program.

Constructing Quality Software, P.G. Hibbard/S.A. Schuman (eds.)

THE PORTABLITIY OF QUALITY SOFTWARE: EXPERIENCES WITH BCPL

J.E.L.Peck and G.F.Schrack
University of British Columbia,
Vanvouver, Canada

This paper reviews problems of compiler transportation, draws attention to some unexpected difficulties and suggests a number of characteristics which portable software should possess.

INTRODUCTION

Quality software should satisfy several requirements. It should, of course, be correct, reliable and robust. It should be readable and well documented both for the user and the maintainer. It should be constructed from small easily understood modules. It should be able to communicate easily with man, with an operating system and with other software. It should be efficient with respect to time and storage and moreover, to prevent much effort from being wasted, it should be portable. This paper will focus upon the aspect of portability.

THE PORTABLITIY HURDLES

The construction (or reconstruction) of quality software faces many hurdles. One of these hurdles is the fact that not all computers have the same architecture. Another hurdle is that some computers become obsolete and newer models take their place. A third hurdle is that many different operating systems exist, each with its own philosophy of how to interact with the user or with his software system.

The existence of these hurdles means that a software system constructed on one computer is not easily moved (or "ported") to another. A good compiler, for example, produced on one computer may require great effort to be ported to another machine, and may even demand considerable effort to be coaxed to work under a new operating system for the same machine. Indeed, if portability is not considered beforehand, it may be easier to rewrite the software system for the new machine or the new operating system rather than to try to modify the old one. For compilers written in assembler language, this could well be the case.

AN INTERMEDIATE LANGUAGE

Many strategies have been devised to alleviate the portability problem. For compilers, one of the most successful is to code it in some well structured language, (preferably its own, e.g., BCPL, PASCAL or ALGOL 68) and to use an intermediate language so that the translation process is sharply divided into two phases. Hopefully, in this way the first phase need not be rewritten. Only the second, or machine dependent phase, will then need modification. But in practice this turns out to be a gross simplification.

With actual experience one may discover that the intermediate language has been designed to match the source machine too closely, leading to difficulties in translating it for another (it is known that the PASCAL effort suffers from this). One may also discover that the intermediate language is conceived at too high a level and as a consequence the second phase of the translation process is a non-trivial task, sufficiently difficult perhaps to encourage abandonment. Another discovery one may make, and this could come as a surprise to those who have not experienced it, is that parts of the first phase will need to be rewritten, because the new operating system may have a philosophy quite different from the old one. Moreover both parts of the compiler must be controlled by some master program module. It is inevitable that most of this module is highly operating-system dependent and, for each new operating system, must be designed and written almost from scratch.

LACK OF DOCUMENTED EXPERIENCE

Unfortunately not many who have attempted to transport a compiler survive with enough energy to describe the experience, while others consider it so much as routine that they do not bother. There are a few descriptions of the porting of PASCAL [WEL 72, RUS 76, GRO 76], but not so many concerning BCPL, although the latter is well known to have a portable compiler [RIC 71]. This lack is regrettable, for the literature then contains only the glowing descriptions of the innovators who, quite naturally, infer that the method they have devised is the solution to all portability problems. In contrast, this paper is not the report of innovators developing a new method, but rather the experience of those who have ported the BCPL compiler to one minicomputer (the NOVA) and are in the process of repeating it for another (the HP). This effort is being made in order to have a good system programming language on the small computers and to gain practical experience. This experience will help to determine where the difficulties of portability lie and perhaps then to suggest how to design software which minimizes these difficulties.

OUR AIM

It is the purpose of this paper to recall the lessons of experience. If in doing this we succeed in placing in perspective the location of the real difficulties and of suggesting how these may be avoided in future, then the effort in writing it will have been rewarded. To anticipate a conclusion, we will discover that the production of a cross compiler, i.e., one which runs on the source machine pruducing code for the target machine, is a relatively minor problem, for which the innovators [RIC 73, WAI 70, 74] have already shown us ways that work quite well. The real difficulty in portability now lies, not so much with the diversity of machine architecture, but with the diversity of operating systems and their many and varied philosophies. Almost all of the effort in porting a compiler is now taken up in trying to find out how to communicate with a new and unfamiliar operating system, and trying to unravel the obscurity of the manufacturer's system manuals.

THE IDEAL MACHINE

We must now show some justification for the remarks made above. For this it will be necessary to describe the method suggested by Richards [RIC 73] for porting the BCPL compiler. This first came to the authors' attention at the Trondheim meeting in 1973. In that paper, Richards describes how the BCPL compiler is constructed in two phases. The first phase translates from the source language to an intermediate language called OCODE [RIC 71], and the second, the machine dependent phase, translates from OCODE to the language of the target machine. He then observes that translation from OCODE was found to be more difficult than expected for one who came at it fresh, for it required a depth of understanding that was not really necessary for successful porting. He therefore devised a lower-level language, the language of a simple machine. This language is called INTCODE, and a translator from OCODE to INTCODE is provided. With this available all that is necessary is to construct an assembler and an interpreter for this very simple machine, written in some software of the actual target machine. This can be done with relatively little effort.

CROSS COMPILERS

One method of solving the portability problem is thus to define a low-level simple ideal machine (which may not exist in hardware) and to have the compiler generate code for that. The method then requires either a) the interpretation of this ideal machine on the target machine, or b) the mapping of the ideal machine instructions to the actual instructions of the target machine. In the case of interpretation, it is only necessary to construct a loader and interpreter in some already available language (possibly assembler) of the target machine. We shall call the result of this exercise an "interpretive cross compiler". In the case of machine mapping, one must alter the last part of the compiler by intercepting calls to the few code generation routines and replacing these routines with routines that generate assembler code for the target machine. We shall call the result of this exercise a "cross compiler". It is important to note that in both these cases the compiler is still dependent on the source machine, and as such has not solved the portability problem.

INDEPENDENT COMPILERS

The next step is to make the compilers run independently of the source machine. In the case of the interpretive cross compiler, it is necessary to run the compiler through itself and to interpret the resulting code on the target machine. A compiler produced in this way we shall call an "interpretive independent compiler". In the case of the cross compiler, if we run the compiler though itself, we obtain a compiler written in the assembler language of the target machine, which may then be assembled and executed. This we shall call an "independent compiler".

THE INTERPRETIVE COMPILERS

The authors have experimented with the interpretive approach, using BCPL, and have verified that it works, but the results were less than satisfying. Because of interpretation of the ideal machine instructions, speed is sacrificed. The interpretive compilers appear therefore to be little more than toys which may be used to study the method. However does such a study reveal useful information on portability problems? If our study is conducted on the source computer alone, without moving to the target computer, then the test is indeed spurious. It proves only that a given compiler may be run interpretively on some ideal machine. If the test includes the interpretation of programs on the target machine, then we have made some progress, for we must then have made contact with the new operating system and solved at least the problem of input and output.

There are, of course, two distinct achievements of quite different magnitude. The first is the interpretive cross compiler. This achievement is relatively easy to attain. The second is the interpretive independent compiler. This is, in theory, a completion of the transportation process, since the compiler is now independent of the source machine. However, this achievement is illusory. Although it tells us about some of the real problems of compiler portability, it is not long before we find that we have constructed only a toy. It usually works too slowly to be a useful tool.

A REAL COMPILER

Our next goal is then to construct a cross compiler (producing assembler code for the target machine). A first look suggests that this involves a rewriting of a large part of the compiler, seemingly a non-trivial task. Closer inspection reveals that the part that produces the assembler code for the ideal machine can easily be isolated. In the case of BCPL, it consists of two or three routines out of twenty or thirty which comprise the translator from OCODE. We discovered that it is easy to replace these few routines with others to produce assembler code for the actual target machine instead.

MACHINE MAPPING

What we have said above is that we examine carefully both the ideal machine and the actual target machine and decide how to map the instruction set of the former onto the latter. In the case of the two minicomputers under consideration, and because of the simple design of the ideal machine, this was found to be an easy task, once the instruction code of the target machine had been mastered. Using this method, we can now confidently state that the production of a cross compiler (without input and output) has indeed been reduced to a task that can be accomplished in two or three weeks. Thus it takes only a short time to produce code that will assemble and run on the new machine, if no input and output is required. The next task is to understand how to receive and to deliver one character at a time from (to) the operating system. A makeshift primitive character transfer interface can usually be accomplished within another week. With this we then have a cross compiler.

WE RUN BUT WE ARE WALKING

If we now wish to run only programs on the target machine that use standard input and output devices, then such a cross compiler can prove to be a very useful tool. In fact, things go so well one is encouraged to think it is only a small step to run the compiler through this process, and a new compiler on the target machine will be available. But this naive view overlooks what now appear to be the major portability problems.

If the target machine is a large one and if its operating system is similar to that of the source machine, then perhaps the completion of the porting will not take long. If this is not the case, then we may be heading for difficulties. The fundamental difficulties then are concerned with size of memory and communication with a new operating system.

SIZE

The problem of size manifests itself early when copying a compiler written for a large (and perhaps virtual) memory to a minicomputer with, say, 32K of 16 bit words. For the large computer, all the intermediate states of the compiler, such as the identifier tables, the program tree and the intermediate code may be held in memory together with all phases of the compiler. Indeed, for a virtual memory system, this is the most natural way. For a minicomputer, however, one may find that even the first phase of the compiler is too large to fit into what memory is left over by the operating system. Fortunately the BCPL compiler is written in such a way that it is easy to isolate three distinct parts, a) that part which builds the program tree, b) that which translates it to OCODE, and c) that part which translates the OCODE to INTCODE.

Our solution for the NOVA (not claimed to be unique) was then to partition the compiler into the three parts indicated above. We have also added a fourth part which is called automatically to translate the assembler code to relocatable binary. The identifier tables and the program tree are passed from the first part to the second in memory, but the OCODE is written to a file and then is read back in again. Of course, the assembler code may eventually be avoided when one has understood enough about the construction of relocatable binary code.

OVERLAY

Such a division may solve the problem of size, but it brings with it other problems. One must now know how to construct a program in several parts using the technique of overlaying (or perhaps swapping). Here it is important to be working with a software system that has a modular construction, to allow for easy decomposition. It is also important that the structure of the software be clear and easily understood so that modules may be torn apart and recombined where necessary. With respect to overlays, there may be several weeks of study involved, for here the operating system manuals may be sketchy at best. One is now working in an area where the supplier did not expect the majority of his users to be, so the explanations are minimal and have not been subjected to the scrutiny of countless readers.

FILE MANIPULATION

Of course, many other techiques such as opening and closing of files need to be learned. Operating systems are often not robust enough for our kind of work, for example, a system that simply crashes when one tries to close a file that has not been opened, is not too helpful. When this happens one must power down and power up again with a complete initial program load. It then involves a painful repetition of crashes to locate the cause of the crash.

One must also discover the structure of a file. Here it is usually not too clear from the manual what the format of a record is and how a new line is signalled, so the answers may have to be determined by costly experiment. Also the input output routines provided by the system may be record (line-at-a-time) oriented, and since BCPL is stream (character-at-a-time) oriented, it can be a non-trivial task to build a system interface to interpret records as streams.

A MINIMAL INTERFACE

The method by which the compiler communicates with the operating system is important. One is tempted at first to write this part in the assembler language of the target machine, especially since the various calling sequences are described in this language in the operating system manuals. This temptation should be strongly resisted. Examination will reveal, as it did for us, both on the NOVA and on the HP, that calls to the operating system can all be unified into one routine that may be written in assembler. We found this to be a happy solution, for it gave immediate power over most of the functions of the system, since each of the individual calls could be set up through small routines written in BCPL itself, with consequent ease of modification, when necessary. Moreover we were not afraid to (and in fact we did) throw away some initial approaches since the effort spent on them was not as great as it would have been if written in assembler.

With this experience we were careful to keep the assembler-written operating-system interface to the barest minimum, even at the cost perhaps of some speed. Having done this for the target machine, we returned to the compiler on the large source machine and performed there the same minimization task. As a result we now have several models, each written in BCPL, of how to interface with an operating system.

GLOBALS

The global vector of BCPL was a source of difficulty. As the reader may know, the language postulates the existence of a large array of cells, numbered consecutively, through which all inter-segment communication passes. This is somewhat like the COMMON of FORTRAN and suffers from the same defects in that if the order is disturbed then the correspondence fails. In the BCPL compiler, as we inherited it, there were almost four hundred of these global cells, for each of which the compiler writer had associated an identifier with an integer.

ENTRIES AND EXTERNALS

Since we found it difficult to coax the system loader to load addresses in some common area, and since we did not wish to set up a global vector of constant size, we abandoned the consideration of globals as a vector and implemented them instead as entries and externals in the usual sense of assembler language. This is a slight departure from the BCPL language, but one which has already been made by others. In one sense, it was a happy decision, for it meant that we can now use the loader provided by the system. We are in the process of changing all our BCPL compilers over to this system. We therefore encourage our users to make use of declarations like

```
EXTERNAL { WRITEF : "WRTF" }
ENTRY    { START : "STRT" }
```

where the string constant is the name which is known to the loader (and may be subject to severe length restriction). We believe that any system that requires the human mind to keep track of the matching of identifiers to integers is inherently error prone. In fact, our experience in porting BCPL (in which there were almost four hundred) showed that the clerical work involved in keeping track of the global numbers was considerable, and was a frequent source of frustrating error.

TOOLS

Some tools necessary for the transportation of software are: a) a good data link from the source computer to the target computer, b) an editor on each system with octal (or hexadecimal) mode, especially on the target computer, c) system software such as assemblers, linkage editors and loaders.

An important factor is the data link. If there is a high speed data line, serviced by existing software, then the task of copying the files many times will be reasonably easy. However, if this data link is not smoothly implemented, then much time will be lost. For example, at some times we were initiating a data link request on the target computer, then running down three flights of stairs and along a corridor to complete the link from the source computer, only to find, on running breathlessly up three flights of stairs again, that the requests did not synchronize. Progress may be even slower if data is to be transported by magnetic tape or paper tape. Why should the data link be so important? The answer is that most operating system manuals are not sufficiently complete or sufficiently clear to enable one to get things right the first time. Progress is usually made by costly experiment. Each individual step in these experiments may involve copying large files from the source machine to the target machine. Any impediment to the transportation of large files will inevitably slow down the compiler porting process.

TRIVIA

What we have outlined above may appear to be trivia and of no technical importance. However one should realise that software transportation is an engineering exercise. It is necessary to have the technical details correct, but it is often the details of the most trivial kind that hold up an engineering project.

THE LESSONS

It is now time to summarize our conclusions. We have found that the translation of BCPL to the language of a simple ideal machine is a definite asset for compiler transportation. Rather than interpret this ideal machine on the target machine, it is better to map it onto the assembler language of the target machine. We have found, however, that these considerations help us only with a small fraction of the portability problems. The real difficulties, as we see them, are the unfamiliarity and obscurity of a new operating system and the time it takes to learn how to communicate with the new system and its file structure.

THE FUTURE

What should we suggest to make portability of compilers easier for the future? Our suggestions fall into two categories, the first concerning compiler construction and the second concerning operating system design. Desirable properties of a portable compiler are

a) it should be for a simple language, otherwise the compiler may be too big and unwieldy,

b) the compiler should be written in its own language, so that it can process itself. This saves learning two languages and provides an automatic test of large portions of the compiler,

c) it should have a modular construction, so that decomposition and recomposition are easier (for this surely will be necessary),

d) it should have an inter-module communication system that is suitable for both humans and for most operating system loaders. BCPL was deficient in this, but we were able to make improvements,

e) the structure of the compiler should be clear and easily understood, for it is likely that one must rearrange it.

The above properties will help, but do not misunderstand our purpose here. These solve only five percent of the problems. The major problem, that which generates ninety-five percent of the work in compiler transportation, is the diversity of operating system construction and philosophy. We believe that if we are to make software of the future more portable, then a necessary condition will be that operating system design should become stable and that operating systems on different machines should not differ radically. A way to ensure this is to concentrate on the creation of portable operating systems. We are currently looking at this possibility with UNIX.

REFERENCES

[GRO 76] C.O.Grosse-Lindemann and H.H.Nagel, Postlude to a PASCAL compiler bootstrap on a DEC system 10, Software Practice and Experience, Vol. 6 (1976) pp. 29-42.

[RIC 71] M.Richards, The portability of the BCPL compiler, Software Practice and Experience, Vol. 1 (1971) pp. 135-146.

[RIC 72] M.Richards, INTCODE, An interpretive machine code for BCPL, University of Cambridge, Dec. 1972.

[RIC 73] M.Richards, Bootstrapping the BCPL compiler using INTCODE, Machine Oriented Higher Level Languages, North-Holland, 1973.

[RUS 76] D.L.Russell and J.Y.Sue, Implementation of a PASCAL compiler for the IBM 360, Software Practice and Experience, VOl. 6 (1976) pp. 371-376.

[WAI 70] W.M.Waite, The mobile programming system: STAGE2, Comm. Assoc. Comp. Mach. 13 (1970) pp. 415-421.

[WAI 74] S.S.Coleman, P.C.Poole and W.M.Waite, The mobile programming system, Janus, Software Practice and Experience, Vol. 4 (1974) pp. 5-23.

[WEL 72] J.Welsh and C.Quinn, A PASCAL compiler for ICL 1900 series computers, Software-Practice and Experience, Vol. 2, (1972) pp. 73-77.

Peck and Schrack : Discussion

Ross: I was so pleased to find you bringing in the real world, but one of the distressing things to me was that when you were listing the practitioners of portability you made no mention at all of AED. The complexity you mention was precisely the real world that we saw, my group and I, 17 years ago. We started in 1960. By 1962 or 1963 we had a major portion of the solutions to those problems in the design of AED. We finished and firmed up the definition of the AED language in 1965. We had already gone through several cycles by 1966 or 1967. We started on the IBM 709 then went to the 7090, then to the 7094. We went from there first to the Univac 1108 and then to the IBM 360 by 1968. In the process we learned that the heart of the matter is something that you haven't even mentioned here yet, and that is how to address all of these problems at the same time, in a practical fashion. That's where the concept of software engineering, to my mind, really came from.

The only way in which we could do this job was to treat it not as a game, not as an academic exercise, but as a major engineering undertaking. I feel a little bit upset at your not having mentioned AED merely because it did not receive recognition in the literature. At the time we were doing these things in this "real world" you cite here, not a single editor would stand up and allow our work to be published without a major rewrite because, they said, it could not be understood. We were interested in doing this work, so we made our MIT publications fully available to anybody who wanted them. And yet, people still come to the subject of portability as though it were brand-new and there were no solution. What I'm saying is that you are overlooking the real solution, which is first to understand how to separate these problems, and then how to solve them all at once by being able to relate the separate solutions. That is, learn what we had to learn, get the practice we had to get and then build the results of that experience into a system.

You gave several guidelines and we could use your points to get this old story told. You say, "Keep the language simple." The first thing about AED is that it is simple. The AED language that now exists is called AED-0 because we were going to tell the world about AED-1; AED-0 was just for our internal use. AED-0 has no modern types at all. In fact, when it started out, it had only integer, Boolean and real, and it wasn't until we had to work with the IBM/360 that we even put in the distinction between integers and pointers. AED-0 doesn't even have the concept of a record, but it does have the concept of a packed component - a portion of a word offset relative to a pointer. By using the language properly you can get the effect of any kind of record structures. Therefore the language is simple and yet fully capable. That's why we were able to do it well.

Next, you say, "Write the compiler in its own language." This was always true of AED, except for the very first compiler, which was written in another language called the Bootstrap Compiler Language. That compiler consisted of only 75 machine instructions and a built-in table of less than 300 words. We wrote that bootstrap compiler for both the TX-0 computer (the first transistorized computer, built by the MIT Lincoln Laboratory) and the IBM 709. The language vocabulary consisted of single punctuation characters found on the keypunch, and handled logic, integer arithmetic and uniform referent notation for the equivalent of record components. A special character appended the just-compiled program to the compiler itself in a standard way, so that the source language following that character was processed by the modified compiler. Hence the name "bootstrap". The last part of the table was used as a built-in symbol table for all of the other characters you could find on the keypunch. It turned out, there were four symbol table entries unused, which could be utilized to write a list-structured, sorted, multi-character symbol table program. That then allowed us to write big programs, leading to the first AED-0 compiler itself. And so, from the very beginning the principles were "keep it simple" and "write in its own language". Both are correct.

Then you say, "Make it well structured and modular." That is the part where there is much more to the story than you've told. That's where the engineering itself comes in. How do you separate out machine independence from machine dependence? In the present AED compiler, for example, 98% of the definition of the AED language is captured in the unchanging source of the compiler. There is no change at all in that defining source when you transport the compiler bodily from one machine to another.

"Translate to a simple ideal machine." We rejected that idea in 1960 because, in effect, it says to the hardware people, "No matter what you may invent in the way of hardware, it's just going to be a simple case of my software machine." We were interested in solving a practical problem, so, "translate to a simple ideal machine" may be OK for the first step of a bootstrap, but what we needed for efficient, professional quality software was to understand the major engineering problem and solve it. We concentrated on systematic code generation techniques to produce what is required for each target machine.

"Keep the system interface to the minimum." That's, of course, exactly counter to the facts of the "real world". You cannot keep the system interface to a minimum. You must solve the real-world problems, which are not simple. And so we did. AED has modular, machine- and device-independent I/O system, storage management system, interface to the operating system system, etc. All of that is done, and it has been done for all these years.

I finish now by saying that it is not just SofTech people or MIT people who can do these things. The best example of portability was a project carried out at the Boeing Company by a group that did not even work with us in the original cooperative program at MIT where we developed AED. This group at Boeing developed the SPS system, the Support Programming System. They invested many man-years to develop a whole system, written in AED, for designing and building assemblers, simulators, testers, etc. for as-yet unbuilt airborn computer hardware. They developed this whole SPS system on the 7094, used it, and then had to move to an 1108 computer when the company changed manufacturers. I may have my numbers mixed up, but I think it took 2 man-months to move those very difficult, high-level system programs and to have SPS operational again on the new machine. They then used SPS to develop several missile systems and then made another change back to an IBM machine, this time to the 360, a 32-bit machine. Again, one month later, or something like that, they had the whole thing operational, and it is still in use. The same process is being continued. For Boeing, SofTech developed a new version of the JOVIAL language for avionics software. This compiler, written in AED within SPS, has the same property of portability. So, there is a very real world out there, that matches exactly your very fine talk. I just wish you could get these new and old things together, and indicate that it is not all in the future. Some of the things in the past can be learned from.

Peck: I don't think that calls for an answer from me. [☺]

Dijkhuis: This is just a short message to inform Mr. Ross that there's a computer science publisher in the room.

Poole: It's about 10 years since I first came into contact with the AED system and I'd like to remark that I think it is one of the most successful of the portability systems. Maybe one of the reasons it isn't widely known is that it quickly moved into a commercial situation.

Ross: No. It is in the public domain, supported by its users and subsidized by SofTech. It is not a proprietary product of SofTech. At one point it was available for $625, the cost of a tape. We could not move it at all at that point. Then when we said for $15,000 you can have a year of maintenance and some help, it started to move. But it has always been the public domain and it will always be available to anybody.

Poole: I do want to make a couple of other points. One is that, to my mind, Waite's STAGE 2 is certainly one of the most portable pieces of software that has ever been produced. It has been exported to almost every country in the world that runs computers, implemented on well over 30 different computers and indeed, you can bring it up on a new machine with about one week's work. On the other hand, the technique used for STAGE 2 broke down once we moved to more complex pieces of software. Consequently, our methods now are based, not on a simple abstract machine, but on a fairly complex one: JANUS is far from simple. It is a very high-level abstract machine, so much so that while it's a very good machine, as the target of compilation process, it's a difficult machine to map onto real machines at the moment. The amount of effort is measured in many, many man-months and part of the research effort is to determine how this can be reduced by a hierarchical approach.

One of the main problems I have found in the portability game is getting the text off the magnetic tape into the system and, if someone could do some research on that, I would be very thankful. Finally, I support strongly Peck's comments about portable operating systems. Presently, we are concentrating on portable compilers for the common languages, but we also have some work in progress on portable operating systems. It appears that UNIX will be one of the first examples of a portable operating system, since I know of two projects which are involved at the moment in moving UNIX from the PDP-11 to other machines, including the Interdata 8/32. So, I think that portable operating systems are really an important area for research at the moment.

Dewar: Since we've started to point out successful examples, it's really a great shame not to mention SNOBOL, because SNOBOL is something that has been ported not by people interested in porting things but by people who are interested in SNOBOL. There, perhaps, lies the significant difference in level of achievement.

Bell: In your opinion is it substantially easier to design a system from scratch to run on two rather different computers than it is to write it for one and afterwards discover that you want to port it to the other?

Peck: If you write it for one and afterwards discover you want to port it to another, then it might be easier to re-write it from scratch for the other one. However, if you begin with the idea that you want to make it portable, then it's probably easier just to write it for one and port it to the other, but you have to begin with that idea.

Kurki-Suonio: I have a question that concerns both portability as described by Peck, at least the toy portability part, and the hybrid programs of Poole. With dynamic microprogramming the distinction between interpretation and execution sort of disappears, since you can write interpretive routines as microprograms. Have you considered what effect this would have on what you are doing?

Peck: Yes, I mentioned that one of our current efforts is to port BCPL to an HP 21MX that is microprogrammable. The next step will be to try to microprogram the INTCODE machine directly so that our problems in porting will be very simple, apart from the operating system.

Poole: I propose that you might have a two-level output for a compiler, but one could even consider three levels: interpreted code, directly executable code and microcode.

Wodon: Our ALGOL 68 compiler has been ported in this way (from the Philips X8 to the P1100) and except, of course, for interfaces, it took five or six months to do it.

Constructing Quality Software, P.G. Hibbard/S.A. Schuman (eds.)

MODULARIZATION OF A MULTI-LANGUAGE OPTIMIZER

by Sergei POKROVSKY

Computing Centre of the Siberian Division
of the USSR Acad. Sci., Novosibirsk 630090, USSR

This is a case study of module split-up and interface design in a multi-language multi-computer optimizing compiler (the BETA System). The paper is written as a confrontation of modular programming systems and "universal" meta-processors, or else, of multi-language compilers and translator writing systems (TWS).

0. INTRODUCTION

There are at least two directions in the attempts to bring more order and generality in programming technology.

The first, which is a natural reflex of the mathematically trained mind, is to try and solve the problem at a meta-level, i.e. to develop a meta-processor that would automatically generate an algorithm on the basis of its specification (e.g. the compiler-compiler concept).

The second is a generalization of the everyday engineering practice of splitting a large system into a set of smaller modules, which facilitates its writing, testing, debugging and maintenance, and under certain conditions makes it possible to re-use previously written modules in a new system.

The first direction is more ambitious, but really works only under (often impractically) severe restrictions; usually these restrictions can be very accurately and concisely formulated. The second approach usually gives excellent results for the particular set of problems that had been envisaged in its design; but the possibility of using a part of such a system in a new application strongly depends on the method used to specify and implement its interfaces. The problem of generalized interface specification may often be viewed as an analogue of meta-language design (though a module is sometimes used with a family of interfaces, so that a further subdivision emerges, which corresponds to the opposition of a "nucleus" versus "envelope" approach to the design of a universal system).

In contrast to earlier BETA publications, which almost exclusively dealt with meta-algorithms, we would like now to restore the proper balance by a somewhat artificial and reactionary emphasis on the more conventional modular approach.

1. MULTI-LANGUAGE COMPILERS AND TWS

Given a family of source languages (and target computers), a multi-language (multi-computer) compiler, or a co-ordinated implementation, is a set of compilers that realize these languages (on the computers in question) and which have the compilation scheme and some algorithms and interfaces in common. Examples are the visionary UNCOL and the more successful ALMO System. A degenerate case is a set of compilers used under one same operating system, which also displays some general merits of co-ordinated implementations: -

- a uniform system of data and program representation;
- a common system of diagnostic messages;
- a common program library;
- easier maintenance;
- effort and space saved by sharing some compiler modules and run-time routines.

A translator-writing system (TWS) is, according to Grushetsky et al. (1975), a comprehensive collection of techniques, rules and utility procedures whose systematic application to any language of a fixed class results in a compiler that implements this language on the given computer.

The notions of TWS and co-ordinated implementation are logically independent: a TWS may contain no real compiler, or produce incompatible compilers without common parts. A TWS user is a systems programmer, who is experimenting with essentially one programming language (or developing an application package on the basis of a single programming language), while a co-ordinated implementation is a more immediate "consumer commodity and may involve radically different languages.

Still, it is desirable to construct a co-ordinated implementation as an open system capable of assimilating further source or target languages; the development of utility procedures which could facilitate this process may be considered as a TWS design.

2. AN OVERVIEW OF THE BETA SYSTEM

Presently the main objective of the BETA Project is the development of a co-ordinated optimizing implementation of the major "general purpose programming languages" (including SIMULA 67, PASCAL, ALGOL 68, PL/1) on a variaty of target computers - see Ershov (1971). This characterization implies at least two kinds of program processing, namely translation and optimization. The possibility to separate them in our System is due to the availability of a suitable Internal Language (IL), which is used as the only form of program representation during the optimization, and as the uniform intermediate language of an Uncol-like compiler.

The development of a self-contained optimizing processor

is the best justification for a joint implementation effort (especially in view of the rising demand for optimization). This point is very important, because unlike standard compilation phases (e.g. parse), optimization is not always envisaged by language designers, and consequently its implementation is no routine matter.

In the sequel the program processing phases of the BETA System will be referred to as

(a) the Parse
(b) the IL Program Generation
(c) the Flow Analysis
(d) the Optimizing Transformations
(e) the Object Program Generation.

Here the Optimizer (c,d) is inserted into the Translator (a, b,e). Their independence is illustrated by the possibility to remove (some) optimizions or to repeat them. Note that even though the IL program generation in the "direct" (non-optimizing) version of the System may seem to be an unnecessary complication, we insist on this process, which makes its debugging and maintenance more reliable.

3. THE TRANSLATOR

We are not much interested here in the parse. In fact, parsing is the best developed field of compiler writing; language designers always pay special attention to its feasibility; finally, the languages included in a co-ordinated implementation are bound to have well documented compilers in which this problem is somehow solved. This is also true of the attribute induction, so that the major difficulty facing us in the development of the translator is in the post-syntactic processing. We formulate it as the following semantic unification problem - see Pokrovsky (1977):

(1) To develop a semantic basis sufficient to uniformly represent constructs of all intended source languages with orientation to each of the target computers (i.e. a machine-oriented machine-independent language).

(2) To standardize the translation into this semantic basis.

One purpose of this standardization is to ensure a clean interlingual assembly at the IL level. Actually the BETA System must allow for two kinds of subprogram integration. The first is the traditional binding of object modules; the second is the integration carried out during translation into the Internal Language of a number of external (sub)routines, possibly written in different languages. Apart from the security issues, the essential difference between these options is due to the availability of powerful optimization, which only in the second case extends across module boundaries, clearing away irrelevant features of a general (e.g. library) procedure.

To implement such interlingual assembly we need some kind of Abstract Hypersyntax, at least for the external-object specifications (types). The word "Abstract" here is a homage to John McCarthy, and the prefix "Hyper-" reflects the superlingual nature of its constituent hypernotions. A hypernotion emerges when a close analogy between some (abstract syntax) notions in at least two source languages enables (requires) a similar treatment by the translation algorithms (this may be mandatory if the notions are made equivalent in interlingual assembly). In this case the hypernotion is constructed more or less as a "direct sum" of the attributes of the individual notions in the particular languages. As a particular notion may enter in more than one association, the Abstract Hypersyntax is not a consistent language, but rather a collection of admissible input formats for a library of compilation modules.

In fact, this standardization of compilation modules and their interfaces is our approach to the problem of generalization of the post-syntactic translation - similar to work by Lancaster and Schneider (1976). We always try to write an IL Generation module for the most general case, even if this is not required for interlingual processing. Such modules are provided with a macro-like mechanism of self-adaptation, which expunges the irrelevant code.

In theory this could be done by a very powerful optimizer as a part of the "static action elaboration" (a generalization of constant propagation) and removal of useless computation. This would simplify the programming (the algorithm being expressed at only one level) and could introduce more (correct) projections of the general algorithm than were anticipated by the programmer.

As an example of a readily constructed hypernotion, consider the "declared variable". The attributes of this hypernotion may be subdivided into three categories: those common to all variables in each of the source languages (among which are "type", "block", "kind", "symbol", "read-only", "external"), the optional ones, which characterize particular kinds of "variables" in some languages, and special attributes which are handled only by language-dependent modules. The "kind" is a good example of direct summation: its values would include "static", "automatic", "controlled" (like in PL/1); various kinds of procedure parameters: "value", "result", "value result", "reference", "procedure" (qualified or not); "record field", "overlayed variable". Now, the latter kind requires two optional attributes for the carrier object and displacement. Although optional, these attributes are known to a general module of the IL Generation Phase, while the special attributes which are necessary to compute them are not (e.g. the equivalence/common links for FORTRAN).

So far we have considered only half of the problem, namely the source-language orientation. In fact the machine orientation is also taken into account during the IL-program generation. This certainly complicates the translation to IL, but we consider it worthwhile because it simplifies the Internal Language and the subsequent phases. After all it seems reasonable to isolate the difficulties at a single phase (rather than to scatter them all through the System).

The machine orientation is achieved in the same way as the adjustment to a source language. In fact this technique is fairly common there, with hypernotions taking the form of formats of (macro) enquiries.

The enquiries of the IL Program Generation Phase are concerned with the representation in the target computer of such machine-dependent features as the file specification format, word size and memory allocation procedures. The result is expressed in terms of the Internal Language, which consequently is a machine-oriented language.

The feasibility of this approach (at least as far as the machine orientation is concerned) was demonstrated by a series of implementations of which the ALMO System seems to be the most successful.

4. THE OPTIMIZER

The optimization algorithms present an example of a much cleaner and more successful generalization. This is due to the invariance of the Internal Language and to a better problem statement.

As it was mentioned earlier, the optimization is an unusual feature, and checking the correctness conditions for an optimizing transformation necessitates a complicated program analysis. It is done at the Analysis Phase, which receives a program written in the "common base" part of the Internal Language and outputs an "annotated" IL program. The latter contains full (covering) information about the flow data and control in the program; this information may also be of interest for other applications, e.g. for discovery of some program irregularities (potential bugs). The "annotations" are kept in a separate file and are easily discarded by a subsequent phase.

Apart from being correct, the transformations we are interested in must improve some run-time properties of the processed program. For so-called <u>machine-independent transformations</u> this may be taken for granted (e.g. the elimination of redundant statements and useless computations, overlaying variables within a block, compile-time elaboration of "static actions"); but most of the traditional optimizations turn out to be machine-oriented.

The application of <u>machine-oriented transformations</u> is governed by a special set of optimization mode enquiries, which originate partly from the description of the target computer and partly from the user's indications. Here are a few examples of such dependencies on properties of the target computer.

- The density of reference may be impaired by code motion, elimination of common subexpressions, space economy across block boundaries.

- Some advantages of a stack architecture may be lost by code motion or making procedure parameters into global variables (e.g. in an attempt to transform a procedure into a subroutine; this expands the code of a stack computer).

- Loop fusion may increase the computation time because a loop may exceed the size of the instruction cache (cf. the optimal segmentation problem).

We need not mention more obvious examples (like register allocation) for which the machine orientation is evident from the very formulation.

The problem of optimal sequencing of optimizing transformations for the BETA System was considered by Pottosin (1977); here we would like only to emphasize the advantages of selecting a small number of powerful primitive transformations over developing a numerous family of algorithms to implement particular cases of a complex construct. Apart from the fact that such casing is done as a part of a translation (which contradicts our conception of optimization as a single language-level processing), this approach has at least two practical disadvantages. First, some dependence on the source language appears, which leads to a more lengthy and less general code; secondly, the System's reliability is decreased, because some cases may happen to occur infrequently.

In the next section we shall consider some properties of the Internal Language which facilitate the generalization of the optimization algorithms.

5. THE INTERNAL LANGUAGE

The Internal Language defines a program representation used by the four phases of the compiler which belong to two very different kinds of program processing. This leads to somewhat contradictory requirements, in particular,

(a) to provide a uniform "semantic basis" sufficient for the uniform representation of constructs of the source languages with orientation to each of the target computers;

(b) to provide maximal explicitness and complete interpretation in cases where this could enhance the effectiveness of optimizing transformations;

(c) to preserve the source program information about some high-level constructs (procedures, loops, case statements), which considerably refines the Analysis and leads to a more efficient Code Generation;

(d) to be convenient for optimizing transformations.

Now let us consider the design principles used to meet these requirements.

5.1. Incomplete Interpretation

The only unquestionable reason behind the point (b) above is the effectiveness of the "static action elaboration" optimization. Other optimizations are performed over (more or less interpreted) program schemata. In fact, a more abstract schematological formulation of optimizing transformations may also contribute to their effectiveness. To facilitate such an abstract formulation the IL specification is modularized into a series of specification levels, which differ in the degree of interpretation: -

- The Syntactic Specification is given in the form of a data base (a set of type definitions written in the implementation language, which closely parallell syntactic productions). The Internal Language is not human-oriented, and this enables us to use fairly complicated graphs to represent IL programs (rather than linear texts which are not suited for the analysis and transformation; for the reader's convenience we shall use a fancy form of ALGOL 68 to represent sample IL programs).
- The Syntactic Specification is sufficient to implement an IL Editor.

- The Schematological Specification describes in addition general concepts of data and control flow and provides interpretation for relevant constructs including types, arguments and results, indirect reference instructions and transfer of control; for other instructions the presence of side-effects is indicated. This level of specification is sufficient for the Analysis and for many machine-independent optimizations.

- The Machine -Independent Interpretation is sufficient to perform most of the "static action elaborations" at compile time.

- The Complete Interpretation is a concretization of the environmental enquiries; it enables the performance of some machine-dependent "static actions" at compile time (e.g. floating-point arithmetic, constant offset calculations); the meta-semantics of these enquiries is explained in terms of a model abstract computer. The enquiries are used by all phases except the Parse.

The Schematological Specification appears to be the most peculiar in the list: the others are present in any system with an intermediate language - cf. the already quoted ALMO, or JANUS system. This is why the subsequent remarks about IL will be centered at this point.

As usual, an IL program specifies actions to be performed over values. The actions are denoted by statements, the values by names (of variables and statements) and by literal constants. Both statements (actions) and values may be atomic or structured.

The structure of a variable is determined by its type. There are atomic and structured types. Values of atomic types are always computed as a whole (this does not prevent them from being of declared, non-standard types). All structured types are declared ones.

Atomic actions are specified by instructions, structured actions are expressed by program fragments.

Any instruction is given a set of operands, which are subdivided into arguments and results. These are names of declared variables, or names of statements which evaluate or use the operand in question. At the Schematological Level the arithmetic and Boolean instructions need not be interpreted, and at that level they do not differ from "black boxes", i.e. pseudo-instructions that represent various run-time library routines and whose specification is not given even at the level of the Machine-Independent Specification. The precise semantics of these instructions is replaced by a series of indications of the possible side-effects, reducibility and of such properties as commutativity, associativeness etc.

The interpreted instructions include all those dealing with access to components of structured objects and transfer of control. The latter involve some constructs of the control graph - a hierarchy of fragments which denote control structures. At the lowest level of the hierarchy we have basic blocks represented as linear lists of consecutively executed instructions. The header of this list represents a label (name); similar names are given to larger fragments, which are composed of subfragments (rather than of instructions).

The last instruction of a basic block must be a transfer of control to an explicitely or indirectly named fragment; this may be a jump, procedure call, swap with a co-routine, or initiation of a parallel process.

The structured statements, represented by fragments, include begin- and procedure-blocks, procedure calls, regular for-statements (like in ALGOL 68) or critical sections (for synchronizations). The Analysis Phase establishes for every fragment the lists of its arguments and results, which enables a uniform treatment of the instructions and some "regular" fragments.

5.2. The Expressive Power

For some languages, the result of the optimizations can mostly be expressed in terms of the language itself, e.g. ALGOL 68. Here we consider only those features which are confined to the IL.

First, in order for some actions to be optimized they must be stated explicitly; the explicit formulation of component access in IL allows the use of common subexpression elimination techniques for "subscript" expression optimization.

Secondly, some <u>machine-dependent</u> optimizations are expressed by means of attributes which govern the casing at the Program Generation Phase (e.g. simplification of procedure calls).

A new feature is introduced in IL, which ensures a correct application of some very powerful optimizations. This is the possibility to associate with some fragments a <u>prologue</u> or an <u>epilogue</u>.

The use of the prologue feature is illustrated by the transformation of the for-statement

```
for i to n do a[i]:=(y:=1/sin(x))↑i od
```

into

```
for i to n
    prolog(y:=1/sin(x))
    do a[i]:=y↑i od
```

The epilogue feature may be used to optimize recursive procedures. Let the original procedure be

```
proc f = void:begin S1; SR; S2 end
```

in which SR is the recursive part; it is equivalent to

```
proc void f:=ff;
proc ff = void:begin f:=fr; S1; SR; S2;
               epilog(f:=ff) end;
proc fr = void:begin SR end;
```

5. CONCLUSION

The relevance of modular programming to the BETA System is at least twofold. First, the most promising application of the System is global intermodular optimization of library procedure calls; secondly, the System structure itself displays a very clear modularity.

The very idea of an intermediate language is due to modularization attempts; the importance of modularization and of having one underlying intermediate language is crucial in a system in which this language forms a standard interface of a large package of universal and specialized optimizations. Implementation of an invariant optimization package is considered by the author to be the only pragmatic justification for the development of such an intricate system instead of a series of direct compilers.

A major advantage of a co-ordinated implementation of this kind over an automatic TWS is due to the possibility of inter-lingual assembly during translation into the Internal Language, which greatly enhances the effectiveness of the optimizations.

On the other hand, concurrent development of a TWS and co-ordinated implementation is very beneficial to the TWS: it would be pointless to include in a TWS oriented towards future languages the anomalies of FORTRAN; but it would be even more foolish to ignore FORTRAN with its immense algorithmic library. Therefore in order to realize a convenient and efficient TWS a symbiosis should be developed, so that irregular features (which usually originate from the old languages) are implemented in the co-ordinated implementation, and a TWS need not worry about them; a restriction of the goals of the TWS to more regular and less ambitious tasks (e.g. the design of application program packages) would enable its designers to concentrate on making the system better suited to its real applications.

REFERENCES

Ershov, A.P. (1971). A Multilanguage Programming System Oriented to Language Description and Universal Optimization Algorithms. "ALGOL 68 Implementation", J.R.L.Peck ed., p. 143 (North-Holland Publ. Co.), Amsterdam-London.

Grushetsky et al. (1975): Грушецкий, В.В., Ершов, А.П., Покровский, С.Б. Метапроцессоры для универсального программирующего процессора. Сб. "Некоторые проблемы вычислительной и прикладной математики", стр. 226 (Наука),

Pokrovsky, S.B. (1977). Semantic Unification in a Multi-Language Compiler. "Lecture Notes in Computer Science", 47 p. 63 (Springer-Verlag).

Pottosin (1975): Поттосин, И.В. Глобальная оптимизация, практический подход. "Труды Всесоюзного симпозиума по методам реализации новых алгоритмических языков", том I, стр. II3 (ВЦ СО АН СССР), Новосибирск.

Lancaster, R.L. and Schneider, V.B. (1976). Quick Compiler Construction Using Uniform Code Generators. "Software - Practice and Experience", 6, No. 1, 83.

Constructing Quality Software, P.G. Hibbard/S.A. Schuman (eds.)

DESIGN SPECIFICATIONS FOR A QUALITY COMPILER FACTORY

A.P.Ershov
Computing Center, Siberian Division

G.D.Chinin
Novosibirsk Division
S.A.Lebedev Institute for Computing Machinery

USSR Academy of Sciences
Novosibirsk, USSR

Production and creativity are often considered as the inherent but contradictory components of programming. While recognizing this unity of opposites, the authors argue for the necessity of reinforcing the production component in compiler development. Analyzing the general characteristics of the production process, the authors reinterpret them in the framework of compiler development. It is concluded that a compiler, although being a unique engineering construction , nevertheless possesses many properties of a mass product. It is noted that contemporary "translator writing systems" are still inadequate with respect to most requirements of the production of efficient programming systems.

1. INTRODUCTION

The authors make their analysis under the general assumption that during the next several decades the exponential growth of software will continue and its logical complexity will also grow. Seemingly, at each moment, there also will be a big gap between the demand and the intellectual resources available for software development. At least, this will be true if we simply try to "extrapolate" present resources, rather than to multiply them by introducing the principal innovations from computer science and software engineering into practice. In order to properly respond to this challenge we have to undertake a kind of transition from simple manufacturing to large-scale industrial production.

This problem has been debated in our professional and scientific circles for almost 10 years [1,2]. Without claiming either the first or the last word in this discussion, the authors submit their view of this problem and an approach to its solution, as applied to development of programming systems for contemporary algorithmic languages - from FORTRAN and ALGOL to ALPHARD and SETL, some of which will perhaps enter the XXI century.

There are no signs that the proliferation of new languages will slow down. However, some polarization and stratification of languages is expected. So called "universal" programming languages will gradually cease to be end-user languages, becoming more and more base languages for software development or meta-languages for the design of various non-procedural specialized languages destined for use in a well-specified and stable context. The language processors for these base languages will grow into large, integrated systems (with instrumental and technological support), being installed at computer manufacturers, software houses and large scientific or university computation centers.

However, even leaving aside new language development it is clear that most current problems will remain: improvement and modernization of existing programming systems, production and delivery of new versions. For these activities, the severe economic requirement to raise productivity and efficiency will play a decisive role.

Unfortunately, compilers are still too expensive;their development cycle is too long; reliability is achieved (if at all) only by exceptional efforts; quality is usually less than satisfactory and rarely in full accordance with a priori specifications; variety is rather insufficient, both in the number of commercially available languages and the diversity of the compilers.

The joint effect of these negative factors leads to figures for the development of an "average" compiler such as 3-4 years of hard work for 10-20 people, and to situations where even powerful manufacturers support a rather small number of languages.

On the other hand, to be a true consumer product, a programming language must be "packaged" in many forms:

- an educational compiler with a transparent translation scheme, simple debugging facilities and restricted modes of operation;
- a versatile compiler for the mass user, with full maintenance and support;
- a base "OEM" compiler, with transfer of maintenance and modification responsibility to a user;
- a pair of compilers - for checkout and for production runs;
- a series of compilers for a family of compatible sublanguages;
- a cross-compiler for a class of object computers.

For a popular language, even this incomplete list requires at present at least 10 years to be more or less fully supported. So far, there is no software vendor which would undertake the production of such a variety of versions, even though any two of them may well have two-thirds of their code in common.

2.GENERAL MOTIVATIONS

We elaborate here the concept of a "compiler factory", as an ad hoc idea aimed at solving at least some of the difficult problems mentioned in the introduction. We deliberately use the word "factory" to connote concentration of a large-scale production, where quality and mass production are brought into economic equilibrium.

What does it mean to speak of compiler development in a factory-like fashion? It means, first of all,that one has to identify, for compiler development, the fundamental components of any industrial activity:

- the product itself
- users of the product
- raw materials
- semiproducts
- processes and tools
- personnel.

Of course, it is not enough just to map the set of buzz-words used in compiler writing onto another set of buzz-words, those of industrial organizations. The problem is much more fundamental because the concentration of compiler production in the framework of an industrial enterprise becomes technically possible and economically justifiable only under conditions of:

- comprehensive and accurate product specifications;
- existence of stable sources of homogeneous raw materials (standardized descriptions of source languages, object and compiling computers, with maximal identification of common features);
- recognizable quantity of semiproducts for multiple use (libraries of programs and other standard texts);
- existence of stable and universal production processes and the means for their automation.

Looking at the compiler development problem along these lines we can recognize in some points a remarkable readiness for industrial methods, but also some significant gaps which require considerable study. We think, that this series of observations is instructive in itself, for it gives a certain perspective with regard to the future development of the field.

3. FEATURE ANALYSIS

The general feature analysis of the compiler factory concept is a rather broad theme which definitely can't be covered systematically in the framework of a conference paper. So we shall limit ourselves only to points where we feel prepared to say something specific.

3.1. User orientation. Historically, compilers have been the second kind of program product, after subroutine libraries. However, a long time has passed before compilers came to incorporate some features of a user oriented product. Frankly, even now most of programming systems are far from ideal in users' eyes. We distinguish the following categories of people using compiler factory products:

- programmers making conventional use of a compiler for problem solving;
- the personnel of customer organizations or field specialists responsible for maintenance;
- the personnel of field-departments responsible for software sale or lease, its installation, user training and front-end complaint handling;
- the personnel of a factory group responsible for the authorized compiler maintenance;
- the personnel of an acceptance testing department, whether belonging to the factory or to a user organization.

By this list we wish to emphasize that in addition to the well-understood (even if not well implemented) interface with the first category of users, there exist interactions with other "users", such as those concerned solely with maintenance.

3.2. Raw materials. The analog to material in programming is information. The role of raw materials at the compiler factory is played by defining documents for source languages and object machines. These documents originate outside the factory and, taken as given, they exhibit something of a mosaic in taste and style, in methods of description and in overall orientation.

On the other hand, it becomes more and more obvious that these diversities spring from a small number of universal laws of information processing and an equally limited number of basic algorithmic language concepts. Moreover, these can be subjected to a reasonably well motivated classification. This accumulation of scientific insight into programming is still far from saturation, but even now it is becoming more and more evident that there exists the possibility (as well as the necessity) to develop a detailed "atlas" of languages and machines, specifying source languages and object computers in some uniform way. This specification is a real starting point of a continuous process of compiler production at the factory. Thus, machine and language "shops" must be postulated within the compiler factory. Their purpose is to create and maintain the language and computer atlases, which involves extensive processing of primary defining documents.

3.2.1. Processing of raw materials. In contrast to many production situations, the processing of raw materials is, in the case of a compiler factory, merely ongoing background work which provides the input for the start of any specific project. We shall speak here essentially of the problem in relation to the language atlas, although analogous considerations apply to that for the range of object machines.

We adopt the concept of an abstract algorithmic language [6], the operational semantics of which are expressed in relation to its abstract syntax by means of a well-structured high-level language (the semantic base). The high level provides a suitably abstract description of the functional properties of the source language. The structure of the semantic base serves to promote the semantic unification of source languages: at the abstract syntactic level many languages look rather similar to one another; this facilitates identification of similar notions (references, loops, procedures) which then can be treated by common semantic routines.

Specifically, the semantic base may be chosen according to different premises. It may be just a very high-level language expressing the semantics of source languages in terms of mapping over its abstract data. It may be a specially designed language "summing up" the fundamental concepts of algorithmic languages, and accommodating requirements for optimization and machine orientation (for example, INTEL language in BETA project [8, 11]). Finally, it might be just an implementation language adopted as a main technological vehicle for compiler production. The atlas of languages can be maintained at any of these levels and the proper choice is a compromise between generality and efficiency.

While there appear to be only minimal obstacles to semantic unification of linguistic concepts, unified language description can be effective only if the proper diversity of implementation is accommodated. It may come as something of a surprise to realize that we lack a comprehensive understanding of machine orientation in algorithmic languages. We believe, that any language is more or less machine-dependent and that its implementation reflects, in one way or another, a certain machine orientation. However, the kinds of dependencies and the forms of such orientation have not been sufficiently well identified and studied. In our opinion, successful unification within the framework of the atlas so as to enable production of compilers for different machines necessitates (in the absence of ultimate knowledge) some systematic approach to methods of machine orientation.

In particular, such methods should make it possible:
- to define algorithmic languages more rigorously;
- to provide machine orientation of a hardware representation of a source language in a more controllable way;
- to establish a better motivated resolution of the conflict between machine-dependent language features and machine-independent opti-

mization techniques.

It may be seen that there are, in fact, three separate dimensions which enter into the unification advocated above: semantic concepts, machine dependencies and compilation schemes.

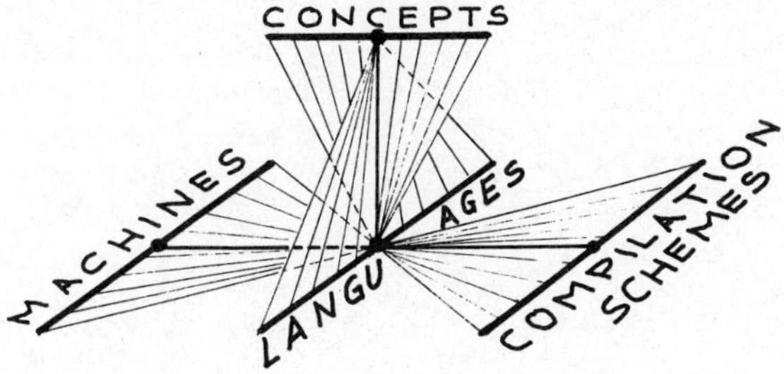

Some statements on the problems of unifying algorithmic language may be found in [7, 10]. The continuing task of establishing and maintaining the atlas of language provides a concrete framework for solving these problems.

3.2.2. Processing of orders. The existence of the atlases represents an accumulation of potential, making it possible for the compiler factory to respond in a "fully informed" fashion to individual orders. Although it is appropriate to anticipate a rather wide variation in demand for specific products, it has already been noted that compilers nevertheless possess some attributes of mass products. These characteristics, together with a certain "inertia" in users' habits, permit reliable information about the needs of experienced users to be collected, so as to predict or even influence the habits of new users. This knowledge can well be formulated as detailed "check-lists" (see, for example, the well known work by R. Bemer [5]). Such check-lists greatly facilitate the preparation of proper design specifications. Work of this kind is unfortunately almost ignored in the technical literature, but it seems that purposeful research could result in a well-elaborated and stable typology of languages, compilers and users.

An inseparable complement to requirements specification are validation, quality control and other feed-back mechanisms. In this respect, there is another surprise: the problem of finding real and objective means to evaluate compiler quality is addressed by only a few specialists, among which must be mentioned especially the work by B. Wichmann [20]. We have made some experimental measurements following this methodology and obtained promising results, which give us some optimism about developing a comprehensive technique of compiler validation. The establishment of these complementary methods is another aspect of the accumulation of potential.

3.3. Semiproducts. One of the most important components of the compiler factory is the production and centralization of all kinds of prefabricated programs which can serve several projects [9]:
- i/o libraries;
- mathematical functions and other basic operations present in many languages;
- basic procedures used in language processing (pack/unpack information, hash-functions, access functions, etc);

- universal syntactic processors (grammar transformers, scanners, parsers);
- general optimizers;
- common semantic routines serving similar constructs in language families.

Such semiproducts probably justify a factory-like approach to compiler development more than any other reason. This is the main source of economy of efforts when implementing many languages.

The efficiency and usefulness of program semiproducts directly depends on uniformity in the contents of the atlas of languages and machines, as well as on the overall strategy of compiler design.

3.4. Universal translating algorithms. The next source of generality is "universal" language processing technology, applicable to many diverse languages. Certainly, automatic processors have to be available in many variants at a compiler factory. There are syntactic processors of various kinds which have a fully developed theoretical basis [12]. Recently, considerable progress has been achieved in optimizing program transformations [13,14] although the picture is still something of a mosaic. The idea of a universal optimizer has emerged and been elaborated [15,16].

Universal processors of any kind inherently introduce some redundancy with respect to any specific language but we are eager to advocate the idea of "mixed computation" as a general powerful mechanism for automatically adapting universal processors to specific constraints.

There is a well known mathematical procedure for partial binding of of free variables of a function by substituting specific values for them:

$$F(x,y)\Big|_{x=a} \Rightarrow f(y) \quad .$$

We observe that partial binding is a mixed process consisting of (1) some computation using the given value "a" and (2) some mapping of F into f. Mixed computation is an extrapolation of this procedure over any program P in a language L, where V is a general (conventional) computation in the language L (Z=V(P,W)). More precisely, mixed computation is a universal computation **M** in L applicable to any program P for which the object domain W=(X, Y) is partially bound, say X=a; values of Y are then said to be "frozen", i.e., they are unavailable during the mixed computation. This process produces

(1) some residual program P'_X, and

(2) an intermediate memory state which is just its frozen part, Y. This will be denoted:

$$M(P,(X,Y)) \begin{array}{l} \nearrow P'_X \\ \searrow Y \end{array} \quad .$$

If mixed computation is properly defined then the residual program, starting with intermediate memory state will successively finalize the computation:

$$Z=V(P,(X,Y))=V(P'_X,Y).$$

It is interesting to note that the mixed computation (or partial evaluation) concept is more than 10 years old and has been rediscovered several times. It is nonetheless far from compiler practice and theory, but it seems, at least for us, to be the "golden key" to many painful problems of compiler theory and construction.

We shall not go into details , referring the reader to [17,18]. We only indicate here those parts of compilation where the unifying strength of mixed compilation appears to be specifically effective.

- Obtaining object code from interpretive semantics.
  Let S_L be the semantics of a language L represented by an interpreter expressed in some implementation language. Let P be a program in L and X be its data. It can be shown that, freezing X in the mixed computation $M(S_L, (P,X))$, we will obtain an object code S'_P for the program P as the residual program and X (source data for the object code) as the intermediate memory state.
- Obtaining the object code generator from the interpretive semantics.
  There exists a straightforward transformation which, for every program P , yields such a program G(P) that

$$M(P,W) = V(G(P),W).$$

  If S_L is the semantics of a language L, then $G(S_L)$ is the object code generator for that language.
- Having a "continuous" spectrum of compilation schemes.

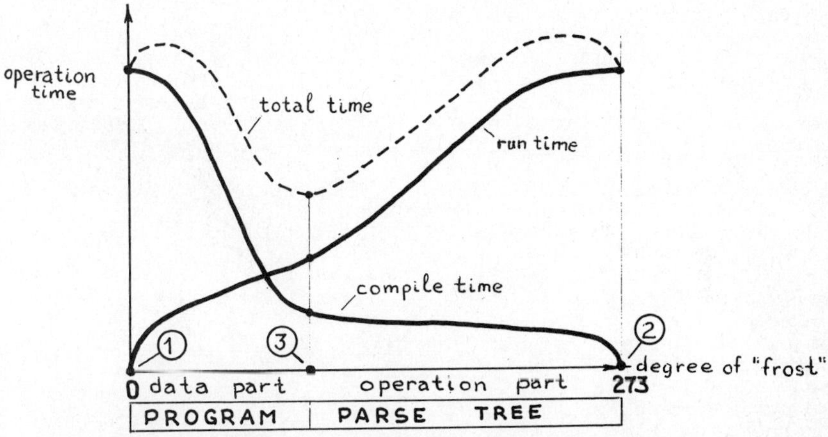

(1) If nothing is frozen during mixed computation ① , then the program will be completely interpreted at the compile time.

(2) If everything is frozen, then nothing will happen at the compile time and the object code will coincide with the language interpreter, so that all computations will take place at run time ② .

(3) If only data is frozen, then the standard compilation scheme will be accomplished ③ .

Seemingly, all conceivable compilation schemes may be expressed in terms of a proportion of frozen components in the program parse tree.

- Unification of optimizing transformations.
  Some optimizations(procedure integration,loop unrolling, constant propagation and dead code elimination) are just special cases of mixed computation.
- Elimination of casing when implementing composite constructs of large programming languages.
- Unification of generator construction.
  Mixed computation would seem to constitute a universal principle, proving the basis for a broad spectrum of automatic tools to support systematic compiler construction.

3.5. Personnel. Personnel organization, i.e. qualification and position identification, formulation and division of responsibilities, personnel grouping, either by administrative hierarchy or by relations of production, is one of the least understood aspects of system programming. We shall not go deeply into this complicated subject, noting only that, in our opinion, a worker at a compiler factory has, at any moment, two attachments: (1) belonging to a service characterizing his professional qualification, and (2) belonging to a specific project group. Which line corresponds to administrative hierarchy depends on a character of the service or profession. For example, the validation service can be administratively independent of the project leader. In other cases, quite contrarily, professional responsibility is not personified at all, but has the form of written regulations and manuals or standards the interpretation of which is solely up to the specialist.

In general, we consider a reasonably large number of specialized services as one sign of mature production. The variety of approaches and evaluation procedures during compiler design and implementation has to adequately reflect the view of all those who are concerned with the compiler as a product. Without trying to be exhaustive, we shall list some important specializations involved in compiler production:

- souce language;
- machine orientation of the source language;
- selection and adaptation of program semiproducts;
- technological support (many specializations);
- library preludes;
- dynamic support in a compiler;
- compiler messages;
- syntactic phase;
- optimization phase;
- generation phase;
- project data base;
- project bookkeeping;
- general standards;
- project standards;
- validation;
- user documentation (many specializations).

Let us note that many of these specializations deal with prepared texts and written programs, and thus, do not demand especially high creative capabilities on the part of such personnel.

3.6. Creativity vs production. The foregoing raises one general issue which we would like to project onto our account of the compiler factory concept, that is how to reconcile the conflict between the creative and the routine,well-controlled activities involved in the process of software development.

In the working of a compiler factory we strictly distinguish (both essentially and organizationally) two kinds of activity: (1) accumulation of the scientific, informational and technological potential, and (2) its realization and discharge in producing specific compilers. In turn, compiler production is divided into a design phase (in which we distinguish (a) logical design, and (b) technological design) and the implementation phases.

We collect below all aspects that we refer to as potential accumulation (the categorization is, of course, somewhat arbitrary).

A. Scientific potential:
- new and better algorithmic languages;
- description methods;
- mathematical models;
- compilation algorithms;
- types of computers;
- typology of languages and machines.

B. Information potential:
- maintenance of the atlas of languages and machines;
- extension of test banks for specific languages;
- accumulation of the feedback information from users;
- accumulation of the internal feedback information from technological lines at the factory.

C. Technological potential:
- development of checklists, instructions, standards and other regulations;
- autonomous implementation of universal compilation algorithms, libraries for multiple use, metaprocessors;
- development and modernization of the technological production facilities.

A special part embracing all the three categories is devoted to experimental projects and trial implementations.

These activities subsume most of the creative efforts undertaken in compiler development. The secret of success lies in the fact that potential accumulation is <u>stochastic</u> and <u>not</u> tied to time constraints - the first enemy of any project. The advanced development of potential is achieved by an early start of the corresponding work and proper resource allocation. The second and decisive component of success is a constructive materialization of this potential in the atlas of languages and machines, in universal language processors and metaprocessors, well developed test banks, numerous libraries and other textual material stored in the data base of the production complex.

The watershed between creative design and reliably regulated implementation is the logical design specification. This is a compact document which is written essentially by the project leader. It results from:
- the initial specifications;
- the principal properties of the language and the machine;
- an initial checklist;
- the leader's experience and intuition.

Roughly speaking, the logical design says WHAT, though containing some hypothesis about HOW. The HOW is filled out by the technological design specification, the main role of which is to resolve problems posed or left open in the logical design. The most important quality of the technological design is its trustworthiness. A very illuminating treatment of the logical and technological phases can be found in F. Brook's book [19].

We have emphasized above the separation between accumulation of potential as opposed to production. It is, however, of critical importance that these two essentially different activities are carried out under the same roof.

4. CONCLUSION

The foregoing analysis is incomplete in many ways. In particular, there are many aspects of a compiler factory which are in no way specific to that application but involve consideration of software production in general, as discussed in [3] and [4]. However, from the standpoint of engineering disciplines as a whole, there is nothing new in such consideration. Nevertheless, this mode of thinking extremely slowly penetrates into programming circles, where it still requires substantial defense. In this regard, programming badly needs well educated managers, as well as specialists in production organization, systems theory and general engineering.

In discussing more rational approaches to compiler production, we must make some comments concerning the notion of translator writing systems as introduced into the literature in the well-known review paper by J. Feldman and D. Gries [21]. Various experiments and theoretical works which advocate one or another global approach to development of programming processors are still vulnerable to the critique by G. Seegmüller at IFIP - 74 in Stockholm [22]. We also are working on translator writing systems. We do not intend to diminish either our own work nor the achievements of our colleagues, which have, in our opinion, contributed to raising the overall scientific and technological potential. However, without exception, translator writing systems are still based upon rather idealized compilation schemes, ignoring many significant and practically important features of programming systems. Most of them lack the synthetic character and versatility which are so necessary for a good compiler factory.

We have introduced the idea of compiler factory as an ad hoc concept. Now we take the liberty to give some more subjective motivations about the chosen theme. The reader may believe or disbelieve the concept of factory-like compiler production. He can think of it as speculation about the future or interpret it as an urgent contemporary problem. But it is impossible to ignore the fact that the idea gives a <u>direction</u> to the evolution of a field as a whole. Furthermore, we have found that this direction has some merits of its own right.

The inspiration for this work came to one of the authors when he recently happened to visit a huge Hawker-Siddley aviation plant in England, where they produce among other things wings for the European-Airbus. He remembered the small mechanical shops of 1910 where the first airplanes

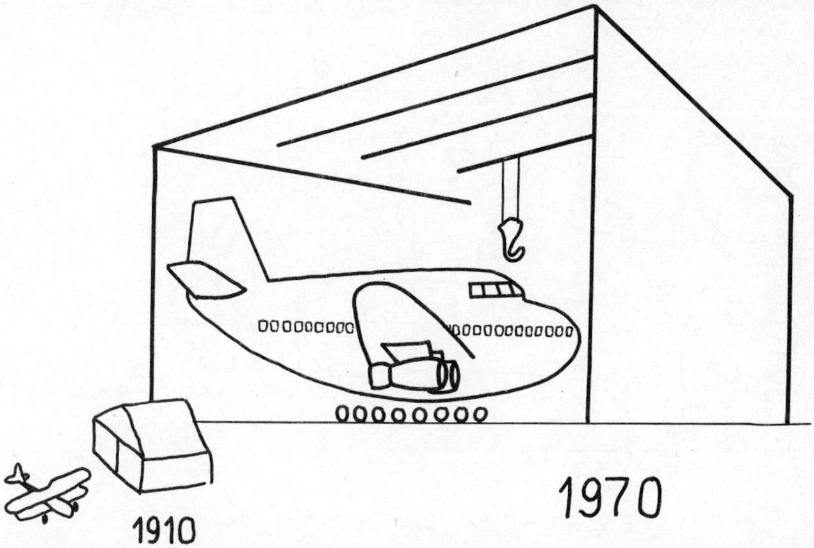

were produced. Though there was almost nothing in common between these engineering undertakings, an understanding of the continuity in the development over the last 60 years of such a well-established industry as aviation made him reflect upon the evolution of our own field.

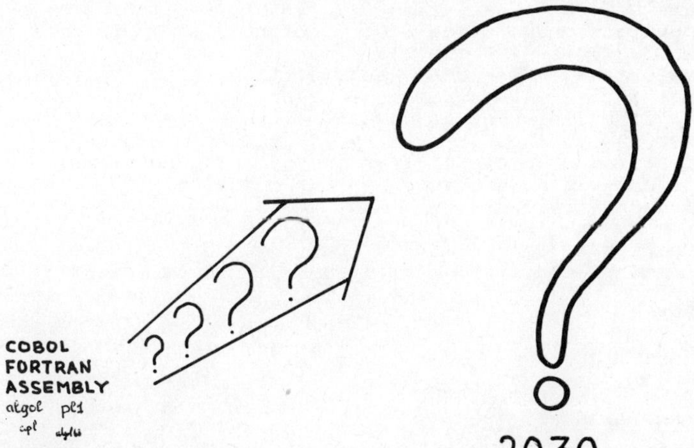

We are afraid that this picture is more truthful than any of us would wish.

But, since we are starting 60 years later, why not to try to anticipate the enormous development of our industry, in which, hopefully, we all believe? We are now educating the students who will design the systems of 2030. How do we make sure that their education will be their life-long friend and assistant in their work?

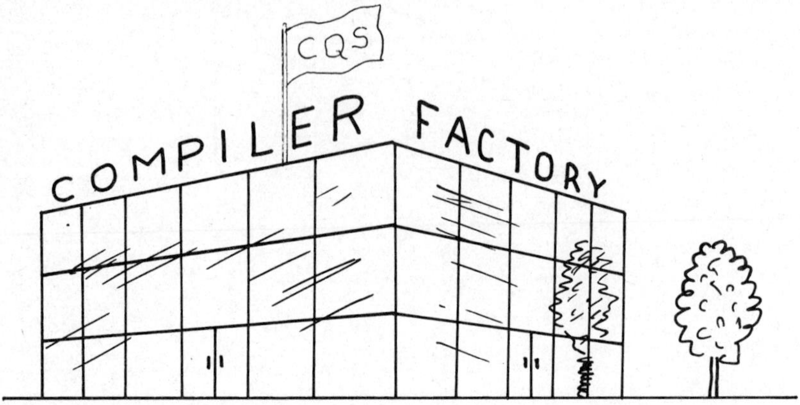

This is an artist's rendering of a compiler factory.

But, believing in the magic of numbers, we would like to supplement the picture (and conclude this paper) with some quantitative projections.

A proper compiler factory is an independent enterprise with a central staff of about 600 people, plus 200 people in the field (about 2 engineers per 20 installations). 40% of the staff are involved in the potential accumulation (10% - science, 15% - information, 15% - technology), 60% of the staff develop and maintain compilers (25% - development, 15% - user documentation, 10% - validation, 10% - maintenance). The atlas of languages contains about 100 languages including dialects; about half of them are in use. The factory carries out no less than fifty projects simultaneously, each having a development cycle of from one half to two years. The factory supports a big manufacturer installing over 1000 data processing systems annually.

The authors wish to express their gratitude to the referees whose thorough comments greatly contributed to the improvement of the paper.

REFERENCES

[1] P. Naur and B. Randell, Ed. Software Engineering. NATO Science Committee, Brussel, 1969.

[2] J.N. Buxton and B. Randell, Ed. Software Engineering Techniques. NATO Science Committee, Brussel, 1970.

[3] H. Bratman and T. Court. The software factory. Computer, May 1975, 28-37.

[4] System design laboratory: preliminary design report. Preliminary working paper. Naval Electronics Lab. Center, TN-3145, March 1976.

[5] R.W. Bemer. Checklist for planning software system production. In [1], 165-180.

[6] A.P. Ershov and V.V. Grushetsky. On a language description method oriented to implementation. A talk to be delivered to IFIP Congress 77, Toronto, Canada, August 1977.

[7] S. Pokrovsky. Semantic unification in a multi-language compiler. Methods of algorithmic language implementation. Lecture Notes in Comp. Sci., 47, Springer-Verlag, Heidelberg, 1977, 63-79.

[8] A.P. Ershov. Problems in many-language systems. Language hierarchies and interfaces. Lecture Notes in Comp. Sci., 46, Springer-Verlag, Heidelberg, 1976, 358-410.

[9] R.L. Lancaster, V.B. Schneider. Quick compiler construction using uniform code generators. Software - practice and experience, 6, no. 1, 1976, 83-93.

[10] Jean E. Sammet. Programming languages: history and fundamentals. Prentice-Hall, Englewood Cliffs, 1969.

[11] S.B. Pokrovsky. Modularization of a multi-language optimizer. A talk delivered to IFIP Working Conference on Constructing Quality Software, Novosibirsk, USSR, 1977.

[12] A. Aho and J.D. Ullman. The theory of parsing, translation and compiling. Vol. 1. Parsing. Prentice-Hall, Englewood-Cliffs, 1972.

[13] A.P. Ershov, Ed. The ALPHA automatic programming system. Academic Press, London, 1971.

[14] E.E. Allen and J. Cocke. A catalogue of optimizing transformations. IBM Research, RC 3548, Yorktown Heights, 1971.

[15] I.V. Pottosin. Global optimization - a practical approach. Proceedings of the All-Union Symposium on Algorithmic Language Implementation Methods. Part I, USSR Acad. Sci. Sib. Div. Computing Center, Novosibirsk, 1975, 113-128.

[16] W. Harrison. A new strategy for code generation - the general purpose optimizing compiler. Preprint. IBM Research Center, Yorktown Heights, 1976.

[17] A.P. Ershov. On the partial computation principle. Information Processing Letters, no. 2, 1977.

[18] A.P. Ershov. On the essence of compilation. A talk to be delivered to IFIP Working Conference on Formal Description of Programming Concepts. St.Andrews, Canada, August 1977.

[19] F. Brooks. The mythical man-month and other essays on software engineering. University of North California, Chapel Hill, 1972.

[20] B.A. Wichmann. The performance of some ALGOL systems. Information Processing 71. North Holland, Amsterdam, 1972;
B.A. Wichmann. Five ALGOL compilers. Computer Journal, Febr. 1972, 8-12.

[21] J.A. Feldman and D. Gries. Translator writing systems. CACM, 11, no. 2, 1968, 77-113.

[22] G. Seegmüller. Systems programming as an emerging discipline. Information Processing 74. North Holland, Amsterdam, 1975.

Session 2b : Discussion

Correll: I would like to ask Ershov whether this multi-language implementation approach isn't some kind of revival of the aged UNCOL idea, where one tries to build some kind of monster which can sometimes be used as a spacecraft and sometimes as a portable tunnel. If so, what does it contribute to constructing quality software?

Ershov: The question probably relates more to Pokrovsky's talk, but I shall reply partially. Our Internal Language does not simply implement the multiplicity of languages and machines as the direct product of language and machine variants, resulting in a monstrous piece of object code for a specific language construct. Rather, the Internal Language provides, for the pair (language, machine), a channel (or tunnel, if you like) through which incompletely defined language features may be properly specialized to a particular machine.

Ross: The idea of mixed computations is very closely related to the semi-products to which you have referred. I wonder how you see these coming together?

Ershov: I have to say that mixed computation has not yet been sufficiently studied, but I consider it to be a good technological device for converting a semi-product into the particular final product.

Sintzoff: I have a comment and then a question. First, the comment. I very much like the principle of mixed computation, and it is a golden key indeed. And I think that you are too modest in saying that it is 10 years old. What is old is the idea of partial or abstract evaluation of the program. But now the new component you are bringing in is that of the partial working out of the program text itself, and this I very much appreciate. Now I have my question. I had an uneasy feeling when you showed us the existence of hundreds of languages in use. Should we also extrapolate with respect to the complexity of each language? Myself, I barely know one language. How will you find the thousands of people needed for teaching this heap of languages?

Ershov: In my opinion, there are indications of the proliferation of simpler, highly specialized languages for stable groups of users, and of languages caused by the proliferation of microcomputers and other devices for individual and specialized use. However, the number of really universal, complicated languages in use will hopefully decrease.

Goos: I am not quite sure whether the atlas of language features will be particularly helpful in determining which language concepts are useful. Very often a careful analysis of possible applications yields more insight than a comparison of many languages.

Ershov: This is a high-level methodological problem. What is the most instructive source of knowledge: analyzing application fields or studying the essence of algorithmic processes, regardless of the problem orientation? Certainly we have to analyze application fields, but I believe that there exist fundamental laws of information processing which many algorithmic languages exhibit. Hopefully these can be expressed in a limited number of concepts. How to discover them properly is a scientific problem.

Bell: I think there are some interesting observations in your illustration showing a factory for producing large airplanes, because mass production started with automobiles, for which the unit volumes were three orders of magnitude larger. In spite of the fact that far more applications programs are needed than systems programs, whenever system programmers talk about software factories they focus on software factories for systems programs. My question is this: would we not be better advised to focus our efforts on factories for application programs?

Ershov: Quite probably you are right. We speak about compiler factories because our real experience has been with compilers. It would be easy for me to support your opinion but more difficult to elaborate it.

Tseytin: I have three questions for Ershov. The first is as follows. A factory requires a relatively uniform flow of raw materials and of orders, but if it is too uniform, then no factory is needed because everything can be done by a single piece of software, a sort of compiler-compiler. Where is the boundary?

Ershov: It is impossible to delineate the boundary in objective terms. I will just express my strong disbelief in a fully automated process of compiler construction from specifications. It will always be a manual process, supported by available tools, because the flow is not as uniform as such approaches require.

Tseytin: My second question is that some factories are involved in mass production, and some work for individual orders. Would you compare your software factory with these two types?

Ershov: A software factory is, in some sense, unique. The design and production phases deal with an individual product, but after that, by merely copying the tapes, you turn that single compiler into a mass-produced item. So there is a peculiar combination of these two types of factory.

Tseytin: My last question is that we have some idea of the qualifications necessary for a computer scientist working as a research programmer. Can you describe the qualifications for a software factory worker?

Ershov: Oversimplifying, I would say that everything is displaced by one level in this kind of intellectual production. So the role of worker would be played by an engineer, that of engineer by a researcher . . .

Turski: And that of researcher?

Ershov: By a philosopher! [☺]

Peck: I would like to recall a question that was raised before but not quite answered. I'm curious about your choice of the name "compiler factory". Wouldn't it have been more in keeping to call it an "institute for compiler generation"? Did you choose the word factory because you believe that for the vast majority of workers, individual creativity might have to be suppressed in the interests of overall productivity?

Ershov: Well, in some sense this is merely a rhetorical figure, just to emphasize some ideas. I prefer to call it "factory", since there are so many characteristics of a production-style environment: schedules, planning, resources, management, routine work, etc. These are hardly consistent with the concept of an institute. As for individual creativity, it should not be suppressed at all, but simply subjugated to the ultimate goals.

Goos: I think the figures which you gave at the end come from some ideal world which is not the existing one. Surely devoting only 10% to maintenance seems to me to be extremely low. It is much higher in practice. Also, I think you grossly underestimated the expense of telling people about certain languages and what they are good for. In the West, we have many so-called sales representatives. Perhaps you do not need them, but nevertheless you will need people who fulfil the function of sales representatives, to tell people about the products and why they are good for them.

Ershov: First of all, please do not take these figures very seriously since they are really imaginary figures taken from a non-existent world. With respect to maintenance, 10% relates to the whole number of workers, including accumulation of potential. Speaking only about the production part, that 10% becomes 20%. And certainly there is no specific figure for interfacing this glass cube with the external world except for the 200 field engineers who just transport and deliver compilers.

Rajlich: I would like to take issue with the proposed size of the factory. You said that the factory should have 600 people. It seems to me that an institution that large can only produce software of mediocre quality, and that high quality software can be produced only by small and dedicated groups. Could you please comment on that?

Ershov: If the quality of the product is poor, the factory will cease to exist. It seems to me that 600 is better for having proper potential than having a very specialized team of 30-50 people doing specialized work but not on such a grand scale.

Král: I think the development of large programming groups is really necessary now. I have a firm impression, caused by my experience during the development of an ALGOL 68 compiler, that some products must be done by quite large groups. But I think there are two problems connected with this matter. First, it is really difficult to attract good managers and good programmers to head the groups. Secondly, they must have enough creative work, and I think that this is a very difficult condition to fulfil. Moreover, the factory is more or less an office and if the choice of people is not made properly, it can easily happen that this factory will do nothing whatsoever.

Turski: It also seems that we are falling into the trap of believing that mass production methods lead to increased quality. Whoever believes that is advised to go for dinner to McDonald's rather than to eat a home-cooked meal. I don't have anything more to say. [Exit, pursued by a bear.]

onstructing Quality Software, P.G. Hibbard/S.A. Schuman (eds.)
©IFIP, North-Holland Publishing Company, (1978)

Generic Mode Facilities in Mary

by

Per Holager
Afdeling Informatika
Katholieke Universiteit
Nijmegen, Nederland (*)

BSTRACT

number of facilities for handling classes of modes are outined. Some of these have been implemented in the programming anguage Mary, namely parametrized modes and mode fragments. he facilities implemented allow the user to define procedures hat work on parameters of a class of modes. These constructs re described in the context of Mary, and their implementation nd use are discussed. Their usefulness has in fact been found o be rather moderate. In the description of the implementation notation is used which may also be of interest.

. INTRODUCTION

t has become widely accepted that the main problems in advaning the arts of software construction are concerned with proesses in the minds of programmers, rather than with processes f machines (1). Programming languages play an important part n these mental processes as they form the interface to the utside world, the vehicle into which ideas must be concretized. ndeed, in the humanities it is a fundamental assumption that ne can only think what can be expressed in one's language. xperience in software construction indicates that this may also pply to programming and its languages.

his will necessarily render programming languages the major omponent of any set of tools and methods for software producion. New programming language elements that encourage clearer bstractions and more complete concepts, may contribute signiicantly to a methodology for constructing software of better uality.

his paper outlines a number of possibilities for increasing the ower and flexibility of declarations, in fully, statically yped programming languages. As generality and flexibility may e taken as the antithesis of structure, this is not necessarly desireable. A specific set of facilities is therefore preented, along with experience obtained with their use. Their mplementation is also explained, to allow their cost-effectiveess to be judged. Current research in this area does not

---

*) Most of the research underlying this paper was performed while the author was employed at RUNIT, Trondheim, Norway; it was in part supported by the Royal Norwegian Council for Technical and Scientific Research, grant no. B.0406.3722.

appear to be as widely known as it should be, see e.g. (2). The primary purpose is therefore to point out that some possible lanes of research have been tried and found not very fruitful. Secondly it will note some other possibilities that show more promise.

The facilities will be discussed in the framework of Mary (3). This is a high-level machine independent, yet machine oriented programming language, primarily aimed at systems implementation. The language resembles Algol-68 (4) to a large extent, with two major exceptions: Language constructs requiring extensive run-time support routines have been omitted. Secondly, the mode concept (but not the mode syntax) closely resembles that of Pascal (5). In particular, each mode describes a physically contiguous data format. This is different from Algol-68 where array objects, in particular, will usually be implemented as several disjoint physical objects. Another difference from Algol-68 is, of course, the generic modes and related facilities.

2. GENERALITIES ON GENERIC MODES

2.1. Concepts

Modes correspond roughly to the data types and data structure definitions of the better known programming languages. More precisely the term "mode" is used as defined in the Algol-68 tradition (6). A mode is a characterization of a class of values and the operations that may be performed upon them (in particular the built-in, intrinsic operations). There exists a syntax defining how modes may be constructed from simpler modes and primitive constructs. (We are of course not primarily concerned with the precise notation of modes, but rather with the immediately underlying meaning). In fully statically typed programming languages every value has a mode as an attribute; the mode is statically known information about the dynamically occurring values of variables, expressions etc. The information of the mode is not (directly) available during execution.

Some operations, both built-in and user-defined, may be applied to operands of more than one mode. Such an operation will then define a class of modes. The indexing operation, for instance, is defined for all array modes. It may be hoped that such classes of modes may be useful abstractions over simple modes; particularly when the operation or operations delimiting the class are user-defined. In this paper such a class of modes is called a generic mode. "Generic" means, "relating to, or characteristic of a whole group or class" (7). In Algol-68 circles generic modes, or rather some special forms of them have been called modals (8). Algol-68-R (9) and Alphard (10) have related facilities. In Simula (11) class prefixing gives similar effect (Note that the term "class" in Simula has approximately the same meaning as "mode" and "generic mode" in this paper).

Note that coercions (implicit type conversions) do not define generic mode classes. The fact that these conversion operations are not written explicitly must mean they are meant to be of negligible importance. (Programming language syntax must be taken at face value). The unimportance of the conversion must in turn mean, the a priori mode is thought to be essentially equivalent to the resulting mode. Coercions define equivalence classes, which appear to be less useful as abstractions precisely because the members are so similar: There is very little room for variation, no flexibility for expressing anything.

Programs must of course be taken at face value: The syntax of a programming language is an interface whose purpose is to display the semantics of programs in a comprehensible fashion. Programming mainly seems to consist of stretching to the utmost ones ability to comprehend complexity. That is, the syntax should be as clear and straightforward as possible, there is no room for euphemisms or innuendoes. If two constructs look alike, this must mean they have similar semantics. Something being left implicit, must mean it is of no concern to the reader.

2.2. Forms of Generic Modes

The idea underlying the concept of generic modes is that it should be possible to write one procedure, or other operation definition, which should "work" for a number of otherwise incompatible modes. It might for instance be possible to write one simple collection of procedure (and other) definitions that implement singly linked linear lists of arbitrary elements. That is, each procedure should work for all kinds of list elements; provided say, their first machine word contains the pointer to the next element in the list. The members of this generic mode are then all modes whose values have a pointer to next in the first machine word, and arbitrary continuation.

In general such an operation definition will depend on certain more basic operations being applicable to the (formal) parameter values. A value may be given as actual parameter when these operations are defined for its mode. But it is not necessarily enough to have these operations available in some abstract sense. The implementation of generic modes may put severe requirements on concrete details in the specifications of these operations. Note that the generic mode is defined equivalently as the domain of the new operation definition, and as the modes for which this collection of basic operations is defined.

The most restrictive generic mode implementations require that the same compiled machine code sequence work for values of the different modes. One is then typically limited to manipulate pointers to objects of arbitrary mode, or structured objects where the front part has a fixed form, the rest being arbitrary. The list handling package mentioned above might typically be produced under these restrictions.

The least restrictive implementation appear to be, passing the necessary basic operations as parameters (procedure or macro-) along with the parameter value to be operated upon. Lindsey proposes this be done implicitly (8). (The collection of operation parameters may then be thought of as a concretization of the mode being passed as parameter).

In this form, generic modes are available in many current languages, those in fact that are able to pass operations as parameters. In Algol, for instance, one could write a procedure for sorting, which takes two procedure parameters: The first should test whether element number "i" of the list to be sorted has a smaller value than element number "j"; giving a boolean result. The second parameter procedure should exchange the values of element number "k" and "l"; "k", "l", "i" and "j" being integer parameters to these procedures. Given these two operations on the list to be sorted plus its length, one can e.g. write a quick-sort algorithm. Note, however, that it would be possible to supply nonsense procedure parameters to such a sort algorithm: This form does not impart any structure to the generic modes being defined.

One can imagine many forms of generic mode implementations of intermediate restrictiveness. A main class are those where the common operation definitions are compiled into different machine code sequences for each different use. The members of its generic mode are then those for which basic operations of the indicated textual form are defined.

Other forms start out by defining a more or less open-ended class of modes, by some syntactic scheme. From this definition a collection of operations is made available, implicitly and/or explicitly. Particular member modes are then produced by refining and specializing this general mode framework. The operations from the common definition are applicable to all these member modes. That is, this class of modes is a generic mode. This scheme is amongst others used by Simula.

2.3. The Generic Mode System of Mary

A number of such facilities have been considered in Mary, not all of them have been fully implemented yet. The are,

- parametrized modes
  - statically parametrized modes
  - dynamically parametrized modes
- mode fragments
  - mysterious mode fragments
  - fillable mode fragments
- generic operators.

Parametrized modes are modes that take (sub-) modes as parameters. There are two forms: Statically parametrized modes, where a specific actual parameter mode must be given on each application, so that the modes are completely known during compilation. The other form is (reasonable enough) the dynamically parametrized modes, where the actual mode of the parameter may only be determined during execution. This mode must, however, be one of a list known during compilation. A parametrized mode is then a class of modes, the members of which are obtained by supplying actual mode parameters. The common operations of the generic mode are those that would be defined for the parametrized mode had the formal parameters been ordinary modes, excepting those operations that rely on some specific property of these formal parameters. Dynamically parametrized modes furthermore give the capabilities of unions of Algol-68, and variant records of Pascal.

Mode fragments are incompletely specified modes. These also come in two flavours, the mysterious and the fillable. When mysterious mode fragments are used, the incompletely specified part may not be interpreted or relied upon in any way. Their purpose is to allow the compiler to generate one machine code body for a procedure, and guarantee that this will work for all actual parameters, regardless of which mode occurs in the place of the mysterious mode fragment. Fillable mode fragments, on the other hand, will be filled in with information from the context in which they are used. These mode fragments are used in the definition of operators. When an operator is applied, the incomplete part is filled in with the corresponding information from the mode of the actual parameter. The operator body is then (re-) compiled into machine code for each application, in a macro-like manner.

Generic operators are operators identified by their name (or indicant) and by the context in which that indicant is used. This is mainly the same as in Algol-68 (12). One may e.g. declare a "+" working on "int"'s and another "+" working on "real"'s. The purpose of using the same indicant for different operators must obviously be that the designer of the program does not want the reader of the program to keep track of which of the operations is in fact being used in each case. Unless that designer is sabotaging his project, this means the operations are identical at some level of abstraction. Which means the collection of modes for which these operators are defined may be considered one generic mode. When "+" etc. are defined for both "int" and "real" operands, this means we are urged to consider them special forms of some more abstract numeric mode.

There is, however, nothing in the formalism of the declarations that tends to enforce any common properties on the group of generic operators, nor any reasonable structure in the resulting generic mode. Unless the language makes it possible to specify (and enforce) some common axioms for such a group of generic operators, the facility is open to abuse. Note that the schemes where a generic mode is produced by specializations from a common framework, tend to impart some structure on what is produced.

Space does not permit an in-depth presentation of all these constructs in this paper. The rest of this discussion shall be limited to statically parametrized modes and mysterious mode fragments. These form a complete facility with which considerable experience has been obtained.

3. STATICALLY PARAMETRIZED MODES

3.1. The language facility

The syntax for this in Mary is -

statically parametrized mode definition:

"*mode*", identifier, "(", identifier list, ")", "=", mode.

This defines the first identifier as the (name of) a new parametrized mode. The formal parameter names are given in the identifier list. These names may be used as (sub-) mode names in the right-hand side mode. For instance:

mode list(p) = struct(ref list(p) next, p info);

When such a parametrized mode is used (i.e. applied) a list (in parentheses) of corresponding actual parameter modes must be supplied. We may for instance write a variable declaration:

list(real)qhead := (nil, 0.0);

This has the same effect as:

mode reallist = struct(ref reallist next, real info);

reallist qhead := (nil, 0.0);

3.2. Representing Modes in a Compiler

Writing a compiler in its own language presents a few paradoxes we need to clear away before we contine on our main tale. In a compiler for a language with modes, the modes being compiled must be represented as data structures. These data structure must in turn be composed from data values of some set of modes. For each alternative in the syntax of the language being compiled, we shall have to be able to store the information present/not present. When a major component is optional, we need the possibility of including an entire data structure subcomponent. This subcomponent should then be one or more values, of one or more modes. Let us as example consider a fragment of a syntax for modes similar to Mary's:

```
mode:
   multiple mode; structure mode; reference mode; union mode
structure mode:
   "struct(", subfield list, ")".
subfield:
   "pack" option, mode, identifier.
```

To represent actual occurrences of such modes, we would in the compiler need values of something like the following modes:

```
mode modedescription =
   ref union (multiplemodedescription,
        structuremodedescription,
        referencemodedescription,
        unionmodedescription);
mode structuremodedescription =
```

```
    ref subfielddescription;
  mode subfielddescription =
    struct (ref subfielddescription next,
        bool packed,
        modedescription subfieldmode,
        identifier subfieldname);
```

We see that the modes of the values needed to represent the information given in a string in a language, is just an obvious reformulation of the syntax of that language. Modes are in fact closely analogous to syntax, and syntax notation may in general be used as a better mode notation. This implies we abstract away from details of "*ref*"'s and the like, which is perhaps the greatest advantage of this notation.

It is similarly clear that the original text of the program part being compiled may be used as a better, more abstract notation for the data structures actually set up in the compiler to represent it. Instead of some kind of picture of machine storage, e.g.:

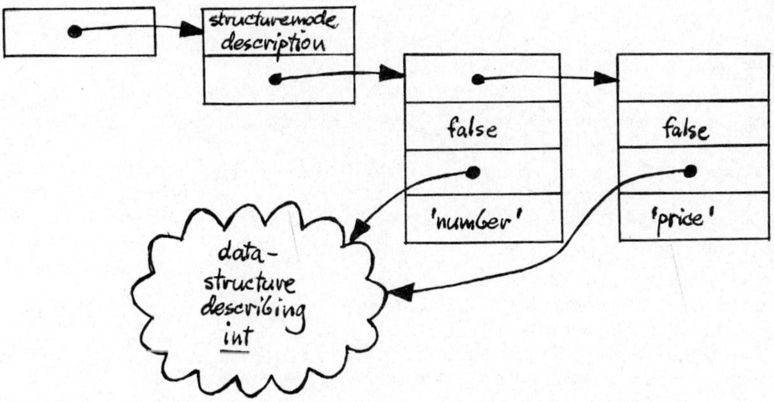

We shall prefer to write the more abstract equivalent:

```
  struct (int number, int price)
```

A competent reader will be able to reconstruct most systems programming kinds of algorithms, given some appropriate example of its effect, and a description of the modes used. This is to some extent relied upon in the following sections. The current section then serves to point out that no elaborate descriptions of modes will be needed, the interested reader can find the required information in the syntax of the language definition. Also note that the following sections are purposely vague concerning many implementation details, like where to insert ref's in data structures.

3.3. Implementation of Statically Parametrized Modes

Even though the semantics appear to be very straightforward, their implementation is not trivial. The main cause of this is the possibility of having recursive mode definitions. That is, the name of the parametrized mode being declared may be referred in the body of its own definition, possibly indirectly through other declared modes. This of course also makes the facility more powerful than the simple macro mechanism it resembles. Consider an example:

mode m(p, q) = struct(p a, ref m(ref q, ref p) b);

This declares the parametrized mode "*m*", which has two parameters "*p*" and "*q*". "*m*" is a *struct* with fields "*a*" and "*b*". The mode of "*a*" is simply the first parameter mode. "*b*" is a *ref* to an object of the same parametrized mode "*m*", but with different, more complicated parameters. That is, the modes of an "*m*" object and the "*m*" object it points to will not be compatible. The example is not very meaningful, but does illustrate the implementation problems one may encounter in "real" sets of mode definitions, where parametrized modes are defined in terms of each other.

Once defined, the name of a declared mode may be used an unlimited number of times, also recursively as noted. That means it is very desireable, if not mandatory, to have a mode represented by one unchanging data structure. This applies as well for parametrized modes, even though the list of actual parameters in general will be different for each point of use. That is, in the compiler there must be a special data object describ ing each use of a parametrized mode. This object must contain a reference to the data structure describing the declared mode, and a list of descriptions of the actual parameter modes. Given the declaration of "*m*" above, we may for instance write:

m(int, real) v := (1, nil);

This declares a variable "*v*" of mode "*m(int, real)*", and initializes it to the value "*(1, nil)*". Observe that the notation "*m(int, real)*" nicely suggests a pointer to what "*m*" is declare to be, and a list of (two) actual parameters.

These mode representing data structures are used to control the application of operations to data objects in the program being compiled. One or two mode representations will be traversed in a manner which in this context is best considered fully collateral. The components of the modes will be inspected, and possibly compared. When a component of the body of a parametrized mode is being inspected, it may be found that it is a formal parameter representation. That is, the thing that should really be inspected is a mode from a specific position in an actual parameter list. The actual parameter list will in general be different for different traversals, whereas the mode body representation itself will be the same. Which means the complete description of the components of a mode body must be composed of two parts, a pointer to that part in the mode representation and a context, which is (a pointer to) the list of the current actual parameter modes.

Except for formal parameters, the components of parametrized mode bodies are modes like all others. It is therefore very desireable to have one kind of mode descriptor which the compiler may use for all modes in all cases. Which means that every mode description in the compiler should have these two parts, the context being empty unless parametrized mode bodies are being handled. The compiler will be maintaining an unknown number of mode descriptions simultaneously, which means this cannot be optimized by setting the list up in some global "context" variable.

The list of current actual parameters will stay the same most of the time during traversal, like when going from the representation of a structure to the representation of the mode of one of the subfields. A new current parameter list is set up when, and only when a data object is encountered which represents the use of a parametrized mode. That is, when the compiler found a use of a parametrized mode, and starts on the inspection of its body. The new list will almost be the same as the list of actual parameters given in the parametrized mode usage representation.

When a parametrized mode is used in the body of a parametrized mode definition, the actual parameters of the usage may refer the formal parameters of the surrounding definition. That is, the actual parameters of the usage must have a context, the same in fact as the context of the mode descriptor referring that usage representation. Note that the context in general will be different each time a given usage is encountered, and that the same usage may be collaterally traversed in another context. That implies, every time a usage is traversed, a physically new list of actuals-with-context must be set up. This new list will then be the context used when traversing the new mode body, the one referred by the usage.

An example might perhaps make this a little more clear. To denote complete modes with context, we will write the mode structure proper, followed by "where", followed by the list of actual parameter modes. These parameters might again each have a context (which will be the same for all), denoted by "where"'s followed by their list(s) of actuals. Now consider a continuation of our example, the program fragment -

real *r* := *v*.*b*.*a* ;

This declares a *real* variable "*r*", and initializes it to the value of "*v*.*b*.*a*". "*v*.*b*.*a*" means, the subfield "*a*" of the subfield "*b*" of the variable "*v*". The compiler must check a number of things here, namely that ".*b*" is appliccable to "*v*", that ".*a*" is applicable to "*v*.*b*", and that a *real* value may be obtained from "*v*.*b*.*a*" to be assigned to "*r*". The mode of "*v*" is:

m(*int*, *real*) ;

To be able to proceed, we must inspect the declared mode, i.e. replace "*m*" by the mode it is declared to be. As part of this operation, a context representation must be built. That is, the mode of "*v*" is essentially -

$$\underline{struct}(\underline{p}\ a,\ \underline{ref}\ \underline{m}(\underline{ref}\ \underline{q},\ \underline{ref}\ \underline{p})\ b\ )\quad \underline{where}\begin{cases}\underline{p}\ \underline{is}\ \underline{int}\\ \underline{q}\ \underline{is}\ \underline{real}\end{cases}$$

The mode of "*v.b*" is then clearly -

$$\underline{ref}\ \underline{m}(\underline{ref}\ \underline{q},\ \underline{ref}\ \underline{p})\quad \underline{where}\begin{cases}\underline{p}\ \underline{is}\ \underline{int}\\ \underline{q}\ \underline{is}\ \underline{real}\end{cases}$$

To be able to proceed further with the analysis of "*v.b.a*", thi must be dereferenced. (This operation will generate executable code, namely an idirect addressing step; as opposed to the inspection of delcared modes and mode parameters that do not affect the generated machine code directly). After the dereferencing, we shall have to inspect "$\underline{m}$" again, yielding for "*v.b*"

$$\underline{struct}(\underline{p}\ a,\ \underline{ref}\ \underline{m}(\underline{ref}\ \underline{q},\ \underline{ref}\ \underline{p})\ b\ )$$

$$\underline{where}\begin{cases}\underline{p}\ \underline{is}\ \underline{ref}\ \underline{q}\ \underline{where}\\ \underline{q}\ \underline{is}\ \underline{ref}\ \underline{p}\ \underline{where}\end{cases}\begin{cases}\underline{p}\ \underline{is}\ \underline{int}\\ \underline{q}\ \underline{is}\ \underline{real}\end{cases}$$

Clearly, the mode of "*v.b.a*" is -

$$\underline{p}\ \underline{where}\begin{cases}\underline{p}\ \underline{is}\ \underline{ref}\ \underline{q}\ \underline{where}\\ \underline{q}\ \underline{is}\ \underline{ref}\ \underline{p}\ \underline{where}\end{cases}\begin{cases}\underline{p}\ \underline{is}\ \underline{int}\\ \underline{q}\ \underline{is}\ \underline{real}\end{cases}$$

But this is not too illuminating. The mode is "$\underline{p}$", which is just a formal parameter of "$\underline{m}$". We shall have to inspect "$\underline{p}$", which yields -

$$\underline{ref}\ \underline{q}\ \underline{where}\begin{cases}\underline{p}\ \underline{is}\ \underline{int}\\ \underline{q}\ \underline{is}\ \underline{real}\end{cases}$$

Observe that inspecting a parameter mode is a sort of inverse of the inspection of a declared parametrized mode; it brings us "down" one level of environments. That is, parameter-inspection brings us back to the environment existing before the last inspection-of-mode.

The purpose of all this was to obtain a "$\underline{real}$" value from "*v.b.a*". We shall first have dereference this, then inspect the parameter "$\underline{q}$". This yields -

$$\underline{real}$$

(- without any parameter environment). Which means, we have succeeded. (In fact, a "$\underline{real}$" may be obtained from "*v*" by selecting the subfield "*b*", dereferencing the value obtained, selecting the subfield "*a*" of the object arrived at, and dereferencing this).

Note that in the context of this section, ordinary unparametrized modes should be considered parametrized modes with zero parameters. Observe (13) that this implementation is in part similar to the dynamic execution of Algol-60 procedures (14) (15). The unchanging mode representation is analogous to the procedure code bodies, the context lists are analogous to procedure activation records, but without anyting similar to local or global variables. The mode parameters are in fact similar to "by name" parameters.

Mode declarations might be textually nested by having an array mode in a mode definition, and supplying as array bound a closed clause containing another mode declaration. But the closed clause should be completely evaluated before analysis of the outer mode declaration starts. At that time all analysis of the inner mode definition must be terminated, making the two definitions completely disjoint. Lastly, it should be noted that the implementation described here is not quite the one used in the current Mary compilers.

4. MYSTERIOUS MODE FRAGMENTS AND THE GENERALIZED CODE SEQUENCE

4.1. The Language Facility

Mode fragments are incompletely specified modes. One might for instance consider having a *struct* where the first subfield is defined; where there should be more subfields, but where these have not been specified. Or an array mode where the index bounds have been left out. Devising a notation for this is easy, for instance "*mode s = struct(ref s next, mysterious);*" and "*array(mysterious)real*".

Mysterious mode fragments have arbitrarily been given a more limited form, however. No details may be given about a mysterious mode fragment, the whole mode is mysterious. So they are usually called just mysterious modes, and work as a kind of place-holder for some, as yet unknown set of ordinary modes.

The purpose of this facility is to make it possible to write procedures that will work for parameters of a class of modes. Each class will be defined as a mode where some component submode is represented by a mysterious mode; this mysterious mode may therefore only be defined in the routine header (i.e. parameters and result specification) of procedures. This is again an arbitrary, though reasonable design decision. The relevant syntax is -

routine header:

"*% (*", parameter description, "*)*", mode, "*:*".

parameter description:

mysterious mode declaration option, parameter list option.

mysterious mode declaration:

"*mode*", identifier list, ",".

That is, a mysterious mode declaration is part of the parameter description in the routine header, which is usually part of a procedure declaration. The mysterious mode declaration will declare one or more identifiers to be names of modes, of this special quality.

Consider an example:

```
proc swap = % (mode m, ref ref m m1, m2):
    begin
        m1 :=: m2 =: m1 ;
    end;
```

This procedure "*swap*" takes two pointers-to-pointers-to-something as parameters, and exchanges the value of the two pointer to-something. Note that Mary does not have the abominable ref of Algol-68, that is, an integer variable has the mode "*int*" not "*ref int*". "*:=:*" is the special assignment operator, assigning the value of the left hand expression to the variable on the right, yielding the old value of the right hand variable (that is, the value which was overwritten in the assignment).

When such a procedure is called, actual modes must be given for each of the mysterious ones. The syntax is pretty obvious; in a call -

actual parameters:

actual modes option, expression list option.

actual modes:

mode list, ",".

That is, we may call "swap" as in -

```
mode string = array (6) char ;
ref string s1 := 'flies' heap string,
    s2 := 'time ' heap string ;
swap(string, s1, s2) ;
```

This declares two variables "*s1*" and "*s2*" to be references to strings, which are arrays of 6 characters. Both variables are initialized to point to initialized strings on the heap. The call on "*swap*" will interchange the reference-to-string values of "*s1*" and "*s2*". There is full mode checking at the call; "*string*" is inserted for the formal "*m*", and coercion will produce two "*ref ref string*" values from "*s1*" and "*s2*". Note that there is a referencing coercion in Mary; the a priori modes are just "*ref string*".

Mysterious modes in the restricted form of procedure parameters have been called "modals" by a number of other authors, in particular Lindsey. Classifying them as a special form of parameters is of course quite valid. We have nevertheless chosen to stress the analogy with fillable mode fragments, as this suggests a wider range of applicability.

4.2. Implementation

This is all done in the compiler, of course, and it is really very simple: No intrinsic operations are defined for such modes, not even assignation. The size of an object of mysterious mode, is not defined, so they cannot be declared. A mysterious mode is not compatible with, nor coercible to anything except itself. The only "real" things one can do with them is, manipulating pointers to objects of such modes (all pointers have the same implementation regardless of what mode objects they refer), or have a mysterious mode object as the (untouched) end of a structure. A special case of this latter use is to have a mysterious mode as (unused) alternative in a union mode.

There is furthermore the possibility of having any specific mode accepted in place of, or as a specification for the mysterious mode at the points of application, Without this the facility would be inaccessible, of course.

The restrictions on use are quite severe. But they seem to be the most general under which a straightforward compiler can produce one efficient machine code sequence with the required general properties. Indeed, one might well argue that this approach shoves the implementation problems over onto the user. Mary is, however, a machine-oriented language where the programmer is expected to have control over such matters.

A less restrictive definition would either require a very elaborate run-time system; or a compiler smart enough to generate more than one machine-code subroutine for such a procedure to handle incompatible actual-modes. Or the compiler might generate in-line code at each point of use (which is what macroes are for in Mary); or some kind of heuristic combination of these possibilities.

A run-time system able to handle this might implicitly handle everything by reference (which may be taken as a concretization of D.T. Ross' object oriented view of data (16)). This would make implementation of generalized code almost trivial, but will in general have implications for the language, particularly for the semantics of the assignment to a component of a data structure. Another possibility is to compile machine code routines which generate, copy etc. values of the actual mode at the point of call, and pass these as parameters to the generalized routines, as suggested by Lindsey (9). This may quite neatly be viewed as passing the mode as parameter to the generalized routine; the representation of a mode being the set of operations that are defined for it! Note, however, that both possibilities are quite inefficient compared with ordinary,in-lined code.

When generalized code procedures are called, a complete, fully defined mode is supplied for the mysterious mode. That implies the modes of parameters and result values will be completely, conventionally defined. Internally in the compiler, one might set up these complete mode descriptions in the ordinary manner. It has been found convenient (indeed, see comment at the end of sec. 4.1), to use the mechanisms of statically parametrized modes; regarding the mysterious modes as formal mode parameters for this purpose.

5. EXAMPLE OF COMBINED USE

In practice it turns out that mysterious modes are used in combination with statically parametrized modes. Let us consider a typical example:

```
mode link(p) = struct(ref link(p) next, ref p info),
     stack(p) = ref link(p) ;
```

That declares two statically parametrized modes, the first of which will be used for the links in a singly linked list. Note that the "*info*" field has the mode "*ref p*" rather than just "*p*". This anticipates that the actual parameter given for "*p*" will be a mysterious mode. "*stack*" is the mode of the head of the list, used to represent the entire list; and its name suggests the list will be used in a stack fashion (last in - first out).

Then consider a procedure operating on such objects:

```
proc tostack = %(mode m, ref stack(m) s, ref m i) :
     begin
         (s, i) heap link(m)
         =: s:-stack(m)
     end ;
```

This procedure takes a stack of something and a pointer to something, and places the something pointed at on top of the stack. This is done by producing a "*link*" object, linking it in next to the list header, and setting it to point to the new object.

The first line of the procedure body calls the "*heap*" generator to get a "*link(m)*" object, and then initializes it to the value "*(s,i)*". That is, the "*next*" field will point at the "*link*" "*s*" is pointing at; the "*info*" field at the "*m*" given as parameter. The result of this is a reference to the object. Observe that all of this can be done in a straightforward manner, handling only physical data objects whose properties are known. The second line of the body sets the list header pointing to the new "*link*" object. (The "*:-stack(m)*" is a cast working on "*s*", to make the assignment occur at the correct level of dereferencing).

Consider a trivial program fragment using the above declarations

```
stack(string) texts := nil ;
string nextext := 'arrow ' ;
tostack(string, texts, nextext) ;
```

This declares a stack of strings by name of "*texts*", initialized to *nil*. Next line declares a string variable named "*nextext*", which in the last line is placed as first element on the stack "*texts*" by the call on "*tostack*". Note that it is impossible to place anything except "*string*"'s on the "*texts*" stack. In the body of "*tostack*", only "*m*" objects will be accepted; mysterious modes are compatible only with themselves (meaning two different mysterious modes are also incompatible). The call of "*tostack*" is also safe, the modes required from the actual parameters are uniquely determined once the actual mode (s) have been indicated.

6. STATUS AND EXPERIENCE

Parametrized modes, mysterious modes and general procedures have been implemented and available in Trondheim since the beginning of 1974. Experience has shown, however, that they are much less useful than anticipated. The single significant application remains the user interface of the inter-process message system of the Mary Runsys timesharing operating system (17).

These facilities are clearly only useful in bottom-up programming: The whole point of it all is to be able to write one set of definitions which can be flexibly applied in a number of conventionally incompatible contexts. The reason for the low utility seems to be a combination of factors. Primarily, there just is not much bottom-up programming in large "system" programs. Secondly, the restrictions on use are very noticeable. Programming a file system interface, for instance, one is primarily interested in the variably-sized objects themselves, not in some abstract representation which can be implemented as a reference. In this application the user interface is best made with some kind of macro, hiding the fact that punning is used to step outside the limitations of the mode checking.

Thirdly, for small, simple constructs this apparatus seems a little too elaborate - it is usually better to duplicate code in-line,or use a macro. There is a textual macro mechanism in Mary which also gives a simple but very limited generic facility: A macro may be applied to any operand for which the text of the macro makes sense.

And fourthly, large complicated constructs embody a large number of specialized design decisions. Finding two nearly compatible, large constructs in one program is just very improbable. Very few compilers use more than one symbol table, for instance.

This might be different in a system aiming more at bottom-up programming, like the writing of service libraries. In a library for compiler writers one would e.g. want a generalized symbol table definition capable of being used in a number of different compilers. As bottom-up programming and libraries mainly have been found useful in the relatively simple world of mathematics, these generic facilities might be found worthwhile in languages for numerical computations or formula manipulation. Systems programs, however, seem to mirror the complexities of human systems, and top-down programming prevails.

This also appears to be the experience from other languages. The class prefixing facilites of Simula give the power of both mysterious mode fragments, useful for bottom-up work, and dynamically parametrized modes (or unions, variant records) which are mainly used for top-down programming. The bottom-up facility is used for the built-in simulation, text handling and i/o facilities of the language, but little elsewhere, it seems.

There is, then, strong reasons to doubt the general utility of statically parametrized modes and mysterious modes. In Mary they are clearly not useful enough to justify the cost of implementation, and the addition to the language description. The other generic mode facilities presented in the introduction show more promise, but have not as yet been properly implemented

ACKNOWLEDGEMENTS

The language constructs described were defined by Mark Rain, implemented by Mark Rain, Ole Solberg and the author. The Mary Runsys operating system has been implemented by Mark Rain and Reidar Conradi, all while working at RUNIT, Trondheim, I also thank Karl Kleine and C.H.A. Koster, both of the Katholieke Universiteit Nijmegen, and the referees for valuable suggestions and comments. Lastly, I would like to thank Veronica Hempel and Michael Stahl for providing food and shelter, without which this article would certainly not have been written.

REFERENCES

(1) G.M. Weinberg; The Psychology of Computer Programming; Van Nostrand Reinhold Company, New York (1971)

and O.J. Dahl, E.W. Dijkstra, C.A.R. Hoare; Structured Programming; Academic Press, London (1972)

(2) D. Gries, N. Gehani; Some Ideas on Data Types in High Level Languages; ACM Conference on Data: Abstraction, Definition and Structure; Salt Lake City, Utah , March 1976

(3) R. Conradi and P. Holager; Mary Textbook; RUNIT, Trondheim (1975)

(4) A. van Wijngaarden et al. (ed.s); Revised Report on the Algorithmic Language Algol 68; Springer Verlag, Berlin-Heidelberg-New York (1976)

(5) K. Jensen, N. Wirth; Pascal User Manual and Report; Springer Verlag, Berlin-Heidelberg-New York (1974)

(6) C.H.A. Koster; The Mode-System in ALGOL68; In New directions in Algorithmic Languages, Stephen A. Schuman

(ed.), p. 99-114; IRIA, Le Chesnay (1975)

(7) H.B. Woolf (ed. in chief); Webster's New Collegiate Dictionary; G. & C. Merriam Company, Springfield, Mass. (1976)

(8) C.H. Lindsey; Modals; Algol Bulletin 37 p. 26-29
and C.H. Lindsey and F.D. Foster; Quasi-modals; Report CHL 74-08-08, presented at the August meeting 1974 of the IFIP WG. 2.1 in Utrecht, Netherlands

(9) P.M. Woodward, S.G. Bond; Algol-68-R Users Guide; Her Majesty's Stationery Office, London (1974)

(10) W.A. Wulf; Alphard: Towards a Language to Support Structured Programs; Dept. of Computer Science, Carnegie Mellon Univ. Pittsburgh, Pennsylvania (April 1974)

(11) O.J. Dahl, B. Myrhaug and K. Nygaard; Simula Common Base Language; Norsk Regnesentral, Oslo (1970)

(12) Stephen A. Schumann; On Generic Functions; In New Directions in Algorithmic Languages; Stephen A. Schumann (ed.), p. 169-192; IRIA, Le Chesnay (1975)

(13) M. Rain, Private Communication, 1972

(14) B. Randell and D.J. Russel; Algol-60 Implementation; Academic Press, London (1964)

(15) P. Naur; Revised Report on the Algorithmic Language Algol-60; Regnesentralen, Copenhagen (1964)

(16) D.T. Ross, Private communication at the May 1974 meeting of the IFIP WG. 2.4 in La Grande Motte, France

(17) P. Holager; A Consolidation of Synchronization Primitives; Machine Oriented Languages Bulletin no. 2, april 1973, RUNIT, Trondheim

Constructing Quality Software, P.G. Hibbard/S.A. Schuman (eds.)

LANGUAGE STRATIFICATION WITHOUT LOSS OF EFFICIENCY

G.D.Chinin
Novosibirsk Division
S.A.Lebedev Institute for Computing Machinery
USSR Academy of Sciences
Novosibirsk 630090, USSR

Adequacy of large-scale programming system construction, considered as a combination of comprehensibility, expressiveness and reliability is achievable when using high level system implementation languages. On the other hand, high level language does not often provide desirable efficiency of the programs, especially with respect to the operating system. This paper deals with the pragmatic method of removing the contradiction between adequacy and efficiency, these principal constituents, which provide programming product quality.

1. INTRODUCTION

The purpose of this paper is to find any constructive solution of the problem of practical combination of the conflicting requirements of efficiency and adequacy, considered as main characteristics of software quality in the working and stable discipline of software design and implementation.

The term "adequacy" means "comprehensibility + expressiveness + reliability". Both comprehensibility and expressiveness are provided by means of language implementation facilities which allow a program description in terms close either to the essence of the program or to the algorithm. Reliability results from the availability of static data checking, limited number of control structures, name protection and modular program construction.

It is quite obvious that the availability of these features determining the adequacy of the programs greatly depends on the level of the system implementation language. The adequacy mainly characterizes the external part of the program and reflects the step-wise processes of its design, implementation, checkout and documentation.

Program efficiency in our presentation is determined by the quantitive characteristics of the resources, which are necessary for static internal program representation and its dynamic execution. The efficiency function decreases according to the increase of the quantity of any necessary resources.

It is possible to say, that there is an optimally efficient representation of any program in the system, but there is no constructive way of realizing it. In general the efficiency of representation provided by a system implementation language tends to decrease with the increase of the language level. Program quality is defined by a "reasonable" correlation between adequacy and efficiency. Fig.1 shows this correlation for sufficiently large programs.

An integrated program project has a number of components with essentially different adequacy treatment. The quality level of each particular component directly influences on the quality of the system on the whole.

Our approach to getting over the adequacy - efficiency conflict in large-scale programming projects has two main features:
(1) hierarchy of language levels of implementation allowing the achievement of high average adequacy, and
(2) controllable representation of language constructs allowing the increase of the efficiency.

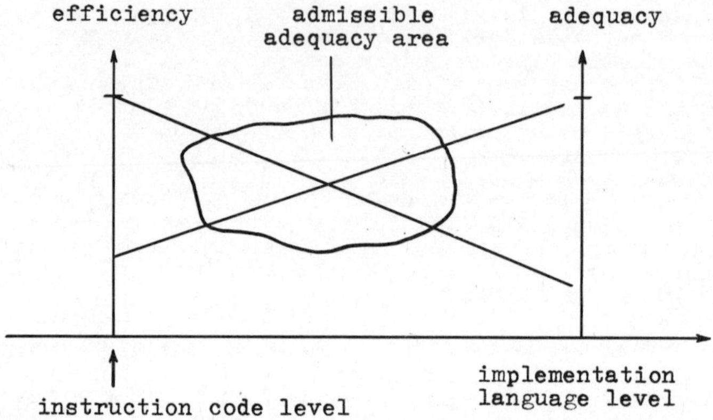

Fig.1. Adequacy - efficiency tradeoff

Below we suggest the more developed interpretation of these théses on the basis of the actual experience in the design and implementation of general-purpose software system for the BESM-6 computer. This system includes sufficiently large number of components:
- supervisor;
- data management system;
- system and front-end programming language compiler;
- service programs.

So that it can be called a large-scale programming system.

2. LANGUAGE HIERARCHY IN A PROGRAMMING SYSTEM

Program components of our system, as in many others [1,2] are divided into ordered layers. Each layer contains a set of components which are either "private" to the layer or provide some external interface. The partition into layers and their ordering is performed by representing a layer in terms of the interface components of the preceding layer. The same hierarchy is also possible within a layer, as, for instance, in [3].

A partition into layers may be rather arbitrary. It greatly depends on implementor's skills and wishes and reflects the phasing of the system implementation.

In our case a layer of program components which support peripheral devices is the lowest one. This layer is based on the machine instruction code and some private components which provide a unified format of transput facilities in the instruction code. At this layer called "absolute", the control is performed in terms of physical addresses of the main memory, channels and i/o devices.

The next layer of program components is called "virtual". It provides virtual memory and logical i/o device facilities. All programs expressed in relocatable code get an access to particular devices including the core memory through means of the virtual layer. This layer is expanded in terms of the instruction code and interface components of the preceding layer.

The absolute and virtual layers are followed by a "logical" layer. It provides with:
- interrupt handling facility;
- processes and coroutines;
- synchronization;
- operations over arrays in the core memory;
- file handling;
- access to formatted transput editor and interpreter;
- a unified static and dynamic linkage between object code segments.

It should be noted that means of the logical layer sometimes do not enable to achieve both proper efficiency and expressive power.

For example, the mechanisms of branching and synchronization for PL/I may be more effectively and economically implemented in some special manner different from those embedded into logical layer. On the other hand the standard mechanism is effective in a multiprogramming mode. Let us take another example. A developed programming system supporting the process of compiler construction prefers to use files of finer structure than that is provided by the logical layer. In these cases some problem-oriented layer extending the logical layer facilities may be built (as was actually done). The implementation of the problem-oriented layer may be based not only on logical layer facilities but may refer to the virtual and absolute layers when necessary. So it is an outline of the layered structure of the system in question.

In summary, a software system is presented in terms of a hierarchy of layers. The interface of each layer creates the set of notions characterizing the properties of the next layer. It must be pointed out that this layering is made in order to strictly emphasize the levels of the system implementation as a whole.

Slightly shifting emphasis, we may consider each layer as defining some language used for the implementation of the next layer. Furthermore, the set of program components of a layer creates a programmed model of an executing machine which corresponds to the language. Then a hierarchy of executing machines (or internal languages) may be spoken about. If each internal language is considered to have a corresponding external programming language, then its executing machine looks like a dynamic support system for programs written in this language. Now there are grounds to present the software system (from outside) as hierarchy of system implementation languages and (from inside) as a set of corresponding language processors including program models of executing machines.

Each implementation language is built on the basis of a single base language. On the one hand this allows their straightforward implementation by reducing them to base language constructs by means of either preprocessors or internal facilities of the base language. On the other hand it makes possible a description of the internal relations (1) between system components or (2) between the system itself and the environment, expressing these relations by means of one single metasystem of notations and concepts provided by the base language.

3. EFFICIENCY, ADEQUACY AND OPTIMIZATION

There are a lot of arguments for the use of high level languages in systems programming, and the expected low efficiency of object programs may be regarded as the only but rather serious practical argument against it. Indeed, this is a serious problem. It is most probable that a straightforward reliable compiler for a sufficiently high level systems programming language will not provide for the required efficiency level when implementing a large programming system. Even if an optimizing compiler is available, it seems unreasonable that it could produce an optimal allocation of data and program segments in the main and external memories, which appears to be one of the most essential parameters affecting the system efficiency.

Optimizing transformations of high level language programs are divided into language level optimizations and machine level optimizations. The first class of optimizations is such that an optimized program may be expressed in the source language. Applying such optimizing program transformation techniques, a user may try to achieve the desired program efficiency.

Machine level optimizations do not have an adequate source language representation. They are usually applied to those source language constructs which have no directly corresponding execution means in the instruction code. As a rule they are concerned with the implementation of the bodies and calls of procedures and with the access to elements of structured values. It seems that the problem of automatic and efficient implementation of such constructs in a large program allocated among a number of memory levels hardly has any solution in practice.

So the essential constructs of high level languages - namely procedures and complex data structures - may be considered as the main origin of inefficiency. It is explained by the fact that most computers do not have special hardware facilities for the direct support of procedure calls and large complex-structured data operations. It is partially explainable by the fact that optimal programming access facilities and procedure body calls for large segmented programs have to take into account not only static but, to a greater extent, dynamic program properties.

On the other hand it is these constructs that contribute most of all to the adequacy of the programming product. They enable the programmer to create a data and operational base for a clear and concise programming of the problem, that additionally increases the software reliability.

An achievement of a reasonable correlation between the level of expressive power and the efficiency of its automatic implementation may be considered as one of the main problems of system programming language design.

The assembler languages with their programs written in the format close to the machine representation, may be regarded as an extreme concession to efficiency requirements. Practically all (not only complex) constructs of the developed programming languages are not available in assembler languages. A more interesting and useful language appears when the principle of control over the object program is combined with the external expressive facilities inherent to the high level programming languages [4].

Another approach to the factual elimination of the contradiction between the efficiency and the expressive power is suggested in[5]. Following this approach, in all cases where a language processor cannot itself select an appropriate implementation it is forced by means of facilities for control over the generation of the object program. One of the first programming languages based on these ideas is presented in [6]. These works have essentially influenced our approach.

Thus one of the main features of a high level systems programming language is the possibility of control over the object program efficiency depending upon reasons external to the program, for example, dynamically allocated resources. So that it is necessary to explicitly point out the implementation aspect of the system programming language as it has been done, for example, in [7].

4. BASE LANGUAGE

4.1. Initial remarks

As far as programming language concerned, it is necessary to distinguish its external and internal aspects. The external aspects are provided by the expressive means of the language and they are intended for the description of the algorithm. The internal aspects are represented by the executing machine revealing the meaning of the program.

With the language implemented on a particular object machine the executing machine has to be expressed in terms of its instructions and data. In general it can be realized in various ways. And the greater the difference between the object and the executing machines, the higher the degree of freedom. At this level optimization possibility appears due to alternatives in the object code representation of some constructs of the language (or its executing machine). As a rule it is related to the implementation of procedures and composite dynamic data.

The problem of an optimal static and dynamic allocation of program components among the memory levels arises when a large program is considered. It is hardly possible to find any optimal and automatic solution of this problem in conjunction with the optimization and data access problem.

Providing such a facility, represented in terms of the source language, may be regarded as a reasonable and acceptable solution to the problem.

Efficiency requirements of object programs may be provided by controlling all essential choices. This means, in particular, that a qualified user has to be able to design and implement facilities of the executing machine which allow more efficient implementation of his specific problem.

The base language is built by a mutual projection of the instruction code and an "ideal" high level language with sufficiently convenient and conventional expressive means. "Projection intersection" provides an outline of the language kernel directly mappable into the instruction code. These source language constructs, which either have natural and adequate representation in machine or control the efficiency of all possible representations, form the kernel. Let us consider the characteristics of the base language beginning from its kernel.

4.2. Kernel

Values and operations. The basic set of the types of values and operations is dependent upon the computer capabilities. Types are associated with operations rather than with data. Data value is interpreted with respect to the applied operation.

"Bit" type. A value of one word size is treated as a bit vector. Componentwise Boolean operations, shift operations and value field selection are defined over bit values. There is a comparison operation (equal/nonequal). All operations except the value field selection are supported by corresponding machine instructions.

"Floating" type. A bit vector of one word size is treated as a floating point value. The usual arithmetic operations and comparison operations are permitted. All operations are supported by machine instructions.

"Integer" type. The instruction code contains no direct operations over integer values but allows their concise presentation in terms of other instructions.

Value denotation. The base language permits sufficiently wide value denotations, and appropriate ones may be selected for any specific task. They include denotations in the form of integer and floating decimal numbers, bit, octal, hexadecimal and byte sequences of the left and right orientation.

Data. There are simple variables mapping into one machine word. The simple variable value type is treated with respect to its use, especially to the basic operations applied.

Although the basic operations, supported by the instruction code, deal with one word size values, the necessity of "short" data packed into one machine word is quite obvious. This results in simple (scalar) structured (field-composed) data with single atomic elements being less than one word long and packed into one or any adjacent memory word in any desired way. When a short value plays the role of source value (or destination), unpacking (packing) command sequences are inserted automatically.

There is a special set of operations in the language allowing in some cases to obtain more concise object programs for handling short data.

Scalar (simple or structured) data may be organized into one-dimensional fixed-size arrays.

Formulas. Formula construction rules admit as operands almost all those language constructs yielding values. Such a generality allows the reduction of intermediate data.

Control. The control facilities comprise the serial, conditional, case and loop statements. "Forced" completion of the statement execution from any internal point is available.

Program structure. Blocks and procedures are the main units of the representation of the static program structure. They have all standard properties. Besides the blocks and procedures, modules are used for this purpose. A module, as well as a block, provides a new localization level for names not accessible outside, but unlike the block, it may contain a number of objects specified as interfaces and accessed outside the module. Thus modules give an adequate representation of software layered system. Besides, the module concept gives in natural way a concise representation of program components which constitute an executing machine.

4.3. Language superstructure

Procedure properties. Let us consider in more detail the admissible procedure nomenclature in a real large program with respect to their object representation. As to memory allocation, procedures may be resident or non-resident. The addressing may be absolute or relative. And as to memory areas occupied by the program, procedures may be:

- relocatable in non-active condition (i.e. if it does not enter in any dynamic chain, then the procedure may be relocated in another memory area if necessary);
- relocatable in any condition;
- non-erasable in any condition (i.e. their memory areas can not be used for any other purpose);
- erasable in non-active condition;
- erasable in any condition.

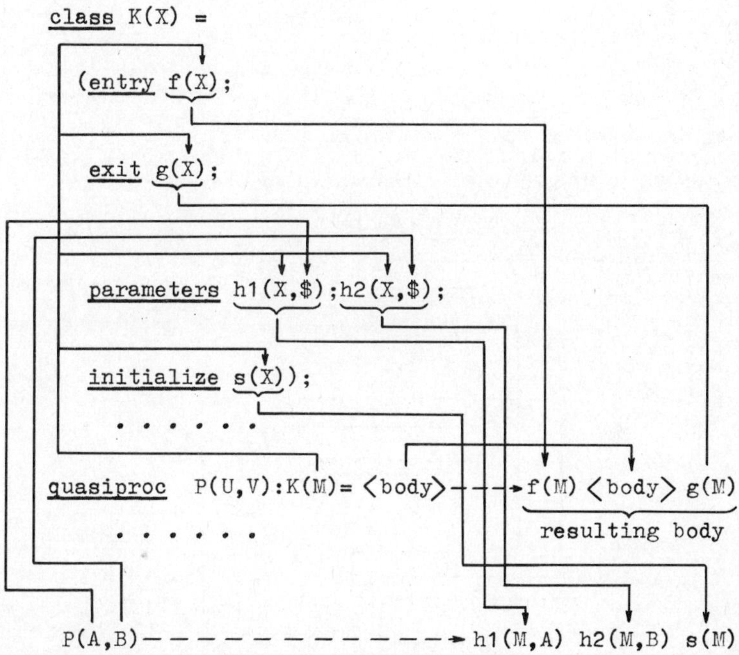

Fig. 2.

Besides, there is a number of different methods of parameter passing and local memory allocation. It is clear that all above-mentioned circumstances have their influence on the manner of coding procedure bodies and their calls. The corresponding language facilities permit to point out the required coding methods.

Classes and quasiprocedures. Specification of these facilities can be related both to one procedure and to a number of procedures. In

the latter case this specification is concentrated in the description of a procedure class. Class declaration sections determine
- local memory addressing method;
- entry/exit coding for the procedure body;
- methods of passing actual parameters and of initiating procedure body execution.

The minimal description of a procedure related to some class contains information about formal procedure parameters and the procedure body only. Such a partial description is called a quasi-procedure description.

Fig.2 shows the layout of interrelations between class declaration, quasiprocedure declaration and body calls.

<u>Programmable data access</u>. The similar efficiency considerations are related to dynamic data of complicated structure or indefinitely large size. Implementation of an efficient access to such data elements depends on the following factors:
- constituent element size (one word, a part of the word, a number of words);
- usage mode (read only/writing admitted);
- mapping of data structure onto main or external memory.

The implementation of data access sequences essentially depends on the representation and usage of the data. The availability of explicit data allocation facilities and corresponding swapping mechanism may be regarded as the main origin of program efficiency. Special programmable access facilities for solving these problems are provided in the language.

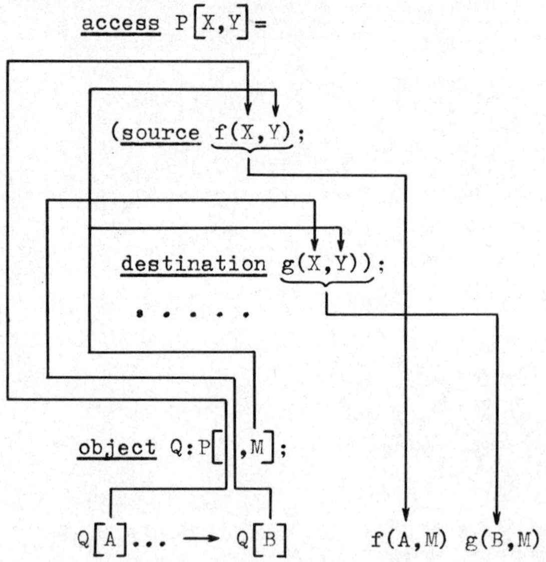

Fig. 3.

<u>Memory access</u>. This description contains two sections according to the data usage - as a value source or as a value destination. When an element of a composed value is in the syntactic position of a

primary, data access is implemented as that of a value source,when it is in a destination position, data access is implemented as that of a value destination. Besides, memory access declaration may include the declaration of necessary memory resources.
Data. Data name is bound with an access by means of object declaration. Thus, particular parameters may be fixed in the memory access declaration. Parameter transfer from the data usage points to the object declaration and to the access declaration is presented on Fig.3.

Classes, quasiprocedure calls and complex data accesses are implemented by means of syntax-controlled macrosubstitutions.

The availability of such completely controlled facilities for the handling of procedures and multivalues would make difficult to use the language in cases when efficiency requirements do not play a prevailing role. Therefore the language base contains some built-in techniques for processing of the static arrays and for procedure implementation (including recursion). These built-in facilities prescribe an executing machine with more powerful functions than those in the instruction code. As long as the capabilities of this machine provide efficient programming there is no necessity to fall outside the limits of the base language and computer facilities.

In general, the language superstructure allows the definition of an executing machine which is specific for a given problem and differs from the basic one. Moreover, reconfiguration of the executing machine can be made within a program. As the program consists of declaration and execution sections, a redefinition of the executing machine is concentrated in the definition sections and has no influence on the text of the execution section.

These properties of the base language provide a two-stage program development process. At first the program is appropriately formulated. At this stage one can use standard methods only, taking no care of the concrete embodiment of program object, programming at a machine-independent level. After the completion of a correct program at this level one can increase its efficiency by developing a machine-oriented part, i.e. create an efficient executing machine by means of the language superstructure facilities. It is essential that the executing machine definition is concentrated within the declaration sections and the execution sections representation does not depend on the declaration sections. From this point of view the superstructure facilities can be called machine-dependent features of the language.

4.4. Special language facilities

The language allows programming at the instruction code level in order to facilitate the proper use of the hardware capabilities. This provides efficient methods for implementation of quasiprocedures and memory accesses.

5. EXAMPLES

```
¢ 1 ¢
access ARR2 [I1,I2,L1,L2]=       ¢ Access to two-dimensional array
                                   without index checking.I1,I2 are
                                   indices, L1 is the number of
                                   rows, L2 is the number of co-
                                   lumns ¢
```

```
(variable V[|L1*L2|];                 ¢ L1*L2 variable for storing ar-
                                        ray components. |...| is a
                                        compile-time expression ¢
 source V[(I1-1)*S2+I2];
 destination );                       ¢ Access function is the same
                                        for destination position and
                                        source position ¢
object MATRIX:ARR2 [, ,10,20];        ¢ 10*20 rectangular matrix ¢
¢ 2 ¢
access RANGE [MIN,MAX,IDENT]=         ¢ Access declaration of variable
                                        assuming values in the range
                                        MIN,MAX ¢
 (variable INTERVAL:(VALUE,           ¢ Variable INTERVAL with compo-
                                        nents ¢
      L:[25:48],R:[1:24])=            ¢ L(eft) and R(ight) are packed
                                        in one word, bound bits are
                                        prescribed ¢
      (MIN,MIN,MAX),                  ¢ Initial field values are gi-
                                        ven ¢
      R,MARKER=IDENT;                 ¢ Variable for permanent storing
                                        of values; variable with the
                                        marker ¢
  procedure ERROR(MARK,VAL)=        ( ¢ Prints the marker, if the new
                                        value is outside the admissib-
                                        le range; and prints the value
                                        of the assignment source ¢) ;
  source INTERVAL.VALUE;
  destination R;
        if INTERVAL.L ≤ R&
           (R ≤ INTERVAL.R)
        then R→ INTERVAL.VALUE
        else ERROR (MARKER,R)
        fi ) ;
object INDEX:RANGE[1,20,'INDEX']; ¢ Object INDEX of the range [1,20]
                                    with the 'INDEX' marker ¢
```

6. BASE LANGUAGE EXTENSIONS

The scheme of the base language and compiler application proposed here offers a natural basis for developing special-purpose languages as extensions of the base language. A system language which includes all the facilities for a convenient presentation of programs composing the functional level of an operating system may be considered as an interesting example. In particular, these facilities provide file handling, memory management, parallel execution, synchronization and input/output. Externally, the system language differs from the base language by the availability of some standard class and procedure identifiers as well as some constructs easily reducible to the base language fragments. A program expressed in the system language is compiled by the base compiler in the context of the logical layer. A module, representing a program of logical layer, contains all necessary objects which implement the system language facilities in the description of the module.

Compiler-writing metalanguage may be regarded as another example of such an extension. This metalanguage includes facilities allowing the adequate definition of the syntax of a source language, its static semantics (context dependencies) and code generators. The syntactic part of the definition is transformed by a preprocessor into data structures used by the lexical and syntactic analysers.

Semantic definition allows a concise and expressive representation of declaration processing, identification and static evaluation of modes. The semantic definitions are transformed by a preprocessor into base language constructs which are supported by a corresponding problem layer.

7. CONCLUSION

Summing up, we can say that base language facilities, which are oriented to the support of large system implementation (modular program structure, programmable data accesses and the quasiprocedure and class mechanism) are intensively used at all the stages of the development of a large system. This relates to the design of a single module, development and application of system layers, the construction of specialized, problem-oriented language superstructures and the assembling of object programs, etc. The programmable data access facilities together with the class and quasiprocedure mechanisms seem especially efficient when implementing problem-oriented languages.

REFERENCES

1. E.W.Dijkstra. The structure of the "THE" multiprogramming system. Comm. ACM 11(1968).
2. P.Brinch Hansen. The Solo operating system: processes, monitors and classes. Software - Practice and Experience. 1976.
3. C.H.A.Koster. Visibility and Types. SIGPLAN Notices. March,1976.
4. N.Wirth. PL/360, a programming language for the 360 computers. JACM 15(1968).
5. W.A.Wulf. Issues in higher - level machine-oriented languages. Machine Oriented Higher Level Languages. North-Holland 1974.
6. W.A.Wulf, D.B.Russel, A.N.Haberman. BLISS: a language for systems programming. Comm. ACM 14(1971).
7. J.D.Ichbiah, J.P.Rissen, J.C.Heliard. The two-level approach to data independent programming in LIS. Machine Oriented Higher Level Languages. North-Holland, Amsterdam, 1974.

Constructing Quality Software, P.G. Hibbard/S.A. Schuman (eds.)

PROBLEMS OF A MODULE INTERCONNECTION LANGUAGE

Václav Rajlich
Research Institute for Mathematical Machines
Loretánské nám. 3, 118 55 Prague 1
Czechoslovakia

In the paper, issues of modular structure for large software systems are discussed. Relationships among modules are classified as call, access, and protection. Rules governing the relationships are proposed and discussed.

INTRODUCTION

For the development of large and reliable software systems, modular structure is probably the best known methodology. Good and logical modular structure enables the user to split the whole system into several largely independent modules. This helps to break the whole design/testing process into several smaller and more manageable ones, without excessive overhead required by integration of modules into the systems.

Modular structure should enable the user to progress both in top-down and bottom-up directions, i.e. from over-all specifications to implementation details and from simple constructs to integration of the whole system, respectively. Then according to circumstances, the user will be free to choose what is for him the best strategy. Another natural requirement is that modular structure should facilitate accumulation of knowledge in programming, both at individual programmer's level, computing center's level, or even computer industry's level. Succesful modules from old projects should be usable and used in new projects.

In the literature, several modularity concepts and proposals appeared, see for example Dahl /1972/, Liskov, Zilles /1975/, DeRemmer, Kron /1975/, Wirth /1976/, Brinch Hansen /1975/, and others. In this paper we shall investigate properties modular structure ought to have, in order to deal with the requirements listed above. The ideas expressed here are related to a project in progress whose goals and general description were published in Rajlich /1975/.

We shall concentrate our attention on basic principles of modular structure and its functioning, i.e. on semantic issues. Issues of syntax and implementation were omitted.

TERMINOLOGY

Let us start with a brief review of terminology.

We shall suppose that the whole system is written in a language which consists of two largely independent portions: One is base language consisting of basic executable commands /for example assignment, if statement, loop statement/ and basic decl rations like variable declarations, array declarations, etc. The other portion is decomposition language, which decomposes the whole system into smaller units. Such units are blocks and procedures in Algol 60, main program and subroutines in Fortran, etc. We shall deal with a proposed decomposition language and avoid assumptions about base language.

Basic building block of the decomposition language is module. Semantics of modules has been standardized to a large degree, cfr. Dahl /1972/, Liskov et al. /1976/, Wirth /1976/, Brinch Hansen/1975/. Module consists of two parts: Global data declaration and procedures declaration. Global data are staticall allocated and their initial values are set at the beginning of program execution. Procedures of the module may use the global data and they implement actions designed by the programmer.

Within procedures, local data may be declared. These are always dynamically allocated and are activated when the procedur is called. No other procedure has access to them. Moreover proce dure may have formal parameters. Within procedure body, base language statements and procedure calls do appear. Three kinds o data may appear within statements of the procedure body: local data, formal parameters, and global data.

Modular structure consists of several modules. Our main attention will be given to relationships of modules within modular structure. We shall consider four kinds of relationship:

Module A calls module B /abbreviated $A \Rightarrow B$/ if procedures of module A contain calls of procedures from module B. This involves parameter passing, either by name or by reference. For other aspects, see concluding remarks.

Module A has access to module B /abbreviated $A \twoheadrightarrow B$/ if procedures of module A use global data of module B.

Module A reads module B /abbreviated $A \rightarrow B$/ if procedures of module A read global data of B, but do not change them. Relationship of access and reading means direct access to the data of the other module which avoids parameter passing mechanizm, something like COMMON in Fortran. It should be used whenever great amount of data is to be shared by two modules, and to pass all data as parameters is inconvenient.

Module A is protected from module B /abbreviated $A \dashrightarrow B$/ if no action within module B may gain information stored in data of A, or change it.

Example of a graph of a modular structure is on fig.1. The tructure consists of four modules A, B, C, and D.

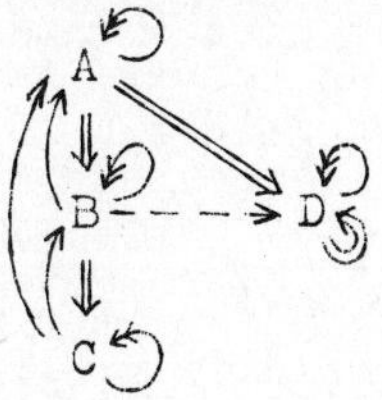

Fig. 1

XIOMS

Let us introduce the following notation:Let A, B be modu-es, then define inductively the following relationships:

$A \Rightarrow^{0} B$ iff $A = B$ and $A \Rightarrow^{i+1} B$ iff there exists module C such hat $A \Rightarrow^{i} C$ and $C \Rightarrow B$. Then:

$A \Rightarrow^{+} B$ iff there exists $j \geq 1$ such that $A \Rightarrow^{j} B$,

$A \Rightarrow^{*} B$ iff there exists $i \geq 0$ such that $A \Rightarrow^{i} B$.

We shall say module A is <u>higher</u> than B and B is <u>lower</u> than if $A \Rightarrow^{+} B$ where $A \neq B$, respectively.

In order to achieve its objectives, modular structure must atisfy certain axioms. Let us introduce the axioms formally. iscussion of their intuitive meaning follows.

A0. For every module A, $A \twoheadrightarrow A$.
A1. If $A \twoheadrightarrow B$, then $A \rightarrow B$.
A2. If $A \rightarrow B$ and $B \Rightarrow^{*} C$, then $C \rightarrow A$ does not hold.
A3. If $A \Rightarrow^{+} B$ and $B \neq A$, then $B \Rightarrow^{+} A$ does not hold.
A4. If $A \Rightarrow^{+} B$ and $B \neq A$, then $A \rightarrow B$ does not hold.

Example in fig. 1 fulfills all axioms A0 - A4.

Intuitively, axiom A0 says that procedures may always use lobal data of the module they are part of. Axiom A1 says that henever a module is accessible, it must be also readable. Axiom 2 is a rewritten characterization of the term "protection" as ntroduced above. Axiom A3 states that procedures of higher modu-es may call procedures of lower modules but forbids the opposite. ote that recursive procedure call is limited to one module only, .e. $A \Rightarrow A$ may be acceptable in certain modular structures. Hence ithin a module, recursive procedure call is allowed and all con-iderations of a recursion are localized within one module. Axi-m A4 says that higher modules may not use data of lower modules irectly. Instead, they must call some procedures which have ac-ess to these data.

Axioms A3 and A4 are the very heart of modular structure.

They embody intuitive principles of hierarchical ordering and information hiding, respectively, see Dijkstra /1971/. We want the modular structure to decompose the system into virtual machi nes. Each virtual machine is in fact an interface between higher and lower portions of the system, respectively. The virtual mach ne code consists of procedures of all lower level modules. Imple mentation details like data structures used for virtual machine implementation are hidden from the user. Higher level modules ar implemented by programming the corresponding virtual machines, while lower level modules are implemented as a refinement of hig level modules. This leads to both axioms A3 and A4.

For example, virtual machines in modular structure of fig are: module C, module D, modules C + D, modules C + B, modules C + B + D, etc. Module B was implemented by programming virtual machine C, module A was implemented by programming virtual machi B + C + D, etc. In short, axioms A3 and A4 allow virtual machine decomposition of the system, and simultaneously they place as li tle constraints on the user as is compatible with the concept of virtual machines decomposition.

All rules given by axioms A0 - A4 can be checked by a com piler on a static modular structure. In our opinion, they create an adequate system for all-purpose modular structure. Neverthele in certain special circumstances, modular structures with additional constraints may be needed.

Axioms A1 - A4 allowed access between modules. However in certain situations, this may lead to undesirable effects, when procedures called change some data of the calling module not spe cified by actual parameters. This was found particularly burdensome in relation to parallel programming, where nondeterminism checks are complicated by this fact, see Souček /1977/. The answer might be the following additional axiom:

A5. If $A \neq B$ then $A \twoheadrightarrow B$ does not hold.
Readability among modules still may be allowed.

Data abstraction technique is a special case of modularit and it needs to exclude not only access but also readability amo modules, see Liskov et al. /1976/. Hence it satisfies the follow additional axiom:

A5'. If $A \neq B$ then $A \rightarrow B$ does not hold.

A syntactically simple modular structure arises when the following axiom is applied:

A5''. Relationship $\Rightarrow$ is a linear ordering of modules, an if $A \Rightarrow B$ then $B \twoheadrightarrow A$.

The modular structure which arises in this way is a sequence of modules where higher modules precede all lower modules A higher module may call any procedure within lower modules whil a lower module has access to all data of all higher modules. Suc arrangement has an easy syntax to check.

CONCLUDING REMARKS

We have discussed some of the semantic issues of module interconnection. Relationship of "call" between modules however contains more aspects than we were able to cover. When A⇛B, then the following may be true:

i/ Procedures of A contain calls of procedures of B.

ii/ Declarations of data in A are defined in B in terms of some "lower" data declaration. This aspect is particularly important in relation to data abstraction technique, cfr. Liskov et al. /1976/.

iii/ Exceptions arising in B, i.e. various overflows and underflows, may have handler in A which resolves the problem. For exceptions handling in block structure, see Goodenough /1975/. Exceptions handling mechanism makes modular structure and virtual machines decomposition much more flexible.

None of the additional points ii/ and iii/ requires revision of axioms of the previous chapter.

The paper has left many questions concerning modularity open. Let us state at least some of them explicitly:

In terms of this paper, data abstractions form a special kind of modularity and they are characterized by additional axiom A5''. In the all-purpose modular structures, should axiom A5'' be mandatory, or should we use milder forms of modularity and make axiom A5'' a voluntary one?

Is modularity compatible with present-day languages like Assembler, Fortran, etc? Is it realistic to expect one universal modularity language for several distinct base languages? Or should each language have its own modular dialect?

These and related questions must be solved before modularity can reach everyday programming practice.

LITERATURE

Dahl,O.J. /1972/, Hierarchical program structures, in Dahl et al., Structured programming, Academic Press.

Dijkstra, E.W. /1971/, Hierarchical ordering of sequential processes, Acta Informatica 1, pp. 115-138.

Liskov, B., Snyder, A., Atkinson, R., Schaffert, C. /1976/, Abstraction mechanisms in CLU, Computations structures group memo 144, MIT laboratory for computer science, Cambridge, Mass.

Liskov, B.H., Zilles, S.N. /1975/, Specifications techniques for data abstractions, IEEE Trans. on Software Engineering, SE-1, pp. 7-19.

DeRemmer, F., Kron, H., Programming-in-the-large versus programming-in-the-small, Sigplan 10, pp. 114-121 /1975/

Wirth, N. /1976/, MODULA: A language for modular multiprogramming, Institut für Informatik Eidgenösische Technische Hochschule Zürich, Report No. 18

Brinch Hansen, P. /1975/, Concurrent Pascal report, Information Science, California Institute for Technology

Goodenough, J.B. /1975/, Exception handling: Issues and a proposed notation, Comm. ACM, pp. 683-696.

Rajlich, V. /1975/, A CAD system for unified hardware-software design, Proc. 12th Design Automation Conference, Boston.

Rajlich, V. /1977/, The theory of computing machines /in Czech/, to be published by SNTL, Prague

Souček, J., Rajlich, V. /1977/, A CAD system for computer architecture design, to be published in Proc. of 2. Hungarian Computer Science Conf., Budapest.

Souček, J. /1977/, Modularity and analysis of parallel processes doctoral dissertation, in preparation, in Czech.

Voda, P. /1975/, Machine oriented languages, Proc. of SOFSEM Conf., in Slovak.

Constructing Quality Software, P.G. Hibbard/S.A. Schuman (eds.)

Programming Languages and the Design of Modular Programs

G. Goos, U. Kastens
University of Karlsruhe, Germany

Abstract: We give a survey on several kinds of modules under functional aspects. Schemes for formulating modules in SIMULA, LIS, MODULA, EUCLID and BALG are discussed and illustrated by examples. Especially questions of how to describe interfaces and scope rules are treated.

1. Introduction

A modular decomposition of a problem and the corresponding modular structure of a program may follow various criteria, e.g.:

- a module should be separately compilable (physical modularity);
- the size of a module should vary only within certain limits;
- the interface, the quantities visible to other modules, should be as small as possible;
- a module may serve to keep related definitions together and separate them from definitions concerned with other issues (conceptual modularity);
- the correctness of a module may be verified with a minimum of assumptions about the environment into which the module is embedded (cf. also [Pa 72b]).

These criteria do not always lead to the same modular structure. Moreover, except for the first two, they are qualitative in nature. It is not uniquely decidable whether a criterion is met. To a certain degree the judgement of this question depends on the taste and experience of the people involved. Finally, the given criteria can not be applied to guide the design process. All they can be used for is to judge whether a proposed modularization is suitable or not. They do not a priori tell what functions or data should be put together into a module. Such a priori criteria may be obtained by viewing modules as abstractions of data types and operations.

Modularity in programming serves various purposes. We build programs from smaller units, the modules, and reduce the overall complexity by this step. An appropriate modularization is also an important means for easier maintenance, portability and similar properties of programs. Verification is based on a modular decomposition of programs.

Modularization could be considered independently of the programming language involved. The separation of these issues, however, requires additional effort for documenting the modularization. It also increases the probability that the modularity might be destroyed during maintenance. It is therefore advisable to have constructs in a programming language which correspond to the notion of module. Procedures alone are not sufficient. They do not allow for representing data abstractions. The required constructs should moreover allow a formulation of the relationship (input/output relations, interfaces) between modules within a programming language in a way which may be controlled by the compiler.

We discuss in this paper several constructs for introducing modules taken from languages such as SIMULA [DMN 71], LIS [Ic 75], BALG [Go 75], MODULA [Wi 76] and EUCLID [LHLMP 76]. We compare the descriptions of interfaces, and how they are associated with modules. The methods are related to strategies for system design and the communication in a programming project.

2. The Specification of Program Modules

The introduction of program modules as intermediate units splits the construction of a program into two steps: The building of the program from modules as basic building blocks and the construction of the modules. By applying the method repeatedly we may split each of these steps again. We may thus view each module from two sides. The <u>external specification</u> specifies the a module as seen by the user. The <u>internal specification</u> specifies the module as seen by the implementor.

The external specification is concerned with the externally visible functions, data, and other properties of a module. It is advisable to describe the data by specifying the operations which may be applied to them rather then by specifying them as accessible objects. Additionally, performance characteristics such as speed, storage requirements, maximum capacity, precision (in case of numeric functions) may be included.

An external specification of a function must describe its input parameters, their admissible ranges and relationships, the possible ranges of the results and their dependence on the input-parameters and other data. The module can only be used reliably if the actions taken in case of incorrect inputs or of malfunction of the base system are specified also. (Complete fulfillment of this requirement is usually very difficult.) Part of the effect of a function may be a change of the internal state of the module which may influence the results of subsequent function calls.

In practice, specifications are usually given informally. The reasons mostly lie in the difficulty of constructing more formal specifications. These, however, are necessary if we wish to apply verification or other validation techniques. Parnas [Pa 72a] showed how to specify the interdependence of different function calls without mentioning the concept of state of a module. A completely formal specification could for instance describe each operation in terms of pre- and postconditions [WLS 75] or we could try to use algebraic specification techniques ([LZ 75] gives an overview on several formal specification techniques). Note that the use of states of a module in an external specification usually results in an overspecification. It suggests that state variables as used in the specification actually exist which may not be the case. It also violates the principle of information hiding ([Pa 71], see also [Ko 76]).

The internal specification describes the functions and data actually provided by the implementation of the module.

It accompanies the module during its lifetime. The module may be designed for reuse in other environments or for other modules. Hence, its functions and data might be more general than actually required by the original external specification. If the module is reused in another context, we have to check, that the internal specification will meet the new external specification. If the module shall be adapted to run in another environment we first must adapt the internal specification.

In simple cases the internal specification may coincide with the external one. Sometimes the internal specification may specify the actually appearing state variables and the internal representation of data structures to such a degree that implementation is only a straightforward coding of the specification.

To show that a given module actually solves a given problem we have therefore to go through the following steps:

- Derive an external specification and show that any module by fulfilling these specifications will solve the problem.
- Show that the internal and external specification agree.
- Show that the implementation meets the internal specification.

The proof may be done by verification or other validation techniques (the first step naturally causes difficulty). If we replace the module together with its internal specification by another one or if we modify the implementation of the module but not its specification, we have to repeat only one of these steps. The effect of modifications is thus limited and controllable.

The step from external to internal specification often corresponds to a substantial change in the conceptual view of a module and the interests and goals of the people involved. This change is particularly significant if it corresponds to a change of levels in a hierarchic system. A prominent example is the difference between the views of an user and a system designer on the functions provided by an operating system. Another example are error messages from a compiler. They are often given in terms of states of the parser. The designer of the compiler has obviously forgotten that the user has another picture of the compiler then he has: States of the parser are internal details which do not occur in the external specification of the compiler and thus cannot be understood by the user.

3. Program Modules and Data Structures

Subsequently we consider modules which are functionally closed units (<u>functional modularity</u>); global data or functions are used only if they must be considered as elements of the underlying base system on which the module is running. Questions of separate compilability etc. are of less interest to us. We may classify such modules into 5 categories. The one extreme is a function without permanent data, the other extreme is a set of data without associated functions.

The first category consists of modules providing one single function without any relationship between distinct calls. Most mathematical functions and numerical algorithms belong to this class. Typical examples are modules for computing exp(x) or the zeroes of a function using Newton´s iteration.

The second category consists of single functions whose results depend on common data. Typical examples are random number generators. Their results depend on state variables whose values were modified in previous calls.

Sets of several functions operating on common data belong to a third category. The results of such functions may depend on preceeding calls of some other functions of the set. Modules of this category are used to structure programs by building groups of functions which solve problems of the same area or provide a set of basic operations for the next higher level of abstraction. Examples are the symbol table module in a compiler with functions for coding and decoding identifiers, or an interpreter for a command language.

The characteristics of modules of the fourth category are nearly the same as above. However, the conceptual view is more oriented towards data than based on the functional aspect. Such a module defines a class of objects together with the applicable operations. An example for this category is the stack module providing the usual operations for manipulating stacks. It represents an abstract data type [LZ 75]. If we also consider modules of the third category as types then typically only one object of such a type is needed. However, the number of objects belonging to a class of the fourth category is conceptually not restricted.

The last (fifth) category consists of modules for which the data type aspect is dominating. Implicitly defined functions exist for accessing the value of objects and their components. Other functions are not directly related to the module definition. These modules correspond to record definitions in the PASCAL sense.

This classification of modules is based mostly on their external specifications and their conceptual usage. From a purist's point of view the first and the fourth category are the most important classes. All other classes may be derived from simple functions or from abstract data types.

A similar classification may be based on the internal specification of a module. The differences between the categories are much more significant in this case because different implementation techniques are applicable to different categories. In many cases this classification will put a module in another category. E.g., sin(x) and cos(x) are independent functions when seen from the outside. They may, however, be implemented by two routines which, after range reduction, use the same polynomial with the same table of coefficients.

4. Modules in High Level Languages

Language constructs for expressing modules of the both extreme categories are well known and exist in several high level languages. Procedures and records in ALGOL 68 or PASCAL may serve as an example. Constructs for expressing more general modules do not exist in these languages. For discussing such constructs we shall first compare the usage and the implementation of procedures and records.

A procedure call dynamically leads to the creation of an activation record containing the local data of the procedure. There is only one function operating on this record, namely the procedure itself. If the procedure is non-recursive, there exists at most one instance of the activation record at a time; otherwise the lifetimes for recursive invocations are nested. Storage may be allocated by stacking the records.

On the other hand the number of instances of an arbitrary record and their lifetimes are not given by the definition of the record type. They are determined by the usage of the objects. Because the number of objects and their lifetimes are generally unpredictable, dynamic creation and deletion of records may cause technical problems with storage allocation and garbage collection. Other difficulties may arise if functions associated to a record type are additionally bound to some environment, i.e., they use data from that environment. In that case we must guarantee that the function is applied neither to nonexistent records nor outside the specified environment.

Language concepts for expressing all categories of modules discussed in section 3 may now be derived from the following considerations:

A module consists of several functions associated with a record describing the commonly used data objects. For modules of category 1 to 3 the number of invocations in a given context and their lifetimes are statically fixed. The number of instances of such modules may dynamically vary only by creating or deleting new contexts. These modules are used for structuring a program.

On the other hand modules of category 4 represent abstract data types. The rules about (dynamic) creation and lifetimes of such objects as well as the naming conventions should be the same as for all other data types. Finally, records of category 5 are of interest as building stones for modules of all other categories. We need them for representing activation records of procedures as well as for representing the nodes of an arbitrary graph (as an example of an abstract type).

For clarity of programming, ease of compilation, and run-time organisation it will be useful in a concrete programming language to explicitly distinguish between modules for structuring a program and for building objects.

5. Modules in SIMULA, LIS, MODULA, EUCLID, and BALG

Let us now consider the module concepts of some newer high level languages. (The appendix contains examples for the definition of a module implementing a queue in each of these languages.)

The class concept of SIMULA models modules of all categories of the previous section - even both extremes. Procedures are necessary only for representing functions; proper procedures are superfluous since they may be replaced by classes. Since the language does not restrict the usage of classes in any direction discussed above the concept is much more powerful than actually required. E.g., for a class which is (mis-)used for representing a proper procedure the retention strategy for the activation record is superfluous. The price for this high degree of freedom is a large overhead at run-time: for all objects - activation records included - storage is allocated on a heap and a garbage collection scheme is used. On the other hand SIMULA does not distinguish between data and functions which are globally visible and those which are for internal use only. It therefore does not achieve the necessary security (see [Ko 76] for a more detailed discussion of this criticism).

The system implementation language LIS [Ic 75] provides two entirely different constructs for defining modules besides procedures. A program is hierarchically structured into a set of partitions. Each partition consists of a data partition and an associated program partition. The latter describes the implementation of the data partition. The functions are also defined in the data partition. By elaborating the declaration of a partition an instance of this partition is created. In the given context this is the only instance. Only by recursive or parallel activations of a procedure segment in which the partition is declared several instances of the partition may simultaneously come into existence. Hence, partitions are category 3 modules.

The second concept in LIS is an extension of PASCAL's records: LIS-records, called plexes, may include functions operating on the components of the plex. The functions can additionally be bound to an enclosing environment. Plexes may be created by declaring variables of the plex type. They may be generated dynamically using an additional language construct, the "domain", which provides storage for allocation of objects of a single plex type.

Plexes may contain private components which can only be accessed by the functions in the plex type. The problem of protecting local information is much better solved than in SIMULA. Plexes truly are category 4 modules.

The module concept of MODULA, a language for modular multiprogramming [Wi 76], covers modules of the categories 2 and 3. Similar to LIS the invocation of such a module is automatically implied by its declaration in an environment. Hence, each environment can contain only one invocation of a module. Procedures and records as defined in PASCAL are included in MODULA too.

The language EUCLID [LHLMP 76] (and similarly ALPHARD [WLS 75]) provides for procedures and an additional module concept that is convenient for program structuring as well as for defining abstract data types. For dynamic storage allocation of these modules EUCLID provides zones similar to the domains of LIS. In case of procedures EUCLID distinguishes between proper procedures and functions delivering a result. The latter may not have any side effect whatsoever. They therefore cannot be used for representing operations on a data structure which change the internal state of a structure. In particular functions such as a random number generator which deliver a result and at the same time necessarily change the value of a state variable cannot be expressed by functions in EUCLID but must be formulated as a proper procedure.

The system implementation language BALG [Go 75] provides constructs for category 1 and 5 modules (procedures and records). A third language construct, the structure module, is used for modules which primarily serve to structure the program (categories 2 and 3 of section 3). It may also be used for representing data structures (category 4) as long as all such structures are introduced by declarations. Restrictions as proposed above apply: The number of module invocations within a given context is statically fixed. Each invocation is represented by a declaration introducing a name for the created instance of the module which is called a (data-) structure. The lifetime of a structure is limited by the lifetime of the environment in which it is created. Structure modules can therefore be implemented using the conventional stack discipline for activation records without any additional language construct or overhead. BALG does not contain a construct for representing modules of category 4 (records with functions) if the number of objects in a given context is only known dynamically.

6. Modules and their Environment

Consider modules of category 1, 2 or 3. A program may be built from such modules in two differing ways. On the one hand we can put the modules one besides the other. There is no restriction on which functions module A may import from a given module B. The "environment" of a module consists of all exported functions and data of all other modules. This building principle is basically used in FORTRAN and in assembler languages. It may lead to programs consisting of a large unstructured set of modules. Additional structure may be imposed only by means not supported by the underlying language. We do not consider this idea any further.

On the other hand we may order modules hierarchically by nesting them similarly to the nesting of blocks and procedures in ALGOL. The environment then consists of all data and functions which the module may import from the surrounding module. In such a structure, nesting may be interpreted in two ways: $A \subseteq B$ could mean that A is a submodule of B realizing some functions or data needed in the implementation of B. $A \subseteq B$ could, however, also mean that A is a module which is built on the basis of the functions and data provided by B; B then plays the role of the underlying layer and A is implemented on the abstract machine defined by

B. In both cases the functions and data provided by B form the environment for the working of A. In the first case A itself enlarges the set of functions and data provided by its environment. In the second case B supplies the building blocks from which the functions of A are constructed; we have therefore the opposite relation: B contributes to the functions and data provided by A for third parties.

The two interpretations of nested modules ask for distinct properties of visibility in the underlying language (cf. also [IC 74]).

In the first case module A may freely import all data and functions available within its environment. It should, however, restrict the access to its local data from the outside in order to hide implementation dependent details. For some applications, access to local data may even be further classified. For example, consider two interrelated data structures D_1, D_2 embedded in a common environment E. Then D_1 exports some general functions visible to everybody and additionally it exports some specific access functions which may only be used for establishing the relationship with D_2.

The visibility or scope rules in this first case are thus the following: Global data are visible to nested modules in the same way as global data in an ALGOL-program are visible to inner blocks. Unlike ALGOL we may, however, also see some of the local data of an nested module from the outside. Unlike SIMULA the set of visible local data is a subset of all local data.

In the second case module A may import a subset of the set of all data and functions defined within B, namely the abstract machine provided by B. Unlike the first case we should therefore not have complete visibility of global data from B to A; the scope rules of ALGOL are not in order here. On the other hand B may not use any data or functions whatsoever of A unless they are explicitly transmitted as parameters to an operation invoked by A. For the direction inside -> outside the scope rule of ALGOL (no visibility at all) is therefore in order.

Altogether, a concept for representing modules in a programming language must therefore allow for restricting access in both ways: Import of global data may be restricted as well as export of local data, and we must introduce into the language means to express these restrictions. The problem has, however, still another dimension: Even if we allow for access to certain data we might ask what kind of access. For example, EUCLID excludes side effects of functions by having read-only access to global data. In general, it should be possible not only to restrict access in a yes/no fashion, but to distinguish between different kinds of access and to specify which kind is forbidden and which is allowed (cf. [Go 74]).

Finally, since modules are mostly compiled separately and may be put into different contexts, it would be convenient to carry the internal specification with the module. The contexts in which we want to use the module then should carrry the external specification of the module. This would make the module self-contained in that its text does not only specify its implementation, but also how it is used. On embedding a module into a context we can attempt to verify automatically that the module is used in accordance with its specification. The language ALPHARD [Wu 75] is trying to achieve that goal but its success remains to be proven. The minimum requirement in this direction is, however, that we provide information about the interface which the compiler can check in a conventional manner on embedding a module. In a typed language this information comprises at least the number, names and types of parameters and other quantities to be transmitted.

Hence, we arrive at the conclusion, that with each module we should supply an interface description which for every quantity declared on one side of the interface specifies whether it is visible on the other side of the interface and if so, shows the access rights and the type.

7. Interface Specifications

Corresponding to the external and internal specifications discussed in section 2 we can consider the interface of a module from two sides. If E is the set of quantities defined in the environment of a module M, and E' a subset of E containing all quantities which are free for use inside of M, then E' corresponds to the external specification of global quantities for M. The module M may define in its internal specification the set E'' of global quantities which it actually uses (import list). If both specifications are supplied then naturally $E'' \subseteq E' \subseteq E$ must hold. The restrictions expressed by these inclusions are conceptually distinct: $E'' \subseteq E'$ expresses the principle of minimizing external references, $E' \subseteq E$ expresses information hiding. Accordingly for F'', the set of local quantities of M used in the environment, F' those visible to the environment, and F those actually defined in M, $F'' \subseteq F' \subseteq F$ must hold.

Usually the modules of large programming systems are textually separated pieces of program, developed by different people. (Textually embedded modules are of minor interest for this discussion.) The interface specifications reflect the communication between them. By putting the interface specification at a specific place, e.g. into a module A, we assign to the programmer responsible for A also the responsibility for the interface specification: he can cause trouble by secretly changing the interface, but nobody else can change the interface against his will. Likewise, if we assume that an interface is frozen at the same time the module containing the interface specification is frozen then the placement of that specification influences the order of system development: The module containing must be designed first. We may distinguish the following cases.

(a) The specification of the interface is placed in the surrounding module where the inner module will be embedded. The surrounding module therefore will be designed first. There is only one kind of restriction possible: The interface specifies the global quantities which are visible to the inner module and the local quantities that module must provide to the outside. This technique implies a top-down development if the inner module is a submodule of its environment, not a new layer. As the inner module has to fit to the given interface, the hierarchy of modules also corresponds to the hierarchy of responsibilities in the system. If the inner module is a new layer, we have a bottom-up development.

(b) The interface is specified within the inner module. This module is designed first. As in (a) there is only one kind of restriction. The module specifies the local quantities which are visible to the outside but it can arbitrarily select quantities from the environment for internal use. The environment just consists of the collection of all global quantities visible in some submodules. This construction corresponds to a top-down system design if the inner module is a new layer.

(c) This case is the combination of (a) and (b): Interface descriptions are placed both in the environment and in the inner module. Here both kinds of inclusion mentioned above may be expressed. A discussion between the participating programmers is needed to agree about the interface. This construct leads to a high degree of clarity and safety of the interfaces, because all quantities are specified on both sides. Due to the complete description of the relationships between modules any order of development, separate compilation and integration is possible.

(d) A different approach recommended in [DRK 75] separates the interface descriptions from the modules and collects them in one or more pieces of program. These parts of the program then define the (static) system structure and the interrelationships between modules. The properties of the interfaces are comparable to those of (c). A special organization of the project is suggested by this solution: Prior to the development of any module the whole structure of the system and the interactions between the modules are to be specified. During the system development there must be a central supervisor for maintaining the interface descriptions.

We will now consider constructs for the specification of interfaces in different languages which support modular programming.

The LIS approach is similar to case (d). Each partition consists of a public part, the data partition, and a local part, the program partition. The data partition says which quantities will be imported by referencing other data partitions. It also specifies the quantities visible to the outside. Lastly it specifies the local (private) data. The program partition specifies again its own data partition but also all other data partitions to which it wishes to get access. The collection of data partitions show the overall system structure as far as visibility is concerned. As a counterpart the program partitions repeat their import requirements. Thus LIS to a certain extent offers case (c) also.

EUCLID doesn´t provide facilities for separate compilation of modules. The common scope rules for identifiers declared in textually nested modules are restricted by the following constructs: Every module contains an interface desciption, where all quantities a module imports from or exports to the environment are listed. Additionally a quantity may be declared to be "pervasive". Then it is visible on the next inner nesting level without mentioning it in an import list. Except for the pervasive construct the same concepts appear in MODULA. In both languages abstract data types can be defined by modules. The operations applicable to objects of such a type (e.g. access functions for record fields) must be mentioned in the exportlist of the module together with the type identifier.

Interface specifications in BALG in its general form are a bilateral construction, corresponding to case (c) above. The environment contains a specific "outer" interface specification for each nested module. The latter starts with a corresponding "inner" interface specification. Each module of a system can be compiles separately. The compiler and the linkage editor automatically check the validity and the inclusion relation of the interfaces during integration of the modules. If the inner module is textually included both interface specifications coincide. An additional construct similar to the LIS concept is provided for the nesting of a module into a completely specified environment. It is used especially for standard environments.

8. Conclusions

Modularisation is not yet sufficiently supported in most common programming languages. From a methodological point of view we have seen in this paper, that modules represent a wide spectrum of concepts ranging from procedures to abstract data types and records. For making the programmer aware of the different concepts, it seems advisable to have distinct language constructs corresponding to these concepts. From the programmer´s point of view 3 constructs would suffice which correspond to procedures (and functions), abstract data types, and records. From the implementation point of view, abstract data types do cause problems: when simplicity of the run-time system or efficiency are of concern, we want to avoid the issues of dynamic storage allocation on a heap and of garbage collection as far as possible. On the other hand, if we want to construct complex structures from objects of such types we must be able to put these objects on a heap. We suggest therefore to implement modules, which do not require this, in a simpler way by allowing only for a fixed number of invocations of such a module in any environment.

The issue of information hiding for modules naturally leads to much more elaborate rules for defining the scope of names and more generally the access rights to objects than are available in current ALGOL-based languages. The main idea is to attach an interface specification to each module which is responsible for extending the scope of local names to the outside and for admitting the use of global names inside the module. By asking for two specifications in case of separate compilation we may control the interface from both sides and we control the communication between the two programmers involved. By including more information - at least the types of the data perhaps even the complete specification - into the interface specification and by automatically controlling the interfaces at binding-time we may greatly enhance the reliability of the resulting programs.

9. An Example

In this section we shall demonstrate some of the discussed ideas by a structural overview of the BALG-compiler. It was developed as a student project at the University of Karlsruhe. About 15 students were involved. A modular design and precise interface descriptions were thus indispensable. BALG was used as design language. The BALG modules were translated manually into the implementation language Burroughs Extended Algol [Bur 74] and run on a Burroughs B6700.

```
            balg_compiler
                   |
                   |
symbol_table <-----+-----> syntactical_analysis
                   |          |
constant_table <---+          +--> lexical_scanner
                   |          |
definition_table <-+          +--> parser
                   |
type_table <-------+
                   |
program_tree <-----+-----> semantical_analysis
                   |
linkage_editor <---+-----> code_generation
```

The compiler has three passes. Their main functions are: Lexical and syntactic analysis (pass 1), semantic analysis (pass 2) and code generation (pass 3). Between passes the program is represented in two different intermediate languages. The intermediate languages are given by several category 3 modules: Symbol table, constant table, definition table, type table, program tree and linkage editor. Each module corresponds to data structure (e.g. a table, tree or file) for a specific class of information. It provides procedures for storing and extracting information in this data structure. The declaration table, for example, defines functions that enter or access attributes of declared objects or identify applied and defined occurrences of identifiers.

These modules encapsulate the representation of the intermediate languages. Therefore the representation is hidden from those modules which are not responsible for it. This property is needed, because the different modules are designed and implemented by different programmers. The internal representation was changed in two cases (constant table, type table) during implementation without affecting other modules.

The passes are category 1 modules (procedures), which perform only one complex task: The transformation of the program. Each pass consists of several modules, e.g. the lexical scanner and the parser are components of pass 1.

Most of the before mentioned category 3 modules represent information for both intermediate languages (e.g. program tree and attributed program tree) and their functions are used in different passes. So these modules are defined on the same level as the passes.

The scanner is a typical category 2 module: A procedure which scans one basic symbol at each call. Data objects, such as a line buffer and a position pointer, are kept between subsequent calls.

On the outmost level of the compiler a category 3 module is defined, which implements stacks with different element types. It is invoked at several instances of the compiler, especially for complex data transfers between other modules (e.g. parser <-> definition table). Category 4 modules (records) are used for numerous purposes (e.g. table entries, nodes of the program tree).

The structure of the compiler reflects the organization of the project: One member of the team was responsible for the overall structure, the system integration and the global error handling. Other members implemented the passes and the modules which represent the intermediate languages.

Each team member produced a separately compilable module. Its internal interface specification contains all quantities, which can be used by any other module or which are imported from the environment.

The root of the hierarchical compiler structure is a module which contains formal definitions for all seperately compilable modules. They are integrated on different levels:

Pass 2 and 3 and the modules for the intermediate languages are placed on the outermost level, the scanner and the parser within pass 1. In the external interface specifications the quantities imported by a module are bound to the invokation of the module, which exports that quantity:

For example the invokation of the module definition_table is named "dt". The procedure "dt.identification" is bound to the procedure "identify" within the external interface specification of the semantic analysis.

The use of these language constructs for specifying interfaces exactly reflects the communication within the project: The programmers responsible for semantic analysis and for the definition table agreed on the specification of the procedure "identify" and put them into their internal interface descriptions. The team member responsible for module integration documented their decisions by means of the external interface descriptions in the outermost module.

```
    % BALG-compiler as BALG module
    %%%%%%%%%%%%%%%%%%%%%%%%%%%%%%

            % An executable BALG-main-program is
            % nested either in a standard environment
            % which provides some implementation
            % dependent quantities (e.g. max_int)
            % or in the hardware environment.
ENVIRONMENT standard #
MODULE : balg_compiler =
BEGIN
                      % Global procedure for global error
                      % treatment
  PROC : error(...) = BEGIN ... END;

                      % External interface specification
                      % of the separately compiled module
                      % implementing the symbol table
  EXTERNAL PROC (...) : error;
  PUBLIC   PROC (...) : encode_identifier;
           PROC (...) : decode_identifier #
  MODULE : symbol_table (CONST INT : max_length) = INNER;

  EXTERNAL PROC (...) : error;
           PROC (...) : interface = link.interface;
  PUBLIC   PROC (...) : enter_definition;
           PROC (...) : identification;
           PROC (...) : give_object_address #
  MODULE : definition_table (CONST INT : max_length) = INNER;

                      % The definitions of the modules
                      % constant_table and type_table are
                      % omitted here.
  EXTERNAL PROC (...) : error;
  PUBLIC   PROC (...) : enter_node;
           MODE       : node = RECORD(...) #
  MODULE : program_tree (CONST INT : max_length) = INNER;
```

```
          % Definition of pass 1
          % Only those global quantities mentioned
          % in the external list are visible
          % within the module.
EXTERNAL PROC (...) : error;
          % The procedure encode_identifier of
          % the invocation st of the module
          % symbol_table is bound to the identifier
                    % encode_id, which is used within
                    % the syntactical_analysis.
         PROC (...) : encode_id = st.encode_identifier;
         PROC (...) : enter_def = dt.enter_definition;
         PROC (...) : enter_node = pt.enter_node;
         MODE       : node = pt.node =  RECORD(...) #
PROC : syntactic_analysis =
BEGIN

  EXTERNAL PROC (...)  : error;
           PROC (...)  : encode_id;
  PUBLIC   PROC symbol : next_symbol;
           MODE        : symbol = RECORD(...) #
  MODULE : lexical_scanner = INNER;

  EXTERNAL PROC (...)  : error;
           PROC symbol : next_symbol = scan.next_symbol;
           MODE        : symbol =
                            scan.symbol = RECORD(...) ;
           PROC (...)  : enter_node = pt.enter_node;
           MODE        : node = pt.node =  RECORD(...) #
  PROC : parser = INNER;

          % The module lexical_scanner is invoked.
                    % The invokation is named scan.
  STRUCT lexical_scanner : scan;

          % statement part of pass 1
  parser

END; % syntactic_analysis
```

```
              % Definition of the separately compiled
              % passes 2 and 3 and of the linkage editor
  EXTERNAL PROC (...) : error;
        PROC (...) : identify = dt.identification;
        MODE       : node = pt.node =  RECORD(...) #
  PROC : semantic_analysis = INNER;

  EXTERNAL PROC (...) : error;
        PROC (...) : give_address = dt.give_object_address;
        MODE       : node = pt.node =  RECORD(...) #
  PROC : code_generation = INNER;

  EXTERNAL PROC (...) : error;
        PROC (...) : give_identifier = st.decode_identifier;
        PROC (...) : give_address = dt.give_object_address;
  PUBLIC   PROC (...) : interface #
  MODULE : linkage_editor = INNER;



               % Invokations of the global modules
  STRUCT symbol_table (100)       : st;
  STRUCT definition_table (2000)  : dt;
  STRUCT program_tree (10000)     : pt;
  STRUCT linkage_editor           : link;


                        % Statement part of the compiler
                        % (calls of the three passes)
  syntactic_analysis;
  semantic_analysis;
  code_generation

END % balg_compiler
```


Acknowledgements

J.D.Ichbiah and C.H.A.Koster read an earlier draft of this paper and made many fruitful remarks.

Literature

Bur 74 Burroughs Corp., B6700/B7700 ALGOL
Language Reference Manual
Form No. 50 00 649, 1974

DMN 71 Dahl,O.J., Myhrhaug,B., Nygaard,K: SIMULA 67
Common Base Language
Norwegian Computing Center, pub. S-22, 1971

DRK 75 DeRemer,F., Kron,H.
Programming-in-the-Large versus
Programming-in-the-Small
International Conference on Reliable Software
Los Angeles, 1975. Also SIGPLAN Notices 10, 6
pages 114 - 121, 1975

Go 74 Goos,G.
Some Thoughts on Variables
Universität Karlsruhe, Fakultät für Informatik
Bericht 19/74, 1975

Go 75 Goos,G.
Die Programmiersprache BALG, vorläufige Fassung
Universität Karlsruhe, Fakultät für Informatik
Bericht 6/75, 1975

Gu 75 Guttag,J.V.
The Specification and Application to Programming
of Abstract Data Types
University of Toronto, CSRG-59, 1975

IC 74 Ichbiah,J.D., Cousot,P.
Visibility and separate compilations
WG2.4, Working Paper, La Grande Motte,
M.O.L. Bulletin 4, 129-132 (1974)

IRHC 75 Ichbiah,J.D, Rissen, Heliard, J.P., Cousot,P.
The System Implementation Language LIS,
ref. manual CII, 4549 E/EN, July 1975

Ko 76 Koster,C.H.A.
Visibility and Types
Conference on Data: Abstraction, Definition, and

Structure, Salt Lake City 1976. SIGPLAN Notices 11, Special Issue, 179-190 (1976)

LHLMP 76 Lampson,B.W., Horning,J.J., London,R.L., Mitchell,J.G., Popek,G.J.
Report on the Programming Language EUCLID
SIGPLAN Notices 12, Febr. 1977

LZ 75 Liskov,B.H., Zilles,S.
Specification Techniques for Data Abstractions
International Conference on Reliable Software Los Angeles, 1975. Also SIGPLAN Notices 10,6, 72 - 87, 1975

Pa 71 Parnas,D.L.
Information distribution aspects of design methodology
IFIP Congress 1971, Ljubljana

Pa 72a Parnas,D.L.
A Technique for Software Module Specification with Examples
CACM vol. 15, No.5, pp.330-336, 1972

Pa 72b Parnas,D.L.
On the Criteria to be used in decomposing Systems into Modules
CACM vol.15, No.12, pp.1053-1058, 1972

Wi 76 Wirth,N.
MODULA: A language for multiprogramming
ETH Zűrich, Institut fűr Informatik, Bericht Nr. 18, März 1976

WLS 75 Wulf,W., London,R.L., Shaw,M.
Abstraction and Verification in Alphard
in S.Schumann (ed.): New directions in algorithmic Languages
IFIP WG 2.1 Working Conference Munich 1975, IRIA, Rocquencourt 1976

Appendix: Examples

We shall demonstrate the module constructs of the different languages by an example for a module implementing a queue. The unlimited queve may be specified by an axiomatic definition of the abstract data type queue taken from [Gu 75].

```
Type queue

Operations: empty_queue : ->  queue
            add         : queue X item -> queue
            remove      : queue -> queue
            front       : queue -> item
            empty       : queue -> boolean

Axioms: empty(empty_queue) = true
        empty(add(q,i)) = false
        front(empty_queue) = error
        front(add(q,i)) =
             IF empty(q) THEN i ELSE front(q) FI
        remove(empty_queue) = error
        remove(add(q,i)) =
              IF empty(q) THEN empty_queue
              ELSE add(remove(q),i) FI
```

The module queue may be implemented in SIMULA by the following class declaration. The type of the elements of the queue must be specified in the class declaration. (For variable element types one may use the type of a reference to a prefix class.)

```
CLASS queue(max_length,error,full);
VALUE max_length; INTEGER max_length; PROCEDURE error,full;

BEGIN INTEGER ARRAY store(0:max_length-1);
      INTEGER first_elem, next_free;
      BOOLEAN empty;

      PROCEDURE add(i); VALUE i; INTEGER i;
      BEGIN IF first_elem = next_free AND NOT empty THEN full;
            store(next_free):= i;
            next_free:= MOD(next_free+1, max_length);
            empty:= FALSE
      END;

      PROCEDURE remove;
      BEGIN IF empty THEN error;
            first_elem:=MOD(first_elem+1,max_length);
            empty:= first_elem = next_free
      END;

      INTEGER PROCEDURE front;
      BEGIN IF empty THEN error;
            front:= store(first_elem)
      END;

      COMMENT Initialization;
      first_elem:= next_free:= 0;
      empty:= TRUE
END;
```

With the declaration

```
REF(queue) qq
```

and suitable procedures error and full the statement

```
qq :- NEW queue(100,error,full)
```

dynamically generates an object of the class queue. An element may be added by

```
qq . add (i) .
```

The example may be formulated using LIS-partitions if there is exactly one queue needed in the whole program:

```
USE DATA environment;$provides: item,max_length,error,full$
DATA PARTITION queue;
     empty  : BOOLEAN == TRUE;
     add    : ACTION(i: IN item);
     remove : ACTION;
     front  : item ACTION;
END;

USE DATA environment, queue;
PROGRAM PARTITION queue;
    TYPE queue_range = (Ø..max_length-1);
    store       : ARRAY queue_range OF item;
    first_elem,
    next_free   : queue_range == Ø;

    PROGRAM add;
    BEGIN IF (first_elem = next_free) AND NOT empty
          THEN full; END;
          store(next_free):= i;
          next_free:= (next_free+1) MODULO max_length;
          empty:= FALSE;
    END;

    PROGRAM remove;
    BEGIN IF empty THEN error; END;
          first_elem:= (first_elem+1) MODULO max_length;
          empty:= first_elem = next_free;
    END;

    PROGRAM front;
    BEGIN IF empty THEN error; END;
          RETURN store(first_elem);
    END;
END
```

These partitions also create one instance of a queue. All imported quantities including the element type are statically bound in the environment.

The environment in which the queue module is declared and used can have the following form:

```
DATA SEGMENT environment;
     TYPE item    = INTEGER ;
     max_length : CONSTANT INTEGER == 20;
     queue      : PARTITION ;
     error,
     full       : SEGMENT ACTION;
END;
```

An element may be added by

```
     add(1)
```

in a context where queue is visible.

```
USE DATA environment;
PROGRAM SEGMENT error;
  BEGIN . . . END;

USE DATA environment;
PROGRAM SEGMENT full;
  BEGIN . . . END;

USE DATA environment, queue;
PROGRAM SEGMENT environment;
BEGIN
  . . .
  add(1)
  . . .
END;
```

If more than one invocation is needed in an environment, the queue must be defined as a plex type. The element type is statically defined in the environment and is identical for all invocations.

```
USE DATA environment;            $provides item, error, full$
DATA PARTITION queues;
TYPE queue =
   PLEX empty      : BOOLEAN;
        add        : ACTION (i: IN item);
        remove     : ACTION;
        front      : item ACTION;
        max_length : CONSTANT INTEGER;
        store      : PRIVATE ARRAY(Ø..max_length-1) OF item;
        first_elem,
        next_free  : PRIVATE INTEGER;
   END;
END;

USE DATA queues, environment;
PROGRAM PARTITION queues;
PROGRAM queue.add:    BEGIN $ as before $ END;
PROGRAM queue.remove; BEGIN $ as before $ END;
PROGRAM queue.front;  BEGIN $ as before $ END;
PROGRAM queue.init;   BEGIN empty:=TRUE;
                            first_elem:=Ø;
                            next_free:=Ø;
                      END;
END;
```

The definition of this partitions in the environment can be written as before. An object of the type queue may be allocated in a domain

```
queues: DOMAIN OF queue;
q: REF queues;
```

by the statement

```
ALLOCATE q == (max_length == 1ØØ) .
```

An element may be added by

```
q . add(i) .
```

In MODULA the queue is defined as a module, which will be invoked implicitly in the environment containing its definition.

```
MODULE queue;
   DEFINE empty, add, remove, front;
   USE max_length, error, full, item;
   VAR store      : ARRAY Ø: max_length OF item;
       first_elem,
       next_free  : integer;
       empty      : boolean;

   PROCEDURE add(i:item);
   BEGIN IF first_elem = next_free AND NOT empty THEN full;
         store[next_free]:= i;
         next_free:= (next_free+1) MOD max_length;
         empty:= FALSE
   END add;

   PROCEDURE remove;
   BEGIN IF empty THEN error;
         first_elem:= (first_elem+1) MOD max_length;
         empty:= first_elem = next_free
   END remove;

   PROCEDURE front: item;
   BEGIN IF empty THEN error;
         front:= store[first_elem]
   END front;

   VALUE first_elem = Ø
         next_free = Ø
         empty = true

BEGIN
END queue
```

As with LIS partitions these declarations implicitly create a queue. An element may be added by

```
   add(i) .
```

In EUCLID the queue is defined as a module type:

```
TYPE queue(max_length:unsigned_int)
   IMPORTS item,error,full =
   MODULE EXPORTS(empty, add, remove, front)
              VAR store       : ARRAY 0: max_length-1 OF item
              VAR next_free   : unsigned_int := 0
   PERVASIVE VAR first_elem : unsigned_int := 0
   PERVASIVE VAR empty      : boolean      := true

   PROCEDURE add(i:item)
   IMPORTS(item,store,next_free,max_length,full) =
   BEGIN IF first_elem = next_free AND NOT empty
         THEN full ENDIF
         store(next_free):= i
         next_free:= (next_free+1) MOD max_length
         empty:= FALSE
   END add

   PROCEDURE remove
   IMPORTS(next_free,max_length, error) =
   BEGIN IF empty THEN error ENDIF
         first_elem:= (first_elem+1) MOD max_length
         empty:= first_elem = next_free
   END remove

   FUNCTION front
   IMPORTS(store, error) RETURNS item =
   BEGIN IF empty THEN error ENDIF
         RETURN store(first_elem)
   END front

END queue
```

In BALG the example is formulated as a separately compilable module definition:

```
                  % internal interface specification
EXTERNAL SITUATION : error, full;
PUBLIC CONST BOOL  : empty;
                  % outside the module empty may only be read
                  % but not changed
       PROC (item) : add;
       PROC        : remove;
       PROC  item  : front #

MODULE : queue (CONST INT: max_length) item =
                  % item is a type parameter of the module
BEGIN VAR ARRAY [0:max_length-1] item : store
      &   INT  : first_elem := 0, next_free := 0
      &   BOOL : empty := TRUE;

      PROC: add(CONST item:i) =
      BEGIN IF first_elem = next_free AND NOT empty
            THEN full FI;
            store[next_free]:= i;
            next_free:= (next_free+1) MOD max_length;
            empty:= FALSE
      END;

      PROC: remove =
      BEGIN IF empty THEN error FI;
            first_elem:= (first_elem+1) MOD max_length;
            empty:= first_elem = next_free
      END;

      PROC: front item =
      BEGIN IF empty THEN error FI;
            store[first_elem]
      END;

      SKIP
END
```

The external and public lists form the internal interface specification of the module.

The module can be invoked at any place of the program where its external specification is visible:

```
                 % situation clause for the situations
         % error and full
UNTIL error, full:
     . . .
     . . .
         % external interface description of the module
  EXTERNAL SITUATION : error, full;
  PUBLIC CONST BOOL  : empty;
         PROC (item) : add;
         PROC  item  : front #
  MODULE : queue (CONST INT : max_length) item = INNER;
     . . .
     . . .
  STRUCT queue (100) REAL : q;
                 % invokation of the module
                 % REAL is the actual type parameter
                 % q identifies the invokation
     . . .
     . . .
  q.add(2.3)
     . . .
     . . .
ON error, full : . . .
                 % definition of the action to be activated
                 % when error or full occurs
END % of the situation clause
```

In the module definition the type of the queue elements is a formal type parameter, which is bound at the time of invoking the module.

Session 3a : Discussion

Ross: I missed in this session's presentations any mention of the words "quality" and "quality software". This seems to me to be the reason for modularity, the topic we have talked about, so it ought to be mentioned. I consider all of these papers to be very much at the implementation level, rather than being concerned with what is to be achieved by modularity. The only way I see of relating these matters to the question of quality would be to address the real problems of building systems. The structure must answer to some desired aim or objective. Only then do we have modularity that is useful in practice.

Goos: I certainly agree that modularity is interesting only as a means of achieving quality software. There are many points to be mentioned here but there is not enough time to go into details. As I have pointed out, modularity is a basis for subdividing work and so good organization depends on modularity. This is one side. On the other side, it is the basis for correctness, reliability and other properties. I think this is the main point in speaking about modularity. Modularity means that we produce the software in pieces which are reusable, and therefore it is a facility to construct parts which are used over and over again; presumably they are improved in the process, so that in the end they have such properties as reliability. One of the main reasons why it is difficult to speak about modularity is that we don't have good facilities for modularity in most programming languages. Programming languages are the framework for thinking and therefore it is necessary to have the proper syntactic form for these notions.

Holager: I would also like to answer Ross's challenge. We want to make quality software and it seems that the major task is to program. If we observe that we are trying to make large programs cheaply, with few bugs, then it is quite clear that the main problem of programming is handling complexity. The only possible way of helping our minds to do this seems to be to split programs into a system of pieces. This seems to be something which models the processes in the minds of people. It seems to be a natural way of going about it. And that is the basis of the module construct. My discussion was trying even to specialize a little more. I wanted not only to have modules, I wanted to have modules which were in some respects better than current concepts, in the sense of corresponding to a particular pattern in people's minds. We had this idea of module, we tried it; it came out moderately well, but proved to be less useful than we had thought.

Ershov: I have a semi-remark or a question to Goos, concerning the module concept. You have mentioned that a highly desirable maximum size for a module is one sheet of paper. I would like to discuss this point technically. How heuristic is such a proposal? Is there some powerful justification for it? Could this be formalized in the sense that one page of text is the most that can be proved, or operated upon in any other way? Certainly this must depend on the system of axioms or assumptions that serves as the basis for your reasoning. I am afraid it would be rather difficult or impossible to avoid the real complexity of this basis. If you contrive to hide this complexity artificially in a proper hierarchy of modules, it means that you have a rather short text on the higher level of the hierarchy but you have a lot of rather complicated and maybe not very convenient assumptions about the lower level. I have the feeling that such a restriction on the size of a software module could be dangerous, unless it's really possible to limit the space for writing and reasoning to one page of text. If so, then there is no serious problem, because it will not be so necessary to computerize the corresponding logical verification and so forth. Do you really believe that with such modularization the human will be able to cope, by human means alone, with the complexity of his programs? Or will he have to be supported by automatic aids as a consequence of this restriction?

Goos: I put a question mark after that statement on my transparency because I am not convinced of this one page restriction. I think the problem is basically one of restricting the quantum of complexity within a module; the one page restriction is an inadequate way of expressing this intent. In system programs the complexity which we achieve on one page is normally high, so that when the page ends and the module has not yet ended then we should think about subdividing the whole thing into two parts. If I look to numeric programs, the restriction to one page is silly because one page might be only half of the initialization of the variables. If I look to programs which are automatically generated by some macrogenerator, the restriction is also silly. So there are different sides to this coin.

Mráz: Experiments in psychology say that the human being is capable of concentrating simultaneously on no more than five to eleven different subjects. That means that if complexity of the module is higher than this, it is not possible to concentrate effectively on what is going on. If the module is 10 pages of assignment statements it may be all right, but if the module has some decision-making or more complex structure, then it should be shorter.

Turski: The problem of module size, one page or more, cannot be decided because the criterion for a module size has to be defined (if at all) in a space of two variables. You see, the size of the module is a trade-off between two conflicting objectives. On one hand we want to have modules as small as possible because in this way we gain flexibility. If we consider modules as reusable objects, as building blocks, then the smaller they are the larger the variety of shapes you can build from them. Thus we want to reduce their size. On the other hand, again in very simplistic terms, the smaller the module the larger the traffic of information into and out of it. The "intermodular friction", to use a physical term, becomes higher. Therefore, we would like to increase the module size in order to lessen intermodular friction. These are quite contradictory desires. It means that in each particular case we have to compromise and the optimal size of the module would be determined by the trade-off between flexibility and the amount of information that would flow in and out of it.

Goos: A remark to that. I think that the question of flexibility and reusability of modules is intimately connected with standardization. It took a long time, for instance, to standardize upon the interface of a stack. Only after standardization did we really come to reusable stacks. As long as everybody is inventing his own data structures, flexibility is not a question of whether a data structure is described in half a page, one page or two pages; such a data structure is not reusable because it has usually been designed too specifically for a given purpose.

Rajlich: I agree very much with Turski. I would like to add that in our experience, we always preferred the second objective, that is reducing the "friction" between modules. Modularity has an organizing influence on the programming team. We always try to minimize the interfaces, which means minimizing the amount of information which people must interchange while working on different modules. Size of the modules is not that important; we decide upon the interfaces between modules without any regard to their size.

Holager: There is another principle, a third principle, which can bring together Turski's two objectives: it is possible to select the "right" modules. This is, of course, a self-recursive definition, the "right" module is the one which gives both small size and little traffic. I never know how this "right" modularization should be achieved, but, on a number of occasions, I have had the experience of suddenly finding it. And I think modules are not useful unless we start thinking about the "right" modules. Just clipping a program into pieces doesn't make sense. Computer printers have been doing that for years, but those are not modules. We have to have the "right" modules.

Sintzoff: My feeling is that this discussion is unbelievable. [☺] Goos, you gave us two constructive criteria for building modules. A module is either a function or it is an abstract data type. Marvellous. Now all the questions about size disappear, because the size of the module is defined by the size of the function or the abstract data type. But you called these criteria constructive! The central problem is to find out what are the functions and what are the abstract data types. This is the question which we should address, not at all the question of how to code the "right" module in some AED or whatever silly language. [👍] [To Ross:] I am sorry. [To Goos:] I have just one question: when you are designing a system how do you discover the functions and the data types?

Koster: You have 10 minutes . . . [☺]

Goos: I will not answer that question. [👎] Sorry. I think this is the creative part of the whole game of designing a system, but it's completely out of the problem area which I addressed. My point was that if you are to find abstract data types or the abstract machine which underlies the solution to your problem, then you must have the appropriate means at your disposal for expressing this abstract machine. Commonly available programming languages provide only inadequate means for expressing such abstract machines, and therefore we should analyze the real requirements. It's true that I was concentrating only on the representation or the implementation. But I think that this is very important, from practical experience. People who have learned only FORTRAN will not usually think about recursive programs. Recursivity is just not a tool for them, because they don't know how to express it. And in the same way abstract data types are not a tool for people who are unable to express them because their programming language does not allow it.

Sintzoff: Sorry, I came to the middle of Siberia and I want to learn something. [☺] Now the game is up. My question again: how do you find modules when you are designing a system?

Wodon: I think we are missing one point here: software is an artificial product and, like any other such product, at least two things are needed to produce it. One is the raw material, the machine and also the languages. The second is the know-how. Since there's no magic about how to modularize or to structure and things like that, we have to rely on solid engineering techniques; that's all we have to go on. To have solid engineering techniques you need good education in engineering.

Goos: Wodon has said part of what I want to say. In the construction process we need several things. One is the know-how about the problem area and experience in solving problems of the given type. We cannot avoid that requirement. The second thing is creativity. Mathematics can construct a theorem prover, but it cannot construct a theorem deriver. There is no such term. And there is no such notion as a program deriver, starting from problem specifications as given by the user. At least I do not believe in such a solution. But I believe that programming languages can help in a constructive way. Modularity, when correctly presented, is a concept which may lead the programmer to ask the right questions. For instance, if you are able to express data abstractions in the right way, then whenever you have to design a procedure and you find you need global variables, you may think that perhaps you have a wrong modularization. Maybe it would have been better to describe a module which comprises not only the given function which you had in mind but also its global data. This is the type of question that you might be led to ask. I cannot do anything more. I do not see any way of re-educating a FORTRAN programmer in such a way that he is forced to construct better programs without actually giving him these more advanced tools.

Rajlich: I would like to comment, too. I think there are three different things involved in finding the right modules. One is simply the ability of the programmer, the second one is his experience and the third one is luck. In my estimation, out of 100 programmers there are perhaps 10 who are able to modularize programs effectively. Fortunately it's enough to have one such programmer in a group of say 10, because it's enough for the project leader to make the modularity decisions. Then there is the factor of experience. In all our attempts to modularize any system we never came up with a good and efficient modularization in the first attempt. It was always on the second attempt at the earliest that we came up with the right abstractions or the right modularization. Then there is this third ingredient: luck. We must realize that modular programming is indeed a new and different programming style from what we learned with FORTRAN and ALGOL 60 or similar languages.

Koster: If you will allow me, I would like to provoke our grand master, Ross, to answer the same question. [☺]

Ross: I'm suitably provoked. While Sintzoff was apologizing for making those bad remarks about AED, I was prodding him and saying that he was giving this year's story. The AED story was the one from 10 years ago. We've been down the road of asking what is modularity, how do I implement it, how do I get experience with it and so forth, and we came right smack up against the problem that you're now talking about, namely, how do you encourage insight. You're quite right that it's a creative process, to actually do the design. This is where the Structure Analysis methods apply. We bring them into the design process. So now we talk about Structured Analysis and Design Techniques: SADT [(TM)]. The point is to try to focus one's attention, to achieve an appropriate separation of interests, purposes and details, to address each aspect properly and then put them all back together. I don't know whether my presentation is going to be very helpful in this regard, but I have been making some notes to address a few of these things at that time. The key thing is that you must have clarity of purpose and clarity of exposition in order to have understanding between people and establish an environment in the minds of people so that they have creative insight. There's no way you can replace creativity. But you can certainly augment it and you can teach people better methods to make it work.

Constructing Quality Software, P.G. Hibbard/S.A. Schuman (eds.)

CONSTRUCTION OF A SYNCHRONIZATION SCHEME BY INDEPENDENT DEFINITION OF PARALLELISM

Y. BEKKERS, J. BRIAT, J.P. VERJUS

ENSIMAG, BP 53, 38041 Grenoble, France

This paper briefly presents an original method to separate the sequential description of the processes from the description of the control of parallelism. This method is used to construct methodically and rigorously a satisfactory synchronization scheme for the kernel system MAS (MAS is a research project under development at the Grenoble University Computing Center).

1. INTRODUCTION

Most current operating systems are written using multiprogramming techniques. Unfortunately, very few system implementation languages offer "real" multiprogramming facilities. Attempts have been made by P. BRINCH HANSEN [BRI 75] and N. WIRTH [WIR 77A] to introduce multiprogramming facilities into a language. The above two methods rely on the idea of associating the specification of access synchronization to a shared object with the shared object itself. This idea (suggested by E.W. DIJKSTRA [DIJ 68]) has numerous advantages (readability, maintainability, ..) which are due to the separation of the description of sequential processes from the description of shared objects.

The method which is presented in this paper permits synchronizing schemes to be constructed by completely separating the sequential description of the shared object itself (i.e. the description of its access procedures) from the description of synchronization. It is therefore a further step toward modular decomposition of parallel programs.

1.1. Purpose of the paper

The concepts, which are presented herein, have not yet been introduced within any language ; however we believe that this could be easily done and we hope that the paper will show that it is worth trying.

We do not intend to show how the extension of the language could be accomplished, nor do we intend to compare (in abstracto) this technique with others, such as monitors [HOA 74] or path expressions [CAM 74] ; rather we will use our experience in the design of a multiprogramming system to show how and why the technique really applies to the problems encountered while designing and implementing the "system kernel MAS" [BRV 76].

(MAS is part of a larger research project called OURS which is under development at the Grenoble University Computing Center).

What we would like to emphasize is that, despite (or because of ?) its conceptual simplicity, the technique is sufficient to solve all our specific problems.

1.2. Implementation methodology of the system kernel MAS

The program which implements the system kernel MAS is divided into a small number of large and completely independent modules. Each module provides a particular set of services (for example, the *paging module* is responsible for the realization of a large virtual memory support and offers services such as *lock a page, request a page*).

A module M1 requests a service, offered by another module M2, by sending a service request to the module M2. Each module runs independently of the others ; therefore a service request is delayed until the serving module is able to perform the service. For this reason, each module possesses a queue where service requests are chained.

A module realizes a fixed number of processes sharing the global state variables of the module (for example, the list of allocated central memory pages). Whenever a process of a module is free, it pulls a service request from the queue and executes the function corresponding to the requested service.

A module acts as if it was a set of identical specialized processors sharing a common memory. Therefore, the system kernel MAS can be viewed as a small number of specialized multiprocessors (one per module) associated with their waiting queues (cf. figure 1). This particular structure of the system is one of the underlying ideas of the project MAS ; the reason is that such software multiprocessors could be easily replaced by real hardware multiprocessors.

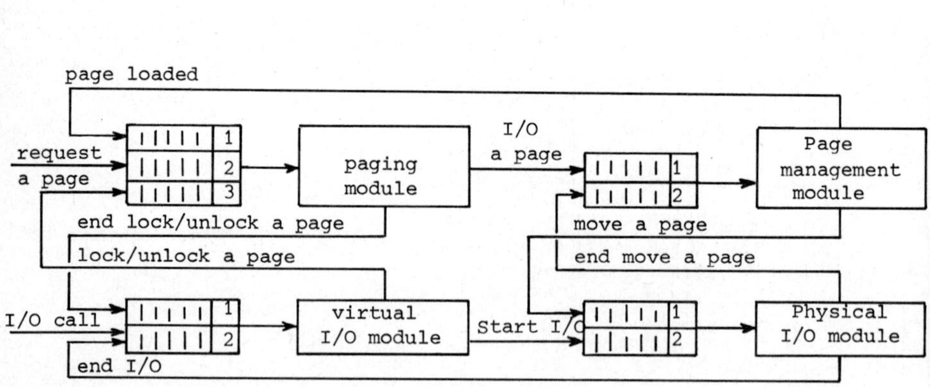

Figure 1 : Example of modules and their relation in the system kernel MAS

The system kernel MAS does not run directly on a bare machine ; there exists basic software, which is considered as a "hardware extension" and which implements the communication mechanisms between the processes of the kernel system MAS. This "hardware extension" is also responsible for interrupt handling : it receives the interrupts and creates foreach interrupt a message which is injected into the current flow of messages and put into the relevant queue. Therefore, communications between the physical I/O modules and the I/O devices are done in a standard manner, and the I/O devices appear to be no more than "hardware modules" integrated within the structure of the kernel system MAS.
To guarantee a satisfactory response time for our system, each process of the system kernel MAS may be created with an associated priority (obviously I/O processes will have high priority).

1.3. The parallelism constraints in the system kernel MAS

From this brief description of the implementation methodology of the system kernel MAS, we will retain four important facts :

(i) a module realises a certain number of processes, the number being defined during the system initialization ; this is called the *degree of parallelism* (it is chosen according to the system load constraints) ;

(ii) there are data which are shared amongst the processes of a module, the accesses to these data have to be synchronized (in the present implementation of MAS, this synchronizing problem is solved by means of *locks*) ;

(iii) a module executes services in an asynchronous manner ; therefore, one can establish a priority among the services offered by a module (for example, it is possible to give the priority to the *unlock page* operation) ; such a priority mechanism is realized in MAS by implementing each queue as a multiple queue ;

(iv) there exists a *priority* among processes of different modules. Presently the priority is attached to a module and all the processes realized within that module have the same priority.

In the present implementation of MAS, the four problems mentioned above have been solved by means of four separate tools ; the methodology that we present in this paper has proved sufficiently powerful to solve all of these four problems. As we said earlier, the tools which are presented herein have not yet been implemented within a language, therefore the following description of a module of the system kernel MAS in terms of control modules is meant to show the adequacy of the method when applied to our specific (but nevertheless general) problems. Moreover, we hope that such a description will show that the method provides good specification and documentation tools.

This paper is divided into two parts : after a presentation of the control module technique, a description of a module of the system kernel MAS in terms of control modules is given.

2. SYNCHRONIZING BY MEANS OF A SEPARATE CONTROL MODULE

The mechanism we intend to present has been introduced by Robert and Verjus [ROB 77]. The following discussion is divided into two parts : firstly, we place their proposal in the context of on-going research on the subject (§ 2.1), secondly, we give a description of their mechanism (§ 2.2).

2.1. On-going research on high-level synchronization tools

2.1.1. The concept of secreatry

In 1968, E.W. DIJKSTRA [DIJ 68] suggested putting cooperating sequential processes under the control of a *secretary process*. This suggestion was the first step towards modular decomposition of parallel programs. Since that suggestion, all high-level synchronization tools, such as *monitors* [HOA 76] and *path expressions* [CAM 74], have been designed in such a way as to permit separate description of shared objects.

However, the high-level synchronization tools may be classified according to the technique which they use to describe the synchronization rules. The concept of monitor uses all the algorithmic facilities offered by the language in which it is introduced. On the contrary, the concept of path expression is based on a simple specific language which has to be introduced within the language to be extended ; this simple language permits a description of the order in which a certain number of procedures (shared among several processes) may be executed.

The proposal by Robert & Verjus (*control modules*) is very much like the path expression mechanism (it permits the control of the parallel execution of procedures), but we will see that the control language has been chosen to be as natural as possible and as close as possible to the formal expressions of synchronization problems.

2.1.2. Separation of the descriptions of processing and control

Tools such as *path expressions* and *control modules* have two important characteristics :

(1) the basic execution unit concerned with synchronization is the procedure ; this means that suspension and reactivation of processes will only occur when entering or leaving procedures ;

(2) the description of the synchronization rules is separated from the description of the access procedures for shared objects ; therefore, objects are split into two parts (a sequential part and a control part).

These characteristics have two important consequences : first, they allow a better decomposition of parallel programs, therefore increasing the quality of programs; secondly, they allow an independent description of the synchronization rules and this increases the maintainability of parallel programs (it is possible to change the control attached to a specific shared object without changing its access procedures, which is not possible with monitors, unless special arrangements are made).

The first characteristic may appear rather restrictive, but we trust that this paper will show that it is not. Besides, this characteristic seems to permit the designing of synchronization tools which have no explicit waiting primitives. Therefore, it can be hoped that these tools will lead to more structured parallel programs.

One of the principal objective of Robert & Verjus was to permit more structured programs to be written. Therefore, it is not surprising that they have adopted the restriction (1) for the definition of their tool.

2.1.3. On the choice of a control language for control modules

The only difference which exists between path expression and control modules comes from the choice of the control language. Robert & Verjus noticed that the control language offered by the path expression technique, gives messy solutions (see the Readers and Writers problem in [CAM 74]) and necessitates unpleasant creation of empty procedures ; therefore, they looked for a new control language.

The originality of the control module proposal is that "history variables" are not only used to prove parallel programs (as it is done in [HOW 76]), but to completely express and implement synchronization rules. Therefore, if the compiler is correct and if the conditions given by the programmer are correct, there is no need to prove the program correct ; hence reliability is increased. Such a language is not only more reliable than the path expression language, but is also more natural because it is very close to the formal expression of synchronization problems.

2.2. Basic concepts of the control module mechanism

We do not intend to describe an implementation scheme for the control module mechanism ; the following paragraph is intended to give an abstract view of the mechanism. After a brief presentation of the logical functioning of the mechansim, we present a discussion about the choice of the *history variables*. Then two types of control modules are presented according to the history variables which they contain.

2.2.1. Functioning of the mechanism : the concept of condition

The mechanism relies on the fact that the compiler knows a certain number of predeclared variables and that it knows how and when the variables are to be modified. Note that a good compiler would optimize the implementation of these variables : only a subset or a combination of these variables will appear within the generated code (see § 2.4 in [ROB 77]).

The logical functioning of the mechanism is very simple and can be explained as follows : a certain number of *history variables* are assigned to a control module (which means that these variables are known by the compiler). The programmer defines for each of the controlled procedures a boolean expression, expressed by means of these history variables. Each boolean expression gives the *condition* which is necessary to give authorizations for executing the corresponding procedure.

Whenever a process calls a controlled procedure, this process is suspended until the attached condition is true. The implemented history variables are only modified at three significant points of the execution of the controlled procedures : at request time, at the beginning of the execution of a procedure, and at the end of the execution of a procedure. These history variables are implicitely updated by the control module, and if the modification of the state of an history variable makes an execution condition become true, then a corresponding waiting process (if it exists) is activated.

Example 1 :

Let P be a shared procedure, to be executed exclusively. Its execution condition could be written as follows :

cond(P) ≡ non active(P)

In this example, the history variable "active(P)" is a boolean variable, it represents the fact that a process is currently executing P. It is the programmer which gives the condition, thefore the compiler should contain a predeclaration of the variable "active(P)", moreover the compiler should generate the code which is necessary to modify the value of this implicit variable.

With this example, we see that the compiler has to know a certain number of predefined so-called "history variables". The choice of the predefined "history variables" is very important, because this choice will determine the information which is to be accumulated pertaining to the history of the use of the shared object ; then according to this information, some synchronizing policy will be allowed and others will be forbidden.

2.2.2. A simple type of control module

It is possible to represent the state of a control module by means of two boolean variables for each controlled procedure. For a procedure P these history variables are :

active(P) : is true when a process is executing P
waiting(P) : is true when a process is waiting for an execution of P.

With such a variable, a programmer could write a condition such as the condition given in the example 1.

Example 2 :

Consider the Readers and Writers problem. The following conditions resolve the problem with priority to the Writers :

cond(read) ≡ non(active(write) or waiting(write))
cond(write) ≡ non(active(write) or active(read))

Unfortunately, boolean variables such as active(P) and waiting(P) do not contain sufficient information about the history of the use of the controlled procedures : these variables only denote the present state of the control module.

The problem of expressing the execution conditions for two procedures P and V, representing the activity of a boolean semaphore, cannot be solved by means of these two variables ; on the other hand, the type of control module suggested by Robert & Verjus permits it to be solved.

2.2.3. A more sophisticated type of control module

The state of the control module may be represented by means of three integer variables for each controlled procedure P ; these variables are :

requested(P) : the number of requests for an execution of procedure P recorded since the beginning of execution,

authorized(P) : the number of authorized executions of P,

terminated(P) : the number of recorded terminations of execution of P.

Note that these variables correspond respectively to the counters $\rho(P)$, $\alpha(P)$, $\lambda(P)$ defined in [ROB 77]. Robert & Verjus have chosen this type of control module although they knew its limitations (see their conclusion). The use of additional predeclared history variables may reduce these limitations, but they consider that this type of control module solves a sufficiently large number of problems. We also are going to use this type to describe the synchronization scheme for the system kernel MAS, therefore we will show that it can be sufficient for the design of a system.

The two following examples show solutions for boolean and general semaphores.

Example 3 :

The condition for the execution of the procedure P simulating the primitive P of a boolean semaphore can be expressed as follows :

<u>cond</u>(P) ≡ authorized(P) - terminated(V) < 0

<u>cond</u>(V) ≡ <u>true</u>

Example 4 :

generalized semaphores :

<u>cond</u>(P) ≡ authorized(P) - terminated(V) < n

<u>cond</u>(V) ≡ <u>true</u>

Note that it is easy to prove that this type of control module is more general than the former one : the two boolean variables used in § 2.2.2 may be expressed by means of boolean expressions on the present *history variables* :

active(P) ≡ terminated(P) - authorized(P) > 0

waiting(P) ≡ authorized(P) - requested(P) > 0

Therefore all the problems which are solved by scheme 1 may be solved by scheme 2, hence scheme 2 is more general than scheme 1.

2.2.4. Remarks on the implementation of the queues of processes

It is possible to implement one queue per controlled procedure. These queues establish an implicit synchronization scheme among the processes calling a given procedure. For example, it is possible to ensure that there will have no "overtaking" amongst processes calling a given procedure (a FIFO queue would ensure that).

Unfortunately, an ambiguity may occur when two execution conditions become true at the same time. The programmer should be aware that such ambiguities may exist.

In their proposal, Robert & Verjus have permitted the definition of combined queues (i.e. where processes awaiting authorizations for executing two different procedures may be grouped). This technique permits the processes waiting for two different conditions to be reordered implicitely, hence the ambiguity may be removed. The following notation will be used :

<u>queue</u> P,Q ; <u>co</u> a single queue is implemented for processes requesting execution of procedures P and Q <u>co</u>

3. CONSTRUCTION OF A SYNCHRONIZATION SCHEME FOR THE SYSTEM MAS

3.1. A module and its two levels of synchronization problems

The synchronization problems that we meet in the system kernel MAS are of two different types : on one hand, we have to solve the problems introduced by the sharing of status variables amongst the processes of a module (see § 1.3.ii) ; on the other hand, we have to offer the possibility of ordering (§ 1.3.iii and 1.3.iv) and regulating (§ 1.3.i) the execution requests of the module functions.

Note that we don't have any "real-time" requirements ; the only time critical operations are the operations related to peripheral devices (this is true for all current operating systems, see [WIR 77B]). As we said earlier, these operations are hidden within the "hardware extension" ; therefore, the system kernel MAS does not know anything about interrupts. However, we must have a mechanism which permits the creation of high priority functions (see § 1.3.iv). In the following, a solution will be given to this problem.

As an example, we will construct a synchronization scheme for the *paging module*. This module implements four functions : *lock a page*, *unlock a page*, *request a page* and *page loaded*. As we saw earlier, several processes might execute these functions at the same time.

Therefore, these processes may concurrently access common variables. In the following section, we are going to construct a synchronization scheme for the shared data problem.

3.2. A synchronization scheme for accessing shared data

Let us first consider the problem of accessing shared data. The simplest solution to this problem is to enforce a mutual exclusion policy. The functions of the *paging module* are naturally dependent (otherwise we would have several modules). This means that it exists at least one common variable which is accessed by all the four functions of the module. Therefore the execution conditions, which enforce that these four functions never access the common variable at the same time, should be :

```
cond(lock a page)    ≡ ¬(active(unlock a page) or active
   (request a page) or active(page loaded) or active
   (lock a page)
cond(unlock a page) ≡ cond (lock a page)
cond(page loaded)    ≡ cond (lock a page)
cond(request a page)≡ cond (lock a page)
```

Such conditions would drastically limit the degree of parallelism within the module (it will be equal to one !), therefore this solution is not acceptable. It is possible to avoid the above limitation by not placing this synchronization problem to the level of the module functions.

For that purpose, all shared data and their elementary access functions may be grouped within "sub-modules". Synchronization can then be expressed at the level of these functions. Let us consider such a "sub-module" called *communication module*. It can be described as follows :

```
module communication module
  int i,j; bool b;
  proc P; co accesses i and b co ;
  proc Q; co accesses j and b co ;
end;
```

P and *Q* are the elementary access procedures which permit access to the shared variables i, j and b. The conditions for *P* and *Q* may be written as follows :

```
cond(P) ≡ non(active(P) or active(Q))
cond(Q) ≡ cond(P)
```

There exists an ambiguity on the choice of the queue in which one has to look first to find the next process to be activated. Therefore, as suggested in § 2.2.4 we will use a combined queue. Hence, the control module for the *communication module* may be written as follows :

```
control module communication synchronizer
begin
   proc P, Q;
   queue P, Q;
   cond(P) ≡ non(active(P) or active(Q));
   cond(Q) ≡ cond(P);
end;
```

The *communication synchronizer* imposes that the procedures *P* and *Q* be executed in mutual exclusion. It is the policy that has been chosen in MAS, but the reader will certainly notice how easy a change of policy would be. Such change would not require any alteration of the *communication module*. The *communication module* and its control module constitute the first level of synchronization. We are going now to construct the second level of synchronization.

3.3. Ordering and regulating the executions of the *paging module* functions

The *paging module* and its four functions may be declared as follows :

```
module paging module ;
begin proc request a page ; ... ;
      proc page loaded ; ... ;
      proc lock a page ; ... ;
      proc unlock a page ; ... ;
end;
```

The four procedures (*request a page*, ...) execute calls on procedures *P* and *Q* of the *communication module*. The first synchronization problem we are going to solve is the problem of limiting the degree of parallelism (§ 1.3.i within a module. Let "degree of parallelism" be the choosen maximum number of processes executing any of the *paging module* functions. According to the definition given in § 2.2.3, the number of processes which are currentl executing a procedure P is

authorized(P) - terminated(P)

Hence the total number of processes currently executing either of the *paging module* functions is (let $\mathcal{P}$ the set of the paging module functions) :

$$\text{number of processes} = \sum_{P\in\mathcal{P}} (\text{authorized}(P) - \text{terminated}(P))$$

Therefore the necessary conditions to execute the paging module functions and to respect the maximum number of allowed parallel processes is :

(1)
<u>cond</u>(*request a page*) ≡ number of processes ⩽ degree of parallelism;
<u>cond</u>(*lock a page*) ≡ <u>cond</u>(*request a page*) ;
<u>cond</u>(*unlock a page*) ≡ <u>cond</u>(*request a page*) ;
<u>cond</u>(*page loaded*) ≡ <u>cond</u>(*request a page*) ;

So far we have not yet solved the problem of the priority among the request for the execution of the paging module functions. The functions *lock a page* and *unlock a page* are tightly linked to the I/O operations. Therefore we would like to give them a higher priority than the two other functions of the module. These two former functions should never be executed if there exists processes waiting for an execution of either functions *lock a page* or *unlock a page*. If such processes exist then the following expression is true :

waiting(*lock a page*) <u>or</u> waiting(*unlock a page*)

(The reader is encouraged to verify that this expression is easily written by mean of an expression on the three integer variables defined in 2.2.3).

Now it is possible to state the new execution conditions as follows :

(2)
<u>cond</u>(*request a page*) ≡ number of processes ⩽ degree of parallelism <u>and</u> <u>non</u>(waiting(*lock a page*) <u>or</u> waiting (*unlock a page*));
<u>cond</u>(*page loaded*) ≡ <u>cond</u>(*request a page*) ;
<u>cond</u>(*lock a page*) ≡ number of processes ⩽ degree of parallelism ;
<u>cond</u>(*unlock a page*) ≡ <u>cond</u>(*lock a page*) ;

The procedures *request a page* and *page loaded* have the same execution conditions ; therefore processes waiting for executing these procedures may be chained within the same queue. Processes waiting for executing *lock a page* and *unlock a page* may also be chained within the same queue.

Hence the control module *paging controller* may be declared as follows :

```
control module paging controller :
begin
   procedures page loaded, request a page, lock a page,
       unlock a page ;
   queue page loaded, request a page ;
   queue lock a page, unlock a page ;
   co declaration of conditions(2) co ;
end
```

3.4. Intermodule priority mechanism

There is still another problem which has not yet been solved : it concerns the problem of the priority among the functions of separate modules (see § 1.3.iv). For example, the priority of the functions of the *paging module* should have a lower priority than the functions implemented by the *physical I/O module* (*start I/O* and *move a page*).

We suggest solving this problem with a separate control module. This control module must control all the executions of the *paging module functions* (called *paging functions*), as well as all the executions of the *physical I/O module* (called *phI/O function*). It is possible to write the control module as follows :

```
control module system regulator :
begin
    proc paging function, phI/O function ;
    queue paging function ;
    queue phI/O function ;
    cond (paging function) ≡ non waiting(ph I/O function);
end;
```

The procedure *paging function* should be declared as follows (the procedure *phI/O function* is analogous) :

```
proc paging function (I : integer) ;
begin case I of 1 : page loaded ;
                2 : request a page ;
                3 : lock a page ;
                4 : unlock a page ;
      endcase;
end;
```

In this case the processes should not directly call the procedures *page loaded*, *request a page*, .. but should rather call the procedure *paging function* (I) ; this is to enforce that the system regulation will work properly. This method is interesting because the present abstract decomposition of the control of parallelism is conserved within the execution structure of the system.

It is possible to introduce within the compiler an automatic generator to which the two following commands may be furnished :

```
paging function ::= page loaded | request a page | lock a
        page | unlock a page ;
phI/O function ::= start I/O | move a page ;
```

With the help of these commands, the automatic generator combines the description of the control modules concerned (*paging controller*, *phI/O controller*, and *system regulator*) and constructs a single (but general) equivalent control module. In this case, the abstract decomposition of the solution is not conserved during the execution.

3.5. Development of a more refined synchronization scheme

It is very easy to establish other types of control. The following example is intended to exhibit the adequacy of the control module method for such refinements.

We would like to ensure that the number of pages locked in central memory be less than a certain percentage (P) of the total number of pages contained in central memory (MAXPAGES). The following expression gives the number of pages locked in central memory :

pages locked = authorized(*lock a page*) - terminated(*unlock a page*)

Therefore conditions for *lock a page* and *unlock a page* should be restated ; therefore, conditions (2) become :

cond(*lock a page*) ≡ number of processes ⩽ degree of parallelism and pages locked < MAXPAGES * P/100;

cond(*unlock a page*) ≡ number of processes ⩽ degree of parallelism

cond(*request a page*) ≡ number of processes ⩽ degree of parallelism and non waiting(*lock a page*) or waiting (*unlock a page*))

cond(*page loaded*) ≡ cond(*request a page*)

4. CONCLUSION

What we would like to emphasize is that there is a need for system implementation languages in which real multiprogramming facilities are introduced. The mechanism that we have presented seems to have a certain number of qualities which we would like to find. Its advantages are multiple and can be summarized as follows :

1) modular decomposition can be better carried out. This is true as much for the processing problems (a module of the system kernel MAS is divided into two independent sub-modules, the *paging module* and the *communication module* in our example), as for the control problem where each problem is solved independently (see the control modules *communication controller* and *paging controller*) ;

2) a uniform solution is given for each kind of synchronization problem (the same tool applies for each problem, see the *paging controller*, the *system regulator* and the *communication controller* ;

3) this method seems to be a powerful specification tool because the expression of the control has been chosen to be simple and rigorous (see § 2.1) ;

4) the compilation of such control module seems to be easy [ROB 76].

Finally, we would like to state that, even though the control module mechanism is limited, it has proved to be sufficient to solve all the synchronization problems which were met while implementing the system kernel MAS.

REFERENCES

[BRI 76] BRINCH HANSEN P., The programming language concurrent Pascal, IEEE Transactions on Software Engineering, 1 N° 2, 1975.

[BRV 76] BRIAT J., ROUSSET DE PINA X., VERJUS J.P., Le projet OURS : ses principes, Congrès AFCET, Gif S/Yvette, November 1976.

[CAM 74] CAMPBELL R.M. & HABERMANN A.N., The specification of process synchronization by path expressions, Technical Report N55, Computing Laboratory, University of Newcastle upon Tyne, 1974.

[DIJ 68] DIJKSTRA E.W., Cooperating sequential processes, in Programming Languages (Ed. F. Genuys), Academic Press, New York, 1968.

[HOA 74] HOARE C.A.R., Monitors : an operating system structuring concept, C.ACM (17,10), October 1974, pp. 549-557.

[HOW 76] HOWARD J.H., Proving monitors, C.ACM (19,5), May 1976, pp. 273-279.

[ROB 77] ROBERT P. & VERJUS J.P., Towards autonomous descriptions of synchronization modules, IFIP 77, Toronto.

[WIR 77A] WIRTH N., Modula : a language for modular multiprogramming, Software Practice and Experience (7,1), January 1977.

[WIR 77B] WIRTH N., Towards a discipline for real time programming, SIGPLAN Notices (V.12,N.3), March 1977, pp; 190-195, (Proceedings of L.D.R.S., March 28-30, 1977).

Constructing Quality Software, P.G. Hibbard/S.A. Schuman (eds.)

CONCURRENT PROGRAMMING WITH CONTROL TYPES

V. E. Kotov

Computing Center
Siberian Division of USSR Acad. Sci.
Novosibirsk 630090, USSR

The problem of structured concurrent programming is approached via the elaboration of a concept of extensible high-level control structures. This concept permits the program structure to be suited both to the structure of the problem to be solved and the available computer system. Three main principles are developed as the basis of the proposed approach, these principles are: (i) to go from the a priori fully parallel program to the specific control structures defined by imposing appropriate restrictions on the initial "chaos"; (ii) to abstract the extensible control types as in the classical manner for data types; (iii) to compose "structured" concurrent programs by the superposition of regular, well-structured control layers. These principles are discussed in terms of the control structure of a simple concurrent language.

1. INTRODUCTION

Structuring, higher levels, modularity and concurrency (parallelism) are some main trends in contemporary programming which aim at the design and production of quality software, and at improved efficiency of computations. These trends force a revision of traditional methods and program primitives intended for controlling computations. The growing number of papers related to control structures in programming languages is evidence of the urgent interest in this area. Progress in control structures is particulary essential for the successful implementation of concurrent programming. It is well known that the problem is quite difficult in such cases, since it is necessary to combine structuring with the adequate description of complex control interactions between concurrent processes (see the survey [1]). Hence, "none of these [suggested structuring methods for concurrent programs] are wholly satisfactory in themselves; and yet their combination would be even more problematic" [2]. Instead of tackling the problem of structuring concurrent programs by the introduction of new control primitives, we would like, here, to investigate how much that problem could be solved via the development of extensible control structures, giving the possibility to adjust the program structure both to the mathematical problem to be solved and to the available computer architecture.

We would like to concentrate our attention on basic, "microcontrol" primitives, rather than on macroprimitives such as subroutines, procedures and other composed constructions. We classify the control primitives and structures into three groups:

- the unconditional ones, which do not depend on the dynamic, actual values of variables; this is the case, for example, of the classical sequential ordering or of the unconditional jump;

- the conditional ones, which depend on the data, essentially because of conditions to be tested dynamically; classical examples are the conditional statements or the critical regions
<u>when</u> p <u>do</u> S <u>end</u>;

- the data-driven ones, which also depend dynamically on the data, but in a completely implicit way; these data-driven control structures favour the distribution of control or permit the use of data structures, such as queues or lists, as a means of organized communication between concurrent processes; in the present paper, we do not treat the case of these data-driven structures because we focus here on computations which share a common memory.

Below we develop three main principles which are at the basis of our work. These principles are (i) to go from chaos to order, (ii) to abstract the extencible control types, and (iii) to compose programs by the superposition of control "layers".

P r i n c i p l e 1 . From chaos to order.

Initially, we assume that the program statements cause computations which a priori are fully parallel and can be performed any number of times. Any possible, specific structuring of the control is then defined by "laying" specific restrictions on this chaos. For example, a purely sequential order of execution can be obtained by imposing restrictions expressed through unconditional control primitives. Thus, our philosophy tends to specify the special case "do sequential" rather than "do parallel".

P r i n c i p l e 2 . Abstract control types.

We completely separate the unconditional control structures from the conditional ones. We then express and construct the unconditional structures in terms of high-level formulas corresponding to some generalized version of Petri nets [3]. The conditional structures are formed using the "trigger function" constructs [4]. The formulas describing unconditional structures are built using composition rules over control structures. It is then natural to introduce the notion of control type as an abstraction or generalization of these formulas: informally, a control type characterizes some regular family of control structures. As it is classical for data types, a control type may be declared by the programmer and the declaration is constructed with formal parameters, operations, formulas and other control types. Thanks to these tools, the programmer can compose the various control patterns which are necessary or convenient in the program he constructs; in particular, the known control structures of sequential programs can be obtained that way. Assume, for example, we construct a control type, identified by "seq" and defining sequential composition of actions; in this case, if A, B and C are statements in some part of the program, then the expression seq(A,B,C) directly requires the pure sequential execution of A,B,C. We may as well define a control type "condexp" to force a set of conditions-actions to be evaluated as a McCarthy conditional: we then write condexp(p→A,q→B,r→C) in order to guarantee that specific type of evaluation for, say, given conditions p,q,r and given actions A,B,C. As a last example, we mention the possibility of constructing a type "par" which, if used in par(A,B,C), permits A, B and C to be executed in parallel but only once. We see how the explicit definition of such abstract control types allows for a better understanding of the program composition, and for the autonomous construction, transformation and verification of control structures. The control type concept resembles that of the path expression [5,6], but, as will be seen later, a control type differs in the way it is used and constructed.

Principle 3. Superposition of control layers.

The basic idea is *to separate* the design of each program section from the specification of various control interactions *between* these program sections and to split these interactions into more simple ones. More precisely, we associate a so-called "layer" with each necessary, semantically monolithic, control constraint, and then we "superpose" the layers thereby obtained on the crude program skeleton given initially. This superposition of well-structured layers may result in a rich structure; yet, this rich structure is constructed in a stepwise way, each component being designed independently. Consider, for example, the statements A,B,C,D and the following control requirements:

(1) A and B must be evaluated sequentially, i.e. A before B;
(2) the executions of A and C must be mutually exclusive;
(3) the executions of C and D must also be mutually exclusive.

The first stage in the design of the program is the independent programming of the actions A,B,C,D: this yields a set Q of statements A,B,C,D. The next stages consist in expressing independently each control requirement; we obtain then three control layers:

```
(1)  seq(A,B)
(2)  mutex(A,C)
(3)  mutex(C,D) .
```

The final program P is simply obtained by superposing these three layers on the initial program Q; note that superposition is denoted by a comma:

```
P = (Q,seq(A,B),mutex(A,C),mutex(C,D)).
```

The mechanism of superposition is the most important component of the proposed algebra of control structures.

The concepts of structured programming with control types will be explained in terms of the control structure of a simple language. To focus attention on control structure, we shall simplify other aspects of the language as much as possible.

2. THE GENERAL STRUCTURE OF PROGRAMS WITH CONTROL TYPES

A program with control types consists of two main parts: first, the declarations of the control types, and, second, the instruction part which can be a hierarchy of modules; the simplest modules, viz those which are at the bottom of the hierarchy, are regarded as indivisible elementary actions; this is the case, for example, of assignment statements.

Moreover, the instruction part of a program with control types can itself be split into two layers, obtained by separating the unconditional control structure from the conditional one.

An unconditional layer, which can themself be split into simpler ones, includes the structure designators defining the unconditional control structure with the help of the declared control types. The syntax and the semantics of the control type declarations and of the structure designators are detailed in Sections 4 and 5.

A conditional layer is a concurrent trigger-function-program [4], TF-program for short. Each module of a TF-program is a collection of submodules each of which is supplemented with a name and a condition; each such submodule is called a "framed module" and the associated condition is called a "trigger function".

Let us consider the special case of programs which have no level of unconditional control: such programs are just TF-programs.

<u>Example 1.</u> The concurrent TF-program which sets output values of x,y,z equal to maximal input value of x,y,z:

```
do  x<y → x:=x+1,
    y<z → y:=y+1,
    z<x → z:=z+1  od
```

This program is a module which simply consists of three framed submodules conditioned by the trigger functions x<y, y<z, z<x, respectively.

The informal semantics of a TF-program may be presented as the following general control procedure for the execution of a module. As the TF-program is a concurrent program, the execution of the module must be described in (discrete) time. After initiation the module is in the active state. Termination, if it occurs, returns the module to the passive state.

The execution of a simple module proceeds in some conventional way and always terminates.

When a compound module is initiated, its internal control takes effect. All input variables of the module are given input values. (We assume the existence of some explicit descriptions of input and output variables.) The control tests the trigger functions of a l l p a s s i v e submodules. These tests are performed cyclically, as caused by some events like terminations of modules or releasing of resources, etc. No submodule is allowed to start or terminate during a test. After a test is completed, some arbitrary nonempty subset of submodules with true trigger functions is selected and the selected submodules are initiated. If there are no active submodules and a current test results in empty set of true trigger functions, then the compound module terminates.

Trigger functions are the only explicit control primitives in TF-program. They are general-purpose control primitives in the sense that any other basic control primitives of parallel or sequential computations can be simulated by trigger functions. For the sake of structuring, however, it is more convenient to express the unconditional control links between modules explicitly and to represent them by means of simpler, more suggestive constructs. In the approach under consideration the unconditional control structures are defined with the help of structure designators which, in turn, are built by the use of control types.

Here is now an example to intuitively show how the unconditional and conditional structures interact.

Example 2. The following program with a declared control type is derived from the previous one, i.e. the conditional layer is formed by the TF-program in Example 1. The unconditional layer we introduce upon that conditional one defines the mutual exclusion of the three submodules: this is achieved by a suitable definition of a control type "mutex3" and by the structure designator mutex3(a,b,c):

```
type mutex3(u,v,t) = 1→*(u▯v▯t),
  do mutex3(a,b,c),
     a: x<y → x:=x+1,
     b: y<z → y:=y+1,
     c: z<x → z:=z+1  od
```

The first line in the program is a control type declaration with formal parameters u,v,t; the right side of the declaration is a type formula which will be explained in the sequel. The structure designator uses the names a,b,c which label the submodules. This new program differs from the original one in Example 1 as follows: it is nondeterministic but it is n o t concurrent, since the designator mutex3(a,b,c) forbids any parallel execution. Thus, the conditional and unconditional layers have been constructed independently and the resulting, actual control structure is automatically obtained when the program is executed. A more detailed discussion is developed in Sections 4 and 5.

To conclude this Section we give a more formal definition of the general structure of a program with control types, using BNF notation. In addition, the symbols ⦃...⦄ are used to frame optional components in BNF productions. A list is a sequence of its elements separated by commas.

```
<program>
      ::= <control type declarations list> <module>
<module>
      ::= <simple module> | <compound module>
<compound module>
      ::= do <components list> od
<component>
      ::= ⦃<component name> :⦄ <unlabelled component>
<component name>
      ::= <identifier>
<unlabelled component>
      ::= <framed module> | <structure designator>
```

<framed module>

    ::= <trigger function> → <module>

<trigger function>

    ::= <Boolean expression>

3. STRUCTURED NETS AND OPERATIONS OVER NETS

Unconditional control structures are defined by well-formed formulas composed of the operations over abstract structures. The semantics of control structures, control types and operations over structures will be described with the help of structured nets which are derived from Petri nets.

A Petri net is a tuple $N=(P,T,F,B,M_0)$, where

P is a finite set of symbols (or sets of symbols) called places,
T is a finite set of symbols called transitions,
$F:P\times T - \{0,1\}$ is a forward incidence function,
$B:P\times T - \{0,1\}$ is a backward incidence function,
$M_0:P - \{0,1,2,\ldots\}$ is an initial marking.

A Petri net is a well-known object, so we cease further explanations To suit this model to our purposes we shall make some generalizations. First of all, to arrange a one-to-one correspondence between modules and transitions we consider firing as a time consuming action (rather than an instantaneous event). The firing is split into three sequential subactions:

- initiation with the change of marking in the following way

$$M'(p) = \begin{cases} M(p), \text{ if } F(p,t)=0, \\ M(p)\dot{-}1, \text{ if } F(p,t)=1 \end{cases} ;$$

- active state;

- termination with the change of marking

$$M'(p) = \begin{cases} M(p), \text{ if } B(p,t)=0, \\ M(p)+1, \text{ if } B(p,t)=1. \end{cases}$$

A compound module is represented by a nested Petri net, which is the same tuple with the following difference: T is a set of generalized transitions. The generalized transition is a symbol (simple transition) or a nested Petri net (compound transition). A nested net is shown in Example 3b. The functioning of a nested net is controlled by the same control as in TF-schemes. The firing of a compound transition includes the following actions: after the transition is initiated, the "internal" net is operated; when the internal net stops, the compound transition terminates and the initial marking of the internal net is restored.

We will restrict ourselves to well-structured nets which are obtained from the class of atomic nets applying operations over nets. The atomic net is the following net:

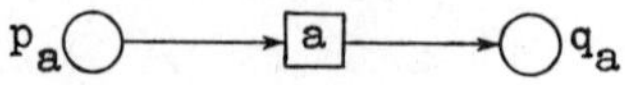

The place p_a is a head place, the place q_a is a tail place of the atomic net.

The operations over nets are defined with the help of two suboperations: union of nets and merging of places. The union operation is almost the usual graph theory union:

If $N_1=(P_1,T_1,F_1,B_1,M_{01})$ and $N_2=(P_2,T_2,F_2,B_2,M_{02})$ then $N=N_1 \cup N_2=(P_1 \cup P_2,\ T_1 \cup T_2,\ F_1 \cup F_2,\ B_1 \cup B_2,\ M_0)$, where

$$M_0(p) = \begin{cases} M_{0i}(p), \text{ if } p \notin P_1 \cap P_2,\ p \in P_i,\ i=1,2, \\ \min(M_{01}(p),\ M_{02}(p)), \text{ if } p \in P_1 \cap P_2 . \end{cases}$$

E.G.:

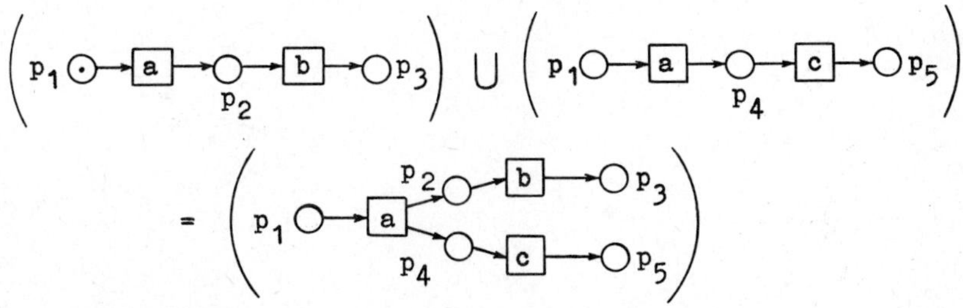

Let $P_1=\{p_1^1,p_2^1,\ldots,p_n^1\}$ and $P_2=\{p_1^2,p_2^2,\ldots,p_m^2\}$ be two disjoint subsets of places of a net N. Then, N'= <u>merge</u>(N,P_1,P_2) is a new net constructed in two steps. Firstly, each place p_i^1, $1 \leq i \leq n$, is split into m copies (together with the incident arcs and marking), each place p_j^2, $1 \leq j \leq m$, is split into n copies. Then each pair p_{ij}^1 and p_{ji}^2 is replaced by new place $p=(p_i^1 \cup p_j^2)$ with the marking $M'(p) = M_0(p_i^1)+M_0(p_j^2)$.

E.G.:

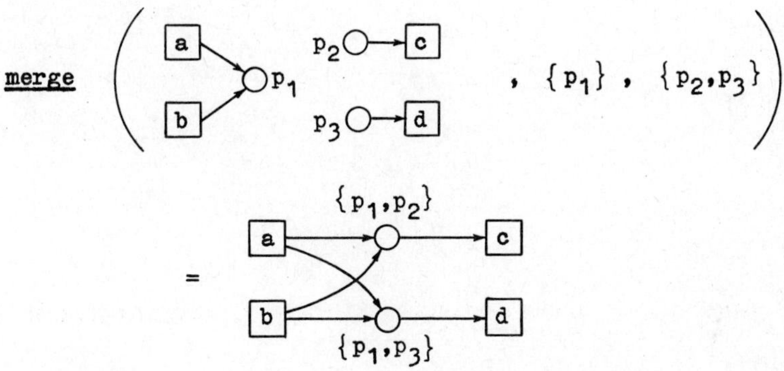

Definition of operations over nets:

Let $H(N)$ be a set of head places of a net N and $L(N)$ be a set of tail places of this net.

a) Binary superposition operation "," .

$$N=(N_1,N_2)=N_1 \cup N_2.$$

By definition, $H(N)=H(N_1) \cup H(N_2)$, $L(N)=L(N_1) \cup L(N_2)$.

The superposition operation "lays" a net on another net.

b) Binary join operation ";" .

$$N=(N_1;N_2)=\underline{merge}((N_1 \cup N_2), L(N_1), H(N_2)).$$

By definition, $H(N)=H(N_1)$, $L(N)=L(N_2)$.

E.g.:

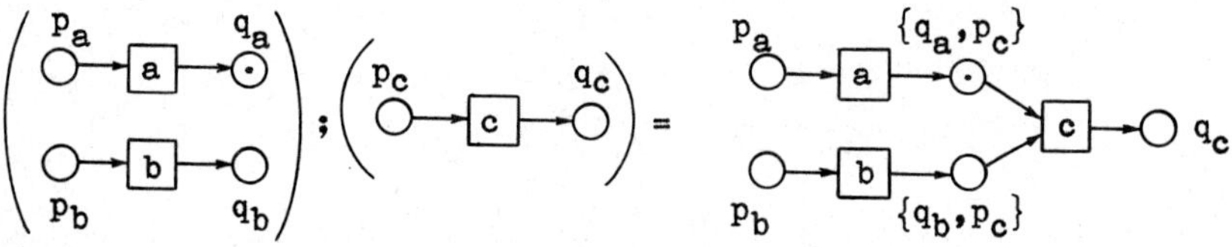

Thus, the join operation puts together two nets, merging the tail places of the first net with the head places of the second one.

c) Binary exclusion operation "▯" .

$H=(N_1 ▯ N_2)=\underline{merge}(\underline{merge}((N_1 \cup N_2),H(N_1),H(N_2)),L(N_1),L(N_2)))$.

$H(N)=H(N_1) \otimes H(N_2)$; $L(N)=L(N_1) \otimes L(N_2)$, where

$P_1 \otimes P_2=\{\{p_1 \cup p_2\} \mid p_1 \in P_1,\ p_2 \in P_2\}$.

E.g.:

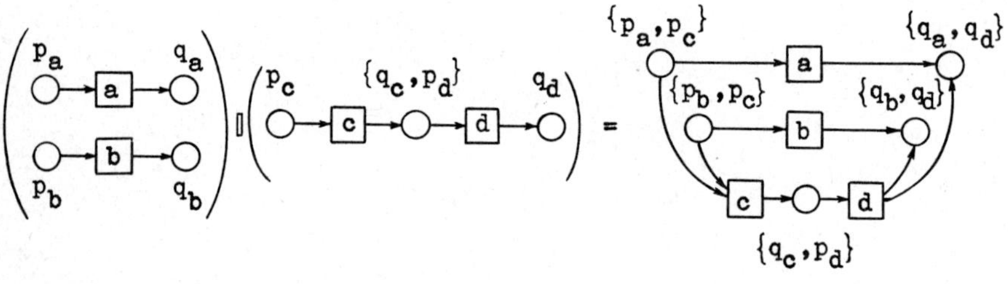

Thus, the exclusion operation unites two nets, merging respectively their head places and their tail places.

d) Unary iteration operation "*" .

N'=*(N)=<u>merge</u>(N,H(N),L(N)).

H(N')=L(N')=H(N)$\otimes$L(N).

E.g.:

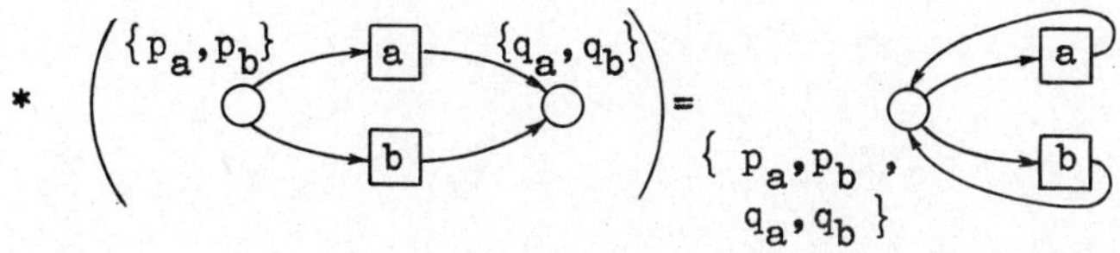

The iteration operation merges the tail places of a net with its head places.

e) Unary operation "n→", where n is a nonnegative integer. N'=n→(N) is the same (topologically) net N with changed marking of the head places:

$$M_0'(p) = \begin{cases} n+M_0(p), \text{ if } p \in H(N), \\ M_0(p), \text{ if } p \notin H(N). \end{cases}$$

This operation increases the number of tokens in each head place by n.

f) Closure operation "<u>do</u>...<u>od</u>".

The net N'= <u>do</u> N <u>od</u> is an atomic net with generalized transition and the net $\overline{N}$ is an internal net of this transition.

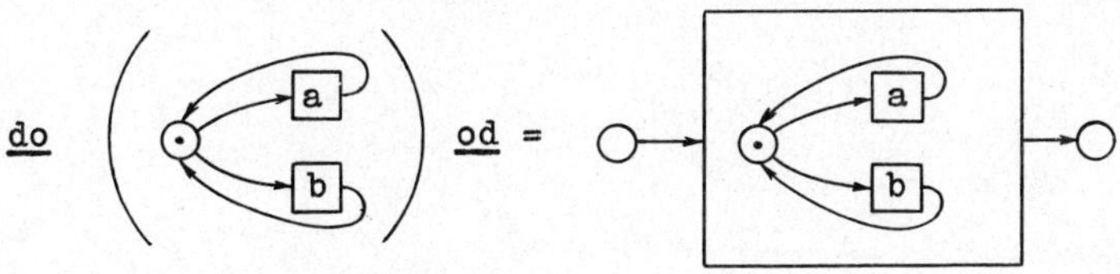

The structured net is a net defined by a well-formed formula (wff):

<wff>

::= <operand>|<unary operation> (<wff>)|

(<wff> <binary operation> <wff>)

<operand>

::= <atomic net symbol>

The context restriction: there are no entries of the same atomic net symbol in the left-hand and in the right-hand part of any formula (<wff> <binary operation> <wff>) if the binary operation is ";" or "▯".

The properties of structured nets and operations over nets are not discussed here because they are the subject of more formal consideration which will be available elsewhere. Now we just note that all binary operations are associative; the operations "," and "▯" are commutative; the operations ";" and "▯" are distributive relative to ",". (These properties of operations and the following ranking - unary operations bind closer than binary ones; the operations ";" and "▯" bind closer than the operation "," - help us to avoid extra parentheses in the further examples.)

<u>Example 3.</u> Well-formed formulas

a) 1 → *(a▯b▯c)

b) 1 → <u>do</u> 1 → *(a,b,c) <u>od</u>, 1 → <u>do</u> 3 → (d,e); i <u>od</u>, 1 → ((b;c)▯d)

and the nets defined by these formulas:

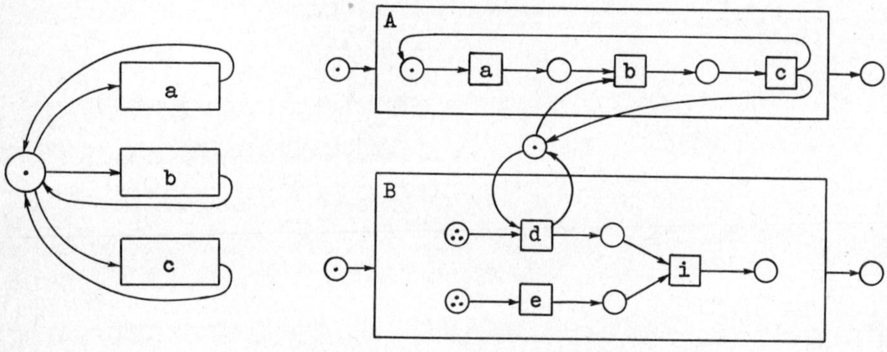

a) b)

Structured nets provide an easy form of expression and checking of deadlocks, etc. Any bounded net (i.e. a net in which the number of tokens in any place at any reachable marking never exceeds some integer) can be transformed into structured form. Any Petri net can be transformed into such a form if the operation "n→" is extended as follows. The integers are augmented by the symbol ω and the operation "ω→" sets the marking of all head places "equal to infinity"; that is equivalent to deleting these places together with the incident arcs.

E.g.:

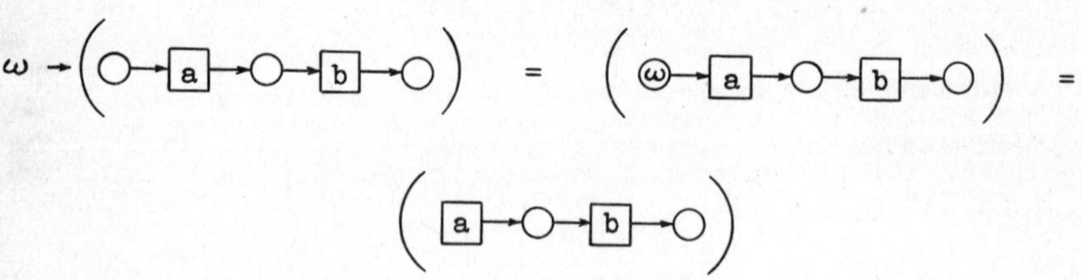

4. CONTROL TYPE DECLARATIONS

A control type defines a regular abstract family of control structures. It may be standard, or it may be defined and named by a declaration. Once declared, a control type can be used within the instruction part in so-called "structure designators"; it can also be used in "type designators" to declare other, new control types. The semantics of the declaration and use of control types will be given in terms of structured nets.

We now give a short summary of the syntactical structure of the declaration of control types:

⟨control type declaration⟩

  ::= <u>type</u> ⟨type identifier⟩ (⟨formal parameters list⟩)

    = ⟨type formula⟩

⟨formal parameter⟩

  ::= ⟨identifier⟩ | ⟨dynamic parameter⟩

⟨dynamic parameter⟩

  ::= <u>var</u> ⟨formal parameter⟩

A control type is "static" if all its formal parameters are just identifiers, viz. static parameters. Type formulas, and similar ones to be discussed later, are well-formed formulas which differ from those in Section 3 only by the nature of the operands. Let us consider for a while the particular case where the operands are simply parameter-identifiers or designators of static types.

<u>Example 4.</u> To describe the mutual exclusion of two modules we may declare a control type "mutex2" by

<u>type</u> mutex2(a,b) = 1→*(a▯b)

where a and b are formal parameters.

We may also declare the type "parseq4" to require the parallel execution of the two sequences of actions:

<u>type</u> parseq4(a,b,c,d) = 1→((a;b),(c;d))

The semantics of these static control types can easily be precised by the following nets:

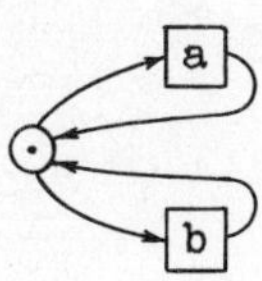

mutex2

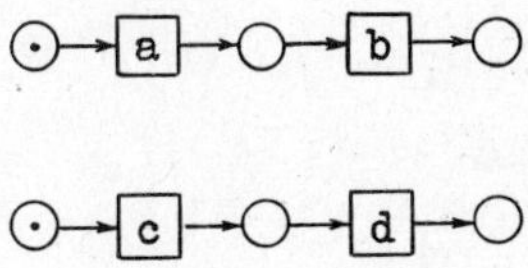

parseq4

We may now declare still another type, "parex4" using the two types we just defined:

<u>type</u> parex4(a,b,c,d) = (parseq4(a,b,c,d),mutex2(a,c),mutex2(b,d))

In this type formula, the operands are type designators. The corresponding net is

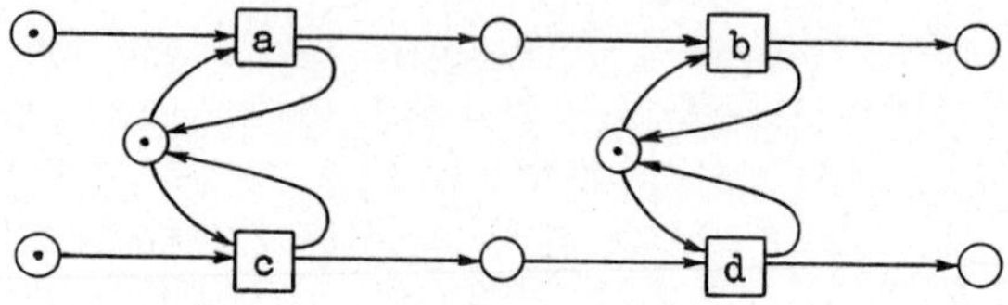

Remark that the last type has been constructed by superposing layers: we have earmarked two sorts of simple control situations, we have declared two types for these situations, and we formed the final type by superposing three layers.

A static control type defines a concrete structure with fixed number of modules. However, there are cases where it is necessary to design a control type characterizing "similar" control structures with a "similar" topology but applicable on a d y n a m i c a l l y v a r y i n g number of controlled modules. If all types were static, we would then be forced to declare a large collection of "similar" static types; this is, in fact, why we had to declare "mutex2" although "mutex3" was already defined in Example 2. It is to avoid such difficulties that we introduce dynamic control types. Thus, each dynamic type defines a set of structures having a similar topology but differing in the number of modules accepted as parameters. In the declaration of a dynamic type, the dynamic parameters in the formal parameters list are indicated by the special symbol <u>var</u>; the number of the symbols <u>var</u> immediately preceding a given parameter is called the dynamic rank of that parameter. When the dynamic control types are used in designators, a dynamic formal parameter is replaced by an actual parameter which may be an arbitrarily long vector of formulas, and which is called a "segment". To illustrate these rules, we introduce three standard dynamic control types, called <u>join</u>, <u>excl</u> and <u>comb</u>, for "join", "exclude" and "combine", respectively. Each of these three types has one implicit dynamic parameter <u>var</u> x, and thus defines on infinite set of formulas. A formula is obtained by the replacement of the parameter <u>var</u> x with a segment. Hence, for any segment $[x_1,x_2,\ldots,x_i]$ the designator

$$\underline{\text{join}}([x_1,x_2,\ldots,x_i])$$

defines the formula $(x_1;x_2;\ldots;x_i)$,

designator <u>excl</u>($[x_1,x_2,\ldots,x_i]$)

defines the formula $(x_1 \| x_2 \| \ldots \| x_i)$,

designator <u>comb</u>($[x_1,x_2,\ldots,x_i]$)

defines the formula $(x_1,x_2,\ldots,x_i)$.

Example 5. Let us declare the dynamic control type

type mutex(var x) = 1→* excl(var x)

We may then use the type "mutex" in a type designator mutex([a,b]) where the actual parameter is the segment[a,b] of length two; this type designator is equivalent to the formula 1→*(a▯b), i.e. to the same formula used to declare the type mutex2. Similarly, the designator mutex([a,b,c]) defines the control structure represented by the formula 1→*(a▯b▯c), i.e. the formula used in Example 2.

The use of segments needs a few more comments. Since a segment is a vector of formulas, it is useful to extend the operations as follows:

$$\underline{o}[x_1,x_2,\ldots,x_i] = [\underline{o}x_1,\underline{o}x_2,\ldots,\underline{o}x_i]$$

where $\underline{o}$ is an unary operation, x_i are formulas;

$$[x_1,x_2,\ldots,x_i]\,\underline{\underline{o}}\,[y_1,y_2,\ldots,y_i,y_{i+1},\ldots,y_j] =$$
$$=[(x_1\underline{\underline{o}}y_1),(x_2\underline{\underline{o}}y_2),\ldots,(x_i\underline{\underline{o}}y_i),y_{i+1},\ldots,y_j]$$

where $\underline{\underline{o}}$ is a binary operation.

We now give a slightly more elaborate example to show expressive power of proposed techniques as well as to illustrate the rules of substitution for dynamic parameters having a rank equal to one.

Example 6. We consider a dynamic control type defined as follows:

type parex(var x,var y) = 1→(join(var x),join(var y),
comb(*(var x▯ var y)))

The designator parex([a,b,c],[d,e,f]) defines the following structure:

parex([a,b,c],[d,e,f]) =
1→(join([a,b,c]),join([d,e,f]),comb(*([a,b,c]▯[d,e,f]))) =
1→((a;b;c),(d;e;f),comb(*[(a▯d),(b▯e),(c▯f)])) =
1→((a;b;c),(d;e;f),comb([*(a▯d),*(b▯e),*(c▯f)])) =
1→((a;b;c),(d;e;f),*(a▯d),*(b▯e),*(c▯f)).

The corresponding net is

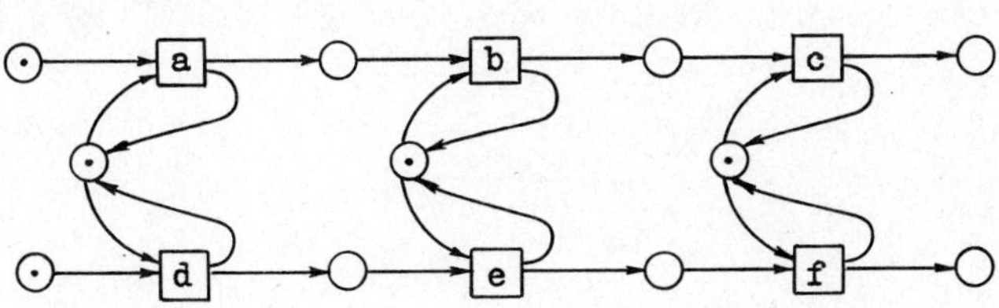

We conclude this section with the more precise definition of the syntactical form of a type designator and one more example of a dynamic control type:

```
⟨type designator⟩
      ::= ⟨type name⟩(⟨actual parameters list⟩)
⟨type name⟩
      ::= ⟨type identifier⟩ | join | excl | comb
⟨actual parameter⟩
      ::= ⟨type formula⟩|⟨segment⟩
⟨segment⟩
      ::= [⟨type formulas list⟩] | [⟨segments list⟩]
```

The syntactical rules for the control type declarations and designators must be augmented by some context restrictions. Some of the restrictions are classical for such constructions; for example the right side of a declaration does not contain parameters not mentioned in the left side; the number of actual parameters in a type designator is equal to the number of formal parameters in the type declaration, etc. Any recursion in type declarations is not allowed. The restriction which concerns the use of symbols (parameter-identifiers) in the well-formed formulas (see Section 3) is valid for the type formulas. Let us define the rank of a parameter identifier in a type formula as follows:

- the rank of the identifier is 0;
- each immediately preceding symbol var increases the rank by 1;
- each pair of enclosing segment brackets increases the rank by 1;
- each "enclosing" type designator decreases the rank by n, where n is a declared dynamic rank of the corresponding formal parameter of that type.

Then, in a type declaration, the declared dynamic rank of a formal parameter must be equal to the rank of that specific parameter in the right-side type formula.

Example 7. This example as well as Example 9 in Section 6 are intended to clear up the rules of the substitution of parameters with dynamic ranks which are greater than one. These parameters help to construct multi-dimensional dynamic structures.

Let us declare the dynamic type

```
type seqex(var var x) = 1 → join([excl(var x)])
```

The structure defined by the designator seqex([[a,b,c],[d,e,f]]) is obtained as follows:

```
seqex([[a,b,c],[d,e,f]]) =
1 → join([excl([a,b,c]),excl([d,e,f])]) =
1 → join([(a▯b▯c),(d▯e▯f)]) =
1 → ((a▯b▯c);(d▯e▯f))
```

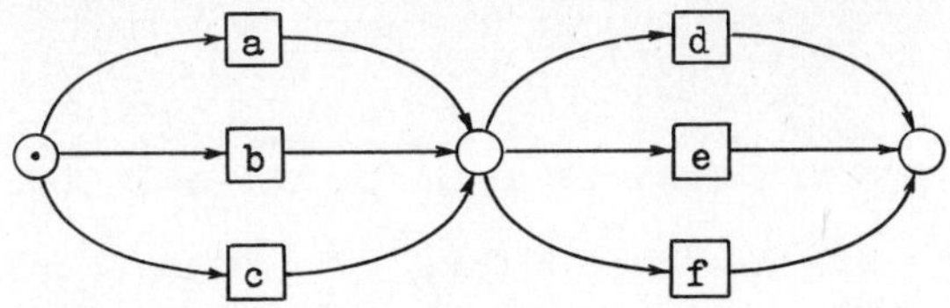

The same type permits us to construct another structure which is defined by the designator seqex([[a,b],[c,d],[e,f]]) and is represented by the following net:

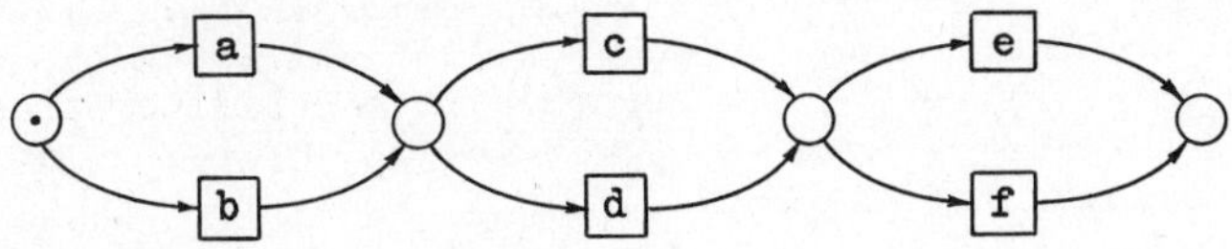

5. STRUCTURE OF A COMPOUND MODULE

We would remind that a compound module has a form of <u>do</u> $C_1,C_2,\ldots$ $\ldots,C_n$ <u>od</u> , where C_i are components, viz. framed modules or structure designators, possibly labelled. Structure designators define concrete control configurations and are structured in the same way as type designators, except that the latter have actual parameters of another kind. To simplify the discussion we shall begin by considering a "canonical" syntactical structure. In this case, a component is a labelled (framed) module or an unlabelled "simple" structure designator :

⟨structure designator⟩

    ::= ⟨type name⟩(⟨actual parameters list⟩)

⟨actual parameter of simple structure designator⟩

    ::= ⟨module reference⟩|⟨segment of module references⟩

⟨module reference⟩

    ::= ⟨module name⟩

Restrictions:

- all the modules must be labelled by different names;
- any structure designator which is a component of a module contains only the references to modules which are present inside that module;
- no actual parameter of a structure designator occurs inside <u>do</u>...<u>od</u> indirectly, i.e. after conversion of the designator into a structure formula;
- the rank of module name in a structure designator, which is considered as a formula, must be equal to 0.

The structure of a canonical module may be displayed by a sort of labelled structured net which resembles a flow-chart.

Each labelled framed module $a:\pi \rightarrow s$, where a is the module name, π is a trigger function, s is a module, is presented as a labelled net:

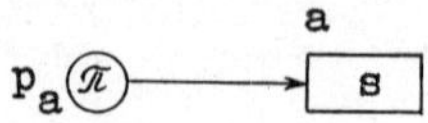

If the module a is simple then a is a simple transition otherwise it is a generalized transition.

A structure designator defines a net with the transitions marked by the module name. Let some module <u>do</u> $C_1,C_2,\ldots,C_n$ <u>od</u> consist of components which are framed modules and structure designators. A set of nets $N_1,N_2,\ldots,N_n$ corresponds to the list of components. The commas in the list are regarded as symbols of the operation ",". So, the resulting net $N=(N_1,N_2,\ldots,N_n)$ is a flow-chart representation of the module; this representation is obtained through superposition of layers $N_1,N_2,\ldots,N_n$.

<u>Example 8.</u> For the program

```
type mutex(var x) = 1→*excl(var x),
do mutex([a,b,c]),
      a: x<y → x:=x+1,
      b: y<z → y:=y+1,
      c: z<x → z:=z+1  od
```

the flow-chart of the module is obtained by the superposition of nets

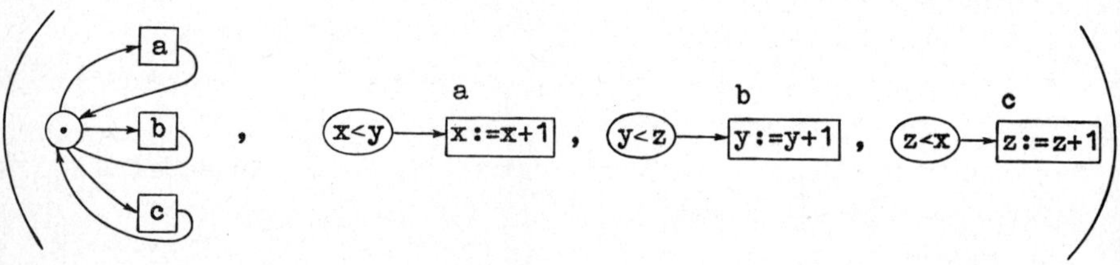

and has a form

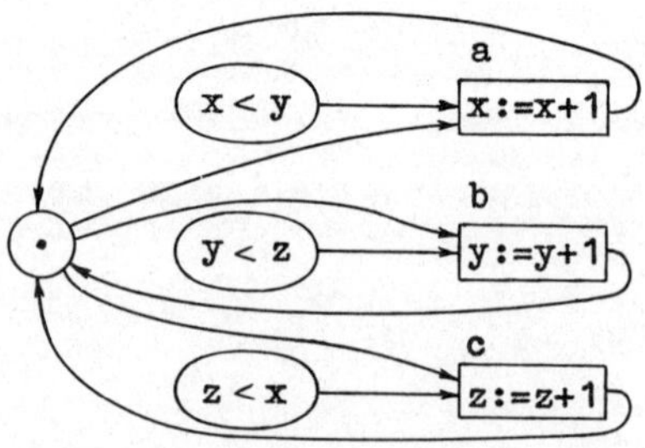

Note, that the concept of a control structure formula built by the use of control types and structure designators differs from the concept of a path expression. A path expression is a procedure-oriented construct: two entries of the same name in a path expression cause two different actions during a program execution, namely, two calls of a procedure. Two entries of the same name in a control structure formula serve the purpose of the layered design of a program and they denote one action.

The execution of a module with structure designators is based on the execution of a TF-module. It is convenient to explain additional actions with the use of flow-charts. When a compound module is initiated, the control structure of the module is formed (see Example 8). The input places $p_1,\ldots,p_n$ of a submodule-transition with a trigger function $\mathcal{T}$ are considered to be conjunctive components of the extended trigger function

$$\mathcal{T} \;\&\; M(p_1) > 0 \;\&\ldots\&\; M(p_n) > 0$$

where M is a current marking of the places. (The extended trigger function is arranged at the initiation of the compound module.) These trigger functions are tested in the same way as the trigger functions of TF-programs. Each test includes two steps. At the first step, the values of extended trigger functions of passive submodules are computed and the markings of all non-zero places are decreased by one. At the second step, submodules are selected for initiation. If some module with the true trigger function is not selected, its input places are increased back by one.

The tests of "global" places (see Example 3b) require some special arbiter-like actions of an enclosing module. A termination of a compound module occurs only if some "local" places or trigger functions disable all submodules. If the "local" parts of extended trigger functions permit the continuation of the execution of some submodules but some "global" places have no tokens, then the module stays in an active, waiting state. In other words, a termination can be caused only by "internal" reasons.

To make the program writing less restrictive, we could generalize the syntactical structure of compound modules in the following way. Structure designators are allowed to be labelled and their actual parameters are more diverse:

<actual parameter of structure designator>
    ::= <component>|<component reference>|
        <segment of actual parameters>
<component reference>
    ::= <component name>

Some additional restrictions on the syntax should be imposed to provide the reducibility of a general syntactical form to the canonical one.

For example, the following program may be transformed into the canonical program in Example 8, hence both programs have the same flow-chart:

```
type mutex(var x) = 1→*excl(var x),
do mutex([x<y→x:=x+1, y<z→y:=y+1, z<x→z:=z+1]) od
```

6. STRUCTURING WITH CONTROL TYPES

Extensible control types give the opportunity to construct various control structures and control primitives of different levels. Specifically, the control type technique allows to convey the known control facilities of sequential and parallel programming languages. (Note should be taken that the sequential primitives sometimes take a more complex form than parallel ones, for the asynchronous parallelism is at the basis of this approach.) After the programmer has prepared a collection of abstract control types, he may verify them by formal methods and write different fragments of his program as a sequential program, or as a parbegin...parend program with semaphores, or as a TF-program [4], or as a Dijkstra's guarded commands program [5], etc. (The TF-program in Example 1 was converted into the nondeterministic guarded commands program in Examples 2 and 8 with the use of the control type "mutex".)

We conclude with some examples illustrating the possibilities granted by the control type description of program structures.

Example 9. A lattice structure with a changing number of modules may be defined by the following dynamic control type:

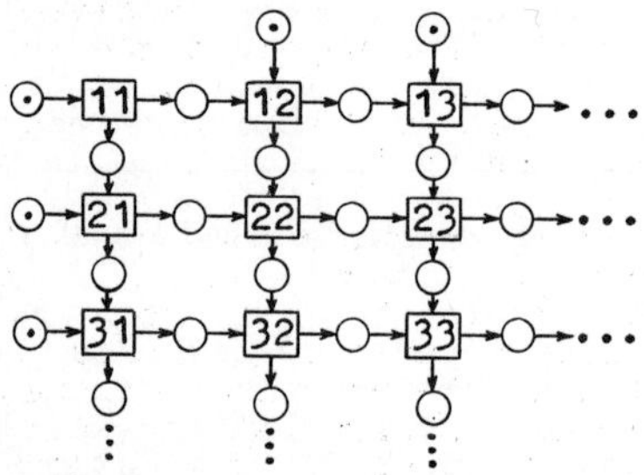


```
type lattice(var var x) =
    1→(comb([join(var x)]),
    comb(join(var var x)))
```

Here is a derivation of a structure formula for the case of a matrix with 3×3 elements:

```
lattice([[11,12,13],[21,22,23],[31,32,33]]) =
1→(comb([join([11,12,13]),join([21,22,23]),join([31,32,33])]),
comb(join([[11,12,13],[21,22,23],[31,32,33]]))) =
1→(comb([(11;12;13),(21;22;23),(31;32;33)]),
comb([(11;21;31),(12;22;32),(13;23;33)])) =
1→((11;12;13),(21;22;23),(31;32;33) ,
(11;21;31),(12;22;32),(13;23;33))
```

Layered structuring and control types allow construction of a program in a stepwise manner. To some extent, the process of program writing resembles conversational programming: a programmer analyses a problem, splits it into components and simpler layers, then he programs the components and adds more and more information about the control interactions, verifying along the way separate layers and results of superposition of layers.

Example 10. Consider the simplified readers-writers problem. A writer thinks and, then, writes into a buffer; a reader reads some information from the buffer, erases this information and then thinks. They act independently, exept that they have no simultaneous access to the buffer and the buffer is of the finite length, say, n.

The subsequent programming steps are the following:

(1) Abstract control types are prepared:

type loop(var x) = 1→*join(var x)

to describe a cyclic sequence of actions,

type mutex(var x) = 1→*excl(var x)

to describe the mutual exclusiveness of concurrent actions,

type buffer(a,b) = n-1 → loop([a,b])

to describe a cyclic "pipeline" sequence of two actions with the volume of a buffer equal to n.

(2) The set of actions with names allocated is formed as a compound module:

do WT: writer thinks,
   WW: writer writes,
   RR: reader reads (and erases),
   RT: reader thinks od

(3) The sequence of action for both writer and reader is described by the following structure designators:

writer: loop([WT,WW]),
reader: loop([RR,RT])

(4) The restriction which excludes simultaneous writing and reading is added:

mutex([WW,RR])

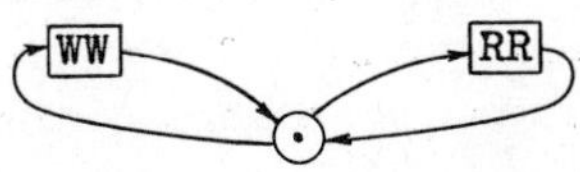

(5) Reading is possible if there is information in the buffer; writing is possible if there is space in the buffer which is of length n:

buffer(WW,RR)

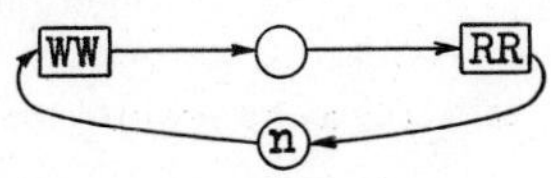

(6) The final program is the result of superposition of the previously constructed layers (control type declarations are omitted):

```
            do  WT: writer thinks,
                WW: writer writes,
                RR: reader reads,
                RT: reader thinks,
        writer: loop([WT,WW]),
        reader: loop([RR,RT]),
                mutex([WW,RR]),
                buffer(WW,RR)  od
```

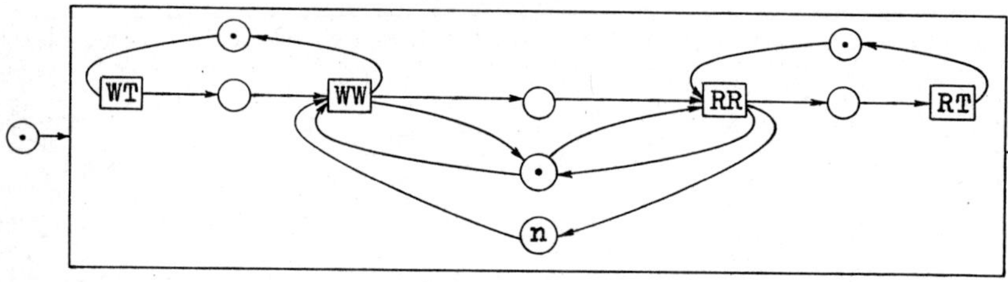

Example 11. The five philosophers problem.

Let the actions of the i-th philosopher be represented by modules with the following names:

IN_i - the philosopher enters the room,
TL_i - he takes the left fork,
TR_i - he takes the right fork,
ET_i - he eats spagetti,
PL_i - he puts down the left fork,
PR_i - he puts down the right fork,
OUT_i - he leaves the room.

We will use the types defined above and a new type

type fourres(**var** x) = 3 → mutex(**var** x)

which permits not more than 4 actions concur in parallel.

The subsequent steps of the programming of the problem solution (no more than four philosophers are allowed to be in the room) are:

a) The action sequence of the i-th philosopher is described by the structure designators

Ph_i:loop([IN_i,**comb**(TL_i,TR_i),ET_i,**comb**(PL_i,PR_i),OUT_i]),
where i=1,2,...,5.

b) Since there is only one fork between two philosophers, the actions

connected with that fork must be mutually exclusive
F_i : mutex([<u>join</u>(TL_i,ET_i,PL_i),<u>join</u>(TR_i,ET_i,PR_i)]),
where i=1,2,...,5, j=i+1 (mod 5).

c) Only four philosophers are allowed to be in the room
R: fourres([Ph_1,Ph_2,Ph_3,Ph_4,Ph_5]).

These designators, written in any order, separated by commas, enclosed by <u>do</u>...<u>od</u>, form the resulting program:

<u>do</u> Ph_i : ...., $(1 \leqslant i \leqslant 5)$
F_i : ...., $(1 \leqslant i \leqslant 5)$
R : .... <u>od</u>

Here is a fragment of the net which pictures the program structure:

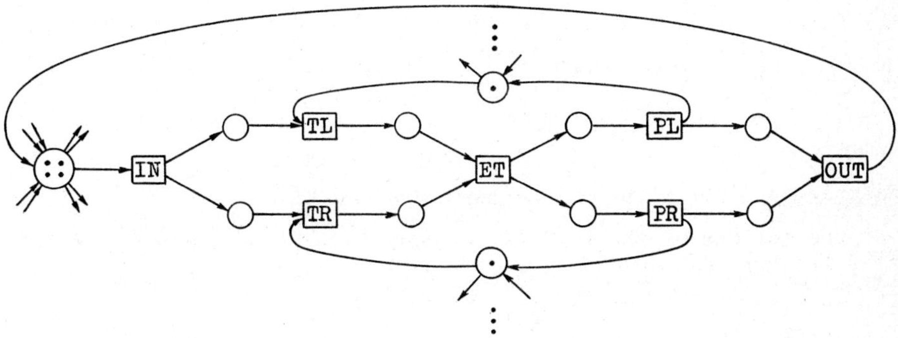

CONCLUSION

In this paper we suggest that it is necessary to revise the traditional methodology of concurrent control structure design. The purpose of this revision is to give a programmer convenient ways of adequately expressing the various control structures and relations inherent in problems, as is already common for data structures. Such an approach is particularly suited for the programming of complex multicomponent dynamic systems, such as operating systems, production models, etc.

The approach considered here is based on three main principles (i) to go from chaos to order; (ii) to declare abstract control types; (iii) to structure in a layered manner. All three principles are closely associated with one another and together form a single unit. In this paper we have only treated basic control primitives which make it possible to construct a wide class of control structures and control relations. As both conditional and unconditional layers of a program with control types are based upon asynchronous control, there are some control situations which are not expressible in the proposed mechanism. For example, control types do not contain the means of forcing all "ready" submodules to be initiated simultaneously or the means of allocating priorities, etc. We assume now that these facilities can be located in the internal control. However, they can be explicitly shown in control type declarations, if we augment the declarations by some extra control information. For example, we can define a type as follows

<u>type</u> primutex(a,b,c) = mutex(a,b,c) <u>priority</u> <u>to</u> a

to declare mutual exclusiveness with the highest priority given to the module a.

The considered sample language can be augmented by classical macroprimitives, like procedures, in a straightforward manner. A more interesting problem is to find a way to express some known high level implicit control primitives in terms of control types. Also, it is of interest to develop some general concept which combines the philosophy of abstract control types with that of abstract data types.

As a final remark, we mention that the proposed approach can be applied to distributed data-driven computations, but the semantics and methods of construction of the program control and data-flow structures must be revised.

ACKNOWLEDGEMENTS

The author wish to thank Alexander Bystrov for helpful discussions. Special thanks go to Stephen A. Schuman and Michel Sintzoff for valuable comments, criticisms, suggestions and much practical assistance which have expanded the volume of the paper but substantially improved its readibility.

REFERENCES

[1] Brinch Hansen,P. Concurrent Programming Concepts. Computer Survey, <u>5</u>, 4, 1973, pp. 223-245.

[2] Hoare, C.A.R. Communicating Sequential Processes. The Queen's University, Belfast, 1976.

[3] Petri, C.A. Kommunikation mit Automaten. Ph.D, Thesis, University of Bonn, 1962 (in German).

[4] Kotov, V.E., Narinyani, A.S. Asynchronous Computational Processes on Shared Memory. Kibernetika, No. 3, Kiev, 1966, pp. 64-71 (in Russian).

[5] Campbell, R.H., Habermann, A.N. The Specification of Process Synchronization by Path Expressions. Lecture Notes in Computer Science, vol. 16, Springer, Berlin, Heidelberg, New York, 1974.

[6] Lauer, P.E. and Campbell, R.H. Formal Semantics of a Class of High-Level Primitives for Coordinating Concurrent Processes. Acta Informatica, 5, 1975, pp. 297-332.

[7] Dijkstra, E.W. Guarded Commands, Nondeterminacy and Formal Derivation of Programs. Comm. ACM, <u>18</u>, 8, 1975, pp. 453-457.

Constructing Quality Software, P.G. Hibbard/S.A. Schuman (eds.)

COMBINING ASSERTIONS AND STATES FOR THE VALIDATION OF PROCESS COMMUNICATION

Gregor V. Bochmann
Département d'Informatique
et de Recherche Opérationnelle
Université de Montréal
Montreal, Canada

INTRODUCTION

Methods for the formal specification and logical validation of systems seem to be of much greater practical importance for the design and implementation of communication protocols than in the case of most other software products. This is because the following typical difficulties arise in the design and implementation of communication protocols:

(a) Without a formal model, it is very difficult to foresee all possible modes of operation that can occur due to varying synchronization between the communicating subsystems, possible malfunction of the communication medium, and/or error recovery actions initiated by one or both subsystems.

(b) A protocol involves several interdependent parallel processes. In this context, faults in the design and programming can give rise to time dependent errors which are very difficult to detect and locate by run time tests. Therefore the logical validation of a protocol can be very useful for detecting any design errors, thus complementing the usual testing methods.

(c) Communication protocols must be implemented in a compatible way on all communicating subsystems. Often, the different subsystems are implemented on different hardware, different operating systems, by different groups of people, and in different organizations. Without a clear and non-ambiguous protocol specification, this would be impossible.

This paper contains an introductory exposition of a protocol specification method that involves finite state diagrams and programming variables for the description of each of the communicating subsystems. Such a description can be used as the basis for logical validation of the communication procedures. The advantages of this method are shortly discussed.

VALIDATION METHODS

Traditionally, data communication protocols are specified in a kind of natural language description which often leads to the problems of ambiguous meaning and incompatible implementations. The need for more formal specification methods has been realized, and different methods have been proposed for this purpose. Such methods must not only provide a framework for a non-ambiguous and clear definition of the protocol, but also facilitate the validation of the definition, and lead to a correct implementation, usually in software.

A well-known method is the use of finite-state transition diagrams for the specification of the communicating subsystems (Bartlett et al. 1969; Merlin 1976). The main advantage of this technique is the simplicity of the model, and the possibility of using algorithms for deriving such properties as liveness of particular states or deadlock-freeness, which are useful for the validation of the defined protocol. We showed that the communication medium used by the communicating subsystems can often be described by a finite state model as well (1976). If one considers the medium as a resource which is shared between the communicating subsystems, one obtains a model which is much related to the description of synchronization properties for shared resources by path expressions (Campbell 1974).

The main limitation of the finite state approach for protocol specification is, again, its simplicity. For describing realistic protocols one usually needs a very large number of states (which makes the description less readable), unless one introduces hierarchical structuring of states and/or program variables, as used by Bochmann and Chung (1977) for the description of HDLC procedures. Another approach consists of describing each communicating subsystem in terms of a process specified in a high-level programming language. In this case, no algorithms are available for the automatic validation of liveness and deadlock-freeness, however, properties of the specified protocol can be verified by using program assertions and invariants, as shown by Bochmann (1975) and Stenning (1976).

COMBINING ASSERTIONS AND STATES

Validation of the interaction between two communicating subsystems usually implies the verification of some global assertions, sometimes invariants, involving the variables of both subsystems. However, in certain circumstances, the global assertions involve not only the subsystem variables, but also the process of execution in each subsystem. Such a situation occurs in particular when each subsystem may execute recovery actions as considered by Randell (1975).

Two methods come to the mind for describing the process of execution in a subsystem: (1) the introduction of additional variables indicating the process of execution of each subsystem, and (2) the use of a finite state program structure with specified transitions from one state to another. We believe that the second method leads often to a more readable description of communication protocols. Apart from readability, this approach presents the following advantages:

(a) The validation algorithms of the finite state approach mentioned above can be used for the finite state aspects of the communication protocol.

(b) Different assertions can be associated with the different states of a subsystem, and different global assertions can be associated with different pairs of states of the two subsystems.

(c) The combination of variables with the finite state approach and the association of executable statements with the transitions of a subsystem is an approach which integrates the complementary methods of finite-state description and programming language description into a powerful and flexible model for the specification of interacting subsystems.

A particular formalism of this kind, related to the one of Keller (1976), is proposed by Bochmann and Gecsei (1977) and has been successfully applied to the description of a more complex protocol (Bochmann and Chung, 1977).

DISCUSSION

For the validation of interacting finite state subsystems one usually has to consider the product state space consisting of all pairs of states in subsystem 1 and 2, respectively (see for example Gilbert and Chandler (1972) or Merlin, 1976). It has been argued that this leads to a very large number of states to be considered, the number of states in the product space being essentially equal to n^2, where n is the number of states in each subsystem. We have however noticed (1976) that in most practical examples the number of reachable pairs of states is much smaller because the nature of the communication medium restricts the possible transitions of the two subsystems.

Assertions that involve the process of execution of both subsystems cannot be associated with a given place in the program text of one subsystem, as is usually done for assertions involving only one process. However, they can be associated with a pair (or a set of pairs) of states in the product space. In the case that the assertion associated with all pairs is the same, it is called a "system invariant".

A simple inductive method for verifying the assertions Q_p associated with the state pairs p is as follows:

1°: Verify Q_{p_o} for the pair p_o of initial states.

2°: For each possible transition t of subsystem 1 or 2 respectively, leading from the state pair p to the pair p', verify that

$$Q_p \wedge P_t \{S_t\} Q_{p'}$$

holds, where P_t is the enabling predicate of the transition t which must hold for the transition to be enabled, S_t is the statement executed during the transition t, which may change the values of the variables, and the notation $Q \{S\} Q'$ means that "Q holds immediately before the execution of statement S" implies that "Q' holds immediately after the execution of S".

REFERENCES

Bartlett, K.A., Scantlebury, R.A., and Wilkinson, P.T. (1969). A note on reliable full-duplex transmission over half-duplex links, CACM 12, 260.

Bochmann, G.V., and Chung, R.J. (1977). A formalized description of HDLC classes of procedures, to be presented at the Nat. Telecommunication Conf., Los Angeles, Dec. 1977.

Bochmann, G.V., and Gecsei, J. (1977). A unified method for the specification and verification of protocols, to be presented at IFIP Congress 1977, Toronto.

Bochmann, G.V. (1976). Finite State Description of Communication Protocols. Publication # 236, Dép. d'Informatique, Université de Montréal.

Bochmann, G.V. (1975). Logical verification and implementation of protocols, Proc. Fourth Data Communications Symposium (ACM/IEEE).

Brinch-Hansen, P. (1973). Operating Systems Principles, Englewood Cliffs, Prentice Hall.

Campbell, R.H. (1974). The specification of process synchronization by path expressions, in Colloque sur les Aspects Théoriques et Pratiques des Systèmes d'Exploitation, IRIA, Paris, pp. 93-106; and Campbell, R.H., and Habermann, A.N., idem, Technical Report No. 55, Computing Laboratory, Univ. of Newcastle upon Tyne.

Dijkstra, E.W. (1975). Guarded commands, non-determinacy and formal derivation of programs, CACM 18, p. 453-457.

Gilbert, P., and Chandler, W.J. (1972). Interference between communicating parallel processes, Comm. ACM 15, p. 427.

Keller, R.M. (1976). Formal Verification of Parallel Programs, CACM, 7, pp. 371-384.

Kotov, V.E. (1977). Concurrent programming with control types, in these proceedings.

Merlin, P.M. (1976). A methodology for the design and implementation of communication protocols, IEEE Transactions on Comm., Vol. COM-24, pp. 614-621.

Randell, B. (1975). System structure for software fault tolerance, Proc. Int. Conf. on Reliable Software, ACM Sigplan Notices Vol. 10, No. 6, p. 437.

Stenning, N.V. (1976). A data transfer protocol, Computer Networks, Vol. 1, No. 2, pp. 99-110.

Vaucher, J. (1973). A WAIT-UNTIL algorithm for general purpose simulation languages, Proc. Winter Simulation Conf., pp. 77-83, San Francisco.

Session 3b : Discussion

Nehmer: I'd like to pose some general questions concerning the state-of-the-art in concurrent programming. The languages which provide concurrent programming tools, such as Concurrent PASCAL and MODULA, adopt some controversial attitudes with respect to concepts such as processes, classes, monitors and modules. What do you think will be the future trend in the development of these languages? In the light of your presentations, do processes as such still have any justification? What should be the ideal relation among modules, processes, monitors, etc.?

Bekkers: I can't answer those questions completely; however, I can say that in our system "processes" do not occur in programs. The execution structure is not expressed in the language, but instead in the way the modules are linked together.

Kotov: My approach differs from that of Bekkers because attention is focused on controlling processes. Monitors and classes are more high-level than the execution-oriented primitives I presented.

Bochmann: I think the notions of shared resources and processes are complementary and we need both. For example, the order in which actions are performed is not completely specified by either path expressions or the control modules of Robert and Verjus, since these simply give certain restrictions on the order in which actions can be executed. However, some processes may access resources, and within each process there is an algorithm that determines in which order the process performs these actions. Therefore both together, resources and processes, determine the order in which the actions are executed.

Král: Kotov's example was very impressive but I have doubts whether the system works so well in cases where complicated synchronizing procedures and conditions are needed, or where explicit synchronized access to queues must be implemented. Do you think that your system is able to cope with such problems?

Kotov: That is a difficult question because some problems concerning simple shared memory can be solved, and some others not. I think that distributed computations, real-time accesses to complex data structures, etc. must be treated in a similar manner but they may require additional components which must be introduced into the system.

Král: That means that the system is not suited for the deadlock problem concerning memory allocation for example?

Kotov: No, I think we must find how to express precisely our problems in this basic set of notions and after that we could say what we can do and what we can't do.

Bekkers: I think your mechanism is more a theoretical tool which can serve as support for documentation and for discussion among researchers. I don't think it is a tool which can be used as a high-level synchronization tool.

Kotov: It is not true that my approach is entirely theoretical. We are developing a language based on these principles. I am against splitting the theoretical and practical approaches and methodology. Why not put them together and try to synthesize practical systems after some theoretical analysis and consideration?

Wodon: I quite agree with Kotov that theory and practice should stay together as closely as possible; however, I don't see a notation derived from Petri nets as being very suitable for programming. Have you any experience in having programmers write programs that way? Can they really do that without making many mistakes?

Kotov: Remember that Petri nets only serve as a semantic base. My paper describes splitting the static and dynamic control structures. Petri nets are sufficient for a description of the wide class of static control structures, and with some features added, like generalized transitions, they are as powerful as Turing machines.

Bochmann: I think Kotov's formalism may very naturally be used to describe the synchronizing control module for shared resources. The language proposed by Verjus and Robert and path expressions are other proposals for this purpose.

Sintzoff: I would like to ask Bekkers a few questions. Do you think that there is a possible conflict between, on the one hand, separating synchronization into distinct control modules and, on the other hand, distributing control throughout the system? When you have a control module you are in fact centralizing the control.

Bekkers: I don't think we are centralizing the control. I think we give the programmer the possibility of distributing the control within the program. From the point of view of the programmer the control is distributed.

Wodon: I don't think I agree with you because Sintzoff was talking about the processes which are exercising the control and here you have a set of history variables which are controlled by some other process.

Bekkers: I think it is an implementation problem. You can either implement a process checking all the conditions for every other process or generate within each process the code to check the conditions. In the latter case whenever a process changes the value of a history variable it checks that no other process is waiting to start again. I think that this second implementation gives decentralized control.

Nehmer: I believe that process synchronization using message mechanisms is more time consuming than using shared variables. The approach you took is only justified if communication between different modules occurs less frequently than communication between processes via shared variables within one module.

Bekkers: Again I think that is an implementation problem. You can implement the communication using messages or using procedure call mechanisms. If you have a great deal of communication it may be better to use a procedure call, whereas if you do not have much communication it may be better to use a message mechanism. I don't think our proposal imposes any prejudice. Our mechanism is in the interface between the programmer and his program, and the interface between the program and the machine is the implementation structure.

Constructing Quality Software, P.G. Hibbard/S.A. Schuman (eds.)

APPLICATION OF OPTIMIZATION TECHNIQUES TO CORRECTNESS PROBLEMS

V.N.Kasyanov and I.V.Pottosin

Computing Center
Siberian Division of USSR Acad. Sci.
Novosibirsk 630090, USSR

The notion of program plausibility is introduced as the absence of meaningless executions of a program and the absence of discrepancies between the program text and the set of executions which it represents. The connection between this notion and program correctness is discussed and ways in which program plausibility can be used for the construction of reliable software are described. It is shown that an automatic program implausibility checking system can be based on program optimization techniques.

INTRODUCTION

This brief position paper discusses a pragmatic approach to obtaining correct programs. Two trends in checking program correctness can be distinguished:

- the design of languages and tools to provide some particular executions of programs, giving detailed information about their behaviour and data (testing). This information can be used by programmers to check program correctness and to localize errors if any.

- the design of systems which either provide some specifications about programs and their data or prove that programs are in fact implementation consistent with their specifications (verification). These systems require no program execution at all and can be used to conclude about correctness or applicability of programs and to localize errors as well.

In both cases some information about the problem being solved is required to decide in favor of or against program correctness. In the first case the programmer chooses some program executions and compares actual program behaviour with that which he expected from the problem. In the second case the programmer either gives specifications describing what the program is supposed to do or compares them with derived ones.

At the same time it is known that, in practice, an experienced programmer looking at an unfamiliar incorrect program detects its implausibility rather than discrepancies with the problem to be solved. The property of plausibility differs from that of correctness, though it includes a number of the essential concepts of correctness.

More precisely, a correct program can be either plausible or implausible. The latter however is reasonable to expect only when a programmer tries to write an implausible and correct program. But writing such programs is always less profitable and more arduous than writing plausible correct programs. Thus, it seems that correct programs would tend to be plausible.

Let us consider a short example - a fragment of an implausible program in ALGOL 68. We have chosen this language as a model to show that even using such a safe language does not prevent a programmer from writing implausible programs, and also to show that program implausibility cannot be detected by syntactic techniques.

The following example contains a collection of horrors:

```
begin int i,k;
      while abs(m) ≤ abs(n) do i+:=1;
      k:=(n-1)*(i-1)+n;
      begin [1:k] int g; int s:=1, j:=1;
            proc ZERO = (ref int a,b,c,int e, ref [] int d):
            begin to ⌈ d-1 do
                  d[a+:=1] := if a≤b then Ø
                  else q[b+:=e, c+:=1] fi;
                  print(d)
            end;
            g[s] := q[j]; ZERO(s,i,j,i-1,q)
end end
```

Example 1.

We give only the program fragment but assume that the whole program is a legitimate one in ALGOL 68. Nevertheless, it is easy to see that this fragment contains a number of anomalies. Thus, considering this fragment only, we may assume that the whole program is not the expected representation of the programmer's algorithm. We list here some of these anomalies:

- The abs(m) ≤ abs(n) test in the first repetitive statement is independent of i. This means that either the i+:=1 statement is never executed or its execution repeats indefinitely.

- The first execution of i+:=1 refers to i before any value has been assigned to that variable.

- The evaluation of the left-hand side of the statement d[a+:=1]:= if a≤b then Ø else q[b+:=c, e+:=1] fi affects the evaluation of its right-hand side. Since left-hand and right-hand sides of the ALGOL 68 assignment statement should be evaluated collateraly, this leads to an ambiguity.

- g is declared as an array but only g[1] is actually referred to (by the statement g[s]:=q[j]).

- In the program there are no references to those values of g[s] which are obtained through the g[s]:=q[j] statement. Thus, this statement does not affect results of any program executions.

The given example is a combination of real incorrect programs and now we list those mistakes and reasons which made the program into an implausible one:

- the multiplication of abs(m) by i was omitted;
- the initialization of i was omitted (a frequent error);
- there is a mistake in the call statement, i.e., q is used in the place of g;
- the semantics of the ALGOL 68 assignment statement was misunderstood.

This list was given only to indicate some types of errors which enter into program plausibility. It should be noted that, for a given program, it is not in general possible to understand the reasons for its implausibility, if only the program text is known. As can be seen above, this requires additional knowledge about the problem to be solved and the algorithm to be represented.

We may observe that the notion of program plausibility is based on the following pragmatic considerations:

- a correct program contains no constructions that are useless with respect to the algorithm to be represented;

- programming features chosen for representation of the algorithm by a correct program are applied in a natural way;

- results of a correct program do not depend on the way in which semantically undefined actions are performed.

Thus, the notion of plausibility is related to the formal treatment of a program as a static representation of its executions for all possible inputs (without any knowledge of the actual problem being solved, in particular without any knowledge of the actual inputs). Intuitively, the <u>plausibility</u> of a given program means that all executions which it represents are reasonable and conform to the program text.

Though it is clear that a static proof of the plausibility of system programs would lead to improved software reliability, this would require an algorithm which proves plausibility, which this would necessitate determining whether an arbitrarily selected path in program is executable. However, it is well known that this problem is undecidable.

In practice, we are obligated to consider a set of executions which is "large enough" to contain all real executions, but we don't know how close this approximation is. As a result we may find, on one hand, some implausible executions which are in fact impossible and, on the other hand, extraneous executions (which are not really possible) may make implausible program constructions into plausible ones.

Hence, we cannot prove the plausibility of a given program nor can we have confidence in a plausibility proof for the extended set of program executions.

In such circumstances checking <u>implausibility</u> rather than proving plausibility the only effective way in which we can attempt to use the notion of plausibility in practice.

It must be observed, moreover, that this is only a step toward the localization of errors. In our opinion, it is nevertheless a significant one.

It should be noted that program optimization* also deals with a program in the way described above. Thus, it is natural to try to use conventional methods of program optimization for checking program implausibility. For example, all anomalies of the program fragment of the example 1 could be discovered by well-known techniques of program optimization such as control and data flow analysis, elimination of redundant actions and performing run-time actions at compile-time, where possible.

Let us consider in more detail the properties of implausible programs. Note, that this list is incomplete and chosen from the point of view how often it is reasonable to expect a property in actual incorrect programs. It should also be noted that for each of these properties a particular algorithm can be formulated. But, as we will demonstrate later, all these properties can be detected by using the three optimization techniques mentioned above. Note that we will use the term "executions" of a given program to mean all executions which are assumed by program optimization rather than only the potentially possible ones.

1. NON-INITIALIZED VARIABLES

This means that there is an "information incomplete" execution, having the property that the value of a variable is referred to before any assignment to that variable. In example 1 there is a simple illustration of this property.

The more complicated case of reference to a non-initialized variable is shown in example 2. Here, in every execution of the y:=xx statement the value of x is referred to before any assignment to this variable.

```
begin ref int xx; int x,y:=3;
   xx:=x;
   y:=xx;
   ...
end
```

Example 2.

---

* The application of various particular transformations to the compiled programs in order to produce more efficient object code.

Another example of an execution being information incomplete is one in which a non-initialized element of a compound variable (array, etc.) is referred to.

The detection of statements using non-initialized variables can be performed by control and data flow analysis. This analysis should be preceded by application of optimization to perform run-time actions at compile-time (for example, the evaluation of index expressions for compound variables).

2. INFINITE EXECUTION

This means that a given program is unable to traverse some of its points in any finite execution.

This property is connected with

- infinite recursion, where every execution of a procedure body contains a call of this procedure;
- deadlock, when synchronization of parallel executions obviously leads to them waiting for each other;
- infinite loops, where every execution of a loop structure leads to its infinite repetition, i.e. either the loop structure has no exit or all conditions which control its repeated execution are independent of the results of its executions (as in example 1).

This property can be detected by the control and data flow analysis. But, as for non-initialized variables, performing some run-time actions at compile-time increases the possibilities for detecting this kind of error.

3. USELESS OBJECTS

This means that either

- a variable (or procedure, mode and so on) has explicit declaration but no uses, or
- a statement belongs to none of the program executions, e.g. the a[i]:=0 statement of the example 3.

```
n:=Ø;
for i:=2 to n do a[i]:=Ø;
```

Example 3.

This property can also be discovered by control and data flow analysis of the program obtained after application of such optimizations as performing run-time actions at compile-time and eleminating redundant actions.

4. REDUNDANT ACTIONS

This means that a given program contains a statement which does not affect the results of any program executions. For example, considering the following program fragment

```
read(x,y); x:=2; p:=x>y;
print((real a;(p|a:=y↑2; 2|3)))
```

Example 4.

we see that reading x and evaluating a are evidently redundant (note, that all other statements of this example affect the printed values).

The presence of such statements is detected by the particular optimization which would eliminate them.

5. NONNATURAL CONSTRUCTIONS

This means disproportions between language constructions and their actual uses in a given program. The disproportion arises when the construction which is used is more universal and complicated then the program actions which are represented by this construction. To clarify this property we list some instances.

5.1. Overcomplicated structure of control.

This disproportion arises when every execution of a loop statement leads to no more than one execution of its body or when a case statement has only one nonempty alternative (a switch list has only one element) and so on. It may seem that this disproportion can be detected by a syntactic technique. But as it can be seen from the example 5 the application of such optimizationtions as performing run-time actions at compile-time and eliminating redundant actions is useful for detection of this disproportion.

```
i:=2;
case i in error, result esac;
```

Example 5.

5.2. Redundant labels.

This disproportion arises when a labeled statement is traversed by program executions only in natural order, e.g. the program has no branch to this label. Redundant labels are detected by control and data flow analysis. It should be noted that using a label as a comment leads to redundant labels. But it seems that the detection of redundant labels is nevertheless useful.

5.3. Overcomplicated data organization.

This disproportion arises when objects used in isolation are declared as parts of a compound object:

- if a record is referred to only by its fields,
- if an array not used as a whole has such a dimension that all index expressions are constants (see example 1).

A simple linear scan of optimized program text detects such disproportions.

5.4. Redundant levels of indirection.

This disproportion arises when a variable label (or variable procedure, pointer and so on) has only a single value. Redundant levels of indirection are detected by control and data flow analysis.

This list can be extended with respect to each individual programming language (the list that was given is essentially language-independent).

6. CONFLICTING EXECUTIONS

This means that results of some collaterally evaluated fragments can depend on the way in which their evaluations are merged. Example 1 gives a simple illustration of such an ambiguity, due to an informatiom connection between collaterally evaluated fragments. A more complicated information connection is shown by example 6, due to Ch. Lindsey.

```
being int i;
      proc p = int:(i:=1;i:=2;i);
      proc q = (int ii,jj) int:ii+jj;
      print(q(p,p))
end
```

Example 6.

Conflicting executions also arise when one of two collaterally evaluated fragments assigns a value to a non-local variable and the other contains a transfer of control out of the construct.

This property can be detected by control and data flow analysis.

7. SEMANTICALLY INADMISSIBLE OR UNDEFINED CONSTRUCTIONS

It is known that a conventional compiler performs correctness checks for some part of the semantics. However the complete discovery of all semantic errors in a given program requires actually running it for all possible cases. The during debugging one may test a program for only a limited number of selected test cases; hence a semantic error can penetrate into the final product.

Furthermore, a language may allow semantically undefined combinations of notions. It is clear that, while these combinations are syntactically legal, it is not reasonable to expect them to be written by a programmer. Indeed, a compiler which was able to detect such combinations would interpret them as errors. Thus, a program containing such semantically undefined combinations is, in fact, incorrect.

Optimization deals with program executions and hence is able to discover some of these semantic violations. For example, it can detect an execution in which an index does not lie within the bounds of an array (or illegal recursion, illegal side-effects, etc.). It can be seen that this detection basically depends on a given language, but the techniques are language-independent.

8. ABSOLUTE IMPLAUSIBILITY

We have listed above a number of program properties that testify to possible errors. These properties are connected with the existence of meaningless executions of a given program, such as information incomplete execution (property 1), infinite execution (property 2), execution without outside effect (property 4) and semantically inadmissible or undefined executions (property 7).

A given program is absolutely implausible if it has only meaningless executions (note, that any absolutely implausible program is an incorrect one). For example, this property is satisfied by the programs of the examples 2 and 6 and the program fragment in example 1. It is clear that absoluteness of implausibility can be detected by the optimization techniques discussed above.

CONCLUSION

The notion of program plausibility has been discussed and a list of some properties of implausible program has been given. It has been observed that all these properties can be detected by well-known techniques of program optimization.

In fact we say that a given program is an implausible one either if meaningless executions can be discovered or if there is a discrepancy between the program text and the set of all program executions that can be assumed. On the other hand, program optimization includes the analysis of a given program to detect as exactly as possible the set of program executions and includes the particular optimizations to convert a given program from its source form to one which conforms to the set of the program executions which is obtained. This is the basis for applying program optimization techniques to checking program plausibility automatically. Furthermore, any progress in plausibility checking techniques corresponds to progress in program optimization as well.

We distinguish between two sources of redundancies in a correct program, which create some difficulties for immediate implementation of this approach.

A program assembled in a high level language from universal fragments can contain redundancies. In this case it is not reasonable to decide on program implausibility after every detection of an anomaly. In other words, it is natural to indicate only absolute implausibility (i.e., incorrectness) associated with the use of a library fragment, but to signal all anomalies in fragments written by the user.

Further, an intermediate or object program can contain redundancies connected with universal compiling technique for some language constructions. But such redundancies can be formally distinguished from those of the source program.

It must be stressed that in our approach we deal with a superset of program executions rather than with actual ones (the difference between these sets depends on both the programming language and the analysis algorithms). This means that some anomalies not existing in actual executions of a given program might be detected; moreover some discrepancies between the given program and its actual executions might not be detected. It is necessary to bear this fact in mind. But it seems that, in practice, the actual difference is small - the success of program optimization tends to substantiate this view.

So, it seems that the given approach serves to provide a useful tool for improving software reliability. Utilization of this tool can be proposed as a necessary step in the process of constructing reliable software. Some experiments using DAVE (L.J.Osterwell, L.D.Fosdick "DAVE - A Validation Error Detection and Documentation System for Fortran Programs", Software-Practice and Experience, v. 6, 1976) tend to support this opinion. Plausibility checking in DAVE is limited to detecting non-initialized and useless variables, but the authors give examples of discovering errors in programs which "have been in use for several months and were though to be error free." The tool can be a part of an optimizing compiler, as well as an autonomous system based on optimization techniques (as is DAVE).

Most of the properties of implausibility listed here are language-independent. Thus, it is possible to implement the given approach as universal (language-independent) tool based on an universal intermediate language.

We see some disadvantages to the approach described, which are due to the incomplete reliability in discovering program errors. But this approach permits us to detect dynamic errors statically and informal errors formally. Thus, it is our position that such a tool can make a practical contribution to constructing quality software.

Kasyanov and Pottosin : Discussion

Bochmann: In practice many programming errors are found by syntax analysis, type checking and other error detection facilities of usual compilers. Do you know how many of the remaining errors would be detected by the additional facilities of your system?

Pottosin: It is very difficult to estimate a percentage of such errors, but it seems to me that these are very "heavy" errors, if errors have some weight. Syntax errors are very cheap, and these errors are very expensive.

King, J.: I have assumed that your system would print out diagnostic messages when it encounters a program that has one of these problems. Is that correct?

Pottosin: Yes.

King, J.: With the system DAVE, Fosdick and Osterweil found that some of the checks were fairly conservative, so they were swamped with warnings. They had to put in a feature to turn off some of the messages. Do you think that your proposal would have the same problem?

Pottosin: It's true. We have not taken a definite decision in this respect, and it's clear that we are in a worse position because our system is much more suspicious than the DAVE system.

King, J.: Then my question becomes a warning.

Turski: Which can be suppressed! [☺]

Wichmann: I should like to relate our NPL experience. People roughly divided themselves into two categories when such diagnostics were introduced: those who welcomed the ability to make their programs even more rigorously correct and continued to use the system, and those who got so annoyed with the system that they ceased to use it at all.

Correll: I don't understand why a program which contains redundant statements should be considered to be implausible. It may be very plausible. You put in redundancy to make the program more readable and checkable.

Pottosin: Logically you are correct, but statistically detection of the redundant actions in a program can give you necessary hints about possible mistakes in this program.

Holager: It seems to me that in large systems it is almost impossible to make absolutely sure you have exactly as much code as you need. In large programs a very common error is that some module does not handle all cases presented to it through its data. Now, it's better to handle too many cases than too few cases. It is safest to write a redundant alternative in a CASE statement, when we are not absolutely sure the case will never occur.

Pottosin: It's necessary to distinguish a generalized, multiple use routine from a specific algorithm which may use this general routine. A programmer ought to know (or be told) what parts of the program written by himself are implausible. This same verification serves to detect the situation in which the generalized procedure is impossible (i.e. when it is absolutely implausible). But it is also very important to detect that the utilization of this general procedure by a programmer leads to implausibilities.

Meertens: I should like to relate some experience I had in using a PL/I optimizing compiler on a program. After the syntax errors had been corrected, there were several warnings, none of which, when carefully considered, corresponded to errors. There were also some remarks by the optimizing part, each of which turned out to correspond to an error in my program.

Turski: My comment is twofold. First, I would like to state that I like the paper very much, because it's to my knowledge the first goal-directed attempt described at this conference to do something to improve the quality of software. This the first part of my comment. The second part is that I would like to elaborate on what Correll picked up before. Some of the optimization work seems in principle contrary to what some people call defensive or security-minded programming. For instance, I teach my students always to verify on input to their modules the conditions under which a given module is supposed to operate. Such checks are obviously redundant by design. I don't want to pick on the technicality of suppressible messages. What bothers me is that perhaps here we see something deeper, namely that the optimality of code is not in the same plane as quality or security of code, that perhaps these goals are orthogonal, and if this should be the case, there is absolutely no hope of achieving one as you try to reach the other.

Constructing Quality Software, P.G. Hibbard/S.A. Schuman (eds.)

STATIC SEMANTIC CHECKS IN AN OPEN-ENDED LANGUAGE

by

Hartmut Feuerhahn
(Technische Universität Berlin)

Cornelis H.A. Koster
(Katholieke Universiteit Nijmegen)

March 1977

ABSTRACT

Static semantic checking is the investigation by the compiler of the plausibility of a syntactically correct program. This paper discusses the nature and limitations of static semantic checking, especially when applied to an open-ended language, using the semantic checks in the CDL2 compiler as an example.

KEYWORDS

Static semantics, semantic checking, open-ended languages, extensible languages.

0. INTRODUCTION

By "static semantic checking" we mean the investigation of the plausibility of a syntactically correct program, based on an analysis of the flow-of-control and flow-of-data in the program, verifying semantic properties of the program that can be verified statically, i.e. at compile time.

This check may (classically) answer such questions as:

- do all applied identifiers have a defining occurrence?
- are, in all assignations, the types of source and destination compatible?
- is the result of dereferencing a reference compatible with the use made of it?

but for some languages it may also determine:

- do all variables have defined values upon being used?
- are various parts of the program free from side effects upon one another?

and other questions pertaining to the execution of the program but answerable at compile time.

Such a static semantic check attempts to catch semantic errors which would otherwise be detected only dynamically, which will

- shorten the test phase and the whole implementation process
- increase the reliability of the product, and
- improve maintainability.

In this paper, we will be concerned with the feasibility of static semantic checking, and with aspects of the design of a language that affect the effectiveness and the efficiency of such a check.
In particular, we will discuss the question how such a check can be made for an open-ended language, i.e. a language which allows in its programs the application of algorithms, objects and types defined outside the framework of the language itself. The techniques described here are not new, but both their actual feasibility and the design choices made in the open-ended implementation language CDL2 may be of interest.

1. OPEN-ENDED LANGUAGES

It will be necessary to first clarify our notion of open-endedness, and its relation to extensibility.

The constructs occurring in a programming language may be classified as follows:

- elementary constructs forming the kernel of the language
  - elementary algorithms
    e.g. assignation, jump, selection, subscription
  - elementary datatypes
    e.g. *bool* or *1..32767* or *BIN FIXED(32)*
- construction mechanisms for building composed constructs
  - control structures for constructing a composed algorithm out of other algorithms e.g. the classical Dijkstra control-structures, or LISP conditionals
  - data structures for constructing a composed datatype out of other datatypes
    e.g. *ref amode* or [ ] *amode* or *struct(amode a, b)*
- abstraction mechanisms for building new elementary constructs out of others through
  - naming
    e.g. in declarations for procedures, operations, types and objects
  - hiding and encapsulation
    e.g. class declarations, or modules with interfaces.

A language with well-developed abstraction mechanisms we will call an extensible language. Historically, extensible languages were conceived as a means to build (starting from the kernel of the language) a language level suitable for programming some specific class of programs. Therefore the emphasis was on syntactic extension (as, e.g. in GPL and ALGOL N). An example of syntactic extension is the addition of a *while*...*do* ..*od* statement to a language, expressing its semantics in terms of conditional jumps.

By an open-ended language we will mean an extensible language whose kernel is not (totally) fixed. In using an open-ended language, a suitable kernel is postulated and implemented separately (e.g. through a macro mechanism). The emphasis is therefore on semantic extension.

Examples of semantic extension are the borrowing of input/output procedures from a library by a language that lacks i/o primitives, or the addition to FORTRAN of subroutines for dynamic memory management written in assembly language.

There are many examples of extensible languages that are not open-ended since they have a fixed kernel: languages like ALGOL 68 among the high level languages, the macro assembly languages among the low level languages. A classical open-ended high level language is Strachey's GPM (General Purpose Macroprocessor).

1.1. OPEN-ENDED LANGUAGES AS SIL's

Programming in a language without a fixed kernel poses some problems, asking for sophisticated users. Their usage seems to be restricted to systems implementation, where they are of help in portability and adaptability: since the language kernel is not fixed, it can be chosen to suit the application and with one eye on portability. Also, open-endedness furnishes a systematic solution for the need expressed by machine oriented programmers to "have access to every bit and every instruction of their machine" in a SIL. Any general macro processor (e.g. STAGE2, ML/1) can be used as an open-ended language. Examples of partially open-ended languages there are many: in fact, library facilities and provisions for machine code procedures can be and have been used for semantic extension, adding features to a language that cannot usefully be expressed in the language itself (e.g. FORTRAN + assembly language patches).

MARY is a partially open-ended language because of its facility for the inclusion of arbitrary instructions from the target machine; this facility is used in the "implementation prelude" to provide machine-orientation and thus enhance efficiency, and also gives the programmer access to the interrupt system, status bits and other odds and ends. The open-endedness of MARY was considered unsafe and undesireable by its authors, but has clearly been found unavoidable.

An extreme example of an open-ended language is CDL [1,2], whose kernel language is practically empty: all operations and data access primitives have to be borrowed from the target language by means of macros and can then be composed by built-in control structures and abstracted by procedures. This extreme position has proved very illuminating, forcing the programmers to be aware of the fundamental questions of portability, adaptability and efficiency.

2. SEMANTIC CHECKS

By a static semantic check we mean an investigation by the compiler of the plausibility of a syntactically correct program, taking into account only those properties of the program which can be analyzed statically, i.e. without actually executing it.

Such a check is by no means a proof of the correctness of the program, which would necessitate checking the program against some specification. In most cases, no suitable specification is available. The program can only be checked against itself: it can be checked for the absence of contradictions and patent impossibilities, making use of any useful redundancy present in it.

2.1. USEFUL REDUNDANCY

What constitutes useful redundancy?
The prime example of redundancy in programming languages is the presence of typed declarations.

Although such declarations are often not necessary (declarations by default as in FORTRAN or dynamic typing as in APL can be implemented just as well) they provide for redundancy, allowing:

1) the detection of most spelling errors in identifiers which, in languages with default declarations, might lead to surprising program behaviour whose cause may be hard to find by testing
2) the static attribution of a type to objects, allowing the prohibition of assignations to unsuitable variables and the applications of unsuitable operations.

That is, declarations introduce useful redundancy.
Redundancy is not useful when it cannot be checked, (e.g. comments), when it is not mandatory (like the optional *goto* symbol in ALGOL 68) or when it serves merely to check whether the programmer at one place in his program can repeat what he has said at another, e.g. the destination list in an assigned goto in FORTRAN.

A useful redundancy specifies abstractly the intention of the programmer, in such a way that it can be checked against his concrete actions elsewhere in the program.

In designing a programming language, useful redundancy should be introduced systematically. As an example, we will discuss the redundancies introduced into CDL2 in chapter 3.

In the next sections we will discuss some limitations and problems in static checking.

2.2. INCOMPLETENESS OF A STATIC SEMANTIC CHECK

A static semantic check can of necessity not be complete: the compiler knows only the static properties of the program and will therefore have to make worst-case assumptions ("if something can go wrong, it will").
In the first place, the knowledge of the flow-of-control may be insufficient.

As an example, consider the following piece of program:

```
if (p * p)mod 4 = 2
then real a; # uninitialized # print (a)
fi
```

It is not reasonable to demand from the compiler that it knows that the square of an integer number modulo four can assume only the values 0 or 1 (did you know it?), and that therefore the condition always yields false. The semantic check should report a potential error, even though the clever programmer might have known that the error cannot occur.

In competently written programs, such cleverness should be infrequent, and since the behaviour of programs depends critically on their input, we will have to assume that all paths through a program are taken, and therefore report all potential errors. This may mean, especially for the tricky programs, that some pieces of a program which are not obviously correct are indicated as potential errors. From an engineering standpoint this makes good sense, since a program which is not obviously correct may be a source of pitfalls in maintenance. A program, like Caesar's wife, should be above suspicion.

Apart from the lack of knowledge about the dynamic flow of control, another reason for incompleteness of static semantic checks may be the lack of knowledge about the identity of variables.

In order to answer e.g. the question "does each variable have a defined value upon being used", the compiler has to know what variables are assigned to. We will term a variable x an alias for a variable y if an assignment to y affects the value of x, as in

```
begin real x;
      procedure f(y); y := 0;
      procedure p; f(x);
      procedure t(z); z;
      t(p);
      print (x)
end
```

Whether such questions are statically decideable depends on the presence in the language of such alias-makers as the FORTRAN EQUIVALENCE statement, the PASCAL pointer assignment or the ALGOL 68 identity declarations of the form

<u>ref</u> <u>amode</u> *x* = *y*

To make matters worse, aliasing may be dynamic as in

<u>ref</u> <u>amode</u> *x* = *y1*[*i*]

making it under circumstances impossible to decide statically whether the array *y1* has been properly initialized.
The systematic avoidance of any dangerous aliasing has been the primary design goal of the language EUCLID [10].
In [3] it is discussed in the context of ALGOL 60 how the presence or absence of certain language properties may affect the static decideability of specific properties of programs; in particular this article shows the necessity of full specification of formal parameters.

2.3. INCOMPLETENESS CAUSED BY OPEN-ENDEDNESS OF THE LANGUAGE

Open-endedness of the language is another cause of incompleteness of the static semantic check. Fundamentally, the semantics of borrowed algorithms is outside the scope of the check, and any knowledge about the effect of such algorithms has to be introduced explicitly by a specification under the responsibility of the programmer. Without such a specification, it would be impossible to write meaningful programs. The correctness of the specification itself cannot be decided within the framework of the language, but has to be trusted.

As an example, the specification of a library routine

<u>proc</u>(<u>real</u>)<u>real</u> *sin* = <u>fromlib</u>

allows a modicum of security in calling that routine, provided the specification adequately and correctly captures the relevant properties of the corresponding library routine.

In designing an open-ended language, the necessary redundancy has to be carefully tailored in, to minimize the unavoidable risks.

Specifications of a borrowed algorithm can include

1) its logical effect, given in the form of logical or algebraic axioms (not pursued in this paper)
2) the type of its result
3) the number, order and types of its parameters
4) its calling mode (e.g. an algorithm borrowed from PL/1 may have to be called differently than one borrowed from LISP)
5) the presence or absence of side-effects.

The obvious way to include such specifications into a language is to demand the writing of a heading for each algorithm to be borrowed.

Whether the semantics of the algorithm borrowed fits the heading is lastly the responsibility of the programmer writing the algorithm, who will have to program in a disciplined fashion.

Open-endedness should be used to introduce a small number of primitives, whose relevant properties are specified as precisely as possible, and *not* for the promiscuous spread of code inserts all over the program demanded by ill-informed assembly programmers as a precondition for reluctantly writing their programs in a systems implementation language.

3. STATIC SEMANTIC CHECKING IN CDL2: A CASE STUDY

As an illustration of the ideas and problems treated in the previous sections, we will discuss the semantic check implemented for CDL2. Since CDL2 has been described in other publications, only those of its properties relevant for the semantic investigation are outlined, in order to show how decisions taken in the design of the language influence the feasibility of static semantic checks.

3.1. PROGRAM STRUCTURE

Apart from constructs for modularization and information hiding which are not discussed here, CDL2 programs consist of a collection of declarations, followed by a sequence of calls. The objects declared are:

- *procedures* with parameters and local variables
- *macros* that serve as a means for semantic extension by means of borrowing from a target language
- *variables*; named *constants*; and fixed size *arrays*.

The macros and procedures together will be termed the *algorithms*.

At the end of the program there are one or more *root calls*, which serve as start calls for the program. In addition, *prelude calls* may be defined, which are performed before the first root call and serve for initializing. *Postlude calls*, which finalize the program, are called after the last root call. Preludes and postludes are not essential for a CDL2-program, but facilitate such tasks as the opening and closing of files, initializing of stack pointers etc. - routines of a low level of abstraction, which otherwise had to be passed through the whole hierarchy to the root.

3.2. PROCEDURE STRUCTURE

All procedures yield a boolean result which is used to guide the flow of control. The body of a procedure consists of a number of *alternatives*, interconnected with the "McCarthy *or*" (i.e. not evaluating the second operand if the first yields *true*). An alternative consists of a number of calls of algorithms (the *members*) interconnected with the "McCarthy *and*" (i.e. not evaluating the second operand if the first yields *false*).

The grouping of a number of alternatives by enclosing them between brackets, a repetition operator and leave operators complete the control structures. The resulting algorithm structure could hardly be more concise. It may be modelled by a binary graph [5]. Furthermore, due to the absence of jumps, it has the properties claimed by Dijkstra [9] for structured programming. The flow graphs are "reducible" [8, 10] and easily analyzable and optimizable.

3.3. SPECIFICATIONS

The basis for the semantic checking possibilities in CDL2 are the concise specifications of attributes of each algorithm with regards to its result, its global effect and its parameters.

3.3.1. SPECIFICATION OF THE RESULT

The body of an algorithm may be structured such that the algorithm always returns true (it always succeeds), or it may be such that it can also return false (it may fail). The programmer specifies for each algorithm whether it (according to her) may fail - this introduces redundancy. For a macro, such a specification is essential, since the desired information cannot be deduced automatically. For a procedure, this specification is redundant. The consistency of the calls and the procedure specifications throughout the program is checked in terms of the specifications of the algorithms.

3.3.2. SPECIFICATION OF THE GLOBAL EFFECT

Let us define as the environment of the program the set of all global variables, arrays and input/output files. A change to this environment is termed an activity. Any algorithm may perform an activity upon success, a so-called effect, or upon failure, which we then call a defect. As a consequence of the original idea of considering all procedures as parsing procedures, we consider defects as unwanted side-effects. In CDL2 defects are forbidden and effects must be specified explicitly

In connection with the result attribute, we distinguish four classes of algorithms:

failure possible, no effect - test
failure possible, effect - predicate
failure impossible, no effect - function
failure impossible, effect - action

3.3.3. SPECIFICATION OF PARAMETERS

In CDL2, parameters are passed via a copy/restore-mechanism, i.e. on each call, local variables are set up, which may be initialized with the value of the corresponding actual parameter (copy) and whose value may be passed to the corresponding actual parameter after elaboration of the procedure (restore). The restoring takes place only after succesful elaboration of the algorithm. Upon failure, no restoring is done. It must be specified whether the parameters are copied on entry, restored upon success, or both. Furthermore, a procedure or macro may have _local_ variables. Parameters and local variables together are termed _affixes_. Each affix has one of the following four types according to its specification:

inherited	copied, not restored
derived	not copied, restored upon success
transient	copied, restored upon success
free	not copied, not restored (local variable).

It should be noted that in CDL2 only simple variables and constants can be used as actual parameters: neither arrays nor procedures can be passed as parameters, in order to ensure that the alias problem for simple variables is decideable.

3.4. VISIBILITY RULES

There are just two scope levels in CDL2 on which variables may be declared. The _program level_ consists of the (global) variables, constants and arrays, whose extent is the program. Restrictions on visibility are imposed by a partition of the programs into _layers_ and _sections_ (see [1] and [4]). Variables and arrays can only be accessed in the section in which they are declared, and they cannot be passed through an interface.

On the _algorithm level_, affixes are declared whose scope is the algorithm. Their extent is the incarnation of the procedure or macro that they are local to. There is no nesting of procedure declarations, there is no passing of procedures as parameters, there is no block structure within procedures.

4. LOCAL SEMANTIC CHECK

This part of the semantic check deals with one procedure at a time, checking its body against its heading, i.e. checking the programmer's actions against his intentions.

The body of the procedure is represented by its _control graph_ (see 4.1). For every affix and every node of the graph an _abstract value_ is calculated denoting properties of the values the affix may take at execution time upon reaching the node (see 4.2). The environment and changes to that environment are modelled by one extra pseudo affix with type _global_. Using these terms, we may formulate certain conditions on the use of affix values, which are to be checked (see 4.3).

4.1. THE STRUCTURE OF THE CONTROL GRAPH

The nodes of the control graph are the members of the body of the procedure, i.e. calls for algorithms. If the algorithm called may succeed or fail, two edges leave the member, one labelled t and one labelled f (the _true edge_ and the _false edge_). If the algorithm called cannot fail, it is only left by a true edge. All members of one alternative are interconnected sequentially by their true edges, while all false edges point to the first member of the next alternative. The true edge of the last member of each alternative points to the *true exit*, while the false edges of all members of the last alternative point to the *false exit*. This structure may be modified by the use of operators for repetition and leave and by grouping. The graphs in question can be composed out of four kinds of elements:

call for a *test* or *predicate*: 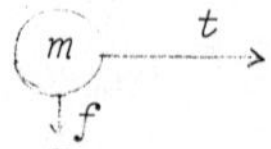

call for a *function* or *action*: 

true exit 

false exit 

One of the members is reached upon entering the rule. We call the corresponding node the *entrance*. The *true successor* of a member m is the node pointed to by m's true edge, its *false successor* is the node pointed to by its false edge.

4.2. ABSTRACT VALUES

The *abstract value* of an affix denotes properties of the set of values the affix may take at execution time. The properties we are interested in, are:

- is the value *undefined*?
- is the value the one given by copying the actual parameter before elaboration of the rule (value *inherited* from caller)?
- has the value been assigned by some call for an algorithm (value *derived* from called), and if so, by which one?

Since some paths through the program graph may join, more than one of the cases above may in general occur at a node. Thus the abstract values are modelled by sets which are constructed by union of the following elementary abstract values:

$$\{undef\},\ \{inherited\},\ \{der_m \mid m \text{ member of the rule}\}$$

We say a value is *assigned* to an affix a by some member m if m has that affix at a derived or transient position. A value is assigned to the pseudo affix modelling the environment if m has some global variable at a derived or transient position or if m is a call for an *action* or *predicate* (thus, all global variables are lumped together).

An affix is *used* by a member m if m has the affix at an inherited or transient position. An affix is used by the *true exit* if it has the type *derived* or *transient*. The pseudo affix is used by every node.

The calculation of the abstract values AV may then proceed iteratively as follows, using well-known techniques (see e.g. [7]).

step_1

for all nodes n and for all affixes a: $AV(a,n) := \emptyset$

step_2

for all affixes a with type free or derived:

$AV(a, entrance) := \{undef\}$

for all affixes a with type inherited, transient and global: $AV(a, entrance) := \{inherited\}$

step_3

We now have to walk through the graph starting at the entrance and performing calculations of the abstract values at each node. In the case of loops, parts of the graph will have to be considered more than once; the walk ends, if in any step no abstract value has been changed anymore. Termination of the algorithm is guaranteed by the fact that abstract values are only changed by adding elements to them.

Upon passing a member m the following calculations have to be done for every affix a:

$$AV(a, falsesucc(m)) := AV(a,m) \cup AV(a, falsesucc(m))$$

a is not assigned to by m

$$AV(a, truesucc(m)) := AV(a,m) \cup AV(a, truesucc(m))$$

a is assigned to by m

$$AV(a, truesucc(m)) := \{der_m\} \cup AV(a, truesucc(m))$$

.3. CONDITIONS ON THE USE OF ABSTRACT VALUES

Using the abstract values calculated above and some additional information obtainable from the graph, the following conditions are checked:

- no undefined value may be used neither by assigning it to the input parameter of a called algorithm nor by restoring it upon success. If a node n uses an affix a, then

  $$\{undef\} \cap AV(a,n) \overset{!}{=} \emptyset$$

  The sign "$\overset{!}{=}$" is to be read as "must be".
- every value that is not undefined, should be used somewhere, otherwise its computation was superfluous.

  We may model this be constructing for each affix a possibly used abstract value PAV, which is the union of all abstract values of the affix ommitting $\{undef\}$. Then we can construct the used abstract value UAV as the union of all abstract values which are used.

  $$PAV(a) := \cup_n AV(a,n) \setminus \{undef\}$$

  $$UAV(a) := \cup_n (AV(a,n) \mid n \text{ uses } a)$$

  $$PAV(a) \overset{!}{=} UAV(a)$$

- no value, that has been created by an assignment in one alternative, may be passed to any alternative following it (<u>independence of alternatives</u> within a procedure body).

  $AV(a,n) \cap \{ der_m \mid m \text{ is in a previous alternative} \} \overset{!}{=} \emptyset$

- a transient affix must obtain a value somewhere. For all affixes a with type <u>transient</u>:

  $AV(a, \textit{true exit}) \overset{!}{\neq} \{\textit{inherited}\}$

- no activity may be performed upon failure (defect). For the pseudo affix *global* :

  $AV(\textit{global}, \textit{false exit}) \overset{!}{=} \{\textit{inherited}\}$

- if the procedure has one of the types <u>action</u> or <u>predicate</u>, it must have an effect. For the pseudo affix *global*:

  $AV(\textit{global}, \textit{true exit}) \overset{!}{\neq} \{\textit{inherited}\}$

- if the procedure has one of the types <u>function</u> or <u>test</u>, it must not have an effect.

  $AV(\textit{global}, \textit{true exit}) \overset{!}{=} \{\textit{inherited}\}$

5. GLOBAL SEMANTIC CHECK

Due to the large amount of time and space which would be necessary for a complete analysis, the control over the use of global variables will not be made as tight as the control over affixes. It is checked, whether undefined values of global variables may be used somewhere. Notice that this check is concerned with simple variables only, since access to composed variables (e.g. arrays or structures) does not belong to CDL2 but is borrowed, and can therefore not be checked.

5.1. CONTROL OVER INITIALIZATION VERSUS STATIC INITIALIZATION

Some languages (e.g. BCPL) force the programmer to initialize all global variables when declaring them. For CDL2, this does not seem to be the right way, since the variables may then only be initialized by constants or by previously defined variables. Firstly, this is sensitive to the specific order of the declarations, which we would like to avoid. Secondly, even though for some kinds of variables the static initialization may work (initialize with "zero" or "nil"), for others they make no sense (how to initialize a global variable that is to hold some attribute of the current element of a huge data structure?). Even if in such a case the programmer initializes the variable with an "impossible" value and checks for that, he has to perform runtime tests in order to find out if there exists some path in his program leading to the use of this "impossible" value. The compiler can carry a big part of this work on its shoulders, testing statically if a variable may be used uninitialized - provided the language does not enforce static initialization in those cases where this makes no sense.

5.2. GLOBAL SEMANTIC CHECK IN CDL2

CDL2 has some properties that simplify a global check:

- the impossibility of exporting variables from one section to another and the parameter mechanism by copy/restore decrease the number of global variables to be treated at any time.
- most of the variables - at least those used throughout the program - are initialized in the prelude part and thus need not be considered in the main part of the program.
- the structure of CDL2 programs as a hierarchy of rules gives rise to a rather efficient "bottom-up" analysis hardly applicable to languages with a more complicated structure.
- due to the copy/restore parameter mechanism and the absence of formal procedures, the alias problem is for simple variables decideable, so that the flow of data can easily be analyzed.

The global check could be extended to keep track of not only the defined/undefined values, but also of the range of a (defined) value. The mechanism should not be entirely different (see [7] and [12]).

5.3. THE METHOD

For every procedure, it is possible to calculate the set of variables that must be initialized before calling it. Let us call this set the use of the procedure. It is also possible to calculate the set of variables that are initialized by the procedure: this is the set of global variables that obtain values on all possible paths through its body to the success exit, but which are not contained in its use. This set is called the yield of the procedure.

If we calculate these two sets for all procedures, including a quasi-procedure constructed from the prelude, root and postlude-calls of the program, all variables which are in the use of that quasi-procedure are used somewhere without initialization.

We can improve this algorithm by performing the calculation just for the first prelude call and then disregarding the variables which are in the yield of that prelude call. Repeating these steps for all prelude, root and postlude-calls, we get a decreasing number of variables for each step. Since our experience shows that most of the global variables are initialized in the prelude-part, the analysis of roots, which contain most of the rules, does not have to consider many variables.

5.4. GLOBAL SEMANTIC CHECK AND SEPARATE COMPILATION

Allowing separate compilation and, therefore, also separate checking of program parts prevents such a complete global semantic check as described above.

Within the framework of our checks, it is especially interesting if some provided algorithm uses variables, which have to be initialized by either another imported algorithm or by some prelude or root-call. The conditions that have to be fulfilled between modules are simple as long as no mutual intermodule communication is allowed, e.g. if the modules form a hierarchy. Having completely unrestricted communication between modules, the conditions obtain such a complexity that they may hardly be checked.

A typical problem is the following:

defining module	applying module
exports *get first, get next*	imports *get first, get next*
⋮	⋮

In some defining module we have implemented the access procedures *get first* and *get next* . The procedure *get next* uses the value of some hidden variables that have first to get a value by a call of *get first* . Thus, the question whether those hidden variables can have an undefined value upon being used depends on the order in which these procedures are called in the applying module.

As long as we compile the two modules together, it is possible to check globally that no uninitialized variables are used.

When separately compiling these two modules we have a problem - in compiling the defining module we do not know the order of the calls; in compiling the applying module we do not know the restrictions on the order of calls.

We see two possible ways of retaining the global check even when separately compiling:

5.4.1. ADDING REDUNDANCY

In the spirit of this paper we introduce redundancy to specify order, in a form resembling path-expressions but checked at compile time, e.g.

order *get first, get next*★.

Adding this meta-algorithmic specification of the order of the calls to the defining module would allow a check that, under this ordering of calls, no uninitialized variable is used.

Adding this specification to the applying environment would allow a check that this order of calls is adhered to.

It is hard to prove statically that calls take place in a specific order, especially due to incomplete knowledge of the flow of control, but one can again take the position that only programs that are obviously and provably correct should be accepted

5.4.2. CHECKING DONE BY A HIGH-LEVEL LINKER

An alternative solution is to leave the problem altogether to such a high-level linker: in compiling either module we may extract information modelling the module interdependencies which could not be checked. These extracts should not be too complex and too big. Their consistency can be checked incrementally in separately compiling and linking modules.

6. CONCLUSION

In using implementation languages, the presence of a static semantic check can catch a great many errors which would otherwise be found only by runtime tests.

Of the semantic checks for CDL2 described here, the local check has been in use since early 1976. It has been improved several times, and is now in a secure and balanced stage. The global check is currently being implemented and has not yet been tested with users.

After initial resistance from our (quite conservative) users, and improvements to its human engineering, the semantic checker has come to be accepted as an extremely useful production tool. One reason why each CDL2 program is now routinely checked, is the speed at which it is performed. The local check needs about 16 seconds of CPU time for a 5000 lines program on an IBM 370/158. This contrasts favourably to the 0.3 to 0.5 seconds per FORTRAN statement mentioned for a similar (but weaker) checker implemented on a CDC 6400 by Fosdickand Osterweil [11], which in that form seems hardly applicable to large programs.

The methods given should be of value to implementation languages in general. Some properties seem to be essential for the application of the checks:

- the copy/restore parameter mechanism and the absence of procedures as parameters are necessary (even though not sufficient) for solving the Alias-problem and simplifying the checks on data flow
- tight visibility control and a simplified blockstructure enhance the perspicuity of the program and reduce the complexity of the calculations involved in the checks
- in designing an open-ended implementation language, useful redundancy should carefully be introduced.

ACKNOWLEDGEMENT

The authors are grateful to the referees for their strongly voiced constructive and destructive criticism of the first draft of this paper.

REFERENCES

[1] J.-P. Dehottay, H. Feuerhahn, C.H.A. Koster, H.M. Stahl, Syntaktische Beschreibung von CDL2, TU Berlin, Informatik, September 1976

[2] C.H.A. Koster, CDL - A Compiler Implementation Language, In Methods of Algorithmic Language Implementation, Lecture notes in Computer Science 47, Springer Verlag, Berlin 1977

[3] H. Langmaack, On Correct procedure parameter transmission in higher programming Languages, Acta Informatica 2, 1973

[4] C.H.A. Koster, Visibility and Types, In Proceedings of an ACM Conference on Data Abstraction, SIGPLAN Notices vol 8 no 2, March 1976

[5] H. Feuerhahn, A Binary Control Structure and its Relationship to Grammars and Side-Effects, In Proceedings of the 4th annual GI Meeting, Lecture Notes in Computer Science 26, Springer-Verlag, Berlin 1975

[6] H. Feuerhahn, Semantische Oberprüfung und Optimierung von CDL-Programmen, TU Berlin, FB 20, Diplomarbeit, June 75

[7] P. Cousot, R. Cousot, Static Verification of Dynamic Type Properties of Variables, In Proceedings 4th ACM SIGACT-SIGPLAN Symposium on Principles of Programming Languages St. Monica, CA, Jan. 1977

[8] F.E. Allen, Control Flow Analysis, SIGPLAN Notices 5/7, July 1970

[9] O.J. Dahl, E.W. Dijkstra, C.A.R. Hoare, Structured Programming, Academic Press, London, 1972

[10] B.W. Lampson, J.J. Horning, R.L. London, J.G. Mitchel, and G.L. Popek, Report On The Programming Language Euclid, SIGPLAN Notices vol 12, no 2, February 1977

[11] L.D. Fosdick, L.J. Osterweil, Data Flow Analysis in Software Reliability, ACM Computing Surveys 8/3, Sept. 76

[12] G.A. Killdal, A Unified Approach to Global Program Optimization, ACM Symposium on Principles of Programming Languages, Boston, October 1973

Feuerhahn and Koster : Discussion

King, J.: I asked the last speaker about the chance of the user being overwhelmed by unnecessary warning messages and I'd like to ask you the same question.

Koster: It is a difficult matter of human engineering to make the right interface between your inhumanly clever compiler and your users. This has also for us been a matter of care. We have redefined the interface a number of times, and I'm not at all happy. One thing is to try to keep the number of error messages down which you can do by a number of techniques. The "axe method" of course is to suppress messages. I would suggest a slightly gentler method, namely to classify errors into classes. For instance, we are using the classes fatal error, warning and hint, and we never show more than two classes, starting with the most dangerous one. While it's true that some information is lacking at first, at least the programmer can bring his program into order sequentially. Secondly, you have to take measures to prevent secondary errors, and I think that the main point there is that you have to adopt the following philosophy. At the definition you check what the programmer says. For instance, if he says that thing does not have side effects, then you check him damn well. But, at the application, you believe him. So, if he has said that it has no side effects and you know it has, you still check on under the assumption that it had none. So this partitions the errors into global ones and local ones and gives an approximation to the right place for the detection of a specific error. Still, I would dearly like this kind of thing, namely the careful and sensible design of a human interface, to be a matter of academic study.

King, J.: Let me state that I think that this and the previous paper are obviously related to the topic of this conference. [☺] If a compiler with the additional features they've discussed will find more errors in my program than one that doesn't have them, it seems to me that there is no way that this can't be beneficial. But if I'm right and these are perhaps the first two papers which have really addressed the theme of the conference, then it's a shame that they are such a small part of it, even if this particular error detection is only a very small part of the whole process of constructing quality software. I have three questions that I would like to address to both authors.

The first was dealt with to some extent by Koster. It concerns the cost of doing all this. There seems to be a paradox in this work, in that the time when we are interested in detecting errors is when we want to run a fast compiler, doing check-out. The ideal situation is to run the optimizing compiler just once, at the end, to get good code for production purposes. If I use these systems, I will have to run the optimizing compiler all the time, because I will need it to find these errors early. It seems that that may increase the cost.

Koster: Allow me one remark on the question of cost. Let me tell you that the bottleneck in the CDL2 system on the IBM 360 is the assembler. Therefore, the default of our compiler is optimize, because if we do not optimize, we lose more time in assembly.

Ershov: I have an immediate counter-question to King. If you speak about the cost, what is your prospective estimate? What is more beneficial: for a programmer to spend three days in making plausible conclusions or semantic checks of his program in his office for three times his daily salary, or to spend one hour of computer time getting his results immediately?

King, J.: I don't think it would be that bad.

Bell: I'd like to add a couple of points on the question of costs. The first is that I think people often overestimate the cost of global flow analysis or optimization or other techniques based upon it. Our experience with production quality compilers is that global flow analysis only adds about 50% to the run time on the average. The second point is that since it's well known that most runs of a compiler encounter errors, that says to me that sooner or later the errors are going to have to be discovered and so that one is probably better advised to spend the machine time finding the errors sooner rather than later, and that even from the point of view of net machine time, time will be saved by doing the checking early. My final point is that it's really axiomatic that the cost of machine time and of machines is going down, and that nothing else connected with the production of quality software is.

Dewar: I should like to point out that these techniques of optimization that lead to suggested implausibilities I think are also useful with respect to low-level programming in either very low-level systems implementation languages or assembly language itself: places where you wouldn't normally consider doing global flow tracing. An enormously large percentage of assembly language errors could in fact be detected by this kind of static checking. In some sample code that I have looked at, well over half of ordinary bugs could be found that way.

King, J.: My second question concerns the fact that checking schemes seem to involve a lot of worst-case analysis; they have to assume that the worst possible case could occur. This is one thing that leads to the large number of warning messages you get. Can't we do better than that? Perhaps we can use some of the techniques which have been developed for proving correctness of programs. We could ask the users to give us a little more information, perhaps some inductive information, to help us check some of these things, and thereby avoid a worst-case analysis.

Koster: How to avoid worst case? It's very simple really. If you want to have more intelligence, introduce it. Add redundancy indicating further information about your program which is checkable. There you can have a complete continuous spectrum between say APL programs, where essentially nothing is statically checkable, and for instance ALPHARD. I would also like to take issue with you that it is bad to have worst case. Actually, if you have designed such a system sensibly, the simplifications are often quite acceptable. But the assumption, that if something can conceivably go wrong it will go wrong (because some stupid idiot will later modify the program out of all resemblance to the previous structure), is a worthy assumption. So I think that the discipline which is enforced by such a checker, if well designed, can and should be lived with.

Sintzoff: I would like to ask a naive question concerning precisely the quality of the checks which are made. For the first such systems, the great number of warnings which were generated show that very crude approximations were used. Now my question is the following: couldn't we think of increasing the quality of the approximation in some sense, still keeping it quite feasible but thereby making a significant improvement in the quality of the result or the warnings?

Koster: Generally I would say that doing that with existing programming languages may be very difficult if they are not designed for the purpose. If you take the example of FORTRAN, then the static alias problem is decidable, but dynamic aliasing, when the correctness of a piece of program depends on the actual values of indices for instance, is just not within your grasp. The only language that I can mention for which these techniques would be applicable to the dynamic case is EUCLID. I am actually making my point not so much in the attempt to save existing languages, but to argue for extending new languages right from the beginning with the necessary mechanisms which make this check worthwhile.

King, J.: I asked the question about doing better than worst casing because I have an answer. My work has been in proving correctness of programs. Lately we've been working on symbolic execution of programs to analyze them. I find that people who have traditionally written compilers don't like that at all, because they say, "I have to do theorem proving," or "I have to do formula manipulation – you don't put that in a compiler; what's wrong with you?" Compilers do global flow analysis and they make graphs and they abstract and throw information away so that they can get the analysis done. It seems to me that both proving correctness and optimizing compiler people can learn from one another. I don't find it objectionable to think that I might have a theorem prover in the bowels of my optimizing compiler, and that it might attempt to prove theorems and do formula manipulation. There are many examples where the typical optimizing compiler built today can't detect certain cases that are fairly easy to detect if you do something like symbolically executing down particular paths. Suppose we test if x is positive, and then change x by adding 1 or 2 or multiplying or applying some simple arithmetic function to x. If we then check if some other expression involving x is positive, an optimizing compiler typically won't pick that up unless it's something very simple like x+1 or x-1; but with a very small amount of symbolic execution you can pick it up right away.

Goos: My real question concerns the perspectives of this method and verification. I agree that verification requires specification which very often is difficult or unpleasant. Secondly, it's clear that this method is applicable immediately while verification has still a way to go. However I see certain cases where this method is applicable, but verification will not be applicable; for instance, when you have open-endedness and you borrow semantics. Whenever you take semantics from somewhere, you have also to bring in the rules, which is a much more difficult task. I cannot see how you solve that.

King, J.: You said that verification requires a specification, so it seems to me that I would just borrow the specification as well, and then I can do it - verify it. The relation I see between verification and plausibility checking was explained I think fairly well by Koster in his transparencies. He said that it is a matter of checking redundancy. He is willing to check the redundancy that is there in the code without having any specifications; verification is essentially checking redundancy between the specifications and the code. So it's just a matter of what you are doing a consistency check between. In the compiler case it's between different aspects of the programming language and in verification it's between the specification and the programming language. It gets fuzzy what is a programming language and what is a specification language in lots of cases. A particular case is if you want to define a type as positive integer, then it's in the programming language. If you put an assertion in the program that says $x \geq 0$, then it's in the specification, and it seems to me that these things can move back and forth. So I see it as a spectrum of things you can do.

Holager: It seems to me ,that in large systems, there is one type of error which is particularly hard to catch. That is when you have a piece of algorithm that inputs complex data. Its function should be to handle a number of different cases characterized by combinations of values in the data. A very typical and unpleasant type of error is that the algorithm is not handling one of the cases which in fact is present in the data. I don't think any of the checking systems we have been hearing about can catch that. And mode typing schemes are not able to catch it. Does anyone have any idea of what we can do to catch this sort of error?

King, J.: At some point you are going to start calling this "proving correctness of programs". It just depends at which point you want to change the name. If you keep saying, "I want to catch this error, I want to catch that error," pretty soon you will say, "I want to show that the program meets its specifications exactly." It just depends upon where you want to stop. Actually, proving correctness of programs is probably the wrong name. Often people talk about proving assertions about programs. You can put in an assertion to that effect, and try to verify it. It's just a matter of degree as far as I'm concerned. I mean, whatever name you want to call it, static checking or program verification, it ultimately amounts to very similar work.

Holager: But is that practical now and if so, with which system? Where can we find a system for handling this particular class of error, which in my experience has been particularly difficult?

King, J.: I think that in limited cases you can do it now. There was a paper I heard recently, by Cousot of Grenoble, about checking pointers using static analysis. It seems to me he has carried some of this stuff a lot further. There are a number of things you can do with proving assertions about programs. The question is primarily how complicated the assertions are, and how much effort you are willing to put into a theorem prover.

Dewar: I think the concept that there is a continuum here is a very important one. I don't like the use of the phrase "absolutely correct". I think I can give convincing examples of programs which are reliable and definitely not correct by any possible interpretation of that word. But if you think in terms of proving certain things about programs, with more or less effort, with more or less perseverance, then the entire concept is a more plausible one.

King, J.: My third and final question is one that interests me very much. It seems to me that systems such as those presented here can be built: CDL2 is operational, Fosdick and Osterweil's system runs. But how many practicing programmers have the benefit of these systems? There seems to be a gap between what we know how to do, what we have developed, and what is really in practice. This question I would ask of everyone. When we get a technique like this that is obviously going to be of some help, how can we get it to be used, how can we put it into the field and really make it useful?

Koster: For CDL2 I can tell you how many users there are: three generations of 70 students and at the moment, I would say about 30 university and even industrial users. All in Germany. Would any of you like the system? [The response is underwhelming.] Seriously, if this kind of technology is going to get into use, it is only because somebody uses it. If everybody waits for somebody else to use it, then we will wait till the end of the world. There is a dangerous tendency with computer scientists to write their own systems from scratch rather than to try out somebody else's. I think that is dangerous, insofar as we never reach the point where we seriously criticize somebody else's work from direct experience. We are so polite to one another; why not be impolite and try it out?

Constructing Quality Software, P.G. Hibbard/S.A. Schuman (eds.)

PROGRAM TEXT AND PROGRAM STRUCTURE*

Lambert Meertens
Mathematical Centre, Amsterdam

Even if a program has been developed in a structured way, its structure need not be reflected in the final program text. Modifications, which are an important part of programming, should be applied at the highest appropriate level of abstraction and worked out downward from there. It is hard to enforce this discipline if a low-level program text is available: such a text lacks the proper structure and thus invites patches. This implies that the program text, as kept around, should reflect the structure of program development. A language feature is proposed for making the structure explicit that is introduced by the method of stepwise refinement.

0. INTRODUCTION

The deplorable quality of many software products is doubtlessly related to the complexity of the task of designing and developing programs. We have witnessed during the last ten years the emergence of a methodology to reduce such complexity by using structure. And yet, in spite of a widespread acceptance of the ideas involved, it appears that the general situation has not substantially improved. It may be that it is too early to notice the effects, but my assessment is different. The method of structured programming is much older than the notion: it is as old as the computer field. Generations of programmers have made use of structuring techniques without being aware that they were doing so. The merit of the prophets of Structured Programming is that they have described the method explicitly, have created the terminology for discussing the design process and have thereby done the groundwork for turning the art into a discipline. But it is one thing to accept a discipline, and another thing to apply it. Most larger software products are developed by teams that are under some kind of pressure to present tangible results, such as an "operational" system (for which it may suffice that it ostensibly does something, though nobody knows what and there is no way to find out).

For a radical improvement we need more than a method or discipline: we need tools with which the willing spirit can enforce the discipline upon his weak flesh. To be sure, already many such tools exist: in fact, each high-level programming language is one to some extent. But it is reasonable to expect that a tool will provide an appropriate support for a given task only

---

*This paper is registered at the Mathematical Centre as IW 78/77.

if it has explicitly been designed for that purpose. What we need are programming languages that have been designed with an explicit model of the program construction process in mind.

1. STRUCTURED PROGRAMMING

The term "structured programming" refers to the _process_ of program construction, rather than to any intrinsic property of program texts constructed in that fashion. It is theoretically possible - though highly unlikely - that a programmer who constructs his program in a most unsystematic way, eventually produces a program text identical to one developed by a colleague in the most structured way possible.

When I use the word "program", it means a program text _together with_ the structure implied by the way in which the text was constructed.

The task of a programmer is to bridge a gap between a top and a bottom: at the top he has a very abstract algorithm ("solve this problem") and at the bottom he has a collection of concrete types and operations supported by his machinery. His task is to implement the top algorithm in terms of the bottom operations. Two important principles he may use to bring structure in this task are:

(a) _Layers of abstraction_ (Dijkstra (1968)): Design a collection of data types with corresponding operations, and possibly some other operations. This collection describes an interface which factors the original task into two new tasks: (i) implement the top algorithm in terms of the operations of the interface, and (ii) implement the operations of the interface in terms of the bottom operations. The design of an interface is in a sense the design of a new, more problem-oriented, programming language.

(b) _Stepwise refinement_ (Wirth (1971)): Factor the original algorithm into a number of sub-algorithms. The program is then composed from the implementations of the sub-algorithms. This is clearly a top-down method.

It is tempting to view stepwise refinement as a special case of (a), since one might consider the sub-algorithms as operations of a new language. For example, if "interpret command" is refined to "IF command ok THEN execute command ELSE error message FI", this may be considered as the design of a new language with operations "command ok", "execute command" and "error message". This is, however, hardly helpful. The essential difference between the operations of a layer and such sub-algorithms, is that the operations of a programming language must have their semantics as simple as possible and be of general applicability, whereas the semantics of the sub-algorithms is in general quite complicated, and the applicability is limited to one (or once in a while perhaps two or three) occurrences, and only in conjunction with the other sub-algorithms.

It is better to consider (a) and (b) as different principles which support and supplement each other. Both create hierarchies, but of different natures: in one case an essentially linear hierarchy of layers (or programming languages), in the other case a (hierarchical) tree structure with the resulting program text as terminal nodes, where the intermediate nodes are labelled with the intermediate sub-algorithms. In either case the ordering in the hierarchy corresponds to the level of abstraction, but these hierarchies should not be confused with each other.

To illustrate the process of stepwise refinement I will spend some time on the problem of finding sentences of a context-free language that are palindromes. (The choice of problem is rather immaterial for the purpose of this paper. This problem has been selected since it has no obvious solution, for it is undecidable whether a given context-free language contains palindromes or not. For some languages, of course, the question is settled easy enough, but no general method to solve the matter is conceivable.) At this moment, I have only a vague notion how to attack such a problem, but an approach is suggested by the following consideration. The given problem is a special instance of the general problem to find common elements of two sets (which, in this case, are a context-free language and the set of palindromes). A procedure to solve this problem is to generate members from one set successively, and to test each element for membership of the other set.

The fact that the test for palindromicity is quite simple, whereas even the order n^3 test for membership of a general context-free language is rather complicated (generating the elements of a context-free language is in comparison almost trivial), and the fact that there are probably many more palindromes of a given length than sentences of the language of that length, both point in one direction: to generate sentences and to test for palindromicity. It is silly, of course, to generate a sentence completely if the first production step, say, already displays different terminal symbols at the front and at the end. This suggests a process where the generation process is guided by whatever terminal symbols have already appeared or may still appear at the front and at the end. The process should maintain a list of possible sentential forms (unfinished potential palindromes) and each time select productions conforming to the present findings, more or less like predictive parsing. Rather than taking the reader by the hand and developing the program "together", I immediately give some developmental steps as they occur to me now.

After the very first steps, the algorithm reads as follows:

```
read grammar;
determine possible first and last terminal symbols for productions;
initialize sentential form list;
WHILE neither list nor patience exhausted
DO develop promising form OD.
```

An obvious candidate for refinement is "develop promising form", and a possible text is:

```
select promising {short} form;
determine its kernel {i.e., what is left of the form if matching
    terminal symbols are deleted};
IF kernel is empty THEN solution found
ELSE develop form
FI;
remove form from list.
```

Next, "develop form" may be refined by replacing it by:

```
determine intersection between possible first and last terminal
    symbols of kernel;
FOR each terminal symbol in intersection
DO select corresponding productions;
   add developed forms to list
OD.
```

The following text has now been constructed:

```
read grammar;
determine possible first and last terminal symbols for productions;
initialize sentential form list;
WHILE neither list nor patience exhausted
DO select promising {short} form;
   determine its kernel {i.e., what is left of the form if matching
        terminal symbols are deleted};
   IF kernel is empty THEN solution found
   ELSE determine intersection between possible first and last
             terminal symbols of kernel;
        FOR each terminal symbol in intersection
        DO select corresponding productions;
           add developed forms to list
        OD
   FI;
   remove form from list
OD.
```

Although this is still a very simple piece of program, the structure is already starting to become less obvious, since some of the abstractions involved are no longer explicitly stated. When eventually all sub-algorithms have been worked out and have replaced their indicators in the above text, the tree-like way in which it was constructed will have been obscured completely. The conceptual units of the program will no longer be visible.

(It is too early for commitment as to an intermediate layer, but some outlines are becoming visible. A priority queue is needed, i.e., a list type to which elements may easily be added, and whose shortest element can easily be extracted. Alternatively, a simple queue could be used, in which case "promising" means: derived in few production steps).

2. MODIFIABILITY

As in any model, the ideal situation depicted above is a simplification The less ideal but more common case is that the programmer is not so lucky that he can plan his future steps in a surprise-free way. Even if he is quite experienced and very careful, many decisions will turn out to have such undesirable consequences that it is preferable to go back and change the decision (and the careful application of the above structuring principles tends to minimize the scope of the effects). If, however, the program is properly modified - a matter of discipline - it will eventually have the structure it would have had if the programmer had made the correct decisions immediately!

It is not only during program development that modifications are necessary. The situation that a large program has to be modified after it has been written is also extremely common. For example, a design requirement for all software products is that they behave "reasonably" even when the user exceeds the limits of the specifications. What "reasonable" means is a matter of user expectations and of human factors and cannot be defined formally. Anyone who has been exposed to software products will be able to supply a list of unreasonable properties that, though not bugs, are still intolerable. One cannot blame (at least, in many cases) the designers for not having foreseen the unfortunate consequences of the combined working of a number of decisions each of which is reasonable enough on its own. One ca only require that the product be modified.

It should be clear that the quality of a program depends strongly on its modifiability, if only because it is the result of a long sequence of modifications. If these modifications are done poorly, the quality of the program will be no better, however well designed the original program may have been.

If a program has to be modified, knowledge of the program structure is extremely important. The structure makes it possible to see if a proposed modification would have farther-reaching consequences than was intended. Alas, reconstruction from the program text of the way the program was constructed is in general an impossible task.

The reason for introducing the notion of program structure was to cater for the situation where the program is too complex to see and understand all elements and their interrelationships simultaneously. For the validity of the argument that knowledge of its structure is important, it is therefore completely irrelevant whether the modifier coincides with the original author.

. STRUCTURING PROGRAM TEXT

I hope the reader is convinced that the program structure must be described explicitly. But this is not enough. Not only must the program structure be made explicit, but this explicit description must also be modified in parallel with the program. It is better not to have any documentation than to have the documentation of a former version. Without documentation it is at least clear that to modify the program reliably one should discard the old text and start from scratch.

The most common reason for obsolescence of documentation is probably that it is just too easy to modify a program without corresponding modification of the documentation, or, to put it differently, that it is not easy enough to modify the documentation at the same time. It is not very realistic to expect that the quality of software will dramatically improve as long as this situation persists. The conclusion is that the structure of the program must be documented in the program text. In that way the documentation can be updated as a routine part of the modification of the program. Also, a description of the structure is always at hand when the program text is looked at. (Remember that the program structure was not an intrinsic part of the program text.)

For example, the "normal" way to implement a layer is to replace the abstract operations textually by the text of their implementations. In that case the structure is lost. What is needed is an explicit description of the interface that can be understood by the receiver of the high-level program text. The attention among language designers is now focussed to such an extent upon this issue (under the name of "abstract data types") that I shall spend no more words on it.

The same problem occurs with stepwise refinements. The normal way to perform a refinement step is to substitute the refinement body *in situ*. The final text is no longer reminiscent of the derivation process.

The solution should be obvious. Simply never perform a refinement step by literal in-situ substitution, but always *retain* the refinement as a functional part of the program. Of course! Why should such a clerical task as textual substitution be performed by the programmer, especially when it is harmful to him? The start of the palindrome program from Section 1 could then run exactly as it was developed there. The program text becomes a linearization of the program tree, with repetition of the node labels ("develop promising form", "develop form") serving as a pointer. Since now no low level text exists, it becomes even difficult to make a patch.

This requires of course new programming languages (or very simple extensions of existing ones.)

Several questions arise. The first question is whether one could not us procedures for refinements. The general answer is that procedures are a completely different language feature: procedures govern the dynamic flow o control, whereas refinements are intended to control the static program structure. Refinements are possible (and sensible) for languages that do no have procedures at all (e.g., specification languages) or for program parts not involving the flow of control (e.g., declarations). Moreover, for languages that do have procedures we may ask the question: if procedures would do, why, then, are they not used for the purpose? A probable reason i that a procedure call, even without parameters, is rather expensive. This i of course an implementation-dependent property and it is imaginable that an implementation would make the obvious optimization for a parameterless procedure that is called only once. But this makes the implementation more complicated, and we should not encourage programming language features whic require an optimization for special cases. It appears that procedures are too general a mechanism. If we look at the way procedures are used in practice, a rough division in three classes can be made: procedures for refinement purposes, which are called from one position without parameters and are not recursive (seldomly used and then only at a high level, near th top), procedures as building blocks for a layer, usually called from many places with parameters but also not recursive (except for the case where they traverse a recursive data structure), and finally procedures to "divid and conquer" a problem that can be expressed recursively, such as quicksort backtracking or formula manipulation. It is unlikely that one feature is th best way of serving such different uses. Anyway, procedures may have parameters and be called recursively, and both possibilities should be excluded for refinements. Another problem with procedures is that one certainly does not want procedures to inherit access rights from their environment automatically, whereas a refinement should inherit everything. For at the time the refinement is written, we do not even yet know what there is to be inherited. (This is in complete contrast with the operation of a layer, which should inherit nothing whatsoever across the interface, that is, statically.) Finally, many languages require definition of procedures before application, an acceptable restriction, except for refinements.

The next question (having settled that refinements are a language feature on their own) is the syntactic form of their "handle". I have chos the good old identifier. One reason is that it is an established way of naming programmer-defined entities. Another reason is that a good choice o identifiers is a better support to documentation than any other form I can think of. Identifiers almost compel a natural language choice, which, for not extremely formally inclined people, is a natural way to express the meaning of a sub-program on the proper level of abstraction. Even if a handle such as "$I := \{x \mid \exists u \in V_T\ [k \Rightarrow^* xu]\} \cap \{x \mid \exists v \in V_T\ [k \Rightarrow^* vx]\}$" wer allowed, the effect at best would be that the reader would blink a few tim and then exclaim: Oh! he means "determine intersection between possible first and last terminal symbols of k". Such formal expressions have a valu at the places where they belong - in the assertions of a formal correctnes proof. Another, admittedly weak, argument in favour of identifiers is the possibility to write a very simple preprocessor to handle refinements as a extension to an existing programming language.

Programmers are usually well-advised not to use very long identifiers. Handles of refinements, however, occur only twice in the text and the obvious argument against long identifiers does not apply. It makes sense to make them long enough to convey some information as to the meaning of the algorithm they stand for.

A research problem is what syntactic positions may be taken by refinement handles. Obvious cases are statements and expressions. Formal parameters, on the other hand, would be a bad idea. As can be seen from the example in Section 4, it may be desirable to allow refinements for declarations also. A definitive answer can only be developed with respect to specific programming languages, however.

Various programming _systems_ have been developed that aid in stepwise refinement by taking over the clerical tasks of textual replacement (see, e.g., Henderson and Snowdon (1975) or Cunningham and Pugh (1976)). These systems may also have the possibility to run an incomplete program. I do not think this offers a solution. In the first place, the proper and obvious tool for aiding the programming process is the programming language. Programs are what we use to communicate algorithms to ourselves, to other programmers and even to computers. The main reason, however, is rather more down to earth: even with the best conventions possible for indicating modifications, the pencil-and-paper method will remain an order of magnitude simpler. As long as the program is in its development phase, each impediment to easy modification is an impediment to obtaining a reliable program. The value of _describing_ an algorithm incompletely (down to a certain level of abstraction) is obvious, but the value of _running_ an incomplete program escapes me.

4. AN EXAMPLE

The use of abstract data types to simplify program modifications is discussed by Linden (1976). He rewrites the sieve-of-Eratosthenes program of Hoare (1972) using abstract data types. But from his program it is apparent that the main gain in readability stems from the choice of identifiers for the operations on his abstract type "sieve set". His program would have been better structured if refinements had been used. The implementation of the operations is rather repetitious and it is as difficult to see that they are correct as in Hoare´s version. A change of representation would involve the major part of the program. Worse yet, there is a rather obscure correspondence between the high-level integer "next" in the program, and the low-level value "xindex". Although Linden states: "this program is a direct translation of the English definition of the algorithm", the coarse structure of the English definition he gives and that of his program are different! The structure of the core of the English definition is:

```
core:
    FOR each integer FROM two through the
        square root of n
    DO remove all multiples from the set OD,
```

whereas that of his program is (slightly simplified):

```
core:
    INT next:= 2;
    WHILE next not exceeding the square root of n
    DO remove multiples of next from the set;
```

```
        find next member
    OD.
find next member:
    REPEAT next:= next + 1
    UNTIL next in set.
```

The correctness proof of the second version requires, unlike the first version, an existence proof, given a prime p, of a second prime p′ with $p < p' \leq p^2$. This proof is not completely trivial. The optimization involved is justified by the statement: "it is not necessary to remove the multiples of any number which has already been removed from the set". This corresponds, however, to a refinement

```
remove multiples if necessary:
    IF multiples already removed
    THEN SKIP
    ELSE remove multiples
    FI.
```

Below I give a version of the algorithm, in accordance with the ideas of this paper. The problem is that the table of primes has to be implemented using a bit map. Primitives for setting and testing one of the bits 0 through wordsize-1 in a "WORD" are assumed available, as is the upper bound n of the primes to be computed. The straightforward solution would involve a division per table access, which is considered unacceptable.

Some notations are employed below that are an immature attempt to express some ideas for the emancipation of abstract data types, taken from EL1, Wegbreit (1974), namely the fact that for a new mode the primitive ways of access have to be described explicitly. Operators may also be anonymous (type conversion functions) or 3-adic (used to define a "generator" in the sense of Alphard, Shaw et al. (1976)).

Two new layers are used, a very simple one for the integral square root, and a larger one for indexing. The definitions are not definitions of the class type, but of the module type as described by Schuman (1974), where details of the implementation are made invisible outside the module.

```
sieve of eratosthenes USING integral square root, indexing.

sieve of eratosthenes:
    declare sieve of size n;
    FOR each integer FROM two through the square root of n
    DO remove multiples if necessary OD;
    print table.
remove multiples if necessary:
    IF multiples already removed
    THEN SKIP
    ELSE remove multiples
    FI.

declare sieve of size n:
    [n] BOOL prime;
    fill prime.
fill prime:
    FOR INDEX p FROM 2 BY 1 TO n
    DO prime[p]:= TRUE OD.
print table:
    FOR INDEX p FROM 2 BY 1 TO n
```

```
    DO IF prime[p] THEN print (p) FI OD.

each integer:
    INDEX p.
two through the square root of n:
    2 BY 1 TO intsqrt (n).
multiples already removed:
    ¬ prime[p].
remove multiples:
    FOR INDEX mult FROM p * p BY p TO n
    DO remove multiple OD.
remove multiple:
    prime[mult]:= FALSE.

DEF integral square root:
BEGIN PROC (INT a) INT intsqrt:
      IF a < 0 THEN ERROR
      ELIF a = 0 THEN 0
      ELSE INT rt:= a ÷ 2 + 1;
           {a < (rt + 1)²}
           WHILE rt > a ÷ rt
           {a < rt²}
           DO rt:= (rt + a ÷ rt) ÷ 2 OD;
           {rt² ≤ a < (rt + 1)²}
           rt
      FI
END.

DEF indexing:
BEGIN PRIMITIVE MODE INDEX:
          (repr: STRUCT (INT intval, word, bit)
              {invariant: intval = word * wordsize + bit},
           assign (v): repr:= v,
           val: repr);

      {type conversion functions}
      OP (INT a) INDEX:
          (intval: a,
           word: a ÷ wordsize,
           bit: a MOD wordsize);
      OP (INDEX a) INT:
          a.intval;

      OP (INDEX a, b) INDEX +:
          IF a.bit + b.bit < wordsize
          THEN (intval: a.intval + b.intval,
                word: a.word + b.word,
                bit: a.bit + b.bit)
          ELSE (intval: a.intval + b.intval,
                word: a.word + b.word + 1,
                bit: a.bit + b.bit - wordsize)
          FI;

      OP (INDEX a, b, c) GENERATOR(INDEX) BY TO:
```

```
            (init: a,
             cont (i): i.intval ≤ c.intval,
             next (i): i + b);

        PRIMITIVE MODE [INDEX] BOOL:
            (repr (size): [0 : size.word] WORD,
             assign (i, v): setbit (i.bit, repr[i.word], ABS v),
             val (i): getbit (i.bit, repr[i.word]) = 0)
    END.
```

5. CONCLUSION

Let me first point out that I do not think that structured program texts are a panacea for the software crisis. If the structure of a program is abominable, it is not particularly helpful to faithfully mirror its structure in the program text (except that a recipient of the program is in a better position not to place unjustified confidence in the program). Similarly, structuring program texts cannot replace the task of proving correctness (but it may be of help). The main advantage of making the program structure explicit as advocated here is that this provides documentation as an integral part of the program text. All necessary modifications can easily be made in the proper way, and updating this documentation in parallel with the program becomes almost automatic (making patches may become hard indeed). In short, future languages should support explicit structuring of program texts and thereby increase the quality of programs.

Of the two major principles introducing program structure, only one, layers of abstraction, is receiving due attention from language designers. The other one, stepwise refinement, seems more or less neglected. The purpose of this paper has been to show that the introduction of refinements as a language feature is desirable and feasible (in fact, SLAN, Hommel et al. (1976), already has a refinement facility, and the standard control structure of CDL and its offsprings CDL2, Dehottay et al. (1976), and ALEPH, Bosch et al. (1974), is very similar). Since the refinements correspond closely to the way a program is developed, they should prove a natural instrument for the programmer.

ACKNOWLEDGEMENTS

The idea of structuring a program text according to the program structure could not have evolved without the work of Dijkstra, Naur, Wirth, Hoare, and too many others to mention. I am indebted to Kees Koster for several suggestions about the content and organization of this paper.

REFERENCES

Bosch, R., Grune, D., and Meertens, L.G.L.T. (1974). ALEPH, A Language Encouraging Program Hierarchy, The International Computing Symposium 1973, Davos, 73-79. (North-Holland, Amsterdam.)

Cunningham, R.J., and Pugh, C.G. (1976). A language-independent system to aid the development of structured programs, Software - Practice & Experience 6, 487-503.

Dehottay, J.-P., Feuerhahn, H., Koster, C.H.A., and Stahl, H.M. (1976). Syntaktische Beschreibung von CDL2, Forschungsgruppe Softwaretechnik,

Technische Universität Berlin.
Dijkstra, E.W. (1968). The structure of the "THE" multiprogramming system, Comm. ACM 11, 341-346.
Henderson, P., and Snowdon, R.A. (1975). A tool for structured programming development, Information Processing 74 (Proceedings of IFIP Congress 1974), 204-207. (North-Holland, Amsterdam.)
Hoare, C.A.R.. (1972). Notes on data structuring, in O.-J. Dahl, E.W. Dijkstra and C.A.R. Hoare, Structured Programming. (Academic Press.)
Hommel, G., Jähnichen, S., and Koch, W. (1976). SLAN - Eine erweiterbare Sprache zur Unterstützung der strukturierten und modularen Programmierung, in Programmiersprachen Fachtagung 1976, Informatik Fachberichte 1. (Springer-Verlag, Heidelberg.)
Linden, T.A. (1976). The use of abstract data types to simplify program modifications, Proceedings of Conference on Data: Abstraction, Definition and Structure, SIGPLAN Notices 11, special issue, 12-23.
Schuman, S.A. (1974). Toward modular programming in high-level languages, ALGOL Bulletin 37.4.1, 30-53.
Shaw, M., Wulf., W.A., and London, R.L. (1976). Abstraction and verification in Alphard: Iteration and generators, Technical Report, Carnegie-Mellon University and University of Southern California Information Sciences Institute.
Wegbreit, B. (1974). The treatment of data types in EL1, Comm. ACM 17, 251-264.
Wirth, N. (1971). Program development by stepwise refinement, Comm. ACM 14, 221-227.

Meertens : Discussion

Correll: You have procedures and functions in many programming languages. Why do you not use them?

Meertens: [Shows transparency prepared beforehand, provoking ☺, and repeats points in paper.]

Koster: One point should be stressed, namely the communications overhead. If you use the normal procedure mechanism then you get all problems of parameters (or globals), the necessity of specifications, the problem of matching lists and so on. The natural communication mechanism between a refinement and the calling environment is by just having them in one same scope.

Meertens: The visibility problem should be solved independently of refinements. There must be some rules for visibility in each language and the visibility from within the body of a refinement should be just as though it were a block present at that place. That is of course also a problem if you use a procedure, unless you are very careful to put the procedure in exactly the right scope.

Meyer: Would you allow parameters?

Meertens: Surely not!

Meyer: In the name of generality, you will naturally be tempted to introduce parameters and then you will go on to invent again the whole concept of procedures. Whether you implement a procedure call or a macro-expansion is not relevant then.

Meertens: A general remark: the quest for generality is sometimes harmful and on some occasions you must restrain yourself. It's not generality for its own sake that you should seek.

Koster: There is a natural distinction between the two mechanisms and their use. While programming top-down you are constructing abstract algorithms all the time. These can be classified into general ones, which are of some universal use, and journalistic ones, fleeting abstractions that you need only in passing. For those fleeting abstractions you should use the proposed refinement mechanism. For the general abstractions, which are of more than local value, you should use the procedure mechanism. This is so simple that it might even be teachable.

Meertens: Furthermore you may use an intermediate layer for general abstractions.

Sintzoff: I have a question, a quite naive one. Earlier we heard much about modular structures. Can you relate what you want with the use of modules?

Meertens: So that my point will be lost in the ineluctable modularity discussion?

Sintzoff: No, but many questions you raised have to be raised for modules.

Meertens: Before you start talking about modules you should define exactly what you mean by modules. The obvious thing for putting into a module is an intermediate layer. You don't have too many problems with interface specifications. You only need to pass to the user, that is, to the top level, the properties which are made available by this intermediate layer. Such modules also are obvious candidates for separate compilation (just as for a programming language the compiler is not recompiled each time). Of course, if I have this top-town refinement I could hope, especially if it is a very large program, to cut it up and also compile separately. For example, this could be a compiler defining an environment, a lexical pass, a parsing pass and a code generator and then I want to have some means to cut it up into pieces, but I think it's independent of the question which I have tried to address here.

Wodon: What is the difference between the feature you propose and a macrogenerator?

Meertens: Of course, it is something which is very similar to macro-expansion, but usually that is not a feature of programming languages. If a programming language comes along and has this macro-expansion capability as an integrated feature, then fine, I can use that as the refinement mechanism in this language. But if I have a programming language, say ALGOL 68, and I am referred to some facility in the operating system for macro-expansion then I'm not happy; it should be an integral part of the programming language itself.

Dewar: I think it is worth pointing out that COBOL has exactly this feature in the PERFORM, which is one of the reasons why well-written COBOL programs are often significantly better than programs written in other languages. I think it's a little appreciated feature of COBOL.

Meertens: Or maybe a greatly appreciated feature of little appreciated COBOL.

King, J.: What about %INCLUDE in PL/I? Would it also give the same facility?

Meertens: There are many languages that in some way or other have features that you can use or abuse to obtain the effect. In general I think this is not the proper approach. One should not say, "This is the programming language, these are the features, how can I use this for what I want?" One should say, "This is what I want, so how do I design the programming language to have these features I need?"

Constructing Quality Software, P.G. Hibbard/S.A. Schuman (eds.)

SOME REMARKS ON SOFTWARE MORPHOLOGY

Jacques André, Jean Bézivin, Jean-Louis Nebut, Robert Rannou
IRISA-Université de Rennes, France

Stephen A. Schuman
IRIA-Laboria, Rocquencourt, France

Abstract. This position paper raises the question of what is the most appropriate *form* for the texts of programs. Our remarks stem from the observation that there is a tendency to incorporate more and more information into a program text, particularly in the context of professionally produced software. This demand arises out of continuing efforts to rationalize the software production process and, especially, to institute a suitable division of labor. We propose a physical structure which directly reflects the different activities involved in the software development cycle; we then explore some further implications of these criteria so as to achieve a more general separation of concerns in programming. Our purpose is to suggest guidelines for future programming languages and, if possible, to orient research in this area towards the requirements of large-scale software production.

1. *Introduction*

Software production isn't what it used to be! Gone are the days when it was the exclusive preserve of a small circle of proud artisans, deploying unlimited amounts of blood, sweat, tears and black magic in singlehanded displays of unbridled "creativity", and (occasionally) achieving almost miraculous results in the form of fully functional finished products. While there persists a certain nostalgia for this earlier, more heroic era, few will be found to mourn its final passing, especially among those who had in one way or another to foot the bill. The emerging "age of reason" is heralded with near unanimity, even though the impetus has been purely economic. From its former status as a secondary concern, subordinate to the manufacture or procurement of computing machinery, software has progressively acquired major commercial significance in its own right, perhaps to the point of reversing its relative position with respect to hardware. As with any such "growth sector", the increasing importance of software has led to concerted efforts to "industrialize" the production process: to subject it to the imperatives of rational planning, to apply reasonable cost-effectiveness criteria, etc. By far the most evident manifestation of this trend is the widespread institution of classical divisions of labor - the hallmark of every industrial revolution.

In the context of commercial software production (as opposed to programming as an academic exercise or a recreational pastime), this division of labor has been carried well beyond the traditional functional decomposition of the programming task (into subroutines, modules or whatever). It has become customary to further subdivide the development of each individual component into a number of separate, ever more specialized activities:

- specification of the initial requirements,
- implementation of a suitable solution,
- validation of that implementation,
- optimization to improve its performance,
- integration into some larger environment,
- documentation for a variety of purposes,
- etc.

Moreover, it is extremely rare for a (successful) software product to remain in a stable state once its original development has been completed. Hence a substantial proportion of production resources must in fact be devoted to efforts collectively referred to as maintenance:

- correction of the inevitable errors,
- revision to upgrade the product,
- extension to provide new capabilities,
- adaptation to meet different requirements,
- etc.

These latter tasks involve modifying what was supposedly a finished product. Whereas it has often been stated that such problems should be approached by "starting over" from some appropriate state and then reiterating the development cycle, this advice is seldom followed in practice. Instead, maintenance is usually carried out quite separately from development, which gives rise to additional specialized activities within the overall production process. In most large-scale, highly structured production environments, the various activities are performed by many different people, executed whenever possible in parallel and iterated in a more or less cyclic fashion. In many respects, such a "system" behaves like a collection of cooperating processes (so much so that one may expect a multitute of "models" for software production, expressed in familiar programming terminology, to be forthcoming in the near future).

One effect of this increasingly complex organization is that more and more information goes into or is generated in the course of the production process. In order to coordinate the different activities, this information must be kept in a complete and consistent state, which can easily become a major preoccupation in and of itself. Not surprisingly, one hears a great deal of speculation about generalized "data bases", in conjunction with ever more sophisticated technological support, as being the ultimate solution to the problems of program development and maintenance. Although much of this can be dismissed as characteristic hyperbole, the intrinsic problem of coping with large amounts of information remains, and the need for some systematic approach is becoming more apparent to all concerned.

The present situation might best be described as a pragmatic compromise, but the reasoning upon which it is based is difficult to refute. The argument goes as follows: since the final program is the primary objective of the software production process, the obvious place to reflect each and every aspect of the finished product is *within the program text itself*. Accordingly, the final program can be seen as a composite projection, consisting of information contributed by each of the different activities involved in its development (fig. 1); a very similar viewpoint could be adopted with regard to the maintenance phase.

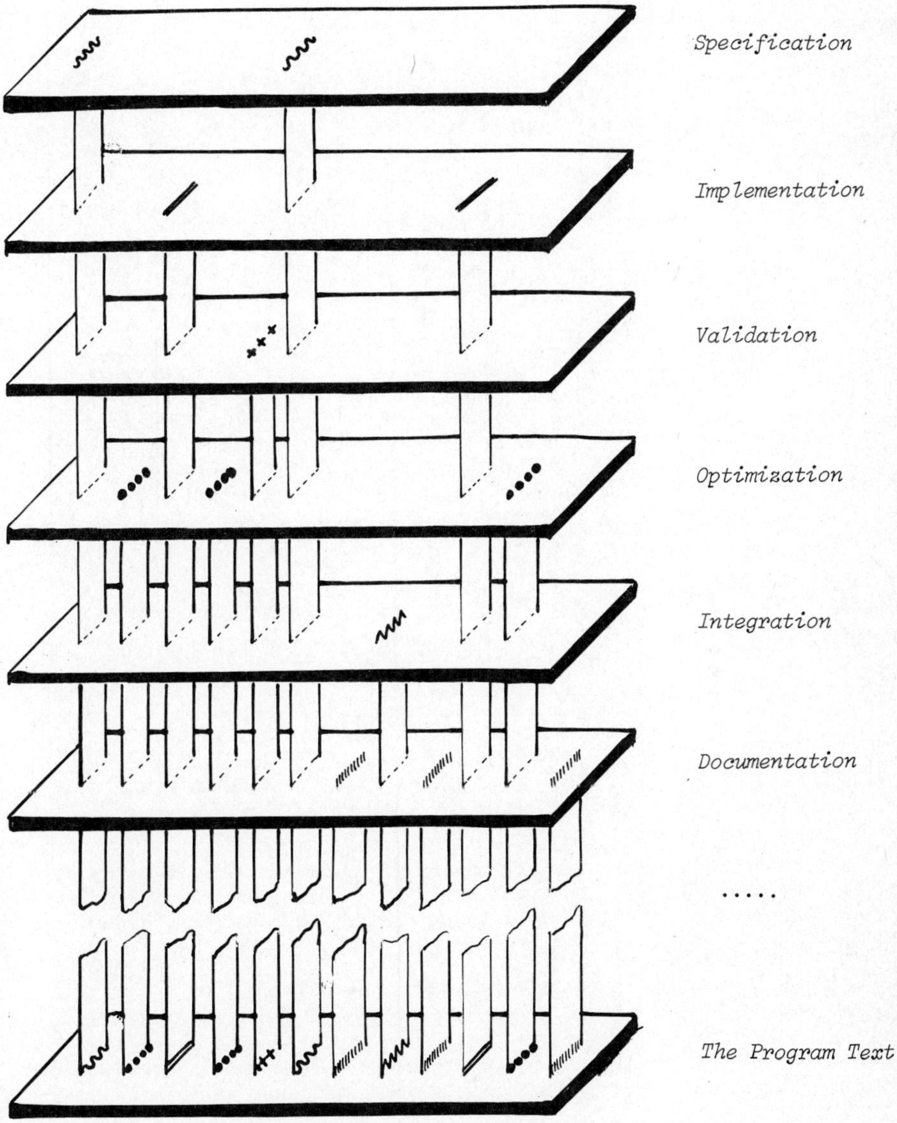

Figure 1. Each activity contributes information to the final program text.

We do not dispute the contention that the program text is the proper place for all such information to reside. Within the context of current production practices, however, we believe that it is both legitimate and pertinent to raise the question of what is the most appropriate *form* for the text of a program. Following the Structuralist School, we refer to this study of the physical structure of programs as *software morphology*.

2. *The programming language in a production environment*

If the program text is to serve as a vehicle for conveying all of the information that enters into obtaining a finished product, then it is almost axiomatic that it must be possible to express this information within the "language" in which that program is written. It appears to be the case that more and more commercially produced software is written in a (relatively) high-level language. (It would probably be a mistake to interpret this as an enthusiastic commitment to improving the quality of the resulting products; it seems more like a grudging concession, which has been made solely in the interests of increasing productivity during the development phase while at the same time reducing the costs subsequently incurred for maintenance.) Somewhat surprisingly, most of these higher-level languages (even those which have been specifically designed for system implementation or are currently being developed for that purpose) stop far short of providing all of the facilities that are required by the various activities involved in the production process. In order to accommodate these demands, compilers intended for use in an "industrial" context must therefore implement not only the standard capabilities of a "pure" algorithmic language (as supposedly advocated by the academic community), but also a host of "special features" catering to the particular requirements of a production environment.

A rather broad range of techniques is used to make such features available. The most common of these approaches will be briefly discussed below.

- Building the desired features into the language into the language (often in the guise of extensions or "ameliorations" to some existing language taken as a basis). This approach is obviously the most general, since it is tantamount to defining a new language and producing the corresponding compiler. It is most appropriate when the features in question have many ramifications throughout the compilation process or when they are considered crucial from a methodological standpoint. Purposes for which this technique is typically employed include:

- to facilitate large-scale programming (e.g., mechanisms for supporting modularity and separate compilation, for describing interfaces and linkage conventions, for providing selective access to and renaming of identifiers);

- to encourage (and enforce) the systematic use of "structured programming", stepwise refinement, levels of abstraction or other constructive methods;

- to reduce the probability of (undetected) programming errors, for instance by means of syntactic constructs which serve to introduce redundancy, to enforce semantic restrictions or to define properties that can be automatically propagated or verified;

- to allow explicit control over the mapping onto an underlying hardware configuration, i.e., making it possible to specifiy data structure allocation and representation, to establish particular register conventions, to exploit capabilities directly implemented by the hardware (such as input/

output operations or priority levels) and, in general, to introduce a host of different machine-dependent considerations;

- to fulfill an important requirement in some area where existing languages are conspicuously inadequate or deficient (parallelism and synchronization or exception handling could be cited as current examples of where such a situation might arise).

• Making available a minimal number of "escape mechanisms" whereby various non-standard features (not present in the language) may nevertheless be used in a program. The classic example is the ability to embed fragments of assembly language coding within a high-level language text. A somewhat more general approach is to provide a suitable interface so that programs in a variety of other languages may be invoked as needed, which means that the language in question is essentially "open ended". Such a technique is, in some sense, the antithesis of the "building in" approach; although it is potentially very powerful, its effectiveness is often severely compromised because of poor integration (e.g., the inability to ensure consistency or to perform optimization across such interfaces). Some more sophisticated forms of this notion have been introduced in newer languages, for instance the possibility to locally override the "strong typing" conventions imposed elsewhere within the language, or the use of keywords to delimit portions of a program wherein certain special features are employed; this latter corresponds to "partitioning" the language according to distinctions such as "safe/unsafe", "portable/non-portable", etc.

• Implementing a variety of "compile-time options", allowing the user to select from among a certain set of capabilities by specifying the values of various parameters for each individual run. This technique is most frequently employed to give some amount of control over the output which is received from the compilation process: the different listings to be produced and their formats; the kinds of analysis to be performed or the types of diagnostics that are desired; the nature of the object code to be generated, whether in interpretive or intermediate form or, alternatively, machine code that has been optimized to a greater or lesser degree; the particular variant of the target machine and/or configuration for which code is to be compiled; the specific run-time environment which is to be assumed, and whether such possibilities as code for dynamic error checking or calls to special monitoring routines are to be included; the sorts of auxiliary data to be recorded, e.g., descriptive information for subsequent (separate) compilation, statistical information for project management purposes, etc. In conjunction with suitable support for separate compilation, this approach can also be used to accomplish much of what would otherwise have to be achieved by means of escape mechanisms. The proliferation of such options reflects the fact that the traditional compiler is coming to be regarded more and more as a multi-purpose tool.

• Providing a repertoire of compiler directives or so-called "pragmatic remarks", which serve to invoke particular functions during the compilation process or to give additional "guidance" with respect to the code that is to be generated. This sort of approach is typically adopted for purposes such as directing the format of the source listing output as a by-product of the compilation, supplying parameters which depend on the conventions of a certain filing system or on some other aspect of a local environment, indicating the required interpretation for critical constructions (e.g., in-line implementation of procedures, generation of non-standard calling sequences and special purpose or priveleged instructions, establishing the correct interface with an operating system, controlling secondary storage usage), enabling or disabling error detection or exception handling procedures, furnishing information needed for optimization (for instance "safe" assumptions which cannot otherwise be deduced and probabilities or frequency indications which may be of interest), etc. This technique is closely related to that of compile-time options and may be used for many of the same purposes; it has the added advantage of allowing greater selectivity than can be achieved by simply setting global parameters for the entire compilation. It is to be observed that such directives can be construed as an alternative to building various features into the language, the difference being that they are then considered as capabilities of one specific compiler rather than as part of the language proper (this distinction is admittedly somewhat academic in most production environments).

- Relying upon a standardized set of "compile-time facilities" or some other variation on the classical theme of macro-expansion, so as to introduce complicated or frequently required extensions in a relatively convenient form. If such a general purpose capability is already present as an integral part of the language, then this approach is usually the most economical means of obtaining a wide variety of additional features (so long as the interpretation of these extensions can ultimately be expressed in terms of the given language, and provided that the problems of error reporting can be overcome in an acceptable fashion). In addition, because of the possibility for conditional compilation, this technique is especially suitable for introducing code and data serving solely for debugging, tracing, measuring, testing and related purposes, since this information may then be selectively eliminated from the final product. This same facility makes it possible to accommodate a certain range of requirements within a single program, in such a way that it can then be adapted to a variety of special cases; this is the approach generally associated with "system generation". More prosaically, macro-generation has often proven to be an expedient method of imposing specific programming conventions. Even when not properly a part of the language, such techniques have been employed to construct a variety of preprocessors for traditional languages (cf. the recent rash of "structured" dialects). An approach of this sort is, once again, essentially equivalent to defining a new language and producing (at least one phase of) the corresponding compiler. Depending upon one's ambitions, the task is usually just as difficult, but the result is frequently an unfortunate compromise at best, since the carefully constructed "facade" does not fully hide the "defects" of the underlying language, which means that the desired discipline is effectively unenforcable.

- Insisting that the necessary information be included in the program text in the form of comments (often to be expressed in increasingly stylized notations - the proud inventions of a new breed of programming managers). Whereas comments have been the traditional vehicle for such purposes as documentation, they must nevertheless be considered as a "last resort" and should not be relied upon for conveying information which is in any way crucial to the production process, owing primarily to the difficulty of ensuring that this information is actually present and always up to date. In part to alleviate this particular problem, there is a growing tendency to process (and even generate) certain kinds of comments in a semi-automatic fashion, whether by means of a conventional text editor or with the aid of other tools specifically conceived for that purpose. However far one may go in this direction, until such time as this "extra information" is effectively integrated into the language proper, a far more fundamental problem is likely to persist: that of guaranteeing consistency between the comments (serving for instance as some sort of specification) and the program itself (which purports to implement those specifications).

The various techniques described above constitute the most common approaches for accommodating the different demands of software production, at least in so far as the programming language is concerned. It must be remembered, however, that many of the steps involved in obtaining a finished product are not directly formulated in any programming language whatsoever. Rather they appear, if at all, as commands expressed in some job control language, as directives to or parameters for a variety of other processors which serve to support the production process: text editors, program librarians, linkage editors, debugging monitors, test case generators, simulators, analytical routines, report generators, documentation systems, etc. Consequently, some significant part of the information associated with the development cycle is directed to or produced by these additional support tools. Finally, there are always a certain number of purely manual procedures, for which the corresponding indications are not available in machine-readable form, if indeed they are written down at all. Since all of this is in conflict with the goal of explicitly reflecting as many aspects of the production process as possible within the actual program text, one may predict that the present trend (towards integrating further features into the programming language and providing additional capabilities in conjunction with its compiler) will continue indefinitely. In the meantime, it would seem prudent to adopt a much broader perspective than is customary with regard to what should and should not be considered as part of the "programming language", particularly when speaking about a production environment.

3. *On the increasing entropy of programs*

It is not our intention to call into question the need for this panoply of "added features", nor to disparage the techniques and ingenuity which have been deployed in order to make the necessary facilities available to the production programmer (whatever his actual title and responsibilities). Rather, we should merely like to suggest that the net effect of this unchecked "urge to ameliorate" is possibly somewhat counter-productive. As evidence we offer, in the form of a parody, the text of a (totally insignificant) production program (see fig. 2 on the next page); we leave it to the reader to decide whether this caricature is in fact unduly exaggerated.

In any case it would hardly be an overstatement to say that such a text requires a certain amount of study before one is able to discern the content of the program in question, let alone be satisfied that it is actually correct. Considerable further effort must be invested in order to understand the purpose of the various constituent constructs, to say nothing of their interrelationships. After sufficient inspection, it will probably be easy to master this relatively trivial example, but one can well imagine the problem of being "unable to see the forest for the trees" when confronted with the text of a life-sized production program. For a real program text to be so visually unintelligible would perhaps be forgivable if it had been entirely generated by machine, on the condition that the only intended readers were also machines! But in so far as human beings still have some role left to play within the software production process, the degree to which the texts of programs can become cluttered with too much information, thereby making them essentially unreadable, must be regarded as a serious problem (or, at the very least, a rather disturbing symptom). Readability of programs has been widely recognized as the key to reducing maintenance costs, and this was probably the principal justification for the shift to higher-level

```
$MANAGEMENT
     MODULE:         RATIO
     AUTHOR:         JOHN N.M.I. DUPOND
     DESIGNED:       75/12/25
     INTEGRATED:     76/01/25
     MODIFIED:       76/01/26  BUG
                     76/02/17  CHANGE IN FORMAT
$
$DOCUMENTATION
*DUC       RATIO
*DU        PURPOSE
*1         THIS MODULE PRINTS THE RATIO Q[I]/SIGMA(Q[I]) WHEN IT IS >=.5
*          AND EACH CORRESPONDING NAME.
*2U        CALL/RETURN
*          CALL IS RATIO(T,N) WHERE T IS THE ARRAY ADDRESS AND N IS ITS SIZE VALUE
*          T IS ASSUMED TO BE IN REGISTER 1 AND N IN REGISTER 2
*2U        ABNORMAL EXIT
*          NONE
     ...
*$
RATIO: PROC(T,N) REAL;
    N: VALUE INT;
     CONTROL N IN R2;
     T: REF[1:] STRUCTURE SERIAL[2];
     BEGIN
          NAME: CHAR, WORD(0), BYTE(0,7);
          Q   : INT, WORD(1) , BIT(25,32);
     END $ STRUCTURE T $;
     CONTROL T IN R1;
     CONTROL SPACE(5);
     TIMING: BOOL CONSTANT= FALSE; $ CHANGE TO TRUE TO ACTIVATE TIMING$
     TRACING:BOOL CONSTANT= FALSE; $ CHANGE TO TRUE TO ACTIVATE TRACING $
     CONTROL EJECT;
     PRINT : PROC XREF;
     %IF TIMING %THEN CLOCK: PROC REAL XREF;
     CONTROL SPACE(2);
     %IF TIMING %THEN TIME: REAL;
     CONTROL EJECT;
     &MAXLENGTH := 1;
     %IF TRACING %THEN
          %BEGIN PRINT(FT1);
               FT1: FORMAT("/* RATIO ENTERED*");
          %END;
     %IF TIMING %THEN TIME := CLOCK;
     &DUMP := 1;
     SUM: INT;
     SUM := 0;
     $ COMPUTE SUM = SIGMA( Q[I] ) $
     I : INT;
     CONTROL FAST LOOP;
     FOR I := 1 STEP 1 UNTIL N DO SUM := SUM+Q[I];
     CONTROL SPACE(2);
     $ PRINT ONLY RELEVANT NAMES AND Q/SIGMA $
     RAT: REAL;
     FOR I := 1 STEP 1 UNTIL N DO
          BEGIN
          ASSERT I <= N;
               RAT  := Q[I]/SUM;
               ON UNDERFLOW THEN PRINT(F1,I);
                    F1: FORMAT("/*UNDERFLOW I=*,2ZD");
               %IF TRACING %THEN
                    %BEGIN PRINT(FT2,I,Q[I],RAT);
                         FT2: FORMAT("/*TRACE I=*,3ZD,*Q=*,3ZD,*R=*,ZD.DD");
                    %END;
               IF RAT >=.5 THEN PRINT(F2, RAT, NAME[I]);
                    F2: FORMAT("/,ZD.DD,7C");
          END;
     %IF TIMING %THEN
          %BEGIN
               TIME := CLOCK-TIME;
               PRINT(FC,TIME);
               FC: FORMAT("/*TIME IN RATIO: *,D.3DE-D");
          %END;
     %IF TRACING %THEN
          %BEGIN PRINT(FT3);
               FT3: FORMAT("/*RATIO EXITED*");
          %END;
END
```

Figure 2. A caricature of a production program

languages in commercial software production. It is therefore somewhat surprising to find that, because of the need for so much extra information, this objective has been severely compromised in the actual usage of these languages. Moreover, owing to the inherent difficulties of seeing thatt all of this information is present, in its proper place and up to date during the development phase, one suspects that the projected improvements in productivity have also failed to materialize in practice.

In all fairness it should be pointed out that this phenomenon of "program pollution" is by no means a monopoly of the industrial environment. One need only consider the extent to which recent proposals from the research community have as their premise the inclusion of additional information within the program text, whether for the sake of automatic verification or for any number of other (potential) advances in the state-of-the-art.

There is an obvious need for a common frame of reference for expressing the different types of information associated with a program. The program text itself is the natural choice, because it is the focus for all of the activities involved in the software production cycle. Unfortunately, it seems that the amount of this information tends to grow (at least) in proportion to the number of distinct activities, so that the physical organization of this information takes on greater and greater importance as the production process becomes more highly evolved and complex. Reflecting upon the problems of large-scale software development, Belady and Lehman [1976] have attempted to formulate certain "laws of program evolution dynamics". The second of these states:

> "The entropy of a system (its unstucturedness) increases with time unless specific work is executed to maintain or reduce it."

It appears to be virtually impossible to effectively reduce the "entropy" of a software product by any after-the-fact approach. The work in question must therefore be performed as an integral part of the development process. Beginning at the earliest possible stage, one of the main objectives of any project should be to establish a comprehensible *visible* structure that clearly exhibits the essential characteristics of each and every aspect of the program under development, as well as the ways in which these aspects are related. Furthermore, this structure must then be rigorously preserved throughout the entire life-cycle of the product, particularly during the maintenance phase - the period when any program is most susceptible to "spontaneous destructuration".

Since the physical structure of the program text is (or ought to be) such a central concern in software production, one might expect that the primary development tool, the programming language, would provide positive support for organizing the different kinds of information which enter into the final product. Instead, however, one finds that even the most modern languages for system implementation cling stubbornly to the conception that the program text should reflect as closely as possible what might be called the *underlying program*. Indeed, it is a point of pride with some of these languages that the text of a program provides an explicit image of the corresponding executable code. Whereas this was probably justified in the days when the listing of the program was the only available guide for interpreting otherwise undecipherable dumps of core memory, the whole idea seems curiously outdated in this age of ever more sophisticated support tools. This supposed advantage is, in any case, almost irrelevant where so much of the information in a program text is of a strictly definitional or documentary nature and, as such, has only an indirect effect at most on the generated code.

A further incongruity of these languages is to be found in the fact that the physical disposition of the different types of information, the way in which it must be interspersed throughout the program, is seemingly imposed *solely for the convenience of the compiler*. There is essentially no attempt to facilitate the tasks of the human beings who must deal in one capacity or another with the actual texts of programs. It is difficult to imagine a more striking example of false economy, especially in light of the premium that is presently placed on programmer productivity.

The necessity of incorporating more and more information into program texts appears to be a fact of life, which may be seen as a direct consequence of the continuing efforts to rationalize the software production process. Even if one fully accepts the legitimacy of this need, it nevertheless looks like something of an excercise in futility to keep on trying to satisfy these demands by "grafting" additional features onto programming languages as they are currently conceived. Perhaps we have reached the point where it would be far more fruitful to begin to explore some fundamentally new departures, taking into account from the outset the requirements for accommodating a diversity of information and paying particular attention to reducing the "entropy" of the resulting program products. Therein seems to lie a worthwhile (and quite possibly urgent) task for the research community.

4. *In search of a suitable form for production programs*

In seeking some means of coping with the "information explosion" discussed above, one guiding principle springs immediately to mind, namely imposing a *physical* separation according to certain, judiciously chosen criteria. The most direct way of applying this principle to the problem at hand would be to segregate the different types of information into physically disjoint parts of the program.

There is, of course, one very well known example where such an approach has been adopted (see fig. 3). Although this form was rather original in its time and now has the added advantage of having been extensively tried in practice, the familiar divisions of a COBOL program cannot seriously be considered to constitute a suitable starting point for the new departure which is sought. This conclusion is essentially based on two reasons. The first is the fact that the underlying rule for the overall decomposition may not be applied *recursively*, so that it would be possible for instance to define data structures in terms of procedures as well as vice versa. It was in part to overcome this obvious limitation that block structure was introduced. In this latter framework, different sorts of declarations could again be intermixed indiscriminately, but there was at least the possibility to nest these definitions (not only textually but also logically) to as many levels as necessary. While even this more general approach has recently been found wanting, the deficiencies in question are of quite another nature. (Block structure is, above all, a means for establishing a particularly simple runtime storage management discipline; it is not very surprising that this criterion has come to be considered a bit too low-level to serve as the primary basis for system decomposition.) Every one of the more modern proposals (oriented mainly towards "modular programming") has the property that the basic structuring principle is recursively applicable, thus rejecting the notion that a strict ordering of the dependencies among the different types of definitions in a program is an acceptable restriction. The second reason why COBOL is not especially useful as a source of inspiration is much less technical though perhaps more important, at least in the present context. This

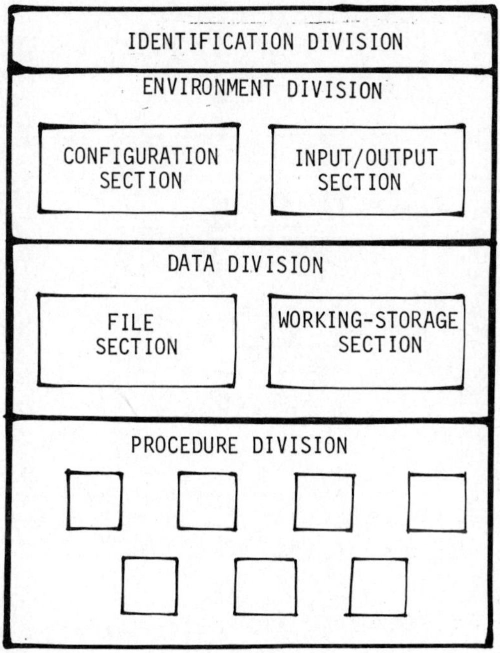

Figure 3. The physical structure of a COBOL program.

reason is that the divisions adopted therein do not really correspond to meaningful distinctions in terms of the software production process. It is indeed difficult to imagine what might be learned about a program by looking, for example, at all of its constituent *procedures* simultaneously and in isolation, without regard to the data on which they operate and in the absence of some larger view of the way in which they are interrelated. The same argument would probably hold for any similar partitioning. In general it is the case that some *combination* of the available programming tools, as embodied in specific linguistic constructs, must be used to solve any given problem. It is therefore hard to see how segregating the different kinds of language constructions within the program text could conceivably facilitate the various tasks involved in the software production cycle.

The second of these critiques is perhaps more constructive than it may at first appear. This is because it strongly suggests an alternative approach: *to separate the information within a program text on the basis of the particular activity to which it pertains*. Thus, if one were to consider the activities traditionally associated with the software production process, this guideline might lead to a structure like that depicted in fig. 4.

One immediately obvious advantage of adopting such a form is that the basis for organizing the information within a program would be independent of (or "orthogonal" to) the criteria used for decomposing a system into modules. Therefore this principle is potentially applicable to large-scale software development (where it is most relevant), irrespective of the specific structuring concepts that are considered appropriate for a particular program product (see fig. 5a). The logical "units" in question might correspond

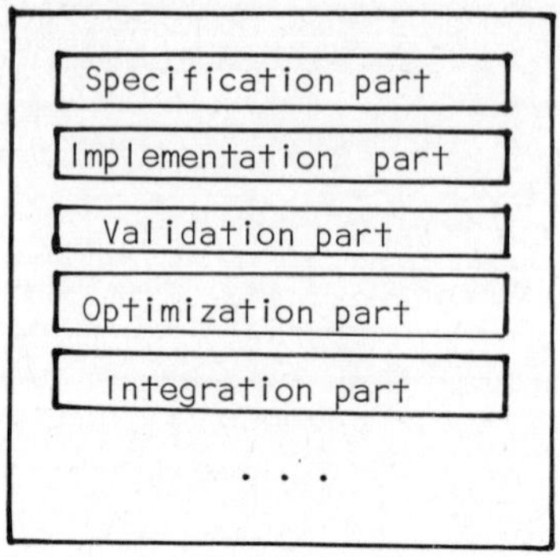

Figure 4. An alternative structure, based on program development activities.

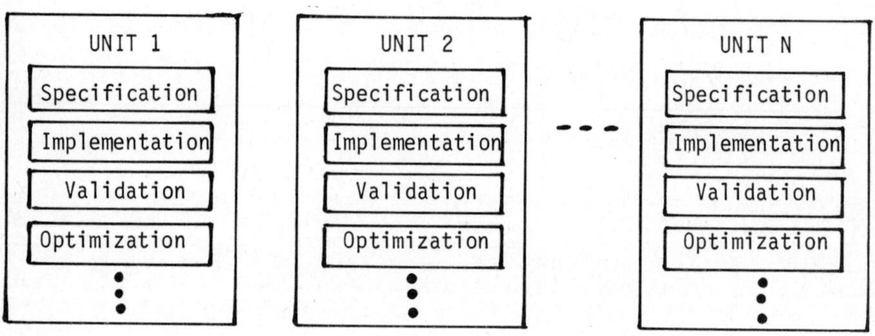

Figure 5a. Logical decomposition of a system, with the various aspects of each component being described separately.

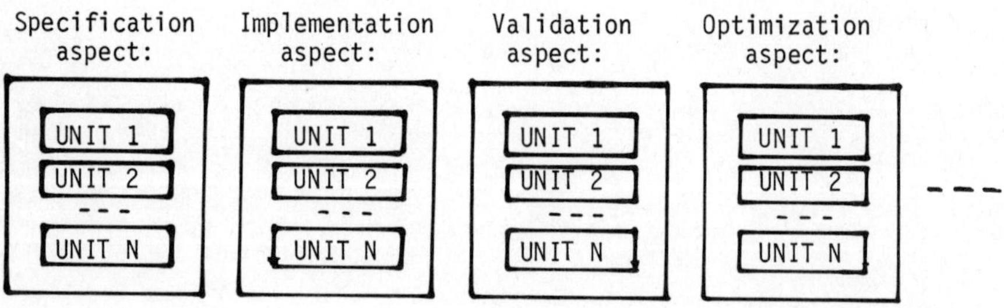

Figure 5b. Dual decomposition of the same system, with each separate aspect of the whole being presented in isolation.

to procedures, classes, clusters, forms, domains, modules, capsules (or "baskets", if that should prove to be more convenient...). It is certainly more realistic to assume that most complex software systems will have to be characterized in terms of some combination of these different structuring concepts. At the same time, however, it seems quite reasonable to consider each individual component, regardless of it nature, to be the "product" of the information associated with the different activities contributing to its development, and to organize the program text accordingly.

A second, compelling reason for adopting such a physical structure is that it directly lends itself to an alternative presentation of the given system, wherein the information is grouped on the basis of the separate activities involved in the development process (see fig. 5b). If indeed the division of labor in software production is to be taken seriously, then this second image must surely correspond to a meaningful view of the program product, in so far as it explicitly reflects the various tasks that are performed as part of the development cycle. Presumably, any approach which directly supports such a presentation would go a long way towards facilitating the work involved in that process. While there may well exist other useful forms in which to present the same information, we feel that this two-dimensional partitioning, on the basis of the logical structure and according to the different activities, would probably be sufficient, at least as a starting point. In any case, we are convinced that such an approach would represent a significant improvement over the present situation, where the different kinds of information within a program are intermixed in an almost arbitrary fashion.

By way of anticipating some of the initial objections that may be raised, it should be stated at once that the specific "aspects" of a program referred to above were chosen solely for purposes of illustration. They correspond to certain of the activities traditionally identified as part of the software development process, but this was only intended to be indicative of the sort of distinctions that might be relevant. The delimitation of the different activities involved in software development is itself somewhat arbitrary, and to a large extent subjective. (For instance, no mention of "documentation" was made in figs. 5a and 5b, perhaps reflecting the authors' prejudice that this should not be carried out as a separate activity in its own right.) Moreover, the "ideal" division of labor may very well depend upon both the type of application that is of interest and the organizational structure of a particular environment, which could give rise to considerable variation from one context to another. It is apparent that to discuss software morphology in such terms is ultimately to speak of *software ergonomy*, an area in which there is practically no scientific basis at present. The divisions of labor which are typical in current practice have grown up out of accumulated experience with classical production techniques and tools. One cannot help but feel, however, that the distinctions among various tasks are at times rather artificial and that they represent, more often than not, an ad hoc response to the problems posed by existing technology. To further complicate matters, the question of which development activities should be singled out as separate aspects within the program text must be resolved within the broader context of an overall programming methodology (an area which is not without controversy at the moment). It may therefore be infered that a number of variations will probably have to be tried out before a fully satisfactory approach can be agreed upon. The need for a certain amount of experimentation does not, in our opinion, invalidate the general guideline proposed here.

Some further implications of the criteria suggested above will be explored in the next section. It is to be noted from the outset, however, that any progress towards the sort of approach proposed here will depend on finding solutions to two, interrelated technical problems:

(1) Appropriate *descriptive techniques* must be developed, so as to allow the the various aspects of a system to be completely characterized *in isolation*, rather than requiring the different kinds of information to be interspersed throughout the program text (in effect forcing the programmer to express himself in terms of the underlying program). This is essentially a matter of language design, but the objectives to be achieved imply a significant departure from the traditional (compiler-oriented) criteria that have heretofore been applied in this domain. It should be observed that, for certain aspects which are of interest (e.g., specification, implementation and optimization), the problem is one of formulating the same solution at several different "levels of abstraction" or, perhaps more appropriately, of supplying further constraints, implicitly associated with such levels. Since "abstraction" is the focus of a great deal of current research, there is already some basis for arriving at adequate linguistic mechanisms. For other aspects (such as analysis and measurement), however, it is much more a question of introducing additional information into an existing program. To date there has been very little work on language constructs for describing this kind of facility independently; the usual approach is simply to (manually) insert instructions into the code.

(2) The corresponding *constructive methods* must also be developed, whereby the different, separately descibed aspects of a system are combined in order to create the final (executable) product (or intermediate versions thereof). The objective is, of course, to fully *automate* the process of constructing the underlying program, instead of obliging the programmer to perform what amounts to the same task, but in a manual (and characteristically error-prone) fashion. There are two complementary facets to this problem. The first is to find, for each separate aspect, the relevant *validation* techniques, serving to ensure not only the internal consistency of the individual definitions but also their mutual compatibility; in so far as possible, this control must be exercised statically, i.e., at the time the constituent descriptions are first introduced. The second facet concerns the actual *generation* techniques to be employed. Because of the overhead involved, it is obviously unacceptable to impose an "interpretive interface" between the various aspects (that is, to accommodate all conceivable possibilities by means of cascaded calls on general purpose procedures). In all probability, methods more akin to those used in system generation will ultimately prove to be the most effective. More generally, it seems clear that the whole compilation process will have to be seen in a much differnt light than at present, owing to the premise that the requisite information arrives "piecemeal" rather than being presented in such a way as to make life easy for the compiler!

The principle of physically separating the information in a program according to the activities involved in its development is strongly related to a recurrent theme in many recent proposals: that the program text should reflect the development history. This process may be seen as a coordinated series of actions - making decisions (and meeting constraints) - which contribute to the construction of the final program product. Of course, it is not the exact sequence in which those actions were carried out that is of interest. However, the essence of the approach we are advocating is that the program text should constitute a record of the decisions themselves, rather than exhibiting their consequences. It is preferable to leave the task of working out all of the ramifications of each decision to more reliable mechanical devices. The indispensible corallary to this argument is that *the underlying program should be inaccessible to the programmer*; its properties should only be detectable by "measurements". This stipulation is necessary in the face of human frailty, to forestall any temptation to modify the underlying program instead of the original program text, thereby creating chaos.We contend that there is really nothing to be learned by inspecting the resultant product (or the executable code) that could not better be determined by a suitable analytical tool.

For the morphological approach outlined above, only the activities involved in the program development cycle were taken into consideration. It should be evident, however, that this general guideline could readily be extended to the maintenance phase as well, so as to encompass the software production process in its entirety. Perhaps we may look forward to the day when the text of a program product will consist (at least at some stage) of a clearly organized original together with an appropriate list of modifications. The propagation of such changes appears to be yet another tedious and error-prone task that is better performed by machines rather than by human beings.

5. *Towards a further separation of concerns in programming*

Although the principle of separating the information in a program text on the basis of distinct activities embodies, in our opinion, a desirable objective, the criteria suggested in the previous section represent something of an over-simplification. The traditional division of labor in software production serves as a suitable point of departure, but to be truly effective the guideline of *separation of concerns* should be systematically extended to all aspects of the programming process. In large-scale system development, it is often appropriate to further subdivide the work into a number of relatively specialized technical tasks, amongst which one may identify (at least) the following domains:

- overall organization and decomposition,
- communication and synchronization conventions,
- data structures and their representation,
- algorithms and their implementation.

(It is to be noted that, whereas conventional programming languages cater almost exclusively to the latter two aspects, the issues associated with the former are frequently far more crucial in terms of their effect on the quality of the finished product.) Within the context of such additional distinctions, one might adopt the point of view that the usual activities (specification, implementation, validation, optimization, etc.) should then be carried out in some sense for *each* of the different domains involved. Below, we shall briefly consider a number of current proposals in these and other areas from the standpoint of their potential contribution to achieving the desired separation of concerns.

● *Overall organization and decomposition*. This area has come to be recognized as perhaps the central preoccupation in system design, owing to its pervasive role in determining the shape of the finished program product. Possibly the most conspicuous result of the recent concern with programming methodology, aside from the ubiquitous "structured" control constructs, is the proliferation of specific linguistic mechanisms aimed at supporting the proper "modularization" of programs [cf. Goos and Kastens,1977]. Encompassing such concepts as procedures, co-routines, processes, monitors and abstract data types, the facilities that have been proposed range from the SIMULA class (which tries to be all of these things at once) to the Modula module (which directly corresponds to none of them). All of these proposals, however, tend to regard modularization as a matter of establishing a suitabl "skeleton", and therefore take the form of special "brackets" for enclosing certain portions of the program text:

```
module M1:
        <...other constructions...>
        module M2:
                <...other constructions...>
        end M2;
        <...other constructions...>
end M1;
```

While this approach may be appropriate at the level of the underlying program, it seems particularly ill suited to the problem of formulating either the skeleton itself or its relevant properties, since these aspects must generally be conceived long before the "other constructions" in question are completely known (or even envisioned). Some efforts have been made in the direction of permitting such decisions to be expressed in an independent fashion, notably the "module interconnection language" of De Remer and Kron [1976] (cf. also [Cheval et al.1977] where separate languages are used for defining and interconnecting modules). More generally, these issues should probably be addressed in the context of a "design language", wherein the basic framework of the entire system is first formulated, together with the fundamental constraints to be respected (and therefore propagated automatically) throughout subsequent phases of the development (and the program). While there has been some work towards this goal, particularly by Parnas [1977] and by Ross [1977], the problem of how best to describe such considerations (to say nothing about how to arrive at the "right" decomposition in the first place) is still very much of an open question. To single these issues out as a separate concern is only the first, but a very significant step in the search for a satisfactory solution.

• *Communication and synchronization conventions*. This area encompasses a number of difficult problems, which collectively constitute the heart of most software design efforts. Despite the central importance of these issues however, there is no systematic approach that is applicable to the entire spectrum of such questions, at least not in common usage. Instead the practicing programmer is confronted with a rather bewildering variety of distin (and sometimes conceptually incompatible) mechanisms and then left to cope best he can. Global variables are the most traditional means of communicati (e.g., between procedures or in the nested modules shown above), though the have come to be considered as somewhat suspect, if not totally "harmful". A the level of the underlying program, such intentions must generally be expressed indirectly, by declaring the variables in the proper scope relative to the static structure of the program (blocks or some derivative thereof). This serves mainly to obscure the basic patterns of communication, especially since nesting is a notoriously awkward and restrictive framework within which to work. A further consequence of adopting low-level approaches of this sort is to create what is essentially an artificial problem, that of "visibility":

```
begin var V1, V2; ...
      proc P1: ...V1... end P1; ...
      proc P2: ...V2... end P2; ...
      proc P3: ...V1...V2... end P3; ...
end
```

(How does one indicate that V1 is only meant to be "seen" in P1 and P3, while V2 should only be visible in P2 and P3 ?) More seriously, nowhere is there any mechanism for specifying the implicit assumptions about the way in which such variables are used to exchange information (e.g., the sequence of values taken on). Of course, the situation is even worse on the larger scale, where the task of sorting out the patterns of communication is most frequently left to some linkage editor; the intentions are not only obscure in such cases, they are practically invisible! Another basic method of establishing communication between different components of a program is by means of conventional formal parameter mechanisms. Although this approach can lead to a certain confusion between static and dynamic dependencies, it does offer the advantage of imposing (to some extent) explicitly stated interfaces, which may therefore be verified; unfortunately this facility also tends to break down on the larger scale unless the linkage editor incorporates essentially the same checking capabilities as are present in the compiler. The fundamental disadvantage of such an approach, however, is that the "data-flow" is inextricably interwoven with the flow of control, making it necessary to laboriously follow the latter in order to comprehend the former. While this is in certain respects a characteristic of algorithmic systems, the patterns of communication are surely of sufficient importance in many applications to merit being described in a more direct fashion. There exists a substantial body of work on so-called data-flow languages (often of a rather "picturesque" style), but to date there has been very little effort to exploit the intrinsic duality between a data-flow description and one based on flow of control so as to provide the programmer with more convenient forms for expressing, as a separate consideration, the way in which information is to be communicated. Moreover, it is well known that the complexity of this class of problems increases dramatically whenever it becomes necessary to synchronize accesses to "critical" data items or, more generally, to interpose a specific "protocol" for coordinating the exchange of information (this usually arises in connection with trying to take advantage of potential concurrency, and is especially crucial in the context of "distributed systems"). Early mechanisms for this purpose (mainly semaphores) typically involved interspersing the corresponding special instructions at properly chosen places within the normal (sequential) control structure. Later proposals (primarily monitors) still have this property, though to a lesser extent, since they have gone a long way towards providing a more convenient framework for structuring the definition of such interactions. These more recent techniques, however, remain open to the same criticisms evoked above with regard to modularization. A more promising avenue of approach (in terms of the objectives advocated here) is perhaps to be found in variants on the concept of path-expressions or in a number of analogous notions that have been proposed for independently defining such control and synchronization constraints (cf. in particular Bekkers et al.[1977] and Kotov [1977]). Even in the light of these proposals, the feeling nevertheless persists that we are still rather far from a comprehensive method of specifying desired patterns of communication, especially if this aspect is to be described in isolation.

• *Data structures and their representation.* In this area there exists a considerable body of work which could serve as the basis for achieving the sort of separation of concerns advocated in this paper. In part, this is because the fundamental requirement, the ability to define the desired data structures independently of their subsequent usage, is already firmly established and directly supported by most higher-level languages in the form of appropriate declarations: the principle is to specify the relevant propertie at the "defining occurrence" of the name used to denote a given data structure, whereby they are then implicitly associated with each individual "applied occurrence" of that identifier; the independence is preserved so long as the notation used to refer to such data structures does not vary as a function of the particular properties which were declared (i.e., the language provides for "uniform referents", to use the term coined by D. Ross). Building upon this foundation, there have been a number of proposals leading towards an even further separation of the various aspects involved in data structure definition. For instance, one of the design objectives in the language LIS [Ichbiah et al. 1974] was to physically isolate certain low-level, machine dependent aspects of such definitions within a separate "implementation part" (thus providing a concrete example of the morphological approac suggested in the previous section). A rather more sophisticated example of isolating data structure representation decisions is to be found in the SETI "representation sublanguage" [Dewar et al. 1977]. There is also the much mor general concept of defining new data *types* (a class of objects rather than one individual instance), which was initially developed in the context of work on extensible languages; in particular, the experimental language EL1 [Wegbreit,1974] permitted the user to specify the corresponding implementat for the "built-in" operations of the language (generation, selection, assignment, etc.) as part of the new type definition. Carrying this principle one step further, the thrust of the current work on "abstract data types" is to provide linguistic mechanisms for defining the "logical behaivior" of so class of objects in such a way as to render their subsequent utilization essentially independent of the underlying representation (cf. languages like CLU, Alphard, Euclid and Mesa - among many others). A predictable outgrowth of these efforts is the emerging emphasis on formally describing the data types of interest solely in terms of their desired behavior, implying a distinct "specification language" (whether "operational" in nature [London et al. 1977] or, perhaps more appropriately, in "algebraic" form [Guttag,1977] While most of this work has so far been oriented towards the verification problem, there have also been some preliminary attempts aimed at developing an alternative approach, namely to automatically derive the actual implementation from the specifications themselves and some indication of the key representation decisions [e.g., King,1977]. It should be evident that there is no shortage of ideas as to how to go about separating the various aspect connected with data structures. The problem is much more one of "distilling existing proposals in order to come up with an approach that can be applied in practice.

• *Algorithms and their implementation.* Whereas the basic mechanisms for encapsulating this aspect of programs (procedures and the like) have been wit us almost from the outset of computing, to this day there are practically n effective methods for separating the various concerns involved in the development of algorithms (with the possible exception of the information introduced for purposes of validation and/or verification, though this is of course traditionally interspersed throughout the program text). This situation persists despite (or perhaps because of) the fact that algorithmics is usually regarded as the most fundamental aspect of programming. There ar two possible interpretations: either present programming languages have evolved to the point that, on the whole, they are now considered to be fully satisfactory vehicles for expressing the algorithmic aspects of programs, and their compilers to be completely adequate tools for producing the finished products which are of interest (but why then are there so many different languages proposed or in use, with such a wide variation in "level", and why is there a need to supply so much guidance and other extra information in order to arrive at the desired result?); alternatively, it may be that once the level and style of the basic algorithmic component have been fixed, the ramifications of this choice are so pervasive that there is really nothing else to do but to "live with" the limitations inherent in this framework, and to resort to whatever expedients are at hand when problems arise. With regard to the formulation of algorithms, a great deal of attention has recently been focused on stepwise refinement and analogous constructive approaches. However, even among the advocates of such techniques, very few have bothered to take the additional step of providing the corresponding linguistic support, so as to preserve some trace of the actual development strategy as part of the program text instead of throwing away this invaluable information in the process. While we strongly concur with Meertens [1977] on the necessity of explicitly accommodating these constructive methods, it should be recognized that such facilities represent only a partial solution. In particular, it is well known that they do not allow certain low-level considerations (e.g., access times) to be conveniently introduced in an after-the-fact fashion, since the consequences of such constraints have an annoying tendency to "percolate up" to the highest levels of the algorithm in question. Moreover, these simple refinement mechanisms do not by themselves constitute a suitable framework for expressing the fact that the desired algorithm is to be obtained by "adapting" some more basic one, especially in the context of quite substantial modifications as would be the case, for instance, when introducing a significant degree of parallelism. Although there has been considerable progress towards automating effective transformation methods, both for purposes of program "improvement" and even for the "synthesis" of a suitable implementation from some set of specifications [e.g., Burstall and Darlington,1977], it has not yet been accepted that one should regard the corresponding directives (and the other information which must be supplied) as proper components of the program text, rather than looking at the results. Perhaps we may ultimately look forward to the day when a program will consist solely of the statement of an extremely "naive" algorithm, together with a set of "construction rules" to be applied [Sintzoff, 1977]. In the meantime, however, it appears that the algorithmic aspect of programming, albeit the most familiar, would stand to benefit greatly from a more systematic separation of concerns.

The different domains discussed above are those most commonly encountered in practice. As such, they constitute obvious points of departure for any effort aimed at developing programming techniques and tools that promote a more appropriate division of labor in large-scale software production. There exist, however, a number of other areas where the guideline suggested here would seem to be particularly applicable. We shall briefly mention certain of these, which correspond to current (and relatively crucial) problems in software development:

- *Real-time constraints*. Wirth [1977] quite convincingly argues that real-time programs are yet another order of magnitude more complicated than ordinary multiprograms". He advocates a discipline whereby the former are first formulated in terms of the latter, with the additional constraints being introduced afterwards as the final step in the construction process.

Within such a context, it seems clear that the constraints in question ought to be expressed as part of the program itself, especially since most of the analytical effort required to ensure that they will be met can be performed automatically (and in general will have to be!); it is then a relatively straightforward extension to generate the underlying real-time program in the course of carrying out this analysis.

- *Exception handling*. Recognizing and responding to exceptional conditions is frequently one of the overriding concerns in the design of complex systems; for instance, over 30% of the code in a computerized switchboard is devoted to error handling. The treatment of errors is the most common, but far from the only context where such a need may arise. Furthermore, the problems involved in this domain are among the most difficult ones encountered in both design and implementation (to say nothing of validation). Despite this situation (which is generally acknowledged), very few languages offer facilities specifically conceived for this class of problems. The "ON conditions" of PL/I were an early effort to satisfy certain requirements in this area, but by now the shortcomings of this mechanism are well known. Goodenough [1975] has attempted to put these issues into perspective and then to propose a more comprehensive approach; he succeeds mainly however in convincing many readers that it is perhaps unwise to adopt a viewpoint that is too all-encompassing. Surely, the nature of exception conditions is that they are *exceptional*. As such, it seems rather ill advised to assimilate various "normal" communication conventions (e.g., between co-routines, on exits from loops or procedures, etc.) within this framework and, in general, to indiscriminately intermix out-of-the-ordinary considerations into the structure which characterizes the expected pattern of operation. The potential confusion comes, to a large extent, from trying to deal with such problems at the level of the underlying program. These difficulties, together with the diversity of implementation techniques which may be required in different cases, constitute strong arguments in favor of developing some means of describing exception handling as a separate concern.

- *Reliability and redundancy*. At the present moment, "reliability" is probably the predominate preoccupation in software production (if not always from the viewpoint of the producer, then certainly from that of the consumer). For all practical purposes, redundancy is the only known method for increasing reliability. Whereas, in the words of B. Randell, "reliability i *not* an add-on feature," redundancy by its very definition is a matter of adding something (often by means of simple duplication). In this regard, it is useful to distinguish between "linguistic redundancy", the purpose of which is to reduce the probability of undetected programming errors, and "operational redundancy", which serves to ensure the integrity of a system and to enhance the likelihood that it will continue to function satisfactorily even under adverse conditions of operation. While considerable attentio has been devoted to the former problem in the context of current language design efforts, with the notable exception of the work at Newcastle [Randel 1975] there have been almost no attempts to provide linguistic facilities for introducing operational redundancy. Given the fact that such redundancy (which, in the opinion of some, wholely subsumes the problems of exception handling) is by nature a separate concern, this domain would seem to be particularly amenable to the sort of approach advocated here.

Each of the different areas discussed in this section corresponds, in some sense, to a "general purpose" aspect of programming. We have deliberately chosen to focus our attention upon these broader questions, but the possibility of introducing a variety of application specific or "problem oriente aspects should not be overlooked. In effect, the principle of separation of concerns can be seen as the first step towards accommodating an arbitrary number of special purpose components within a particular program. To a certain extent, the familiar FORTRAN formats could be regarded as one instance where such facilities might be more appropriate. A more convincing example is to be found in compiler writing, where some variant on BNF notation is usually employed to define the syntax of the source language to be processed; it is indeed difficult to imagine why the programmer should be concerned with this information in any other form, since there exist perfectly good algorithms for constructing the corresponding syntactic analyzer.

Whereas, in the final analysis, it is always possible to express every aspect of interest at the level of the underlying program (or in terms of the resultant machine code, if one so wishes), there are well established and widely accepted reasons for avoiding this option wherever a viable alternative is available. The need to accommodate a further division of labor in software production is but another argument which tends to reinforce this position. Even in the realm of higher-level languages, however, a general purpose, monolithic approach (PL/I still stands as a monument in this regard) seems inevitably to reduce all forms of expression to the "lowest common denominator": the underlying program. Partly in reaction against the excesses committed in the name of "universality" (without even mentioning the associated costs), there is at present a growing concensus in favor of simpler, more sober programming languages, in particular the "Pascal School". Unfortunately, the number of "ameliorated" dialects spawned by such languages is becoming phenomenal, One suspects, however, that this process will have to be continued through many iterations before arriving at a tool which is truly adequate for production purposes; at the moment there is no basis whatsoever for believing that the final result will be any simpler or more appropriate than its "rococo" predecessors. The principle of separation of concerns put forth in this paper may be seen as one way out of this dilemma. In essence, the proposed approach could be construed as a coordinated collection of special purpose languages. The motto might be: *better a complex of simple languages than a single complex language*. While it is hoped that this objective might provide the point of departure for renewed efforts in language design, it must be remembered that the development of suitable descriptive techniques is not sufficient by itself; the success or failure of any such "multi-language approach" will ultimately depend upon the adequacy of the corresponding constructive methods.

. *Conclusion*

The remarks presented here, though possibly provocative, were hopefully thought provoking. They were offered with the intention of stimulating serious reflection upon the fundamental options to be pursued in the development of future programming languages (whence the absence of specific technical proposals as to how the objectives in question might be realized, which we feel would be wholely premature). Whatever the response to the particular guidelines suggested here, it seems clear that research in this domain must recognize and make a concerted effort to accommodate the requirements of large-scale software production, lest the rapidly widening gap between theory and practice become an abyss.

Acknowledgements. We wish to express our thanks to the BIGRE Group in France for constructive discussion of an earlier presentation of these ideas, and to M. Kronental for encouraging us to pursue certain of their implications.

REFERENCES

Y. Bekkers, J. Briat and J.P. Verjus [1977]:
Construction of a synchronization scheme by independent definition of parallelism,
These proceedings.

L.A. Belady and M.M. Lehman [1976]:
A model of large program development,
IBM Systems Journal,1976,3, pp.225-252.

R.M. Burstall and J. Darlington [1977]:
A transformation system for recursive programs,
Journal of the ACM, 24,1, pp.225-252.

J.L. Cheval, F. Christian, S. Krakowiak, J. Montuelle and J. Mossière [1977]
An experiment in modular program design,
Information Processing 77 (B. Gilchrist, ed.), North-Holland, pp.17-21.

F.L. De Remer and H. Kron [1976]:
Programming in the large versus programming in the small,
IEEE Transactions on Software Engineering, SE-2,2, pp.80-86.

R.B.K. Dewar, A. Grand, S.-C. Liu, E. Schonberg and J.T. Schwartz [1977]:
SETL as a tool for generation of quality software,
These proceedings.

J.B. Goodenough [1975]:
Exception handling: issues and a proposed notation,
Communications of the ACM, 18,12, pp.683-696.

G. Goos and U. Kastens [1977]:
Programming languages and the design of modular programs,
These proceedings.

J.V. Guttag [1977]:
Abstract data types and the development of data structures,
Communications of the ACM, 20,6, pp.397-404.

J.D. Ichbiah, J.P. Rissen and J.C. Héliard [1974]:
The two-level approach to data independent programming in the LIS system implementation language,
Machine Oriented Higher Level Languages (W.L. van der Poel and I. Maarssen, eds.), North-Holland, pp.161-169.

P.R. King [1977]:
On the specification and design of abstract data types,
These proceedings.

V.E. Kotov [1977]:
Concurrent programming with control types,
These proceedings.

R.L. London, M. Shaw and W.A. Wulf [1977]:
Abstraction and verification in Alphard: a symbol table example,
These proceedings.

L. Meertens [1977]:
Program text and program structure,
These proceedings.

D.L. Parnas [1977]:
The use of precise specifications in the development of software,
Information Processing 77 (B. Gilchrist, ed.), North-Holland, pp.861-867.

B. Randell [1975]:
System structure for software fault tolerance,
IEEE Transactions on Software Engineering, SE-1,2, pp.220-232.

D.T. Ross [1977]:
Structured Analysis (SA): a language for communicating ideas,
IEEE Transactions on Software Engineering, SE-3,1, pp.16-34.

M. Sintzoff [1977]:
Inventing program construction rules,
These proceedings.

B. Wegbreit [1974]:
The treatment of data types in EL1,
Communications of the ACM, 17,5, pp. 251-264.

N. Wirth [1977]:
Toward a discipline of real-time programming,
Communications of the ACM, 20,8, pp.577-583.

André et al. : Discussion

Correll: You refer to several aspects of a program: specification, implementation, optimization, etc. What I did not understand is the following. Does implementation mean that you write down, for instance in a programming language, a restatement of the same solution you have written down in the specification part, and do you write down in the optimization part a restatement of the same solution you have given in the implementation part? Or do you do it differently, namely writing down in the implementation part transformation rules which should be applied to the specification part and, in the optimization part, optimization rules which should be applied to the implementation part? There are two different things one could do. Which do you suggest?

André: Ideally, the latter.

Correll: This is quite far from what we can do now. It's not so easy to find transformation rules which, when applied to some specification, result in a satisfactory solution. It's easier just to give the corresponding restatement. So I'm not sure if your approach is for the future or is something we could do now.

André: It's not an approach, but an objective. For now, one should see the parts as giving additional information, rather than a complete restatement (for instance, as with the implementation part in the language LIS).

Bekkers: I don't think it's a question of deducing the implementation from the specification. All of these parts are to be seen beside each other. One is not a restatement of another; rather, they are complementary aspects. This is the case in the language LIS, which I am presently using. The same applies to the synchronization proposal presented in our paper here.

Schuman: The point is that, however the program is constructed (by giving a partial restatement, by simply adding information or even by applying transformations), the text should reflect the actual decisions (or actions) which are taken rather than their ramifications.

Meyer: I should like to mention that the approach you seem to advocate is being applied to the development of quite large programs using the language Z, developed by J.-R. Abrial in Paris. This is a multi-layer language, where the first layer is a purely static description of the problem, based on a set theoretic model, without any reference to dynamic execution. This could be seen as the specification part. Then there is a second level of language which is still set theoretic but also algorithmic, that is, you have instructions with assignments, etc. This level is quite close to SETL. You have further layers where you can perform transformations which get you closer and closer to an actual program text in an executable language. So that is, in some sense, a multi-layer approach to the construction of programs.

André: I know Abrial's work, but the message must be heard by the people designing languages today.

Ershov: You have shown a multiple image of a program text and multiple use of these different images. Do you think that it is worthwhile to have a good program text processor which can produce these different images of a program automatically from some canonical text? Should the possibility (or even the existence) of such a processor constitute an objective criterion for the quality of the corresponding programming language?

André: Yes!

King, J.: I'd like to suggest a solution for these problems, namely having an editor and a data-base working in conjunction with each other. Most of the things described are discussed and have been discussed in data base work. For instance, you have projections. Of course, once you project all those things together then you'd like to have the inverse projections, as is done in data bases. The two different views of a program correspond to a file inversion. Throughout the paper, there were all the different things one sees in the data base area. What you really have is a large amount of information which you'd like to query and examine. The only thing that seems to me slightly different in this application is that I would like to see, examine, and change this data probably more in the common context of an editor, but having the data base behind it. For example, I might want to see just the program text that gets compiled and make changes to it. Then I want to see the correctness assertions. At any moment, I would want to look at some particular aspect. For this I need an editor working against a data base.

Wodon: In both Meerten's and André's talks, you have different program parts which are interconnected (levels in one case, aspects in the other). If you want to see the connection, then you have got to see the whole thing; if you want to see only some aspect then you have got to separate it out. I don't see that there is any way out except using a larger sheet of paper when writing the program. [☺] Seriously, the whole is often as important as it's parts. Inside the machine, of course, you can use a data base, but apart from that I see the "larger sheet of paper" as the only possibility.

King, J.: That was exactly my point. You want to see all of this information, but not all at once, and you want to see how it's related. It seems to me easy to use an editor for looking at different aspects. If for one particular point you want to see some related aspect, you need only type a very simple command and, all of a sudden, you have a screen full of other information. So you never look at the whole thing or at a big sheet of paper; you wander across that paper in time, along different axes according to your desires, using an editor with a data base behind it. Moreover, you want to be able to change that information as you explore it.

Meertens: It's not only a matter of looking at already constructed programs, it is also a question of constructing programs. If somebody offered me a programming language without any input statements, but he told me I could use an editor to insert my data into the program, I would not be very satisfied. In fact, at our computing service we have an editor with a data base behind it, with special transformations making it possible to take very high-level specifications and produce a working program. It makes several passes and is customized to the application. It is generally known as an ALGOL 68 Compiler. [☺] The point is that when you are programming, you want to write down a set of specifications or whatever in a way which suits you, which is usable and useful to communicate information to yourself and to other people, i.e., it should be human-oriented. What you would like to do is to present that, without any transformation, to a computer which will then perform mechanical transformations as needed. That is known as a compiler.

Ross: Considerably more than an editor is needed. I hate to keep harking back to AED. There we do have a conditional macro-expander and the mechanics of all these techniques were tried at various times, but it kept coming out unreadable. I'm pretty sure that the answer lies in King's pleading for a data base so you can be selective, together with what really is a whole compiler rather than just an editing process. Only with that kind of combination can you start to achieve these objectives. I think it's a more difficult tool design job than you realize until you start trying it.

Holager: I have now seen a number of presentations advocating that the programming system should record the pieces that the programmer produced when he wrote the program and the sequence in which this was done. I think we should try to take a step backwards now and consider why. Such a record seems to be a pretty good tutorial exposition, for the fellow wanting to read it, debug and modify it. But, it seems to me that the order in which it was written is not necessarily the best order in which to read. As King pointed out, it is quite possible to have a system which allows you to go through your program in just about any order. It is possible to make a tool which allows you to pick out any identifiable set of pieces of your program and to consider them in isolation. I think we should try to think a little more about the needs of the programming process, and about which things must be seen in what order during that process. It seems to me that there are at least four main types of tasks. You write the program, but that's a very small job, really. The first important thing is when you read it to try to learn what this program is all about. Then it seems like a good idea to follow the footsteps of the author. Secondly, you want to fix bugs. Then you probably want to go through it in quite a different manner. Thirdly, you will want to put in new functions to modify it. I really don't know what order you want then. Fourthly (that should have been the second, perhaps), you want to verify it, at least informally. Clearly, when you want to verify it, you very much want a system which automatically forces you through all the relevant aspects.

Constructing Quality Software, P.G. Hibbard/S.A. Schuman (eds.)

AN INTEGRATED TOOL FOR THE BUILDING OF LARGE SOFTWARE SYSTEMS

Andrej Mráz
Computing Research Centre,
Bratislava, Czechoslovakia

The paper describes an integrated tool for the development of large software systems. The system is designed to improve the quality of the software developed and to automate many activities connected with software development. The system described is simultaneously a production tool, an information system and a control system.

INTRODUCTION

In order to achieve a higher quality of software, it is generally accepted that both methods of construction and appropriate tools are necessary.

A wide spectrum of different tools has been developed, but few of them are in general use. The main exceptions are text editors and program librarians. There are many reasons for this situation.

- Most of the above mentioned tools depend on the language which they are supposed to support.
- Many of them are not portable to another operating system or hardware environment.
- They are often incompatible with one another.
- They are clumsy to use.
- The use of some of these tools is deliberately restricted (because of competition among software producers).

These and a lot of other difficulties encountered in program development could be overcome if the various tools were integrated.

It is not a new idea to integrate such support tools. In the last few years, some integrated tools have been designed, built and even used (with varying degrees of success). However, the range of activities automated by existing systems of integrated tools is rather narrow. Nonetheless, it seems to be true that the increased integration of those systems substantially improves the quality of software which is built. Currently almost any institution building large-scale software systems develops its own version of a more or less integrated software development system. This is merely empirical evidence supporting the usefulness of integration. There are also reasons intrinsic to the problem that make the integration desirable.

- The software development process is still rather irrational. Therefore there are many tools which cannot be coherently incorporated into any homogeneous programming language. Still the tools have to be somehow unified.
- Many functionally different tools can use the same program components (e.g. parsing and data- and control-flow analysis can be used for automatic documentation, optimization, static syntax checking, etc.). This economizes on the number of components within the system, guarantees their compatibility and makes the system easier to use.
- By an integrated approach many activities can be controlled, analyzed and checked, as well as automated (i.e., recording the number of "test runs", performing thorough intermodular checking and optimization etc.)

In this paper we describe an integrated system which is being developed at the CRC Bratislava.

DESCRIPTION OF THE SYSTEM

The system is intended to integrate the most important tools which support software systems development, starting from the moment when the architecture of the future software system is specified. Most of the pertinent activities can be mapped onto the following groups of tools:

- the implementation language
- tools producing automatic documentation
- maintenance and modification tools
- testing and debugging tools
- tools ensuring active reliability
- linking mechanisms
- optimization
- data base administrator.

The basis for integrating these tools is the methodology of modular programming.

The implementation language

The implementation language is the core of the system. It has been derived from the programming language MODULA. The main change to the language is the introduction of separate compilation, where all information about modules is stored in the database. The system itself is written in this implementation language.

The system uses a multipass compiler with different intermediate languages. Particular tools are plugged into the system at the appropriate "level of abstraction" corresponding to a particular intermediate language. Multipass design also facilitates porting the system to smaller computers.

The data base

The data base management system stores different types of data having complex inter-relations. Every part of the source program is stored together with other data and information, viz:

- Information about the overall structure of the system under development and information as to where that particular part belongs.
- The program specifications, together with information identifying the author of the specification, indicating who is authorized to make modifications, recording the date when the coding was started and when it is scheduled to be finished, etc.
- The program itself, together with the data used to test it, subroutines for a special testing environment, control results (used for automatic checking of test-runs), other versions of the program, etc.
- A definition of the interface with other program modules, types and objects visible from other modules.

Analysis and evaluation

Some of the stored data may be used immediately whereas the others, which predominate, have to be analyzed beforehand. Many of the analytical activities can be automated. The most important is the analysis of program properties. The results can be used to enhance program efficiency, reliability (testing, debugging), to improve structural properties of programs (legibility, modifiability, etc.), to optimize programs, to create automatic documentation and to produce selected results of analysis and evaluation to suggest to the programmer how to reshape his programs in order to improve their quality. Most of the above mentioned analysis is derived from data and control flow analysis (both static and dynamic).

Moreover, data of a statistical or organizational nature can be obtained, such as simple statistical sums, averages or even correlations, as well as organizational (pert-time) evaluations. Thus the productivity of programmers may be checked, the system itself can evaluate the efficiency of its own components and other important information for the control of the software development process can be extracted.

Modifications and maintenance

The system provides tools ranging from common text editing (of source programs, data associated with scheduling or budgeting, etc.) through more sophisticated syntax-driven program modification all the way to automatic modification (optimization).

Checking

The system allows the user to switch on or off a variety of dynamic checks of his running programs. An exhaustive static checking is also done by the system. Using the information stored in the data base, various intermodular relations are checked.

Full-fledged verification is not incorporated into the system, but many static semantic checks, based on useful redundancy (intermodular type checking, consistency of versions of separately compiled interdependent modules etc.) are provided.

CONCLUSION

At present it is rather difficult to say which tools are effective in practical use or what will happen when these tools are integrated. Therefore the system is of a somewhat experimental nature. Some tools might be deleted from the system and the others may be added or modified.

The CRC plans to deliver the first version of the system to the users at the end of this year.

LITERATURE

1. L. Osterweil and L. D. Fosdick, "DAVE-A Validation, Error Detection and Documentation System for Fortran Programs," University of Colorado, Department of Computer Science, TR No.CU-CS-071-75.

2. L. Clarke, "A System to Generate Test Data and Symbolically Execute Programs," University of Colorado, Department of Computer Science, TR No.Cu-CS-060-75.

3. R. M. Balzer, "Exdams: extensible debugging and monitoring system," AFIPS 1969 SJCC, 34, 567-580, AFIPS Press, Montvale, N.J.

4. N. Wirth, "MODULA" A Language for Modular Multiprogramming," TR.18 ETH Zürich, June 1976.

Mráz : Discussion

Ershov: I would like to clarify the design objectives of this project. Is it intended as a vehicle for your own research or do you have some real or imagined customer?

Mráz: It is basically designed for real use. We have a very fortunate situation. In our centre there are some groups which are building a rather large statistical information system and they are in a sense obliged to use our system.

Turski: That certainly will improve its quality!

Mráz: I believe that. We are learning from this experience. We find that solving the sort of problems that real users have gives us some idea of what is really important, and of what really helps in programming. A system which is designed from "behind a desk" usually does not work in the way which was expected.

Ershov: You use the term "integrated". From your paper I have interpreted this term to mean an integrated collection of tools, but in your presentation you spoke of integrating the implementor and the user as well, so there is some ambiguity.

Mráz: Our main objective is the integration of tools, not the integration of users. But, in the first stages of development it is probably beneficial to integrate the users as well, because the quality of the system will be much better if we know what users need and if they know what we can give them and when. But the main objective is really the integration of tools.

Turski: May I ask you to answer one question? For what is your system being designed? What is the purpose of this system? What is its planned use? What is the specification for this product? What is it for? What is the objective to be achieved?

Mráz: We intend this system to be for anybody who is going to implement a large software system, anybody who has already specified the main functions of his future system and has designed its general architecture. We are trying to give him a tool which will help him in programming. On the other hand, there are two kinds of prospective users. Some are managers and the others are programmers. Most of the tools are for the programmers' benefit. We also believe that this integrated approach allows us to create data which could be helpful to managers, and which could even be useful in finding out what happens in the process of software creation.

Turski: I was rather afraid that I would get an answer like that. The specification is not only incomplete, it is non-existent. There is only one purpose: to design a system in which to try several (I believe) very bright ideas. This is excellent, but we are talking here about the quality of software. We are not talking here about exercises to develop creativity. Now, I would like to ask the author what sort of measures did he have before he set to work, and how is he going to measure success? If the system works, is that success? Or did he have in mind some other criteria? There are dozens of systems in which you can write software which is modular, highly integrated, complex and fully verified. We know such systems. Ross produced about ten of them. Almost anybody can design such systems. It is a challenge to implement them and some of us are lucky enough to have the money to do so. Others do not, but it does not really matter because we do not know why such systems are going to improve the quality of software. I am trying to get at the real qualities of such systems, rather than a lot of buzz words which describe a complex, integrated approach and so on. Now, I am a programmer, too, and I can utter any number of these wonderful words for public relations, like "let the machine do what it is best suited to do". I just want to find out how you know it is going to improve the quality of software? The answer I am getting is because it is integrated, complex and so on. Perhaps I should give up at this stage. [Exits through portable tunnel.]

Koster: I have a partial answer to Turski. The first measure for success is what happens to your own programming when you have that kind of system. The second check is to see what somebody else does with it when he gets it into his hands. I happen to be involved in the development of a similar system and I know the reactions from users, which go in the direction of feeling liberated from the circumstances under which they had to work before. But perhaps this is an irrational response; more rationally, users start undertaking more difficult things than they otherwise would have, and seemingly going about them more competently than expected.

Dewar: I think it is very well to ask what guarantees you have that this approach will improve software quality. It seems that the point is to remove irritations in programming, but it is not clear that the irritations are not beneficial. For example, I give a couple of ways in which such a system may eventually have a bad effect on software quality. In the first place making it easier to program certainly invites more people to program. The easier you make it to program, the more incompetent people are invited to take on tasks which are beyond them. Another possible effect might come from automatic documentation systems which may encourage people to think that they do not need to document, that the machine would be able to do it for them. There may be many other respects in which systems like this would not have the expected effects. We must measure the effects of such systems and not merely assume that they are obviously desirable.

Mráz: We are aware that a large integrated system is not a solution by itself. We have much experience with using more or less complicated systems at our centre. We know from our own experience that the more complicated the systems we have, the greater the temptation for the programmer to use more complicated constructs. Programs are less legible, more difficult to understand, less efficient and so on. But on the other hand, for the programmer who is following some methodology, and who is educated in programming, an integrated tool can be a real help. The system alone would not help anybody; quite the contrary. But if the system is combined with education of programmers in some methodology and strong direction from managers or lead programmers, then some success can be achieved. Another thing: very few people know how to measure the efficiency of any method or the success of any system. We want the system to measure some quality indications such as number of debugging runs and so on. Of course, we know how long it took to write a program with available tools and we can compare it with the performance of those who use our system. We can compare the number of errors. We do believe that we can experiment with the system and we will see how it helps and how it does not.

Ross: I believe that such systems as we are talking about here do form an essential part of a systematic approach to quality software. They don't themselves yield quality software but can give the stability needed to attain the achievement of quality.

Constructing Quality Software, P.G. Hibbard/S.A. Schuman (eds.)

ABSTRACTION and VERIFICATION in ALPHARD: A Symbol Table Example

Ralph L. London, USC Information Sciences Institute

Mary Shaw, Carnegie-Mellon University

Wm. A. Wulf, Carnegie-Mellon University

Abstract: The design of the Alphard programming language has been strongly influenced by ideas from the areas of programming methodology and formal program verification. In this paper we design, implement, and verify a general symbol table mechanism. This example is rich enough to allow us to illustrate the use as well as the definition of programmer-defined abstractions. The verification illustrates the power of the <u>form</u> to simplify proofs by providing strong specifications of such abstractions.

Introduction--The Symbol Table Task

Previous reports [Shaw76b, Wulf76a,b] have described the Alphard programming language and its associated verification methodology. These reports developed Alphard definitions for the canonical examples of data abstractions (stacks, queues, and sets). These examples are sufficiently simple to be grasped readily, and they have appeared often enough in other languages that the reader may compare various approaches to their definition. There is, however, a danger in considering *only* these examples. It is possible that an approach will work for only the easy examples, or that the definition of something more complex will be far less elegant. Therefore, in this report we shall consider a larger, more realistic example: an abstraction of a *symbol table*. For comparison purposes the reader may wish to refer to the similar example given in [Guttag76] and to a hashtable example in [Wegbreit76].

The research described here was supported in part by the National Science Foundation (Grant DCR74-04187) and in part by the Defense Advanced Research Projects Agency (Contracts: F44620-73-C-0074, monitored by the Air Force Office of Scientific Research, and DAHC-15-72-C-0308).

Since the present paper is one of a series, we shall repeat very little of the background, motivations, and design goals (and also syntax and semantics) for Alphard that appear in the previous papers. We presume that the reader is familiar with the use of a form for abstraction and with the verification methodology for a form. The design goals originally were, and remain, concerned with both programming methodology and verification. We wish to produce a programming environment which supports and encourages the development of "well structured" programs, and which also makes the verification of these programs easier than in existing languages. We believe that verification is an important part, but only one part, in constructing or producing quality software. Verification is not something to be done only after the software is finally constructed, but must at least be considered from the first design decisions onward.

Suppose, then, that we must produce a number of compilers, assemblers, and interpreters to operate on several different computers. Each such system will contain a symbol table mechanism; although each system will have its own requirements, many of the gross, *abstract* properties of these symbol tables will be the same. It seems desirable to have a single implementation of these common aspects which is verified; that will be our aim.

But what *are* the common properties? Many texts [e.g., Gries71] describe a symbol table as a *mapping* from identifiers (strings appearing in a source program) to a set of *attributes* associated with those identifiers. Examples of such attributes include "type", "run-time memory address", "number of dimensions" (for arrays), etc. In some cases, the mapping may be sensitive to the context in which the identifier occurs. (Algol-like block structure is the most common example of this context sensitivity; the mapping from identifier to attributes depends upon the block in which the identifier appears. Name qualification, as in field selection from a record, is another example in which the interpretation of the field selector depends upon the type of the record.) The common properties, then, are ones which involve the application and manipulation of this mapping; principally

- some means to apply the mapping, i.e., to find the attributes associated with the occurrence of an identifier.

- some means to alter the mapping, e.g., by inserting and/or deleting entries and signaling changes in context.

Since we want our abstraction to serve a spectrum of languages, system types (e.g., compilers and assemblers), and machines, it would *not* be appropriate to include the specific attributes as part of the abstraction. Rather, we shall presume that the user of our abstraction will define some mechanism for storing and retrieving attributes, e.g., a vector of records; our abstraction will then provide a mapping from an identifier to a unique integer which, for example, may then be used as an index into this vector of attribute records.

Concerning the issue of context sensitivity, we shall provide an abstraction which supports block structure because (1) it is the more general case and (2) with proper implementation, the generality costs very little when it is not used. We shall not explicitly provide for the kind of context sensitivity needed for record selectors, but we shall show how the abstraction may be used to achieve it.

Note that the informal term "block-structured" does not describe a unique name-binding policy. For example, consider the program fragment

```
...
integer k=10;
...
    begin
    vector X[1:k];
    integer k=3;
    ...
```

In the declaration of the vector "X", there is a question about which "k" should be used to define its upper bound. The semantics of some languages specify that the value of the variable "k" defined at the outer block level, i.e., 10, should be used; other languages specify that it is the innermost definition, i.e., "integer k=3", which should be used. To accommodate the second of these schemes requires that a full lexical analysis pass be performed before *any* name binding (symbol table construction) is done.

In order to make our abstraction useful on this pure lexical pass, as well as later when the full symbol table is constructed, we shall define it as a mapping between "things" and integers. In a simple system the "things" will be identifiers and the integers will probably be indices into the vector of attributes described above. In a more complex system, the initial lexical pass may use the abstraction to convert identifiers into integers; these integers may in turn be the "things" mapped into symbol table indices during a later pass. An example of the use of the abstraction will be given later to help clarify this point; for the moment the reader may simply assume that the "things" are identifiers.

Summarizing, then, our abstraction shall provide:

(a) A block-structured mapping from "things" to integers.

(b) A set of six operations to *insert* a new "thing", to *lookup* the integer associated with a specific "thing", to test whether a specific "thing" is *defined* at the current block level, to *enter* and to *leave* a block level, and to test whether the mapping is *full*, i.e., whether there is room for another "thing".

The Symbol Table Abstraction

The preceding section provides an informal description of the symbol table abstraction; in this section we shall be more precise. To do so, we shall choose one particular specification technique from among the existing techniques. As we have stated in more detail elsewhere [Wulf76a,b], we are neither advocating this technique (abstract model) nor rejecting others (such as algebraic axioms). Alphard should accommodate more than one, and we have chosen for the purposes of the papers one with which we are comfortable. While a serious comparison of specification techniques is eventually required, this paper is not the place to do so. Nor shall we provide stepwise refinements or a systematic construction from the informal description of the symbol table abstraction to the precise specification. We do give, using the syntax and format of Alphard, the precise specifications part of the form called "symtab"[1] followed by several explanatory remarks:

```
form symtab(T:form< ←,=,hash(T,k:integer) returns x:integer pre (k>0) post (0≤x<k') >,
        m,n:integer) =
   beginform
   specifications
        requires n≥1 ∧ m≥1;
        let symtab = <block:integer, assoc:{<s:T,bl:integer,ui:integer>}>;
        invariant
            cardinality(assoc)≤n
            ∧ 1≤ui≤n ∧ 1≤bl≤block
            ∧ (t1,t2 ∈ assoc ⊃ (t1.s=t2.s ∧ t1.bl=t2.bl ≡ t1.ui=t2.ui));
        initially symtab = <1,{}>;
        functions
            defined(st:symtab,str:T) returns t:boolean
                post t = ∃i st <str,st.block',i> ∈ st.assoc,
            insert(st:symtab,str:T) returns i:integer
                pre cardinality(st.assoc) < n ∧ ¬defined(st,str)
                post  st = <st.block', st.assoc' ∪ {<str,st.block',i>}>,
            lookup(st:symtab,str:T) returns x:integer
                post if ∃ y ∈ st.assoc st [y.s=str ∧ ∀z ∈ st.assoc, z.s=str ⊃ z.bl ≤ y.bl]
                    then x = y.ui
                    else x = 0,
```

[1] A primed variable (e.g., k') represents the value of that variable prior to the execution of an operation. To shorten the pre, post, in, and out conditions in our papers, we often, by convention, omit assertions about variables which are completely unchanged. Thus for example, we have omitted st = st' from the post condition of *defined.*

```
enterblock(st:symtab)
    post st = <st.block'+1,st.assoc'>,
leaveblock(st:symtab)
    pre st.block > 1
    post st = <st.block'-1, st.assoc' - {<s,x,ui> st x≥st.block'}>,
full(st:symtab) returns t:boolean
    post t = (cardinality(st.assoc) = n);
```

Note that, abstractly, a symbol table consists of a pair: an integer, "block", and a set, "assoc". The integer denotes the current block level, has the initial value 1, and is altered only by the operations *enterblock* and *leaveblock*. The set, initially empty, consists of triples containing the "thing" defined, the block level at which it was defined, and the unique integer ("ui") associated with the <thing,block level> pair.

The parameters of the form specify the type, "T" (usually strings), of "things" to be entered in the table, and the maximum number, "n", of simultaneous entries permitted. The parameter "m" is a bit more difficult to explain, and we shall for a moment defer it, together with the discussion of the required rights of T.

Since the symbol table contains only currently defined things, the block level of each entry must be legitimate (e.g., between 1 and the current value of "block"). Further, since a maximum of n entries is allowed, the "associated integer" must lie between 1 and n. The let clause and the abstract invariant express these restrictions (the last line of the invariant expresses the uniqueness of the integer associations). The remainder of the specifications states that the initial symbol table has a block level of 1 and an empty "assoc" set, and then lists the symbol table functions and their abstract pre and post conditions.

Now, let us return to the issue of the parameter m and the required rights on T. As may be seen from the requires clause of the specifications, the only requirement on m is that its value be strictly positive; it does not enter into any of the other parts of the formal specification. Hence, one may properly conclude that its precise value is immaterial and the abstraction will function correctly with any positive value.

The value of m does, however, affect the *performance* of the abstraction. Neither Alphard nor other languages with similar goals have yet found an appropriate way to specify performance properties. In practical systems, of course, such properties are of paramount importance. Since we now have no formal way of specifying them, we must give a small peek into the representation in order to explain the significance of m. (Indeed, the need to have m and the hash function name in the specifications has essentially revealed the techniques used in the implementation of the abstraction.) The representation uses a hash table, with collisions resolved by chaining, and m specifies the size of this table, i.e., the number of values that the hash function may assume. Although any positive value of m will work, larger values will tend to provide faster searches at the expense of some additional storage.

In addition, the value of m may affect the distribution of "hits" on any particular hash table entry; see [Knuth73] for a discussion of hashing functions and their properties. We will not discuss these properties here, but note that the form T which defines the things stored in the symbol table is required to provide a hashing function which, given an object of type T and an integer k, returns an integer in the range 0 to k-1. Thus, an appropriate choice of m depends in part on the properties of this function.

Implementation of Symbol Table

In choosing the implementation of the symbol table abstraction, we have been careful to pick a practical one; it is, in fact, one which is used in several commercial compilers. We chose to do this rather than, for example, to use a direct implementation in terms of sets (e.g., the *simpleset* form defined in [Shaw76b]). We have done this in order to emphasize that both the language and verification methodology are intended to be used for practical, production quality systems. The more direct implementation, and also its proof, would have been straightforward and clear. However, it would not have been a production quality implementation and thus would not have been useful in a real system. We shall comment on this point further in the conclusion, but we feel strongly that language, methodology, and verification *must* respond to the requirements of practical, efficient systems.

We shall obtain the implementation in two steps. We shall define an intermediate abstraction (form) in the process of obtaining the complete implementation. This intermediate abstraction will support a restricted, but not uncommon, style of list-processing.

Now, whenever a system implementation is described, one is faced with a presentation problem: whether the description should be "top-down" or "bottom-up". Both have advantages. In this case we have chosen to make the presentation predominantly top-down -- primarily to emphasize that the implementation of lower level abstractions is irrelevant to the correctness of the higher level ones. The next paragraph, however, is an exception to the predominant flavor of the presentation; it describes the implementation of the symbol table in low-level terms, as it will exist after compilation of the *forms*. It is included for those of us (including the authors) who still need concrete representations to aid their reasoning; purists may simply skip the next paragraph.

The symbol table will be implemented as a hash table with explicit entries for the symbol and its declaration block level, but an implicit encoding of the integer mapping.

Hash collisions are resolved by associating a linked list of symbol table entries with each value of the hash function. Each new entry is inserted at the head of the appropriate list. The entries on the lists are therefore ordered by block level (innermost block first). To find the innermost instance of a symbol, *lookup* need only perform a linear search of the list associated with the hash value of the symbol; the first instance of the symbol in the list is necessarily the one declared at the innermost block level. It is a simple matter for *leaveblock* to delete the proper entries from the heads of these lists.

The implementation of symtab presumes the existence of a form called "condis" (collection of named, disjoint integer sequences). The explanation of the symtab implementation will require that we first understand (i.e., specify) condis. Although condis is intended to support a group of linear lists, its abstract specification is stated in terms of more mathematically tractable entities, namely sets and sequences.[2] The verification of symtab will use the abstract specification from condis but nothing else. The verification of condis will be independent of symtab and its verification. The specifications part of condis is (followed by additional explanation):

```
form condis(n,m:integer) =
beginform
specifications
   requires n≥1 ∧ m≥1;
   let condis = L:{sq_i:<e_i1,e_i2, . . . , e_in_i> | 0≤i≤m-1 ∧ e_ik is integer};
   invariant 1≤e_ik≤n ∧ ∀i,j ∈ [0..m-1](e_ik1=e_jk2 ⊃ i=j ∧ k1=k2);
   initially ∀i ∈ [0..m-1] sq_i = <>;
   functions
      xtnd(s:condis,i:integer) returns j:integer
         pre i ∈ [0..m-1] ∧ SIGMA_j∈[0..m-1] length(s.sq_j)<n,
         post s.sq_i = <j>~s.sq_i',          ! note j is a new value not in any sq (by I_a)
      del(s:condis, i,j:integer)
         pre s.sq_i = < . . . , j, . . . > ∧ i∈[0..m-1]
         post s.sq_i = <j, . . . >,
      delall(s:condis,i:integer)
         pre i ∈ [0..m-1]
         post s.sq_i = <>,
      full(s:condis) returns t:boolean
         post t = SIGMA_j∈[0..m-1] length(s.sq_j) = n;
```

[2] Definitions and properties of sets appear in [Halmos60] and those of sequences in [Wulf76a,b].

```
generator indis(s:condis,i:integer) extends x:integer
    requires 0≤i≤m-1
    let indis = s.sq_i where indis≠<> ⊃
            (indis = c~<x>~d and c, <x>, and d are disjoint);
    rule for(I, x, <s,i>, ST) =
        premise s.sq_i=c~<x>~d ∧ I(c) {ST} I(c~<x>);
    rule first(P, x, <s,i>, β, S_1, S_2, Q) =
        premise s.sq_i=c~<x>~d ∧ P ∧ ∀y ∈ c(¬β(y)) ∧ β(x) {S_1} Q,
        premise P ∧ ∀y ∈ s.sq_i¬β(y) {S_2} Q;
auxiliary predicates
    follows(s:condis,i,j:integer) ≡df ∃k st sq_k = <. . ., i, . . ., j, . . .>,
    mbr(s:condis,i,j:integer) ≡df sq_i = <. . ., j, . . .>;
```

A condis is abstractly described as a set of precisely m sequences of integers; these sequences are named sq_0 through sq_{m-1}. The abstract invariant asserts that: (1) each integer in any of the sequences lies in the range 1 to n and (2) a particular integer appears as a sequence element at most once in the entire set of sequences. From these two facts we can observe that the sum of the lengths of the sequences is at most n; moreover, in the case that this sum is n, each of the integers 1 through n will appear (precisely once) in one of the sequences.

As a practical matter, each of the sequences in the condis will represent a linear list; specifically, sq_i will be associated with the value i produced by the hash function. The sequence elements will be the (integer) indices into a vector of information within symtab; thus the sequence sq_i (and the corresponding entries in the vector of information) will represent the linear list of triples in the abstract "assoc" set of symtab which have the hash function value i.

Four functions and a generator are provided by the condis form. Function *xtnd* extends the head of a specified sequence by one element; the abstract invariant prevents this integer from being one which already appears in some sequence. Function *del* permits the initial elements of a specified sequence to be deleted, and function *delall* permits all the elements of a specified sequence to be deleted. Function *full* tests whether all of the integers already are in some sequence. Generator *indis* produces the elements of a specified sequence in order, starting with the head. The specification of condis also gives two auxiliary predicates (*follows* and *mbr*). These may be used in proofs, but are not actually implemented as executable functions; they should be viewed as an extension to the abstract vocabulary.

At first sight, the condis abstraction may seem unusual; however, we chose to define it in this way for two reasons:

- By using integers to denote elements, we can obtain an efficient encoding of the unique integer mapping required by symtab. This encoding is one which might be selected in actual practice.

- This definition allows us to skirt the issue of pointers (references) for purposes of this paper.[3]

Now we can present the complete definition of the symtab form.

```
form symtab(T:form< ←,=,hash(T,k:integer) returns x:integer pre (k>0) post (0≤x<k') >,
        m,n:integer) =
    beginform
    specifications
        requires n≥1 ∧ m≥1;
        let symtab = <block:integer, assoc:{<s:T,bl:integer,ui:integer>}>;
        invariant
            cardinality(assoc)≤n
            ∧ 1≤ui≤n ∧ 1≤bl≤block
            ∧ (t1,t2 ∈ assoc ⊃ (t1.s=t2.s ∧ t1.bl=t2.bl ≡ t1.ui=t2.ui));
        initially symtab = <1,{}>;
        functions
            defined(st:symtab,str:T) returns t:boolean
                post t = ∃i st <str,st.block',i> ∈ st.assoc,
            insert(st:symtab,str:T) returns i:integer
                pre cardinality(st.assoc) < n ∧ ¬defined(st,str)
                post  st = <st.block', st.assoc' ∪ {<str,st.block',i>}>,
            lookup(st:symtab,str:T) returns x:integer
                post if ∃ y ∈ st.assoc st [y.s=str ∧ ∀z ∈ st.assoc, z.s=str ⊃ z.bl ≤ y.bl]
                    then x = y.ui
                    else x = 0,
            enterblock(st:symtab)
                post st = <st.block'+1,st.assoc'>,
            leaveblock(st:symtab)
                pre st.block > 1
                post st = <st.block'-1, st.assoc' - {<s,x,ui> st x≥st.block'}>,
            full(st:symtab) returns t:boolean
                post t = (cardinality(st.assoc) = n);
```

---

3 As most people who have followed the recent literature on programming methodology and verification are aware, the presence of references (unconstrained pointers) in a programming language interferes with our ability to understand and verify programs that use them. While we believe we have made significant progress in Alphard toward resolving the problems introduced by the unconstrained pointer, we will not complicate this paper with pointer issues.

```
representation
    unique
        blvl: integer,
        info: vector(record(s:T,bl:integer),1,n),
        as: condis(n,m)
            init blvl ← 1;
    rep(as,info,blvl) = <blvl, {<info[i].s,info[i].bl,i> | ∃j ∈ [0..m-1] st mbr(as,j,i)}>;
    invariant
        (mbr(as,i,j) ⊃ hash(info[j].s,m) = i)
        ∧ (follows(as,i,j) ⊃ blvl ≥ info[i].bl ≥ info[j].bl ≥ 1 ∧ (info[i]=info[j] ⊃ i=j))

implementation
    body defined out (t = ∃j st st.info[j]=<str,st.blvl> ∧ mbr(st.as,hash(str,m),j)) =
        first j:indis(st.as,hash(str,m)) suchthat st.info[j].s=str
            then t ← st.info[j].bl=st.blvl else t ← false;

    body insert in ¬full(st.as) ∧ ¬defined(st,str)
            out (st.info[i]=<str,st.blvl> ∧ sq_hash(str,m) = <i>~sq'_hash(str,m)) =
        begin
        i ← xtnd(st.as,hash(str,m));
        st.info[i] ← <str,st.blvl>;
        end;

    body lookup out (x=0 ⊃ (j ∈ [1..n] ∧ ∃i ∈ [0..m-1](mbr(st.as,i,j)) ⊃
            st.info[j].s ≠ str)) ∧ (x>0 ⊃ st.info[x].s=str ∧ (st.info[j].s=str ⊃
             j=x ∨ st.info[x].bl > st.info[j].bl)) =
        first j:indis(st.as,hash(str,m)) suchthat st.info[j].s=str
            then x ← j else x ← 0;

    body enterblock out (st.blvl = st.blvl' + 1) =
        st.blvl ← st.blvl+1;

    body leaveblock in st.blvl > 1
            out (st.blvl = st.blvl' - 1 ∧ (j ∈ [1..n] ∧ i ∈ [0..m-1] ⊃
                (mbr(st.as,i,j) ≡ mbr(st.as',i,j) ∧ st.info[j].bl < st.blvl'))) =
        begin
        st.blvl ← st.blvl-1;
        for i: upto(0,m-1) do                ! the generator upto is defined in [Shaw76b]
            first j:indis(st.as,i) suchthat st.info[j].bl ≤ st.blvl
                then del(st.as,i,j) else delall(st.as,i);
        end;
```

```
    body full out (t = SIGMA_{j∈[0..m-1]} length(s.sq_j) = n) =
        t ← full(st.as);
endform
```

Note that the representation of a symtab consists of three objects: (1) *blvl*, an integer, is a direct representation of the abstract entity *block*, and is initialized to 1. (2) *info* is a vector of records which hold the "thing" (usually a string) and the block level at which it was declared. Each of these records is, in effect, one of the triples in the abstract "assoc" set; the third element of the triple, the unique integer, is not explicitly represented -- rather, it is implicitly encoded as the index of this record in the vector. (3) *as* is a condis, and as explained above, it represents a set of lists of indices into this vector of records; each such list is uniquely associated with a hash function value.

A point which may not be obvious is worth noting. It is rare that all *info* entries will be in use; we thus have a potential problem in maintaining the free storage of this vector. This problem is handled by the condis abstraction. The uniqueness of the integers in condis sequences guarantees that no *info* entry will be used simultaneously by different members of assoc. In essence, the integer values which are in the condis sequences correspond to occupied entries, and all other integers in the range 1 to n correspond to unoccupied, or free, entries. Specifically, the abstract invariant of condis and the post condition of *xtnd* together provide a safe allocation of new *info* entries. Similarly, *del* and *delall* provide a safe deallocation mechanism.

To illustrate the operation of the implementation, consider the interaction of the bodies of *insert* and *lookup*. When a new symbol is to be inserted, we first invoke the condis operation *xtnd*. This has the effect of extending the head of the sequence associated with the hash value of the symbol by a new, unique, integer. This integer is then used as the index into the vector *info* and the symbol and current block level are recorded in this entry. When a later *lookup* is performed on this symbol, the *indis* generator is used to find the first integer, j, in the sequence associated with the hash value of the symbol for which "info[j].s" matches. Since *xtnd* extends the sequence at its head, this match is necessarily the most recently declared instance of the symbol.

Verification of the form Symtab

A form is verified by proving four properties as described in [Wulf76a,b] and summarized in Appendix A. As promised earlier, the verification below uses only the abstract specification of the form condis, including the auxiliary predicates. The implementation of condis is, as desired, irrelevant to symtab. All uses of the generator indis satisfy the independence assumption provided that in leaveblock we regard both the then and else clauses as being outside the first generator.[4]

For the form

1. Representation validity

   Show: I_c(as,info,blvl) ⊃ I_a(rep(as,info,blvl))

   Proof: cardinality(assoc) ≤ n follows from I_a for condis, namely, $1 \le e_{ik} \le n$ and no duplicate e_{ik}'s means at most n elements in assoc. The relation 1≤ui≤n holds because of mbr in the rep function and $1 \le e_{ik} \le n$ in I_a for condis. The relation 1≤bl≤block follows by setting j=i in follows(as,i,j) in I_c. To show uniqueness in assoc, first note that identical s and identical bl means, letting hash(t1.s,m) = hash(t2.s,m) = k, that mbr(as,k,t1.ui) and mbr(as,k,t2.ui), whence we have either follows(as,t1.ui,t2.ui) or follows(as,t2.ui,t1.ui). In either case, since info[t1.ui]=info[t2.ui], then t1.ui = t2.ui as required. The converse of the uniqueness clause holds since I_a for condis means no duplicates.

2. Initialization

   Show: n≥1 ∧ m≥1 { blvl←1 } <1,{}> = rep(as,info,blvl) ∧ I_c

   Proof: This holds since initially of condis says each sq_i=<>, i.e., ¬mbr(as,j,i) and ¬follows(as,i,j). Note that n≥1 ∧ m≥1 permits the declaration as:condis.

For the function defined

3. Concrete operation

   Show: I_c { first j:indis(st.as,hash(str,m)) suchthat st.info[j].s=str then t ← st.info[j].bl=st.blvl else t←false } β_{out} ∧ I_c

   Proof: I_c holds since it is unchanged. Indis may be called since 0≤hash(str,m)<m. By the first term of I_c, str can only be located from $sq_{hash(str,m)}$. For the then clause, the second term of I_c gives β_{out}. (Note that mbr(st.as,hash(str,m),j) holds by the definition of indis.) For the else clause str was not located from $sq_{hash(str,m)}$, whence t is false as required.

4a. β_{in} holds

   β_{in} is true

4b. β_{post} holds

   Show: I_c ∧ β_{out} ⊃ t = ∃i *st* <str,st.block',i> ∈ st.assoc

   Proof: If t is true in β_{out}, then <st.info[j].s, st.info(j).bl,j> =

---

[4] Strictly speaking, this violates the definition of the first statement in [Shaw76b], a definition which we must modify to permit, for example, finalization statements and the leaveblock usage. We must also weaken the independence assumption. With the strict interpretation, however, an ad hoc argument shows that there are no problems in this case because indis does not modify the generated sequence and no further generation is attempted after the then and else clauses.

<str,st.block',i> $\in$ st.assoc, i.e., choose i to be j. If t is false in β_{out}, there will be no i and t is false as required.

For the function insert

3. Concrete operation

Show: $\beta_{in} \wedge I_c$ { i←xtnd(st.as,hash(str,m)); st.info[i]←<str,st.blvl> } $\beta_{out} \wedge I_c$

Proof: The pre of xtnd holds because hash(str,m) $\in$ [0..m−1] and because ¬full(st.as) means cardinality(st.assoc) < n whence the SIGMA term < n. The first term of β_{out} is clear. Since the hash(str,m)th sequence of as is extended, $sq_{hash(str,m)}$ = <i>~$sq'_{hash(str,m)}$ where i is the appended new element. The first term of I_c follows by the call to xtnd and st.info[i].s=str; the second term of I_c follows by I_c and ¬defined(st,str), i.e., str is not defined at the current block.

4a. β_{in} holds

Show: $I_c \wedge$ cardinality(st.assoc)<n $\wedge$ ¬defined(st,str) $\supset \beta_{in}$

Proof: cardinality(st.assoc) < n means ¬full(st.as).

4b. β_{post} holds

Show: $I_c \wedge \beta_{pre} \wedge \beta_{out} \supset \beta_{post}$

Proof: The new triple <st.info[i].s,st.info[i].bl,i> is added to st.assoc.

For the function lookup

3. Concrete operation

Show: I_c { first j:indis(st.as,hash(str,m)) suchthat st.info[j].s=str then x←j else x←0 } $\beta_{out} \wedge I_c$

Proof: I_c is unchanged. As in the operation defined, str can only be located from $sq_{hash(str,m)}$. By indis, j $\in$ [1..n]. Hence only the else clause makes x=0 and, as required in this case, j $\in$ [1..n] $\wedge$ $\exists$i $\in$ [0..m−1](mbr(st.as,i,j)) $\supset$ st.info[j].s≠str. For the then clause, the first term after x>0 holds by the suchthat clause. For the second term after x>0, suppose j≠x. Using the second term of I_c (note that follows(st.as,x,j) holds) rules out the possibility that st.info[x].bl=st.info[j].bl since otherwise j=x. Hence st.info[x].bl > st.info[j].bl.

4a. β_{in} holds

β_{in} is true

4b. β_{post} holds

Show: $I_c \wedge \beta_{out} \supset \beta_{post}$

Proof: x=0 means ¬$\exists$y *st* y.s=str. x>0 means x = y.ui, i.e., y = <st.info[j].s,st.info[j].bl,j>.

For the function enterblock

3. Concrete operation

Show: I_c { st.blvl ← st.blvl+1 } $\beta_{out} \wedge I_c$

Proof: β_{out} is clear. Since st.blvl increases, I_c still holds.

4a. β_{in} holds

β_{in} is true

4b. β_{post} holds

Show: $I_c \wedge \beta_{out} \supset \beta_{post}$

Proof: st.block = st.blvl = st.blvl'+1 = st.block'+1 and st.assoc = st.assoc'.

For the function leaveblock

3. Concrete operation

Show: $\beta_{in} \wedge I_c$ { body } $\beta_{out} \wedge I_c$

Proof: st.blvl = st.blvl'-1 is clear. By the for statement each sq_i for i ∈ [0..m-1] is adjusted by the first statement. For each of indis, del, and delall, we have the pre condition i ∈ [0..m-1] by the for statement. The other part of pre of del, mbr(st.as,i,j), holds by indis. In the then case, del(st.as,i,j) deletes all entries in sq_i up to but not including j. Because j is the first j with st.info[j].bl≤st.blvl<st.blvl', the block level ordering asserted by I_c ensures β_{out}. In the else case all st.info[j].bl>st.blvl whence sq_i should become <>, which delall does. β_{out} follows since st.info[j].bl<st.blvl' ≡ ¬mbr(st.as,i,j). In both the then and else cases, I_c still holds because the lists only get shorter and st.blvl>1 on entry.

4a. β_{in} holds

Show: $I_c \wedge$ st.block >1 ⊃ st.blvl>1

Proof: In the rep function, st.block and st.blvl correspond.

4b. β_{post} holds

Show: $I_c \wedge \beta_{pre} \wedge \beta_{out} \supset \beta_{post}$

Proof: Since st.blvl=st.blvl'-1, we have st.block=st.block'-1 as required. By β_{out} and the rep function, st.assoc=st.assoc' - {<s,x,ui> *st* x≥st.block'}.

For the function full

3. Concrete operation

Show: I_c { t←full(st.as) } $\beta_{out} \wedge I_c$

Proof: β_{out} is exactly the post condition of full in condis. I_c is unchanged.

4a. β_{in} holds

β_{in} is true

4b. β_{post} holds

Show: $I_c \wedge \beta_{out} \supset \beta_{post}$

Proof: t = ($\text{SIGMA}_{j \in [0..m-1]}$ length(s.sq_j) = n) = (cardinality(st.assoc) = n).

QED

Implementation of the form Condis

As discussed earlier, the abstract representation of condis is a set of precisely m sequences of integers. The integers in these sequences are all in the range 1 to n, and a particular integer appears at most once in some sequence.

As one might expect, the sequences will be represented by singly linked lists. In fact we shall use an integer vector, *lt* (for link-table), to store all of the lists which represent sequences in a condis. The fact that an index i into lt is in the kth position of such a list will represent the fact that i appears in the kth position of the corresponding abstract sequence. A separate vector, *sq*, of length m, is used for the heads of the lists. In all cases, zero, which is not a legal condis sequence element, is used to indicate the end of a list; thus, in particular, if sq[j]=0, the jth condis sequence is empty.[5] A separate list of those integers which are not currently members of any sequence is also maintained, and the head of this list is maintained in the simple variable *free*. The following diagram illustrates one possible configuration of a condis object which has been declared with m=3 and n=10:

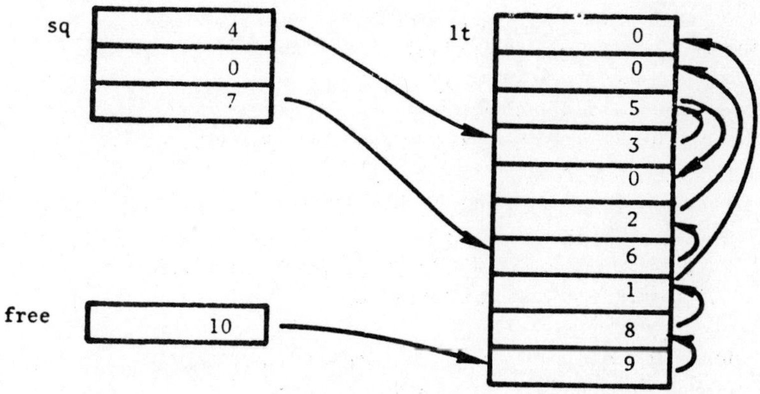

[5] We can now explain why the function delall is *not* redundant. The knowledge that zero ends a list is private to condis, and therefore it is not known in symtab. Hence, in the body of leaveblock of symtab, the operation "delall(as,i)" cannot be replaced by "del(as,i,0)". To do so would violate the pre condition of del because if j is a member of sq_i, it means j≥1.

The full condis form is given below.

```
form condis(n,m:integer) =
beginform
specifications
   requires n≥1 ∧ m≥1;
   let condis = L:{sq_i:<e_i1,e_i2, . . . , e_in_i> | 0≤i≤m-1 ∧ e_ik is integer};
   invariant 1≤e_ik≤n ∧ ∀i,j ∈ [0..m-1](e_ik1=e_jk2 ⊃ i=j ∧ k1=k2);
   initially ∀i ∈ [0..m-1] sq_i = <>;
   functions
       xtnd(s:condis,i:integer) returns j:integer
           pre i ∈ [0..m-1] ∧ SIGMA_j∈[0..m-1] length(s.sq_j)<n,
           post s.sq_i = <j>~s.sq_i',          ! note j is a new value not in any sq (by I_a)
       del(s:condis, i,j:integer)
           pre s.sq_i = < . . . , j, . . . > ∧ i∈[0..m-1]
           post s.sq_i = <j, . . . >,
       delall(s:condis,i:integer)
           pre i ∈ [0..m-1]
           post s.sq_i = <>,
       full(s:condis) returns t:boolean
           post t = SIGMA_j∈[0..m-1] length(s.sq_j) = n;
   generator indis(s:condis,i:integer) extends x:integer
       requires 0≤i≤m-1
       let indis = s.sq_i where indis≠<> ⊃
                   (indis = c~<x>~d and c, <x>, and d are disjoint);
       rule for(I, x, <s,i>, ST) =
           premise s.sq_i=c~<x>~d ∧ I(c) {ST} I(c~<x>);
       rule first(P, x, <s,i>, β, S1, S2, Q) =
           premise s.sq_i=c~<x>~d ∧ P ∧ ∀y ∈ c(¬β(y)) ∧ β(x) {S1} Q,
           premise P ∧ ∀y ∈ s.sq_i¬β(y) {S2} Q;
   auxiliary predicates
       follows(s:condis,i,j:integer) ≡df ∃k st sq_k = < . . ., i, . . ., j, . . . >,
       mbr(s:condis,i,j:integer) ≡df sq_i = < . . ., j, . . . >;
```

```
representation
   unique
        sq: vector(integer,0,m-1),
        lt: vector(integer,1,n),
        free: integer
        init begin free ← 1; for i:upto(1,n-1) do lt[i] ← i+1; lt[n] ← 0;
              for i:upto(0,m-1) do sq[i] ← 0 end;
   rep(sq,lt,free) = {SQ_i | 0≤i≤m-1} where
        if sq[i] = 0 then SQ_i = <> else
        if sq[i] = p_1 ∧ (∀j ∈ [1..k-1] lt[p_j]=p_{j+1}) ∧ lt[p_k]=0 then SQ_i = <p_1, . . . ,p_k>;
   invariant
        0 ≤ free ≤ n
        ∧ ∀j ∈ [0..m-1] 0 ≤ sq[j] ≤ n
        ∧ ∀k ∈ [1..n] 0 ≤ lt[k] ≤ n
        ∧ {free, sq[j], lt[k]} = {m+1 0's, 1, 2, ..., n}      ! this term is a multiset equality
        ∧ ∀i ∈ [1..n](succ(free,i) xor ∃!j(succ(sq[j],i)))
              where succ(i,j) ≡df i=j ∨ (i≠0 cand succ(lt[i],j));

implementation
   body xtnd in s.free≠0 ∧ i ∈ [0..m-1]
              out (succ(s.free',j) ∧ succ(s.sq[i],j) ∧ s.sq[i]=j ∧ s.lt[j] = s.sq'[i]) =
        begin
        j ← s.free; s.free ← s.lt[j];
        s.lt[j] ← s.sq[i]; s.sq[i] ← j;
        end;

   body del in succ(s.sq[i],j) ∧ i ∈ [0..m-1] ∧ j ∈ [0..n] out (s.sq[i]=j) =
        if s.sq[i]≠j then
              begin local k:integer;
              k ← s.sq[i];
              while s.lt[k] ≠ j do k ← s.lt[k];
              s.lt[k] ← s.free; s.free ← s.sq[i]; s.sq[i] ← j;
              end;

   body delall in i ∈ [0..m-1] out (s.sq[i]=0) =
        s.del(s,i,0);         ! a call to the concrete body del, not the abstract function del

   body full out (t = (s.free=0)) =
        t ← s.free=0;
```

```
formbody indis =
beginform
representation
    rep(s.sq,s.lt,i,x) =
        if s.sq[i] = 0 then <> else
        if x = 0 then c~d where c = s.sq_i and d = <> else c~<x>~d
            where c = <p_1, . . ., p_{r-1}>, x=p_r, d = <p_{r+1}, . . ., p_k>,
            p_1 = s.sq[i], s.lt[p_k] = 0, and (∀j ∈ [1..k-1] s.lt[p_j] = p_{j+1});
    invariant true;
implementation
    body &init out (x=s.sq[i] ∧ (&b ≡ s.sq[i]≠0)) =
        (x ← s.sq[i]; &b ← x≠0);

    body &next in succ(s.sq[i],x) ∧ x≠0 out (x=s.lt[x'] ∧ (&b ≡ s.lt[x']≠0)) =
        (x ← s.lt[x]; &b ← x≠0);
endform

endform
```

The implementation of the four operations in condis should be fairly obvious. *xtnd* merely removes an entry from the free list and places it at the head of the appropriate list; note that this entry is returned (in j) as the value of function *xtnd*. *del* is a bit more interesting. It searches the appropriate list for the entry in lt which points to the first entry, j, which is *not* to be removed. It then moves the entire initial portion of the list to the free space list by simply setting the proper pointers. If all the entries are to be removed, *delall* does this; it calls del to search for the list-ending zero and to move the entire list to the free space list. *full* just tests if the free space list is empty.

The predicate *succ* defined in the concrete invariant is closely related to the abstract predicate *follows*. Although the parameterizations of the two predicates are different, they ask the "same" question and are related by

$$\text{follows}(\text{rep}(sq,lt,free),\ i,\ j) = \text{succ}(i,\ j)$$

The form indis(s,i) defines a generator for elements of the integer sequence s_i starting with first(s_i). Abstractly, an indis is composed of three (sub)sequences, the first containing the elements already generated, the second the (singleton) current element, and the third the other elements yet to be seen.

In [Shaw76b] we discussed the proof rules for iteration statements. We showed that certain simplifying assumptions about the generator can yield simple proof rules these assumptions are satisfied by indis, as we will show in the verification of condis. We therefore have a proof rule for the <u>for</u> statement which corresponds closely to Hoare's sequence rule and also a proof rule for the <u>first</u> statement. These proof rules are given in the <u>specifications</u> of indis, and indeed constitute the major part of those specifications. The basis for this specification technique for generators is given in [Shaw76b].

Verification of Condis

We can now verify the <u>form</u> condis.

For the form

1. Representation validity
   Show: I_c(sq,lt,free) ⊃ I_a(rep(sq,lt,free))
   Proof: $1 \le e_{ik} \le n$ holds by the bounds on sq[j] and lt[k] and the fact that the <u>rep</u> function drops the zeroes that indicate the end of a list. The e_{ik}'s are distinct because the multiset {sq[j], lt[k]} contains each of 1, 2, ..., n at most once. The multiset property of I_c implies succ(free,0) and succ(sq[j],0).

2. Initialization
   Show: $n \ge 1 \wedge m \ge 1$ { <u>init</u> } $\forall i \in [0..m-1]$ sq_i=<> $\wedge I_c$
   Proof: After <u>init</u> we have free=1, lt[1]=2, ..., lt[n-1]=n, lt[n]=0, sq[0]=0, ..., sq[m-1]=0. Using the <u>rep</u> function, each sq_i=<> since each sq[i]=0. $n \ge 1$ means $0 \le free \le n$. The bounds on sq[j] and lt[k] and the multiset property are clear. $\forall i \in [1..n]$(succ(free,i) $\wedge$ ¬succ(0,i)).

For the function xtnd

3. Concrete operation
   Show: s.free≠0 $\wedge$ i ∈ [0..m-1] $\wedge I_c$ { body } $\beta_{out} \wedge I_c$
   Proof: The four terms of β_{out} are clear as are the bounds in I_c. The multiset property holds because the body permutes the values s.free', s.sq'[i], and s.lt'[s.free']. Since the head of s.free moves to the head of s.sq[i], each i ∈ [1..n] still satisfies exactly one succ term. β_{in} (and I_c) ensures that the accesses to s.lt and s.sq are within bounds.

4a. β_{in} holds
   Show: $I_c \wedge \beta_{pre} \supset \beta_{in}$
   Proof: i ∈ [0..m-1] is immediate. If s.free=0, then the multiset property

of I_c means, using the rep function, that the SIGMA term is exactly n, a contradiction. Hence s.free≠0.

4b. β_{post} holds
Show: $I_c \wedge \beta_{out} \wedge \beta_{pre} \supset sq_i = \langle j \rangle \sim sq_i'$
Proof: Since s.sq[i]=j and s.lt[j]=s.sq'[i], the rep function gives $sq_i = \langle j \rangle \sim sq_i'$.

For the function del

3. Concrete operation
Show: $\beta_{in} \wedge I_c$ { body } s.sq[i]=j $\wedge I_c$
Proof: If s.sq[i]=j then β_{out} holds and I_c is unchanged. If s.sq[i]≠j then define the set G_p = { x | succ(s.sq[i],x) ∧ succ(x,p)}. Add the ghost operation "H←H ∪ {k}" after "k←s.lt[k]" in the while loop and add "H←{k}" after "k←s.sq[i]". A while-loop invariant (placed before the test) is then $H=G_k$ because $G_{s.sq[i]}$ = {s.sq[i]} and

$$H=G_k \wedge s.lt[k]\neq j \supset H \cup \{s.lt[k]\} = G_{s.lt[k]}$$

The while terminates because succ(s.sq[i],j) and s.sq[i]≠j. At termination s.lt[k]=j and $H=G_k$. The multiset property of I_c holds because the last three statements in the body permute the values s.free', s.sq'[i], and s.lt'[k]. Furthermore, each element in H is now a successor of s.free rather than of s.sq[i]. All other successors of s.sq[i] and all previous successors of s.free remain so, respectively. β_{out} and the bounds in I_c are clear.

4a. β_{in} holds
Show: $I_c \wedge \beta_{pre} \supset \beta_{in}$
Proof: Immediate from β_{pre} and I_a for condis.

4b. β_{post} holds
Show: $I_c \wedge \beta_{pre} \wedge \beta_{out} \supset sq_i = \langle j, \ldots \rangle$
Proof: Only sq_i changes. sq_i now begins with j and there are no other changes to sq_i.

For the function delall

3. Concrete operation
Show: $\beta_{in} \wedge I_c$ { s.del(s,i,0) } s.sq[i]=0 $\wedge I_c$
Proof: β_{in} and the multiset property of I_c imply in holds for s.del. (I_c holds for s.del as required.) The out for s.del gives s.sq[i]=0. I_c after s.del gives I_c after delall.

4a. β_{in} holds
Show: $i \in [0..m-1] \supset i \in [0..m-1]$
Proof: Immediate

4b. β_{post} holds

Show: $I_c \wedge i \in [0..m-1] \wedge s.sq[i]=0 \supset sq_i=<>$

Proof: Only sq_i changes. $s.sq[i]=0$ means $sq_i=<>$.

For the function full

3. Concrete operation

Show: I_c { t←s.free=0 } t = (s.free=0) ∧ I_c

Proof: Immediate

4a. β_{in} holds

β_{in} is true

4b. β_{post} holds

Show: $I_c \wedge \beta_{out} \supset \beta_{post}$

Proof: t = (s.free=0) = (SIGMA . . . = n) using the multiset property of I_c.

To verify the indis generator, we must first reconstruct the pre and post conditions rom the specified proof rules:

&init

<u>post</u> $(\&b \equiv s.sq_i \neq <>) \wedge (\&b \supset x = first(s.sq_i) \wedge c = <>)$

&next

<u>pre</u> mbr(s,i,x)

<u>post</u> $(\&b \equiv d' \neq <>) \wedge (\&b \supset x = first(d') \wedge c = c' \sim <x'>)$

ext, we must show that indis satisfies the *standard aggregate assumptions*:

(a) The indis abstraction is explicated in terms of sequences. The normal empty sequence (<>), concatenation operator (~), and leading element selector (first) are available.

(b) The complete sequence to be generated is $s.sq_i$, which can be decomposed as indicated in the <u>let</u> clause of indis.

(c) The specifications of &init and &next have the required form.

urthermore, indis satisfies the *basic generator assumptions* because (a) &init and &next rminate and (b) &init and &next alter only the indis variable x (and the return value &b).

Since "sq", "lt", and "free" are unchanged by indis, the I_c of condis still holds and ll be used in the proof.

For the form (indis)

1. Representation validity
   Show: $I_c \supset I_a$, i.e., true ⊃ true
   Proof: Immediate

2. Initialization
   Show: 0≤i≤m-1 { } true ∧ true
   Proof: Immediate

For the function &init

3. Concrete operation
   Show: true { x←s.sq[i]; &b←x≠0 } x=s.sq[i] ∧ (&b ≡ s.sq[i]≠0)
   Proof: Clear

4a. β_{in} holds
   β_{in} is true

4b. β_{post} holds
   Show: x=s.sq[i] ∧ (&b ≡ s.sq[i]≠0) ⊃
   (&b ≡ $s.sq_i$≠<>) ∧ (&b ⊃ x = first($s.sq_i$) ∧ c = <>)
   Proof: From the rep function for indis, $s.sq_i$ = (if s.sq[i]=0 then <> else some non-empty sequence). Hence &b ≡ s.sq[i]≠0 ≡ $s.sq_i$≠<>. For the second term of the conclusion, assume &b. Then x=s.sq[i]≠0 and the final clause of rep gives $s.sq_i$ = c~<x>~d. Since x=s.sq[i]=p_1, then c = <> whence also x = first($s.sq_i$).

For the function &next

3. Concrete operation
   Similar to &init.3

4a. β_{in} holds
   Show: mbr(s,i,x) ⊃ succ(s.sq[i],x) ∧ x≠0
   Proof: mbr(s,i,x) means x≠0 by I_a for condis. The term succ(s.sq[i],x) follows from mbr(s,i,x), the rep function, and the definition of succ.

4b. β_{post} holds
   Show: mbr(s,i,x') ∧ x=s.lt[x'] ∧ (&b ≡ s.lt[x']≠0) ⊃
   (&b ≡ d'≠<>) ∧ (&b ⊃ x = first(d') ∧ c = c'~<x'>)
   Proof: mbr(s,i,x') means x'≠0 and $s.sq_i$≠<>, and therefore by the rep function also s.sq[i]≠0. Hence in the final clause of the rep function, &b ≡ s.lt[x']≠0 ≡ d'≠<>. For the second term of the conclusion, assume &b. Then x=s.lt[x']≠0 and the final clause of rep gives $s.sq_i$=c~<x>~d and, because x'≠0, also $s.sq_i$=c'~<x'>~<d'>. Since x=s.lt[x'], it follows that x = first (d') and c = c'~<x'>.

QED

Examples of the Use of Symtab

In this section we shall present a skeletal example which involves three different styles of usage of the symtab abstraction. It is not our intent either to make this example complete or to suggest that the utility of the abstraction is limited to these three cases. Rather, we wish to bolster the reader's intuition about ways in which the abstraction might be used.

The example we have chosen is a multi-pass compiler for an Algol-like (i.e., block-structured) language, and indeed we have restricted ourselves to the first two passes -- lexical and syntactic analysis, respectively. In this scheme, the first pass is responsible for reading units of the source file (identifiers, literals, punctuation marks, etc.) and converting them to an internal form called a "lexeme". These lexemes are written onto a file which will be read again by the second pass. The second pass is responsible for reading the file of lexemes generated by the first pass and performing syntactic analysis. Although it is not important to our example, the output of the second pass will likely be some other intermediate representation (e.g., reverse polish or trees) which is suitable for optimization and code generation.

Here, then, is the skeletal program; more detailed comments on the uses of the symtab abstraction, and on the program in general, follow the example.

```
function compiler (source: file(char))=
  begin
     form condis . . .;
     form symtab . . .;
     form id extends string=
        beginform
        specifications
           function hash (s:id, m:integer) returns k:integer pre m>0 post 0≤k<m';
        . . .
        endform;

     form lex extends integer=
        beginform
        specifications
           function hash (x:lex, m:integer) returns k:integer pre m>0 post 0≤k<m';
        . . .
        endform;
```

```
        local L: file(lex);

        begin   ! pass 1
            local NT: symtab (id, 127, 1000);
            !
            ! pure lexical pass, see discussion below.
            !
        end;

        begin   ! pass 2
            form attributes = . . .        ! see discussion below
            local A: vector (attributes, 1, 2000);
            local ST: symtab (lex, 127, 2000);
            !
            ! syntactic (parse) analysis pass; see discussion below.
            !
        end;

        . . .
    end;
```

This program first defines four <u>forms</u>. Symtab and condis have been defined in detail previously and hence are not repeated. The <u>forms</u> *id* and *lex* are extensions of strings and integers, respectively, and merely add hashing functions; we have not defined the implementations of these functions, since they are not germane to the example. Note too that a file of *lex*es is defined at the outermost block level; this file is the explicit interface between the first and second passes.

As noted earlier, the function of the first pass is to convert the external representation of the program (a file of characters) into a more convenient internal form -- namely a file of lexemes (where each lexeme represents an atom of the language). Since this pass does no syntactic analysis, in particular it does not recognize block structure. This implies that all occurrences of the same atom (e.g., "xyz") will be mapped to the same lexeme. This mapping is accomplished through the use of the NT (for name-table) instantiation of symtab; indeed, the *only* use of NT is to obtain this unique mapping and the instantiation is therefore deleted on exit from the block in which the first pass is accomplished.

In skeletal form, the body of the block for pass 1 might look somewhat as follows:

```
open(source); open(L);
while ¬end of file(source) do
begin
    local i:id, x:lex;
    !
    ! do whatever is appropriate to assemble the next atom
    ! from the source file into "i".
    !
    if (x←lookup(NT,i))=0 ∧ ¬full(NT) then x←insert(NT,i);
    write (L,x);
end;
rewind(L);
```

Note that the operations *enterblock* and *leaveblock* are not used, all *insert* operations are done at the same block level, and only one entry per atom will be made.

The second pass is substantially more complex since it performs the full syntactic analysis; hence we will not even attempt to illustrate its skeletal form. We would, however, like to point out several things about it.

First, notice that this block defines a form named *attributes*. We have not shown the body of this form, since it will be highly language- and machine-specific. However, the notion is that this form provides for the storage and manipulation of whatever information must be retained about a symbol, e.g., its type, run-time storage address, array bounds, and so forth.

Second, we have declared a vector, A, of these attribute objects. As suggested in an earlier section, instances declared at a given block level will be associated with a unique integer, but this integer will be different from the one associated with the same identifier declared at a different block level. These integers will, in turn, be used as indices into the vector A (e.g., to set and retrieve information about the identifier).

Finally, we have declared another instantiation of symtab, ST. This one *will* be used to recognize block structure, and, specifically, will map from the simple lexemes generated in the first pass into indices into the vector, A, of attributes. As the parser detects blocks (begin-end pairs) in the source program, it will invoke *enterblock* and *leaveblock*. The declaration processing routines will invoke *defined* to determine whether an identifier has been declared twice at the same block level (presumably an error), and perform *insert* operations to define the instances of the identifier at the current block level. The rest of the compiler will perform *lookup* operations to obtain the index of the attribute vector entry associated with specific lexemes. (Note, by the way, that by appropriate ordering of *insert* and *lookup* operations the declaration processor can obtain either of the interpretations of "block-structure" discussed in the introduction.)

Before leaving this example, let us return to the form attributes (defined in pass 2) to illustrate another potential use of the symtab abstraction. As was mentioned in the introduction, in general the mapping from identifier to unique integer may be context-sensitive. Block structure is the most familiar form of such sensitivity, but another is name qualification, as in field selectors for records. In many languages one makes a declaration such as

```
x:record(name:string, age:integer, z:integer);
```

and then refers to "x.name", "x.age", and "x.z". A problem arises when, at the same block level, there is another declaration such as

```
y:record(ss:integer, z:boolean);
```

In such a case the identifier "z" is no longer unique -- its interpretation depends upon the name it qualifies.

There are many ways one might treat this, including inserting each of "x", "x.name", "x.age", "x.z", "y", "y.ss", and "y.z" as complete identifiers in ST. An attractive alternative, however, is to include instantiations of symtab in each of the attributes; that is, to make form attributes appear somewhat as follows:

```
form attributes=
   beginform
   . . .
       representation
           . . .
           unique qual:symtab(lex,1,10),
   . . .
   endform;
```

If this is done, then to determine the interpretation of "x.z" one would first search ST for the index, i, associated with the lexeme for "x", then search A[i].qual for the index associated with the lexeme for "z".

Although this compiler example has been sketchy, we hope that it has suggested some of the ways in which the symtab abstraction may be applied. The details of the example are not important, except insofar as they help the reader's intuition; what *is* important is the notion that well-chosen abstractions have many uses. The class of broadly useful abstractions is simply too large to include them all in a single programming language -- hence Alphard has chosen to provide a linguistic facility so that the programmer may define them. Many such (verified) abstractions will find their way into the library, and hence incrementally enhance the "power" available to the programmer --

ithout, at the same time, limiting him to the language designer's preconceived notions of hat constitutes an appropriate set of abstractions (or, for that matter, implementations).

onclusions

A programming language is a tool for the construction and communication of rograms; as such its utility should be measured relative to these tasks. In other words, he language should be *used*, and the quality of that use must be judged. While this is true f any programming language, it is especially so of one such as Alphard, which departs ubstantially from those in common use.

Thus, in this and other reports we are attempting to exhibit Alphard in relatively ealistic contexts and, along with the reader, to judge the practical utility of our creation. t is far too soon to draw definitive conclusions -- that must await the use of Alphard in eal programs -- but we would like to share some of our impressions resulting from these xperiences.

First, the symtab abstraction is about the (conceptual) size we envision for most bstractions; larger programs will be constructed by further "layering". Thus we take our bility to specify and verify this form as fairly strong evidence that larger programs will lso be tractable.

Second, in most respects the implementation is a practical, efficient one. This einforces our intuitions that *no* efficiency need be sacrificed to obtain clear, verifiable rograms. (The one exception to this statement is our use of fixed-sized vectors and, orrespondingly, integers for the unique identification of symbols. A more realistic mplementation would, perhaps, have done true dynamic storage allocation and used eferences. We avoided this implementation primarily because it would have carried us nto portions of Alphard not covered in previous reports, but also because those portions f the language are still in flux. We trust that the reader will forgive this departure from ealism.)

Third, one of the anticipated advantages of an Alphard-like language is that a library f verified abstractions will develop. Both of the forms developed here might well go into hat library so we are getting some evidence that this hoped-for advantage will be ealized.

Fourth, one of our private objectives was to make the form mechanism strong nough to support an extremely broad class of abstractions -- the ultimate target being the spectrum covered by our intuitive notion of the word "abstraction". The evidence is ot conclusive, but we are feeling better about meeting that goal all the time.

Finally, we should say a few words about our experience concerning the effort needed to define a form. It should be clear that the actual code in a form body, i.e., the implementation part, is roughly the same size as the corresponding code in other languages (although the first statement does seem to shorten many of the examples). Moreover, for some reason, the information needed for verification (abstract and concrete invariants, abstract pre and post conditions, rep function, etc.) usually seems about equal to the code size; thus a full form is about twice the size of the code alone. This does not particularly concern us, since these kinds of specifications tend to replace much of the documentation that would otherwise be needed -- and they are certainly more precise.

We find the verification of a form, once the specifications and code have been written, to be more difficult and time-consuming than coding, but not unreasonably so (say by as much as a factor of two or three). Sometimes it is necessary to modify the specifications, or the code, during the verification in order to remove inconsistencies that are uncovered. The verification may also suggest different specifications, usually ones that are more constrained but sometimes simpler ones. In spite of the difficulties, the bodies of functions tend to be small and their proofs correspondingly small, as can be seen from these examples. Moreover, the proofs of the two forms symtab and condis were independent. To date our proofs have been manually generated, but we envision having automated, interactive aids in the future. These should reduce the verification time to approximately the coding time. Since this is less than the time currently spent on debugging, we feel highly encouraged.

The majority of our time goes into designing and specifying the abstraction. There are two related aspects of this: getting the intuitive abstraction "right", and formalizing it (at least sufficiently for it to be verified). The two appear related in that difficulty in formalizing an intuitive abstraction often seems to uncover muddy thinking at the intuitive level. While we seem to be improving our ability to formalize, indicating that it is a learnable skill, we have no easy rules for picking the right abstraction in the first place. While, with practice, our abilities in choosing abstractions may also improve, we suspect that this is a fundamental problem of design and has a significant aesthetic component.

It is clear that we are just learning to use the power of the tools we are creating and exploring. Much remains to be discovered about what is possible or impossible, easy or hard, and reasonable or unreasonable to do with the facilities. In this connection we note that an early version of symtab was a one-level form, used no generator such as indis, and had only some of the same verification information. Although that version of symtab used the same implementation ideas, it was essentially incomprehensible. When we realized that multiple ideas were becoming confused, we separated the maintenance of the lists from the lookup algorithms. The result was that the code, the specifications, and the verification all became much more manageable.

Acknowledgements

We owe a great deal to our colleagues at CMU and ISI, especially Mario Barbacci, Neil Goldman, Donald Good, John Guttag, Paul Hilfinger, David Jefferson, Anita Jones, David Lamb, David Musser, Karla Perdue, Kamesh Ramakrishna, and David Wile. We would also like to thank James Horning and Barbara Liskov and their groups at the University of Toronto and Massachusetts Institute of Technology, respectively, for their critical reviews of Alphard.

References

[Gries71] David Gries, *Compiler Construction for Digital Computers*, Wiley, 1971.

[Guttag76] John Guttag, "Abstract Data Types and the Development of Data Structures", *Supplement to the Proceedings of the SIGPLAN/SIGMOD Conference on Data: Abstraction, Definition, and Structure*, March 1976 (pp. 37-46). Also *Communications of the ACM*, 20, 6, June 1977 (to appear).

[Halmos60] Paul R. Halmos, *Naive Set Theory*, Van Nostrand, 1960.

[Hoare72] C. A. R. Hoare, "Proof of Correctness of Data Representations", *Acta Informatica*, 1, 4, 1972 (pp. 271-281).

[Knuth73] Donald E. Knuth, *The Art of Computer Programming, Volume 3, Sorting and Searching*, Addison-Wesley, 1973.

[Shaw76a] Mary Shaw, "Abstraction and Verification in Alphard: Design and Verification of a Tree Handler", *Proc. Fifth Texas Conference on Computing Systems*, 1976 (pp. 86-94).

[Shaw76b] Mary Shaw, Wm. A. Wulf, and Ralph L. London, "Abstraction and Verification in Alphard: Iteration and Generators", *Carnegie-Mellon University* and *USC Information Sciences Institute Technical Reports*, 1976. Also *Communications of the ACM* (to appear).

[Wegbreit76] Ben Wegbreit and Jay M. Spitzen, "Proving Properties of Complex Data Structures", *Journal of the ACM*, 23, 2, April 1976 (pp. 389-396).

[Wulf76a] Wm. A. Wulf, Ralph L. London, and Mary Shaw, "Abstraction and Verification in Alphard: Introduction to Language and Methodology", *Carnegie-Mellon University* and *USC Information Sciences Institute Technical Reports*, 1976.

[Wulf76b] Wm. A. Wulf, Ralph L. London, and Mary Shaw, "An Introduction to th Construction and Verification of Alphard Programs", *IEEE Transactions on Softwar Engineering*, SE-2, 4, December 1976 (pp. 253-265).

Appendix A
Informal Description of Verification Methodology

Alphard's verification methodology is designed to determine whether a form wi actually behave as promised by its abstract specifications. The methodology depends o explicitly separating the description of how an object behaves from the code tha manipulates the representation in order to achieve that behavior. It is derived fror Hoare's technique for showing correctness of data representations[Hoare72].

The abstract object and its behavior are described in terms of some mathematica entities natural to the problem domain. Graphs are used in [Shaw76a] to describe binar trees; sequences are used in [Wulf76a,b] to describe queues and stacks and in condis t describe list processing, and so on. We appeal to these abstract types

- in the invariant, which explains that an instantiation of the form may be viewed as an object of the abstract type that meets certain restrictions,

- in the initially clause, where a particular abstract object is displayed, and

- in the pre and post conditions for each function, which describe the effect the function has on an abstract object which satisfies the invariant.

The form contains a parallel set of descriptions of the concrete object and how i behaves. In many cases this makes the effect of a function much easier to specify an verify than would the abstract description alone.

Now, although it is useful to distinguish between the behavior we want and the dat structures we operate on, we also need to show a relationship that holds between th two. This is achieved with the representation function rep(x), which gives a mapping fro the concrete representation to the abstract description. The purpose of a for verification is to ensure that the two invariants and the rep(x) relation between them ar preserved.

In order to verify a form we must therefore prove four things. Two relate to th representation itself and two must be shown for each function. Informally, the fou required steps are[6]:

For the <u>*form*</u>

1. Representation validity

   $I_c(x) \supset I_a(rep(x))$

2. Initialization

   <u>requires</u> { *init clause* } <u>initially</u>(rep(x)) $\wedge$ $I_c(x)$

For each function

3. Concrete operation

   <u>in</u>(x) $\wedge$ $I_c(x)$ { *function body* } <u>out</u>(x) $\wedge$ $I_c(x)$

4. Relation between abstract and concrete

   4a. $I_c(x)$ $\wedge$ <u>pre</u>(rep(x)) $\supset$ <u>in</u>(x)

   4b. $I_c(x)$ $\wedge$ <u>pre</u>(rep(x')) $\wedge$ <u>out</u>(x) $\supset$ <u>post</u>(rep(x))

Step 1 shows that any legal state of the concrete representation has a corresponding abstract object (the converse is deducible from the other steps). Step 2 shows that the initial state created by the <u>representation</u> section is legal. Step 3 is the standard verification formula for the concrete operation as a simple program; note that it enforces the preservation of I_c. Step 4 guarantees (a) that the concrete operation is applicable whenever the abstract <u>pre</u> condition holds and (b) that if the operation is performed, the result corresponds properly to the abstract specifications.

---

6 We will use $I_a(rep(x))$ to denote the abstract invariant of an object whose concrete representation is x, $I_c(x)$ to denote the corresponding concrete invariant, italics to refer to code segments, and the names of specification clauses and assertions to refer to those formulas. In step 4b, "<u>pre</u>(rep(x'))" refers to the value of x *before* execution of the function. A complete development of the <u>form</u> verification methodology appears in [Wulf76a,b].

London et al. : Discussion

Nehmer: If I understand correctly you can compile programs and you can verify them. Could you tell us a little more about the verifier?

Hibbard: [who, in the absence of the authors, agreed to make the presentation] No. Definitely not! [☺]

Turski: I like these short answers. [☺] May I ask you whether it it is possible for one FORM to have different representations and different implementations concurrently, in a single program.

Hibbard: Well, one can, of course. When one is inside of the FORM, one can inspect the concrete representation. There is nothing to stop you from supporting two independent implementations inside the FORM. This will, in fact, end up by being specified in the concrete representation.

Turski: Is it possible to have a single specification for stacks, but to define two different representations (as two separate FORMS) in the same program? How would one then define the identity of such objects? And in which FORM?

Hibbard: You are going out of my area of competence. I understand the problem however. It is a problem which I also have.

Král: You said that the aim of the system is to increase productivity. Have you any practical experience in increasing programmer productivity using this tool?

Hibbard: It is not yet an implemented language. In the conclusion, the authors give some indication of the expected effects on productivity.

Wichmann: I like the principles of ALPHARD very much, but the system seems to have one hang-up. It seems that the work that has to be done by the programmer is at least tripled. Moreover, maintenance is not just modifying the programs but changing the specifications in some mysterious way. So the amount of work that has to be done there is also tripled.

Hibbard: I agree with you that if the abstractions that are being used in a program are not yet finalized, then re-specification each time you redesign the interfaces between the FORMs, or redesign the FORMs themselves, will increase the total amount of work. But I do want to make it clear that there is no need to verify a FORM and there is no need to give more than the minimum of specification. So there is no reason why programming in ALPHARD should be any more difficult than programming in any other language at a similar level.

Correll: ALPHARD is certainly a step in the right direction. However, it is not yet "home". ALPHARD gives us data abstraction. The programmer himself has, however, to provide, on all levels, the abstraction in terms of which he wants to think. So there is no support whatsoever in the form of some kind of basic model. SETL, on the contrary, provides us with some very helpful, very general models, namely set theory. There exist quite a lot of programs where you are very happy with set theory for expressing your first thoughts, your first specification of the program. At this stage you just don't worry too much about data abstraction. So I think ALPHARD, together with some basic model like set theory, would be even more helpful.

Hibbard: My answer to that is that SETL and ALPHARD exhibit very much the backgrounds of their creators. SETL is a top-down design language, coming out of mathematical stables. ALPHARD is a bottom-up design language coming from someone who has been interested in machine design and low-level software design. However, I think that both ALPHARD and SETL are capable of the same powers of abstraction. There is the intention that ALPHARD come with a standard prelude of suitable FORMs that have been pre-verified. And for example, the FORMs for set and map could well be the standard library for ALPHARD. One of the points that you raised, though, is that SETL provides convenient interactions, as I understand you, between control structures and data structures, which apparently are lacking in ALPHARD. The control structures of ALPHARD are themselves primitive. I have not had time to show that, in fact, this is not so. But there is a paper on loops in ALPHARD which shows in fact that it is possible to modify the control structures to take account of the data structures on which they are operating. The actual loops in ALPHARD would be very similar to the loops that are present in SETL. I believe that most examples could be written in ALPHARD with very little difference between the languages. Except, of course, that in ALPHARD there would be a whole standard prelude hidden from the sight of the programmer.

Constructing Quality Software, P.G. Hibbard/S.A. Schuman (eds.)

SETL AS A TOOL FOR GENERATION OF QUALITY SOFTWARE *

Robert B. K. Dewar
Arthur Grand
Ssu-Cheng Liu
Edmond Schonberg
Jacob T. Schwartz

Computer Science Department
Courant Institute of Mathematical Sciences
New York University

'Pure' SETL is a language of very high level, allowing algorithms to be programmed rapidly and concisely with minimum attention to specification of detailed data structures. A representation sublanguage adds a system of declarations which allow the user of the language to specify the data structures that will be used to implement an algorithm which has already been written in pure SETL, without necessitating any rewriting of the algorithm itself.

To the extent that programming tools can aid in the development of quality software, there seem to be two possible approaches to their design:

1) Make it harder to write bad programs

2) Make it easier to write good programs

Much of the work in development of very strongly typed languages (e.g. ALPHARD, [1]) which emphasize aids for proof of correctness approaches seems to focus on the first aim of making it hard to write bad programs. The difficulty with this approach is that the syntactic complexity imposed on the programmer often conflicts with the goal of making it easier to write good programs. Thus we may observe that even simple programs in ALPHARD are long and involve a large proportion of text which is not part of the algorithm proper, but rather represents redundant semantic information whose sole purpose is to facilitate formal proofs of program correctness.

The approach of SETL [2] is to focus almost exclusively on the aim of making it easier to write good programs, realizing that this involves omitting some of the built-in redundancy which is characteristic of strongly typed languages. It is interesting to note that two other languages taking a similar approach, APL and SNOBOL4, are proving to be extremly popular despite minimal manufacturer support and despite the fact that both these languages can

* This work was supported by: The National Science Foundation Grant MCS-76-0016, and ERDA Adminstration Agency Contract EY-76-C-02-3077*000.

only be dismissed as jokes by proponents of structured programming concepts. We believe that the success of these two languages is a reflection of the fact that the emphasis on ease of programming is an important one. The SETL language attempts to capitalize on this point, and at the same time demonstrate that this goal can be achieved without sacrificing the basic notions of modularity and structure which are essential to the production of large programs.

To illustrate the SETL approach, we give in Fig. 1 a complete example of a SETL program. This program performs a topological sort using the familiar algorithm which keeps track of the number of predecessors of each node in the graph. The input data consists of pairs of strings, representing the ordering relationship. The output is a list of strings giving one possible linear ordering. For the sake of simplicity, a test for cycles has been omitted.

```
module main;

      /* names is set of names involved        */
      /* succ is a map giving the ordering     */

      names  := nℓ;
      succ   := nℓ;

      /* loop reading pairs giving ordering    */

      loop doing read(a,b) until a = om do
           names with a;
           names with b;
           succ  with [a,b];
      end;

      /* numpred(x) = number of predecessors of x   */
      /* nopred is list of nodes with numpred = 0   */

      numpred := {[n,0] : n in names};
      (forall [a,b] in succ) numpred(b) + 1; end;
      nopred := {n in names | numpred(n) = 0};
      /* this loop picks elements from nopred and   */
      /* removes them, adjusting numpred properly   */
      (while nopred /= nℓ)
           print(next from nopred, newline);
           (forall f in succ{next})
                numpred(f) - 1;
                if numpred(f) = 0 then nopred with f; end
           end;
      end;
end;
```

FIGURE 1. TOPOLOGICAL SORT IN SETL

This example shows how SETL allows specification of an algorithm of this type with a minimum of extraneous details. No declarations are required, all typing being weak, and it is not even necessary to specify the data structures which will be used for the various maps and sets involved. However, the basic details of the algorithm must be provided. SETL makes no attempt to derive clever algorithms automatically from high level specification statements. To illustrate this point, we give another program for the topological sort in Fig. 2. SETL regards this as an (inefficient) algorithm in its own right. The problem of deriving the algorithm of Fig. 1 automatically from that of Fig. 2 is an interesting one, but is not attempted in the current version of SETL, nor envisioned as an integral part of the language. For an approach to this problem using techniques of formal differentiation, see [3].

```
module main;

        names := nℓ;
        succ  := nℓ;

        loop doing read(a,b) until a = om do
             names with a;
             names with b;
             succ  with [a,b];
        end;
        (while is n in names | not(is x in names | [x,n] in succ))
             print(n from names, newline);
        end;
end;
```

FIGURE 2. SLOW TOPOLOGICAL SORT IN SETL

Returning to Fig. 1, this program may be submitted to the SETL compiler and will run as it stands, using a standard hash table structure for all maps and sets. The execution will be efficient in the sense that the algorithm is linear in the number of pairs in succ, and its execution time will be linear when expressed in this manner in SETL, i.e., no hidden 'order N' or worse inefficiencies creep in. However, the running time will be worse (by some constant factor) than the low level expression of the same algorithm due to the basic overhead of accessing hashed structures.

One possible approach to improving the efficiency of the algorithm in Fig. 1 is to recode it in some lower level language where explicit data structure choices, which are more efficient for the problem at hand than hash tables, can be made. To illustrate this we show just the last part of the algorithm (the loop which outputs successive elements) coded in ALGOL-68 with two different data structure choices:

Fig. 3 shows the result of using linked lists to represent the map *succ* and the set *nopred*. This data structure choice ensures linear time behaviour of the algorithm.

Fig. 4 shows the result of using a bit matrix to represent the map *succ*, and a bit string to represent the set *nopred*. This representation is more efficient in terms of storage use, at the expense of added execution time and a departure from linear behaviour.

```
      mode node = struct (string name,
                          int    numpred,
                          ref link succ);
      mode link = struct  (ref node node,
                          ref link link);
      ref link nopred;
comment (while nopred /= nℓ) comment
      while nopred :/=: ref link (nil) do
comment print(next from nopred, newline); comment
      ref node next = node of nopred;
      nopred := link of nopred;
      print ((string of next, newline));
comment (forall f in succ{next}) comment
      ref node fn := succ of next;
      while fn :/=: ref link (nil) do
           ref node f = node of fn;
           fn := next of fn;
comment numpred(f)-1; comment
           numpred of f -:= 1;
comment if numpred(f) = 0 then nopred with f; end; comment
      if numpred of f = 0
      then
           nopred := heap link := (f, nopred)
      fi
    od
 od
```

FIGURE 3. ALGOL-68 TRANSLATION (LINKED LISTS)

```
      int n := # number of items involved #;
      [n,n] bool succ;
      [n] int numpred;
      [n] string name;
      [n] bool nopred;
comment (while nopred /= nℓ) comment
```

```
      while
      int next;
      bool found := false;
      for j to n while not found do
           if nopred(j) then found := true fi
      od;
      found
      do;
comment print(next from nopred, newline); comment
      nopred[next] := false;
      print((name [next], newline));
comment (forall f in succ{next}) comment
      for f to n do
           if succ[next, f] then
comment numpred(f)-1; comment
           numpred[f] -:= 1;
comment if numpred(f)=0 then nopred with f; end; comment
      if numpred[f]=0 then nopred[f] := true fi;
    fi
  od
od
```

FIGURE 4. ALGOL-68 TRANSLATION (BIT STRINGS)

From these examples we note two important points. First, the expression of the algorithm in ALGOL-68 is greatly affected by the choice of data structures. It is quite difficult to see, from the ALGOL-68 text alone, that the underlying algorithm is identical since its logical structure has been obscured by different data structure choices in the two cases.

Secondly, the derivation of these examples from the basic algorithm as expressed in SETL is essentially mechanical once the data structure choice has been made. To emphasize this point, we have included as comments in the ALGOL-68 text the SETL statements to which sections of the ALGOL-68 text correspond.

The fact that this translation is mechanical suggests that it should be automated, and this is the central idea behind the SETL representation sublanguage, whose purpose is to allow the programmer to gain the efficiency made possible by detailed specification of data structures, without requiring the time consuming and error prone process of translating the entire algorithm.

The declarations of the representation sublanguage are completely separate from the SETL program itself, which is not modified in any way. The normal procedure is to create these declarations as a separate file, which the compiler merges with the original program by matching up module and procedure names.

At its simplest level, the representation language allows datatype declarations which are syntactically similar to the ordinary declarations of an ALGOL like language. The intention is however focused on gaining efficiency, rather than obtaining the compile time checking available with strong typing. The resulting program will run faster simply because some type checks may be eliminated, and hard code generated for some sequences which required library calls in the original form. However, the program still contains a sufficient number of type checks to ensure its integrity. If there is an assignment statement A: = B; and A has been declared to be an integer, and B has been left undeclared, then if it is not possible to determine by global flow tracing that B has an integer value at the point of the assignment, a type check is made and an execution error occurs if B is not an integer. This ensures that the only possible adverse effect of making such datatype declarations is to cause the resulting program to terminate with an error message. It is never possible to introduce a type error which is undetected and causes erroneous results.

The more complex part of the representation sublanguage is concerned with specifying the data structures for maps and sets. The important concept here is that of a base set. A base set is an auxiliary set which may not appear explicitly as a variable in the program, and in terms of which actual program variables are described.

In the case of the topological sort, the significant base set is the set of names, and a statement:

```
base nodes : string;
```

identifies the base and gives it the name nodes. This name does not appear in the algorithm itself, but will be referenced in other declarations in the representation section.

We then identify the program variable *names* as a set whose elements are elements of this base set:

```
repr names : local set {elmt nodes};
```

The base set will be stored as a linked hash table at run time. The repr declaration for *names* causes it to be represented using a single bit associated with each element of the base set, the bit being on if the element of the base is in names. In this particular case, all such bits will be on, since the base nodes is identical to the set *names*. However, this is a property of the algorithm on which we do not depend when constructing these declarations.

Two other representation are available for sets, and are illustrated by the following possible declarations for the set *nopred*:

```
repr nopred : sparse set {elmt nodes};
repr nopred : remote set {elmt nodes};
```

The sparse representation causes *nopred* to be stored as a hashed linked list of pointers into the base set. Normally SETL does not use pointers to values (an assignment of a set or map value causes the map to be copied, rather than generating a pointer to the same value), however this introduction of pointers is entirely transparent, since the base set is not a program variable. Thus every time a value is added to the set *nopred*, it will be added to the base set nodes if it is not there already, but this side effect is transparent because the value of the base set nodes cannot be inspected by the program. Again it is a property of the algorithm, not used in the construction of the declarations, that whenever a value is added to *nopred*, it is already in the base set. The representation obtained for *nopred* by this declaration is similar to that chosen in the linked lists ALGOL-68 version of the algorithm.

The remote representation causes *nopred* to be stored as a bit string. As a base set is constructed, unique (but arbitrary) integer index values are assigned to its elements. These index values are used to select the bit corresponding to a particular base element from the bit string. This representation corresponds to that chosen for the second ALGOL-68 version. It should be noted that this representation is particularly effective if set union or intersection operations are to be performed on sets stored in this manner, since these operations reduce to bit vector logical operations.

We now turn our attention to the maps *numpred* and *succ*. There are three representations available for maps where the domain of the map corresponds to a base set, analogous to the three representations for sets:

local map	Represented by storing the range value in a dedicated field allocated in each element of the base set.
remote map	Represented by storing a vector of range values, indexed by the index values associated with base elements.
sparse map	Represented by a separate hashed linked list, where the domain value of each entry is a pointer to the corresponding base element.

In addition, the representation declaration distinguish between single valued maps (smap) and multiple valued maps (mmap).

We may now choose representations for the maps *numpred* and *succ* as follows:

```
repr numpred : local smap (elmt nodes) int;
repr succ : local mmap {elmt nodes} sparse set {elmt nodes};
repr succ : remote mmap {elmt nodes} remote set {elmt nodes};
```

The two declarations for *succ* correspond to the two possible choices illustrated by the ALGOL-68 programs. As can be seen, the difference is obtained by altering a single word in the declaration text; no changes whatever are made to the original SETL algorithm, in contrast with the extensive differences in the ALGOL-68 programs. Finally, we have

```
repr n, a, b, f : elmt nodes;
```

This causes these variables to be stored as pointers to the corresponding base elements. Indexing a local map with such a variable corresponds to picking up the appropriate field of the base element using this pointer, which is analogous to a structure selection in

ALGOL-68. Indexing a <u>remote</u> map with such a variable is a vector indexing operation.

The two sets of declarations, corresponding to the two ALGOL-68 examples, are given in their entirely, as they would be submitted to the SETL compiler, in figure 5.

```
Module main;
      /* repr section for list representations */
      base
           nodes : string;
      end;
      repr
           names   : local set {elmt nodes},
           succ    : local mmap {elmt nodes} sparse set {elmt nodes},
           numpred: local map (elmt nodes) int,
           nopred : sparse set {elmt nodes},
           n,a,b,f: elmt nodes;
      end;
end;

Module main;
      /* repr section for bit string representation */
      base
           nodes : string;
      end;
      repr
           names   : local set {elmt nodes},
           succ    : remote mmap {elmt nodes} remote set {elmt nodes},
           numpred: local map (elmt nodes) int,
           nopred : remote set {elmt nodes},
           n,a,b,f: elmt nodes;
      end;
end;
```

FIGURE 5. SETL REPR SECTIONS FOR TOPOLOGICAL SORT

By submitting the original SETL program together with one of the two possible <u>repr</u> sections to the SETL compiler, a resulting program is obtained which closely resembles the corresponding ALGOL-68 program in execution style and efficiency.

The word 'closely' in the above paragraph is worth examining in more detail since it illustrates at the same time the power of the SETL approach and the danger of manual translations such as those given in ALGOL-68 earlier.

The bit string representation in SETL is a very close match for its ALGOL-68 counterpart. The only difference is that the SETL structure for *succ* is a vector of vectors, rather than the two dimensional array which will be obtained from most ALGOL-68 compilers (i.e., it corresponds to declaring *succ* as [] ref [] bool rather than [,] bool).

The 'linked list' representation in SETL is a different matter. SETL will store *nopred* as a hashed linked list, the hashing being required by the fact that *nopred* is a set and sets may not contain duplicate elements. This means that the statement:

```
nopred with f;
```

involves a hashing operation, even in the presence of all the repr statements, causing the program to run more slowly. What went wrong?

The answer is that the ALGOL-68 program is not an exact translation of the SETL algorithm as given. It translates the offending statement without any attempt to eliminate possible duplicate elements. However, it is a fairly subtle property of the algorithm as stated that there never arises a case in which an attempt to insert duplicate elements is made. Thus the ALGOL-68 translator was either clever or lucky, but was in any case doing much more than translating the original algorithm. This is good example of the kind of potential error which can be introduced by manual refinement of algorithms. The correctness of the translation depending on an unstated assumption whose validity, even once stated, is far from obvious. Many program bugs are introduced in similar fashion by basing program transformations on similar assumptions which are not valid in all cases.

The SETL approach guarantees that the program resulting from use of the repr statements is semantically equivalent to the original. In the absence of datatype errors, which will result in error termination, the results obtained will be identical to those obtained from the original program. Therefore it was impossible to use repr statements to convert the SETL program into the (potentially different) version represented by the ALGOL-68 program. It is possible that a clever optimizer could note that such a translation was possible, but this is outside the scope of the current work.

In SETL terms, the approach embodied in the ALGOL-68 linked list translation represents a (slightly) different algorithm, and this difference must be reflected in the original statement. If we use a tuple rather than a set for *nopred*, then the desired semantics (of ignoring equal elements) are obtained. This is achieved simply by changing one statement in the original program:

```
nopred   := {n in names | numpred(n) = 0};

    becomes

nopred   := tuple [n in names | numpred(n) = 0];
```

Repr statements can now be given to generate the linked lists of the ALGOL-68 example essentially exactly. However, the bit string representation for *nopred* is no longer valid and the second ALGOL-68 translation is now "incorrect". Therefore it is no longer possible to generate this translation using repr statements, although the map *succ* could still be represented as a bit matrix.

In conclusion, the SETL approach allows algorithms to be written in a maximally concise manner, without concern for selecting the data structures to be used. A reasonably efficient execution can be obtained from this initial statement. If greater efficiency is desired, then <u>repr</u> statements may be added to the SETL program at selected points to enhance its efficiency without any danger of introducing errors by subtle departures from the semantics of the original program. The resulting program will execute with efficiency comparable to that attainable from a lower level language without the need to entirely recode the algorithm at the lower level. We believe that this approach will be effective in meeting the declared goal of making it easier to write good programs.

REFERENCES

[1] Wulf, W.A., R.L. London & M. Shaw, *Abstraction and verification in Alphard*: in New Directions in Algorithmic Languages 1975 S.A. Schuman (ed.) IRIA, Rocquencourt, 1976.

[2] Schwartz, J.T., *On Programming: An Interim Report on the SETL Project: Part I: Generalities: Part II: The SETL Language and Examples of its Use:* Revised June 1975 Computer Science Department, Courant Institute Of Mathematical Sciences, New York University.

[3] Paige, R. and Schwartz, J.T., *Expression Continuity and the Formal Differentiation of Algorithms*: Proc. Fourth ACM Symposium on Principles of Programming Language, Jan. 1977.

Dewar et al. : Discussion

Holager: It seems to me that sets in the mathematical sense are too general for use in programming. What I think we need is a limited form of sets, in order to get more discipline in the programming process. Have you any comments on that?

Dewar: To some extent, I am put in the position of someone defending APL, trying to argue that the whole world consists of vectors of varying length. I think I have a more secure basis in claiming that all the world is made up of sets and maps, but seriously, I think the test is whether it works in practice. It's certainly not the case that maps are an immediately natural way of thinking, but our experience is that, with some small level of exposure, it quickly becomes a way of thinking which effectively meets the criterion of producing programs in a clear form. I think that it is very hard to demonstrate by any abstract arguments. I'd rather demonstrate it by concrete experience.

Holager: My point was that a set of some limited kind of elements might be a better concept than just a general set of anything.

Dewar: That comment seems related to the question of strong typing in general. There is a very simple answer to that. How can you ever have a set of specific elements without having to say what kind of elements they are? It is a nuisance which does not achieve anything from the point of view of making it easier to write good programs. It may achieve something from the point of view of making it hard to write bad programs, but as I have said, this is not the focus of our objectives.

Wichmann: I don't quite understand how you can change the representation of a procedure parameter, since the representation of the actual parameter may change from call to call. Could you explain please?

Dewar: Each variable that appears in the program has some specific declaration. If there arises a case where you want to give multiple declarations of something, there is a facility for obtaining multiple representations throughout, but there is no facility for saying dynamically represent it sometimes one way and sometimes another way. In most programs a given variable has one use throughout the program. Strong typing does not severely restrict the power of expression. It is, after all, not the case that all variables in an ALGOL 68 program are unions. Although you can construct examples where the latter possibility is wanted, looking at the considerable library of programs which we have collected, that's certainly not a problem.

Koster: If you choose a different representation for your underlying data structures, then you have to change the ALGOL 68 program radically. However, I consider the fact that this program is not invariant under the choices of representation to be a programming error in the original program. The program, in fact, does not have a sufficient degree of uniformity of referents. If you want to change your representation in this way, you have to separate your program out into a functional part and a representational part, and take care that the changes in the representation are all confined to the layer where this representation is defined.

Ross: Could you compare the SETL approach to other forms of abstract data types, as in CLU or ALPHARD? They all seek to raise the abstraction level. In the early 60's we chose not to extend the syntax in these areas, but only to work with the semantic level in terms of hierarchies of functions. High level functional instructions stayed exactly the same in the face of radical changes of the basic functions which effectively implemented them.

Dewar: First of all, I find it strange to put SETL in the same class as ALPHARD because I find them to be two sides of a coin. We are very interested to know which way that coin will fall. [Ross shows that the coin falls on its side. ☺] I would like to take the example from the ALPHARD paper presented here. I wrote the symbol table from that paper as an exercise. It's about 12 lines of SETL which I considered to be very clear. In fact, the level of clarity is, I think, very similar to, or an improvement on, the level of clarity of the ALPHARD specification section. Unfortunately, there is a lot left to do in ALPHARD after writing the specification section, which is itself twice as long. Now, I am willing to believe that the 150 lines that represent the symbol table example in ALPHARD are correct, after much effort in verifying them. But I am also, with much less effort, willing to believe that my 12 lines are correct. I think we have two very different approaches. I consider ALPHARD to be a crystallization of the approach of doing extra work to avoid errors. The reason that I didn't treat a symbol table example in my talk is because its native implementation in SETL was perfectly efficient and didn't require any use of the data structuring mechanism. The important point in SETL is that these mechanisms would be applied in a very limited manner, only where they were needed to improve efficiency.

Correll: I would come back to the comparison with CLU and ALPHARD. What I like about SETL is that it is easier to write programs in this language; it was very hard for me to write programs in CLU and ALPHARD. The reason is that the approach is different. SETL tries to be a high-level language and tries to support automatic translation to lower levels. CLU and ALPHARD leave this translation process to the user and hope that the user can prove that his implementation is correct.

Dewar: Yes, I certainly agree with that. I might say that in preparing my slides, I found the task of translating into ALGOL 68 more difficult than I expected and, in fact, when I showed the slides to someone who knows ALGOL 68 very well, the one with linked lists and references had to be examined very carefully to make sure that it was correct.

Fuksman: Do you have any experience in writing system programs using SETL?

Dewar: The term "system programming" seems to cover a number of possibilities. Certainly for such system components as compilers, SETL is an appropriate choice. The global optimizer for SETL is being written in SETL and we expect it to be adequately efficient. Now if systems programs means operating systems, I think that raises entirely different issues. For example, the question of protection. It is one thing to talk about bad programs; it's quite another to talk about protection in the presence of malicious system components. That problem is not addressed by the current design of the language.

Session 4d : General Discussion

Turski: I hate to be out of tune with the majority of speakers at this conference, but I seem to be posing a question which no one is willing to answer. I am still waiting, hoping that, perhaps tomorrow, Ross will address my points about the users' requirements, specifications and quality. I have lost hope that somebody will consider the relation between quality and redundancy, even though redundancy is the only known means to achieve reliability and robustness in programs (I refer, for instance, to the work at Newcastle). Now I have a distinct feeling that some of our speakers, if not all, believe that designing new programming languages and, in general, building more sophisticated tools leads necessarily to increased quality of the products. I am afraid this is false. I just want to see why anyone believes that increasingly sophisticated tools (which are fun to construct, I grant you) lead to improved quality of the products which are constructed by means of those tools. I might be terribly stupid, but, please, give me at least a shred of evidence, an idea, why increased sophistication of tools leads to increased quality of the products.

Holager: I think that most people buying software will agree that a low price is a very desirable property. It is a debatable point, of course, whether price should be considered as a component of quality. At the least, you will find that, given a fixed amount of money, more sophisticated tools (which increase productivity) will allow you to do a more thorough job, which will then allow you to produce a better quality product.

Dewar: As far as programming languages are concerned, the only empirical evidence available suggests that the sole effect of the language is on the size of the corresponding source program, and that programmers' productivity is about the same in lines per day no matter what programming language they use. What this means is that the effect of a programming language is really rather small, because individual programmers vary in their productivity by a huge factor, perhaps 30 or 40. I think that ultimately, the issue of programming languages is a very small one relative to the issue of programming techniques.

Tseytin: Do high-level languages improve the quality of software? If software is viewed as a communication channel from a human being to the hardware, one of the components of quality may be the efficiency of the system on both ends of the channel. High-level languages are known to decrease hardware efficiency, but it is widely recognized that the loss is well compensated by improved hardware and automatic optimization, so the net gain in efficiency is dramatic. I believe that further development of high-level languages will further increase the efficiency, but the point I would like to make is that the situation is different with respect to software reliability. So far, the impact of high-level languages on reliability has been positive, because complex tasks were separated into layers, some of which could be verified, whether by experience or by formal reasoning, and because the total amount of human input to machines was reduced. But the development of high-level languages continues, and a number of powerful new concepts are proposed. Where do they come from and what purpose do they serve? I think that the characteristic property of a high-level language is that it allows a complex task to be structured and represented in much the same way as in the human mind. Often we think we are inventing new high-level language features when we are just discovering how the appropriate knowledge of a problem is represented in the human mind. Some developments in artificial intelligence seem to confirm this. To simplify the transformation from human knowledge into the expressions of a programming language surely enhances the human's confidence that he has actually said to a computer what he intended to say. But the development of high-level language features is proceeding mainly along the lines of mathematically provable systems, "structured programming", etc. It has become commonplace to abuse FORTRAN and other, mathematically untidy IBMish software, but it must be recognized that those practical languages were the first to incorporate (though not in the best form) some language features that are, to my mind, vital for a really intelligent software. Among these features I mention open-ended design, modularity, defaults, specific uses of symbol processing (keywords, linkage editing, macro generation), etc. I argue that the development of high-level languages should consciously use all of those things, as well as knowledge representation techniques from artificial intelligence, even though some mathematically minded theorists may deplore that. Of course, speaking to a highly intelligent machine may become unreliable, because it may supply the missing information from its default knowledge and the human may not be aware of this or may not know exactly what the default assumptions were. In many cases, however, speaking to a mechanical device appears to be more reliable than speaking to a human. For a trunk call, I prefer to dial rather than to speak to an operator. In submitting a job for computer processing, the use of a job control language is surely safer than giving verbal instructions to a human operator (although even using some JCL you may get a quite unexpected response). I do not say that the development of high-level languages should stop where it is now, or that it should proceed only along the lines of mathematically provable extensions. But I stress that, in these developments, the issue of reliability needs special consideration.

Goos: I would like to address myself to the question of whether we should design new languages. My answer would be both yes and no. We should not only design new languages but also address ourselves to the question of how to make best use of existing languages. Considering the title of this part of the conference, "The programming language as a tool", I have only heard about how to experiment with new languages. I didn't hear very much about how to use existing languages as tools. We must consider the fact that it takes a very long time, about 10 or 15 years, until ideas about new programming languages come into practice. It takes many man years before we have implemented a new programming language so that it can really be used for constructing quality software. All that we've said here applies to quality software which could be constructed in, perhaps, 1982. Do we really believe that, for instance, Nehmer's problem can only be solved in 1982, after we've introduced all these new programming languages? What can we say about the use of existing languages?

Schuman: If I remember rightly, in order to meet the reliability requirements of that particular project, it was decided to design a new language . . .

Holager: I can tell you something about what the group I was previously with did in order to live with an existing language. Firstly, it seems that procedures come in two classes: those produced in a top-down fashion, and those produced in a bottom-up fashion. In the ones produced in a top-down fashion, we tended to put a check on the input data to ensure that the input data conform to some set of assertions, or some reasonability constraints. In the bottom-up procedures there was generally some kind of function value being produced and we checked that for plausibility. Furthermore, we saw it as quite essential that every time we had some form of CASE statement or more complicated IF-THEN-ELIF-THEN ... statements then we made sure there was always an OUT (or ELSE) at the end. This was usually redundant. If we had done our job properly, that part would never be executed. But with a sad regularity we ended up there, in the trap with nothing else to do but stop and report.

Schuman: Turski mentioned earlier that he always taught his students such techniques; he called them redundancy by design. However I would like to suggest that this is possibly a misuse of the traditional conditional statements, in so far as the intention is to indicate the expected conditions of operation rather than to determine the normal flow of control. Perhaps it would be more appropriate to use assertions, or pre- and post-conditions, richer type declarations (for instance, involving predicates), acceptance tests, or any of the more recent linguistic mechanisms which have been proposed for the purpose of improving reliability. We have been attempting to add redundancy, but in ways which can be statically checked or otherwise exploited in some effective fashion. How, tell me, are we to accomplish this if we can neither change existing languages nor design new ones to support these techniques properly? It has been pointed out that there exists an entire spectrum of possibilities, ranging from simple plausibility checks to (semi-)automatic program verification. The more we try to achieve in this respect the more imperative it becomes that the language itself directly support and enforce the constraints which must be imposed. Such an approach is typified by ALPHARD and EUCLID, and is being pursued in a number of other experimental efforts. It is to be observed that the further we try to go in this direction, the more our proposed programming languages take on the attributes of what might instead be called specification languages. Certainly SETL can be seen in that light. Given this tendency, it becomes relevant to speak of automatically generating (or "synthesizing") the corresponding program, thereby ensuring that it is correct by construction rather than by verification. In that case the resulting programs would also be "redundant by design", but only to the extent that the original specification provided for true redundancy, as opposed to information serving solely to reduce the probability of (undetected) programming errors.

Nehmer: I would also like to comment on your remark. I think that, at the present time, it is not possible to generate directly the code from specifications. The specification methods available now do not allow selection of the most appropriate implementation alternative according to some "suitability" criteria. To achieve that we have to add more information at the specification level.

Schuman: That is exactly my point: we find we must add further information. This is accomplished fairly effectively in SETL, by means of the representation sublanguage which Dewar described. That mechanism serves primarily to increase efficiency, but one could imagine a similar approach for introducing redundancy. Allow me to point out that, according to the call-for-papers, the subject matter of this conference is "techniques and tools for Constructing Quality Software". It seems to have become fashionable to insist on the primacy of techniques over tools. While there is an element of truth in this position, to my mind it is rather irresponsible to take an overly militant stand in this regard. Proposed techniques for software construction are, in a great many cases, essentially useless unless they are properly supported by suitable tools. Nine times out of ten, this comes down to incorporating certain facilities into a programming language and into the corresponding compiler or some closely associated processor. And even then, we've only begun. There remains the problem, mentioned earlier by King, of putting these things into practice. There, even more modesty seems to be in order, for I am afraid we don't have the foggiest idea of how to solve that problem.

Goos: In essence, Schuman is saying that we cannot live with existing languages for technical reasons. My point is that there exist other constraints, for instance: your boss likes you to program in FORTRAN and nothing else; you must be compatible with programs written in some strange language; the programmers who are at your disposal do not know any other language; etc. For such reasons, I think, it is not a complete answer to say that for technical reasons we have to abandon present languages and move on. I would like to mention one approach which could improve the situation, namely teaching people how to express new concepts using an existing language. It is not by accident that I also mentioned in my presentation how modularity might be expressed in languages like FORTRAN. Such teaching has a twofold effect. The first one is that people become aware of what kind of programming discipline is needed in those languages, which is not mentioned in the usual books. Secondly, only by showing them the deficiencies of existing languages are you able to convince them gradually, and to prepare them to switch over to some new language. This second point is especially important; it is not enough to say to people that PASCAL or whatever language you like, is much better and that they should therefore go over to this new language — full stop. That just does not suffice.

Rajlich: I wonder why so few people advocate the evolutionary development of dialects. For example, we might try to define modular FORTRAN or something like that. I think this procedure could be quite interesting because it would allow for more changes without creating whole new languages. The best way to entrap users may be to embed those newer techniques progressively into the languages they already know.

Meyer: I'd like to comment a little on what Goos just said. I work in exactly the type of environment he spoke about, that is an industrial environment where almost the only language used is FORTRAN. Any realistic observer can affirm that there is no reason to think that the situation will be much different in the next 10 years. Maybe it might one day be FORTRAN 77 instead of FORTRAN 66, but that's the only change we can expect. We are trying to do precisely the sort of thing Goos was mentioning, that is trying to educate the users, trying to tell them at a really simple level what is good in FORTRAN, what is bad in FORTRAN; well, it's easier to define what is bad FORTRAN than what is good FORTRAN. As for his second point, however, about convincing individual programmers that there are better languages, I'm quite sure that we shall not succeed by trying to convince individual users. The problems of languages are at a much higher level. They are economic problems, and may be even political problems; it is not a problem of convincing the individual programmer.

Meertens: I think that the way in which programs are constructed very much influences the productivity of the programmer and that the programming language may be a great help for constructing programs in a particular way. A response to Goos, who proposes more or less that programs be taught and written in some high-level language and then put into an available language: under the circumstances that is probably a sensible thing to do, but in fact, what you are obliging people to do is to play the role of the compiler from a high-level language into an available language; this may be the best way to live with it but there is a problem, namely that people are not the most reliable compilers. The important thing is that, in order to play that game, you first have to have that high-level language, so I think it remains worthwhile to seek more advanced languages, allowing higher levels of abstraction and supporting better methods of program construction.

Dewar: The question of how we can live with current programming languages is really a misplaced one. We might better ask how we can live with the sea of incompetent programmers who are currently using them.

Correll: What can we do as a research community to improve the quality of programs which are written in industry? I would like to refer to some experience I've had recently with a part of German industry. With respect to the programming languages and the tools they use, it appears that we cannot do very much. There are managers who are trained in using certain languages, in using certain tools, and they don't want to switch. But they are not very good in doing designs. What they sometimes do is to ask the research community to help them in designing systems. So I think that what the research community can do, if it wants to help to improve the quality of programming which is done in industry, is to get into the business of helping to do better designs and specifications. In that way I think we can still have an impact on industry.

Schuman: But is that really the job of the research community?

Holager: Computing science appears to have very little influence on the practice of computing. I should like to argue that the only feasible way of altering this is by presenting measurements of the real efficiencies of our novel tools and methods; measurements would also provide much-needed feedback to the scientific community. [Prepared statement:]

THE AMATEUR

I suppose we all know the typical academic computing amateur. Who will — with great enthusiasm and FORTRAN — proceed to waste an inordinate amount of his own and other people's time. He is, of course, an expert in some other field: ask him what he is doing, and he will answer physics or psychology or physiology or whatever. Observe what he is doing, and you shall find out the truth: he is trying to debug a program. And be his progress ever so slow, he will never question his tools or working methods, which he regards as some wondrous amalgam of high science and black magic. Is it possible to do something about this waste of the time of presumably very talented people, to help them write less haphazard programs and get their data processed with a reasonable expenditure of effort?

THE PRACTITIONER

- is generally not much better off. He is typically producing 1000 machine instructions per year if he is writing very difficult programs in assembly code, or the equivalent of 20,000 instructions per year if he is coding very simple applications in a high-level language. These are the same figures people were reporting 15 years ago; there does not appear to have been any significant progress.

And more harmful: the reliability of new computing applications is as low as it has ever been. The high cost of producing code still keeps organizations from properly tailoring their computer based systems to the needs of humans and society.

There is of course little reason to expect any change as long as the typical programmer still has the same general level of training in much the same tools and techniques as 15 years ago: he is typically the graduate of some one-week course in RPG, COBOL, PL/1, or Assembler. He has heard about structured programming which he considers a very academic idea, to be mentioned now and then to keep his image up. The rest he has learned by trial and error, mostly error.

There is little reason to call him "professional" — "well-paid amateur" is probably more appropriate. Carlson (1) writes, quite appropriately:

> *"The overall impression is that the computing technology does not yet provide a foundation for professional practice. The experience to date indicates that only limited areas of subject matter have reached a stage where two or more experts can refer to, and agree upon, a first set of*

principles in their development or evaluation or practical designs, applications or operations."

In any area of intellectual service, a professional practice appears to have two essential foundations:

- The existence of a set of tools and methods, each being in some sense the best for a subclass of the problems encountered, where the set is complete in the sense that the subclasses cover most of the problems encountered.

- The ability to identify the problem that should be solved, and with some reliability to choose the most effective tool or method for it.

Current practitioners of the art of constructing software clearly cling to their few techniques with the blind love typical of amateurs. Something must be done.

THE SCIENTISTS

-, however, appear to spend most of their time building science for the sake of it, or rather, in an effort to gain academic recognition. And behold, they have already been able to produce the basis for academic respectability: a number of subfields that are hardly able to communicate!

We have the mathematicians, tirelessly trying to prove programs incorrect, or just devising new notations to keep the mind nimble.

We have the systems software engineers, revelling in their Herculean abilities: dismembering Labyrinthean Monster programs, cleaning Augean Stables crawling with bugs, and forever falling for the Siren Songs of their own new programming language.

We have the programming methodologists, misty masters of mysteries forever seeking the magic Philosophers' Stone which will turn the basest mental objects into golden, well-structured programs.

Clearly, a good deal of current activity in the field of informatics has no relevance to quality software construction. Some other research is still in the speculative stages; that is fair enough. But then, what about the vast amount of research which seems relevant, and has been finished? Can some of this contribute to a practical technology for producing quality software, a foundation for professional practice in our field?

The fact is, we do not know. We all have our opinions, which we express with a conviction which often seems inversely proportional to its factual foundations. In the area of programming languages, for instance, fashion seems to be as fleeting and whimsical as in female clothing. What true computer scientist would appear in public with the programming language of five years ago?

THE PRACTICE

Clearly, most practitioners believe informatics cannot contribute anything to their activities. Many programmers see themselves as the ultimate programming technologists (and dread the thought they might not be). Try to sell one of them a language or technique which is less than 15 years old, and he will become very angry: he has no time for such academic toys — he has important work to do.

Many informatics departments are still fighting in vain to avoid FORTRAN in the introductory programming courses. Their universities simply do not believe them when they say they can teach students something more worthwhile. The practitioners of computing simply see no reason to believe that the technology of producing software will change in the next 30 years or so.

THE SCIENCE

What then is accepted as fact in our field? From their usage, it is apparent that RPG, COBOL and FORTRAN are better than assembly languages for their respective fields of application. There appears to be a universal, though very vague feeling that one must think systematically when developing programs, that the structure of the resulting program must in some manner reflect this. And that is really all.

Most computer scientists feel we can do a lot better. But the crucial point is, we have not proved we can do better. It plainly appears that our techniques will not be put into practical use until we take the trouble of documenting how they perform. To do that we shall have to observe the productivity, reliability, cost, etc. of using current methods. We shall then have to measure experimentally the improvement, if any, using our new tools and techniques on a specific kind of task, in a specific kind of environment.

The methodological problems of doing this are great. We must observe how well people do their work: a psychologically touchy subject. Programming work appears to consist mainly of mastering complexity, which means the tasks of the experiments must be large enough that complexity is really encountered, and that trivial beginners' problems do not dominate the results (2). It also seems essential that the participants be experienced in the kind of work to be done. Students and trainees have in some experiments shown a variability much too large to allow meaningful measurements (3). To multiply the costs even further, each experiment must be repeated to allow a rudimentary statistical treatment.

So the costs will be high. But anyone believing novel methods would be significantly better than current practice, should agree that things staying as they are is by far the most expensive alternative. In academic circles this difficult research should of course be promoted and encouraged by accepting the resulting reports for formal publication. To the more glamorously inclined, this may seem like an unbearable price: an unexciting report on a few tedious experiments must get priority over an elegant paper of mathematically cast speculations.

Because we have amassed more than enough speculations and ideas, it is time to start weeding and pruning. Only factual observations can tell which ideas are valuable, and in which context. Only this can supply the basis for a professional attitude towards the utensils of the trade: the ability to coolly choose an economical and convenient set of tools and techniques for each job at hand.

Clearly, we have been going about our science in a very amateurish fashion. It is a very fundamental axiom of cybernetics that a closed, goal-directed system cannot exist without observation of its results. Computer science is a closed system indeed, and has been trying to proceed towards our goal of a technology for producing quality software with only the flimsiest observations.

Indeed, if we are the professionals, then God help the amateurs!

REFERENCES

(1) Carlson, W., Summary Report to the ACM Council - ACM/NBS Action Programs Memo, April 23, 1974 (as quoted in the CACM, Jan. 1975, p. 5).

(2) Gannon, J. D., Language Design to Enhance Programming Reliability, Technical Report CSRG-47, University of Toronto, Jan. 1975.

(3) Weinberg, G. M., The Psychology of Computer Programming, Van Nostrand Reinhold Company, New York (1971).

Dewar: One quick comment: my experience with hobbyists is that they are exactly the people who embrace the newest themes with the greatest pleasure and throw away all the previous work, so I just ask myself who are the amateurs?

Ershov: Holager's statement is a very nice piece of prose, but there is too much irony in it to be really productive and, in my opinion, there are some really misleading points in it. One point: computer science is not closed, it is just the opposite. And another point: practitioners are not so ignorant with respect to computer science. I hope our conference will give some evidence that both are true.

Holager: I think that computer science is remarkably closed; much too closed. One of the symptoms of this is an incomprehensible technical jargon. Very many of the words we are using are unnecessary. We could use ordinary, understandable words instead of something like "real-time", or "compile-time". The latter just means "during compilation". Most of these words seem to be specifically tailored to keep other technical people from understanding what we are doing. Concerning your other point, the ignorance of programmers is often appalling indeed. It may be different here in the Soviet Union from what I was used to in Norway. But the majority of programmers I have met have heard very little about what computer scientists are working on. And they have understood less.

Turski: According to the information I have, the productivity of poets has not increased for the last 5000 years, as measured in the number of lines of verse they produce per day. It is highly irregular, but when integrated over a lifetime, it seems to be about two volumes of collected works. If the number of lines produced by programmers per day has not increased over the last 15 years, it may signify one of two things: that this is the limit of human capacity for solving problems, as measured in that particular measure, or that this measure is meaningless. I'd rather hold to the second concept. According to my observations, and I have been in this field close to 20 years, which easily spans the 15 year period you have mentioned, productivity has increased enormously. The problems I am now giving quite routinely to my students in the second year at the university, which they have to solve within a semester, and 40-50% do it beautifully, are the problems which took me, 15 or 20 years ago, many months of total devotion. I refer here to some technical things like writing compilers. My students write compilers for languages with precedence grammars routinely, as an exercise. Now, 20 years ago we did not know what a precedence grammar was, let alone how to exploit this fact in writing a reliable compiler. So, you see, even though the productivity measured in terms of lines of code per day perhaps has not increased, the productivity measured in terms of problems solved by means of programming per unit of time, has improved, and most spectacularly in these areas where sound mathematical theory has been developed and widely understood.

Dewar: I would like to make a comment with regard to productivity and the counterexample (compilers) that was proposed. I think there is a most staggering example that productivity hasn't changed at all recently. The best FORTRAN compiler I have used is FASTRAN on the 7094 which was written, I believe, by three men in six months in 1963, which is close to 15 years ago, and it's almost completely error free. I never ran into errors, a statement I can't make about any subsequent FORTRAN compiler that I've ever interacted with.

Turski: My second observation relates to the points I made before. It seems that we are too self-conscious, that too often we concentrate on our own problems as being the only proper problems for our professional attention. One can observe a very curious phenomenon: faced with problems of our own making we export them into the application area. One clear example of that, which I already gave, is the "integrity of a data base". This is a purely "in" phenomenon. You see, banking systems, until they applied computers, never had to worry about "integrity" because they never had the invisible update. This invisible update we take to be such a glorious thing: I even read books by prominent computer scientists in which this is considered as the cornerstone of programming! But the assignment statement has no counterpart in real life, in the life of honest book-keepers. And until and unless an invisible update is introduced, there is no problem of data base integrity. Why we should export this problem into the application area is a mystery. The ill of the profession is not that it is so stupid, but that it loses from its view the fact that we are in a profession to serve other people.

Constructing Quality Software, P.G. Hibbard/S.A. Schuman (eds.)

TOWARDS A FORMAL LANGUAGE FOR FUNCTIONAL SPECIFICATIONS

M. Berthaud
CER IBM - La Gaude - France

The current trend in system development is toward improved design methodology, providing testable, unambiguous output, with optimum use of simulation as a design aid.

The use of a formal descriptive language as a partial replacement for natural language at the product design phase promises a major advance toward such improved methodology by favoring more consistent, structured, and testable design representation.

INTRODUCTION

In a traditional development process, architecture and design phases are based on natural language and flowcharts, with feedback to the design phase via design reviews.
One of the major problems arising when writing functional specifications is due to natural language, which is not the adequate tool to communicate precisely in a technical environment. It leads to redundancy, inconsistency, and incompleteness.

Various studies have shown that approximately 50% of valid problems found after release of the product can be attributed to the design phase, and these are the most expensive errors to correct.

Several techniques have been used to improve the development process. The most significant ones are:

- Defect Removal Technique: Design reviews and inspections (I)' during system development phases detect and solve problems. The systematic use of design reviews improves the design, reduces the number of errors and allows a better control of the process.

- Defect Prevention Technique: A series of tools has been developed to improve the functional specifications by reducing ambiguities and inconsistencies.

  Cause and Effect Graphs (CEG)[2] require a careful and exhaustive study of the specifications in order to draw a boolean graph. The CEG drawing may be part of the design job, with the advantage that it helps the designer to produce a more accurate design. The Test Library Design Automation Program (TELDAP) allows generation of test case patterns for functional test.

FUNCTIONAL SPECIFICATION CHARACTERISTICS

Functional specifications are an essential step in the development process. In order to improve the reliability of the product and remove ambiguities from a functional viewpoint, the following requirements must be fulfilled:

- What and not how: At this level, it is important to describe "what must be done" and not "how it should be implemented". This logical view of the overall system should ignore unnecessary details which will be addressed in the low level design phase.

- Structured: In order to reduce the complexity of the product, the functional specifications must define a decomposition framework into logical entities (or components). The interactions between these components must be minimized and completely formalized; such a decomposition makes easier the job distribution to different groups for the following development phases.

- Human readable and non-ambiguous: Functional specifications must not be subject to interpretation by programmers, i.e. no design decisions must be taken at a latter stage.

- Machine readable: Legibility and updating of the specifications may be improved by automatic processing such as text formatting, cross-references, etc... Specific tools to improve design review efficiency can also be developped.

The use of a descriptive language (or Very High Level Language) allows to achieve two additionnal objectives:

- Completeness: The description of the system should provide a functional model that could be tested, using a simulation technique, to ensure conformity to the objectives of the product and to detect internal incoherence.

  Figure 1 compares the traditional development phases with the new approach.

  Note that the time devoted to the low level design phase and the code and desk debug phase is much longer than that spent on equivalent phases in the new approach. Also, modifications to the objectives may be easily included using the descriptive language.

- Conformity to executable code and vice-versa:

  - Directly compile the description in efficient running code, or

  - use inspections to ensure that the code conforms to the specifications, and

  - generate test cases from the description.

In the rest of this paper, we describe a set of programming tools, called Functional Specifications Tools (FST), which could be used by designers in writing more accurate functional specifications.

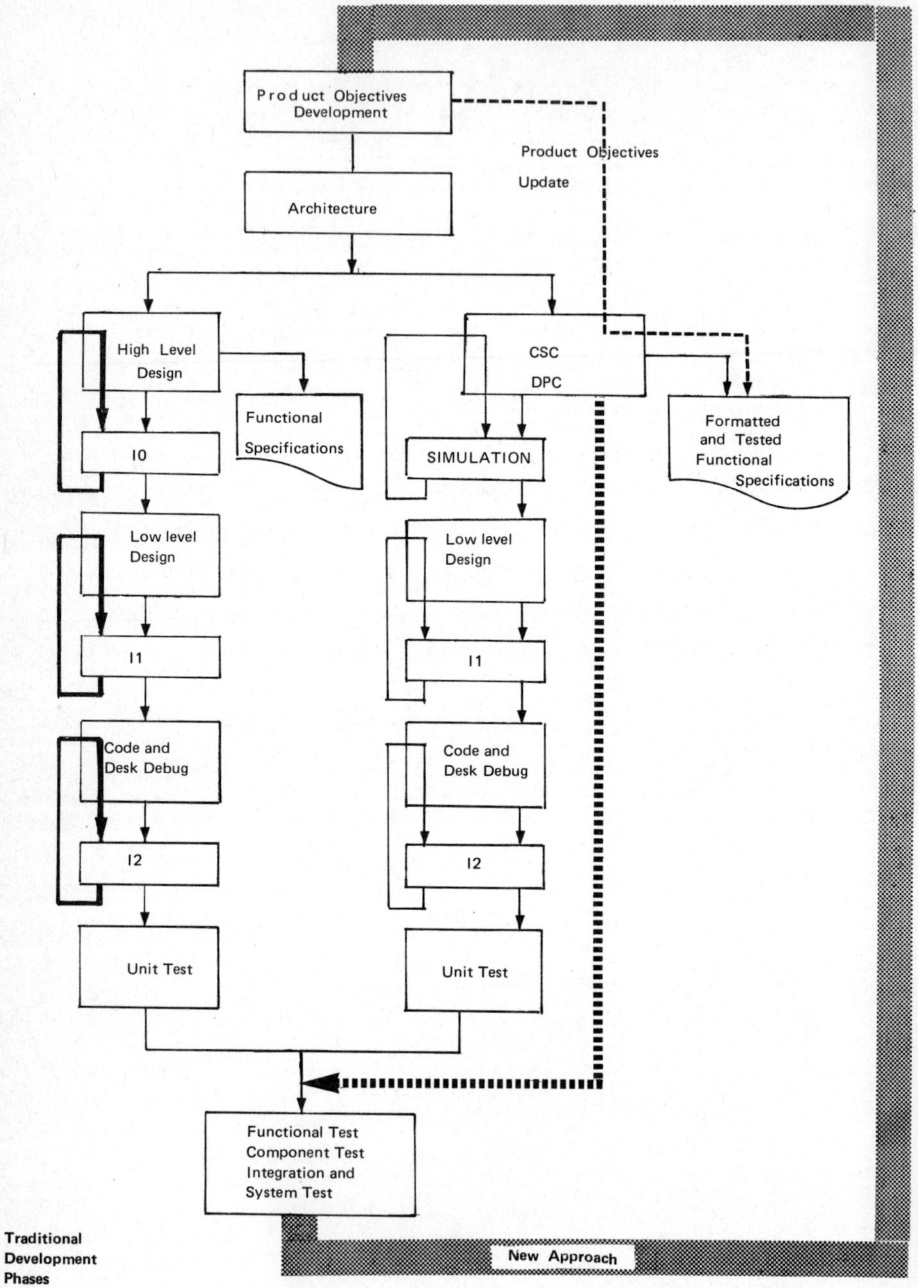

Figure 1. Traditional Development Phases Compared to the New Approach

SYSTEM DECOMPOSITION PRINCIPLES

The System to be described (if complex) has to be decomposed into 'processes' which may be logically concurrent (they can run independently on one or more actual processor). Each process represents a functional entity ; it is equivalent to a sequential machine (or automaton), the behavior of which may be represented in terms of relations between three sets of variables: inputs, outputs and states[3] . So, the overall system consists of a set of automata which communicate and synchronize by exchanging messages.

Each automaton can be described independently. On a given input (e.g. a message coming from another automaton), an action is performed according to the current state and a new state is reached. The state may be considered as a memory that contains information about the past behaviour of the system (figure 2).

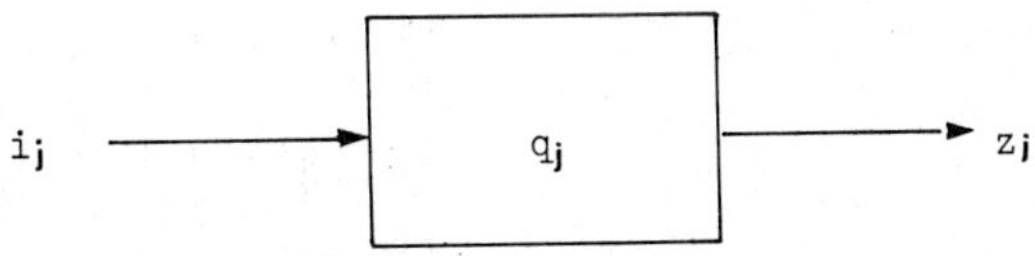

$$\text{with} \quad z_j = f_z\,(i_j\,,\; q_j)$$

$$\text{and} \quad q_{j+1} = f_s\,(i_j\,,\; q_j)$$

Figure 2. System State

In fact, the state is represented by a set of variables ; a particular state Qj corresponds to specific values for these variables. The set of possible states is obtained by the cartesian product of all possible values of all variables (if they are independent). In the case of complex systems, the cardinality of this set is very high.
In order to reduce the complexity, variables belonging to the state can be grouped into classes, according to some criteria; on another hand similar inputs can be gathered under a generic name with additionnal attributes. Thus, a partition of the system may be found; a way to achieve this partition is to divide the system into two components:

- the first one represents the control structure, mainly recognizing valid input sequences

- the second one which is under the control of the previous one, represents data manipulation, i.e. the modifications of variables according to the input.

A similar separation exists in any language between syntax and semantics. However it should be noted that the frontier between these two notions is subjective, and it is the responsibility of the architect (or the designer) to choose the best compromise between the relative complexities of the control structure and data manipulation.

In our approach, the system should be described as two components, using distinct tools:

- the Control Structure Component (CSC) recognizes valid input sequences and invokes the main processing functions and output functions.
- the Data Processing Component (DPC) specifies the logical data organization and describes the main processing functions.

CONTROL STRUCTURE COMPONENT (CSC)

CSC CONCEPT

As soon as an input, referred to as an event, is recognized, definite states are expected that depend on the current state of the system. If the recognized event is expected, the system takes appropriate action and goes to another state.

Two methods may be used to describe valid sequences of events:

- Set up a list of valid sequences
- Create rules to generate valid sequences

The first method requires an exhaustive list of sequences. This seems impossible to define in large systems where many combinations can exist.

CSC adopts the second method. Following established rules, it generates all possible valid sequences of events. Figure 3 illustrates this concept.

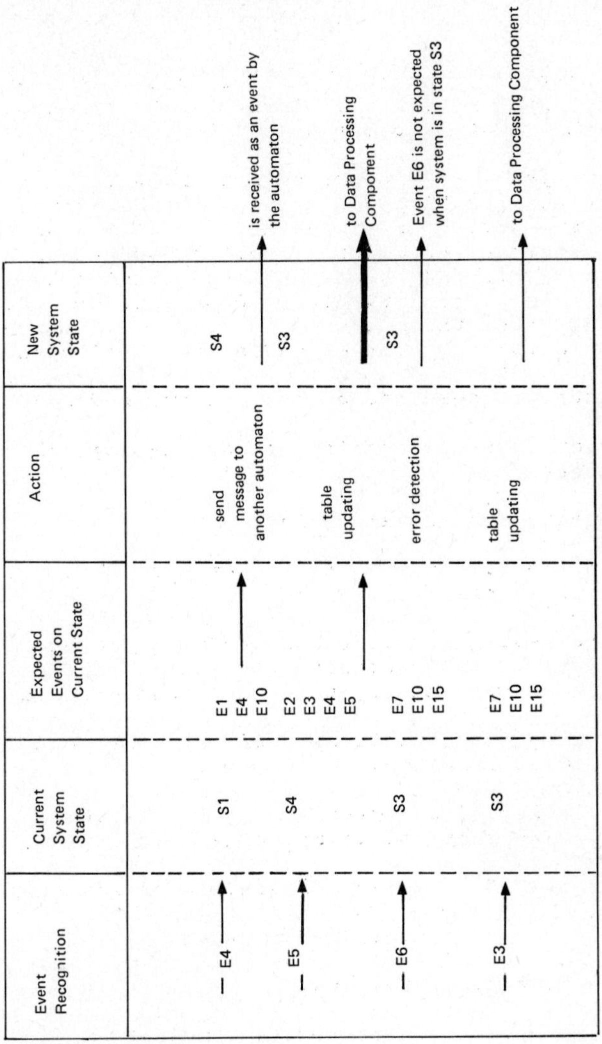

Figure 3. CSC Concept

Note: Since the system is a sequential machine, the next event will not occur before the action is completely executed.

A message sent to an automaton is considered by the latter as an event.

CSC LANGUAGE

Given a set of inputs, the rules define the applicable sequences. Each rule has a name, which represents a part of the state of the automaton.

Several types of automata are known. They differ according to the kind of input sequence they accept. A finite-state automaton is characterized by a unique value for the state at a given time. A push-down automaton associates with the state a stack that memorizes the history. The Control Structure Component of FST accepts input sequences that can be defined by a restricted push-down automaton, corresponding to LL(1) grammars[4].

CSC Language is composed of the following items:

- Events, which are inputs or messages from other automata
- Contexts, which name rules
- Functions, which name actions. Two types of functions exist:
  - Processing functions invoked by CSC but described by the Data Processing Component. These functions can return values, which are considered as events.
  - Connection functions used for the communication between automata.

The description of an automaton consists mainly in a set of rules. The simplest format of a rule is:

```
context-a  >  event-e SEND-automaton-x:message-m

                    F:function-f context-b
```

which can be read as follows:

if event-e occurs in context-a, message-m is sent to automaton-x, function-f is performed and context-b is entered.

EXECUTION OF A CSC DESCRIPTION

A CSC description is machine readable and so can be processed to produce:

- A formatted listing which is part of the functional specifications.
- Intermediate code having simple and portable instruction set.

  The intermediate code may be assembled for a specific machine to produce a code executable through an interpreter. The description of the control structure is first simulated with dummy programs written in DPC language. These are progressively replaced by processing functions as they are described by the Data Processing Component.

  The relative simplicity in the constructs and items of the control structure description allows operational code to be obtained from the intermediate code.

CSC FACILITIES

Two facilities may be included into the Control Structure Component to review the description: a Query facility and a Flow facility.

Query Facility

A Query facility can be used to investigate any CSC description, from a terminal:

- Display all elements of a specified type, such as messages, events, and data
- Display the description of specified rules and functions
- Display all locations of the rules where specified objects are referenced

Flow Facility

A Flow facility can be used to execute symbolically a CSC description, from a terminal:

- Set up the CSC (a certain number of automata)
- Choose a logical event and route it to a selected automaton
- Decide on the return event from a function
- Control the message handler by routing messages to the appropriate automaton

DATA PROCESSING COMPONENT (DPC)

DPC CONCEPT

The purpose of DPC is to give a logical definition of data and to describe how data are processed. In most systems, data exists mainly as information contained in tables and control blocks, and data processing consists in establishing relations between this data. Using this concept, data in FST are described by a Relational Model[5]. This approach, introduced by E. F. Codd for large data bases, does not concentrate on the internal representation of data, but rather on the relations existing between the data.

DPC deals with system data and functions without taking into consideration the physical aspect. This enables designers to focus only on the logical aspects of the system, thus avoiding to consider unnecessary details at their level.

DATA ORGANIZATION

To describe system data, DPC needs to structure data into small entities. It uses the following items:

Object : the atomic piece of data

Category: a collection of objects having the same logical type

Relation and Access-Function: a binary relation[6] establishes a double correspondence between objects of two categories:

the direct access-function and the transposed access-function (Figure 4).

Relation A to B

Objects T N
Y P

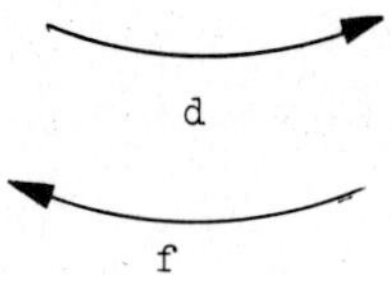

d is the direct access-function
f is the transposed access-function

Figure 4. Relations and Access-Functions

Variables: results of intermediate operations or input/output parameters of a function.

DPC Function: a set of statements executing a logical function of the system.

DPC LANGUAGE

System Design is made up with two phases which are reflected in the DPC language:

- A definition phase
- A manipulation phase

Definition Phase

Categories and relations are defined and new ones are added to the data space. Objects are not entered at this time. The following example illustrates the simplicity of a CREATE function.

```
function-name CREATE;
CATEGORY category-name1,category-name2,category-name3;
RELATION category-name1  TO category-name2
(direct-access-function-name, transposed-access-function-name);
END;
```

Manipulation Phase

Describes how data defined in a CREATE function are handled: updating relations, creating objects, determining which events have to be returned to CSC.

To evaluate the strength of the DPC language, a sample of the statement types you may use in the manipulation phase is given below:

HEADER: to specify the function name and the input/ouptut parameter list.

ASSIGNMENT: to assign a set expression or an arithmetic expression to a variable.

ADD-TO: to add objects to a category or pairs of objects to a relation.

ERASE-FROM: to suppress objects from a category or a pair of objects from a relation.

REPLACE: to replace a pair of objects by another pair in a relation.

CONDITION: This has the following format:

```
IF conditional-expression THEN...;ELSE...;ENDIF;
```

FOR: has the following format:

```
FOR variable-name BELONGING-TO set-expression;
            statement-list;ENDFOR;
```

PERFORM: to call another DPC function.

A DPC function may be processed to produce:

- A formatted listing (another part of the functional specifications)
- Cross-references

- Diagnostics
- Intermediate code, that is, an internal representation of functions ready to be simulated.

FST SIMULATOR

The FST simulator allows the accuracy of the system description to be tested by interpreting the intermediate code obtained after the compilation of CSC and DPC descriptions. CSC and DPC intermediate codes may be tested interactively ; it is possible to test each one separately.

A set of commands is made available to:

- Define the system configuration
- Start simulation
- Collect statistical information

In the simulation process, CSC events are generated either step by step by the user from a terminal, or automatically by an event generator.

Figure 5 illustrates a complete FST Process.

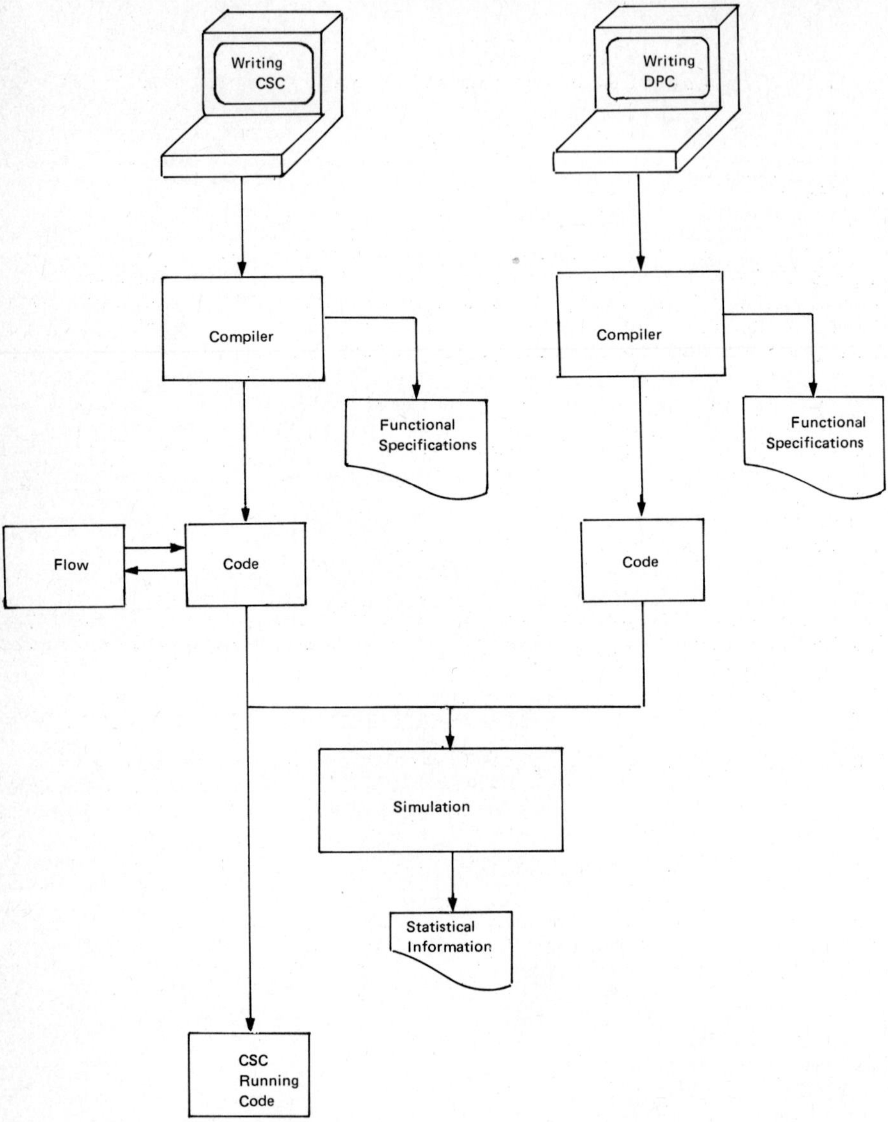

Figure 5. Complete FST Process

FUTURE DEVELOPMENTS

The set of tools we have detailed should improve the quality of functional specifications. Further work is necessary to enlarge the scope of FST to generate automatically test cases and operational code. Both improvements would reduce the time devoted to development and increase the quality of the product.

TEST CASE GENERATOR

The Test Case Generator may be designed to generate from the formal description a series of test patterns, which will be of use at system test. Test patterns would supply an automatic way of verifying the accuracy of the operational system, what has always been difficult to do.

CODE GENERATOR

The Control Structure Component may produce portable running code.

The production of efficient running code by the Data Processing Component is subject to more complex difficulties, the main one being the performance degradation. An optimizer for the language should be based on techniques already described for SETL by J.T. Schwartz[7]. However, it is not sure that performance can be improved automatically in all cases and it seems reasonable to ask the developper to provide information on the physical representation of data.

CONCLUSION

A lot of work is currently done for the improvement of the various levels of product specifications. Two recent papers[8,9] are proposing methodology and automated tools, in order to completely define a product before the development phase.

The approach, presented in this paper, has the same goal with also the ambition to provide a functional simulation of a product. At an early stage, it should allow the detection of deficiencies (e.g. human factors), potential errors (e.g. synchronisation problems) and the determination of critical performance functions. The formalized functional specifications, coupled with inspections techniques during the implementation phase, should insure a coherent development process and reduce the maintenance cost.

Acknowledgement

The work reported in this paper is the result of contributions from several people, in particular Michel Duponchel, Philippe Potin and Max Peltier.

BIBLIOGRAPHY

1 Mike Fagan
Design and Code Inspections and Process Control in the Development of Programs
IBM Kingston - TR25-572

2 W. Elmendorf
Cause-Effect Graphs in Functional Testing
IBM Poughkeepsie - TR00-2487

3 T.L. Booth
Sequential Machines and Automata Theory
Ed. John Wiley and Sons - 1967

4 M. Griffiths, M. Peltier
Grammar Transformation as an Aid to Compiler Production
IBM France, Grenoble Scientific Center - Study FF2-0057, May 1968

5 E.F. Codd
A Relational Model for Large Shared Data Banks
C.ACM, vol 13 nb 6, june 1970

6 J.R. Abrial
Data Semantics
Grenoble University - France

7 J.T. Schwartz
Automatic Data Structure Choice in a Language of Very High Level
C. ACM, vol 18 nb 12, december 1975

8 D. Teichroew, E.A. Hershey III
PSL/PSA: A Computer-Aided technique for Structured Documentation and Analysis of Information Processing Systems
IEEE Transactions on Software Engineering, vol SE-3 nb 1, january 1977

9 D.T. Ross, K.E. Schoman Jr
Structured Analysis for Requirements Definition
IEEE Transactions on Software Engineering, vol SE-3 nb 1, january 1977

Berthaud : Discussion

Fuksman: I would like to see some examples. When you consider, say, a compiler, what is the functional specification of a compiler? What does it mean, "the recognizable inputs and actions"? Is not such a functional specification the compiler itself?

Berthaud: The functional specifications of a compiler are similar to the definition of the language. For example, if you take the definition of ALGOL 60, you have syntactic rules and semantic rules. Syntactic rules can be represented by the Control Structure component, semantic rules are actions called by the Control Structure component. So you could describe the compiler using just these techniques.

Fuksman: Once I've described it in that way, what else must I do? Have I finished my work on the compiler?

Berthaud: You've finished your work if you can obtain the code directly from these specifications.

Ross: The functional specifications of a compiler should correspond more to the specification of the semantics of the metalanguage, independent of the language itself that was to be compiled. And then, how do you do lexical processing? How do you do parsing? How do you do back tracking in the event of error? How do you output the assembly listing? These would be part of the functional specifications for a compiler.

Poole: The project you just described seems to me to be very ambitious because its availability would surely result in the production of high-quality software. I'm very interested in how far you have progressed. What is advertisement and what is operational? Is this a description of a working system or only a functional specification? [☺]

Berthaud: We have implemented the compiler for the Control Structure component. The first version of the compiler for the Data Processing component was also written. The major problem is the inefficiency of the generated code which consists mainly of calls to run-time PL/I routines. The flow-tracing tool for the Control Structure component exists, allowing symbolic execution of the description. It is not very difficult to produce running code from a Control Structure description because it is very similar to your portable compiler; it has a very simple intermediate language and you can generate code from it either for a 370 computer or for some mini-microcomputer. The Abstract Machine Supervisor is also running. To date, no product has been constructed using these tools.

Constructing Quality Software, P.G. Hibbard/S.A. Schuman (eds.)

QUALITY STARTS WITH REQUIREMENTS DEFINITION

Douglas T. Ross
SofTech, Inc.
Waltham, Massachusetts

The thesis of this position paper is that quality of software is relative to the intended application and can only be achieved by a disciplined methodology in which quality requirements are incorporated into the original requirements definition for the problem and are carefully checked and confirmed at every stage in the production process.

THE SYSTEM LIFE CYCLE

How is quality of software to be measured? Against what can the quality of software be compared? How, indeed, can the quality of software be "assured", as "quality control" and "quality assurance" are standard features of every mature manufacturing process? These are a new breed of question and concern for software. Only now that software design and production methodologies are becoming systematized can they finally be addressed.

Figure 1, (drawn from [5]), shows that an ideal system technology would act as a perfect transmission medium to allow the production of an ideal system, which would be the perfect solution to a set of requirements.

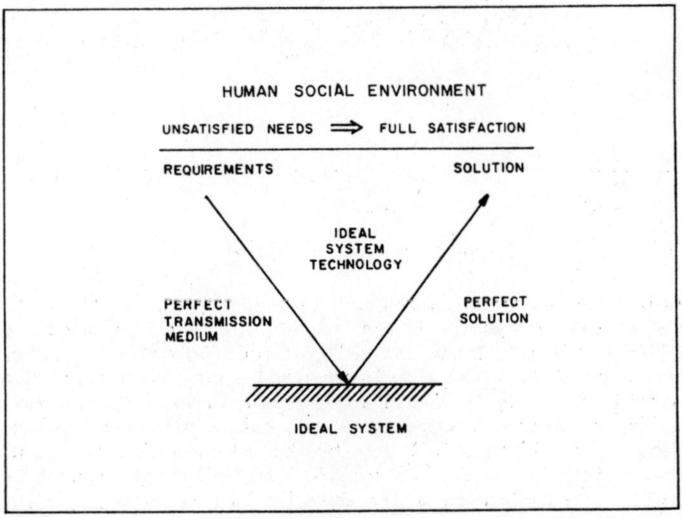

Figure 1
Ideal System Building

Figure 2, (from the same source), shows that our real system technology has imperfections which do not permit perfect recognition and translation of system requirements into perfect solutions. "Those imperfections (see Figure 2) affect our creation of a (non-ideal, imperfect) system by letting in stray unwanted inputs and allowing some important factors to be lost. Those imperfections also affect the delivery of the solution, causing lost capability and distortion of results into unwanted effects." These are the real facts of life that absolutely and inescapably determine the quality of software, even if that quality itself is relative.

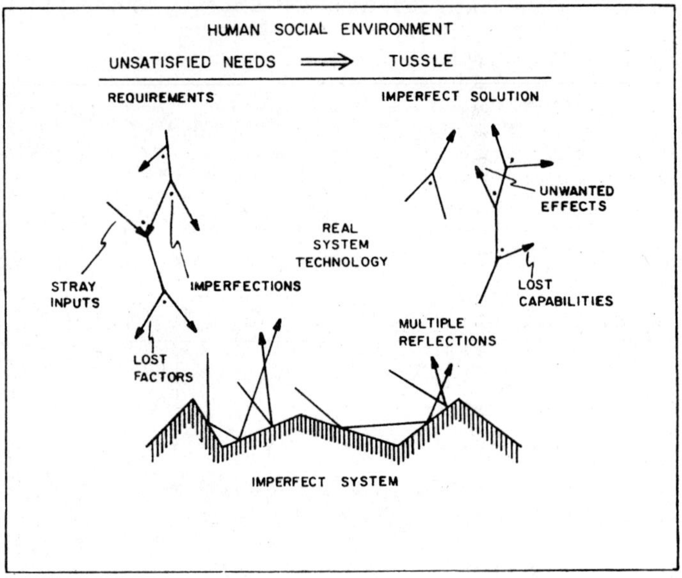

Figure 2

Actual System Building

Figure 3 elaborates an illustration from [6], and shows the basic structure of the system life cycle. In that paper, we were concerned primarily with the WHY, WHAT, HOW of system development. I.e., recognition of a problem says WHY a solution is needed, specification by means of a functional architecture tells WHAT the system is to do, and design leads to a system architecture, stating HOW the solution is to be achieved. As Figure 3 shows, this is then followed by the actual building and use of the system, which yields results, which then can be interpreted and assessed as to their value. Any inadequacies then lead to recognizing an additional, modified problem, causing another cycle.

Each of the activities involved (recognize, analyze, design, build, use interpret) and each of the entities involved (problem, functional architecture, system architecture, operational system, results, and values) inherently have their own sets of imperfections in execution or representation. These cause the deviation from the ideal shown in Figures 1 and 2. Some may be inconsequential, and others may be serious. The life cycle of Figure 3 applies to all kinds of systems, large and small. How important the imperfections in the non-ideal system technology used for its realization are, depends upon the problem.

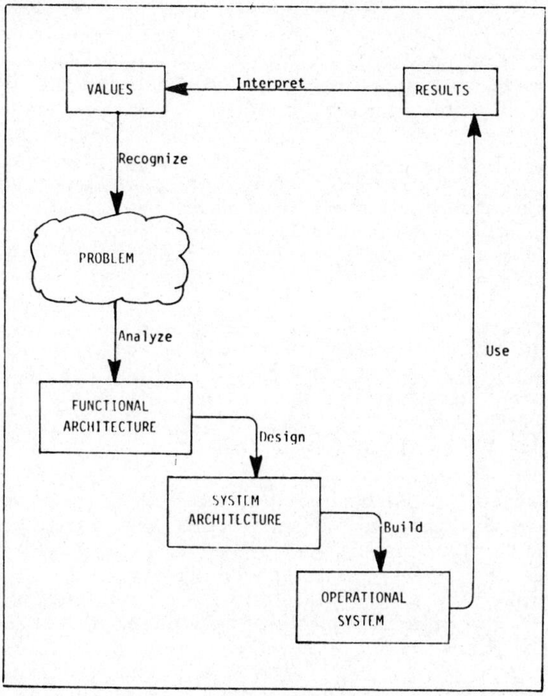

Figure 3

The Software Life Cycle

THE NEED FOR ORDER AND STABILITY

In order to have any sensible treatment of quality at all, every aspect of the system life cycle must be based on an orderly, controlled, and disciplined methodology. This is not to say that all software must be produced with exactly the same set of tools and approaches, for this clearly would be excessive. The rigor and care used for a moon shot or real-time system control, in which lives may be endangered, would be far too elaborate and expensive to use for the preparation of a one-time, inconsequential laboratory experiment. Nonetheless, there is a question of quality in each case. The question cannot even be addressed, much less answered, if the production method used is not orderly, controlled, and disciplined in each case. There may be a broad spectrum of the degree to which the ideal system technology is approached, but even the simplified, streamlined methodologies must be complete and consistent. Each version must be (in some reasonable fashion) a proper degeneration of the elaborate, most advanced state-of-the-art, merely simplified to suit a simpler set of circumstances.

REQUIREMENTS DEFINITION STARTS QUALITY

The System Life Cycle begins with Requirements Definition, which is concerned with WHY, WHAT, and HOW. Quoting from [6], "Requirements Definition must deal with three subjects:

(1) Context analysis: the reasons why the system is to be created and why certain technical, operational, and economical feasibilities are the criteria which form boundary conditions for the system.

(2) Functional specification: a description of what the system is to be, in terms of the functions it must accomplish. Since this is part of the problem statement, it must only present boundary conditions for considerations later to be taken up in system design.

(3) Design constraints: a summary of conditions specifying how the required system is to be constructed and implemented. This does not necessarily specify which things will be in the system. Rather it identifies boundary conditions by which those things may later be selected or created.

Each of these subjects must be fully documented during Requirements Definition." In each case, the WHY, WHAT, HOW, aspects of Requirements Definition firmly establish boundary conditions which the later aspects of development must satisfy. Since we have already established that there is a spectrum of complete and consistent methodologies that can be employed, the primary thesis of this paper should be clear and acceptable. That thesis is:

> Specification of quality must be an integral part of the Context Analysis aspect of Requirements Definition and must be controlled at all stages of the development to yield quality assurance appropriate to the specific system problem.

Notice that Context Analysis presents the total set of reasons why a solution is needed. The Functional Specification and Design Constraints provide further boundary conditions, which elaborate but fit within the boundary conditions laid down by Context Analysis. Therefore, it is appropriate that the question of quality be firmly established from the beginning, and that all questions of quality are properly elaborated in those first two steps. The quality aspects of Functional Specification and Design Constraints quantify the general qualitative expression of value and importance expressed in Context Analysis.

QUALITY CONTROL AND ASSURANCE

It is important to realize that quality is not concerned with testing, itself, but with an assessment of test results. Thus, from the view presented here, the design and execution of tests (or the determination of assertions and execution of proofs) is considered to be an integral part of the production process, itself. Quality assurance for software consists of the formal execution of the required tests and the assessment of results. Enforcement of this monitoring and the adjustment of processes (or rejection, reworking, or downgrading of products, in accordance with test results), is quality control.

Virtually all of the broad range of experience from quality control and quality assurance in manufacturing can be carried over into software development. As is the case in manufacturing, highest quality results most cheaply when a process, itself, is sufficiently reliable and stable to assure the quality of produced product by simple monitoring or controlling of process parameters. Depending upon the level of perfection required, when a process is too variable, it is necessary to test the resulting product, itself. When value is very high relative to the variability of the process, each item produced must individually be inspect and passed. Under less stringent conditions, a testing program in which a selection of products are sampled is adequate, but also is intimately connected to the sensitivity, stability, and work-value involved.

Software quality is, however, different from hardware or physical part quality because there is nothing to wear out or break in software. Therefore, software quality questions hinge almost entirely upon applicability of different ranges of questions and assertions, all of which ultimately revert to a common basis regarding the adequacy of symbolic or numerical representation of intended physical realities. In this sense, questions of software quality are much more subtle and difficult than hardware questions, even though there is nothing to wear out or break.

CONCLUSION

Quality of software can only be assured by a continuing backward reflection (the reverse of that shown in Figure 1) at each stage in the production process. Each step must be orderly, and must be justified and confirmed by the specification of quality imposed in the originating requirements definition. The references cite such a disciplined approach to quality software based on SofTech's Structured Analysis and Design Technique (SADT™). The important features of SADT for quality are its rigor of interconnection of each stage and process, and the incorporation of controlled confirmation cycles for each one. Any method with similar enforced rigor can also yield quality software. But because software quality is almost entirely dependent on the design and production methodology, lack of such rigor and discipline must necessarily yield software of questionable quality.

REFERENCES

[1] Brackett, J. W., and McGowan, C. L. (1977). "Applying SADT to Large System Problems", Proceedings, Symposium on Systems Development Technology, University of Maryland, April 1977

[2] Irvine, C. A., and Brackett, J. W. (1977). "Automated Software Engineering Through Structured Data Management", IEEE Transactions on Software Engineering (IEEETSE), Vol. SE-1 No. 1, pp 34-40

[3] Ross, D. T., Goodenough, J. B., and Irvine, C. A. (1975). "Software Engineering: Process, Principles, and Goals", Computer, Vol. 8, No. 5, pp 17-27.

[4] Ross, D. T., and Brackett, J. W. (1976). "An Approach to Structured Analysis", Computer Decisions, September 1976, pp 40-44.

[5] Ross, D. T. (1977). "Reflections on Requirements", IEEE Transactions on Software Engineering (IEEETSE), Vol. SE-3 No. 1, pp 2-5.

[6] Ross, D. T., and Schoman, K. E., Jr. "Structured Analysis for Requirements Definition", ibid., pp. 6-15.

[7] Ross, D. T., "Structured Analysis (SA): A Language for Communicating Ideas", ibid., pp 16-34.

Ross : Discussion

Schuman: I like very much your definition of model. ["M is a model of A if M can be used to answer questions about A", discovered in a Dutch technical dictionary.] How, though, does one discover the questions one wants to ask?

Ross: From painful experience, among other ways.

Schuman: There is much less of a problem in mastering complexity once you know what you're talking about. The real problem is to find out what it is you want to talk about in the first place, what questions you want to ask, what it is you want to model so that those questions can then be answered.

Ross: I think a start on this is just to take the original decomposition. If you consider the view I gave of the production cycle, each of those stages gives a very well-defined "why", "what" and "how". In fact they overlap. The problem statement is "why", functional architecture is "what", system architecture of the design is "how". But now, once I have that, then the functional architecture becomes "why", the system architecture becomes "what" as I do the actual design, and "how" is the actual architecture of the system. And so it goes chaining right around. Now, if you break down the structure of the specification document, for example, you find that you need different orientations for different submodels in order to cover the area; the most important thing in choosing the models is having in mind who you are trying to communicate with, what's the audience. You need different models for management people, for technical people or for the novice needing basic instruction. One Structured Analysis job we did in Norway had about 42 different models, all hooked together to describe how to produce a family of numerical control systems, hardware and software.

Sintzoff: Now I want to test your model, so I'm going to ask questions. [☺]

Ross: What's the aim?

Sintzoff: Understanding your method. When you cut a box into 6 boxes, how do you effectively find those 6 boxes?

Ross: That's the same question. It has the same answer. One was with respect to the model, and this is with respect to the actual diagrams. They're both the decomposition question. I can give you one more hint, but there's no cook-book. All Structural Analysis does is that it gives you orderly methods for writing out orderly ways of thinking. But there's no magic. It turns out though that the intersecting, separate but inter-related models seem to correspond very closely to the major concepts of levels of abstraction or of abstract machines, to the distinction between hardware and software, and to the distinction between the different roles of people or suborganizations. So, again that's a matter of having an organized view of Nature, because Nature doesn't have problems. You are the one who is seeing problems in it. You must be precise about what each of those views means by itself, and then about how they go together.

Sintzoff: I have another question. How do you ensure that the successive versions you spoke of are converging?

Ross: I can't go into the details now. You cannot do Structural Analysis without having other people involved. There is a requirement for readership and there are very strict rules about how readership is done. There are notations that are written on the diagrams. An author and his reader are not allowed to speak orally until the reader has written comments and the author has in turn written his reactions to the comments. If either one of them feels that there's more that needs to be said, then and only then will they talk. There are also technical committees involved, which check on understanding, on correctness, etc.

Ershov: A question about your practical experience with the human factors of implementing the design and development scheme: how do you coerce people to fit into this system? Is it more a managerial problem or is it one of properly selecting designers? If you have to interpret the rules of the game, is it the manager's or the designer's responsibility to interpret these rules? Do you follow Conway's law that the managerial hierarchy of the project determines the functional or structural hierarchy of the object of the design?

Ross: Starting with the last question first, the managerial and organizational viewpoint is very frequently imposed on both project and product. We do find that it is worthwhile making separate modules for both the product and the project, in order to establish schedules, budget, approval cycles, reporting patterns, etc. As to the type of people involved, it has much less to do with their previous background and training (except for their appropriateness for a given orientation of a model) than with their own innate ability. Some people just find it difficult to think sufficiently abstractly, to make good models. But frequently, you'll find that the same person who has difficulty being trained as a good author will make a very good reader, because he's very meticulous in finding holes and patterns in other people's thoughts. Many people who don't have to have this analytic ability are still involved on the periphery of a project, because you get those people involved on an interview basis and in the readership cycle. You can train them to be commenters easily. And so the disposition of people where they fit seems to be very flexible. The thing that is most intriguing about the methodology is that once people get into it they find that it's no threat.

Rajlich: You have a figure which shows a loop, called the "software life cycle". I understood that in order to achieve a certain quality we have to make several cycles for each software product. What hints do you have to minimize the number of iterations?

Ross: Minimization of the times around the cycle is the experience level with the product. In other words, after you've built dozens of compilers you can build a very good compiler in no time at all, in one cycle around the loop. But the first time you are encountering a problem you will quite probably learn from your first experience. The important thing is to find the proper balance in each project. Frequently, you don't have the opportunity to make more than one cycle, but that's an artifact, since you just don't have the time to do the next round.

Kurki-Suonio: As a user of software products, there's one thing related to requirements analysis and functional specifications that bothers me, which I was trying to touch in my brief contribution. Specifications for software systems are derived from the analysis of what should be done. This means that software designers need a clear idea of the environment of use and purposes of the final product. However, after the product is available, it exists in its own right, and will be used or misused in environments not preconceived by the designers and for purposes for which it was not originally intended. This seems to me to lead to many more implicit assumptions and restrictions in software than in hardware. Therefore one has to be extremely cautious in building software products. When one looks at software product descriptions, they usually consist of examples of user situations and directions of how to use the product in those cases. It is true that the user does need explanatory descriptions but what I'm afraid of is that software designers and implementers also seem to think in terms of such intended situations, not in terms of the functional properties of the product itself. I wonder whether you share these opinions and whether your methods would help in this matter.

Ross: I suspect that I share your concern. Again, to me the key to all of our problems is understanding where they lie. It seems to me that you're describing, in the context of a software producer, the fact that the market place isn't completely under control. I would say that there's no magic for overcoming that. You can't keep the user from loading things into the back of his car and using it as a truck. There's no way you can stop that, but you can give him enough understanding of what's in the car, how strong the springs are, and so forth, so that he won't overly abuse it.

Koster: In our group we looked at SADT [TM] diagrams in some detail and tried your method out in one design. It was, I think, moderately successful. It left me with one suspicion, however, that any other way of intensively and extensively discussing all aspects of the design that came to mind would have done just as well. To mention one alternative, a formalized documentation system used as the center of interaction among various people would, I think, do just as well. Any other form of brainstorming may very well work. The central issue seems to be establishing terminology and identifying components. All the rest, the use of special forms, the beautiful numbering scheme, your dual diagrams, seem to be so much "mumbo-jumbo". I like your ideas, but they are of no help. They tell me what to do, not how to do it. I'm still in the woods. Don't you think that a design methodology is only useful if it can be taught to students?

Ross: Yes.

Koster: Isn't being able to teach it to students the highest form of understanding it yourself?

Ross: We do teach it.

Koster: To students?

Ross: Yes. You are welcome to your opinions about the method, but I think that the other aspect that hasn't been covered is the matter of visibility: the biggest problem in software is that we've been unable to see or envision the structure of the things that we make. That's why hardware people have made faster progress, I think, because every practitioner can tell when he makes a mess, whereas with software people, the stack of printout looks the same whether it has good stuff on it or bad. I think you are overlooking a great deal of what we found to be important in practice. You yourself probably can get along because you probably are practicing most of these things in your own way, as are many people,in the room. But this is a method that can be taught. It does seem to greatly enhance communication and give greater understandability and rigor. We are now proceeding into computer support tools, which is another reason for the compact notations. Things such as simulation are also in the cards for this methodology.

Dewar: Programming methodology reminds me of psychiatry: talking to people about your problems is helpful, but there's no evidence that the specific framework on which this psychiatric discipline is hung has any effect whatever. All presentations on programming methodology follow the same pattern: I have a good idea which will solve the problem; I tried it and it works! But really there's nothing more to it than that it's a good idea to think about what you're doing. I support Koster's remark. The only evidence we have is that structure is useful, but we've no evidence that one specific structure is more useful than another. One can ask for measurements, but these are almost impossible to make, because it's well known that anything at all increases productivity. So, simple comparative measurements won't give us that information. And unless we can get some empirical evidence, we're turning in circles. We can produce an infinite number of models, which may give a rich literature but no hard information.

Ross: I'm sorry, you seem to have misunderstood what I'm saying. I've said nothing about any particular structure. Structured Analysis has no structure, imposes no structure, provides no magic. All it provides are notation, tools, checklists, guidelines, training, suggestions, readable experience, useful pragmatic things learned from a very wide range of products; but it doesn't impose any structure and, as I've said to the original question, the viewpoint of the user is what really matters.

Dewar: But nevertheless, we see components like the magical number six.

Ross: That's a magic number in a sense, yes. You must have an integer, five is too small and seven is too big. [☺]

Constructing Quality Software, P.G. Hibbard/S.A. Schuman (eds.)

ON A CONSTRUCTIVE APPROACH TO THE ARCHITECTURE OF A SPECIAL PURPOSE OPERATING SYSTEM

Claus H. Correll
Leibniz-Rechenzentrum der
Bayerischen Akademie der Wissenschaften
München

1. Introduction. Developing a system through refinement means that the specification of the system proceeds in steps of decreasing abstraction and increasing detail. What is specified about the system in any step remains valid throughout all following steps. All details which are added in later steps have to be consistent with what has in more abstract terms been determined in earlier steps.

Practical experience shows that stepwise refinement is even in the most disciplined efforts not in full purity applied to the construction of a system. This paper contains a case study of a top-down development which employs "stepwise approximation" rather than stepwise refinement. The difference to refinement is that approximation permits the adjustment or revision of specifications of earlier steps in later steps. What is specified in any step may define a simplified solution to the systems requirements or may state some construction principle which helps to understand the system and can be followed in later steps as far as it is useful. The specification of the entire system proceeds in steps which gradually eliminate the simplifications and perfect the accommodation to the systems requirements.

The stepwise development of a systems architecture which is described in this paper as a case study starts from two "orthogonal" construction principles, derives from them two alternative intermediate specifications and combines the suitable elements of each of the two alternatives in such a way as to obtain a systems architecture which meets the environment conditions of the system. The two construction principles introduce different views of the systems structure. By virtue of their simplicity they support the understanding of the system's mechanics. By virtue of their generality they allow to derive different systems architectures each of which reflects the strict application of the underlying construction principle. Unfortunately these derived systems architectures do not, in one way or another, fulfill the requirements of a satisfactory solution. The ultimate reason for this lies in the fact that the construction principles were arrived at through dramatic simplifications of the systems requirements leaving out any consideration of the environment conditions.

The systems architectures derived from the construction principles are specifications of simplified solutions which have to be revised and improved in order to obtain the desired solution. The construction principles on which the simplified solutions are based remain only partially valid for the final solution. It is however due to the employment of such imperfect and simplifying construction principles that we could find the elements for the composition of an acceptable solution and keep this solution comprehensible though it is more complex than each of the intermediate alternatives.

<u>2. The Systems Requirements.</u> Before we further describe the single phases of a stepwise approximation to a systems architecture we shall outline the requirements of the system to be discussed as a case study in this paper.

Under discussion is the operating system of a remote concentrator node in a centralized computer network for remote batch and interactive I/O. All concentrators in the network are linked to a central site computer (network host) via dedicated high speed full-duplex lines. A concentrator supports display terminals, line printers, card readers and plotters (see figure 1). The downline data streams from the host to the remote output devices share the capacity of the line for data transmission from the host to the concentrator. The upline data streams from the remote input devices to the host share the capacity of the line for data transmission from the concentrator to the host. A data stream consists of a sequence of data messages of one and the same kind. A data message may be one of the following: a job deck, a print file, a plot file, an input entered in one piece at a display terminal or an output that can be displayed in one piece on a terminal screen.

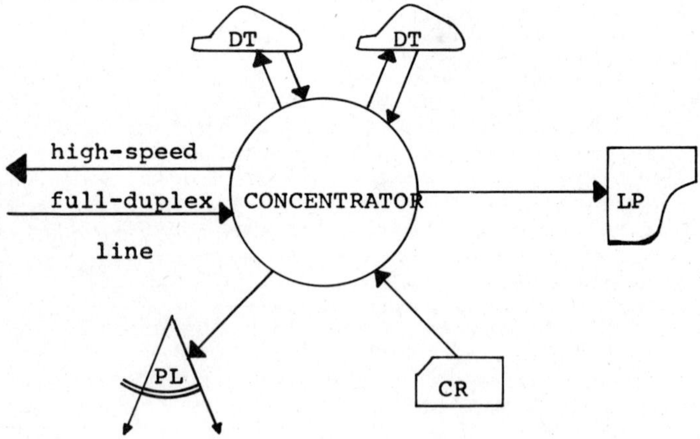

Figure 1: Configuration of a remote concentrator node.

The data messages are multiplexed on the line. This means that the data messages are decomposed into data packets, and the packets of different messages are transmitted in an arbitrary but fair order. Data packets of interactive data streams comprise complete input or output messages. They are limited in size by the character capacity of the display screen. Data packets of batch data streams contain roughly 10 - 40 card images or print lines depending on the information density on the physical medium.

Each transmitted data packet must be acknowledged by its receiver through a packet acknowledgement message (ACK). The acknowledgements are used to adjust the transmission rate of a downline data stream to the speed of the corresponding output device, and to regulate input from a peripheral device in accordance with the transmission rate provided for the corresponding upline data stream.

Besides data message multiplexing (upline) and unravelling (downline) the concentrator has to handle batch data compression (upline) and expansion (downline), code conversion and the mapping between virtual and real terminal characteristics.

3. The Systems Environment. The operating system which has to fulfill the above requirements will be built on top of a previously existing kernel system. The hardware and the kernel system define an environment of which the following aspects are of interest for our case study:

- There exist efficient operations for starting, delaying and resuming sequential processes.
- The maximum size for the address space of such a process is uncomfortably small.
- With each peripheral device there is a queue for I/O requests associated. This queue serves as a channel program. It is executed independently by the channel processor. Unfortunately each such queue permits only a rather small number of entries.
- The machine has only one central processor.

We will see what impact these environment conditions have on the systems architecture.

4. A Stepwise Approximation to the Systems Architecture. Informal, imprecise and incomplete problem specifications like the above requirements description are commonly experienced as the starting points from which a systems architecture has to be developed. In the first step of our top-down approach we try to find construction principles which promise help in structuring the system. Such principles originate in the endeavour of describing the systems requirements in terms of simple and comprehensible models, or of tailoring appropriate software construction techniques to the special requirements of the system under construction. The construction principles put forward fundamental ideas about how the system might operate. Only if the principles are simple can they be applied to the construction of the system. Simplicity is legitimately obtained by mea-

ningful simplification. Each construction principle focusses on one essential aspect of the system and deliberately leaves other aspects out of consideration. The different construction principles are preliminary since in the course of a complete systems analysis they may require restrictions or revisions.

As the next step in developing a systems architecture one derives a proposal for such an architecture from the construction principles. This proposal has to be checked against the systems requirements and environment conditions. Necessary improvements may lead to violations of the construction principles. The structuring effect of the construction principles will however remain visible in many respects.

In the case of the system discussed below two alternative proposals for the systems architecture were derived from two orhtogonal construction principles. Each alternative was the result of a strict application of one of the two principles. Thus we had not only to check both proposals against the requirements and the environment but we could also choose between two alternatives.

Alternatives are useful only if it is feasible to compare them. A comparison is facilitated if the same terms are used in describing the alternatives and if solutions to the same questions are presented. Before deriving alternative architectures we therefore decided on the structuring concepts to be used, and the items to be considered, in defining the systems architecture.

After evaluating the proposals an improved solution to the systems architecture must be constructed which exploits all good partial solutions found in the proposals and succeeds in fulfilling the systems requirements and environment conditions. The method is to stick as close as possible to the construction principles and to make adjustments only as far as they are indispensable. In our example the two alternative proposals could be combined to a satisfactory solution which derived profit from both principles equally well. The principles, though not each completely followed throughout the entire system, proved to be the driving elements in the development process. They illustrate the basic ideas how the final system operates.

The following sections will be devoted to the discussion of our example. Sections 5 through 9 will describe the five phases of the development: 5: the construction principles; 6: the items to occur in each description of an architectural alternative; 7A: the first, 7B: the second alternative; 8: an evaluation of the alternatives; 9: the synthesis. The conclusion in section 10 will relate the constructive approach of approximating a design in steps to the goal of obtaining a quality product.

5. The Construction Principles. The operating system of the remote concentrator has to organize the flow of data between the central site computer (network host) and the remote peripheral devices. There are two different ways of describing the flow of

data through the concentrator:

A) The concentrator has input ports and output ports. The data travelling from the host downline and the data travelling from the input devices upline enter the concentrator through input ports. They leave the concentrator through output ports for output devices or upline transmission. Seen from within the concentrator, the input ports "produce" data and the output ports "consume" data. A construction principle for the operating system of the concentrator would be to mask each port with a process which controls the I/O of the port and either produces or consumes data. A producer process and the corresponding consumer process exchange data through a queue in which produced data are buffered until they can be consumed. It is part of the production process to enter the data into this queue; and it is part of the consumption process to remove the data from this queue.

B) The systems requirements describe the data flow in the network in terms of data streams. The data are transmitted packetwise on the line. Data packets belonging to different data streams are transmitted in an arbitrary (but fair) order. A construction principle for the operating system of the concentrator would be to accordingly have the data streams pass also packetwise and interleaved through the concentrator. The concentrator would operate as a switchboard for data packets. For each packet a connection is switched on which the packet is transferred through the concentrator. The system is structured as a collection of concurrent processes each of which is responsible for all activities concerning the transfer of the data packets of a particular data stream from the input port through the concentrator to the output port.

Figure 2 shows the construction principles A and B in a schematic form. Clearly, the construction principles A and B exclude each other since they give different advice to decompose the system into processes. But they are also powerful and independent enough that two different architectural alternatives can be derived from them. In this sense we call the two construction principles "orthogonal".

6. The Items to Occur in Each Description of an Architectural Alternative. In order to obtain uniform descriptions of alternative architectures which allow for comparison and recombination we wish to use the same structuring concepts in each alternative and to consider solutions to the same questions: Processes being the unitsof processor allocation will be used as structuring concepts; the processor scheduling, the cooperation between the processes and the queues required in the system will be considered in each alternative.

7. The Architectures Derived from the Construction Principles.

A) The first alternative: Construction principle A is applied.

Decomposition into processes: The system is composed of several cooperating processes. Each process is dedicated to control one

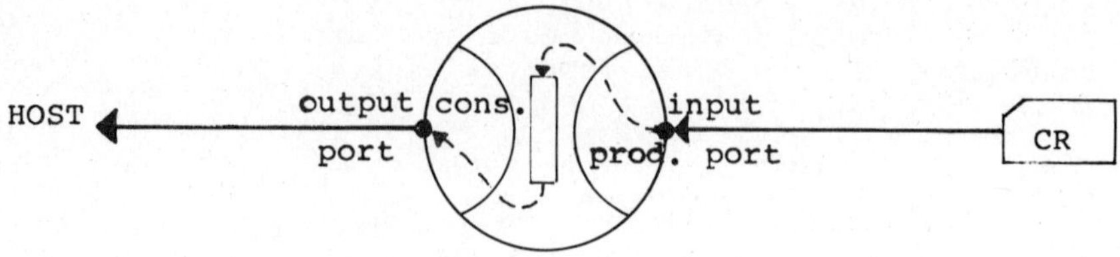

A: producer-consumer relation

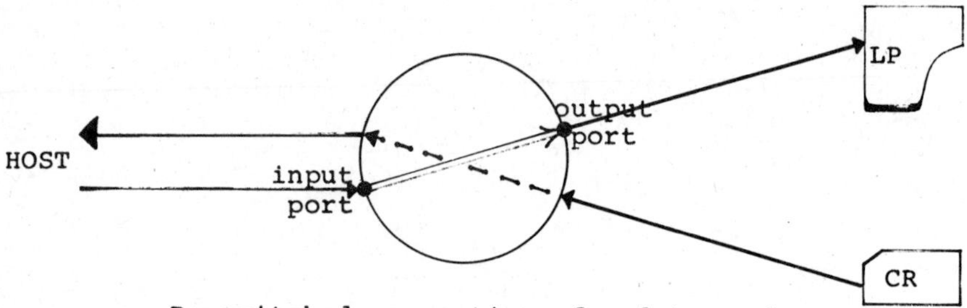

B: switched connections for data packets

Figure 2: Construction principles A and B.

particular kind of I/O: either the I/O of all peripheral devices of one type or the input from the communication line or the output for the communication line. The following processes exist (cf. figure 3):

- DTP - the display terminal process
- LPP - the line printer process
- PLP - the plotter process
- CRP - the card reader process
- CLIP - the communication line input process
- CLOP - the communication line output process.

DTP, LPP, PLP and CRP perform all necessary data compression or expansion, code conversion and transformations between virtual and real device characteristics.
CLIP disentangles the data streams flowing downline into the concentrator and distributes the data packets to DTP, LPP or PLP and the ACKs to DTP or CRP.
CLOP wraps the data which were collected by DTP or CRP up into packets and multiplexes the data streams and ACK messages on the line.

Process cooperation and queues: From the process communications point of view each process produces and/or consumes data packets and ACK messages. Producers and consumers synchronize on shared queues for passing data or ACKs from one process to another. With each of the processes DTP, LPP, PLP and CRP there are two queues associated. Into one queue CLIP enters packets or ACKs to

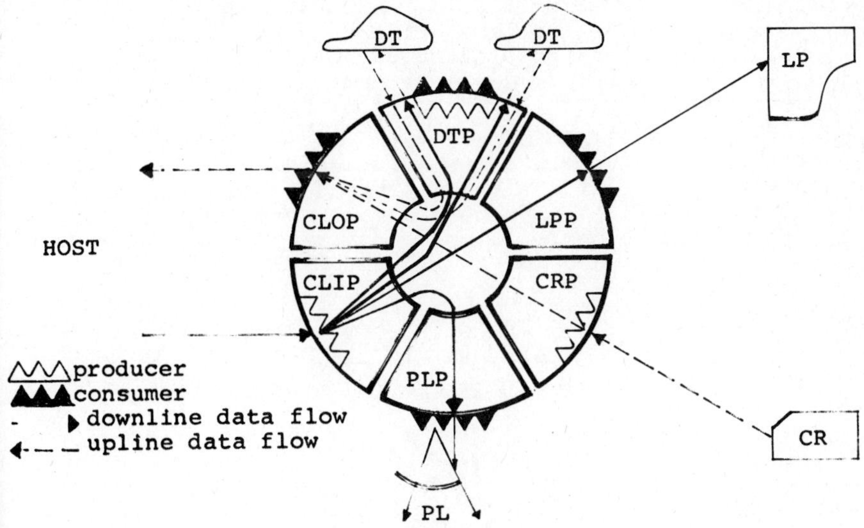

Figure 3: Producers and consumers.

be consumed by the associated process. From the other queue CLOP removes data or ACKs which have been produced by the associated process. (Remark: If one of the processes DTP, LPP, PLP or CRP controls N devices there are 2N queues associated with it.)

Processor scheduling: Whenever an interrupt from an I/O device or from the communication line adapter occurs the associated process is activated and the central processor is rescheduled. So we have an "interrupt-driven" system.

B) The second alternative: Construction principle B is applied.

Decomposition into processes: The system is composed of several concurrent processes. Each process is dedicated to control one particular kind of data stream or ACK stream on its way through the entire concentrator from its source to its sink. Data streams arise from the downline data transmission for remote output devices and from the input of remote input devices. They end in output buffers which can be emptied by the channel processor. The following types of data streams exist (cf. figure 4):

a) downline: display terminal output
b) downline: line printer output
c) downline: plotter output
d) upline : display terminal input
e) upline : card reader input

ACK streams flow in the opposite direction to that of their corresponding data streams. The following types of ACK streams exist:

f) upline : ACKs for display terminal output
g) upline : ACKs for line printer output
h) upline : ACKs for plotter output
i) downline: ACKs for display terminal input
j) downline: ACKs for card reader input

The processes controlling data streams of the types a) through e perform all necessary data compression or expansion, code conversion and transformations between virtual and real terminal characteristics. In addition they do all necessary wrapping and unwrapping of data up into or out of packets.

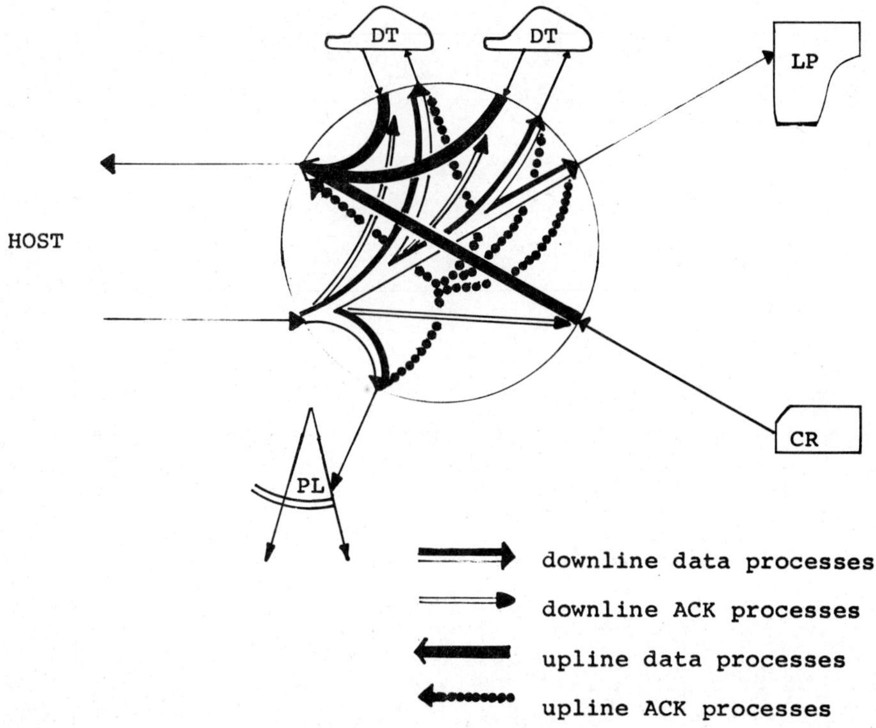

Figure 4: Processes controlling data streams or ACK streams.

Process cooperation and queues: Each process controlling a data stream cooperates with the process that controls the corresponding ACK stream. With each device and each direction of the line there is a queue of I/O buffers and a queue of I/O requests (channel program) associated on which such pairs of cooperating processes and the channel processor synchronize their accesses. Data stream processes enter or remove full buffers, ACK stream processes enter or remove empty buffers into or from the queues of I/O buffers.

Processor scheduling: The central processor is allocated to each process as long as it takes to transfer an entire data packet or ACK message from its source queue to its destination queue. Referring to downline data or ACK processes the entry to be processed next in the queue of input from the communication line determines which downline process has to be activated next. The system may be called "packet-driven".

8. An Evaluation of the Alternatives. Both alternatives fulfill the systems requirements. It is outside the scope of this paper to further check each of the two solutions against other requirements as, for instance, error recovery. We proceed in the top-down development of the systems architecture by selecting those parts of each solution which meet better the environment conditions. To this end we compare three aspects of the alternative systems architectures:

i) size of the processes,
ii) length of the I/O queues,
iii) impact of the processor scheduling policy.

With respect to the environment conditions we found the following advantages and disadvantages of the single alternatives:

i) The second alternative distributes the systems activities on more and smaller processes (separation of data packet and ACK message handling). This would be even more the case if the wrapping and unwrapping of data up into or out of packets would be concentrated in two separate processes as proposed in the first alternative. Since the existing kernel system supports the use of many small processes the solution of the second alternative together with the indicated improvement is the preferred decomposition of the system into processes.
ii) The second alternative requires queues only at the "periphery" of the concentrator; namely as the sources and sinks of the data and ACK streams through the concentrator. These queues might be implemented through the I/O queues which are provided by the pre-existing kernel system. This is however prohibited by the restrictions on the length of the I/O queues. Consequently the data stream processes of alternative two have to digest the data packets piecemeal in order to fill or empty the I/O queues sufficiently frequently.
iii) In the first alternative the compression of data is performed earlier and the expansion of data is performed later than in the second alternative where a process becomes active only when a full packet is there to be compressed or expanded. Thus the "packet-driven" system requires more buffer space than the "interrupt-driven" system.

Certainly, a closer analysis would uncover many more pro's and con's. We conclude this section by listing the elements which we decided to select from the menu of solutions contained in the two alternatives:

i) We have processes to control data streams, ACK streams, the input from the communication line and the output for the communication line. This is a combination of elements from both alternatives.

ii) With each device or line direction we have associated a "short" queue of I/O buffers (basically using an exchange buffer technique) and the corresponding queue of I/O requests (channel program). Furthermore we have "long" queues (similar to those of the first alternative) for the exchange of data and ACKs between the two processes controlling the communication line on the one hand and the processes controlling the data and ACK streams on the other hand.

iii) We have an "interrupt-driven" system.

9. The Synthesis. The elements selected in the previous section can be combined into an integral design of the systems architecture. This architecture better meets the environment conditions than the intermediate alternatives did. The two orthogonal construction principles remain valid in separate parts of the architecture synthesized from the selected elements. The two processes controlling the communication line act in such a way as a producer and a consumer according to construction principle A that the rest of the system can be decomposed into processes which control data packets or ACK messages from their source to their destination according to construction principle B.

10. Conclusion. A constructive approach to a systems design like the one discussed in this paper contributes substantially to the goal of obtaining quality software. To support this claim we have the following arguments:

- Our approach was geared to produce and study design alternatives. It is a common expectation in many engineering disciplines that the competition of different designs enhance the quality of the final product.
- Our approach was a derivative one. This means to start from principles and to construct solutions which employ these principles. In this way ad-hoc solutions, decisions on the wrong things at the wrong time and many inconsistencies can be prevented.
- Our approach attacks the problem of constructing a comprehensible system despite of an awkward system environment. If stepwise refinement contributes to quality - as we do believe - then stepwise approximation is the practical variant which can be used with success in the case of the above problem.

Correll : Discussion

Sintzoff: I think that one of the most significant steps in your method is the last one, the step where you integrate two or more alternative approaches. It has been successful in the one case study you have presented. What are the chances that you will succeed on other problems also?

Correll: The particular problem I have studied is searching for a structure of a system, but I have tried to generalize from this particular problem. For this generalization, your question certainly has to be answered, "Well, I really don't know." In the particular application of operating system construction, I'm quite hopeful that there might be a second example where we can use this technique.

Goos: I have two points. Firstly in certain respects this method of merging different alternatives is comparable to what Michael Jackson proposes in his book when he says that if you have two different files in one program, an input stream and an output stream which do not fit together, then first produce two programs for these two different streams and then try to merge. Of course, what he is doing is something other than what you are doing but the principle is the same. The second point is provocative: what could you do to solve Nehmer's problem?

Correll: I don't know since I've not studied it.

Mráz: While designing our system, we were trying different alternatives too, maybe not as formally as you did but the alternatives were discussed and so on. It often happens that the right solution did not appear in the next hierarchical step, but some three or four steps later, and it was too late by that time. I feel that some way of thinking in alternatives is necessary, but it's not always as easy as it has been here.

Rajlich: I would like to ask you how you have managed to merge two alternatives. In our experience, whenever two alternatives were considered and then finally merged, that meant rewriting the whole system.

Correll: I didn't get much further than outlining the structure of each alternative. I didn't give an implementation or even a complete specification. So it all occurred on a very high level, where it was still possible to merge the alternatives. This was an example of incomplete specifications in the form of construction principles. These are easy to understand and they generate further ideas on how to proceed in realizing the lower levels. Nevertheless they are incomplete. A complete answer requires, in our case, two incomplete specifications which are based on orthogonal ideas. Only both principles together managed to specify completely the solution we were aiming at.

Ross: Exactly. And the whole reason you are so satisfied is that you did a complete job in each of those layers. You left parts with well-defined, structured boundaries within which you could then seek out further specifications or further experience or leave them open for another layer. That is the whole point. Your "incomplete specifications" were more than merely incomplete. They were structured consistently and well-defined in their incompleteness. They therefore give a better-defined problem for the next stage of the specification.

Sintzoff: We have been hearing of levels, modules, atoms, layers, decompositions, architecture, structure, and so on and so on. Now, I have a very naive question: How can we find those decompositions and those structures? I have one element of an answer, one example where scientific method may be of help, which is the field of nearly decomposable systems in system theory.

Correll: I just want to answer one part of your question. How did we obtain different alternatives and different construction principles in my special project? We applied some kind of heuristic method: I studied the problem description and discovered two crucial ways of looking at the whole problem, namely there were ports for data which had to be catered for by some processes, and there were data streams which were to be pumped through the concentrator. Starting from these very simple ideas I worked my way through to the alternatives. So, it's a purely heuristic method.

Sintzoff: OK, you say you are a creative designer, but I'm a stupid one. [☺ ☺]

King, J.: I know which one I would hire. [☺]

Nehmer: I guess we have arrived at the crucial point of the discussion now. The question was raised several times: is creativity necessary? The same question was asked by Sintzoff now. How do we go from a specification to a construction process? How do we go from a specification to the final implementation? I think that basically the idea behind these questions is to formalize the construction process, and to avoid any sort of heuristic within this process. My personal response to that idea is no, I think the construction process will always be heuristic. We could conceivably reduce the heuristics by defining appropriate architectural and structural elements in order to construct our software, but we can never eliminate them.

Correll: I would like to come back to Sintzoff's question. I was looking for general construction principles. I cannot tell you how I came to find these principles. That is certainly heuristic. But in looking for such general construction principles, I tried to find simple ones, easy ones which are not complete answers but at least partial answers. That gives a basis for evaluating the alternatives, to discover which is the better or which is the worse alternative. When the outcome is not decisive, then you must seek some synthesis.

Constructing Quality Software, P.G. Hibbard/S.A. Schuman (eds.)

A METHODOLOGY FOR SIMULTANEOUSLY DEVELOPING AND VERIFYING PASCAL PROGRAMS

D. Bär
Department of Mathematics
Humboldt-University of Berlin
German Democratic Republic

The methodology described here is strongly related to that based on abstract data types. As far as possible, it is tried to incorporate the advantages of these ideas into the process of developing and verifying programs in PASCAL-like languages. Connected with this methodology, a man-machine dialogue strategy for proving programs correct is outlined and demonstrated by examples. In particular, this dialogue strategy supports the guessing of loop invariants and serves to reduce the complexity of the theorems to be proved valid by the theorem prover.

1. INTRODUCTION

This paper is to give a survey of a methodology for simultaneously developing and verifying PASCAL programs step by step. It is not intended to define all the details of this methodology or of its basic concepts in full generality. Instead, we restrict ourselves to summarizing the basic principles and demonstrating them by an example.

The methodology is aimed at constructing PASCAL programs, Jensen, Wirth (1974), which are partially correct with respect to given exit assertions and corresponding entry assertions where the latter are as weak as possible with respect to the former.

The basic ideas of our methodology are very much related to those connected with abstract data types, Hoare (1972),

Liskov, Zilles (1974, 1975a), and, in particular, with those underlying the intentions of ALPHARD, London, Shaw, Wulf (1976 a,b,c,d). The main distinction is that we try to incorporate these ideas as far as possible into the methodology of developing and verifying programs in PASCAL-like programming languages rather than to create completely new languages at once. However, we do agree to the fact that the exhausting of the advantages of these basic ideas eventually demands concepts like classes, clusters, or forms and, thus, languages like SIMULA, Dahl (1970), CLU, Liskov (1975 b), or ALPHARD, respectively.

But, on the other hand, we are convinced that even in the case of PASCAL-like languages the way of developing and verifying programs as well as the quality of the programs obtained can considerably be supported and improved by the basic philosophy of abstract data types.

There are essential <u>interdependences</u> between the processes of developing and verifying programs strongly affecting both of them. Moreover, to a considerable degree the <u>quality</u> of the programs eventually obtained as well as the methods and techniques for providing them with an appropriate <u>documentation</u> can essentially be improved by taking into consideration these mutual dependences as far as possible.

Therefore, from the very beginning, our methodology is aimed at <u>simultaneously</u> developing and verifying PASCAL programs <u>step by step</u>.

Any <u>step</u> of the development and verification process is to reflect

(i) the current stage of the program development (its <u>statement part</u>, in particular),

(ii) the <u>assertions</u> (entry assertion, exit assertion) the statement part is to be proved consistent with, and

(iii) the <u>axioms</u> supporting this correctness proof.

Hence, these <u>steps</u> are defined to be <u>abstract programs</u>

$$p = (P , h_o , h_1 , \mathfrak{H})$$

where P is the statement part of the current stage of the program development, h_o and h_1 are the entry assertion and the exit assertion, respectively, P is to be proved consistent with, and $\mathfrak{H}$ is the axiomatic basis of the proof required. In the following a summary of our methodology will be given (chapter 2) and demonstrated by a tree handling example (chapter 3).

The second main aspect of this paper is aimed at a man-machine dialogue technique (chapter 4) for proving programs correct. In particular, this dialogue technique is to support the guessing of loop invariants and to essentially reduce the complexity of the theorems to be proved valid by the theorem prover.

Finally, in chapter 5, a successful man-machine verification dialogue for the initial program version of the tree handling example is demonstrated.

2. A SUMMARY OF THE METHODOLOGY

In our PASCAL-oriented methodology, the process of both developing and verifying programs is carried out step by step:

$$p_1 , p_2 , \dots , p_k .$$

Each of these steps p_i is a so-called abstract program

$$p = (P , h_o , h_1 , \mathfrak{H})$$

where

P is a statement part of PASCAL.

h_o, h_1 are the entry assertion and the exit assertion, respectively, of p. Assertions are defined to be well-formed formulas of a first-order predicate calculus whose atomic formulas are PASCAL expressions of the type Boolean with the PASCAL variable identifiers as free varibles.

$\mathfrak{H}$ is the axiomatic basis of p consisting of a finite number of axioms $H \in \mathfrak{H}$.

Axioms are defined to be

(i) assertions ,

(ii) PASCAL definitions ,

(iii) PASCAL declarations ,

(iv) constant, function, and procedure specifications, or

(v) obtained from axioms defined by (i), (ii), (iii), or (iv) by connecting them with $\neg$, $\wedge$, $\vee$, $\rightarrow$, or $\leftrightarrow$.

In particular, $\mathfrak{h}$ is supposed to satisfy the following requirements :

(1) For any variable identifier occurring in P, $\mathfrak{h}$ contains exactly one variable declaration.

(2) For any type t, $\mathfrak{h}$ contains at most one type definition.

(3) For any constant, function, or procedure identifier occurring in P, $\mathfrak{h}$ contains either exactly one constant definition, function declaration, or procedure declaration or exactly one constant, function, or procedure specification, respectively.

In extending the PASCAL terminology we introduce constant specifications

$$\text{cid} : t \quad ,$$

function specifications

$$\text{fid} : t_1 \otimes \ldots \otimes t_r \Longrightarrow t \quad , \text{and}$$

procedure specifications

$$\text{pid} : t_1 \otimes \ldots \otimes t_r \Longrightarrow t'_1 \otimes \ldots \otimes t'_n$$

where cid is a constant identifier, fid a function identifier, and pid a procedure identifier. t, t_1, t'_1, are types.

A type t is said to be standard in p if $\mathfrak{h}$ does not contain any type definition for t.

A constant, function, or procedure identifier is said to be standard in p if it is specified (and, thus, not defined or declared, respectively) in $\mathfrak{h}$.

In our methodology, the initial step $p_1 = (P_1 , h_o , h_1 , \mathfrak{h}_1)$ is to reflect most naturally both the problem to be solved and the way of solving this problem. Therefore, all the types of the objects to be operated on and all the constants, predicates, functions, and procedures immedialtely relevant to the problem ought to be considered <u>standard</u> in p_1. Thus, $\mathfrak{h}_1$ should neither contain any type definition nor any function or procedure declaration. In this way, all the components of p_1 can be expressed "really problem oriented".

In order to prove p_1 consistent with its entry and exit assertion all the constant identifiers, function identifers, and procedure identifiers involved must be <u>axiomatically</u> described in $\mathfrak{h}_1$. Notice, however, that the demand for the <u>completeness</u> of these axiomatic descriptions should be considered <u>relative</u> with respect to both the problem to be solved and the ideas supporting the solution implemented in P_1.

Now we can try to verify p_1. To this end a man-machine <u>dialogue technique</u> has been developed which will be described and demonstrated in the chapters 4 and 5

After having proved p_i $(i \geq 1)$ correct we ask if p_i is already compatible with PASCAL, i.e., if all the types, function identifiers, and procedure identifiers considered standard in p_i are really standard in PASCAL. If so, we are ready $(i=k)$.

Otherwise, we must get p_{i+1} from p_i by <u>implementing</u> some of the "pseudo standard" types, constant identifiers, function identifiers, or procedure identifiers.

<u>Types</u> are implemented by PASCAL <u>type definitions</u> in connection with <u>additional axioms</u> describing some of the constant identifiers and function calls occurring in P_i by equivalent <u>constants</u> or <u>variables</u> created by the new type definitions.

Suppose, for instance, the type of a (binary) <u>tree</u> as well as the constant identifier <u>void</u> and the function identifiers <u>tip</u>, <u>weight</u>, <u>content</u>, <u>left</u>, and <u>right</u> with the specifications

$$\text{void} \;:\; \text{tree} \;;$$
$$\text{tip} \;:\; \text{tree} \Longrightarrow \text{Boolean} \;;$$

weight, content : tree $\Longrightarrow$ integer ;
left, right : tree $\Longrightarrow$ tree ;

had been considered standard in p_i and had been described in $\mathfrak{H}_i$ by the axioms

$$T : tree \wedge T \neq void \wedge tip(T) \longrightarrow weight(T) = content(T)$$

and

$$T : tree \wedge T \neq void \wedge \neg tip(T) \longrightarrow weight(T) = weight(left(T)) + weight(right(T)).$$

Then tree can be implemented by the following type definitions :

```
tree = ↑ node ;
node = record case TIP : Boolean
              of true : (CONT : integer) ;
                false : (LEFT,RIGHT : tree) end ;
```

From the basic intention of this type implementation we get the following additional axioms describing the constant identifier void and the calls of the function identifiers tip, content, left, and right by equivalent constants and variables created by these type definitions :

void = nil ;
T : tree ⟶ (tip(T) ⟷ T↑.TIP) ;
T : tree ⟶ content(T) = T↑.CONT ;
T : tree ⟶ left(T) = T↑.RIGHT ;
T : tree ⟶ right(T) = T↑.RIGHT ;

Now $p_{i+1} = (P_{i+1} , h_o , h_1 , \mathfrak{H}_{i+1})$ can be obtained from $p_i = (P_i , h_o , h_1 , \mathfrak{H}_i)$ in the following way :

(1) P_{i+1} is obtained from P_i by simultaneously replacing all the function calls in consideration by their corresponding equivalent variables according to the additional axioms.

(2) $\mathfrak{H}_{i+1}$ is obtained from $\mathfrak{H}_i$ by

(i) incorporating the new type definitions as well as all the constant definitions among the additional axioms ,

(ii) carrying out the same <u>replacements</u> as described in (1) , and

(iii) <u>deleting</u> the specifications of all the constant identifiers and function identifiers affected by the additional axioms.

It can be shown as a theorem that p_{i+1} obtained in this way is (partially or totally) <u>correct</u> if p_i was.

Thus, p_{i+1} need not be reverified. We must only ensure that $\mathfrak{H}_{i+1}$ is left <u>consistent</u> by our implementation.

<u>Function identifiers</u> and <u>procedure identifiers</u> are implemented by function declarations and procedure declarations, respectively.

Suppose P_i contains a <u>function identifier</u> f specified in $\mathfrak{H}_i$ by

$$f : t_1 \otimes t_2 \Longrightarrow t \quad .$$

In order to implement f in the next step a new (nested) development and verification process must be started which is aimed at getting a correct abstract program

$$p = (P , \text{true} , f(x,y) = z, \mathfrak{H})$$

where $\mathfrak{H}$ consists of at least

(i) all the <u>axiomatic descriptions</u>, <u>type definitions</u>, and <u>constant definitions</u> belonging to $\mathfrak{H}_i$,

(ii) the function specification $f : t_1 \otimes t_2 \Longrightarrow t$, and

(iii) the variable declarations $x : t_1$, $y : t_2$, and $z : t$.

Note that none of the declarations belonging to $\mathfrak{H}$ has anything to do with those belonging to $\mathfrak{H}_i$.

Then, proceeding in the original development process, p_{i+1} can be obtained from p_i and p as follows :

(1) P_{i+1} is P_i .

(2) $\mathfrak{H}_{i+1}$ is obtained from $\mathfrak{H}_i$ and $\mathfrak{H}$ by

(i) deleting the function specification

$$f : t_1 \otimes t_2 \Longrightarrow t \qquad \text{and}$$

(ii) adding the function declaration

```
function f(x:t1; y:t2) : t ;
         const C ; type T ; var V ; F
         begin P ; f := z end ;
```

where C, T, V, and F are lists of all constant definitions, type definitions, variable declarations, and function or procedure declarations, respectively, belonging to $\mathfrak{H} \setminus \{x : t_1 ; y : t_2\}$ but not to $\mathfrak{H}_i$.

Again we can show as a (PASCAL) theorem that p_{i+1} obtained in this way is (partially or totally) correct if p_i was and, thus, p_i need not be reverified.

Now suppose we had reached a (partially or totally) correct abstract program $p_k = (P_k , h_o , h_1 , \mathfrak{H}_k)$ which is compatible with PASCAL, i.e., all the types, constant identifiers, function identifiers, and procedure identifiers occurring in P_k were either really standard in PASCAL or given by type definitions, constant definitions, function declarations, and procedure declarations, respectively, belonging to $\mathfrak{H}_k$.

Then we had verified the actual PASCAL program PP given by

```
program const C ; type T ; var V ; F begin Pk end.
```

where C, T, V, and F are lists of all the constant definitions type definitions, variable declarations, and function or procedure declarations, respectively, given by $\mathfrak{H}_k$.

Thus, we had shown with respect to the axiomatic basis $\mathfrak{H}_k$ that PP was consistent with the entry assertion h_o and the exit assertion h_1 :

$$h_o \quad \{PP\} \quad h_1 \quad .$$

Notice that, in general, $\mathfrak{H}_k$ may be further reduced by deleting those axiomatic descriptions all the function and procedure identifiers occurring in them are declared in $\mathfrak{H}_k$. We denote this simplified axiomatic basis by $\mathfrak{H}_k^*$.

Suppose x_i (i=1,...,r) and y_j (j=1,...,n) are to be considered the input variables and the output variables, respectively, of PP with

$$x_i : t_i \in V \qquad \text{and} \qquad y_j : t'_j \in V \quad .$$

Then from PP we can get the following actual PASCAL procedure declaration which is correct with respect to $\mathcal{G}^*_k$:

<u>procedure</u> PPP(x_1:t_1;...;x_r:t_r; <u>var</u> y_1:t'_1;...; <u>var</u> y_n:t'_n) ;
PP* ;

where PP* is obtained from PP by deleting

(i) the word <u>program</u> and the dot ,

(ii) the variable declarations x_i:t_i and y_j:t'_j , and

(iii) the type definitions for $t_1,\ldots,t_r$, $t'_1,\ldots,t'_n$ (which must be given outside this procedure declaration).

If PP has exactly one output variable we can get a <u>correct actual PASCAL function declaration</u> from PP in a very similar way (see the example in chapter 3).

Notice, finally, that the (possibly nested) sequence(s) p_1, p_2, ... , p_k of abstract programs reflecting the entire developing and verifying process can be considered a suitably structured and appropriate <u>documentation</u> of the final program version PP or of the actual PASCAL function or procedure declaration derived from it.

3. AN EXAMPLE DEMONSTRATING THE METHODOLOGY

The following example is based on a problem which is very similar to that considered by London (1975).

Given a <u>binary tree</u> To whose terminal nodes (tips) contain integer values. The <u>weight</u> of To is defined to be the sum of all the integer values stored in the tips of To.

We are looking for a partially correct <u>actual PASCAL function declaration</u> of a totally defined function computing the weights of given binary trees To.
In order to extend the variety of necessary data types by explicitely dealing with stacks of trees we suppose that the function to be developed should be non-recursive.

3.1. THE FIRST STEP

The abstract program to be developed and verified in the first step is

$$p_1 = (P_1 , \text{true} , W = \text{weight}(To) , \mathcal{A}_1)$$

where To (of the type tree) and W (of the type integer) are the only input variable and the only output variable, respectively, of our problem.
The type tree, the auxiliary type stack (of trees), and the function identifier weight (mapping trees into integers) are considered standard in p_1.

We add the auxiliary variables T (of the type tree) and S (of the type stack) and start with the following suggestive statement part P_1 :

```
    W := 0 ;   S := push(empty, To) ;
    while S ≠ empty
       do begin T := top(S) ;   S := pop(S) ;
                while ¬ tip(T)
                   do begin S := push(S, right(T)) ;
                            T := left(T)
                      end ;
                W := W + content(T)
          end
```

The axiomatic basis $\mathcal{A}_1$ of p_1 is given by the following groups of axioms :

(V1) variable declarations

T : tree ; To : tree ; S : stack ; W : integer ;

(S1) specifications

```
     weight, content  :  tree ⟹ integer ;
                 tip  :  tree ⟹ Boolean ;
         left, right  :  tree ⟹ tree ;
               empty  :  stack ;
                 top  :  stack ⟹ tree ;
                 pop  :  stack ⟹ stack ;
                push  :  stack ⊗ tree ⟹ stack ;
         totalweight  :  stack ⟹ integer ;
```

(A1) <u>axiomatic descriptions</u>

(i) T : tree $\wedge$ tip(T) $\longrightarrow$ weight(T) = content(T) ;

(ii) T : tree $\wedge$ $\neg$tip(T)
weight(T) = weight(left(T))+weight(right(T)) ;

(iii) T : tree $\wedge$ S : stack $\wedge$ SS : stack
(SS=push(S,T) $\longleftrightarrow$ SS$\neq$empty $\wedge$ top(SS)=T $\wedge$ pop(SS)=S) ;

(iv) S : stack $\wedge$ S = empty $\longrightarrow$ totalweight(S) = 0 ;

(v) S : stack $\wedge$ S $\neq$ empty $\longrightarrow$
totalweight(S) = weight(top(S)) + totalweight(pop(S)) ;

Note that the axioms (A1iv) and (A1v) are to connect the auxiliary type stack with the result type integer in the most natural way.

Now p_1 must be proved partially correct.
However, we postpone this proof and use it as a demonstration of our man-machine dialogue technique given in chapter 4.

3.2. THE SECOND STEP

The second step p_2 = (P_2 , true , W = weight(To) , $\mathcal{G}_2$) is aimed at <u>implementing the types tree and stack</u>.
We decide for the following <u>type definitions</u> :

```
   tree = ↑ node ;
   node = record case TIP : Boolean
                  of true : (CONT : integer) ;
                    false : (LEFT , RIGHT  :  tree) end ;
   stack = ↑ level ;
   level = record TOP : tree ; POP : stack end ;
```

The basic intentions of these type implementations are described in the following <u>additional axioms</u> introducing variables and constants created by these type definitions and are to replace function calls of tip, content, left, and right as well as the constant identifier empty and the calls of top and pop :

T : tree $\longrightarrow$ (tip(T) $\longleftrightarrow$ T↑.TIP) ;

T : tree $\longrightarrow$ content(T) = T↑.CONT ;

T : tree $\longrightarrow$ left(T) = T↑.LEFT ;

T : tree $\longrightarrow$ right(T) = T↑.RIGHT ;

```
     empty = nil ;
     S : stack ⟶ top(S) = S↑.TOP ;
     S : stack ⟶ pop(S) = S↑.POP .
```

Thuse, we get the following <u>statement part</u> P_2 of the second step:

```
  W := 0 ;   S := push(empty, To) ;
  while S ≠ empty
     do begin T := S↑.TOP ;   S := S↑.POP ;
              while ¬ T↑.TIP
                 do begin S := push(S, T↑.RIGHT) ;
                          T := T↑.LEFT
                    end ;
              W := W + T↑.CONT
        end
```

The <u>axiomatic basis</u> $\mathfrak{G}_2$ of the second step is obtained from $\mathfrak{G}_1$ by (i) incorporating the new type definitions, and the constant definition empty = nil, (ii) carrying out the replacements induced by the additional axioms, and (iii) deleting the specifications of empty, tip, content, left, right, top, and pop.

So we get the following $\mathfrak{G}_2$:

(V2) <u>variable declarations</u>

```
     T : tree ;  To : tree ;  S : stack ;  W : integer ;
```

(S2) <u>specifications</u>

```
          weight  :  tree ⟹ integer ;
            push  :  stack ⊗ tree ⟹ stack ;
     totalweight  :  stack ⟹ integer ;
```

(T2) <u>type definitions</u>

```
     tree = ↑ node ;
     node = record case TIP : Boolean
                   of true : (CONT : integer) ;
                     false : (LEFT , RIGHT : tree) end ;
     stack = ↑ level ;
     level = record TOP : tree ; POP : stack end ;
```

(C2) <u>constant definitions</u>

```
     empty = nil ;
```

(A2) <u>axiomatic descriptions</u>

(i) $T{:}tree \wedge T\uparrow.TIP \longrightarrow weight(T) = T\uparrow.CONT$;

(ii) $T{:}tree \wedge \neg T\uparrow.TIP$
$weight(T) = weight(T\uparrow.LEFT) + weight(T\uparrow.RIGHT)$;

(iii) $T{:}tree \wedge S{:}stack \wedge SS{:}stack \longrightarrow$
$(SS=push(S,T) \longleftrightarrow SS \neq empty \wedge SS\uparrow.TOP=T \wedge SS\uparrow.POP=S)$;

(iv) $S{:}stack \wedge S = empty \longrightarrow totalweight(S) = 0$;

(v) $S{:}stack \wedge S \neq empty \longrightarrow$
$totalweight(S) = weight(S\uparrow.TOP)+totalweight(S\uparrow.POP)$;

Remember that p_2 is (partially or totally) <u>correct</u> if p_1 was.

3.3. THE THIRD STEP

The only remaining problem is to implement the function identifier push specified in $\mathfrak{H}_2$ by

$$push \ : \ stack \otimes tree \Longrightarrow stack \quad .$$

To this end we must look for an abstract program

$$p = (P , true , push(S1, T1) = SS , \mathfrak{H})$$

where

$$\mathfrak{H} = (A2) \cup \{S1{:}stack ; T1{:}tree ; SS{:}stack\} \quad .$$

Due to axiom (A2iii) of $\mathfrak{H}_2$ we get

$$push(S1,T1) = SS \longleftrightarrow SS \neq empty \wedge SS\uparrow.TOP=T1 \wedge SS\uparrow.POP=S1$$

as a theorem following from $\mathfrak{H}$.

Now we easily get the <u>statement part</u> P :

```
new(SS) ;   SS↑.TOP := T1 ;   SS↑.POP := S1      .
```

As P is obviously consistent with the desired exit assertion $SS \neq empty \wedge SS\uparrow.TOP=T1 \wedge SS\uparrow.POP=S1$ we omit this proof.

Thus, according to the rules given in chapter 2 we get the abstract program

$$p_3 = (P_3 , true , W = weight(To) , \mathfrak{H}_3)$$

with $P_3 = P_2$ (see above).

$\mathfrak{H}_3$ is obtained from $\mathfrak{H}_2$ by

(i) deleting the function <u>specification</u>
$push : stack \otimes tree \Longrightarrow stack$ and

(ii) adding the function declaration

```
function push(S1:stack ; T1:tree):stack ;
         var SS:stack ;
         begin new(SS); SS↑.TOP := T1; SS↑.POP := S1;
               push := SS
         end ;
```

Moreover, since p_3 is obviously compatible with PASCAL, $\mathfrak{G}_3$ may be further reduced to $\mathfrak{G}_3^*$ by deleting the axioms (Aiii), (Aiv), and (Av).

So we obtain the correct abstract program

$$p_3 = (P_3 , \text{true} , W = \text{weight}(To) , \mathfrak{G}_3^*)$$

with $P_3 = P_2$ (see above) and the following axiomatic basis $\mathfrak{G}_3^*$:

(V3) variable declarations

```
T : tree ;  To : tree ;  S : stack ; W : integer ;
```

(S3) specifications

```
weight  :  tree ⟹ integer ;
```

(T3) type definitions

```
tree = ↑ node ;
node = record case TIP:Boolean
                of true:(CONT:integer);
                   false:(LEFT, RIGHT : tree) end ;
stack = ↑level ;
level = record TOP:tree ; POP:stack end ;
```

(C3) constant definitions

```
empty = nil  ;
```

(F3) function and procedure declarations

```
function push(S1:stack ; T1:tree):stack ;
         var SS:stack;
         begin new(SS); SS↑.TOP := T1; SS↑.POP := S1;
               push := SS
         end ;
```

(A3) <u>axiomatic descriptions</u>

(i) $T\text{:tree} \wedge T\uparrow.\text{TIP} \longrightarrow \text{weight}(T) = T\uparrow.\text{CONT}$;

(ii) $T\text{:tree} \wedge \neg T\uparrow.\text{TIP}$

$\text{weight}(T) = \text{weight}(T\uparrow.\text{LEFT}) + \text{weight}(T\uparrow.\text{RIGHT})$.

Finally, we get the correct <u>actual PASCAL function declaration</u> wanted by choosing To as the input variable and W as the output variable and by imbedding (C3), (T3), (V3)$\setminus\{$To:tree$\}$, and (F3) as follows :

```
type tree = ↑node ;
    node = record case TIP:Boolean
                  of true : (CONT : integer) ;
                    false : (LEFT, RIGHT : tree) end ;
 :
function weight of a tree (To : tree):integer ;
        const empty = nil ;
        type stack = ↑level ;
            level = record TOP : tree ; POP : stack end ;
        var T : tree ;  S : stack ;  W : integer ;
        function push (S1:stack ; T1:tree):stack ;
                var SS : stack ;
                begin new (SS) ; SS↑.TOP := T1 ;
                      SS↑.POP := S1 ; push := SS
                end ;
        begin
        W := 0;   S := push(empty, To);
        while S ≠ empty
           do begin T := S↑.TOP;   S := S↑.POP;
                   while ¬ T↑.TIP
                      do begin S := push(S, T↑.RIGHT);
                               T := T↑.LEFT
                         end;
                   W := W + T↑.CONT
              end;
        weight of a tree := W
        end.
```

4. A MAN-MACHINE DIALOGUE TECHNIQUE FOR VERIFYING ABSTRACT PROGRAMS

4.1. BASIC CONCEPTS

Verifying of an abstract program $p = (P, h_o, h_1, \mathfrak{H})$ means solving the partial or total correctness problem

$$\Pi(p) = \Pi(P, h_o, h_1, \mathfrak{H})$$

connected with p. Informally, $\Pi(p)$ should be read:

"Under what circumstances is p (partially or totally) correct?"

Solutions of the correctness problem $\Pi(p)$ are assertions describing certain circumstances under which p is correct. Of course, true has to be considered a solution of $\Pi(p)$ if and only if p is correct.

But we are interested in a much more comprehensive range of solutions than simply true (i.e. "yes") or false (i.e. "no").

An assertion h is said to be a solution of the correctness problem $\Pi(p) = \Pi(P, h_o, h_1, \mathfrak{H})$ if and only if the abstract program

$$(P, h_o \wedge h, h_1, \mathfrak{H})$$

is correct, i.e.,

$$h_o \wedge h \ \{P\} \ h_1$$

with respect to $\mathfrak{H}$.

Thus, in particular,

(i) $\Pi(P, \text{true}, h_1, \mathfrak{H})$ asks for an entry assertion h_o providing for the correctness of the abstract program $(P, h_o, h_1, \mathfrak{H})$,

(ii) if h is a solution of $\Pi(p)$ and $h' \rightarrow h$ is valid under $\mathfrak{H}$ then h' is a solution of $\Pi(p)$ as well and, thus,

(iii) false is a solution of any correctness problem.

Of course, we are interested in solutions of $\Pi(p)$ which are as weak as possible.

A solution h^* of $\Pi(p)$ is said to be ideal if, for any solution h of $\Pi(p)$, $h \rightarrow h^*$ is valid under $\mathfrak{H}$.

Notice that the question for an <u>ideal</u> solution of the <u>total</u> correctness problem $\Pi(P, \text{true}, h_1, \mathfrak{h})$ is equivalent to that of Dijkstra's predicate transformer of P (Dijkstra 1973). Correctness problems $\Pi(\text{empty}, h_o, h_1, \mathfrak{h})$ concerning the <u>empty statement</u> are called <u>simple questions</u> and h is a solution of this question if and only if $h_o \wedge h \longrightarrow h_1$ is a <u>theorem</u> under $\mathfrak{h}$.
In particular, the question $\Pi(\text{empty}, \text{true}, h_1, \mathfrak{h})$ is solved by any h with $h \longrightarrow h_1$ being a theorem under $\mathfrak{h}$.

In the following, $\mathfrak{h}$ is fixed and, hence, we omit it in our notations. In particular, we write

$$\begin{aligned} \Pi_P(h_o, h_1) &\quad \text{instead of} \quad \Pi(P, h_o, h_1, \mathfrak{h}), \\ \Pi(h_o, h_1) &\quad \text{instead of} \quad \Pi(\text{empty}, h_o, h_1, \mathfrak{h}), \text{ and} \\ h_1 &\quad \text{instead of} \quad \Pi(\text{empty}, \text{true}, h_1, \mathfrak{h}). \end{aligned}$$

A correctness problem $\Pi_Q(g_o, g_1)$ is said to be a <u>reduction</u> of $\Pi_P(h_o, h_1)$ if any solution of the former is a solution of the latter, as well.

In particular, we are interested in reductions of $\Pi_P(h_o, h_1)$ decomposing the statement part P. We look, for instance, for a reduction of $\Pi_{P;Q}(h_o, h_1)$ in terms of Π_P and Π_Q.

For this, our concept of a correctness problem has to be defined more generally by

(i) admitting correctness problems themselves to be arguments of Π_P and
(ii) considering conjunctions $\Pi_P \wedge \Pi_Q$ of correctness problems to be correctness problems, as well.

An assertion h^* is said to be a <u>solution</u> of $\Pi_P(\Pi_1, \Pi_2)$ if and only if there are solutions h_1^* and h_2^* of Π_1 and Π_2, respectively, such that h^* is a solution of $\Pi_P(h_1^*, h_2^*)$.

h^* is said to be a <u>solution</u> of $\Pi_1 \wedge \Pi_2$ if it is a solution of both Π_1 and Π_2.

Now $\Pi_{P;Q}(h_o, h_1)$ can be reduced to $\Pi_P(h_o, \Pi_Q(\text{true}, h_1))$.

In this example, the latter is an <u>equivalent reduction</u> of the former, i.e., both have got the same range of solutions.

For any correctness problems Π_1 and Π_2 we write

$\Pi_1 \Longrightarrow \Pi_2$ to denote that Π_1 can be reduced to Π_2 and

$\Pi_1 \Longleftrightarrow \Pi_2$ to denote that $\Pi_1 \Longrightarrow \Pi_2$ and $\Pi_2 \Longrightarrow \Pi_1$

(thus, $\Longleftrightarrow$ denotes equivalent reduction).

4.2. A DIALOGUE STRATEGY FOR SOLVING CORRECTNESS PROBLEMS

Solving a correctness problem means constructing a solution which is as weak as possible.

In our man-machine dialogue strategy the man's part should be played by a human being (called "the user") who is familiar with the problem to be solved. The part of the machine can be played by a suitable deterministic automaton (called "the system").

The system's activities are

(i) to reduce the current correctness problem (equivalently as far as possible),

(ii) to address simple questions to the user whenever it is necessary,

(iii) to check the logical admissibility of the answers returned and, suggested by them, proceed reducing or asking.

The user's activity is to decide in each case for one of the following three possibilities:

(i) to answer the system's question strongly by giving solution of that question,

(ii) to answer weakly by returning a reduced question,

(iii) to deny answering at all (i.e., the question itself is returned as an answer) if he does not feel certain of another useful answer.

Fig. 1 is to show the basic principles of our dialogue strategy:

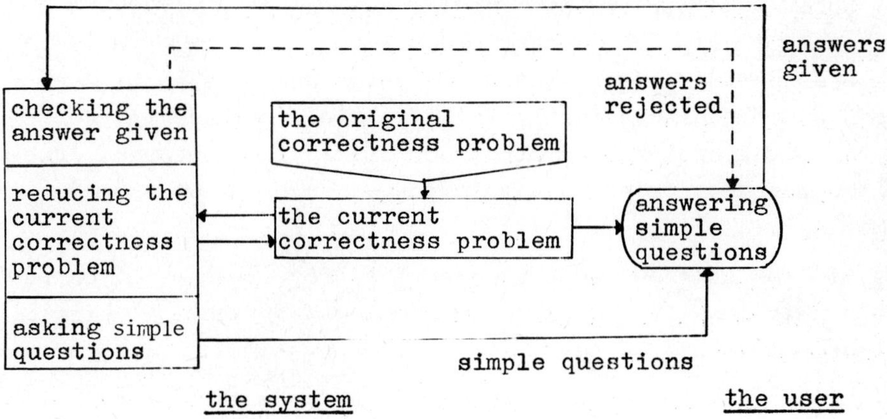

Fig. 1

Fig. 1 can best be explained by the following "program" :

```
begin
current correctness problem := original correctness problem ;
repeat while it could be helpful to have  a simple question
             answered
                {this is decided by the system}
         do begin
            address this question to the user ;
            if the user feels certain of answering
            then begin
                 his answer is returned to the system ;
                 while the system cannot accept the answer given
                    do begin
                       it is turned back ;
                       the user gives another answer
                       end
                 end
         else the question is returned to the system ;
         end ;
     reduce the current correctness problem
until the current correctness problem has become an assertion;
solution := current correctness problem
end
```

Of course, wether or not a dialogue process is really <u>successful</u> or proceeds sufficiently <u>purposively</u> essentially depends on the <u>answers</u> returned by the user. In particular, when a dialogue eventually fails in yielding a useful solution we do not know anything about our original correctness problem (remember that <u>false</u> is a solution of any correctness problem).

But it can be shown as a theorem that for any partial correctness problem $\Pi_P(h_o, h_1)$ our system has got the following reasonable properties:

(i) every dialogue started for the original correctness problem $\Pi_P(h_o, h_1)$ <u>terminates</u> and yields a (possibly useless) solution of $\Pi_P(h_o, h_1)$ and

(ii) for any solution h of $\Pi_P(h_o, h_1)$ there is a dialogue yielding the solution h.

Thus, in order to proceed as purposively as possible the user should deny answering unless he feels certain of giving a <u>useful</u> (i.e., a very natural) answer (see the examples in 4.4 and 5). Moreover, the dialogue strategy has to be overlaid by a <u>backtracking</u> strategy which enables the user to cancel an earlier given answer, to replace it by a more useful one (or to deny answering at that point), and to restart the dialogue from that point.

4.3. REDUCING CORRECTNESS PROBLEMS

In the following, we make available some of the most frequently used <u>rules for reducing correctness problems</u>.

Let H, H_o, and H_1 denote any correctness problems,

(1) $\Pi(H_o, \Pi(H_1, H_2)) \Longleftrightarrow \Pi(H_o \wedge H_1, H_2)$

(2) $\Pi_P(H_o, H_1 \wedge H_2) \Longleftrightarrow \Pi_P(H_o, H_1) \wedge \Pi_P(H_o, H_2)$

(3) If $H_o \rightarrow H$ is valid then $\Pi(H_o, H_1) \Longrightarrow \Pi(H, H_1)$

(4) $\Pi_{\underline{begin}\ P\ \underline{end}}(H_o, H_1) \Longleftrightarrow \Pi_P(H_o, H_1)$

(5) $\Pi_{P;Q}(H_o, H_1) \Longleftrightarrow \Pi_P(H_o, \Pi_Q(true, H_1))$

(6) $\Pi_Q(H_o, H_1) \Longleftrightarrow \Pi(H_o, \Pi_Q(\text{true}, H_1))$

(7) $\Pi_{v:=e}(\text{true}, H) \Longleftrightarrow H|_{v\leftarrow e}$ where $H|_{v\leftarrow e}$ means simultaneous replacing (all free occurrences of) the variable identifier v by the expression e.

(8) $\Pi_{\underline{if}\,cond\,\underline{then}\,P\,\underline{else}\,Q}(\text{true}, H) \Longleftrightarrow \Pi_P(\text{cond}, H) \wedge \Pi_Q(\neg\,\text{cond}, H)$

Rules (1),...,(8) should be evident.
None of them requires any user assistance whereas reducing <u>loop correctness problems</u> does:

(9) An appropriate reduction of the loop correctness problem

$$\Pi_{\underline{while}\,cond\,\underline{do}\,rep}(\text{true}, H)$$

is considered a part of the dialogue and depends essentially on the user's answer to the so-called <u>basic question</u> of that loop:

$$\Pi(\neg\text{cond}, H) \quad .$$

This basic question asks for an assertion h_o^* that implies (any solution of) H <u>whenever the loop terminates</u>. Thus, h_o^* could be considered a promising candidate of a <u>loop invariant</u>:

(9a) If the basic question $\Pi(\neg\,\text{cond}, H)$ of the loop considered can be <u>answered strongly</u>, i.e., by an <u>assertion</u> h_o^* then

$$\Pi_{\underline{while}\,cond\,\underline{do}\,rep}(\text{true}, H) \Longrightarrow \Phi_{rep}^{cond}(h_o^*)$$

where $\Phi_{rep}^{cond}(h_o^*)$ starts a new (sub)dialogue aimed at getting a <u>loop invariant</u> from h_o^*.

For any assertion h^*, Φ_{rep}^{cond} is defined recursively as follows:

$$\Phi_{rep}^{cond}(h^*) = \begin{cases} \text{true} & \text{if } h^* \text{ is theorem over } \mathfrak{h}; \\ h^* \wedge \Phi_{rep}^{cond}(\Pi_{rep}(\text{cond} \wedge h^*, h^*)) & \text{otherwise} \end{cases}$$

Now suppose the basic question $\Pi(\neg\text{cond}, H)$ cannot be answered strongly but is returned (possibly in a reduced form).

Then we must solve the so-called first-order problem of this loop:

$$\prod_{rep}(\text{cond}, H_o^*)$$

where H_o^* is the user's answer to the basic question $\prod(\neg\text{cond}, H)$. Note that getting solutions H_1^* of this first-order problem requires transforming H_o^* once "along the loop body" and, thus, our dialogue will be enriched with information concerning the loop body:

(9b) If the basic question $\prod(\neg\text{cond}, H)$ of the loop considered cannot be answered strongly but by a simple question H_o^* then

$$\prod_{\underline{\text{while}}\,\text{cond}\,\underline{\text{do}}\,\text{rep}}(\text{true}, H) \Longrightarrow$$

$$\Phi^{\text{cond}}_{\text{rep}}(H_1^*) \wedge \prod(\Phi^{\text{cond}}_{\text{rep}}(H_1^*) \wedge \neg\text{cond}, H_o^*)$$

where H_1^* is a solution of the first-order problem $\prod_{rep}(\text{cond}, H_o^*)$ of that loop and $\Phi^{\text{cond}}_{\text{rep}}$ is the same as in (9a).

In 4.4 we give a very simple example demonstrating our dialogue strategy. Finally, in chapter 5, we demonstrate this technique by verifying the first step of the example of chapter 3.

4.4. A VERY SIMPLE EXAMPLE

Consider the well-known problem of determining the integer quotient q and the remainder r in dividing x by y, i.e., the abstract program p = (P, h_o, h_1, $\mathfrak{H}$) with

P : q:=o; r:=x; while y≤r do begin r:=r-y; q:=q+1 end ,

h_o : is to be found out ,

h_1 : $r=q\cdot y+r \wedge o \leq q \wedge o \leq r \wedge r < y$, and

$\mathfrak{H}$: some suitably choosen axioms for integers.

Let us try to find out a domain of the partial correctness of p which is as weak as possible. Thus, we are faced with the partial correctness problem

$$\Pi_P(\text{true},\ x=q\cdot y+r \wedge o \le q \wedge o \le r \wedge r < y) \quad .$$

Referring to the rules given in 4.3, according to (3) we get

$$\Longrightarrow \Pi_{q:=o;r:=x}(\text{true}, \Pi_{\text{while}}(\text{true},\ x=q\cdot y+r \wedge o \le q \wedge o \le r \wedge r < y)\ ).$$

According to (9) we ask the <u>basic question</u> of the while loop:

$$\Pi(r < y\ ,\ x=q\cdot y+r \wedge o \le q \wedge o \le r \wedge r < y).$$

This suggests the <u>strong answer</u>

$$h_o\ :\ \ x=q\cdot y+r \wedge o \le q \wedge o \le r$$

and due to (9a) we get step by step

$$\Longrightarrow \Pi_{q:=o;r:=x}(\text{true}, \oint^{y\le r}_{r:=r-y;q:=q+1}(r=q\cdot y+r \wedge o \le q \wedge o \le r)\ ),$$

$$\Longrightarrow \Pi_{q:=o;r:=x}(\text{true},\ x=q\cdot y+r \wedge o \le q \wedge o \le r \wedge \oint^{\text{cond}}_{\text{rep}}(\Pi_{\text{rep}}(y\le r \wedge x=q\cdot y+r \wedge o\le q \wedge o\le r\ ,\ x=q\cdot y+r \wedge o\le q \wedge o\le r\ ))).$$

Due to (4), (5), and (7) we get

$$\Longrightarrow \Pi_{q:=o;r:=x}(\text{true},\ x=q\cdot y+r \wedge o\le q \wedge o\le r \wedge \oint^{\text{cond}}_{\text{rep}}(\underline{\Pi(y\le r \wedge x=q\cdot y+r \wedge o\le q \wedge o\le r\ ,\ x=(q+1)\cdot y+r-y \wedge o\le q+1 \wedge o\le r-y)})).$$

The underlined simple question can be <u>strongly answered</u> by <u>$o \le r$</u>. After having proved the corresponding simple theorem valid the system accepts this answer and gets

$$\Longrightarrow \Pi_{q:=o;r:=x}(\text{true},\ x=q\cdot y+r \wedge o\le q \wedge o\le r \wedge \oint^{\text{cond}}_{\text{rep}}(\Pi_{\text{rep}}(y\le r \wedge o\le r\ ,\ o\le r))).$$

Applying (4), (5), and (7) again, the system obtains

$$\Longrightarrow \Pi_{q:=o;r:=x}(\text{true},\ x=q\cdot y+r \wedge o\le q \wedge o\le r \wedge \oint^{\text{cond}}_{\text{rep}}(\underline{\Pi(y\le r \wedge o\le r\ ,\ o\le r-y)})).$$

The underlined simple question is passed to the user and can obviously be answered by <u>true</u>. So the system gets

$$\Longrightarrow \Pi_{q:=o;r:=x}(\text{true},\ x=q\cdot y+r \wedge o\le q \wedge o\le r)$$

and, due to (5) and (7), the system reduces to the simple question

$$\underline{\Pi(\text{true},\ x = o \cdot y + x \wedge o \leq o \wedge o \leq x)}$$

which is passed to the user and, of course, answered by $\underline{o \leq x}$. Thus, our original correctness problem has been reduced to the solution

$$o \leq x$$

as the domain of the partial correctness of p.

5. A MORE REALISTIC EXAMPLE OF A VERIFICATION DIALOGUE

Remember the abstract program

$$p_1 = (P_1,\ \text{true},\ W = \text{weight}(To),\ \mathfrak{G}_1)$$

of section 3.1 (the first step of the development of the tip counting example) with P_1:

```
Q1 {     W := 0 ;  S := push(empty, To);
wh1      while S ≠ empty
            do begin
   rep1 (Q2  {T := top(S); S := pop(S);
         wh2 (while ¬tip(t)
                 do begin
             rep2 { S := push(S, right(T)); T := left(T)
                    end;
              W := W + content(T)
              end
```

In the following we write c, w, tw, l, and r instead of content, weight, totalweight, left, and right, respectively. Simple questions addressed to the user are underlined.

Our dialogue has to be started with the initial correctness problem

$\Pi_{Q1;wh1}(\text{true}, W=\text{weight}(To))$. Due to rule (5) in 4.3 the system gets

$\Rightarrow \Pi_{Q1}(\text{true},\ \Pi_{wh1}(\text{true},\ W=w(To)))$. Now the basic question $\underline{\Pi(S=\text{empty},\ W=w(To))}$ is passed to the user.

But the user has not the slightest idea and <u>denies answering</u>. According to (3) and axioms (V1) and (A1iv) the system produces the reduced question

$$\underline{\Pi(tw(S)=0,\ W=w(To))}$$

but the user <u>denies answering</u>, again. Thus, the system has to proceed according to (9b):

$$\Longrightarrow \Pi_{Q1}(true, \oint_{rep1}^{S\neq empty}(H_1^*) \wedge \Pi(\oint_{rep1}^{S\neq empty}(H_1^*) \wedge S=empty\ ,\ H_o^*)) \quad (1)$$

where H_o^* is the reduced basic question $\Pi(tw(S)=0,\ W=w(To))$ of wh1 and H_1^* is a solution of the <u>first-order problem</u>

$$\Pi_{rep1}(S=empty,\ \Pi(tw(S)=0,\ W=w(To))$$

of rep1. After having labelled the reduction obtained by (1) we start a sub-dialogue for solving the first-order problem

$\Pi_{Q2;wh2;W:=W+c(T)}(S=empty,\ \Pi(tw(S)=0,\ W=w(To)))$.

Due to (5), (7), (1):

$$\Longrightarrow \Pi_{Q2;wh2}(S=empty,\ \underline{\Pi(tw(S)=0,\ W+c(T)=w(To))}) \quad .$$

Again the user <u>turnes back</u> the question and according to (5) we get

$$\Longrightarrow \Pi_{Q2}(S=empty,\ \Pi_{wh2}(true,\ \Pi(tw(S)=0,\ W+c(T)=w(To)))).$$

The system reduces the <u>basic question</u> of the inner loop wh2

$\Pi(tip(T),\ \Pi(tw(S)=0,\ W+c(T)=w(To)))$ according to (1):

$\Longrightarrow \underline{\Pi(tip(T) \wedge tw(S)=0,\ W+c(T)=w(To))}$ turned back; (3):

$\Longrightarrow \underline{\Pi(w(T)=c(T) \wedge tw(S)=0,\ W+c(T)=w(To))}$.

Now the user is convinced of his first really helpful answer:

$$\Pi(tw(S)=0\ ,\ W+w(T)=w(To))\ .$$

Thus, again the system has to proceed according to (9b):

$$\Longrightarrow \Pi_{Q2}(S=empty,\ \oint_{rep2}^{\neg tip(T)}(H_1^{**}) \wedge \Pi(\oint_{rep2}^{\neg tip(T)}(H_1^{**}) \wedge tip(T)\ ,\ \Pi(tw(S)=0, W+w(T)=w(To)))). \quad (2)$$

After having labelled this point we try to get a solution

H_1^{**} of the <u>first-order problem</u> of the inner loop wh2:

$$\prod_{S:=push(S,r(T));\ T:=l(T)}(\neg\, tip(T), \prod(tw(S)=0,\ W+w(T)=w(To))).$$

According to (5), (7), and (1) the system gets

$$\Longrightarrow \underline{\prod(\neg\, tip(T) \wedge tw(push(S,\ r(T)))=0\ ,\ W+w(l(T))=(To)\ )}\ .$$

This question is <u>turned back</u> and, according to (3) and the axioms (V1) and (A1ii), it is reduced to

$$\Longrightarrow \underline{\prod(w(T)=w(l(T))+w(r(T)) \wedge tw(push(S,r(T)))=0,\ W+w(l(T))=w(To)\ )}\ .$$

This can be <u>weakly answered</u> by

$\prod(tw(push(S,r(T)))=0,\ W+w(T)-w(r(T))=w(To)\ )$; (1),(V1),(A1):

$$\Longrightarrow \underline{\prod(\ w(r(T))+tw(S)=0\ ,\ W+w(T)-w(r(T))=w(To)\ )}$$

and the user's answer is obviously

$$\underline{W + w(T) + tw(S) = w(To)}\ .$$

Thus, we have got H_1^{**} : $W + w(T) + tw(S) = w(To)$ and can proceed at ② reducing

$$\oint_{rep2}^{\neg tip(T)}(H_1^{**}) = H_1^{**} \wedge \oint_{rep2}^{\neg tip(T)}(\prod_{rep2}(\neg tip(T) \wedge H_1^{**}, H_1^{**})\ ):$$

$$\Rightarrow H_1^{**} \wedge \oint_{rep2}^{\neg tip(T)}(\prod_{rep2}(\neg tip(T) \wedge H_1^{**},\ W+w(T)+tw(S)=w(To)\ )\ )$$

$$\Rightarrow H_1^{**} \wedge \oint_{rep2}^{\neg tip(T)}(\underline{\prod(\neg tip(T) \wedge W+w(T)+tw(S)=w(To)\ ,\ W+w(l(T))+tw(push(S,\ r(T)))=w(To)\ )}\ )\ \text{refused};$$

$$\Rightarrow H_1^{**} \wedge \oint_{rep2}^{\neg tip(T)}(\ \underline{\prod(w(T)=w(l(T))+w(r(T)) \wedge W+w(T)+tw(S)=w(To),\ W+w(l(T))+w(r(T))+tw(S)=w(To)\ )}\ )\ .$$

This question can be obviously answered by <u>true</u> and, hence,

$$\Rightarrow H_1^{**} \wedge \oint_{rep2}^{\neg tip(T)}(true) \Longrightarrow H_1^{**}.$$

Thus, H_1^{**} : $W + w(T) + tw(S) = w(To)$ is an <u>invariant of the inner loop</u> wh2, remember that! Now proceeding from ② we get

$\Longrightarrow \Pi_{Q2}(S \neq \text{empty},\ W+w(T)+tw(S)=w(To) \wedge$
$\wedge \Pi(W+w(T)+tw(S)=w(To) \wedge tip(T), \Pi(tw(S)=0,\ W+w(T)=w(To))))$

$\Longrightarrow \Pi_{Q2}(S \neq \text{empty},\ W\text{ß}w(T)+tw(S)=w(To) \wedge$
$\wedge \underline{\Pi(W+w(T)+tw(S)=w(To) \wedge tip(T) \wedge tw(S)=0,\ W+w(T)=w(To))}\ )$

answer : <u>true</u>

$\Longrightarrow \Pi_{Q2}(S \neq \text{empty},\ W+w(T)+tw(S)=w(To))$

$\Longrightarrow \underline{\Pi(S \neq \text{empty},\ W + w(top(S)) + tw(pop(S)) = w(To))}$

answer : $W + tw(S) = w(To)$ and, thus, we have got

$\underline{H_1^*: W + tw(S) = w(To)}$.

Now we can proceed from ① .
We omit the part of the dialogue reducing

$\Phi^{S=empty}_{rep1}(H_1^*) \Longrightarrow H_1^*$, i.e., showing that H_1^* is an <u>invariant of the outer loop</u> wh1. Notice, however, that this part can be essentially strengthened by remembering that H_1^{**} was an invariant of the inner loop. Then

$\Pi_{Q1;wh1}(\text{true},\ W = w(To))$ can be further reduced as follows:

$\Longrightarrow \Pi_{Q1}(\text{true},\ W+tw(S)=w(To) \wedge \Pi(W+tw(S)=w(To) \wedge S=\text{empty},$
$\Pi(tw(S)=0,\ W=w(To))\ )\ )$,

$\Longrightarrow \Pi_{Q1}(\text{true},\ W+tw(S)=w(To) \wedge \underline{\Pi(W+tw(S)=w(To) \wedge S=\text{empty} \wedge tw(S)=0,}$
$\underline{W=w(To)\ )}\ )$

As the last question should obviously answered by <u>true</u>, we obtain

$\Longrightarrow \Pi_{W:=0;S:=push(empty,To)}(W + tw(S) = w(To))$,

$\Longrightarrow \underline{\Pi(\text{true},\ 0 + tw(push(empty,\ To)) = w(To))}$, refused;

$\Longrightarrow \underline{\Pi(\text{true},\ w(To) = w(To))}$, answered by <u>true</u> and, thus,

$\Pi_{P_1}(\text{true},\ W = w(To)) \Longrightarrow \text{true}$, i.e., <u>p_1 is partially correct</u>.

REFERENCES

Dahl, O.J., Myhrhang, B., and Nygaard, K. (1970). THE SIMULA 67 Common Base Language, Publ. S-22, Norwegian Computing Centre, Oslo.

Dijkstra, E.W. (1973). A Simple Axiomatic Basis for Programming Language Constructs, Technical Report, Technological University, Eindhoven, The Netherlands.

Hoare, C.A.R. (1972). Proof of Correctness of Data Representation, Acta Informatica, No.4, 271-281.

Jensen, K. and Wirth, N. (1974). PASCAL User Manual and Report, Lecture Notes in Computer Science, Vol. 18.

Liskov, B. and Zilles, S. (1974). Programming with Abstract Data Types, SIGPLAN Notices, No.4, 50-59.

Liskov, B. and Zilles, S. (1975a). Specification Techniques for Data Abstractions, IEEE Transactions on Software Engineering, SE-1, No. 1, 7-19.

Liskov,B. (1975b). A Note on CLU, MAC-TR, MIT.

London, R.L. (1975). A View of Program Verification, Proc. Int. Conf. on Reliable Software, Los Angeles.

London, R.L., Shaw, M., and Wulf, W.A. (1976). Abstraction and Verification in ALPHARD, Technical Reports, Carnegie-Mellon University
(1976 a) Introduction to Language and Methodology
(1976 b) Iteration and Generators
(1976 c) A Symbol Table Example
(1976 d) Design and Verification of a Tree Handler

Bär : Discussion

King, J.: You made no mention of inductive assertions in your presentation . . .

Bär: Well, inductive assertions are mainly needed in loops, as loop invariants. I must refer you to the paper. But let me make clear that I only consider entry and exit assertions, not intermediate assertions. If there's a point where an intermediate assertion is needed, perhaps as a loop invariant, then first of all the system tries to guess the loop invariant and if it fails to guess this invariant, it then asks the user to give him a suitable one.

King, J.: I have another comment. I understood you to make the statement that correctness proofs need to say yes or no. There has been work on methods for saying something other than yes or no; I can recall one paper entitled "Proving the Incorrectness of Programs." There is the possibility of a more refined answer than just yes or no.

Bär: I agree, of course. My dialogue strategy can fail in proving correct programs correct. However, it can be shown as a theorem of this methodology that any dialogue process terminates, possibly with the solution of failure. Then I don't know anything. This is the worst case. In other cases it terminates yielding an entry assertion for the entire program which is too strong, too narrow. This is a typical outcome. In this case the entry assertion which is too narrow includes diagnostic information about what could be wrong in that program. And in general this will help you to find the errors, the bugs and so on.

Correll: You make some change to h_0 whenever you find that the program you have given cannot be proved using that assertion. On the other hand, you want to have the weakest pre-condition. Isn't this inconsistent? What you really want is to have one fixed pre-condition and one fixed post-condition, and you want to construct a correct program from those conditions. You are not interested in any weaker conditions, you are not interested in any other pre-conditions, you are just interested in the one you have started out with at the highest level.

Bär: Well, then we must restrict the concept of the correctness problem to a boolean one: you are only interested whether the program meets its specifications or not, yes or no. These special cases, yes or no, are contained in the methodology, but in general you get more. You get information about what could be wrong. It's a little bit more. You are less likely to get false for the first run if the verification is approached in this more general way.

King, J.: Does your method find the weakest h^* ?

Bär: That is impossible in general. You can find the weakest pre-condition h^* if you exclude any kind of recursion, including loops; otherwise you cannot. What you can show about loops or recursive calls essentially depends on the quality of the intermediate assertions or loop invariants that the user puts into the system. I said that it is possible to find the weakest h* in case your program doesn't contain any recursion, but this doesn't mean that determining the weakest h* is the main feature of this methodology.

Holager: Your method relies upon being able to find suitable intermediate abstract programs. It seems to me that this is the same as the problem of finding nice intermediate levels of abstraction (or the "right" modules) which we have been talking about so much, but with the additional constraint that the layers to be found should be suitable for program proving. Would you care to comment on how to define suitable intermediate programs?

Bär: How to define these intermediate steps of the development process? Of course, you can't give an algorithm for developing well-structured programs. The only thing you can do is to give guidelines for heuristic thinking, but you shouldn't prevent people from thinking. [☺]

Dewar: What practical experience have you had with this approach so far?

Bär: What part of the approach, the development of programs or the verification of programs? The methodology for developing programs has arisen out of four years of teaching structured programming based on existing programming languages. For various reasons, we mostly used the programming language PASCAL, but we were primarily interested in teaching our students methods which would be applicable when they start work in industry. The aim was to teach good techniques of developing structured programs so that our students could make use of this experience in practice.

Dewar: You said nothing about the verification part . . .

Bär: As to the second part of the methodology, we have now verified a lot of programs, most of them well known from the literature, the usual set of examples used to illustrate all approaches to program verification: sorting problems, tree-sort, quick-sort, Dijkstra's program. [☺] We have also detected some real programming errors. [☺]

Constructing Quality Software, P.G. Hibbard/S.A. Schuman (eds.)

ON THE SPECIFICATION AND DESIGN OF ABSTRACT DATA TYPES

P. R. King
Department of Computer Science
University of Manitoba
Winnipeg, Manitoba
Canada

The paper discusses an approach to the formal derivation of a concrete data type from its specifications. Means are defined for both the intrinsic (internal) specifications of a type and the extrinsic specifications of one type as a second, more "concrete" type. Given the extrinsic specifications of a user's abstract type T as a primitive abstract type T_0, the intrinsic specifications of T_0 and of a primitive concrete type T_1, and the extrinsic specifications of T_0 as T_1, the problem at hand is to derive an implementation of T in terms of T_1. The derivation proceeds by the application of rewriting rules, axioms, theorems over types and a "calculus" for the derivation of deterministic programs from first order logic specifications. The proposals are illustrated by several common "folk-lore" examples.

1. INTRODUCTION

While it cannot be argued that a correct piece of software is *ipso facto* of high quality, the converse is certainly true. In this paper we are concerned with the derivation of correct software from a given set of specifications. At the outset it must be stated that we do not present more than an approach to one single facet of the production of correct software; we restrict ourselves to the question of deriving correct data structures from their specifications.

1.1. TYPES

Recent languages have come to treat a data structure, or more simply a *type*, as comprising not only a set of values which may be assumed by objects of that type, but also a set of functions and operators (which we will henceforth refer to collectively as "operations") applicable to those values. Thus we observe the *class* mechanism of Simula, [3] and two of its notable successors, the *cluster* of CLU [11] and the *form* of Alphard [18]. In all three cases a type is represented by some sort of program module wherein are defined the set of values and operations in question. Generally, the set of values of a type T is constructed in terms of the set of values of some other possibly more primitive type T_1, and the operations of T in terms of those of T_1. Further, a type T may possess an arbitrary number of parameters. It is this notion of type that we adopt here.

1.2. TYPE VERIFICATION

The Alphard *form* goes one important stage further; the constructive definition of T in terms of T_1 may be supplemented by the specifications of T in terms of some other type T_0, where the relationship between T_0 and T_1 is assumed to be completely known. It is then possible to adapt techniques originally proposed by Hoare [8] to "verify" that the definition of T in terms of T_1 is correct. The verification consists basically in demonstrating that the diagram A in Figure 1 is commutative.

1.3. TYPE DERIVATION

In this paper we are concerned with what is in some sense the complementary task to such verification, namely the formal derivation of the implementation of T in terms of T_1 given the specification of T in terms of T_0 and the implementation of T_0 in terms of T_1. The task is illustrated in diagram B of Figure 1, where the dotted line indicates constructive definitions which are to be derived rather than verified.

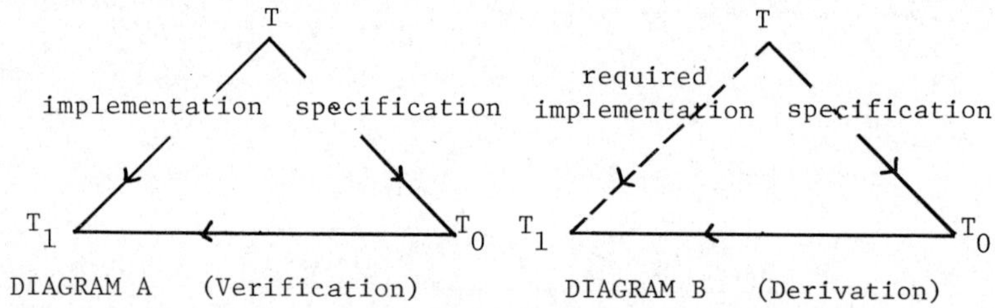

FIGURE 1
Type Verification and Derivation

1.4. TYPES AND LEVELS

In the foregoing three levels of types have been introduced which we now classify more precisely:-

i) T : the type which the user wishes to define and of which he may specify the creation of instances and manipulations. T will be known in the sequel as a "user abstract type" (*usab*)

ii) T_0 : the type used for specifying T. T_0 will be termed a "primitive abstract type" (*primab*) and should be regarded as a "system-supplied" abstract type. A primab must be an entity about which much is known or provable mathematically and which is capable of convenient representation in terms of the concrete types available.

iii) T_1 : a primitive type of the given target language. T_1 will be termed a "primitive concrete type" (*primconc*).

We may also distinguish a fourth level, the implementation of T in terms of T_1, the derivation of which is the task at hand. We will term this a "user concrete type" (*usconc*). This derivation is one component of the overall derivation of what we might term a "user abstract program", which will comprise several such user abstract type definitions together with manipulations on them. It should be remarked how the treatment of types as "modules" has subdivided the overall derivation problem into a number of considerably easier ones, something whose counterpart for verification has been frequently remarked upon.

2. SPECIFICATION OF TYPES

2.1. INTRINSIC and EXTRINSIC SPECIFICATIONS

In order to perform any manipulations on a type T, its internal properties must be well known and fully expressed. These properties will, following Sintzoff [16], be termed the *intrinsic specifications* of the type. Two entities are involved : the "primitives" or base definitions of the set of values, and the list of operations with a specification of each. Further, T may be parametrized, so that in reality we are dealing with sets of types. The specifications of one type T in terms of a type T_0 are, again following Sintzoff, termed the *extrinsic specifications* of T. It is essential to specify the primitives of T, but is frequently convenient to specify the operations as well, provided restrictions of consistency are observed. The situation is clarified in the following diagram:

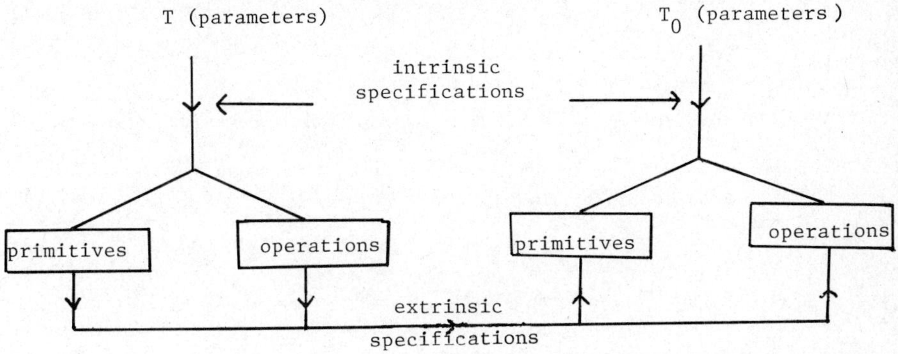

FIGURE 2

Intrinsic and Extrinsic Specifications

We now consider two examples, the intrinsic specifications of the primab *seq* (finite sequence) and the extrinsic specifications of *seq* as *array*. The primab *seq* is adapted from [9] while *array* is taken from CLU [11] with the **changes** that the routine *retracth* returns the shrunken array rather than the deleted element, **and that *similar* tests if two arrays have equal elements, not necessarily in the same order.**

```
MODE  SEQ (TYPE T, INT n)
   PRIMITIVES    nullseq ,    (SEQ s,T x) s ⊕ x ;
   OPERATIONS
      FUNCTION   length =   (SEQ s | s = nullseq) 0,
                            (SEQ s|∇ (SEQ s1,Tx): s=s1 ⊕ x)1+length(s1);
      FUNCTION   leader =   (SEQ s|∇ (SEQ s1,Tx): s=s1 ⊕ x)s1;
      FUNCTION   last   =   (SEQ s|∇ (SEQ s1,Tx): s=s1 ⊕ x)x;
            OP   ⊕      =   (SEQ s1,s2|∇(SEQ s3,Tx):s3=leader(s2) ⊕ x)
                                                     (s1 ⊕ s3) ⊕ x
END
```

Figure 3

Intrinsic specifications of primab *seq*

```
EXTR  SEQ (TYPE T)  AS  ARRAY (T T)v
  WHERE   nullseq  :: create (1),
       (SEQ s, Tx)s ⊕ x :: extendh (v, x);
 BEGIN
     FUNCTION   length = (SEQ s) size (v);
     FUNCTION   leader = (SEQ s |length(s) ≥ 1) retracth (copy(v));
     FUNCTION   last   = (SEQ s |length(s) ≥ 1) fetch (v,high(v))
 END
```

Figure 4

Extrinsic specifications of primab *seq* as primconc *array*

Whereas the overall meaning of these two sets of specifications is probably clear, certain features require elucidation.

i) Of the two general approaches to the provision of formal specifications [10] namely *algebraic* and *operational* specifications, the mechanisms being utilised here lean towards the latter. The pre- and post-conditions for the specified operations make use of Schuman's *generic functions* which will be recalled in detail in §2.2. The reader should compare our style with the algebraic style as in [5] and [6], particularly in relation to the more complex examples given later.

ii) Use is made of the symbol ∇ as a *definitional quantifier* [14] to furnish the conditional definition of an identifier. The simplest form is

$$\nabla x : E(x)$$

This is a logical term yielding *true* if the evaluation of the logical expression E is defined, whereupon the identifier x is defined and denotes the value satisfying E. In all other cases the proposition yields *false*. The scope of x is the context in which the logical term occurs. A type specification of x is permitted, and several identifiers may be conditionally defined. Thus, the most general form is

$$\nabla(P_1x_1,\ldots, P_nx_n) : E(x_1,\ldots,x_n)$$

(iii) The operation ⊕ has not been extrinsically specified in Figure 4; we emphasise that it is strictly unnecessary to specify more than the primitives and that any overspecification, while possibly useful in the derivation process, implies the need for consistency proofs.

We will consider further examples of specifications in §2.3 following a discussion of generic functions.

2.2. GENERIC FUNCTIONS

This term will henceforth refer to Schuman's definitions [14] with notational changes, as now detailed. In abstract terms a generic function G is a set of alternative functions

$$G = \{f_1, f_2, \ldots, f_m\}$$

each having the same external (program) name, g say. The functions f_i although declared or specified separately are not available for explicit individual call; rather a call $g(Y)$ of the generic function implies the deterministic selection and execution of one of the alternatives f_i. Each f_i is defined over a specific domain $\mathcal{D}(f_i) = \mathcal{D}_i$; the most general form of definition is

$$g(P_1x_1, \ldots, P_nx_n \mid q(x_1,\ldots,x_n))E(x_1,\ldots,x_n)$$

where $P_1x_1,\ldots,P_nx_n$ are the formal parameter specifications

$q(x_1,\ldots,x_n)$ is a logical expression

$E(x_1,\ldots,x_n)$ is the body of the function.

In view of the existence of the conditions q the functions f_i are termed *conditioned functions*. The domain of the conditioned function thus defined, f say is

$$\mathcal{D}(f) = \{V = (x_1,\ldots,x_n) \mid \prod_{i=1}^{n} P_ix_i \wedge q(V)\}$$

In terms of the domains $\{\mathcal{D}_i\}$, then at the simplest level the call $g(Y)$ is equivalent to f_i where $Y \in \mathcal{D}_i$. Frequently there will be several domains $\{\mathcal{D}_j\}$ satisfying $\forall_j : Y \in \mathcal{D}_j$, but this potential non-determinacy is resolved by requiring

i) that the domains $\{\mathcal{D}_i\}$ be disjoint or nested (that is, any two domains $\mathcal{D}$ and $\mathcal{D}'$ must be pairwise disjoint or one must be strictly included within the other)

ii) that the function f_i selected from the set $\{f_j\}$ be the one with the narrowest domain.

Stated formally the condition i), which we will denote by DS, is

$$\exists i^* \in I : (\forall_j \in I : j \neq i^* \longrightarrow \mathcal{D}_{i^*} \subset \mathcal{D}_j)$$

where $\quad I = \{i \in [1:m] \mid Y \in \mathcal{D}_i\}$

and the selection ii) is given by

$$g(Y) \equiv f_{i^*}(Y) .$$

In addition to the domain, the *range* of a conditioned function may be defined, as inferred from its body. In employing generic functions to provide specifications, the domain and range are to be considered as (sets defining characteristic conditions which are) pre- and post-conditions (input-output assertions) for the application of the individual conditioned functions. It is felt that the notation introduced provides a particularly convenient way of expressing and manipulating such assertions. (Whether one should regard *(INT i|i > 0)* as comprising a parameter specification and a pre-condition on that formal parameter, or a single precondition in which the specification of the type of *i* is one conjunct, or indeed as the definition of a type as in [1] is largely immaterial here).

2.3. FURTHER SPECIFICATIONS OF "SYSTEM SUPPLIED" TYPES.

In §2.1 we illustrated the specification techniques with one example each of intrinsic and extrinsic specifications. We now introduce the other types treated here and provide six further sets of specifications, which will be used in the derivations of §3.

Our second primab is *set*, adapted from Hoare's "powerset" [9]. The intrinsic specifications of *set* appear in Figure 5 and should need little elucidation beyond the remark that the possibility of defining abbreviations and of deriving or proving useful theorems on the type are illustrated. In addition to the CLU *array* introduced earlier we will make use of a second primitive concrete type, *list*, a linear linked list with provision for removing cells from and returning them to a list *avail* of available space. The intrinsic specifications of the primconc *list* appear in Figure 6; it is sufficient to remark that "hidden" functions (preceded by an "*") may appear to facilitate the specifications. The same device has recently been employed by Guttag [6] to simplify the writing of algebraic specifications. We permit a quite general use of this facility.

Following these two sets of intrinsic specifications, we will give two further illustrations of the extrinsic specifications of primabs as primconcs, by specifying *set* as both *array* and *list*. The former specifications appear as Figure 7; it will be observed that no extrinsic specifications of the operations *IN*, ⊂, ∩, ∪ or - have been given, which will, as noted earlier, complicate any formal derivation making use of these specifications. The specifications of *set* as *list* given in Figure 8 are considerably fuller, implying a more complex task during the consistency checking. Hidden functions are again used.

```
MODE SET (TYPE T, INT n)
   PRIMITIVES Ω, (SET s, T a) s ∪ {a};
  OPERATIONS
     OP IN = (T a, SET s|s = Ω) FALSE,
             (T a, SET s|∇(SET s1):s = s1 ∪ {a}) TRUE,
             (T a, SET s|∇(SET s1, T b): s = s1 ∪ {b} ∧ a ≠ b) a IN s1,
             (T a, SET s) FALSE;
     OP  ⊂ = (SET s1, s2|s1 = Ω) TRUE,
             (SET s1, s2|s1 ≠ Ω  ∧ ∀x:x IN s1 → x IN s2) TRUE,
             (SET s1, s2) FALSE;
     OP  ∪ = (SET s1, s2|s2 = Ω)s1,
             (SET s1, s2|∇(SET s3, T a): s2 = s3 ∪ {a})(s1 ∪ {a}) ∪ s3;
     OP  ∩ = (SET s1, s2|s2 = Ω)Ω,
             (SET s1, s2|∇(T a): s2 = {a} ∧ a IN s1) {a},
             (SET s1, s2|∇(T a): s2 = {a})Ω,
             (SET s1, s2|∇(SET s3): s2 = s3 ∪ {a})(s1 ∩ s3) ∪ (s1 ∩ {a});
     OP  - = (SET s1, s2|s1 = Ω)Ω,
             (SET s1, s2|∇(T a): s1 = {a} ∧ a IN s2)Ω,
             (SET s1, s2|∇(T a): s1 = {a}) {a},
             (SET s1, s2|∇(SET s3,T a):s3≠Ω ∧ s1=s3 ∪{a})(s3-s2)∪({a}-s2);
FUNCTION card = (SET s|s = Ω)0,
                (SET s|∇(set s1, T a): s=s1 ∪{a} ∧ a IN s1) card (s1),
                (SET s|∇(set s1, T a): s=s1 ∪{a})1 + card (s1);
     OP  = = (SET s1, s2)(s1 ⊂ s2) ∧ (s2 ⊂ s1);
DENOTE Ω ∪ {a} BY {a}
     END

  THEOREMS:          i)  t IN {a} ≡ t = a
                    ii)  ∇(T a): s = {a} ≡ card(s) = 1
```

Figure 5

Intrinsic specifications and some theorems for primab *set*

```
MODE LIST (TYPE T, INT n)
    PRIMITIVES  null, avail,
                (LIST s | n ≥ 1) link(s),
                (LIST s | n ≥ 1)T: datum(s),
                (INT i  | i ≥ 0) create (i);
    OPERATIONS
       OP EMPTY = (LIST p)p = null;
       OP FULL  = (LIST p)length(p) = n;
      FUNCTION bottom = (LIST p|EMPTY p) null,
                        (LIST p|EMPTY link(p))p,
                        (LIST p)bottom (link (p));
      FUNCTION equal  = (LIST p,q|EMPTY p ∧ EMPTY q) TRUE,
                        (LIST p,q|length(p) = length(q) ∧
                              datum(p) = datum(q)) equal (link(p), (link(q)),
                        (LIST p,q) FALSE;
      FUNCTION has    = (LIST p, T x|EMPTY p) null,
                        (LIST p, T x|datum(p)=x)p,
                        (LIST p, T x) has (link (p), x);
      FUNCTION length = (LIST p|EMPTY p) 0,
                        (LIST p) 1 + length (link (p));
      FUNCTION  add   = (LIST p, T x| ¬ (FULL p ∨ EMPTY p))
                               link(bottom(p')) = avail ∧ p = putin(p',x),
                        (LIST p, T x| ¬ FULL p) p = putin(p',x);
     *FUNCTION putin  = (LIST p, T x) avail = link(avail') ∧
                               link(bottom(p)) = null ∧ (bottom(p)) = x;
      FUNCTION delete = (LIST p, T x| ¬ EMPTY p; LIST lptr:=p, ptr:=p)
                         p=takeout(p',lptr,ptr,x) ∧ lptr =ptr → p=link(p');
     *FUNCTION takeout= (LIST p, l, r, T x|EMPTY r)p,
                        (LIST p, l, r, T x|datum(l) = x)
                          link(l)=link(r') ∧ link(r) = avail' ∧ avail = r',
                        (LIST p, l, r, T x) takeout (p, link(r), r, x)
END
```

Figure 6

Intrinsic specifications of the primconc *list*

```
EXTR   SET (TYPE T)  AS  ARRAY (T T)v

      WHERE    Ω  :: create (1),
             (SET s, Tx) s ∪{x} :: extendh (v,x);

BEGIN

   FUNCTION card = (SET s) size(v);

        OP    =   = (SET s1,s2) similar (v.s1, v.s2)

END
```

Figure 7

Extrinsic specifications of primab *set* as primconc *array*

```
EXTR SET (TYPE T,INT n) AS LIST (T T)v
     WHERE      Ω :: null,
          (SET s, T x)s ∪ {x} :: add (v,x);

   BEGIN

OP ∪ = (SET a,b|LIST (T, length(v.a)+length(v.b))lc:=null)
                                           fill(fill(lc,v.a),v.b);

OP ⊂ = (SET a,b|card (a ∪ b) = card(a)) TRUE;

OP ∩ = (SET a,b|LIST(T,min(length(v.a),length(v.b)))lc:=null)
                                             and (v.a,v.b,lc);

OP IN = (T x, SET a) has (v.a,x) ≠ null;

OP = = (SET a,b) equal (v.a,v.b);

FUNCTION card = (SET a) length(v);

OP - = (SET a,b|LIST(T, length(v.a))lc:=null) take (fill(lc,v.a),v.b);

*FUNCTION fill = (LIST lc, lb|lb=null)lc,

                 (LIST lc, lb|has (lc,datum(lb))≠null)fill(lc,link(lb)),

                 (LIST lc, lb)fill(add(lc,datum(lb)), link(lb));

*FUNCTION and  = (LIST la,lb,lc|lb = null)lc,

                 (LIST la,lb,lc|has(la,datum(lb))≠null)
                       and (la, link(lb),add(lc,datum(lb))),
                 (LIST la,lb,lc) and (la,link(lb), lc);

*FUNCTION take = (LIST lc,lb|top(lb) = null)lc,

                 (LIST lc,lb|has(lc,datum(lb)) ≠ null)
                       take(delete(lc,datum(lb)), link(lb)),
                 (LIST lc,lb) take (lc,link(lb))

END
```

Figure 8

Extrinsic specifications of primab *set* as primconc *list*

2.4. SPECIFICATION OF USER ABSTRACT TYPES

Since the goal of this work is the derivation of an implementation of a given usab as a designated primconc, we do not require intrinsic specifications to be provided for the usab. The starting point is, rather the extrinsic specifications of the usab as a selected primab. This implies that specification of the primitives be replaced by three other mechanisms as follows:

i) the specification of an initial value to be assigned to all newly created instances of this particular type

ii) a condition which must be satisfied by the environment in order that the creation of an object of this type may proceed

iii) an invariant condition.

Items ii) and iii) correspond exactly to the predicates β_{req} and I_a in Alphard and we adopt the same form. We insist that any non-local object used in any type-module appear as a parameter. Hence both these conditions will be conditions on the formal parameters of the type being extrinsically specified.

We now give the extrinsic specifications of two "classical" usabs, namely, *stack* which is extrinsically specified as the primab *seq* in Fig. 9, and Hoare's "small int set"[8], renamed *simp* and specified extrinsically as *set* in Figure 10.

```
EXTR STACK (INT n, TYPE T) AS SEQ(T T) p:=nullseq
    REQUIRES  n > 0
    INVARIANT  0 ≤ length(p) ≤ n
BEGIN
    FUNCTION push = (STACK s, T x|0 ≤ length(p) < n) p=p' ⊕ x;
    FUNCTION pop  = (STACK s|notempty (s)) p=leader(p');
    FUNCTION top  = (STACK s|notempty (s)) last(p');
   *FUNCTION notempty = (STACK s) 0 < length(p)
END
```

Figure 9

Extrinsic specifications of usab *stack* as primab *seq*

```
EXTR SIMP (INT n, TYPE T) AS SET(T T) m:=Ω
        REQUIRES    n ≥ 0
        INVARIANT   card(m) ≤ n
  BEGIN
    FUNCTION insert = (SIMP s, T x|card(m ∪{x}) ≤ n) m=m' ∪{x};
    FUNCTION remove = (SIMP s, T x|x IN m) m=m'-{x};
    FUNCTION  has   = (SIMP s, T x)x IN m
END
```

Figure 10

Extrinsic specifications of usab *simp* as primab *set*

2.5. CONSISTENCY AND COMPLETENESS OF SPECIFICATIONS

A full discussion of these two topics is beyond the scope of this paper. For our purposes it is sufficient to make the following remarks:

i) Completeness of the specification of an individual operation is equivalent to the validity of the condition *BB* , where

$$BB = \forall y \in \mathcal{D}(y): \exists i \in [1:m] : y \in \mathcal{D}_i$$

where the generic function specifying the operation is $\{f_1,\ldots,f_m\}$ and $\mathcal{D}(y)$ is the domain over which it is required that the operation be specified.

Frequently all the conditioned functions f_i have identical formal parameter specifications and $\mathcal{D}(y)$ is the "universe"; in this case completeness reduces to demonstrating

$$\sum_{i=1}^{m} q_i(y) = TRUE$$

ii) The internal consistency of each individual operation is assured by the domain restrictions on conditioned functions mentioned in §2.2, which imply a deterministic selection from among the alternatives in the specification of an operation.

iii) There remains the question of the interrelated consistency of a set of operation specifications. We have seen that this problem arises when a type is over-specified extrinsically, that is, when some of its operations are specified in addition to its primitives. It is necessary, in such cases, to verify the equivalence of the extrinsic specification of each such operation and what may be inferred from the corresponding intrinsic specification composed with the extrinsic specifications of the primitives. This verification is very similar to the verification methodology of Alphard.

The predicates employed in verifying completeness and consistency require the domains involved to be sets on which the operations of union and intersection can be performed. If these predicates are to form part of an automated system, such a system must comprise a theorem prover capable of handling all the domains used. We will glibly suppose that this can be done, and proceed.

3. DEVELOPMENT OF DATA TYPES

3.1. STATEMENT OF THE PROBLEM

The task of deriving the implementation of a usab as a primconc, outlined briefly in §1.3, is more precisely depicted in Figure 11, where the various levels of types and specifications are included.

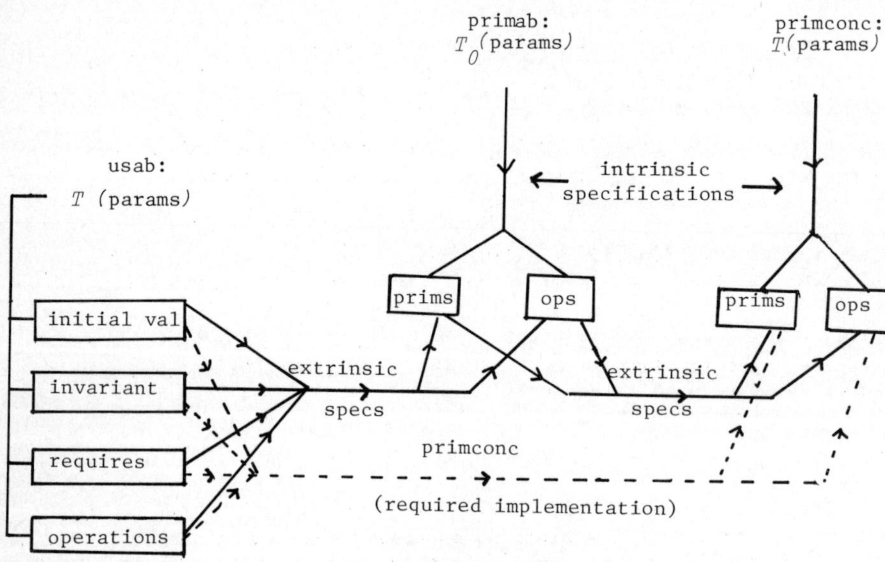

Figure 11

The processes of specification and derivation

The form in which a derived user concrete type appears is entirely target language dependent. While it is not our intention to invent ALGOL 84, we certainly require a notation which is at least plausible, to illustrate the results of the derivation process. In figures 12, 13 and 14 appear the final forms of the three sample derivations comprising the bulk of this section; the reader is urged to consult these briefly before proceeding. It will be observed that the form bears close resemblance to its counterpart in Simula, CLU and Alphard, which will cause no surprise. We have arbitrarily chosen to prefix any abstract quantity with "*a*" or "*A*" to assist the reader; the word *FUNCTION* is also arbitrarily transformed to *PROC*. The operations again employ the generic functions of §2.2. The derivation process will be explained mainly by way of illustration; remarks on its formal definition and possible automation appear in §5.1.

3.2. TWO SIMPLE EXAMPLES

Example 1. Implementation of *stack* as *array* using primab *seq*

The implementation is derived by the application of suitable transformations to Figure 9; non-immediate steps will be expanded within the brackets {...} and portions of text which require further derivation will be enclosed within the brackets «...» . Successive steps in such derivations will be denoted by use of ⇒ ; several steps will be denoted by $\overset{*}{\Rightarrow}$.

```
    CTYPE CSTACK (INT n, CTYPE CT|n > 0)             (uses invariant)
      DCL ARRAY (CTYPE, 1,0) cstackrep;              (uses initial value)
  BEGIN
    PROC cpush = (CSTACK cs, CT cx|¬  «pre») ERROR,
                 (CSTACK cs, CT cx| «0 ≤ length(p) <n» ) «p=p' ⊕ x» ;
```

(In order to ensure that each concrete function is total, the derivation will always supply a conditioned function whose body is *ERROR* and whose condition corresponds to the negation of a condition *pre* which is in turn the disjunction of all preconditions in the specifications)

```
{ ¬ «pre»      ⇒  ¬ « 0 ≤ length(p) < n»
               ⇒  ¬ « 0 ≤ length(p)» ∧ «length(p) <n»
               ⇒  ¬  ( «true» ∧ «length(p)<n»)        (invariant)
               ⇒     size (cstackrep) ≥ n         (specs. of length)
               ⇒     size (cstackrep) = n         (invariant)         }
                  *
{ «0 ≤ length(p)<p»  ⇒ size (cstackrep) < n   (similar to previous
                                                          derivation)}

{ «p=p' ⊕ x»  ⇒   «p» := «p ⊕ x»              (assignment axiom)
              ⇒  cstackrep := «p ⊕ x»
              ⇒  extendh (cstackrep, cx)     (using specs. of a primitive
                                              and specs. of extendh)}

   PROC  cpop = (CSTACK cs|cnotempty(cs))  «p = leader(p')»  ;
```

(Since *notempty* is a total function, ¬*pre* is not needed)

```
                 *
{ «p=leader(p')»  ⇒ cstackrep := «leader(p)»         (as before)
                  ⇒ retracth (cstackrep)         (specs of retracth)}
```

(In fact, the last step is rather more complex than stated; it uses the equivalence of *retracth(b)*
and *ARRAY a,b; b:=copy(a); retracth(b); a:=copy(b)*)

```
PROC  ctop = (CSTACK cs|cnotempty (cs))  «last(p')» ;

{ «last(p')» ⇒ fetch (cstackrep, high (cstackrep))    (specs. of last)
             ⇒ last  (cstackrep)   (using unstated theorem for array)}

   *PROC  cnotempty = (CSTACK cs)  «0 < length(p)»

{ «0 < length(p)»   ⇒ 0 < size (cstackrep)}
```

This completes the derivation; the final form of the usconc *cstack* appears in Figure 12.

```
CTYPE CSTACK(INT n, CTYPE CT|n > 0)
  DCL ARRAY (CTYPE, 1,0) cstackrep;
BEGIN
  PROC cpush = (CSTACK cs,CT cx|size(cstackrep)=n)ERROR,
               (CSTACK cs,CT cx|size(cstackrep)<n) extendh(cstackrep,cx);
  PROC cpop  = (CSTACK cs|cnotempty(cs))retracth(cstackrep);
  PROC ctop  = (CSTACK cs|cnotempty(cs))last(cstackrep);
 *PROC cnotempty = (CSTACK cs) 0 < size(cstackrep)
END
```

Figure 12

Final form of the user concrete type *cstack*

Example 2: Implementation of *simp* as *list* using primab *set*.

This derivation is similar to that of example 1 and will be treated quite rapidly.

```
CTYPE  CSIMPL (INT n, CTYPE CT|n ≥ 0)
    DCL   LIST (CT, n) csimplrep := null ;      (using initial value)
BEGIN
    PROC cinsert = (CSIMPL cs, CT cx|¬ «pre» ) ERROR,
                   (CSIMPL cs, CT cx) «m=m' ∪{x}» ;
```

{ ¬ «pre» $\overset{*}{\Rightarrow}$ *length (csimplrep) = n* (much as in example 1)}
{ «m =m' ∪{x}» ⇒ «m» := «m ∪{x}»
⇒ *cs:=* «m ∪{x}»
⇒ *add (csimplrep, ct)* (primitive specification in Fig.8)}

```
    PROC  cremovel = (CSIMPL cs, CT cx| ¬ «pre» ) ERROR,
                     (CSIMPL cs, CT cx)  «m=m'-{x}» ;
```

{ ¬ «pre» ⇒ ¬ «x IN m»
⇒ ¬ *has (csimplrep, cx) ≠ null*}
{ «m = m'-{x}» $\underset{*}{\Rightarrow}$ *cs:=* «m - {x}»
⇒ *cs:= LIST(CT,length(cs))lc:=null;*
take(fill(lc,csimplrep), «{x}»)
and {x} is an abbreviation for Ω ∪{x} so that
«{x}» ⇒ *add (null, cx)* (specs. for ∪) }

```
    PROC  chasl (CSIMPL cs, CT cx) «x IN m»
```

{ «x IN m» ⇒ *has (csimplrep, cx) ≠ null* (as before) }

The hidden operations require no derivation; the final form of the derived concrete type is given in Figure 13.

```
CTYPE CSIMPL(INT n, CTYPE CT|n ≥ 0)
  DCL LIST(CT, n) csimplrep:=null;
BEGIN
  PROC cinsertl=(CSIMPL cs,CT cx|length(csimplrep)=n)ERROR,
                (CSIMPL cs,CT cx)add(csimplrep,ct);
  PROC cremovel=(CSIMPL cs,CT cx|has(csimplrep,cx)=null)ERROR,
                (CSIMPL cs,CT cx|LIST(CT,length(csimplrep))lc:=null)
                       take(fill(lc,csimplrep), add(null,cx));
  PROC chasl   =(CSIMPL cs, CT cx) has (csimplrep,cx) ≠ null;
 *PROC  fill     ¢ copied from Figure 8 ¢;
 *PROC  take     ¢ copied from Figure 8 ¢
END
```

Figure 13

Final form of the user concrete type *csimpl*

3.2. MORE ELABORATE DERIVATIONS

This final example will illustrate more precisely the range of transformations required to perform such derivations. Five different classes of transformations are utilised

i) application of a simple *rewriting rule*, so that the concrete representation is a valid piece of code in the target language

ii) application of an *axiom*, that is a general theorem which is true of all abstract and concrete types

iii) application of a theorem, an abbreviation or the specification of a primitive of one of the types

iv) application of one step of a "calculus" for program derivation. This calculus is fully defined and illustrated in [10] and starts from specifications expressed in first-order logic, deriving corresponding program segments in terms of generic functions, which are, in general, recursive. It should be observed that since our specifications infrequently use quantifiers explicitly, the recursive relationships introduced by applying this calculus will most often appear in a "canned" form .In derivations involving the search implied by specifications using the quantifier "∇" however, the calculus is used in its full form.

v) the introduction of new hidden functions to facilitate the process.

Example 3. Implementation of *simp* as *array* using primab *set*.

```
CTYPE   CSIMPA (INT n, CTYPE CT|n ≥ 0)
  DCL  ARRAY(CTYPE, 1,0)csimparep; (these 2 lines are derived as in ex.1)
BEGIN
  PROC  cinserta = (CSIMPA cs,CT cx|¬ «pre») ERROR,
                   (CSIMPA cs,CT cx)  «m=m' ∪{x}» ;

{ ¬  «pre»  ⇒ «card(m ∪{x})»  = n                   (using invariant)
            ⇒ size («m ∪{x}») = n          (calculus: specs. of card)
            ⇒ size (extendh (csimparep,cx)) = n  (primitive specs.) }
{ «m = m' ∪{x}» *⇒ extendh (csimparep, cx)          (as before) }.

  PROC cremovea = (CSIMPA cs, CT cx|¬ «pre» ) ERROR,
                  (CSIMPA cs, CT cx) «m=m' - {x}» ;

{ ¬  «pre»  ⇒ notin (cx,cs)         (introducing a new hidden function)
  where  *PROC notin = (CT cx,CSIMPA cs| «s=Ω» ) TRUE,
                       (CT cx,CSIMPA cs| «∇(SET s1):s=s1 ∪{x}») FALSE,
                       (CT cx,CSIMPA cs| «∇(SET s1,Tb):s=s1 ∪{b}∧x≠b» )
                                                       ¬ «x IN s1»,
                       (CT cx,CSIMPA cs) TRUE;
```

(these last 4 lines employ the extrinsic specifications of *notin* in Figure 5, applying the calculus; *s* and *x* are, respectively, those instances of the types *set* and *T* corresponding to *cs* and *cx*)

```
{ «s=Ω» ⇒ similar ( «s», «Ω» ) ⇒ similar (csimparep, create (1)) }
{ «∇(SET s1):s=s1 ∪{x}» *⇒ ∇(ARRAY cm):similar(csimparep,extendh(cm,cx))
```

(using the specs. of = for *set* and the specification of a primitive)

```
                ⇒ cx = last (csimparep)
```

(using an *array* theorem and the calculus to search for the appropriate *array*) }

```
{ «∇(SET s1,T b) : s=s1 ∪{b} ∧ x ≠ b»
      ⇒ ARRAY cm := copy(csimparep); retracth(cm); cx≠last(csimparep)
```

(this derivation is not given in detail since it is identical to the previous step, apart from the fact that, since *z* appears in the output assertion, the initialised declaration of *cm* is retained) }

```
{¬ « x IN s1» *⇒ notin (cx, cm)           (as before)} }
{«m = m' - {x}» *⇒ csimparep :=copy(subtract(cs, cx))  (much as before)
   where *PROC subtract = (CSIMPA cs, CT cx) « s = s'-{x}»
      (using s and x as above)
That is *PROC subtract =(CSIMPA cs, CT cx| «s=Ω» ) «Ω» ,
                        (CSIMPA cs, CT cx|« ∇(T a):s={a}∧a IN{b}» )«Ω» ,
                        (CSIMPA cs, CT cx|«∇ (T a):s={a}» )« {a}» ,
                        (CSIMPA cs, CT cx|«∇ (T a,SET z):z≠Ω∧s=z ∪{a}» )
                                « (z-{b}) ∪ ({a}-{b})» ;
```

(applying the calculus to the specification in Figure 5 and using *s* and *b* to denote the *set* and *T* corresponding to *cs* and *cx* in the usual way).

The derivations for ≪ *s*=Ω≫ and ≪Ω≫ have appeared already.

{≪∇ *(T a):s={a}* ∧ *a IN {b}*≫ $\overset{*}{\Rightarrow}$
≪ *card(s)=1*≫ ∧ *similar(csimparep, extendh(create(1),*≪ *a*≫*))* ∧ ≪ *a*≫ = *cx*

(using the calculus, specifications of primitives and one theorem)

$\overset{*}{\Rightarrow}$ *size(csimparep) = 1* ∧ *csimparep [1] = cx*

(using the calculus for *card*, eliminating ≪ *a*≫ and using *array* theorems)}

{≪ ∇*(T a):s={a}*≫ *)* ≪*a*≫ $\overset{*}{\Rightarrow}$ *size(csimparep)=1)csimparep*

(using a derivation virtually identical to the previous one)}

{≪∇ *(T a,SET z): z≠Ω* ∧ *s=z* ∪*{a}*≫

$\overset{*}{\Rightarrow}$≪ ∇*(CT ca,ARRAY cz):* ¬ *similar(cz,create(1))*∧*similar(csimparep,extendh (cz,ca))*≫

$\overset{*}{\Rightarrow}$ *size(csimparep)>1;ARRAY cz:=copy(csimparep);retracth(cz); CT ca:=last(csimparep)*

(using the calculus and a liberal dosage of *array* theorems)}

{≪ *(z-{b})* ∪ *({a}-{b})* ≫ ⇒ *union* (≪ *z-{b}*≫ , ≪ *{a}-{b}*≫ *)*

where the derivation of the hidden function *union* will not be detailed, since it is both lengthy and introduces no fresh ideas.}

{≪ *z-{b}*≫ $\overset{*}{\Rightarrow}$ *subtract (CSIMPA:cz, cx)*}
{≪ *{a}-{b}*≫ ⇒ *(CSIMPA:extendh(create(1),ca),cx)*}

(These two derivations are simple, but introduce a fresh problem. As suggested in §1 one may not assume *ab initio* that there is an instance of the abstract type *CSIMPA* corresponding to the *ARRAY cz*. The "cast" notation (*CSIMPA:cz*) is used to denote the corresponding value *if one exists*. A consistency check requiring the verification of the existence of a concrete fixed point of any procedure involving such a cast is strictly necessary; the details of this are beyond the scope of this paper, but would involve the abstract execution of such procedures.)}

PROC chasa (CSIMPA cs, CT cx) ≪ *x IN m*≫

{≪ *x IN m*≫ ⇒ ¬ *notin (cx,csimparep)* (as before)}

This completes the derivation; the final form of the concrete type appears as Figure 14.

```
CTYPE CSIMPA(INT n, CTYPE CT|n≥0)
  DCL  ARRAY(CTYPE,1,0)csimparep;
BEGIN
  PROC cinserta=(CSIMPA cs,CT cx|size(extendh(csimparep,cx))=n)ERROR,
                (CSIMPA cs,CT cx) extendh(csimparep,cx);
  PROC cremova =(CSIMPA cs,CT cx|notin (cx,cs))ERROR,
                (CSIMPA cs,CT cx)csimparep:=subtract(cx,cs);
  PROC  chasa  =(CSIMPA cs,CT cx) ¬ notin (cx,csimparep);
 *PROC  notin  =(CT cx, CSIMPA cs|similar (csimparep, create (1)))TRUE,
                (CT cx, CSIMPA cs|cx=last (csimparep))FALSE,
                (CT cx, CSIMPA cs|ARRAY cm:=copy(csimparep); retracth(cm);
                       cx ≠ last(csimparep)) notin (cx,cm),
                (CT cx, CSIMPA cs) TRUE;
 *PROC subtract=(CSIMPA cs,CT cx |similar(csimparep,create(1)))create(1),
                (CSIMPA cs,CT cx |size(csimparep)=1∧csimparep[1]=cx)create(1),
                (CSIMPA cs,CT cx |size(csimparep)=1) csimparep,
                (CSIMPA cs,CT cx |size(csimparep)>1)
                     (ARRAY cz:=retracth (copy(csimparep));
                        CT ca : last (csimparep);
 union(subtract(CSIMPA:cz,cx),subtract(CSIMPA:extendh(create(1),ca),cx)));
 *PROC  union  =(CSIMPA cs1,cs2|similar(csimparep.cs2,create(1)))cs1,
                (CSIMPA cs1,cs2)
         union  (CSIMPA: extendh(csimparep.cs1,last(csimparep.cs2)),
                 CSIMPA: retracth(csimparep.cs2))
END
```

Figure 14

Final form of the user concrete type *csimpa*

4. COMPARISON WITH RELATED WORK

4.1. WORK ON DATA TYPE DERIVATION

In [15], Schwartz discusses the automatic derivation of data structures from their specification in terms of (unordered) sets. The approach taken in SETL is to obtain information about the data structure to be derived by applying techniques of data-flow analysis, regarding the SETL program as being in a "very high level" language. This highly successful approach is therefore more appropriately regarded as optimisation than formal derivation.

In [7] the design of a data-type driven method for program synthesis is described. The specification language is Scott's Logic for Computable Functions (LCF) with the addition of sets, quantifiers and types, which appear as *definition schemes*. Thus, at the specification level, the approach is somewhat related to ours, but the goal in von Henke's system is the generation of control structures, rather than concrete types.

The work which is without doubt closest to our own is that of Spitzen and Wegbreit [17] who attempt to perform data-type synthesis by *machine extension*. The specifications proposed are quite similar to ours, although there is not the same clear distinction made between the three "levels" of types. Their synthesis is, in fact, rather closer to the verification philosophy of Alphard; the user being required to give an "implementation" of a type as well as a "correctness condition". We certainly do not dispute their contention that mechanical verification of types is "within the range of or not too distant from state of the art verification systems", whereas "synthesis seems to be substantially harder", but, nonetheless, have preferred to tackle the latter problem here.

5. CONCLUDING REMARKS

5.1. IMPLEMENTABILITY

Nothing whatever of this proposed system has yet been implemented. Each individual stage of the derivation as listed in §3.2 could be readily implemented, but it is in the provision of a means-end analysis for ordering the individual stages that the major question of implementability arises. Our initial implementation plans are for a highly interactive system; it is hoped that the user will play a steadily decreasing role as heuristics are developed and built in.

In addition to the above, several minor items, such as the introduction of subtypes, the role of protection mechanisms and access control of types (as in Alphard) must be considered. The ultimate goal is the incorporation of the synthesis of types as proposed here in a general system for program synthesis. Means for specifying manipulations on and interaction between objects of specific types, and for extending the current derivation techniques to cover these will be studied further.

5.2. INEFFICIENCY AND IMPROVEMENT

The reader will have remarked upon certain glaring inefficiencies in the concrete types derived in Figures 12, 13 and 14. The derivations illustrated in this paper are to be regarded as the first stage of an overall process. In [2] and [4] Burstall and Darlington have defined methods for the improvement of functions defined by recursion equations, and in [10] the application of such techniques to the improvement of programs synthesised in terms of generic functions is shown. A second phase of any derivation would be improvements of this sort to the operations in the derived concrete types. The details of this phase are beyond the scope of this paper, though it may be of interest that improvement of the concrete type *csimpa* of example 3 has been performed.

Acknowledgements.

The ideas discussed here began to form as a result of discussions with S. A. Schuman at IRIA. I am grateful to Donna Bobbie for her help in their presentation, particularly the specifications involving *list*. I also thank the referee for a number of helpful suggestions, particularly in respect to the notations used and the order of presentation of the material. I am also grateful to Mrs. M. Williams for her speedy and accurate typing.
The work was supported by the National Research Council of Canada under Grant number NRC A7308.

REFERENCES

1.Bauer, C.L. and Gnatz, R. (1973). Mengen in algorithmischen Sprachen oder: Arten und Prädikate. Bericht Nr. 7202, Abt. Mathematik der TU München.

2.Burstall, R.M. and Darlington, J. (1975). Some transformations for developing recursive programs, Proceedings International Conference on Reliable Software, Los Angeles, California, pp. 456-472.

3.Dahl, O.J., Myhrhaug, B. and Nygaard, K. (1970). The SIMULA 67 common base language. Publication S-22, Norwegian Computing Centre, Oslo.

4.Darlington, J. (1975). Applications of program transformation to program synthesis. Proceedings Symposium on Proving and Improving Programs, Arc-et-Senans, France, pp. 133-144.

5.Guttag, J.V., Horowitz, E. and Musser, D.R. (1976). Abstract data types and software validation. ISI/RR-76-48, Univ. of Southern California.

6.Guttag, J.V., Horowitz, E. and Musser, D.R. (1977). Some extensions to algebraic specifications. Proceedings A.C.M. Conference on Language Design for Reliable Software, pp. 63-67.

7.Von Henke, F.W. (1975) On generating programs from data types: an approach to automatic programming. Proceedings Symposium on Proving and Improving Programs, Arc-et-Senans, France, pp. 57-69.

8.Hoare, C.A.R. (1972). Proof of correctness of data representations. Acta Informatica 1, 4, pp; 271-281.

9.Hoare, C.A.R. (1972). Notes on data structuring. In Structured Programmin (Dahl, Dijkstra, Hoare) Academic Press.

10.King, P.R. (1976). La synthèse des programmes déterministes par les fonctions génériques. Congrès AFCET Panorama de la nouveauté informatique en France, Gif-sur Yvette, pp. 371-379.

11.Liskov, B. (1975). An introduction to CLU. in New directions in Algorithmic Languages 1975, S. A. Schuman (Ed), Iria, pp. 139-156.

12.Liskov, B. and Zilles, S. (1975). Specification techniques for data abstractions. IEEE Transactions on Software Engineering, SE-1, 1, pp. 7-

13.Parnas, D.L., Handzel, G. and Würges, H. (1976). Design and Specification of the minimal subset of an operating system family IEEE Transactions on Software Engineering, vol. SE-2, No.4, pp. 301-307.

14.Schuman, S.A. (1975). On generic functions. in New directions in Algorithmic Languages 1975, S. A. Schuman (Ed), Iria, pp. 169-192.

15.Schwartz, J.T. (1975). Automatic data structure choice in a language of very high level. Proc. Second ACM Symposium on Principles of Programming Languages , PP. 36-40.

16.Sintzoff, M. (1975). Composing specifications of information structures. in New directions in Algorithmic Languages 1975, S.S. Schuman (Ed), Iria

17.Spitzen, J. and Wegbreit, B. (1975) The verification and synthesis of data structures. Acta Informatica 4. 2 , pp. 127-144.

18.Wulf, W.A., London, R.L. and Shaw, M. (1976). An introduction to the construction and verification of Alphard programs. IEEE Translations on Software Engineering, SE-2, 4 , pp. 253-265.

P. King : Discussion

Mráz: I don't quite see the nature of your specification language. For instance, in ALPHARD I can see it is more or less the predicate calculus and arithmetic. I don't quite see what is the power of your specification language. Could you compare it to something more common?

King, P.: What we are doing here is using what I might call operational specifications, rather than algebraic specifications as used by Guttag and other people. Though the notation is different, these are quite similar to the specifications that are used in ALPHARD. For each of the functions we define its pre- and post-conditions. The pre-conditions are defined as a domain, but I want to write these in a functional notation and therefore I split up the domain into its parameter specification and the other characteristic conditions. So you may regard it all as the pre-condition. In the case of an extrinsic specification, the post-condition is any expression using either the primitives or defined operations for the type at the lower level. For an intrinsic specification, this will be any expression involving the primitives of the intrinsic type, which may be built up recursively, using its operations. So it is an operational specification giving the pre- and post-conditions and, indeed, it is quite close to the ALPHARD mechanism in intent though not in the notation used.

Mráz: If I understood you rightly, you are allowing just one level of hierarchy in constructing abstract data types, because you have to map your abstract data immediately onto the lowest possible level in the target language. Is that right?

King, P.: Yes and no. The way I presented it here, yes. The way it is discussed in the paper and the way I actually see it, no. I considered that there could be several levels of this.

Mráz: Can you automatically provide the transformation from the highest level to the lowest level?

King, P.: That would be the goal, yes.

Holager: It would appear to me that the implementation issue is really central here. The reason why half of the computer scientists in the world are not working on such approaches could be that they feel they cannot achieve a practical implementation. Could you perhaps talk a bit about the perspectives?

King, P.: I agree that the implementation problem is difficult. May I tell you how I think we will approach the implementation problem in a little more detail? For each of the five mechanisms that I spoke about, implementing them all individually is relatively easy; there is no theoretical difficulty in them. The difficulty is, of course, to perform what I might call the means-end analysis for doing this. Our intention is to provide this initially in an entirely interactive system, the user selecting which transformations he wishes, and as heuristics are developed, to build them in. My feeling is that in computer science today's artificial intelligence is tomorrow's compiler. This is strongly evidenced by the work of Burstall and Darlington on transforming recursive programs. Two or three years ago their system was entirely interactive and heuristic; now it is entirely automatic. I think we should proceed along those lines. There was a remark in a recent paper by Spitzen and Wegbreit on the synthesis and verification of data types that whereas verification is almost within our grasp synthesis is still a long way off. One has to agree. But I do not think that is a reason for not tackling the problem.

Constructing Quality Software, P.G. Hibbard/S.A. Schuman (eds.)

INVENTING PROGRAM CONSTRUCTION RULES

Michel Sintzoff

Centre de Recherche en Informatique de Nancy[(1)]

and

MBLE Research Laboratory, Brussels

A synthesis of various, established or tentative, program construction rules is presented. In this synthesis, the attention is concentrated on the way such rules can be invented, rather than on their formal foundations or their effective usefulness. It is shown that related ideas can yield construction rules for apparently quite different types or properties of programs. The programs considered can be sequential, non-deterministic or parallel. A first family of properties is related to the logic of the programs : absence of finite or infinite blind alleys, assurance of termination, absence of deadlock and of starvation, completeness and correctness of signaling. The second family of properties is concerned with economy : effective feasibility of construction rules, simplifications of the conditions of actions, speeding up of the actions, increased independence of parallel actions. Throughout, an effort is also made to show the relationships between construction rules and proof rules, and the recurring rôle of iteration and approximation.

1. INTRODUCTION.

In the course of constructing any quality software, the design of quality algorithms always remains a central activity : this was the case for compilers and operating systems, and is becoming the case for real-time systems or distributed computing. The present paper investigates some aspects in the discipline of program construction. It is a bit strange and distressing to witness that much energy in designing actual techniques and languages for software support, often remains concentrated on the analysis, the processing or the verification of programs, not primarily their construction as such. Systematic program design was already well advocated ten years ago but, alas,

---

(1) during 1977 and with the support of the Centre National de la Recherche Scientifique, France.

the main axis of the corresponding technical and formal work remained the study of a posteriori proof rules for programs : compare Dijkstra (1968) with Dijkstra (1976). To be sure, many works are concerned with automated or interactive program synthesis and transformation : they are relevant to program design by providing ideas of systematic construction rules, by shedding light on the equivalence between massaged programs, and by showing the difficulty of automation in this field. However, these techniques are often heuristic, their effect on the logic or the economy of programs is either neutral or not measured, and they are applicable mainly for deterministic, iterative and recursive programs. We also need techniques which, by their very nature, *ensure* required global properties, which cover the important types of programs, and which are convergent in the sense that the more they are applied, the better the programs become.

The name of the game in program design is often "proof rule" : we are told to construct a program such that it can be proved to be correct with respect to given initial and final conditions. This too implicit a method of programming is not always helpful. Instead of formally describing properties of programs, we should constructively prescribe properties to programs. We propose to design construction rules by using plain common sense. We start by stating what is the property to be achieved by a program, for example absence of starvation or logarithmic speed ; that statement can well use the expressive tools of verification rules or complexity analysis. We then naïvely deduce from that platonic statement a constructive rule of program formation ; using that rule, even without much ingenuity, we should be able to achieve the desired property ; moreover, that rule should permit to derive programs which are suboptimal , but still adequate, in the case the perfect solutions are too difficult. Our main theses are thus the following ones : many sucessful, effective, by now classical, techniques for program analysis and verification can and must be reconsidered as tools for construction and synthesis ; naïvety and laziness are often the best foundations in finding formation rules ; convergence and approximation seem to be prerequisites for realizability.

The range of the paper being already overextended enough, we shall omit the data component in the well-known equation "Programs = Data + Algorithms", and develop instead the equation "Algorithms = Conditions + Actions". Our programs are made of a set of rules each of which consists of a condition of applicability and an action to be performed. This very pure program structure is classical in the old theory of algorithms; it has been used consistently by workers in parsing, artificial intelligence or Petri nets ; it has been recently promoted in programming methodology circles ; it can partly model sequential, non-deterministic or parallel programs ; it can even be related to ways of expressing axioms for data structures. The program properties we consider correspond not only to the logical soundness of programs but also to the economy of their use. Typical aspects of correctness are, for sequential programs, the assurance of success, and, for parallel programs, the assurance of permanent operation and cooperation. As to the economical qualities, we shall consider, in the sequential case, the simplicity of the conditions and the speed of the actions, whereas, in the parallel programs, we will try to increase the degree of permissible parallelism.

The paper aims at presenting a unified synthesis of various methods which have been already established or are tentatively proposed here. It represents thus a risky snapshot of a research in progress (hopefully), and is intended to study the problems and the principles rather than formal technicalities or great examples of programs. Still, a minimum of formal tools is required to convey the essential ideas : the programs are the most formal objects produced by man since they must be processed by machines, and formal rigour is often an excellent logical parapet. However, in order to prevent premature obscurity and complexity, we shall try to avoid any formal smoke or technical overkilling, and we will justify certain results by the intuitive physics of the problem, in place of detailed proofs ; this perilous approach should be vindicated or contradicted by foundational studies to be made elsewhere or by others. Incidentally, we somewhat misuse here the term "construction rules"; in fact, we form better programs on the basis of crude ones, and human intuition is not at all eliminated : we should rather speak of possibly constructive guidelines for program design; yet, our hope is to reduce the intensity and the density of the necessary intuition.

The main examples of this paper are in fact construction rules as such. The program examples serve only to illustrate the functioning of these rules, and are mostly academic and artificial, if not childish ; nevertheless, various significative examples from the classical folklore have been derived using some of the proposed methods. Each section ends with a discussion intended to show intriguing relationships, to evaluate pros and cons, and to indicate some relevant literature.

The first Sections of the paper are concerned with logical properties of non-deterministic sequential programs : rules are given for constructing programs which successfully reach a given goal, i.e. which avoid finite (Section 2) and infinite (Section 3) blind alleys. Next, the feasibility of the methods proposed is enhanced by using approximation principles in the program construction process (Section 4). The economy of sequential programs is increased by simplifying the conditions of actions when a given origin can be taken into account (Section 5) and, more importantly, by iteratively speeding up the given actions (Section 6). Section 7 summarizes and discusses known techniques for ensuring the logical correctness of parallel programs (deadlock and starvation prevention, correct and complete signaling). Section 8 investigates how the amount of parallelism could be systematically increased. Section 9 presents a number of conclusions. The references given at the end are incomplete : they do not point to important papers in program synthesis, transformation, or verification; yet, they include some related papers on complexity analysis, on distributed control, and on approximation methods.

We list here a few notations and auxiliary definitions for the first Sections. A program $\underline{S}$ is a set $\|_i S_i$ of rules (or conditioned actions) S_i, i=1...N. Each rule S_i has the form "condition → action". Each condition A_i is a boolean expression on the variables. Each action s_i is a set of concurrent assignments such as "x_1:=E_1, x_2:=E_2" : the expressions E_i are first evaluated, and then their values are assigned to the corresponding variables. A goal Q and an origin P are predicates. For example, the gcd program can be formulated as follows :

Program $\underline{S}$: [$x>y \rightarrow x:=x-y \mid x<y \rightarrow y:=y-x$]
Goal Q : $x=y$.
Origin P : $x>0 \wedge y>0$.

Thus, the rules S_i of a program [$A_1 \rightarrow s_1 \mid \ldots \mid A_N \rightarrow s_N$] are applicable iteratively. It is straightforward to rewrite in that form most sequential program built by use of serial composition, non-deterministic choice, and iteration : it suffices to introduce auxiliary variables as program counters and to push all the inside conditions outside. We shall also use the following definitions of old predicate transformers :

$$\text{pre}(\,\|_i\, S_i,\ R) = \bigvee_i \text{pre}(S_i,\ R) \tag{1.1}$$
$$\text{pre}(A \rightarrow s,\ R) = A \wedge \text{pre}(s,\ R)$$
$$\text{pre}(x{:=}E,\ R) = \exists \bar{x}{:}R[\bar{x}/x] \wedge \bar{x}{=}E \equiv R[E/x]$$
$$\text{pre}((x_1{:=}E_1,\ldots,x_m{:=}E_m),\ R) = R[E_1/x_1,\ldots,E_m/x_m]$$

$$\text{post}(\,\|_i\, S_i,\ R) = \bigvee_i \text{post}(S_i,\ R) \tag{1.2}$$
$$\text{post}(A \rightarrow s,\ R) = \text{post}(s,\ A{\wedge}R)$$
$$\text{post}(x{:=}E,\ R) = \exists \hat{x}{:}R[\hat{x}/x] \wedge x{=}E[\hat{x}/x]$$
$$\text{post}((x_1{:=}E_1,\ldots,x_m{:=}E_m),\ R) = \exists\, \hat{x}_1\ldots\hat{x}_m{:}R[\hat{x}_1/x_1,\ldots,\hat{x}_m/x_m] \wedge \bigwedge_j x_j{=}E_j[\hat{x}_1/x_1,\ldots,\hat{x}_m/x_m]$$

The fact that a logical union corresponds to a set $\|_i S_i$ is easy to understand : pre($\underline{S}$,R) defines the initial states from which R *can* be reached by *one* application of $\underline{S}$, and post($\underline{S}$,R) characterizes the final states which can be reached by one application of $\underline{S}$ from a state R. Thus, pre($\underline{S}$,R) differs as follows from the weakest precondition wp($\underline{S}$,R) given in Dijkstra (1976) : wp($\underline{S}$,R) is also defined for iterated applications, and it determines the set of states from which R *can and must* always be reached by repeated applications of $\underline{S}$. It is easy to see that

$$\text{pre}(\underline{S},\ \bigwedge_k R_k) = \bigwedge_k \text{pre}(\underline{S},\ R_k) \text{ if } R_{k+1} \Rightarrow R_k,\quad k=1,\ldots,\infty \tag{1.3}$$
$$\text{pre}(\underline{S},\ \bigvee_k R_k) = \bigvee_k \text{pre}(\underline{S},R_k) \qquad k=1,\ldots,\infty$$

and similarly for post.

2. AVOIDING DEAD-ENDS.

We begin by seeking after rules for constructing programs which are successful, in the sense they *must* eventually reach a given goal when they are applied. We may express this requirement in terms of two other ones : first, there may be no dead-end, or finite blind alley, viz. after any application of any program action the goal is reached or the condition of some action becomes valid ; second, there may be no infinite blind alley, i.e. there is no way to apply the program actions infinitely often without ever reaching the goal. In this Section, we propose a very simple way to form programs which avoid dead-ends, that is which verify the first subrequirement. Moreover, throughout the paper, we assume to be given a set of preliminary rules. This is acceptable because many problems can be stated by defining initial and final conditions and by giving a set of primitive, permissible actions. The drawback of such an assumption is that these initially given actions may lead to very inefficient programs : we shall attack this crucial problem in Sections 5 and 6. Until then, our task boils down to the construction of conditions protecting the given actions in such a way that the logical success is guaranteed.

Thus, our present problem is, given a goal Q and a preliminary set $\underline{S}$ of rules $S_i = A_i \rightarrow s_i$, to derive a program $\underline{T}$ with rules $T_i = B_i \rightarrow s_i$; these differ from the preliminary S_i only in that each A_i is strenghtened into a new condition B_i in such a way that no dead-end can be reached. This means that, after applying any T_i, the goal Q is reached or some T_j can be applied again i.e. some B_j is reached. In short, for i,j=1...N,

$$B_i \Rightarrow A_i$$

$$B_i \Rightarrow \text{pre}(T_i, \bigvee_j B_j \vee Q)$$

These implications amount to $B_i \Rightarrow A_i \wedge \text{pre}(s_i, \bigvee_j B_j \vee Q)$, i.e.

$$B_i \Rightarrow \text{pre}(S_i, BB) \text{ where } BB \equiv \bigvee_j B_j \vee Q \qquad (2.1)$$

It remains to see how to construct decent solutions of the system (2.1). The solutions $B_i \equiv \underline{\text{false}}$ verify (2.1) trivially. We should thus find "good" solutions. Let us then try to find the best ones. We remember that, if f is a continuous function in a lattice, the maximal solution of $x \leq fx$ is the maximal solution of $x=fx$; see, for example, Park (1969). Then, recalling the Picard-Knaster-Kantorovich-Tarski-Birkhoff-Kleene results, we compute

$$\begin{array}{lll} (\text{max}) & B_i = \text{pre}(S_i, BB) & \\ \text{by} & B_i^0 := \underline{\text{true}} & i,j=1...N \\ & B_i^{n+1} := \text{pre}(S_i, BB^n) & BB^n \equiv \bigvee_j B_j^n \vee Q \, . \\ & B_i = \bigwedge_{n=0}^{\infty} B_i^n = \forall n : n \geq 0 : B_i^n & \end{array} \qquad (2.2)$$

Note that all the solutions, i.e. not just the optimal ones, can be constructed by simply building the iterates according to

$$B_i^{n+1} \Rightarrow pre(S_i, BB^n)$$

This will be investigated in Section 4.

As an example, consider the goal $Q \equiv (x=2)$ and the preliminary rules

$$\underline{S} = [\, 0 \leqslant x \leqslant 1 \rightarrow x:=x+2 \mid 0 \leqslant x \leqslant 1 \rightarrow x:=x+1 \mid 0 \leqslant x \leqslant 1 \rightarrow x:=x-1]$$

Then, $B_i^0 := \underline{true}$, $BB^0 := \underline{true}$

$B_i^1 := 0 \leqslant x \leqslant 1$, $BB^1 := 0 \leqslant x \leqslant 2$.

$B_1^2 := x=0$, $B_2^2 := 0 \leqslant x \leqslant 1$, $B_3^2 := x=1$, $BB^2 := 0 \leqslant x \leqslant 2$

Since $BB^1 = BB^2$, we have $B_i^2 = B_i^3 = B_i$. Hence,

$$\underline{T} = [\, x=0 \rightarrow x:=x+2 \mid 0 \leqslant x \leqslant 1 \rightarrow x:=x+1 \mid x=1 \rightarrow x:=x-1] \;.$$

The dead-ends, such as $x=0 \rightarrow x=-1 \rightarrow\ ?$, permitted by $\underline{S}$ are avoided by $\underline{T}$. However, $\underline{T}$ still allows the cycle $x=0 \rightarrow x=1 \rightarrow x=0$: this produces an infinite blind alley which never reaches $x=2$.

If the iteration (2.2) converges in two steps on $B_i \equiv A_i$, then we simply verify that the initial $\underline{S}$ already did avoid dead-ends. If (2.2) yields $B_i \equiv \underline{false}$, this means that no solution can be found: the actions of $\underline{S}$ always fall in a dead-end.;this is the case for $Q=(x=5)$ and $\underline{S} = [\, x < 3 \rightarrow x:=x+1]$.

The problem of avoiding dead-ends was studied in Sintzoff (1976) but then solved by another, approximated method discussed in Section 4. Method (2.2) is surprisingly simple in comparison.

If the B_j are maximal solutions of (2.1),then BB is the maximal solution of

$$BB \Rightarrow Q \vee pre(\underline{S}, BB) \tag{2.3}$$

This begins to remind of the way Dijkstra (1976) builds the weakest precondition ensuring termination on Q of iterated $\underline{S}$: it is the minimal solution of

$$(min) \qquad H = Q \vee wp(\underline{S}', H)$$

where $\underline{S}'$ is $\underline{if}\ A_1' \rightarrow s_1 \parallel \ldots \parallel A_N' \rightarrow s_N\ \underline{fi}$ and $A_i' = A_i \wedge \neg Q$. Let us then see what mean the *minimal* solutions of

$$(min) \qquad B_i = pre(S_i, BB)$$

They are derived by

$$B_i^0 := \underline{\text{false}} \qquad (2.4)$$
$$B_i^{n+1} := \text{pre}\ (S_i, BB^n)$$
$$B_i = \bigvee_{n=0}^{\infty} B_i^n = \exists n : n \geq 0 : B_i^n$$

In this case, BB is the minimal solution of

$$(\text{min}) \qquad BB = Q \vee \text{pre}(\underline{S}, BB) \qquad (2.5)$$

If we develop the first iterates (2.4), we easily see that the minimal B_i say not only that dead-ends are avoided but also that the goal Q *can* always be reached, i.e. there always exists *at least one* path leading to Q by $\underline{T}$ when starting on such a B_i. In case $\underline{S}$ is deterministic ($A_i \Rightarrow \neg A_j$ if $i \neq j$), finding the solutions (2.4) amounts to ensuring Q is always reached, and this can be much harder than the computation of (2.2). Consider for instance $Q=(x=1)$ and the well-known, stumbling-block rules $\underline{S}= [\, x \text{ \underline{mod} } 2=1 \wedge x >1 \rightarrow x:=x/2 \mid x \text{ \underline{mod} } 2=1 \wedge x >1 \rightarrow x:=3x+1]$; applying (2.2) yields immediately $\underline{T}=\underline{S}$, but (2.4) has not been computed. Note finally that it is an exercise in lattice theory to prove that the solutions by (2.4) solve (2.1), and are safely approximated (§4) by $B_i^{n+1} \Rightarrow \text{pre}(S_i, BB^n)$.

3. AVOIDING INFINITE BLIND ALLEYS.

By infinite blind alleys, we mean infinite successions of applications of actions which never reach Q. Recall that to always reach Q amounts to avoid finite blind alleys, viz. dead-ends, as well as infinite ones. Again, we are given a goal Q and a preliminary set $\underline{S}$ of conditioned actions. We now want to derive a program $\underline{T}$, on the basis of Q and $\underline{S}$, such that no infinite blind alley is possible with $\underline{T}$. A naïve approach is to find out what are the infinite blind alleys allowed by $\underline{S}$, and then to eliminate them. When we follow such infinite paths, we go through a set of subconditions C_i of A_i such that each C_i excludes the goal Q and that the corresponding action s_i sends on some C_j again. In a word, there exist C_i which imply A_i, which preserve $\neg Q$ and which are "sendable" on $\bigvee_j C_j$. Formally, any set of C_i permitting infinite blind alleys in $\underline{S}$, is a non-empty solution, for i,j=1...N, of the system

$$C_i \Rightarrow \text{pre}(S_i, CC) \wedge \neg Q \quad \text{where} \quad CC = \bigvee_j C_j \qquad (3.1)$$

But this is only a diagnostic. We still need the cure. A naïve idea is simply to replace A_i by $A_i \wedge \neg C_i$ in $\underline{S}$, and then to look for any remaining infinite unsuccessful path. This idea is too naïve because restricting all the A_i may be excessive : for example, in order to cut a two-step cycle $x=0 \rightarrow x=1 \rightarrow x=0$, it is necessary to delete only one of the transitions $x=0 \rightarrow x=1$ or $x=1 \rightarrow x=0$, not both of them. We are thus led to the following method ; $i,j=1...N$:

Begin : $B_i := A_i$ (3.2)

Iterate: Find some C_i, not all false, such that

$$C_i \Rightarrow pre(B_i \rightarrow s_i, CC) \wedge \neg Q, \text{ with } CC = \bigvee_j C_j \;;$$

Choose some C_i', not all false, such that $C_i' \Rightarrow C_i$;

$B_i := B_i \wedge \neg C_i'$

End when all possible C_i's are false.

This scheme constructs new iterates B_i by "destructing" parts of conditions C_i which are included in the previous iterates B_i and which permit infinite blind paths. Note that these C_i need not at all be maximal.

Let us apply (3.2) for the goal $Q=(x=2)$ and the rules $\underline{S}= [\,0 \rightarrow +2 \mid 0,1 \rightarrow +1 \mid 1 \rightarrow -1 \mid 3 \rightarrow -2\,]$; the second rule, for example, should be read as $x=0 \vee x=1 \rightarrow x:=x+1$.

Begin : $B_1:=0$, $B_2:=0,1$, $B_3:=1$, and $B_4:=3$; read $B_2:=(x=0 \vee x=1)$.

Iteration 1 : We may find

$$C_1 := \underline{false},\ C_2:=0,\ C_3:=1,\ C_4:=3,\ CC:=0,1,3$$

Indeed, $[\,\underline{false} \rightarrow +2 \mid 0 \rightarrow +1 \mid 1 \rightarrow -1 \mid 3 \rightarrow -2\,]$ goes on forever without reaching $(x=2)$. We choose

$$C_1' = C_3' = C_4' = \underline{false} \text{ and } C_2' = (x=0) \;.$$

Hence $B_1:=0$, $B_2:=1$, $B_3:=1$, $B_4:=3$.

Iteration 2 : All possible C_i are now false. Thus, we *end*.

The resulting program $\underline{T}$ is

$$[\,0 \rightarrow +2 \mid 1 \rightarrow +1 \mid 1 \rightarrow -1 \mid 3 \rightarrow -2\,] \;.$$

Consider now other choices of C_i' in *Iteration 1*. If $C_1'=C_4' = \underline{false}$, $C_2'=(x=0)$, $C_3'=(x=1)$, the solution obtained does well avoid infinite blind alleys but is suboptimal : the transition $x=1 \rightarrow x=0$ is unnecessarily excluded. If $C_1' = C_2' = C_4' = \underline{false}$ and $C_3'=(x=1)$, we obtain still another solution which is as optimal as the first one above : no transition can be added without introducing a possibility of cycle ; thus, the problem of avoiding infinite blind alleys has *no unique weakest solutions* in general. Another choice could be $C'_1 = C'_2 = C'_3 =$ false, $C'_4=(x=3)$: it is a bad one because it does not cut the cycle but instead eliminates a state from which Q can be reached ; it would be prevented if the C_i were minimal.

It is wiser not to use the scheme (3.2) . Indeed, to find optimal solutions, it is advisable, at each iteration, to derive only minimal C_i and then to choose $C'_k = C_k$ for one k, and $C'_j =$ false for $j \neq k$. This is slow and not practical. Nevertheless, assume for a while we can use this method to avoid infinite blind alleys. Then, we can obtain as follows a program which reaches Q always : first, we apply (3.2) to eliminate infinite blind alleys from the initial $\underline{S}$, and we obtain, say, $\underline{T}'$; second, we use (2.2) starting with $\underline{T}'$, in order to prevent any dead-end ; the resulting program always reaches Q.

If we simply want to verify that a given $\underline{S} = \|_i \; A_i \rightarrow s_i$ does always reach Q, we just have to verify that $\underline{S}$ avoids finite and infinite blind alleys. Formally, for i=1...N, we verify

$$A_i \Rightarrow BB \wedge \neg CC \tag{3.3}$$

where BB and CC are the maximal solutions of

$$\text{(max)} \qquad BB = Q \vee pre(\underline{S}, BB)$$

$$\text{(max)} \qquad CC = \neg Q \wedge pre(\underline{S}, CC)$$

Moreover, the domain K from which Q is always reached by $\underline{S}$, can be defined in terms of these maximal solutions, viz.

$$K = Q \vee BB \wedge \neg CC$$

Recall that the maximal solution of $BB=Q \vee pre(\underline{S},BB)$ is implied by the minimal solution EE of $EE=Q \vee pre(\underline{S},EE)$. On the other hand, if x is the maximal solution of x=fx and if $y= \neg x$, then y is the minimal solution of $y= \neg f \neg y$. Thus, if $DD= \neg CC$, we know DD is the minimal solution of $DD=Q \vee \neg pre(\underline{S}, \neg DD)$. Let us then consider the minimal solution H' of

$$\text{(min)} \qquad H' = Q \vee pre(\underline{S},H') \wedge \neg\, pre(\underline{S}, \neg H')$$

We remark that, for our simple actions s_i and for "wp" of Dijkstra (1976),

$$\begin{aligned} pre(\underline{S},R) \wedge \neg\, pre(\underline{S}, \neg R) &= \bigvee_i [A_i \wedge pre(s_i,R)] \wedge \bigwedge_i [A_i \Rightarrow \neg pre(s_i, \neg R)] \\ &= (\bigvee_i A_i) \wedge \bigwedge_i [A_i \Rightarrow pre(s_i,R)] \\ &= wp(\text{IF}_i\; A_i \rightarrow s_i,\; R) \end{aligned}$$

Thus H' is equal to the weakest precondition H ensuring termination on Q of the iterated S ; the distinction between terminating on Q and reaching Q is secondary here, and depends only on the replacing of A_i by $A_i \wedge \neg Q$ in S. In spite of these interesting similarities, it remains to find out how or when the equivalence between K and H' can be proved formally.

The system (3.1) is close to the one given in van Lamsweerde and Sintzoff (1976) for preventing deadlocks : then, $Q \equiv$ false and the maximal solutions are the ones to be constructed ; this is quite simple when compared with the iterative destruction (3.2) of minimal solutions.

4. APPROXIMATING THE FORMATION RULES.

We concluded the presentation of the rather crazy method (3.2) by advising not to use it. What can we do ? The naïve answer is to trade perfection and infeasibility for imperfection and feasibility, that is to accept approximated solutions. In Sections 2 and 3, the iterates B_i^n are constructed by starting from the top A_i and by imposing successive restrictions. Now, we start from nothing, viz. false, and we successively add extensions D_i^{n+1} to the iterates B_i^n, yielding B_i^{n+1}. Thus, instead of deleting undesirable states as before, we add desirable ones, and, more importantly, we do it without looking for optimal solutions. Our aim is to have a simple iterative scheme with which we always can derive new conditions ensuring that the goal is reached ; we do accept that these new conditions can be very poor. The basic idea is simple enough. Each addition D_i^{n+1} must be both useful and safe : it should send on one of the previous iterates in order to prevent dead-ends, and it should exclude the creation of infinite paths which avoid the goal. The first requirement is well expressed by the term $pre(S_i, BB^n)$. The second one is the difficult one, as we saw in Section 3. Let us then try to find a sufficient requirement to approximate it. Such an approximation is simply $\neg BB^n$: then, BB^{n+1} contains states (i) from which Q can be reached in n steps or less, because of $pre(S_i, BB^n)$, and (ii) from which Q cannot be reached in more than n steps, because $\neg BB^n$ is imposed on each addition D_i^{n+1}. In summary,

$$B_i^0 := \underline{false}$$

$$B_i^{n+1} := B_i^n \vee D_i^{n+1} \qquad D_i^{n+1} \Rightarrow pre(S_i, BB^n) \wedge \neg BB^n \qquad (4.1)$$

$$BB^n = \bigvee_j B_j^n \vee Q$$

$$B_i = \bigvee_{n=0}^{\infty} B_i^n = \exists n : n \geq 0 : B_i^n$$

Another way to understand the conjunct $\neg BB^n$ is to notice it forbids detours: no state already present in the wave BB^n may be taken in any new addition D_i^{n+1} ; thus, as soon as a path has been established from some state to the goal, no longer path between that state and the goal can be included.
A third way to look at D_i^{n+1} is to consider a predicate gain(S,R) defining in which cases S transforms $\neg R$ into R, viz.

$$\text{gain}(S,R) = \neg R \wedge \text{pre}(S,R) \qquad (4.2)$$

Then :

$$D_i^{n+1} \Rightarrow \text{gain}(S_i, BB^n) \qquad \text{I.e.:} \begin{cases} B_i^n \Rightarrow B_i^{n+1} \\ B_i^{n+1} \Rightarrow B_i^n \vee \text{gain}(S_i, BB^n) \end{cases}$$

The additions D_i^{n+1} must represent an effective progress towards the previous iterates.

Assume $\underline{S} = [0 \rightarrow +2 \mid 0,1 \rightarrow +1 \mid 1 \rightarrow -1]$ and Q : 2 . Read Q ≡ (x=2).
The application of (4.1) yields

B_i^0 := <u>false</u>, BB^0 := 2

$D_1^1 \Rightarrow 0$, $D_2^1 \Rightarrow 1$, $D_3^1 \Rightarrow$ <u>false</u>. We take the maximal D_i^1 , (they are simple) :

$B_1^1 := 0$, $B_2^1 := 1$, B_3^1 := <u>false</u>, $BB^1 := 0,1,2$.

Since all $D_i^2 \Rightarrow$ <u>false</u>, $B_i \equiv B_i^1$. The resulting program

$\underline{T} = [0 \rightarrow +2 \mid 1 \rightarrow +1 \mid \underline{\text{false}} \rightarrow -1]$ unnecessarily excludes the transition $0 \rightarrow +1$ or $1 \rightarrow -1$, but is obtained without much ado.

As an additional exercise, let us consider Q=(x=1) and the stumbling-block
$\underline{S} = [\, x \ \underline{\text{mod}}\ 2{=}0 \rightarrow x{:=}x/2 \mid x\ \underline{\text{mod}}\ 2{=}1 \rightarrow x := 3x+1]$.

B_i^0 := <u>false</u>, BB^0 := (x=1).

$D_1^1 \Rightarrow (x{=}2)$, $D_2^1 \Rightarrow$ <u>false</u>. Choose $D_1^1 := (x{=}2)$, lest a void solution be found:

$B_1^1 := (x{=}2)$, B_2^1 := <u>false</u>, $BB^1 := (x{=}1 \vee x{=}2)$.

$D_1^2 \Rightarrow (x{=}4)$, $D_2^2 \Rightarrow$ <u>false</u>. Choose $D_1^2 := (x{=}4)$, lest a finite solution be foun

$B_1^2 := (x{=}2 \vee x{=}4)$, B_2^2 := <u>false</u>, $BB^2 := (x{=}1 \vee x{=}2 \vee x{=}4)$.

An easy guess is $D_1^n := x{=}2^n$, D_2^n := <u>false</u>

Then $\qquad B_1^n := \bigvee_{k=1}^{n} x{=}2^k$, B_2^n := <u>false</u>, $BB^n = \bigvee_{k=0}^{n} x{=}2^k$.

The quality of such choices depends on the available induction power.
We check the guess :

$$D_1^{n+1} \Rightarrow x{=}2^{n+1},\ D_2^{n+1} \Rightarrow \ldots.$$

Hence, $D_1^{n+1} := (x{=}2^{n+1})$ and D_2^{n+1} :=<u>false</u> are acceptable. The program obtained is

$$[\text{is power of two}(x) \rightarrow x:=x/2 \mid \underline{\text{false}} \rightarrow x:=3x+1] \ .$$

This is a correct but poor solution ; yet, it is better than a perfect but unverified solution.

Various policies are allowed by (4.1). A Jacobi policy would be to choose $D_i^n \neq \underline{\text{false}}$ whenever possible. A Gauss-Seidel policy would be to choose $D_k^n \neq \underline{\text{false}}$ for $k=n$ mod N, if possible, and $D_j^n = \underline{\text{false}}$ for $j \neq n$ mod N. The choice of such policies influence the speed of convergence as well as the nature of the solutions. If, in (4.1), we choose the maximal D_i^{n+1} at each step, then the resulting B_i are obtained by

$$B_i^{n+1} = B_i^n \vee \text{gain}(S_i, BB^n) \quad \text{(Jacobi policy)} \tag{4.3}$$

and BB is thus the minimal solution of

$$\text{(min)} \qquad BB = Q \vee BB \vee \bigvee_i \text{gain}(S_i, BB) \tag{4.4}$$

$$= Q \vee BB \vee \bigvee_i \text{pre}(S_i, BB) \wedge \neg BB \wedge \neg Q$$

$$= Q \vee BB \vee \text{pre}(\underline{S}, BB)$$

This is equivalent to the equation (2.5) since the minimal solution of $x = x \vee fx$ is that of $x=fx$ for f continuous. Thus, (4.3) yields solutions which include all states from which the initial $\underline{S}$ may lead to Q ; of course, transitions can still be unnecessarily excluded. By construction, the iterates BB^n according to (4.1) imply the iterates BB^n by (4.4), and, thus, they yield approximations from below. Indeed, if f is continuous, $u^0=x^0$, $x^{n+1}=fx^n$, $u^n \Rightarrow u^{n+1}$, $u^{n+1} \Rightarrow fu^n$, $x = \bigvee_{n=0}^{\infty} x^n$, and $u = \bigvee_{n=0}^{\infty} u^n$, then $u \Rightarrow x$. Approximations from above would be given by $x^0=v^0$, $v^n \Rightarrow v^{n+1}$, $fv^n \Rightarrow v^{n+1}$, $v = \bigvee_{n=0}^{\infty} v^n$; then, $x \Rightarrow v$. The approximations from above are thus unsafe since they are not necessarily contained in the complete and correct solution. Nevertheless, they can be used for measuring the quality of approximations since an upper bound of the discrepancy between u and x is that between u and v. These matters are investigated by Sintzoff (1977).

The unsafe approximations from above, associated with (4.3), for a Gauss-Seidel policy, were given in Sintzoff (1976) for eliminating dead-ends. Similar approximation principles, established independently for automated static bound checking, are investigated in depth by Cousot and Cousot (1977). A close variant of (4.3) and its properties are developed by van Lamsweerde and Sintzoff (1976) and used by van Lamsweerde (1977). The solutions yielded by method (4.1) should verify the system

$$B_i \Rightarrow H$$

$$\text{(min)} \qquad H = Q \vee wp(\underset{i}{IF}\ B_i \rightarrow s_i, H)$$

See direct, formal proofs of this fact in Scholten (1977). Remark that not all solutions by (4.1) are contained in those by (4.3).

5. SIMPLIFYING THE CONDITIONS GIVEN AN ORIGIN.

Until now, we improved the conditions of actions by taking into account the goal to be reached. The conditions thus obtained can be costly because, in fact, they are invariant conditions valid for many initial states. Let us then assume that an origin P is given in addition. We ask for the weakest conditions ensuring the initially given conditions when starting on *that* origin P. This simplification problem has an easy enough solution, which is refreshing. We are given $S = \underset{i}{\|}\ A_i \rightarrow s_i$ and an origin P, and we want to derive $\underline{T} = \underset{i}{\|}\ B_i \rightarrow s_i$ such that

$$B_i \wedge L \Rightarrow A_i \qquad (5.1)$$

where L expresses the fact the actions of $\underline{S}$ are applied starting on P. This predicate L is nothing but the minimal solution of

$$\text{(min)} \qquad L = P \vee post(\underline{S}, L) \qquad (5.2)$$

computed by

$$L^0 := \underline{false}$$

$$L^{n+1} := P \vee post(\underline{S}, L^n)$$

$$L = \bigvee_{n=0}^{\infty} L^n$$

This L defines the set of all states reachable from P by $\underline{S}$. The solutions B_i of (5.1) are defined as well by

$$B_i \Rightarrow A_i \vee \neg L$$

Note again that, by construction, each B_i implies A_i when P is the initial state ; thus, if the A_i ensure a goal Q is reached, then the B_i ensure that also. If useful, we may approximate L from below by $L^{n+1} \Rightarrow f(L^n)$.

As an exercise, consider an origin $P=(x=1 \wedge y=0)$ and the program $\underline{S} = [\ x<5 \wedge y<5 \rightarrow x:=x+1,\ y:=y+2]$. It is easy to compute

$$L = (x=1 \wedge y=0) \vee (x=2 \wedge y=2) \vee (x=3 \wedge y=4) \vee (x=4 \wedge y=6)$$

Then $B_1 \Rightarrow x\neq 4 \vee y\neq 6$. There are two acceptable weakest conditions : $B_1=(x\neq 4)$ or $B_1=(y\neq 6)$. Thus, we have here another construction problem without unique weakest solution.

Let us now combine the methods (4.1) and (5.1). We are given a goal $Q=(x=\text{factorial}(a))$, an origin $P=(x=1 \wedge i=1)$, and the crude program $\underline{S}$ = [$\underline{\text{true}}$ → x:=x ×(i+1), i := i+1] . We first propagate Q in the condition by the backwards iterations (4.1) and obtain, among others and with $a \geq 1$,

$\underline{S}'$ = [$x=\text{factorial}(i) \wedge 0 < i < a$ → x:=x×(i+1), i:=i+1]

which ensures Q is reached. The new condition is of course unacceptably rich. Let us then diffuse the origin P by the forward iterations (5.2). We obtain

$$L = (x=\text{factorial}(i)) \wedge i \leq a \wedge i > 0$$

and $B_1 \Rightarrow i\neq a \vee x \neq \text{factorial}(i)$.

There are two solutions : $B_1=(i\neq a)$, or $B_1=(x\neq \text{factorial}(i))$.
The second one is degenerate because it satisfies (5.1) vacuously since then $B_1 \wedge L$ = $\underline{\text{false}}$. A simple way to prevent this is to require $P \Rightarrow Q \vee \bigvee_i B_i$.
Our final program is

$\underline{T}$ = [i≠a → x:=x (i+1), i:=i+1] .
P : x=1 ∧ i=1. Q:x = factorial(a).

The method developed hereabove is an alternative to what is often done, namely (i) to discover a decomposition of the goal Q into an invariant part I and a variant part $\overline{B}$, (ii) to deduce actions which preserve I, (ii) to find a termination function in order to prove that $\overline{B}$ always must eventually become true, and (iv) to deduce an initial action for guaranteeing I at the beginning. The method given here can be useful when the problem specifications imply a natural definition of an origin P, and when (4.1) and (5.1) can be used to produce solutions which are non-trivial even if approximated.

6. SPEEDING UP THE ACTIONS.

Sections 2 to 5 were devoted to the iterative improving of conditions of actions on the basis of a given goal and a given origin. Since we assume that the given actions form a part of the initial program specifications, these actions are usually simple-minded and the resulting programs can be very inefficient if the actions are left unchanged. This is a serious problem to face. We naïvely and tentatively propose the following straightforward idea : to replace the given actions by iteratively accelerated ones, in such a way that the new program converges to Q faster than the initial program and that the new actions are equivalent to an iterated composition of the given ones.

More precisely, we can state our objective as follows. We are given a program $\underline{S}$ which, if it is applied, always reaches a goal Q ; the rules of $\underline{S}$ are $A_i \to s_i$; the domain from which $\underline{S}$ can lead to Q is, by (4.4), the minimum solution AA of $AA = Q \vee AA \vee gain(\underline{S}, AA)$, where $gain(\underline{S},R) = \bigvee_i gain(S_i,R)$. The speed of convergence of the iterates AA^n towards AA depends on the rate of growth of $gain(\underline{S},AA^n)$. We shall then aim at deriving from $\underline{S}$ a new program $T = \|_l B_l \to t_l$ such that $gain(\underline{T}, BB^n)$ is significantly greater than $gain(\underline{S},AA^n)$. As to the actions t_l, we want them to represent a finite composition of actions s_i.

Let us now see how these accelerated actions t_l could be derived. To simplify the presentation, which is still tentative anyway, we assume that $\underline{S}$ has only one rule $A \to s$. The new program $\underline{T}$ should essentially consists in an accelerated action $B \to t$ where t is equivalent to some composition (s; s;...;s) of the action s. We may write ϕs for t. The new condition B must simply guarantee that the given condition A holds before each of the successive applications of s contained in ϕs. For example, if $\phi s=(s; s; s)$, then $B=A \wedge pre(s,A) \wedge pre(s,pre(s,A))$. Let us denote B by $\beta(A,\phi,s)$ when $t= \phi s$. The main rule of $\underline{T}$ is thus $\beta(A,\phi,s) \to \phi s$. It remains now to define an acceleration ϕ which should be flexible in two directions : first, ϕ should permit much speed up by representing many compositions of s; second, ϕ must still permit to fall back on the elementary s when accelerated variants become inapplicable. We shall thus include in $\underline{T}$ additional rules which transform ϕ in an adaptative way, starting from an origin where ϕ is the identity. Firstly, there is a rule for speeding up ϕ itself by a transformation F on ϕs as long as this is useful, i.e. as long as $\neg\beta(A,F\phi,s) \wedge \neg Q$ holds. Secondly, another auxiliary rule does slow down ϕ when ϕ is not useful anymore, i.e. when $\neg\beta(A,\phi,s) \wedge \neg Q$ holds ; the action of slowing down can simply be the application on ϕ of the transformation F^{-1} inverse of F. In summary, from

$$\underline{S} = [\, A \to s\,]$$

we derive

$$\underline{T} = [\, \beta(A,F\phi,s) \wedge \neg Q \rightarrow \phi := F\phi \quad | \beta(A,\phi,s) \rightarrow \phi s \quad | \neg\beta(A,\phi,s) \wedge \neg Q \rightarrow \phi := F^{-1}\phi \,] \tag{6.1}$$

according to the scheme

$\underline{T}$ = [speed up the acceleration if useful
| apply the accelerated action if possible
| slow down the acceleration if necessary]

The transformations ϕ and F must be designed in such a way that $F\phi s$ represents more applications of s than ϕs, and that ϕs represents at least one such application. Obviously, the faster ϕs can grow, the greater gain($\underline{T}$,BB^n) is. Note that this expresses an increase in the speed of *static* convergence of the iterates BB^n. This may correspond to an effective improvement of the dynamic execution speed only if ϕ,F, and β can be expressed in terms of economical actions. The present method does not solve the latter question.

Consider

$$\underline{S_0} : [\,\underline{\text{true}} \rightarrow x:=x+1]$$
$$P : x=0 \wedge E\ y : y > 0 \wedge f(y) \leqslant a < f(y+1)$$
$$Q : f(x) \leqslant a < f(x+1)$$

We first derive $\underline{S}$ which always terminates on Q :

$$\underline{S} : [\, f(x+1) \leqslant a \rightarrow x:=x+1]$$

We want to speed up $\underline{S}$. Since k successive applications of x:=x+1 amount to x:=x+k, a reasonable choice for ϕ_k is x:=x+k. We can speed up ϕ_k in various ways ; let us do it by a shift, viz. by a multiplication by two :

$F\phi_k = \phi_{2k}$. The new origin is $P \wedge k=1$ and the resulting program is

$$\underline{T} : [\, f(x+2k) \leqslant a \rightarrow k:=2k \quad | f(x+k) \leqslant a \rightarrow x:=x+k \quad | f(x+k) > a\ k > 1 \rightarrow k:=k/2] \tag{6.2}$$

The $\underline{S_0}$, P and Q as given above represent a rather large class of problems, which can be characterized as follows :

$$P : x=0 \wedge E\ y : R(y) \wedge y > 0$$
$$Q : \text{Min}\ \{x \mid R(x) \wedge x > 0\}$$
$$\underline{S_0} : [\, \neg R(x+1) \rightarrow x:=x+1]$$

We can apply the above derivation in various folklore examples. The first one is the positioning of the given number a in an array f(x) of (N+1) ordered numbers :

$$P \;:\; x=0 \wedge E\, y : 1 \leqslant y \leqslant N \wedge f(y) \leqslant a < f(y+1)$$
$$Q \;:\; 1 \leqslant x \leqslant N \wedge f(x) \leqslant a < f(x+1)$$

The accelerated program is

$$\begin{aligned} \underline{T} \;:\; [\; & x+2k \leqslant N \wedge f(x+2k) \leqslant a \rightarrow k:=2k \\ |\; & x+k \leqslant N \wedge f(x+k) \leqslant a \rightarrow x:=x+k \\ |\; & (x+k > N \vee f(x+k) > a) \wedge k > 1 \rightarrow k:=k/2 \,] \end{aligned}$$

Note that bound checking was not required but is easily ensured by a left-to-right evaluation of the boolean operations in each condition. Note also that the equality k=1, which holds initially, may well remain untouched until the end if the second rule of $\underline{T}$ is always chosen. A simple way to prevent this is to give priority to the first, speeding-up rule by following the textual ordering of the rules as in the McCarthy conditionals. We do not elaborate further on these various matters.

The result (6.2) can also be used for computing the quotient of a by b :

$$P \;:\; x=0 \wedge a > 0 \wedge b > 0$$
$$Q \;:\; bx \leqslant a < b(x+1)$$

The accelerated program is

$$\begin{aligned} \underline{T} \;:\; [\; & b(x+2k) \leqslant a \rightarrow k:=2k \\ |\; & b(x+k) \leqslant a \rightarrow x:=x+k \\ |\; & b(x+k) > a \wedge k > 1 \rightarrow k:=k/2 \,] \end{aligned}$$

As is well-known, $\underline{T}$ can be ameliorated by introducing auxiliary variables and actions, which simplify the evaluation of the conditions. Let us, for example, use

$$bx \equiv y \;,\; bk \equiv z$$

The origin is then $x=0 \wedge k=1 \wedge y=0 \wedge z=b$. The final program is

$$\begin{aligned} [\; & y+2z \leqslant a \rightarrow k:=2k,\; z:=2z \\ |\; & y+z \leqslant a \rightarrow x:=x+k,\; y:=y+z \\ |\; & y+z > a \wedge k > 1 \rightarrow k:=k/2,\; z:=z/2 \,] \end{aligned}$$

As a last application of (6.2), we give an accelerated program computing the integral square root of the integer a :

$$P \;:\; x=0 \wedge a > 0$$
$$Q \;:\; x^2 \leqslant a < (x+1)^2$$

The accelerated program can be written as follows , with $x^2 \equiv y$, $2kx \equiv u$, and $k^2 \equiv v$ to simplify the conditions :

$$[\, y+2u+4v \leqslant a \rightarrow k:=2k,\ u:=2u,\ v:=4v$$
$$|\, y+u+v \leqslant a \rightarrow x:=x+k,\ u:=u+2v,\ y:=y+u+v$$
$$|\, y+u+v > a \wedge k > 1 \rightarrow k:=k/2,\ u:=u/2,\ v:=v/4 \,]$$

Here, we show how to use other ways of speeding up. Let us again consider the case of the quotient :

$$P \ : \ x=0 \wedge a > 0 \wedge b > 0$$
$$Q \ : \ bx \leqslant a < b(x+1)$$

The accelerated action is x:=x+k. Instead of defining k as a power of 2, we can construct it as a Fibonacci number. We just need an additional variable h to remember the Fibonacci number preceding k : the speeding up amounts then to replacing k by k+h and h by k, since F(n)=F(n-1)+F(n-2). Our accelerated program is now

$$[\, b(x+k+h) \leqslant a \rightarrow k:=k+h,\ h:=k$$
$$|\, b(x+k) \leqslant a \rightarrow x:=x+k$$
$$|\, b(x+k) > a \wedge k > 1 \rightarrow k:=h,\ h:=k-h \,]$$

with origin $x=0 \wedge a > 0 \wedge b > 0 \wedge h=0 \wedge k=1$. We simplify the conditions by $bx \equiv y$, $bk \equiv u$, $bk \equiv v$:

$$[\, y+u+v \leqslant a \rightarrow k:=k+h,\ h:=k,\ u:=u+v,\ v:=u$$
$$y+u \leqslant a \rightarrow x:=x+k,\ y:=y+u$$
$$y+u > a \wedge k > 1 \rightarrow k:=h,\ h:=k-h,\ u:=v,\ v:=u-v \,]$$

This accelerated program for the quotient uses only additions and subtractions, without any multiplication or division. At the end, a-y gives the remainder.

In previous Sections, the conditions in programs were strengthened or weakened by iterative, static deductions on the basis of a given goal and a given origin. Here, the actions are improved by introducing actual program rules which accelerate them, iteratively too, but at run time so to speak. Thus, we started to study in a common framework the iterative, formal deductions and the iterative, effective applications of actions.

Various other examples, not copied here, show an interesting problem area: the accelerated program may require the use of an auxiliary memory which functions as a stack with a maximal depth of logarithmic order. Now, the acceleration implied by these programs can sometimes be expressed by a simple transformation of recursive functions which directly implies the same exponential gain in time and in stack-space. We do not know whether or not these simple transformations can be made as straightforward as those in (6.1) for the same programs. Yet, (6.1) may in fact produce lower-level implementations of stacks, and this should make us ponder.

We can think of speeding up the actions in many other ways : we could as well maintain a family of various accelerations for the same action ; we could also try to speed up the speeding-up function itself. All this is omitted here, and requires a preliminary, serious complexity analysis. See, for example, Brent (1976) for an analysis of left-shift and right-shift algorithms which are not unlike the speeding-up and slowing-down phases in (6.1).

7. ENSURING STRONG CORRECTNESS OF PARALLEL PROGRAMS.

The previous Sections were concerned with nondeterministic, sequential programs only. We start now to investigate construction rules for the formation of improved parallel programs. We first summarize, in the present Section, a number of methods which ensure the logical soundness of parallel programs and which were worked out by Sintzoff and van Lamsweerde (1975) and van Lamsweerde and Sintzoff (1976). We shall recall only a minimum of technical details, and instead develop an introductory example and a general discussion ; we also aim at showing various deep relationships with the previous Sections, and at preparing a later Section which studies how to increase the amount of parallelism.

For the time being, we restrict ourselves to sets $\underline{S}$ of critical regions, or monitor procedure calls, S_i such as

$$\underline{\text{with}}\ x\ \underline{\text{when}}\ A_i\ \underline{\text{do}}\ s_i\ \underline{\text{end}}$$

which we abbreviate into

$$[\,.(x).\ A_i? \rightarrow s_i\ .]$$

The dotted brackets indicate indivisible actions, the (x) lists the global variables being accessed, and the question-mark indicates waiting if the condition is false. We want to transform the constructs S_i into a set $\underline{T}$ of improved sections on the form

```
with x begin wait(W_i); s_i ;
             if V_ij then signal(W_j) fi
       end
```

abbreviated as

$$[\,.(x).\ [W_i? \rightarrow s_i]\ ;\ [V_{ij} \rightarrow W_j!]\ .]$$

The improvement must ensure four properties. First, the new conditions W_i must imply the original ones A_i. Second, the W_i do guarantee the absence of deadlocks : this is equivalent to avoiding dead-ends, as in (2.1), when the goal Q is <u>false</u> ; hence the W_i are maximal solutions of $W_i \Rightarrow \text{pre}(S_i, WW)$ where $WW = \bigvee_i W_i$. Third, the W_i prevent any individual starvation. The individual starvation of some S_k is prevented if its entry-condition W_k must always become eventually true whenever the other S_j ($j \neq k$) are evaluated whereas S_k is waiting; this means that, for $j \neq k$,

$$W_j = \text{wait}_k \wedge \neg W_k \wedge B_j \vee (\neg \text{wait}_k \vee W_k) \wedge W'_j \tag{7.1}$$

where $\text{wait}_k \equiv$ <u>**true**</u> iff S_k is waiting, B_j ensures W_k is reached, and W'_j was the entry-condition of S_j before preventing the starvation of S_k. The crucial part is to derive the B'_j s : since $\|_j\ B_j \rightarrow s_j$ must reach the goal W_k, we must solve a system similar to (3.3):

$$B_j \Rightarrow BB \wedge \neg\, CC \wedge W'_j$$

where BB and CC are maximal solutions of

$$BB \Rightarrow \text{pre}(\|_j\ B_j \rightarrow s_j,\ BB) \vee W_k$$

$$CC \Rightarrow \text{pre}(\|_j\ B_j \rightarrow s_j,\ CC) \wedge \neg W_k$$

This has to be done in turn for each k=1...N. The fourth and last property to be ensured by the improved system T is the correctness and completeness of the signaling parts : the V_{ij} must be such that W_j is signaled when and only when necessary. This is quite easy to achieve : V_{ij} is simply $\text{gain}(S_i, W_j)$ expressed in terms of the final state of S_i ; see also (4.2):

$$V_{ij} = \text{post}(S_i, \neg W_j) \wedge W_j\ . \tag{7.2}$$

This completes the summary of these techniques. Note that the hardest part is to solve the highly mutually recursive equations ensuring the absence of individual starvation of each section T_i ; approximated methods appear essential here.

Before developing a typical example, we shall give a few details on the constructs which will be used.

Serial composition of S_1 and S_2	$S_1;S_2$
Concurrent composition of S_1 and S_2	S_1,S_2
Conditioned action	$A \to s$
Choice between S_1 and S_2	$[S_1 \mid S_2]$
Endless repetition of S	[* S *]
Critical section S on globals x	[.(x). S.]
Wait-condition	A?
Signal-action	A!

These stenographic rules should not be taken too seriously. It is a straightforward, although menial, task to translate the above constructs into more elementary ones so that the techniques of Sections 2 to 4 can be applied.

As an illustration, we consider the classical problem of the five philosophers. We shall pinpoint the main steps of the development of a parallel program which is correct, deadlock-free, starvation-free, and signal-complete. We omit all the details of the underlying deductions ; most are given in van Lamsweerde and Sintzoff (1976). The problem is defined by the following specifications ; i=1...5, and the arithmetic is modulo five :

Scheme for $phil_i$: [* $phil_i$ is hungry ;
$phil_i$ eats ;
$phil_i$ thinks
*]

Invariant : for each i, $phil_i$ eats $\wedge$ $phil_{i+1}$ eats = false .

We can represent these specifications by using variables c_i such that

$c_i=1$ iff $phil_i$ is hungry
$c_i=2$ iff $phil_i$ eats
$c_i=0$ iff $phil_i$ thinks

Our problem specifications are then formalized as follows :

$phil_i$ = [* [.(c_i). c_i:=1 .] ;
[.(c_i). c_i:=2 .] ;
[.(c_i). c_i:=0 .]
*]

$$I = \forall i : (c_i=2 \wedge c_{i+1}=2) = \underline{false}$$

We now derive conditions A_j of the actions s_j in order to ensure I is preserved : $A_j = [\, I \Rightarrow pre(s_j,I)]$.

$$\begin{aligned} phil_i = [* & [\,.(c_i).\ c_i:=1.];\\ & [\,.(c_{i-1}, c_i, c_{i+1}).\ c_{i-1}\neq 2 \wedge c_{i+1}\neq 2? \rightarrow c_i:=2.];\\ & [\,.(c_i).\ c_i:=0\ .]\\ *] & \end{aligned}$$

By applying (7.2), we derive conditions preventing deadlock and ensuring complete signaling :

$$\begin{aligned} phil_i = [* & [\,.(c_i).\ c_i:=1.];\\ & [\,.(c_{i-1}, c_i, c_{i+1}).\ c_{i-1}\neq 2 \wedge c_{i+1}\neq 2? \rightarrow c_i:=2.];\\ & [\,.(c_{i-2}, c_{i-1}, c_i, c_{i+1}, c_{i+2}).\\ & \qquad c_i:=0\ ;\ [\,c_{i-1}=1 \wedge c_{i-2}\neq 2 \rightarrow c_{i-2}\neq 2 \wedge c_i\neq 2!],\\ & \qquad\qquad [\,c_{i+1}=1 \wedge c_{i+2}\neq 2 \rightarrow c_i\ \neq 2 \wedge c_{i+2}\neq 2!]\\ & .]\\ *] & \end{aligned} \tag{7.3}$$

In the notations detailed in Sintzoff and van Lamsweerde (1975), the last signaling part would be written as

$$\begin{aligned} \underline{see}\ \ & c_{i-1}=1 \wedge c_{i-2}\neq 2 \rightarrow c_{i-2}\neq 2 \wedge c_i\neq 2,\\ & c_{i+1}=1 \wedge c_{i+2}\neq 2 \rightarrow c_i\neq 2 \wedge c_{i+2}\neq 2! \end{aligned}$$

However, we do not use here the full power of such see-clauses ; our present signals are simple, monitor-like ones. It remains now to prevent individual starvation. Here is a version ensuring that $phil_3$ does not starve; it was obtained by applying (7.1) and (4.3) ; we omit the signaling parts :

$$\begin{aligned} phil_2 = [* & [\,.(c_2, c_3, c_4).\ c_3\neq 1 \wedge c_4\neq 2? \rightarrow c_2:=1.];\\ & [\,.(c_1, c_2, c_3, c_4).\\ & \qquad c_1\neq 2 \wedge c_3\neq 2 \wedge (c_3=0 \vee c_4\neq 2)? \rightarrow c_2:=2.];\\ & (\ldots \text{ the last part as in } (7.3)\ldots)\\ *] & \end{aligned} \tag{7.4}$$

$phil_4 \equiv phil_2$ where the indices 1,2,3,4,5 become 5,4,3,2, 1 respectively.

$phil_1$, $phil_3$, $phil_5$: as in (7.3) except for the signaling parts.

The signaling parts must be adapted because of the newly obtained conditions. The following policy has been derived : $phil_2$ may not start eating when $phil_3$ is hungry whereas $phil_4$ has not yet finished eating ; similarly for $phil_4$ w.r.t. $phil_2$; this indeed prevents the starvation of $phil_3$. We omit the final conditions preventing the starvation of each philosopher.

The solutions obtained by Courtois and Georges (1977) for the same problem are all different from (7.4). These other solutions are necessary and sufficient for the following, strict requirement : each philosopher may only access its immediate neighbours. They were elaborated after a thorough graph-theoretical study. To contrast, (7.4) was derived as an aside exercise without much thinking. It requires each philosopher accesses his neighbours and his neighbours' neighbours, but not more : the control is thus also distributed, although not as much as possible ; the fact this property holds here is an accident, since control distribution was not stated as an objective of the methods (7.1) and (7.2). On the other hand, because of the very use of (4.3) to solve (7.1), the following properties are verified by (7.4) : each state which does not create an effective risk of starvation is allowed, and, as soon as any philosopher becomes hungry, the others act in such a way that he will be authorized to eat as soon as possible ; the second property holds because no detours are allowed by (4.1), and the first one is due to (4.4). It should be interesting to investigate whether the solutions other than (7.4) could be easily derived by using iterations other than (4.3), e.g. (4.3) with a Gauss-Seidel policy, or (4.1), or even (3.2). This comparison with the work by Courtois and Georges suggests that an integrated interplay between general methods and specific theories is recommended in our field too.

Hoare's axiom $I \wedge W$ {signal(W)} I should be used with care because it permits the programming of superfluous signaling actions as well as the omission of necessary ones : for example, given an invariant $x \geqslant 0$ and a condition variable w associated with $x > 0$, it permits to program <u>begin</u> x:=x+1 ; signal(w)<u>end</u> as well as <u>begin</u> x:=x+1 <u>end</u>, whereas the precise solution is <u>begin</u> x:=x+1 ; <u>if</u> x=1 <u>then</u> signal(w) <u>fi</u> <u>end</u>. Highly refined proof rules are studied by Howard (1977) for a large variety of signaling policies. The construction rule (7.2) is both simple and complete, but it remains based on a specific, operational view of the signal-action.

The proposed methods allow the cooperation or synchronization components of parallel sections to be systematically derived. These components remain integrated with each corresponding section. We could well think of separating the synchronization parts altogether, by putting them in a distinct, synchronizing section ; this has been repeatedly suggested, see a recent proposal by Robert and Verjus (1977). For example, consider the following scheme; we omit to indicate the critical variables from now on :

```
producer = [ * [ x=0? → x:=x+1 ;
                 x=1  → x=1!]     *]
consumer = [ * [ x=1? → x:=x-1 ;
                 x=0  → x=0!]     *]
```

These self-synchronizing processes can easily be transformed into two processes plus a separate synchronizer ; we introduce the synchronizing identifiers "p" and "c" corresponding to x=0 and x=1, respectively ; "syn" is associated with the synchronizer :

```
producer = [ * [ p? → x:=x+1; true → syn!] *]
consumer = [ * [ c? → x:=x-1; true → syn!] *]
synchronizer = [ * [ x=0 → p! ; syn? → skip],
                   [ x=1 → c! ; syn? → skip]   *]
```

This uncoupling is essentially based on that proposed by Brinch Hansen (1977); the use of additional notations to hide syn would give

```
producer = [ * [ p?! → x:=x+1] *]
consumer = [ * [ c?! → x:=x-1] *]
synchronizer = [ * [ x=0 → p!?], [ x=1 → c!?] *]
```

It is preferable here and now to evaluate the advantages and the drawbacks of such a separate synchronizer. Each section would access its local variables and its private synchronization-identifier only ; on the other hand, the synchronizer would in fact be a central controller : we thus would increase the independence of parallel sections but could decrease the control distribution. The synchronizer would repeatedly test the conditions allowing signaling-actions, in a sort of high-level busy waiting : this could be acceptable if a network of processors would be used. The problems of concurrent signaling and of dynamic numbers of processes would need careful study. If necessary and sufficient signaling is required, the conditions for signaling in the synchronizer could become intricate ; if superfluous signaling is accepted, the conditions could be simplified but, then, unnecessary delays in the necessary signal-actions could occur because of the redundant signals. Consider for example the synchronization scheme hereafter ; note <u>cor</u> stands for the McCarthy <u>or</u> :

```
producer = [ * [ x+1 < n cor p?! → x:=x+1] *]
consumer = [ * [ x-1 > 0 cor c?! → x:=x-1] *]
synchronizer = [ * [ x+1=n → p!?] ,
                   [ x-1=0 → c!?] *]
```

The synchronization is well tailored since only the critical conditions, e.g. x+1=n , are tested by the synchronizer. Look now at the following, simpler version :

```
producer = [ * [ p?! → x:=x+1]  *]
consumer = [ * [ c?! → x:=x-1]  *]
synchronizer = [ * [ x+1 ≤ n → p!?] ,
                   [ x=1 ≥ 0 → c!?]  *]
```

Here, the synchronizer may send a signal to the producer when $x+1 < n$, which is superfluous and may delay the consumer.

8. INCREASING THE DENSITY OF PARALLELISM.

Up to this point, we have studied how to ensure some logical and economical properties of sequential programs, and some logical characteristics of parallel ones ; we ended the previous Section with a discussion on how to increase the control distribution or to decrease the amount of control interferences between parallel parts. In this Section, we intend to investigate how the density of parallelism could be augmented by reducing the accesses to global data. Indeed, the degree of permitted concurrency between two program sections S_1 and S_2 depends on their logical independence, which is limited by assignments to variables shared by S_1 and S_2. We present here a rather simplistic approach to tackle this problem, namely by creating private copies of global variables in each concurrent section.

Assume we are given two program parts S_1 and S_2, an origin P and a goal Q, such that the repeated application of the non-deterministic program $[\ S_1 | S_2]$ always leads to Q when starting from P. In general, the sections S_1 and S_2 use and update common global variables, and thus only one section at a time can be evaluated. Let us now try to transform S_i into T_i (here, i=1,2) such that T_1 and T_2 can be evaluated concurrently, without any mutual exclusion. The culprit being the accessing of global data, a simple-minded solution is to eliminate any sharing of data altogether : T_i is nothing else than S_i where a new, private variant z_i replaces each variable z shared by S_1 and S_2. The logical independence of $T_1(z_1)$ and $T_2(z_2)$ is of course total. However, the repeated concurrent execution of T_1 and T_2 is not at all guaranteed to lead from P to Q : for one thing, P and Q are defined in terms of the global variables z, not their variants z_i. We have to construct an initial phase, Init, going from P(z) to $P_1(z_1)$ and $P_2(z_2)$, and a final phase, Fin, going from $Q_1(z_1)$ and $Q_2(z_2)$

to Q(z). Our gross scheme is thus

Global, initial, briefing phase : $Init(z, z_1, z_2)$
Independent, parallel, main activities : $T_1(z_1)$, $T_2(z_2)$
Global, final, reporting phase : $Fin(z_1, z_2, z)$

This can be precised as follows, using Hoare's nice notations and indicating parallel repetition by [...‖ ...] :

$$\{P(z)\}\ Init\ \{P_1(z_1) \wedge P_2(z_2)\}\ ;$$
$$[T_1 \parallel T_2]\ ;$$
$$\{Q_1(z_1) \wedge Q_2(z_2)\}\ Fin\ \ \{Q(z)\}$$

It remains to find out what can be P_i, Q_i, Init and Fin. The origin P is a prerequisite for both S_1 and S_2. Hence, the origin P_1 of T_1 can surely be $P[z_1/z]$; yet, this is too much because T_1 disturbs in general only a part of $P[z_1/z]$; we define thus P_1 as that part of $P[z_1/z]$ which can be changed by T_1 ; similarly for P_2. The goal Q_1 is simply the logical result of the ending applications of T_1 starting on P_1 : thus, $Q_1 = L_1 \wedge \neg B_1$, where L_1 is given by (5.2) solved for P_1 and T_1, and where B_1 is the condition of applicability of T_1. To derive the actions Fin, we need adding to Q an interface predicate relating z to z_1 and z_2 : this has to be invented, and will be noted $R(z_1, z_2, z)$. This interface predicate may require an auxiliary invariant $I(z_1, z_2)$ to be guaranteed throughout T_1 and T_2. Our scheme is now, for i=1,2 :

$$\{P\}\ Init\ \{\textstyle\bigwedge_i P_i \wedge I\}\ ;\ [T_1 \parallel T_2]\ ;\ \{\textstyle\bigwedge_i Q_i \wedge I\}\ Fin\{Q \wedge R\}$$

where P_i = part of $P[z_i/z]$ changed by T_i
$Q_i = L_i \wedge \neg B_i$, B_i = applicability condition in T_i
$L_i(min) = P_i \vee post(T_i, L_i)$
R : to be invented
I, Init, Fin : to be derived.

This simple scheme works at least on the following example, which computes factorial(n) from both sides, so to speak :

P : $x=1 \wedge i=0 \wedge j=n+1$
Q : $x=fact(n)$
<u>S</u> : $[\,i+1 < j \rightarrow x:=x\times(i+1),\ i:=i+1$
$\quad |\,j-1 > i \rightarrow x:=x\times(j-1),\ j:=j-1]$

We use the variants x1, x2, i1, i2, j1, j2, and easily deduce

P_1 : $x1=1 \wedge i1=0$. Q_1 : $x1=1.2.\ \ldots\ .(j1-1) \wedge i1+1 = j1 \wedge i1 \geq 0$.
P_2 : $x2=1 \wedge j2=n+1$. Q_2 : $x2=n.(n-1).\ \ldots\ .(i2-1) \wedge j2-1=i2 \wedge j2 \leq n+1$.

Let us now invent an interface between x1, x2, in Q1, Q2, and x in Q. A simple one is

$$R(x1, x2, x) : x = x1 \times x2.$$

We derive then

$$\text{Fin} : x{:=}x1 \times x2$$
$$I \quad : (j1-1)+1 = i2-1, \text{ i.e. } j1=i2-1$$

We obtain thus, for $n \geq 2$ since $1 \leq j1 < i2 \leq n$,

```
     x1:=1, i1:=0, j1:=(n÷2),
     x2:=1, i2:=(n÷2)+1, j2:=n+1 ;
    [ i1+1 < j1 → x1:=x1 × (i1+1), i1:=i1+1
    ‖ j2-1 > i2 → x2:=x2 × (j2-1), j2:=j2-1] ;
     x := x1 × x2 .
```

The principle proposed is very simple, and drastic. It maximizes the degree of interleaving without paying any attention to the cost of creating variants. We could think of being less extreme, for instance by allowing the concurrent reading of global variables or by using forms of critical writing and reading. It would not be too difficult to extend the present scheme in order to derive,e.g., the program of concurrent search verified by Owicki and Gries (1976). However, it is another matter to establish construction rules for deriving programs such as concurrent garbage collectors.

9. CONCLUSIONS.

A programming language should be a language for constructing programs. Its design should thus be based on program construction techniques, then on verification methods, and then on implementation tools : the reverse order of priority is an error of perspective. In other words, a program construct should be included in a language only if a construction rule for its sensible use can be given : a mere proof rule is not sufficient. A benefit of this requirement would be a great simplicity, precision, and expressive power of the language. Indeed, construction rules,to be effective, require extremely pure program structures, much more so than proof rules since constructing is usually more difficult than verifying. The investigation of program design tools forces in fact the introduction of clean and clear notations with which it is a mental and physical pleasure to work.

Programs must be constructed to meet various needs, not only logical adequacy, but also economical properties, be it in time, in space, or in distribution. There exists a wealth of techniques available for analyzing these various properties : we may mention, a. o., verification rules and complexity analysis. These techniques should not be an end by themselves : otherwise, for example, the important field of program correctness would be in danger of degenerating into a verification conference generator, a testbed for futuristic artificial intelligence enterprises, or even a fashionable subject matter for ineffectual discourses. Instead, we should build on the existing analysis methods and transform them into useful program design techniques. It appears that interesting construction rules can be invented on the basis of known techniques for verification or complexity analysis. It is our hope that this approach can be generalized with success.

The present paper is imperfect as already said in the introduction. The technical quality of the various construction methods which have been presented is proportional to the amount of thinking already spent on them : thus, the older problem of avoiding dead-ends is better elaborated than the more recent one of increasing parallelism ; yet, the initial phases of these various investigations are similar in style and spirit. To be really convincing, any proposed construction rule should be applied to yield some big examples, viz. programs which are needed and useful but which have not yet been obtained. The lack of such results is certainly a symptom of the none-too-advanced state of the art in programming technology ; we cannot assert that the present paper is necessarily a step in the right direction. Another problem area which needs systematic study is the ordering or combination of construction rules corresponding to different properties : for instance, we may wish to accelerate a given program as well as to increase the density of parallelism.

Approximations are essential in iterative schemes, lest solutions remain inaccessible. We should thus strive for approximated, iterative schemes which yield suboptimal solutions ; measures should be found to evaluate the quality of these solutions, and these solutions should approximate from the safe side, viz. they should still guarantee the property sought for. Let us justify these claims by a colourful example. Assume we are given two non-deterministic programs $\underline{S} = \|_i S_i = \|_i A_i \rightarrow s_i$ and $\underline{S}' = \|_i S'_i$, a goal Q and a predicate G. The programs $\underline{S}$ and $\underline{S}'$ are executed repeatedly, but each application of S is followed by one of S' : these programs are playing against each other. It is asked to transform S into $\underline{T} = \|_i \ B_i \to s_i$ such that $B_i \Rightarrow A_i$, that G is always preserved, and that, after each application of T, either Q is obtained or T will be able to play again in spite of any possible action of S'. If Q means "checkmate for S'" and G is "not checkmate for S", the problem has no known solution. The defensive strategy asked for corresponds to non-trivial solutions of the following, simple implications :

$$B_i \Rightarrow G \wedge pre(S_i, Q \vee \neg pre(\underline{S}', \neg \bigvee_j B_j))$$

This is related to the system (2.1) for avoiding dead-ends, which was easy to solve compared to other systems. Yet, it would be difficult here to construct optimal solutions ; even very poor ones are not obvious, and they should be the first objectives. This example shows also that the major difficulties are not always in the description of a problem or in the definition of a procedure of solution, but may well be in the effective construction of actual solutions. A more positive justification of approximations is the fact that many successful tools in software design are designed that way : the contexts added in context-free parsing rules to make them successful, are sufficient but need not to the best ones ; the global optimizers of programs look only for simple, sufficient conditions in order to apply the corresponding optimizations. To sum up, the use of approximate iterations, which has been successful in good production software, should also be considered for good software production.

The deep unity underlying apparently various techniques for program verification, compile-time checks or global optimization,was expressed, already seven years ago, in terms of iterative and approximated computations. It is again intellectually satisfactory to see the growing convergence between construction problems apparently as different as the prevention of deadlocks, the acceleration of actions, or the generation of deterministic parsers. Indeed, approximated iterations play a recurring rôle in the formal deductions, the formal iterations begin to be integrated with the actual iterations of the programs, and there is no borderline anymore between the classical derivations of mathematical formulas and the generation of the corresponding programs. Unification should help to face the problem of the tension between theory and practice, and we should strive for the continuing cross-fertilization of ideas and techniques.

Acknowledgements. Parts of this paper have been favourably influenced by the constructive will of IFIP WG2.1, by the probing questioning of IFIP WG2.3, by fruitful discussions with P. Cousot and A. van Lamsweerde, and by activities of new colleagues in Nancy.

REFERENCES.

Brent, R. P. (1977). Analysis of the binary Euclidean algorithm. In : J. T. Traub (ed.), Algorithms and Complexity (Academic Press, New York), 321-374.

Brinch Hansen, P. (1977). Distributed actions : a concurrent programming concept. (Univ. of South. California)

Courtois, P. J., and Georges, J. (1977). On starvation prevention . RAIRO Informatique (in press).

Cousot, P., and Cousot, R. (1977). Fixed point approach to the static analysis of programs. (Univ. of Grenoble).

Dijkstra, E. W. (1968). A constructive approach to the problem of program correctness. BIT 8, 174-186.

Dijkstra, E. W. (1976). A discipline of programming (Prentice-Hall, New Jersey).

Howard, J.H. (1976). Signaling in monitors. Proc. 2nd Int. Conf. Software Engineering (IEEE) 47-52.

Owicki, S., and Gries, D. (1976). An axiomatic proof technique for parallel programs I. Acta Informatica 6, 319-340.

Park, D. (1969). Fixpoint induction and proof of program properties. Machine Intelligence Vol.5 (Edinburgh Univ. Press), 59-78.

Robert, P., and Verjus, J.P. (1977). Towards autonomous description of synchronization modules. Proc. IFIP 77 Congress (North-Holland, Amsterdam).

Scholten, C. S. (1977), Reflections on Sintzoff's method (Philips, Apeldoorn).

Sintzoff, M. (1976). Eliminating blind alleys from backtrack programs. Proc. 3d Int. Coll. Automata, Languages and Programming (Edinburgh Univ. Press) 531-557.

Sintzoff, M. (1977). Iterative and approximated formation of successful programs (CRIN, Nancy).

Sintzoff, M., and van Lamsweerde, A. (1975). Constructing correct and efficient concurrent programs. Proc. Int. Conf. on Reliable Software (ACM-IEEE) 319-326.

van Lamsweerde, A., and Sintzoff, M. (1976). Formal derivation of strongly correct parallel programs (MBLE Research Lab., Brussels)

van Lamsweerde, A. (1977). From verifying termination to guaranteeing it : a case study. Proc. IFIP Working Conf. on Formal Description of Programming Concepts (North-Holland, Amsterdam).

Sintzoff : Discussion

Turski: Can this lucidly described methodology lead to low quality programs as well?

Sintzoff: Yes, oh yes! In fact, it can lead to the worst quality programs [☺] in the following sense: if I am approximating and if I am very tired, I may simply approximate towards nothing and construct a void program. What can we do then? We should measure the quality of the approximation. That's a central problem. It was also discussed in the papers on plausibility checking. I propose the following approach: approximate the unattainable point x from both sides, from below and from above. I know that my ideal solution I cannot obtain lies in between. So I can measure the quality of my approximation by taking the distance between the approximation from below and the approximation from above, and I know that is a majorant of the distance between the safe approximation from below and the ideal solution. So, I can construct two approximate solutions and I can measure the poorness of these solutions.

Turski: Now you have to introduce much more powerful concepts. Before you had just the ordering. Now you have to have the distance.

Sintzoff: I know, I know. I told you I am at the bottom-level of the work. But we have to introduce a distance. I feel this is essential to any scientific progress. We have to be able to measure in some sense the quality of our results.

Session 5c : Closing Discussion

Meertens: My opening contribution to this closing discussion is more or less a moralist view on the theme, "from specification to implementation". Let me begin by showing you one of the noble dreams of mankind, as seen by the artist:

And then one day, engineers came along and made this thing out of it:

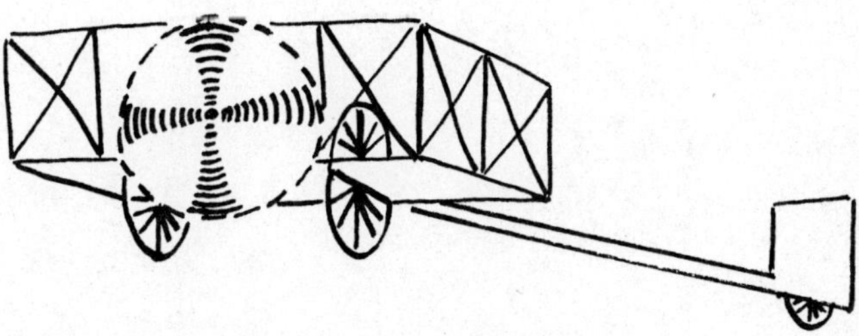

It was flawed, but it flew. And so mankind flew.

Another, more recent dream of mankind, as presented by science fiction is the following:

But now, the computer scientists come along and say, "Oh, you mean this dream:"

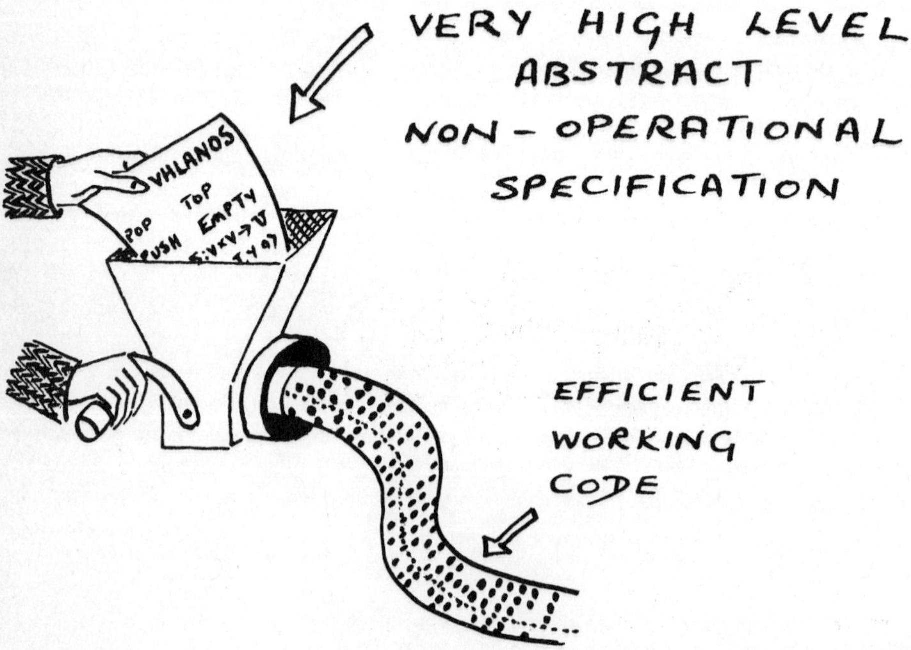

I think this last picture is a Utopia, in fact, which cannot be reached. To convince you of this, I have an example of a piece of a very high-level abstract, non-operational specification that goes like this:

```
Y(I) = A * SINF(OM * X(I) + PHI)
```

You see, that was 20 years ago. Of course now it's completely obvious to anybody that you can transform this into working code, so we no longer think about it as being a very high-level, abstract, non-operational specification, but at one time it was so considered. That's my point. With a plane you know when it flies, since it no longer touches the ground. But when have you reached this very high level of abstraction? I think that's in some sense the problem. In honor of Sintzoff I have two naive questions. First, can we write quality VHLANOS (very high-level, abstract, non-operational specifications)? And to show you I'm not too naive, the second question is: how do we debug very high-level, . . .? Still, I think the situation is not that bad. It is to me more or less obvious (if you look at some approaches) that is much easier to achieve quality on the specificational level than to achieve quality on the level of the working program because you have fewer concerns. There are some things which work like the very high-level abstraction I have just shown you. Just to give you another example, consider these specifications:

```
empty: stack.
push:  (el, stack) -> stack.
top:   stack -> el.
       top(empty) = undefined.
       top(push(a,b)) = a.
pop:   stack -> stack.
       pop(empty) = undefined.
       pop(push(a,b)) = b.
```

I hope it's a familiar example. Of course, these are intrinsic specifications, and there are no extrinsic ones. But if you take a slightly different point of view, they are purely operational. It's very easy to make a compiler for this type of description; you just need simple pattern matching at run-time to find out what to apply if you can no longer simplify and that's it. The implementation would be something like linked lists. I'm sure this is very well known. There are two very valid concerns if you are working along this line. One is the matter of efficiency. There is the answer, "Well, make it go faster", and I've heard several times, "make the hardware go faster". I think that's no answer, because I'm concerned with efficiencies of the order that can only be achieved by significant transformations. There's also the matter of the convergence of these approximations, about which Sintzoff talked. These questions are in general as difficult as any question in mathematics and they require all our ingenuity.

Now, what are the practical implications of this kind of work for constructing quality software? The first requirement is that it works. Well, I have two suggestions (this is where the moralism comes in). The first one is to work out methods for manual construction, using inverted verification methods (to each proof there is a counterpart, which is the synthesis). Many of the methods we see now are trying to go further and further, but the level is still such that they have to be done by hand and not by automated means, although there may be automated assistance. We should work out these methods in such a way that the poor programmer can apply them, otherwise they are of no use. The other suggestion is to single out some cases with guaranteed convergence of approximation and to implement these methods. In general, solving equations is a very hard task, but if you take linear equations we have good methods for that. I have a third suggestion, which is to proceed onwards to Utopia and by so doing to provide input for VHLANOS; but this, of course, makes sense only if there will also be output.

Dewar: Since Meerten's remarks I see in a somewhat clearer light the essential difference between SETL and ALPHARD: what in ALPHARD is considered as specification is regarded in SETL as code. To try to make you believe that, there is at least the claim that it can be executed efficiently, whatever that means. Now to the extent that this claim is true, it means that a lot of verification efforts simply go away. For SETL the question is: did we make a bug in this piece of code, whereas in ALPHARD the question is, in some sense: did we make an error in the specification (if so, there is nothing we can do because, after all, that was the specification). Now obviously there is no way to remove the need for verification altogether, but I think moving the whole discourse to this level where VHLANOS is considered as code makes the possibility of verification more believable because then a lot of the very tedious low-level work that's been seen in most verification efforts just disappears.

Meertens: I hate to take a stand in the great ALPHARD-SETL debate, for fear of being crushed by two giants, but I think both are basically algorithmic languages. SETL obviously starts from a higher point. It supports a higher abstraction level than ALPHARD does initially. But ALPHARD supports an abstraction mechanism, so with some effort you can reach the SETL level and then you have SETL expressed in ALPHARD. On the other hand, in SETL, where these things are part of the language, there is support such as optimization, automatic search for better data structuring, etc., which ALPHARD doesn't have. However, I think it's not fair to compare them on the level, "I can say this, can you say this, too?" You can make the programs look the same, and then try to go on from there (to VHLANOS . . .).

Dewar: I do agree with that. Clearly it's true that ALPHARD can be made to look like anything if you think of it as an extensible language. The point that has not yet been demonstrated by any convincing examples is the power of abstractions at that next level and the need for them.

Correll: It occurs to me that in some sense we have missed the topic of this conference because what we were talking about was a much more general topic, namely "obtaining quality software". I would say obtaining quality software can be subdivided into two parts: "constructing" and "improving". Only the former, constructing quality software, was the announced subject of this conference, but I don't at all regret that we talked on this broader topic because now we can see both approaches. Perhaps there are more, but at least we can identify these two approaches in the effort to do something about obtaining better quality programs. What is the difference between constructing and improving? Well, it seems to me that constructing is to think about the quality aspects of a program before the fact (the fact being that the program has arrived, is there, is operational, is working), whereas improving is something which you do after the fact (once you have the program and find that it has problems, that it doesn't have the quality attributes you'd like). Improvement is going through an existing program and trying to add more quality, as opposed to introducing all the quality aspects during the construction process so that they are already present at the point when you arrive at the final program.

Certainly one thing we might do at this point is to consider which is the better approach, constructing or improving. So we should try to find out the pro and the contra for each approach. I'll start out with pro-construct. Well, the basic idea of constructing is that the very moment we have completed our task we are happy with the final program, we are happy with its quality aspects. We don't have a complete operational program until such time as we have added all our quality interests. Pro-construct is that the feedback loops are shorter (feedback loops in the sense of Ross's talk), since there is some stepwise approach which helps us to find out where the quality problems are at a much earlier stage. And we may hope that constructing can some day be mechanized. So this is certainly pro-construct. Now, I am somewhat unfair. This is my bias. You should tell me what is good about the improving approach. Before that I will give the arguments against improvement as I see them. Well, one problem is, for instance, what to do with incorrect programs. Proving and verification techniques so far don't help too much. They are good if a program was correct in the first place; then you can show it is really correct. There is work on the way to help out in this situation, but I don't think we know much about proving programs incorrect. It seems to be a very hard task, and it might be easier to construct correct programs in the first place. I think trying to do something about incorrect programs is very difficult, and everybody has heard many bad opinions about testing. A second argument against improving is that it is extremely inconvenient to do something about a final program once its development history has been lost. We have heard at least two talks here at the conference which tried to help out in this respect, but the way we construct programs at present, with the programming languages we have today, this difficulty is very likely to occur. So improving after the fact is not the way we should do it. The third argument as to why improving is not the right approach is that having arrived at the final program, one is too easily satisfied. The project is stopped once the system is operational, and one simply never gets around to the essential step, namely improving the program. This is certainly a temptation and therefore, a constructive approach which precludes this possibility would obviously be better. Again, I'm unfair. Where are the contra-constructing arguments? Well, I'm biased in this respect, and I simply say I don't know. Please, give me your opinions.

Holager: I have tried the approach of making a program of not too high quality and then improving upon it. I've found that to be a very bad way of going about it, mainly because the initial programming turned out to be too lax. The complexity and ingenuity of the bugs that were introduced was so staggering that the improvement process turned out to be almost impossible.

Wodon: I'm a bit confused about the meaning you have for improving a program. If you speak about going from incorrect to correct, I'd call that more than improving. Of course, it might be to go from partially correct to correct, which seems to look like improving. Now and then it may be necessary to introduce some added qualities, but often that is more a matter of economics than of philosophy or whatever. Would you please specify what you mean by improving?

Correll: If you talk about optimization, for instance, that does not fall within my very strict meaning of improving because I hope to have a constructive or automatic approach. I would like to see optimization (where you start from some specification which is not optimal and then apply some mechanical tool to enhance the performance), as a constructive approach.

Mráz: I think that, in speaking of improving, you were starting from the wrong assumption, namely, that one would be improving programs which were badly structured initially. I think that if we speak of improving programs which were constructed on good principles to begin with then we stand some chance of succeeding, so there is something to be said for this method.

Ross: I believe that whether one constructs or improves, the game should be played in an equally structured manner, and if one does so, then I believe that both methods, in fact, come together.

King, J.: The thing I find surprising is the different views people have about program verification. When it was first promoted people got very excited and decided that this would solve all kinds of problems: "Wouldn't it be nice to just put my program into a machine and have it come out and confirm that indeed I have all the bugs out of it?" But as things developed in the program verification field, people began to work in the area more realistically and realized that it's a very difficult problem and, in my opinion, a long range problem. So now we have one school of people saying, "Forget it, it's not worth looking at." I think we have to be much more realistic. This is a very useful notion. It probably will prove useful in the future sometime, but it doesn't offer any golden key. Basically, a correctness proof is just some kind of consistency check. In its strictest form, verification is a redundancy check between the code and some specification. The code tells us how to accomplish the results we want, and the specification tells us what results we want to achieve. This strict view is I think very productive because the distinction between "how" and "what" seems to me to draw on different parts of the thought process. I find that I do quite different kinds of thinking when I'm thinking about what I want to do as opposed to how I want to do it. But I don't think that this distinction should be interpreted restrictively. Basically I see program verification as a way of checking any redundancy that's in a program. A lot of what has been going on here is essentially trying to discover exactly what form that redundancy should take to be useful. As far as abstraction is concerned, it's a popular thing to introduce into the programming languages, and it goes hand in hand with verification. I feel it's impossible to prove that a program is correct if you can't understand it. The notion that I might be able to verify a program that's so bad I don't know what it does seems very far fetched. I've often found in program verification work that the place where I'd like the verifier to help me most is exactly where it could do least and the place where I don't need it, is the place where it's best. But I view this morbid checking mechanism as a last little confirmation after you've done a good job. A program is not like a mathematical theorem, where you have to get a few hundred people to agree that it's right. It runs on a machine and there is a final judge of whether it's right or wrong (in terms of accomplishing a given job), which is not quite the same as getting someone else to agree. So you really would like a last little check to make sure that it will indeed run correctly on the machine. As for the difference between the constructive approach and the after-the-fact approach, I feel that the constructive approach doesn't really exist. What's happening is that the people are doing their work so simply, so carefully that the proofs of correctness are obvious and they do them in their heads. The proofs are not done explicitly, but they are there and so I see very little difference between the two approaches. The constructive approach just doesn't make the proofs explicit. As for the automatic generation of programs from their specifications, it does not seem to me to be an alternative to any of the other methods. In fact, most of the different methods are not really alternatives to one another, they are techniques that can all be used. The constructive approach, or the approach of automatically generating programs, just seems to me very difficult, even more difficult than proving the correctness of programs, at least in general. For special cases it's probably very much easier.

Holager: There is a difference between constructive methods and after-the-fact verification. It is the difference between having complete redundancy which you have if you do after-the-fact verification and just a nice well-structured single thought on the subject when you have a constructive proof.

King, J.: If you use some constructive method and arrive at a program you feel very confident in, and it's a large program, where did the confidence come from? My claim is that it came from careful implicit step-by-step proofs, as you went along. That is not much different from taking programs afterwards, and going back through them and carefully constructing the proof step-by-step.

Holager: No, there is a difference. A number of times I have been completely convinced that a program I had constructed was really reliable, but I was wrong every time. The problem is that once you've been led into an incorrect thought pattern you can easily repeat it both in the program and in the immediate constructive proof. But if there is a good time lag between those two, then there is a good chance you'll not make the same error.

Dewar: I believe that everyone does have a proof in his mind as he programs, but I think it's a proof more in the sense that mathematicians talk about a proof. And I don't notice much enthusiasm among mathematicians for computer verification of proofs, despite the fact that they have severe problems in the accuracy of proofs. I think this may reflect a more realistic attitude on the part of mathematicians than the one we have as computer scientists.

Holager: We have been talking about how to make reliable software. One of the basic means for getting reliability is full redundancy, so that no single error in any component will cause the system to fail. There seems to be one general and obvious way of doing this, which has been used for thousands of years. That is: do the job, evaluate the results independently, and repeat in a different manner if the job was a failure. We can indicate some special cases. Most work on verification fits into this mold. We program with the assertions and invariants needed for the proof, and then we check them. We go back to the beginning and modify the program if the proof shows it to be incorrect. On the other hand, if we start off with the specification and somehow get the code compiled automatically, then we do not get this kind of reliability. If we construct our program in parallel with the proof, then again the two processes are too coupled to give the reliability which full redundancy is supposed to give. One obvious way of achieving this is the following: do the job in several different ways, and then choose two or three that agree. There is a very simple procedure that could be applied: have two groups do the same job independently of each other, and have them meet periodically, when some subcomponent of the total job has been done, locking them in until they agree. This should at least give the advantages that people are trying to obtain by verification, and in a very simple straightforward manner. The problems are purely human or organizational. How does one make people agree? A member of one group might be very domineering and so be able to prevail every time. Now, that won't work. It is necessary to have groups which are, in some human sense, balanced. On the other hand, if they are too incompatible, they'll just end up fighting and nothing will come out. Another problem is that if the work done between sessions is too large, then the chance of merging alternatives is very low. I suppose it would be best to have small groups of people selected for their ability to co-operate yet different enough so that they won't make the same errors, and then have them meet every week or so. On the whole this seems to be much more practical than the highly mathematical, very beautiful things that have been proposed by many researchers. I've been criticized for being too negative, so consider this proposal as my positive contribution at this conference.

Koster: I think that you don't take into account human nature. There are further problems. One is collusion, or that one group will slowly wear the other down, so that they will agree on something. The second problem is that of politics. You might also say that this system has been tried and has worked in practice, namely in choosing popes, where all the cardinals are put together into a closed, confined part of the Vatican and then one waits for a white puff of smoke to come out.

Hibbard: That shows the problem: is agreement quality? [☺]

Holager: It is hoped that these groups will have thought enough about the problem so that agreement would be, in a sense, objective. But in formal terms, it would mean that the solution agreed upon is right.

Bell: The disadvantage of your suggestion is that people won't want to spend extra effort to do it twice. However, your method is well suited to an experiment in practice. For instance a payroll program in a commercial environment will from time to time need to be re-written anyway, so it would be possible to treat the second version as an independent effort, and then see where they disagree.

Holager: I would object to saying that the amount of work is inordinate. I think that, altogether, this would involve approximately three times the work of just producing one version in a straightforward fashion. And I think it is accepted that producing high-quality software is at least three times the amount of work in any case.

Correll: I made use of such a technique to come up with the structure for an operating system. However, the reason I had two approaches was not that I wanted to apply such a method, but because my analysis of the problem resulted in two completely different ideas on how to do it. There could be situations where I have more than two, and there are many situations where there is only one idea of how to do it.

Holager: It is hoped that the groups would not produce different solutions. It is hoped that the basic algorithms would be the same. But it is hoped that, collectively they won't overlook anything.

Kurki-Suonio: Could you tell me what is the essential difference between your proposal and the way in which PL/I was designed? [☺]

Holager: I think that in the PL/I design there was too much collaboration between participants. You have to make sure that the errors they make are not correlated.

Dewar: A quick comment on why it did not work for PL/I: N was not 2, it was considerably more than 2. Since nobody likes an idea which isn't his own, all good ideas remain in the minority. So this approach is only practical if the number of participants is exactly two.

Wichmann: I have a counterexample for your method, I think, which is related to the problem of underspecification. Namely, if you had two ALGOL compilers working on the same machine, it would be very unlikely that they would produce the same object code. But they may be equally acceptable in some sense.

Holager: I think that if you make two different ALGOL compilers, then it will be quite impossible to merge them after the fact. That is why I said you'll have to repeat this once a week or once every two weeks. The difficulty here seems to be that the size of the jobs is quite critical. If they are too large, you'll never be able to merge; if they are too small, then there will probably be collusion. The point is that the difference between the proposals should mainly consist in errors, so that you can merge them into a perfect program. Furthermore, you'll have to determine the composition of the groups carefully, as well as the stages in which the work should proceed. Ultimately we want to make machine code, but clearly we shall also have to make some high-level specification, a medium-level specification, etc.

Ross: I believe that this phenomenon occurs with great regularity in the scheme used by Structured Analysis where you find differences of opinion about what is the next stage of the decomposition. That's considered a natural part of the readership cycle. Sometimes a reader will come back with a re-drawn diagram as a response to the author. I think the big mistake would be allowing this to happen with respect to the entire system design. If you have competing designs for the entire system, then you should take time out to come up with the criteria for quality, and to enhance your understanding of the context analysis and the requirements definition, etc. Then you will have the basis for an agreement that makes progress towards a single goal.

King, J.: I'd like to make some comments based on my first impressions of this conference, even though I feel better about it than I did at the beginning. It seems we are to talk about constructing quality software by analogy. I would talk about constructing quality tunnels, but they're dark, they're dull and all the interesting parts are inside where I can't see them. So I'd rather talk about constructing quality bridges, since Turski has also given us that metaphor.If we had to construct a quality bridge, what would we do if we didn't know how to go about it? I would go look at some quality bridges and examine them. I would ask the people who built the quality bridges: "How did you build a quality bridge? Could you show me your diagrams? Could you show me the planning process you went through? How did you get a quality bridge?" It would be nice if that's what we'd found here. Perhaps Ross could show us some of his quality software. I'd like to see some quality software. We should have a conference on "look at my beautiful program". There was a series at Carnegie-Mellon University a few years ago entitled "The Ideal ...", and then they filled in the blank: "The Ideal Computer", "The Ideal Program", etc., and had someone come and speak on that topic. I think a conference like that might be very interesting. That's one thought. Another thought that occurred to me was that there's a big difference between Computer Science and Programming. What we've primarily been talking about here is Programming, but I think most of us are computer scientists. Now I doubt that someone constructing production programs would be concerned about how to do it better. He's too busy, he doesn't have the time. So it's reasonable that computer scientists try to worry about how to write good programs. When I look at the affiliations of the participants here (universities and research institutes, primarily), I don't picture any of these people doing production programming. Now computer scientists have good ideas and they develop prototype tools. And I respect the people in this room, I think we have a collection of very renowned computer scientists from all over the world. However, I came to one conclusion as to why we had so many papers about tools. If you have an idea about how software ought to be developed, but have never really done it, then it's very hard to explain your idea and be heard. The busy people won't stop to listen. So what you do is build a tool and see if you can get them to use that tool. Another problem has to do with the education of production programmers. In my country the people who write the production programs have not been trained by computer scientists. Computer scientists don't write the programs nor do they train the people who do. These are two completely different worlds. It seems there is a big gap, but computer scientists with good ideas should try to get these busy people to stop for a moment and listen a little bit more. So I have two requests: bring me a quality program next time; and let's try to develop some dialogue with production programmers and see if we can get them to use our good ideas. [♪]

Ershov: I have a general question to the audience, which I'd like to ask in both Russian and English. [English translation:] I kindly request those participants at this conference who during the last five years were involved in writing or preparing production software to raise their hands. [About 80% do so.] Not so bad!

King, J.: I'm surprised, pleasantly surprised.

Turski: At the beginning of this conference I tried, albeit very unsuccessfully, to bring into our consideration the poor users' view of software. As the discussion developed, it dawned on me quite early that there are two notions of quality: internal quality and external quality. The internal quality is the "best" with respect to the programmers' understanding of the problem and the boundary conditions. The external quality is the "best" with respect to the users' needs. The real problem as I see it, and I stand here as someone who has worked both as a theoretician and as a practitioner, is to try to bridge the gap between these two models. I remember very vividly, from the closing session of the IFIP Congress in New York, an invited talk by Marvin Minsky, who devoted most of his time to saying that to be a model of a thing is not a binary relation as most people tend to think, but a ternary relation involving an object, a model and an observer. So the model is always relative to an observer or, as Ross mentioned, to a particular question you ask. What this beautiful question from the Dutch dictionary failed to mention was that for various questions you may need various models. That seems to explain what has been occurring this week. We have been concerned primarily (perhaps with the exception of one or two papers) with the programmers' model of quality software.

So, how are we going to bridge this gap? (I note that many people say it's a gap which is better left unbridged.) But it's quite obvious that if we are going to bridge this gap, we cannot stay on the ground of one or the other of these two models. It's like the notion of truth in meta-mathematics, where it has been demonstrated that semantical truth cannot be expressed in terms of the same language in which you make the statement; you have to drag in a meta-language.Therefore you have to have some means, some encompassing methodology in which to think about these two models. I believe that it is hopelessly unrealistic to assume that users will start to formulate their specifications or their requirements in terms of ALPHARD, or SETL or any other of these approaches. This is not because of the complexity of expression which we've been speaking of (this can be remedied), but because the users are not interested in queues, stacks or what not. They are interested in bank accounts, airline seat reservations and a variety of things which have nothing to do with the notions we use in building our models.I really would like you to ponder a while...I don't expect any answer at this conference on how this gap can be bridged. I think that what Ross shows goes a long way in this direction, even though it certainly is, to use Koster's elegant term, a "mumbo-jumbo". It's mumbo-jumbo, but it is implemented mumbo-jumbo. You see, there is absolutely no way in which you can formally decide whether driving on the lefthand side or on the righthand side is better. On the other hand you had better implement one of these policies. [☺] It can't be proven, it can't be established which is better, but a lot of ridiculous rules had to be implemented to get drivers to obey some order. It's not because there's any magic in the particular form of the forms Ross was showing. But the existence of such forms, the fact that they must be filled out and that no progress is mechanically made possible unless these forms are agreed, signed and counter-signed is a big step towards systematic solution of users' problems.

I don't know how we can achieve this coupling between the two models. There are several possible approaches (some of which, I think, are slightly too pornographic to be mentioned in this room). But some ideas from so-called automatic programming could bear on it. Perhaps some research in artificial intelligence can bear on it, for instance, the analysis of specifications presented in say, slightly formalized natural language (slightly formalized by being put on forms), where we try to find out the objects and the operations. Most of what we've been hearing today about specifications and so on is, to a mathematician, extremely simple. We are talking about abstract algebras and morphisms between various abstract algebras. Now, it took us programmers about 20 years to discover that we too have to learn abstract algebras. Perhaps, if we go slightly further, we shall realize that there is a lot of abstract algebra in the everyday way people talk. We just have to find it. Much of that could be done. If it cannot be done completely, then at least we can identify those things which are missing, those points without completion of which we cannot progress any further. That would be an extremely big step towards bridging the gap. Not because we would be able to do any automatic construction of programs, but because at least we would be able to handle formally these semi-formal specifications, at least to find out what is missing there.

I observed that we are very much preoccupied with building tools. Of course, building tools is necessary in every craft, but I believe we could do with some motivation in building our tools. That is, we should try to specify for what we are building a new language. It would be ideal if this were specified not in terms of our own model but in terms of where this new language or this linguistic tool would fit in the "terra intacta" between the two models. I don't think it's a great effort, but again one of those silly things. We should set to work trying to see how it is going to be used.

Finally I see that from day to day we have been changing our collective opinion about optimization and reliability or redundancy. One day we all seem to agree that redundancy is a good thing; the day before we all agreed that optimization, which gets rid of redundancy, is a good thing. Now, this slight inconsistency in the collective opinion of those present in this room indicates that perhaps we should not be taking strong positions on issues like optimization and redundancy. They are relative and we'll discover that they are relative. We'll do much better when we specify relative to what.

Ross: My comment goes back to the earlier stages of what Turski said. With respect to the definition of the models that we heard from the Dutch dictionary, I didn't go into a slight variant that we added to it for use in this field, which could have some relevance with respect to the question of quality. By adding to the definition of model (M is a model of A if M can be used to answer questions about A) the concept of a well-defined question set, you do, in fact, convert the concept of model into a binary relation again. A given construct is or is not a model with respect to the given question set, and this again relates back to the idea of structuring of questions, through Structured Analysis. Again, what is the question set, what is the orientation, what is the standpoint, viewpoint, and purposes of the model, what determines the nature of the modelling process itself? Finally, the loop is closed by carrying this idea of making things into binary form one step further. And this is what I am trying to do, which I think is worth mentioning in the context of constructing quality software. I am attempting to come up with a logical system of tolerance, so that you would be able to say that a given subject matter is exactly within tolerance or not. Then you could convert the range of imprecision into a binary specification of exactness. And then this allows you to have proof procedures using mathematical logic, applicable to the inevitable gap that must always remain between a model and the actual thing being modeled. There's also the problem of structuring the question sets and organizing your thought processes in a structured fashion, and carrying the details of the model through to narrow the gap to an acceptable degree. And then, I believe, we will be in the position of being able to have constructive methods which inherently include constructive proof and verification, and which ensure that the quality matches our needs.

Meertens: We are talking now about bridging a gap, probably with a quality bridge, for which we must have engineering techniques. Since I think the gap is to some extent verbal, I'll try a verbal attempt at closing it somewhat. First, I have two naive questions, and these are questions to which we get answers only by approximation. The first question is: Who is the User? I've already asked Turski, "Is the pedestrian run down by a car a user?" And the answer was: "Yes, he's an accidental user." [☺] I think, for software it must be the same. The second naive question is: Who is judging the specifications and in what position are we to change this situation? To narrow the gap, some 15 years ago, when all these notions of structured programming were not expressed verbally, there were uneasy feelings amongst programmers that certain techniques of programming were unaesthetical, that some tricks were "dirty", and if you look back now, it was an expression of the fact that those techniques were unreliable in the sense that they were not robust in the context of modification, and modifications were considered a part of the normal production process. What concerns the programmer concerns the user, and unreliable products can concern the user very greatly. Once I was involved in writing a program which had something to do with controlling a reservoir in a small town in Switzerland. You can imagine my feelings when on some Sunday morning I learned on the radio that a dam in that city had broken down, and it took two days to find out that it was a different dam from the one for which I performed computations. In the meantime I had desperately tried to verify my program, but didn't succeed during those two days; in fact, I found many errors. [☺]

Turski: I cannot resist the temptation to close on a non-constructive note. One of my mathematical colleagues once remarked that there is really no sense in devising any mathematical proofs for theorems because, you see, either a theorem is correct, and the proof is not going to help it, or a theorem is incorrect, in which case you can't make the proof. [Last exit: to banquet.]

List of Participants

S. A. Ananievski	Polytechnical Institute, Kiev, USSR
J. André	IRISA, University of Rennes, France
D. Bär	Humboldt University, Berlin, GDR
Á. Bedö	Research Institute for Applied Computer Science, Hungary
J. R. Bell	Digital Equipment Corporation, USA
Y. Bekkers	University of Grenoble, France
M. Berthaud	IBM Laboratory, La Gaude, France
G. V. Bochmann	University of Montreal, Canada
G. D. Chinin	Lebedev Institute for Computing Machinery, Novosibirsk, USSR
C. H. Correll	Bavarian Academy of Sciences, FRG
G. Dávid	Academy of Sciences, Hungary
J. Demner	Institute of Computational Techniques, CSSR
R. B. K. Dewar	Courant Institute, New York University, USA
W. Dijkhuis	North-Holland Publishing Company, The Netherlands
B. Dömölki	Institute for Coordination in Computer Science, Hungary
J. Duplinsky	Computing Research Centre, CSSR
A. P. Ershov	Academy of Sciences, Novosibirsk, USSR
A. Fuksman	Rostov State University, USSR
G. Goos	University of Karlsruhe, FRG
P. G. Hibbard	Carnegie-Mellon University, USA
P. Holager	University of Nijmegen, The Netherlands
V. N. Kasyanov	Academy of Sciences, Novosibirsk, USSR
V. Katkov	Academy of Sciences, Novosibirsk, USSR
I. O. Kerner	Wilhelm Pieck University, Rostock, GDR
J. C. King	IBM Research, Yorktown Heights, USA
P. R. King	University of Manitoba, Canada
C. H. A. Koster	University of Nijmegen, The Netherlands
V. E. Kotov	Academy of Sciences, Novosibirsk, USSR
J. Král	Institute of Computation Techniques, CSSR
R. Kurki-Suonio	University of Tampere, Finland
V. Kurochkin	Academy of Sciences, Moscow, USSR
A. A. Letichevski	Institute of Cybernetics, Kiev, USSR
J. Maluszynski	Academy of Sciences, Poland
L. Meertens	Mathematical Centre, The Netherlands
B. Meyer	EDF-Etudes et Recherches, France
M. Miyakawa	ETL, Tokyo, Japan
A. P. Mráz	Computing Research Centre, CSSR
J. Nehmer	Nuclear Research Centre, Karlsruhe, FRG
M. E. Nemenman	Institute of Electronic Computers, Minsk, USSR
J. E. L. Peck	University of British Columbia, Canada
P. Petrov	Bulgarian Academy of Sciences, Sofia, Bulgaria
S. Pokrovsky	Academy of Sciences, Novosibirsk, USSR
P. C. Poole	University of Melbourne, Australia
I. V. Pottosin	Academy of Sciences, Novosibirsk, USSR

L. Raikov	Institute of Radioelectricity, Moscow, USSR
V. Rajlich	Research Institute for Mathematical Machines, CSSR
D. T. Ross	SofTech Incorporated, USA
A. Sárközy	Academy of Sciences, Hungary
J. Schlichting	Control Data Corporation, The Netherlands
S. A. Schuman	IRIA-Laboria, France
S. Shtarkman	Institute of Applied Mathematics, Moscow, USSR
M. Sintzoff	MBLE Research Laboratory, Belgium
G. Tseytin	Leningrad State University, USSR
W. M. Turski	University of Warsaw, Poland
E. Tyugu	Estonian Academy of Sciences, USSR
I. V. Velbitsky	Institute of Cybernetics, Kiev, USSR
B. A. Wichmann	National Physical Laboratory, UK
P. Wodon	MBLE Research Laboratory, Belgium

Index to Discussions